Ninth Edition

PROACTIVE POLICE MANAGEMENT

Edward A. Thibault
State University of New York College at Oswego (Ret.)

Lawrence M. Lynch
Onondaga Community College (Ret.)

R. Bruce McBride
New York State University Police

Gregory Walsh
Utica College

PEARSON

Boston   Columbus   Indianapolis   New York   San Francisco   Hoboken
Amsterdam   Cape Town   Dubai   London   Madrid   Milan   Munich   Paris   Montreal   Toronto
Delhi   Mexico City   Sao Paulo   Sydney   Hong Kong   Seoul   Singapore   Taipei   Tokyo

Editorial Director: Vernon Anthony
Executive Editor: Gary Bauer
Editorial Assistant: Lynda Cramer
Director of Marketing: David Gesell
Marketing Manager: Mary Salzman
Senior Marketing Coordinator: Alicia Wozniak
Marking Assistant: Les Roberts
Team Lead, Project Management: JoEllen Gohr
Procurement Specialist: Deidra Skahill
Media Project Manager: April Cleland
Project Manager: Linda Cupp
Creative Director: Jayne Conte
Cover: Getty Images
Cover Designer: Suzanne Behnke
Full-Service Project Management Composition: Mansi Negi, Aptara®, Inc.
Printer/Binder: RR Donnelley, Harrisonburg, VA
Cover Printer: RR Donnelley, Harrisonburg, VA
Text Font: Minion Pro

Library of Congress Cataloging-in-Publication Data

Thibault, Edward A.
    Proactive police management / Edward A. Thibault, State University of New York College at Oswego, Lawrence M. Lynch, Onondaga Community College, R. Bruce McBride, State University of New York Gregory Walsh, Utica College.—Ninth edition.
        p. cm.
    ISBN 978-0-13-359843-8
    ISBN 0-13-359843-8
    1. Police administration.   2. Police administration—United States.   III. Title.
HV7935.T47 2014
363.2068—dc23   2013048291

ISBN 13: 978-0-13-359843-8
ISBN 10:   0-13-359843-8

CONTENTS

PREFACE

The theme of this book is that police managers must be proactive. While the term has many business connotations, for our purposes the word *proactive* means foreseeing events, situations, and potential threats before they become major issues through the use of long and short-term planning. Proactive police managers go out of their way to have open consultations and communication on crime and community issues with major stakeholders, which include members of the department who serve the community, the community that the department serves, and other agencies that interact with the department on a daily basis. There is reliance on both human beings and technology to achieve agency objectives. In all, the main management objectives are to reduce crime and to improve the quality of life in the community that the department services.

This proactive concept is not new. In the preface of the 1829 duty manual of the recently organized London Metropolitan Police, Commissioners Rowan and Mayne wrote,

> It should be understood, at the outset, that the object to be obtained is the prevention of crime. To this great end every effort of the police is to be directed. The security of person and property, the preservation of public tranquility, and all other objects of a police establishment will thus be better effected than by the detection and punishment of the offender after he has succeeded in committing the crime.
>
> Every member of the police force, as the guide for personal and professional conduct should constantly keep this in mind. Officers and police constables should endeavor by such vigilance and activity as may render it impossible for anyone to commit a crime within that portion of the town under their charge.

Thus, proactive policing is a grand and noble tradition of the first modern police force and policing throughout the ages.

Based on the authors' experience in education, policing, and management, three important considerations must be made before discussing proactive management for American policing. First, we believe that sound management is management based on a combination of theory and practice. Practice without analysis causes us to repeat the mistakes of history, so our theoretical analysis must be directed toward the practical for implementation into the day-to-day rigors of operating a police department.

Second, we reject complete adherence to the authoritarian as well as to the purely participatory styles of management. In the authoritarian model, which dominates many police organizations, important elements of planning and communications are eliminated or lost. In the full participatory model, response to emergency and life-threatening situations is hampered because too many people are involved, and decisions take too long. In crisis management, for example, one person has to be in charge of the crisis management team, with subordinates responding to this top administrator.

Third, we rely to a great extent on the consultative style of management. As will be shown, the consultative style leaves room for change and "doors open" throughout all elements of the police organization. It can be an efficient and dynamic style of management, provided that the necessary elements of a well-run law enforcement agency are met. Consultation also includes discussions with the community on law enforcement and safety problems. It is one of the key ingredients for community-oriented and problem-oriented policing, which are being publicly advanced by police and community leaders. Proactive planning to deal with an infrastructure attack or activity by a "spree" sniper has to be done in consultation with private and public agencies and the community.

This edition of *Proactive Police Management* provides a review, analysis, and synthesis of the various approaches to police management, including traditional scientific management, the behavioral/systems approach, and the human relations approach. There is enough detail concerning basic organization and management skills that police managers and students of police management will find the text useful. At the same time, major conceptual contributions from the behavioral sciences and human relations are explored in the context of police management. Most important is the constant theme of being proactive: planning ahead, anticipating the future, and attempting to establish some control by police managers over those future events.

Community policing—which over the past decade appeared to becoming phased out due to federal funding considerations—still exists as an important concept for national policing policy. Overall, community policing echoes the relationship between police and the community before automobiles and wireless radios. In fact, the rise of social media is contributing to greater police and citizen interactions.

Much attention is also paid to evolving theories, such as the notion of giving and total quality management and reengineering, along with new applications of computer technology, such as the spatial and time analysis of crime events. This combination of new proactive management concepts and the application of new technology continues to revolutionize policing as well as other private and public services in the United States.

In the first edition, we wrote that most police departments operate on traditional organization principles as stated in O.W. Wilson's classic police administration text from the 1950s. Since the 1990s, college-educated and professionally trained managers have become concerned with twenty-first-century proactive communication advances and organizational theories that can be readily applied to their departments.

Policing today remains in the limelight in terms of ethics, the use of authority and force, the crime problem as related to increased drug use and trafficking, and repeated calls by state and national leaders for dealing with crime and terrorism problems. Correspondingly, many police managers complain that they must do more with less under the burden of reduced budgets from the current economic turndown that began in 2008. From the viewpoint of the general public, there is widespread support for police to contain crime. The events of September 11, 2001, still have had a profound background that we present the proactive style of management.

NEW TO THIS EDITION

- Chapter 1 on history perspective gives a broad overview of issues, trends, and personalities that have shaped American policing. We added President Theodore Roosevelt, who served as New York City Police Commissioner, brought many new initiatives to law enforcement, including a civil service system.

- Chapter 2 on, "Police Culture," updates the subcultural norms of secrecy, solidarity, and social isolation. A review of female executives in law enforcement has been moved to this chapter, where contemporary issues and the continued advancement of females in law enforcement are discussed.

- Chapter 3 builds on past reviews on police leadership, adding a new examination by James Grant, who found that leadership includes the notion of being a giving leader.

- Chapter 4 highlights how police success is often measured through statistics and productivity. A repeating issue in the many measurement areas is how police leaders have continued to address the vast responsibilities of a 21st Century police agency under the new post-2008 municipal budget realities.

- Chapter 5 highlights the current reality of doing more with less, and making tough priority decisions for the agency.

- Chapter 6 discusses how the ever-changing electronic media impacts policing such as Facebook, Twitter, Instagram, Tumbler, or Vine.

- Chapter 7 presents police technology beyond communications in such areas as report writing, data bases, internal administrative documentation, dispatching and vehicle monitoring.

- Chapter 8 contains an update on staff deployment and new initiatives in patrol such as predictive policing.

- Chapter 9's presents a look at the practicalities of illegal gambling investigations, such as during large national sporting events, and a fresh look at the once popular DARE Program, and a new look at police-prosecutor relations. A new section on law enforcement's anti-terrorism efforts has been added to the chapter, as well.

- Chapter 10 now includes a discussion on police lawsuits and how damaging one successful suit can be to a police agency and municipality.

- Chapter 11 provides a fresh review of document storage and take-home vehicles.

- Chapter 12 recommends increased educational requirements for new hires in law enforcement, with the goal of having a nationwide college-educated police force. The stress of being a police officer is discussed, including the alarming suicide rate in law enforcement.

- Chapter 13 presents a review of a police study on international anti-terrorism training, and updates to virtual simulation capabilities.

- Chapter 14 recommends that police leaders conform emergency planning according to National Incident Management System (NIMS) guidelines. Contemporary events, such as the April, 2013 Boston Marathon Bombing is brought into this edition.

- Chapter 15 includes recent events in Wisconsin, when the state legislature and governor successfully rolled back many powers given to public union.

- Chapter 16 again focuses on the future of policing and current trends brought about by technology and government fiscal crisis and the continued increase in global crimes.

PROACTIVE POLICE MANAGEMENT (NINTH EDITION) HIGHLIGHTS

Proactive Police Management is widely used both as a textbook for college and university classes in police management and as a reference text for police managers in dealing with operational issues in their departments. It is also used for training police supervisors and administrators and is required reading for civil service promotional examinations. As a result, we receive a number of ideas from readers and keep abreast of new developments through our work with professional associations and interactions with police managers. National data and technological trends have been added throughout the book. While the original purpose of this textbook—providing a historical perspective of police management, and the issues that have, are, and will face policing—is still intact, it also relates that history to contemporary issues occurring right up to this textbook's going to press.

First we would like to introduce Gregory Walsh, the fourth author. Dr Walsh teaches and writes in the areas of police management, homeland security, and emergency management and joined the faculty after a 25-year career with the New York State Police. Before retiring as captain with the Bureau of Criminal Investigation, he was also responsible for counter-terrorism planning as it related to critical infrastructure.

Ironically, during the past year Bruce McBride retired from the faculty and decided to return to the law enforcement field as Commissioner of Police for the State University of New York. He now coordinates law enforcement operations for the University's 28 campuses.

Edward Thibault and Larry Lynch are enjoying their lives as "academic retirees" and remain active in a wide number of criminal justice associations. Ed was the director of the public justice program at Oswego, and Larry was director of the criminal justice program at Onondaga Community College and Chief of Police for Town of Dewitt. Thus, it comes as no surprise that this book is written through the eyes of working administrators.

In this edition, Chapter 1 on historical perspective gives a broad overview of issues, trends, and personalities that have shaped American policing. In terms of contributions to police leadership, we added President Theodore Roosevelt, who served as New York City Police Commissioner and brought many new initiatives to law enforcement, including a civil service system. A review of female executives in law enforcement has been moved to Chapter 2, where contemporary issues and the continued advancement of females in law enforcement are discussed.

Chapter 2, "Police Culture," updates the subcultural norms of secrecy, solidarity, and social isolation. It also discusses the impact on policing by black, Hispanic, and female officers. The importance of informal group structure to inter-agency and intra-agency effectiveness is reviewed.

Chapter 3 builds on past reviews on police leadership, adding a new examination by James Grant, who found that leadership includes the notion of being a giving leader.

Chapter 4 highlights how police success is often measured through statistics and productivity. A repeating issue in the many measurement areas is how police leaders have continued to address the vast responsibilities of a twenty-first century police agency under the new post-2008 municipal budget realities.

As with Chapter 4, police executives doing more with less and making tough priority decisions for the agency are the focus of Chapter 5, which reviews the basic operating principles for police organizations. Is committing limited personnel resources to traffic safety more important to the respective community than a vice unit? Ongoing evaluations of special unit activities will help a police chief balance resources with community needs.

New to Chapter 6 is how the ever-changing electronic media impacts policing. Just as parents can fall behind in their desire to monitor their children's online communications through Facebook, managers need to be aware of the ever-newer instant communications trends, such as Twitter, Instagram, Tumbler, or Vine, as well as making wise decisions on implementing some or all new media as potential investigative or community service resources.

Police technology beyond communications is presented in Chapter 7. Report writing, databases, internal administrative documentation, dispatching, and vehicle monitoring—they can all be enhanced by proactive, forward-thinking police leaders.

Patrol operations are discussed in Chapter 8. Should a police squad leader, who has eight officers available for patrol on today's evening shift, put out eight squad cars with one officer in each, four two-officers units, or maybe four one-officer units, one two-officer unit, and two officers on foot patrol? On what would the squad leader base that decision? Decisions such as these and many more policing initiatives are discussed.

New to Chapter 9's review of the basic line functions of policing is a look at the practicalities of illegal gambling investigations, such as during large national sporting events; a fresh look at the once popular DARE program; and a new look at police–prosecutor relations. A new section on law enforcement's anti-terrorism efforts has been added to the chapter, as well.

A new discussion of police lawsuits and how damaging one successful suit can be to a police agency and municipality can be found in Chapter 10, which covers administrative and staff issues. Auxiliary functions are the topic of Chapter 11, which provides a fresh review of document storage and take-home vehicles.

Chapter 12 discusses human resources management. One of the recommendations the authors make in this new edition is to increase educational requirements for new hires in law enforcement, with the goal of having a nationwide college-educated police force. The stress of being a police officer is discussed, including the alarming suicide rate in law enforcement.

Training is presented in Chapter 13. New to this edition is a review of a police study on international anti-terrorism training, and updates to virtual simulation capabilities.

Proactive planning, discussed in Chapter 14, adds to the last edition's revamp of the chapter with the recommendation for police leaders to conform their agencies to National Incident Management System (NIMS) compliance. Contemporary events, such as the April 2013 Boston Marathon bombing, are brought into this edition.

Collective bargaining and police management are the topics of Chapter 15. The chapter reviews current trends in this area such as the events in Wisconsin, when the state legislature and governor successfully rolled back many powers given to public union. Chapter 16 again focuses on the future of policing and current trends brought about by technology and government fiscal crisis. Crime and police activity are becoming more globally based on the worldwide economy, terrorism, and criminal activity.

INSTRUCTOR SUPPLEMENTS

Instructor's Manual with Test Bank Includes content outlines for classroom discussion, teaching suggestions, and answers to selected end-of-chapter questions from the text. This also contains a Word document version of the test bank.

MyTest This computerized test generation system gives you maximum flexibility in preparing tests. It can create custom tests and print scrambled versions of a test at one time, as well as build tests randomly by chapter, level of difficulty, or question type. The software also allows online testing and record-keeping and the ability to add problems to the database. This test bank can also be delivered formatted for use in popular learning management platforms, such as BlackBoard, WebCT, Moodle, Angel, D2L, and Sakai. Visit www.PearsonMyTest.com to begin building your tests.

PowerPoint Presentations Our presentations offer clear, straightforward outlines and notes to use for class lectures or study materials. Photos, illustrations, charts, and tables from the book are included in the presentations when applicable.

To access supplementary materials online, instructors need to request an instructor access code. Go to **www.pearsonhighered.com/irc**, where you can register for an instructor access code.

Within 48 hours after registering, you will receive a confirming email, including an instructor access code. Once you have received your code, go to the site and log on for full instructions on downloading the materials you wish to use.

ALTERNATE VERSIONS

eBooks This text is also available in multiple eBook formats including Adobe Reader and CourseSmart. *CourseSmart* is an exciting new choice for students looking to save money. As an alternative to purchasing the printed textbook, students can purchase an electronic version of the same content. With a *CourseSmart* eTextbook, students can search the text, make notes online, print out reading assignments that incorporate lecture notes, and bookmark important passages for later review. For more information, or to purchase access to the *CourseSmart* eTextbook, visit **www.coursesmart.com**.

ACKNOWLEDGMENTS

In closing, we would like to acknowledge the hundreds of students we have taught over the past two decades. Today, many former students are police and public administrators, and their comments and questions on the topics in this book have been invaluable. We also thank the many faculty members who adopted this book and gave us critical comments.

We would like to thank the many police administrators who have used this book for administrative and educational purposes, and provided information on new training and operational developments in police services.

We also thank the training and management staff at the New York State Office of Public Safety; the police chiefs in the State University of New York System; and our friends and colleagues all over the world with the International Association of Chiefs of Police and the International Association of Campus Law Enforcement Administrators.

Special thanks go to former chief and now Professor Raymond Philo of the New Hartford, New York, Police Department for his operational insights on intelligence-led policing, technology, and agency accreditation. Special acknowledgment goes to Jay Berman, Professor, New Jersey City University, and George Curtis, retired Dean of Business and Justice Studies, Utica College.

Edward A. Thibault gives thanks to Korni Swaroop Kumar, colleague, friend, and international scholar, who shared his thoughts on global policing, and to his wife, Marianne Pampuch, for her love, support, and affection.

Lawrence Lynch gives thanks to Marilyn Lynch for her patience and support especially during his recent illness.

R. Bruce McBride gives thanks to his loving family—Barbara, Robbie, Megan, and Brian McBride. He also says thanks to his colleagues and students at Utica College for their constructive comments over these past years. This edition also acknowledges the memory of Al Cali, of the University at Albany, who was a kind teacher and friend.

In addition to thanking his new co-authors for having him join them for this new edition of *Proactive Police Management*, Greg Walsh would like to thank the many Criminal Justice students at Utica College whom he had the pleasure of having pass through his classroom, as they have taught him as many lessons as he has shared with them.

We would also like to thank the staff at Pearson for their continuing support and for publishing the ninth edition of *Proactive Police Management*.

Edward A. Thibault, Ph.D
Baldwinsville, New York

Lawrence M. Lynch, M.P.A
Escondido, California

R. Bruce McBride, Ed.D
Delmar, New York

Gregory Walsh
New York

1 Historical Perspective

KEY TERMS

bureaucracy

common culture

empowerment

human relations

Law Enforcement Assistance
    Administration (LEAA)

local control

Metropolitan Police Act

modus operandi

Pendleton Act

proactive

scientific management

The origins of the modern police force can be traced to the creation of the Metropolitan Police in London, England, in the year 1829. The social and economic conditions created by the Industrial Revolution caused a great surge in the number of people migrating to the cities of England, and this largely uneducated and poorly trained population brought with it the chaos of poverty, unemployment, and crime. This, in turn, led to a proliferation of private and special police forces designed to serve the needs of the diverse interest groups prevalent at the time. The merchant police were hired to protect the individual store owners and shopkeepers, a parochial police force protected churchgoers and church property, and special police were hired to protect the harbor front and shipping interests on the Thames, just to mention a few.

The organization of these special groups was at best haphazard and self-serving. The people of the big cities had no organized group to serve the general interests of the total population. The home secretary at the time, Sir Robert Peel, lobbied intensively in Parliament for a professional organized police force under government control. His Act for Improving the Police In and Near the Metropolis of London, commonly known as the **Metropolitan Police Act**, was approved in 1829. Its main purpose, as outlined in the first duty manual, was to prevent crime and to protect property.

Lieutenant Colonel Charles Rowan and Richard Maynes, Esq., the authors of the first instruction manual, adapted their text from the 1803 military manual of the Irish constabulary police, entitled *Military Training and Moral Training*. The force was organized into ranks of superintendent, inspectors, sergeants, and police constables (Reith, 1975: 135–36). Some 11,000 recruits were screened to arrive at the final 1,000 officers who made up the semimilitary structure of the forerunner of our modern police organizations.

Before we examine the historical development of police management theory, we should trace the main stages of development of the present managerial systems of law enforcement in the United States. The history can be roughly divided into six periods. As shown in Table 1-1, these periods are actually cumulative; that is, many characteristics from one era persist into subsequent periods.

TABLE 1-1   Periods of History in Police Management

Years	Period	Major Leaders and Authors	Major Contributions to Police Management
1750–1900	Industrial Revolution, traditional management model	Sir Robert Peel, Charles Rowan, Richard Maynes, John Moore, Henry Fielding, John Fielding, Theodore Roosevelt	Economic man, centralized administration, semimilitary model, ranks, strong leadership, crime prevention objective of policing
1900 to present	Scientific management	Max Weber, O.W. Wilson, Frederick Taylor, Henry Fayol, Raymond Fosdick, Elmer D. Graper, Bruce Smith, August Vollmer, V.A. Leonard, Dwight Waldo, William Parker	Modern bureaucracy, unity of command, civil service, division of labor, specialization, one-way authority, narrow span of control, omnipresent patrol officer, hierarchy
1925 to present	Human relations and participative management	Elton Mayo, Chester I. Barnard, Leonard Fuld, Frederick Herzberg, R.R. Blake, J.S. Mouton, Rensis Likert, W. Edwards Deming	Focus on personnel management, motivation techniques, morale, stress management, participatory and democratic management with team approach, communication models, TQM[a]
1945 to present	Behavioral management	Herbert Simon, Douglas Murray McGregor	PPB, organizational development, PERT, STAR[b]
1960 to present	Systems management	Patrick Murphy, James McNamara	Zero-based budgeting, interfacing of subsystems
1980 to present	Proactive police management	James Q. Wilson, George Kelling, Herman Goldstein, William Bratton, Lee Brown, Robert Trojanowicz	Emphasis on forward planning, consultative management, problem solving, high-technology information systems, data-driven departments, preventing crime, communities deciding the police agenda

[a]TQM, total quality management.

[b]PPB, programming, planning, and budgeting; PERT, program evaluation and review techniques; STAR, system training and analysis of requirements.

THE INDUSTRIAL REVOLUTION AND TRADITIONAL MANAGEMENT, 1750–1900

One of the major management principles of the Metropolitan Police Act that appeared in the original 1829 duty manual was Principle 9 (Reith, 1975: 166), namely, *the test of police efficiency is the absence of crime and disorder and not the visible evidence of police action in dealing with them.* Today, this principle becomes increasingly important as police managers look toward the proactive management model and utilize more planning and research to provide a more efficient delivery of services.

The force's authorized strength of 3,295 men in 1829 was arrived at by attempting to determine, in as logical a fashion as possible, the relationship between disorder and crime in each section of London and the personnel necessary to deal with it. During its first four years of existence, this police force was not only engaged in all-night battles with rioting mobs, but was also under constant threat of being eliminated by the government. However, strong leadership coupled with an excellent command structure and a semimilitary organizational model brought order to the streets of London, along with diminished evidence of crime in general. This model, which continued to have a solid history of success in the later nineteenth and early twentieth centuries, was gradually extended to all parts of England.

Another important component of this fledgling force was the principle of **local control**. As Reith (1975: 169) points out in his history of police, "In England, each separate police force in the provinces is established under local authority which in the boroughs is the Watch Committee of the town or city council and in the counties the Standing Joint Committee of the county council, comprising justices of the peace and county councillors in equal numbers. . . . There is no central headquarters, no minister or chief of police." The British were very proud of the local control of their police forces, and this concept was exported to America. As a result, the selection of constables and the election of sheriffs in the United States have to this day been strictly controlled and zealously guarded by their respective communities. The political need for local control and the federal system of government severely curtailed the creation of countrywide or metropolitan police agencies in the United States. This reluctance to consolidate or combine forces in light of modern-day economics is a major issue for proactive police managers.

Today, Great Britain's police have traded local control for centralized administration and services, especially in the area of supervisory and command-level policies. At present, it is the policy of most constabularies to transfer a newly appointed officer to a different constabulary after an appropriate training period. The policy of not promoting police managers to take charge in their local districts eliminates a great deal of local influence and control over the police force.

In the United States, the lack of lateral entry between agencies has created a career ladder within the agency that has had the opposite effect: increased local control. The American promotional system leads to some special management problems in the areas of both training and control. The demand for local control by communities in many areas continues and the creation of special police authorities, for example, campus, transportation, and environmental, results in the overlap of jurisdictional authority and duplication of services.

With the passing of the **Pendleton Act** of 1870, many federal employees were placed under a civil service merit system governing conditions of their employment in an effort to reduce the political interference that had prevailed since the Jacksonian era. Shortly thereafter, civil service reform spread throughout the states. The new era, created by the scientific management writers and leaders after 1900, gave rise to civil service reforms in policing.

Theodore Roosevelt

Theodore Roosevelt, the 26th president of the United States, served as police commissioner for the City of New York from May 1895 to April 1897. Similar to other American cities at this time, New York was undergoing unprecedented growth as a result of the increased manufacturing, trade, and increased immigration from Europe. It was, however, a city of great wealth and abject poverty. City services, including police, were grossly corrupt and inefficient and under the control of a political machine known as Tammany Hall.

Historians classify Roosevelt as a good example of a class of reform-minded administrators and writers, who became known as progressives. The progressives felt that municipal services needed to be organized and responsive to public needs especially the police, who were the cornerstone for public safety. They also had a strong sense of morality and viewed unregulated alcohol sales and widespread prostitution as evil. Similar to Robert Peel, Berman (1987: 8) discusses that Roosevelt initiated a number of reforms that focused on the following:

- Adoption of military titles and traditions, such as rank titles and uniforms, to improve the image and identity of the department
- Centralized control under one command structure starting with the commissioner to address the system of fiefdoms under a politically connected precinct captain
- A system of discipline to weed out corrupt and ineffective officers and supervisors
- Hiring standards based on competitive testing and a civil service system rather than political connections
- Increased training to address job tasks and improve performance
- Reduction of nonpolice tasks, such as overseeing boarding houses

Although his tenure as commissioner was brief, he was able to accomplish many goals. Throughout his term, Roosevelt was president of the bipartisan four-member police board but it was acknowledged by the press and the public that he was the head of the department. He would go out on patrol at nights to check on officers and the workings of each precinct. At central headquarters, business practices were initiated for payroll and supplies, including the use of sealed bids for major purchase, and a system of funds for informants. Despite intense political opposition, the board under his leadership was able to remove a number of corrupt supervisors and officers, including the superintendent of police. Based on his previous experience as a Civil Service commissioner, new personnel standards were introduced, including the use of written and physical examinations.

As described by Berman (1987), by March 1897 he became very frustrated as he was unable to capture department and public support for enforcement of laws prohibiting the sale of alcohol on Sunday. His tenure as commissioner concluded in April. His organizational initiatives, however, set the blueprint for administrative and operating standards for other major police departments in the United States that continued into the twentieth century and formed the basis for the professional law enforcement model.

SCIENTIFIC MANAGEMENT, 1900 TO PRESENT

In their classic textbook on public administration, Nigro and Nigro (1973: 92–96) refer to **scientific management** as the machine model, where emphasis is on efficiency, orderliness, and output. They cite Frederick Taylor as providing the four basic principles of this approach:

1. Division of labor and specialization
2. Unity of command and centralization of decision making

3. One-way authority
4. Narrow span of control

This, along with the monocratically organized bureaucracy developed by Max Weber (see Chapter 4 for a discussion of Weber's principles), became the basic conceptual structure for scientific management. As Nigro and Nigro (1973: 97) point out, the emphasis was on "rationality, predictability, impersonality, technical competence, and authoritarianism." This model fit well with the already existing semimilitary model of police organization, where the manager was definitely in charge of the organizational machinery.

In their early study of **bureaucracy**, Blau and Meyer (1971: 34) give us three stages of developing bureaucracies that are also characteristics of police organizations. First, cash salaries replace unpaid work by family members. Then a clerical component is added, and the owners are separated from management. Finally, managers are expected to have professional qualifications. This has had further implications that are distinctly nondemocratic, namely, that "bureaucratic authority . . . prevents the group itself from conferring the position of leadership upon the member of their choice" (1971: 66). If the group itself cannot pick its leaders, then a rationale has to be developed for another selection process. This is also true of the surrounding political context. One of the thrusts of scientific management is to have professional police managers replace political appointees, whereby authority is then conferred by expertise and professional standards.

Other parts of this book examine specific contributions of this approach to police management in some detail. Rather than introduce material that will be examined later in a variety of contexts, let's take two major figures steeped in this tradition and examine them as typical examples of the scientific management approach: O.W. Wilson and William H. Parker.

O.W. Wilson

Orlando Winfield Wilson served as a patrol officer under August Vollmer, chief of the Berkeley, California, Police Department, from 1921 to 1925. His career included being chief of police in Fullerton, California (1925–1928), and Wichita, Kansas (1928–1939); professor of criminology at the University of California at Berkeley (1939–1960); and then dean (1950–1960). In World War II, Colonel Wilson served as chief public safety officer in Italy, England, and Germany (1943–1947). From 1960 to 1967, he was the reform-minded chief of police in the Chicago Police Department. His book, *Police Administration*, first published in 1950, became the most influential management textbook for use by modern police managers and police management faculties in the United States.

Basically, Wilson carried on Vollmer's sound approach to police management under the main principles of encouraging the following:

1. A professional police department divorced from politics
2. Rigorous police personnel selection and training processes
3. Use of the latest technological innovations available for law enforcement (e.g., maximum use of patrol cars, radio systems, and computerized record keeping)

Interestingly, Wilson was both committed to the professionalization of policing and opposed to civil service. He felt that civil service tests and rules of seniority hampered the police chief in selecting the most qualified personnel for law enforcement and promotion to leadership positions.

Wilson organized his book around three basic administrative processes: (1) planning, (2) activating, and (3) controlling. In 1963, he wrote, "Wisely conceived plans are the keystones of administration; without them the entire venture may fail" (p. 89). He went on to explain the key part planning has in his organizational scheme. Good planning, based on the study of needs and used as a continuing process, serves to bind an organization together, to implement the policy underlying its aims and purposes, to direct its efforts into the proper channels, and to guide in both training and performance. He saw the process of activating as one primarily of organization and leadership. Accordingly, "the essence of leadership is the ability to obtain from each member of the force the highest quality of service that he has the capacity to render" (1963: 9). Wilson stressed that this leadership was a positive force and that relying on punishments ultimately means a failure of leadership.

His third process of control related to police organizations was accountability. He opposed the creation of civilian review boards since police leadership should be accountable for all officers' actions. He was concerned with punishing officers who used excessive force. As Gazell (1974: 373) states in his excellent biographical article, Chief Wilson was "worried about what is sometimes called lawlessness in law enforcement." He considered this to be a definite police management problem that should be handled internally. As discussed by Gazel (1974), Wilson is best remembered as a main contributor to American policing through his various leadership practices and writings.

William H. Parker

Between 1927 and 1939, William Henry Parker rose from the position of a police officer to captain in the Los Angeles Police Department (LAPD), earned an LLB degree, and uncovered a scandal in the police promotion process that resulted in a grand jury investigation and general cleanup of the department. During World War II, working under Colonel Wilson, Parker developed the police and prison plans for the invasion of Europe and organized democratic police departments in Frankfurt and Munich (Gazell, 1976: 29).

Parker shared many of Wilson's concerns. Basically, Parker's main contribution was to the implementation of scientific management in the LAPD, one of the largest police departments in the country, during his tenure as chief from 1950 to 1968. Parker was known for his strong stand on effective law enforcement, accountability, technocratic innovations, and commitment to police professionalism. Besides the normal background investigation, Chief Parker also demanded that recruits have IQs of 110 or above, undertake a closely supervised one-year probation period, and undergo a thorough psychiatric examination. He also created an exhaustive **modus operandi** (method of procedure) file made up of over 2 million cards, one of the finest police laboratories in the world, and a planning and research division that used and still uses state-of-the-art computer technology. Gazell (1976) summed up Parker's internal changes to police organizations with many examples such as the creation of internal affairs and planning units. He also spearheaded the use of one-person patrols, the need for traffic enforcement, and the need to deal with alcoholism among police officers.

Under Parker's leadership, the LAPD became a model for the country in terms of standards of excellence for police personnel recruitment and training, sophisticated planning, and a solid image for professional law enforcement. His willingness to take on technological and some organizational innovation in the spirit of scientific management served to encourage other departments throughout the country to accept these innovations. This became especially true when the **Law Enforcement Assistance Administration (LEAA)** was willing to provide startup costs and basic capital throughout the 1970s.

Other Contributors

Other noted works on police organization based on the scientific approach appearing throughout this period were Elmer D. Graper's *American Police Administration* (1921), August Vollmer's *The Police and Modern Society* (1936), Raymond B. Fosdick's *European Police*

Systems (1915) and *American Police Systems* (1920), *Municipal Police Administration* (1943) published by the International City Managers Association, and Bruce Smith's *Police Systems in the United States* (1940). What appears in the writings of these early observers is skepticism toward municipal police operations and a willingness of police officials to blame immigrants and other public officials for crime problems. One theme that is most common, however, is the resistance to change by police officials. For example, Fosdick (1920: 306) wrote that uniformed patrol in many cities was outdated since patrol zones had not changed over the course of 20–40 years. Smith, who wrote a comprehensive review of American policing after World War II, had in 1923 addressed operational and ethical problems with the New Orleans police. When he returned in 1946, he found many of the same problems he had encountered in his first study.

Nevertheless, the contributions of these early observers collectively forge the basis for the present study and discussion on crime and policing. Wilson's classical approach, which emphasizes the traditional elements of the unity of action, division of labor, and centralization of authority, continues to serve as the benchmark for American police administration.

HUMAN RELATIONS AND PARTICIPATIVE MANAGEMENT, 1925 TO PRESENT

Basically, this model does not exist in any one department. It has some of the personnel thrust of the scientific management model and some of the democratization of the team policing approach and its variations.

The **human relations** approach considers the police executive to be a team leader who creates a cooperative effort among line officers through the use of a management team. In Maslow's terms, the police executive is a self-actualizing individual who helps fulfill the social security, self-esteem, and autonomy needs of the personnel in his or her police organization. As found in McGregor's Theory X and Theory Y approach, the manager is responsible for motivating personnel and developing talent. This is done organizationally by having the manager create opportunities and provide guidance so that all members can realize their potential in contributing to the organization. The theme here is that management should be group centered. According to Tannenbaum and Schmidt (1975), the manager would basically operate from two premises:

1. The manager defines limits within which the group makes decisions.
2. The manager and the group jointly make decisions within limits defined by organizational constraints.

The team policing approach, in theory, views the police manager acting as a *primus inter pares* (first among equals) rather than as a traditional autocratic administrator. The human relations approach is especially germane to the participatory management model where full-service and multispecialist teams operate with strong community commitment. In other words, team policing is an adaptation of McGregor's Theory Y to the field.

When we examine the components causing stress among police officers, the twin Maslow needs of autonomy and security come into play. Basically, the police officer needs to feel that he or she has the prospect of a promotion along a reasonable career line and that his or her job is relatively stable and free from potentially capricious management. Personnel grievance and promotion matters play as large a role in producing stress on the job as does the work on the streets. With the strong perception of danger and the need for alertness to deal with the unexpected in the field, police officers have a special drive and a need for security on the job. Participatory management, when applied correctly, may solve these problems. Traditional, autocratic scientific management often fails to deal with these human relations problems in a satisfactory manner.

Departmental participatory management models, in which mid-level and line personnel have an important say on how to address local crime problems, become an essential element of community policing, which is discussed in Chapter 8. What comes into play is the formation of a new working relationship between line officers and police administrators that reduces the traditional concept of centralized authority. Participatory management results in more individualized accountability to discipline and rewards. Allied to this is the term **empowerment**, which is commonly found in many police articles on participatory management. By definition, empowerment is a condition whereby employees have the authority to make decisions and to take action in their work areas without prior approval.

In recent years, there have been a number of organizational theory books that are modern versions of the 1930s' human relations school. Based on operations in large Japanese and Scandinavian corporations, many observers discuss the positive aspects of employee–management work teams. This includes the production of high-quality products and the creation of positive employee relations in a noncollective bargaining atmosphere. Theorists such as James March and Karl Weick have concluded that it is the informal structures that generally result in getting things done.

Popular in this vein were a series of "prescriptions" based on work by Tom Peters and coauthors (*In Search of Excellence: Lessons from America's Best Run Companies* (1982) and *A Passion for Excellence: The Leadership Difference* (1985)) that veer away from traditional management models and recommend people-oriented, humanistic systems as the basis for future national and international competition by U.S. businesses. Key terms such as "management by wandering around," "entrepreneurship," and "client satisfaction" are related to the traditional concepts of planning, forecasting, and budgeting based on the authors' observations of successful companies.

The successful companies discussed by the Peters group are primarily in the private sector, and some from their first book do not exist today. Among the key concepts that can be applied to police management is the idea of a **common culture**, where the mission of the organization is culturally shared between management and employees. The concept of a corporate culture is much like the concept of the police culture, which has been explored thoroughly by writers on policing.

The successful companies that were studies at that time, today have dealt with the hard realities of reorganization and downsizing, which have occurred in both corporate and public sector organizations that sought to decrease levels of middle management or to combine work sites to reduce operating and personnel costs. In the private sector, many multinational corporations have "farmed out" or "outsourced" the production of certain units of work to countries or nonunion concerns with lower wage rates. If anything, this trend has resulted in the establishment of smaller business enterprises and the demise of worker loyalty to the norms and values of common culture found in large companies.

Allied with the participative management model is the concept of quality teams or project teams created by management to address a certain problem. This forms the basis of total quality management (TQM), which uses the participative approach among employees to improve products or service. These concepts are also discussed in Chapter 3. It is important to note that companies using these approaches retain, for the most part, the traditional hierarchy model.

Both management and employees are brought into this corporate culture through vigorous training, constant employee recognition, and reform of organization processes that have a negative impact on employee performance. As discussed in Chapter 2, the police occupational subculture can be used in a positive manner to achieve organizational goals.

BEHAVIORAL MANAGEMENT, 1945 TO PRESENT, AND SYSTEMS MANAGEMENT, 1960 TO PRESENT

These approaches have had their most significant impact in the areas of fiscal organization, day-to-day budgeting, and short- and long-range planning. Although often seen as competing with the human relations approach, as both systems have evolved in the 1980s, the systems–behavioral management approach complements much of the human relations approach, having developed mechanisms for accountability as it integrated quantitative measures for both fiscal and human behavior goals.

A behavioral goal has three major components:

1. A goal stated in an empirical manner so that any ordinary person would be able to see, hear, taste, smell, or feel something
2. A criterion of success that is normally less than 100 percent
3. A context in which to measure the goal developed in empirical terms

Here are two examples:

> The patrol officer will increase the time spent on foot patrol each shift by one hour from his or her radio car. The location and time is to be based on the crime situation of the community. Time is to be logged as special foot patrol and will be exclusive of routine property and business area checks. (A realistic goal is to attempt an increase in preventive patrol, apprehension, and community relations.)
>
> The investigator shall interview on an average three to five suspects for every 40-hour tour of duty and shall document these interviews in a written report within one 8-hour tour of duty of the documented end of each interview. (This would constitute an increase in the productivity of an officer whose main duties consist of such interviews.)

Where possible, such behavioral objectives can develop into excellent tools of accountability for management. However, there is a risk of creating goals that are too detailed and involve an inordinate amount of paperwork compared with the amount needed to get the job done.

Proponents of the systems–behavioral approach developed a number of systems for accountability, forward planning, and fiscal organization:

1. Management by objectives (MBO)
2. Program evaluation and review techniques (PERT)
3. Programming, planning, and budgeting (PPB)
4. Organizational development (OD)
5. Zero-based budgeting (ZBB)

The various approaches will be reviewed in the appropriate chapters.

Community Policing, Problem-Solving Policing, and Intelligence-Led Policing

Community policing, which involves the community in police decision making on general policy affecting the community and crime, continues to be a widely used approach in theory. It incorporates problem-solving policing, which attempts to solve specific crime problems in the community. Along with these two approaches is what has been called the "broken windows" approach, which attempts to improve a neighborhood in terms of trash pickup, clean streets, good lighting, and so on. These approaches were funded with millions of dollars and are used throughout the nation. A new approach is intelligence-led policing, which focuses on the criminal and crime analysis. These approaches are described in the patrol chapter (Chapter 8) and incorporate many of the elements of proactive policing.

PROACTIVE POLICE MANAGEMENT, 1980 TO PRESENT

The **proactive** approach is the focus of this book. Various aspects of this approach are discussed throughout the chapters and reviewed in detail. However, the most significant elements can be outlined here:

1. Objective of policing is crime prevention
2. Strong commitment to community involvement
3. Modern bureaucracy, range of control techniques
4. Full-service department with multispecialist teams
5. Full use of modern communication models (both technological/computer and human relations techniques)
6. Modern budgeting and accounting systems in full use
7. Great emphasis on forward emergency and crisis management planning
8. Consultative management approach (all elements of organization consulted; management team makes final decisions and organizes the implementation of policy decisions)
9. Data-driven department with optimal use of modern technology
10. Emphasis on art of the possible and operational utility of management approaches

Scholars who advocate this approach in their work with community policing include James Q. Wilson, Robert Trojanowicz, George Kelling, and Herman Goldstein. Police managers who serve as recognized leaders in the proactive approach are Lee Brown, former head of the Houston and New York City police departments and former head of the Police Foundation; David Couper, former chief of the Madison, Wisconsin, Police Department; Steven Bishop, former chief of Kansas City; and William Bratton, Chief of the Los Angeles Police Department.

William Bratton

William Bratton started as a patrol officer in the Boston, Massachusetts, Police Department, and attained the rank of superintendent in 1980, the highest ranking position. He was awarded the Boston Police Department's highest medal for valor, which he earned by facing down a bank robber and rescuing a hostage in 1975.

From 1990 to 1992, he served as chief of the New York City Transit Police. He was instrumental in merging the Transit Police and New York City's Housing Police with the New York City Police Department (NYPD). In 1993, he was elected president of the Police Executive Research Forum and was commissioner of the Boston Police (1993–1994). As New York City police commissioner from 1994 to 1996, he was responsible for reengineering the NYPD by decentralizing responsibility to New York City's 76 precinct commanders and institutionalizing Compstat. (See Chapter 7 for a description of Compstat.)

Doing this resulted in crime dropping dramatically in New York City while the quality of life improved. In the past, he indicated, the department was too reactive, too centralized. He discovered that random patrol did not scare criminals. His major goals were to reduce fear in the neighborhoods and to prevent crime from happening. In the previous 20 years, "the Department had focused on arrest numbers." Using reengineering, a corporation model, he created 12 task forces to shake up the department to deal with overall crime reduction, which should be the major product of any police department.

He also took the concept of "broken windows" to heart and states how pleased he was with increasing the quality of life and disorder control. He embraced community policing and problem solving as major efforts in dealing with the community in individual precincts. He sends a clear message for one of the major goals of community policing: "Police can return to the role for which we were invented: preventing crime. . . . Police can control behavior with crime prevention" (Anonymous, 2000: 2). According to Bratton, the NYPD must work in partnership with the community through precinct councils and precinct commanders (Bratton and Knobler, 1998).

The crime-patrol planning model Compstat was his major success when he was commissioner of the NYPD. Compstat is based on four major principles:

1. Timely, accurate intelligence: He emphasized that old information did not work; only up-to-date information worked.
2. Rapid response: He gives an example of target hardening a site to stop terrorists from blowing it up, in other words, crime prevention.
3. Effective tactics: To stop drug dealers, for example, the focus should be on a place where there have been a great number of shootings.
4. Relentless follow-up: Review programs and strategies and keep them updated.

Under Commissioner Howard Safire, who took over from Bratton, the system that Bratton had put in place has, for the most part, been working very well. From 1996 to 1998, the crime rates continued their dramatic downward trend. Commissioner Bratton used these concepts in Los Angeles, where he was appointed in 2002. Today he also serves as consultant and media spokesperson on national and global police issues. In December 2012 he was once again appointed as Commissoner for New York City.

Lee P. Brown

Lee Brown began his career in 1960 as a patrol officer in San Jose, California. He was sheriff of Mulnomah County, Oregon; commissioner of public safety in Atlanta; chief of the Houston Police Department, 1982–1990; New York City police commissioner, 1990–1992; and director of national drug policy, 1993–1995. He held a cabinet position in the federal government and became the first African American mayor of Houston in 1998.

The son of farmworkers, Lee Brown earned a bachelor's degree from Fresno State University, a master's degree from San Jose State University, and a PhD from the University of California at Berkeley in 1970. He was a professor at Texas Southern University and Rice University.

> While he was chief of the Houston Police Department, Brown initiated one of the early models of community policing, which he called neighborhood-oriented policing (NOP). He wanted to involve citizens directly with the police. He wanted to change the police officer from an enforcer of neighborhood beats to an officer who would become involved with problem solving with the community (Oettmeier and Brown, 1988).

The beats were redesigned to conform to neighborhoods, and beat officers were permanently assigned to specific neighborhoods. Some investigation was decentralized. Police supervisors and managers were encouraged to support beat officers in solving neighborhood problems. The deterrence of crime became the criteria for evaluating the beat officer. This meant that there should be less crime, traffic accidents, and calls for service because the beat officers were solving problems.

In New York City, Commissioner Brown continued with his philosophy of community policing, initiating problem-oriented policing (POP). He claims that his earlier work with community policing with NYPD set the stage for the success of Compstat and the crime-attack planning model.

Raymond W. Kelly

Raymond Kelly is the first person to serve twice as police commissioner of New York City: 37th commissioner, 1992–1994, and 41st commissioner, 2002 to present. Based on the experiences of the World Trade Center bombings, the department has focused on terrorism from a city and worldwide perspective. Over 1,000 detectives are specifically assigned for counterterrorism and NYPD personnel are stationed in major cities around the world. During the 2004 Madrid terrorist bombings and 2005 London bombings, NYPD detectives arrived there within a day. In 2007, under Commissioner Kelly's leadership, NYPD issued a report on homegrown terrorism that showed the various steps in radicalizing a person into a terrorist.

Commissioner Kelly holds several degrees, including a Master of Laws degree from New York University and a Master in Business Administration from the Kennedy School at Harvard. He graduated first in his class from the NYPD Police Academy in 1960. By 1990 he was promoted to deputy commissioner under Lee Brown. As the 37th commissioner, he emphasized crime reduction and quality-of-life issues such as eliminating "squeegee men" annoying drivers and improving the quality of life in neighborhoods, which became a hallmark of community policing. Upon the election of Rudolf Giuliani in 1994, William Bratton became commissioner, replacing Kelly.

After his first stint as commissioner, he served in a number of federal and international capacities. From 1996 to 1998, as U.S. Undersecretary for Enforcement at Treasury, his duties included supervising the U.S. Customs; the Secret Service; Bureau of Alcohol, Tobacco, and Fire Arms; and other federal police services. He also served as the director of the International Police Monitors in Haiti and was commissioner for Customs for the United States from 1998 to 2001. He also retired as colonel from the Marine Corps Reserves after 30 years of service, including service in the Vietnam War.

Kelly was reappointed Commissioner by Mayor Blumburg. During his second tenure, there were a number of controversies including the use of aggressive arrest and use of force tactics at the Republican National Convention in 2004. At this time, he is a vocal proponent on the use of "stop and frisk" by officers as a means of controlling street crime and illegal gun use. In New York State, police officers can stop a person and then conduct a pat-down of the person if there is probable cause to believe that the person might be carrying a weapon. This practice is widely condemned by many civil rights and community groups as it is viewed as being disproportionately used against persons of color. For the mayoral elections of November 2013, Kelly stepped down and was replaced by William Bratton, who had also served as commissioner before Kelly.

Conclusion

The history of police management is an evolving field of study. Every theoretical approach offers something of operational and theoretical use to the modern police executive. The secret of success is to select and synthesize the approaches that will work for a particular department, given its specific problems and political context. The proactive approach is meant to be flexible and utilitarian yet adheres to principles that will give coherence to police management as it responds in the world of the twenty-first century. The proactive model, of course, incorporates many of the previous schools of theory presented, including community-oriented policing (COP), POP, and TQM, which are being applied to police operations today.

Police management evolved from the rather rigid (semimilitary) organizational model of the late nineteenth century to a more flexible approach that emphasizes human relations skills. Proactive police managers who have been professionally trained and college educated synthesize contributions from all periods of police management.

From the traditional model, these managers develop a finely honed sense of bureaucratic organization. The organization itself has to be created, and this means the creation of a hierarchical organization. The scientific management period focused on goals and the placing of these goals in organizational context. O.W. Wilson and William H. Parker adapted the basic bureaucratic model from Max Weber to make Weber's model functional in today's communication-sophisticated society. The approach depends on having a central organization along with the ability to respond rapidly to ordinary as well as unusual crises.

Although the human relations approach tended to overemphasize the importance of democratic management, its emphasis on the vital importance of human relations and personnel skills contributed significantly to modern police administration. One finding from this movement is the recognition of the need for training in human relations skills for both middle managers and supervising personnel. Besides having a good sense of leadership and organization, sergeants and lieutenants must be able to persuade police officers to do their jobs with the utmost efficiency. Sergeants especially are important to the morale and the optimal use of personnel.

Our modern manager grounds himself or herself in behavioral reality by utilizing the contribution of the behavioral management movement. After becoming firmly grounded in achievable practical behavioral objectives, the police organization can adopt the proactive police community management model of anticipation and the forward planning needed in all aspects of police management: personnel, fiscal, community, and operations.

Questions for Review

1. Discuss the basic principles of the following managerial models: traditional, scientific, human relations, behavioral, systems, and proactive.
2. Explain the significance of the following individuals to police management: Sir Robert Peel, Frederick Taylor, Theodore Roosevelt, O.W. Wilson, William H. Parker, William Bratton, Lee Brown, and Raymond Kelly.
3. Discuss the contributions of the English police system to the American system of policing.
4. Explain why the American system of policing has evolved into the existing complex structure of overlapping authorities and jurisdictions.

Class Project

History provides a useful means to understand the current state of a community or organization. Review the history of a local or state police department and list the major benchmarks of the department's development. Departments in large cities have formal department histories that are found in books or journals and are often available on the Internet. In some cases, interviewing the senior officer of a local department provides an interesting oral history.

Web Works

There are a number of Web sites that have information on police operations and management. Many students first look up Google; while a good first step, Google often has a number of sites with undocumented opinions and data. What follows are the main Web sites for the U.S. Department of Justice. Most federal agencies can also be found by typing in their abbreviations followed by ".gov," such as fbi.gov for the Federal Bureau of Investigation. Many departments and organizations also participate on Facebook and Twitter.

The main site for the Department of Justice is usdoj.gov, which gives you access to other DOJ Web sites:

Bureau of Justice Assistance	ojp.usdoj.gov/bja
Bureau of Justice Statistics	ojp.usdoj.gov/bjs
Enforcement Education	ojp.usdoj.gov/opclee
Federal Bureau of Investigation	fbi.gov
National Criminal Justice Reference Service	ncjrs.org
National Institute of Justice	ojp.usdoj.gov/nij
National Law Enforcement and Corrections Technology Center	nlectc.org
Office of Community Oriented Police Services	cops.usdoj.gov
Office of Juvenile Justice and Delinquency Prevention Programs	ojjdp.ncjrs.org
Office of Police Corps and Law	ojp.usdoj.gov/opclee

References

Anonymous. On Patrol Web site (onpatrol.com/brantin/html), January 26, 2000.

Berman, J.S. *Police Administration and Progessive Reform: Theodore Roosevelt as Police Commissioner of New York*. New York: Greenwood Press, 1987.

Blau, Peter M., and Marshall W. Meyer. *Bureaucracy in Modern Society* (2nd ed.). New York: Random House, 1971.

Bratton, William, and Peter Knobler. *How America's Top Cop Reversed the Crime Epidemic*. New York: Random House, 1998.

Brown, Lee P. *Community Policing: A Practical Guide for Police Officials*. Washington, D.C.: National Institute of Justice, 1989.

Brown, Lee P., and Mary Ann Wycoff. "Policing Houston: Recycling Fear and Improving Service." *Crime and Delinquency*, 35 (January 1986), pp. 71–89.

————. "Policing Houston." In Larry Sherman et al., eds., *Preventing Crime*. College Park, Md.: University of Maryland, 1997.

Fosdick, Raymond B. *European Police Systems*. Montclair, N.J.: Patterson Smith, 1915, reprinted 1969.

————. *American Police Systems*. Montclair, N.J.: Patterson Smith, 1920, reprinted 1969.

Gazell, James A. "O.W. Wilson's Essential Legacy for Police Administrators." *Journal of Police Science and Administration*, 2, no. 4 (December 1974), pp. 365–375.

————. "William H. Parker, Police Professionalism and the Public: An Assessment." *Journal of Police Science and Administration*, 4, no. 1 (March 1976), pp. 28–37.

Graper, Elmer D. *American Police Administration*. Montclair, N.J.: Patterson Smith, 1921, reprinted 1969.

International City Managers Association. *Municipal Police Administration*. Chicago: International City Managers Association, 1943, reprinted 1969.

New York City Police Department. Administration— Police Commissioner, Raymond W. Kelly. Web posted at nyc.gov/html/administration/headquarters_co. shtml. Accessed November 29, 2013

Nigro, Felix A., and Lloyd G. Nigro. *Modern Public Administration* (3rd ed.). New York: Harper and Row, 1973.

Oettmeier, T.N., and L.P. Brown. "Role Expectations and the Concept of Neighborhood-Oriented Police." In *Development of Neighborhood Oriented Policing*. Arlington, Va.: International Association of Chiefs of Police, 1988.

Peters, Thomas J., and Nancy Austin. *A Passion for Excellence: The Leadership Difference*. New York: Random House, 1985.

Peters, Thomas J., and Robert H. Waterman. *In Search of Excellence: Lessons from America's Best Run Companies*. New York: Harper and Row, 1982.

Reith, Charles. *A New Study of Police History*. Edinburgh: Oliver and Boyd, 1956.

————. *The Blind Eye of History*. Montclair, N.J.: Patterson Smith, 1952, reprinted 1975.

Rosen, Marie Simonetti. "A LEN Interview with Commissioner Bratton of New York." *Law Enforcement News*, June 30, 1995, pp. 8–10, 14.

Schultz, Dorothy. "Law Enforcement Leaders: A Survey of Women Police Chiefs in the United States." *Police Chief* (March 2002), pp. 25–28.

Smith, Bruce. *Police Systems in the United States*. New York: Harper and Row, 1940, revised 1960.

Tannenbaum, R., and W.H. Schmidt. "How to Choose a Leadership Pattern." *Harvard Business Review* (March/April 1958), p. 36; reprinted in *Business Classics: Fifteen Key Concepts for Managerial Success*. Cambridge, Mass.: Harvard University Press, 1975.

Trojanowicz, Robert, et al. *Community Policing: A Contemporary Perspective* (2nd ed.). Cincinnati: Anderson, 1998.

Vollmer, August. *The Police and Modern Society*. Montclair, N.J.: Patterson Smith, 1936, reprinted 1970.

Wilson, O.W. *Police Administration* (2nd ed.). New York: McGraw Hill, 1963.

2   Police Culture

KEY TERMS

argot

blue minority

coop

culture

cynicism

esoteric knowledge

gemeinschaft

gesellschaft

Guardians

hook

horse

informal structure

main man

meat eater

National Association of Women Law
   Enforcement Executives (NAWLEE)

peer group

police personality types

Postulates of Invisibility

rabbi

role entrapment

secrecy

social isolation

solidarity

subculture

tin

Uncle Tom

Police management operates within the context of one of the strongest vocational subcultures existing in American society. In this chapter, we have two objectives. First, we are going to look at the police subculture and examine its effect on day-to-day business and on police managers. Then we will consider the informal organization that exists in all police departments and that all managers must reckon with. The informal organization can be used to increase effectiveness and efficiency, or it can be turned to managerial sabotage.

THE CONCEPT: POLICE SUBCULTURE

Culture means many things to many people, but common components that come into play in the context of this textbook include morals, customs, and norms.

The police, although part of the American culture, form a distinctive **subculture** because of characteristics of their particular vocation: law enforcement.

A subculture is "a group that shares in the overall culture of the society but also has its own distinctive values, norms, and lifestyle" (Robertson, 1987: 76). Police subculture has its own set of cultural norms. Robertson defines *norms* as "shared rules or guidelines that proscribe the behavior appropriate in a given situation" (1987: 62). These norms create a lifestyle for a police officer both on and off the job. The traditional major norms of the police subculture are **secrecy**, **solidarity**, and **social isolation** that define the subculture.

Secrecy

Police deal with people's valuable reputations, which can be destroyed by routine police investigations. A school official might be the target of an investigation in which a young woman was raped in a van. Any public knowledge of the investigation can destroy the official's reputation, even if the investigation is proved to have been unfounded. Many months can go into a drug investigation. Talking about the investigation, even to a spouse, means jeopardizing lives. In his book on police culture, Crank (2004: 276) writes that the code of secrecy is an important element in police organizations. "Those who violate the principles of secrecy may encounter ostracism, loss of friends and a shortage of back up in dangerous street encounters," he stated.

Solidarity

The officer is part of a police family. The children are police children. The spouse is a police wife or a police husband. Police officers stick together. They protect the brother and sister officer from a hostile public and from their own brass. The operating norm is "You are never alone."

Social Isolation

The perception of a hostile public is part of what makes police officers feel alone (Shernock, 1988). Officers carry a gun and arrest people. They know they can trust a cop but never an outsider. Every day, officers deal with the underclass in society—people who steal, drunks and drug dealers, people who sell dope to children, and child molesters who prey on the weak and innocent. Police officers are doing "dirty work." This is work that deals with an undesirable population. Officers in the public eye can take on the stigma of that population. So the officer's friends and family are other cops and people in the "business."

This is a theme that runs through most contemporary texts on police. For example, in *Contemporary Municipal Policing*, McCamey et al. (2003: 167–68) write, "Thus police officers tend to socialize with other police officers . . . their identities as police officers sometimes make them socially unacceptable even when off-duty. . . . Thus, officers tend to divide the world between 'us' and 'them,' the former consisting of other police officers, the latter encompassing most everybody else." Kappler et al. (2005: 236) write about the police worldview, which they note is also an occupational "self-perception that is internalized." They write that the world is often viewed as those who are police officers and those who are not. Many police officers are unaware of the cultural norms that affect their daily lives. Still, all officers have to take these norms into account—for example, the role of secrecy, the norms of police unity and loyalty, and the perception of danger and suspicion that pervades this subculture.

CHARACTERISTICS OF THE POLICE SUBCULTURE

A. B. Hollingshead has given us the basic definition of a vocational subculture and its major characteristics (Arnold, 1970: 22): "a group of specialists recognized by society, as well as by themselves, who possess an identifiable complex of common culture, values, communication devices (argot or other symbols), techniques, and appropriate behavior patterns." Two forces in American society have a monopoly on the use of legal force: (1) the armed forces concerning outside threats and (2) the law enforcement community concerning internal social control. The police department is a human service agency that specializes in the use of legitimate force and is recognized as such by law. The police themselves make a great distinction between those who have a "tin" and those who are civilians. Those who have a piece of **tin**—that is, a police badge—are sworn police officers and have the right to carry a gun.

Argot

Police officers in every region of the nation have developed an **argot** (specialized vocabulary of a profession) that is generally not shared by outsiders. This stems, in part, from the nature of normal communication between officers. Police officers spend considerable time riding in patrol cars or patrolling on foot with portable radios and cell phones. They are also continually involved with their state's penal law and department operating codes. Much of police argot revolves around (1) citations to the penal law, (2) words and phrases that are coded and phrased so that they can be heard without ambiguity over a radio, and (3) criminal and street jargon laced liberally with obscenities.

Examples of argot from the major police forces have become well known. In the New York City Police Department (NYPD), officers may have a **rabbi** (a highly placed police official) who can help them out if they get caught cooping (sleeping on duty). In other departments, the rabbi might be called a **hook** or a **horse**. Argot from the black community also creeps in, such as when a rabbi becomes a **main man**.

Esoteric Knowledge

Hollingshead's second major characteristic of a vocational subculture is an excellent description of what researchers refer to as the transition from the police academy recruit to police officer, which he calls "the acquisition by initiates of the body of **esoteric knowledge** and appropriate behavior patterns before the novices are accepted by the initiated" (Arnold, 1970: 22). Today the recruit police academy spends hundreds of hours teaching such subjects as firearms, law, unarmed combat, preservation of a crime scene, and basic investigation techniques. Today, increasing time is being spent on human relations, family crisis intervention, and other human service subjects, such as child and drug abuse. The objective of the police academy, over and above teaching basic knowledge and skills, is to instill into the recruit an acceptance of the police role model. This means an acceptance of both the formal and informal codes and discipline making up a police officer.

Cynicism

In his classic work *Behind the Shield*, Arthur Niederhoffer (1969: 104) showed the stages of **cynicism** as the police recruit moves from the idealistic role models of the police academy to the street. The first stage, *pseudo-cynicism*, occurs at the training school/recruit level and is an attitude that "barely conceals the idealism and commitment beneath the surface." The second stage, *romantic cynicism*, comes within the first five years of an officer's career. The third stage, *aggressive cynicism*, is evident at the 10-year mark, when "resentment and hostility become obvious." At this stage, Niederhoffer talks about a subculture of cynicism. The end of the police officer's career is what Niederhoffer calls *resigned cynicism*, when an officer accepts the flaws of the system. Forty years later, Van Brocklin (2009) advanced Niederhoffer's conclusions by looking at the medical consequences of sustained cynicism, calling it the *death of the spirit*. Interestingly, Van Brocklin also reflects on the positive side of cynicism, in that the perpetual distrust of the public that tends to develop in a police officer could also be a tool that helps that officer survive dangerous encounters.

Crank (2004: 275–76) summed up this approach in what he called **Postulates of Invisibility**:

1. Do not give up another cop. Regardless of the case . . . never provide information to the public or superior officers.
2. Watch out for your partner first and then for the rest of the shift . . . inform a fellow officer if he or she is being investigated by internal affairs.
3. If you get caught off base, do not implicate anybody else . . . do not involve other cops who might also be punished.
4. Hold up your end of the work. Malingering draws attention to everyone on the shift.
5. Do not suck up to the bosses for special favors.

Internal Sanctions

Hollingshead's final point on the characteristics of a vocational subculture focuses on the internal social control that helps describe how a police department's informal structure actually works (Arnold, 1970: 22): "Appropriate sanctions [are] applied by the membership to control members in their relations with one another and with the larger society and to control nonmembers in their relations with members." **Peer group** pressure concerning loyalty to the police profession is enormous and overwhelming. William Westley (1970), an earlier researcher in the sociology of the police, showed that the police in Gary, Indiana, would even be willing to perjure themselves to protect a brother officer. Although the research was done in the 1950s, the conclusions hold for today's police culture. As a vocational subculture, police officers must depend on one another especially in dangerous situations, Terrill, Paoline, and Manning (2003) revisited this subject with a multiagency analysis of the coercive nature of police culture. Interestingly, they found police officers fit into several different attitudinal areas, rather than just one standard "culture," with respective agency leadership playing a significant role in that culture.

Solidarity

As has been shown, there is a great deal of pressure for conformity among police officers. Reiser (1974: 138) considers peer influence to be "one of the most profound pressures operating in police organizations." He shows how it functions: "It bolsters and supports the individual officer's esteem and confidence, which then allows him to tolerate higher levels of anger, hostility and abuse from external sources." Reiser, who served as department psychologist for the Los Angeles Police Department (LAPD), has pointed out an important factor concerning peer pressure: It can be a positive force in the life of the individual police officer. One of the most profound statements that any police officer can make is that he or she is never alone once having become a sworn officer. On the job, the call for "officer in trouble" will mean that officers in and outside the immediate vicinity will normally drop what they are doing and rush to that officer's aid. Even officers who are off duty will feel compelled to come to that officer's aid, even from a distance. Reiser stresses the cost of this group support (1974: 138): the "loss of autonomy in the areas of values and attitudes." It seems that group values become shared while there is a great deal of rationalization created to support conformity to the police group.

The importance of common sense was further discussed by Sever (2008), including the imposing role that culture and police subculture play on decision making and the development of what is considered to be common sense in policing.

The most frequent example of this feeling of unity, besides the officer-in-trouble call and the need for backup in potentially dangerous situations, is probably seen in the area of professional courtesy. Professional courtesy is normally not discussed in textbooks and articles, but it is practiced every day in police forces. When civilians are stopped for a traffic infraction, they expect a traffic citation. When police officers are stopped, they do not expect a traffic ticket; they expect to be let go because of professional courtesy. When professional courtesy does not occur, it is a story carried from jurisdiction to jurisdiction and can lead to a feud between police officers in two different jurisdictions.

When a police officer has an automobile breakdown, he or she does not necessarily call a garage mechanic but may, in fact, call the nearest police department or highway patrol. Help from the local officers may range from driving the officer to a good garage that will give special service and rates to police to having the police mechanic fix the private auto while the stranded officer has coffee with the other officers. With the evolution of policing accountability and higher ethical standards, however, such practices as these are growing increasingly unacceptable, resulting in internal investigations and sanctions. Wambaugh addressed this long overdue cultural change in policing in his novel, *Hollywood Station* (2006), which finds the police officers in the story often afraid to make decisions for fear of the *Monday morning quarterbacking* of those decisions by supervisors, internal affairs, the media, and the public.

THE ULTIMATE SYMBOL OF SOLIDARITY: THE POLICE FUNERAL   This is based on "Good-by in a Sea of Blue" (Lord et al., 2004: 353–63) and refers to officers killed in the line of duty. "Being a cop is solidarity personified. A cop killing rolls through a sea of blue like a tidal wave," they state.

In a funeral given to an officer, police officers gather from jurisdictions across America, standing together rank on rank with a black ribbon over the top of their badge. They are there, in person, to honor their blood comrade, a fallen officer, with the most powerful religious and national symbols in the country in a rigidly formal ceremony. They are there to show, in a public ceremony, every person in America the might and power of law enforcement, the thin blue line: Bagpipes and drums play "Amazing Grace" and "Taps" while the officer is surrounded by hundreds of flags; there is a 21-gun salute; wreaths bear the badge number of the fallen officer; police motorcycles escort the coffin; and major roads are closed.

Social Isolation

Most researchers concerned with police culture agree that police are isolated from the rest of American society (Clark, 1965; Skolnick, 1966; Tauber, 1967; Westley, 1970; Savitz, 1971). A typical response to the question: "What do you do for a living?" in a social gathering often evokes this "hazy" response if you are the only police officer in a social gathering.

When asked at a party what he or she does, the police officer often says that he is a government worker. When pressed, the officer may walk away. Why does this happen? As many officers have said, "If I tell them that I am a cop, they'll want to give me a hard time about some traffic ticket they got. Next will come some bull concerning police corruption and then they'll hold me personally responsible for some court letting some killer loose on the street. What do you want me to do, spoil all the parties I go to that have civilians there, spoil these parties for myself and my wife? It's really better if you stick to your own." And stick to their own, they do. There are police bars, police picnics, and police poker parties. From these and other social activities dominated by fellow officers and their family, police officers create a feeling that each one of them is part of the **blue minority**. This social isolation has made many police officers consider themselves a persecuted minority. Stan Shernock surveyed 11 police departments and concluded, "As a result of police perception of public hostility toward them, police officers have assumed many of the characteristics of a minority group" (1988: 184). Shernock showed, as Westley did in the 1950s, that police socialize almost exclusively with police. Since Westley did his research, there have been no changes in the fundamental police norms of secrecy, solidarity, and social isolation, despite law enforcement's many advances. Wasilewski and Olson (2010) wrote that not only does police isolation impact negatively on the officer, largely due to the imbalance of the day-to-day experiences unique to the profession, but that same isolation also has a bearing on the community and ultimately the police mission. Even with significant advances in the educational levels of police officers of all ranks, minority hiring, and fast-paced technological advances, the police are still a blue minority with slow-to-change subcultural norms.

Perception of Violence and Psychological Distance

There is a positive functional aspect to this social isolation, and that is the need for psychological distance between the police officer and many of his or her clients.

When a teacher becomes too involved emotionally with students, the job becomes untenable because he or she is not able to make objective judgments. The same thing can happen to a police officer. Police are not always dealing with citizens of goodwill who are unafraid, calm, and friendly. Sometimes they have to deal with drunken drivers who throw up on their uniforms and urinate in the backseat of their patrol car.

Picture yourself going into a low-income neighborhood on what is called "mother's day," the day when welfare checks arrive in the mail. Here is an actual incident. Two officers answered the call for a domestic dispute. Using good police procedure, they separated the shouting husband and wife, one to the living room and one to the kitchen. The wife was shouting to the officers that her husband tried to beat her up. Her language was obscene, as was her husband's. Both had been drinking alcohol.

The officers returned to the living room and positioned themselves between the husband and wife to try to calm them down. The wife took out a small-caliber handgun and managed to fire a shot at her husband. She was disarmed and taken to police headquarters, but both officers never forgot that incident.

In another case, one of the authors of this book was responding to a domestic dispute call. He approached the front door of the house and promptly encountered a loaded shotgun being thrust into his body. The homeowner explained that he didn't want the officer on his property. After a good deal of talk, the shotgun was withdrawn, and the fight was dealt with. But the author will never forget the incident.

Dr. John Stratton, former director of psychological services for the Los Angeles County sheriff's office, shows what happens to officers who are involved in traumatic events, such as killing another human being. Roughly one-third develop major problems that affect their family, and they may leave the profession because of the trauma; about one-third have moderate problems, such as waking up screaming at night, but they recover; and about one-third have minimal problems (Stratton, 1984).

A number of police officers have put the situation this way: "You are at the scene of a fatal auto accident on a busy high-speed highway. Spread before you is a young person with a limb cut off, blood flowing across the highway, and guts spilled out. This person is dead, and there is an auto blocking traffic. You don't have time to gag; you have to save lives, you have to make sure there is a call for help, take care of any other injured, and direct traffic so that there are no more bodies spilled out on the highway." This is not a normal experience for a civilian, but it is a normal one for a police officer. You need to have objectivity and distance if you are to be able to go home at night, love your spouse, and hug your children.

Vincent E. Henry (2004), one of the creators of Compstat at NYPD, published a very intense and personal book titled *Death Work*, about officers dealing with death and the dead bodies of people who had their lives cut short. The death of children who had lived in poverty and deplorable conditions was especially stressful. He shows how police solidarity is alive and well and is an important cultural norm of support for police officers.

> It takes time for new recruits to be accepted into police culture. At the same time, it can be devastating to confront your first murder, death from drugs, and so on. Henry noted that it takes time for relationships to develop amongst officers. Rookies often do not receive the full benefit of an established relationship with other officers, such as when one officer at a traumatic scene looks after the emotional needs of another.

Henry quotes officers about depression and despair, considering threats to their own mortality.

He gives us a feeling for the detectives in the Crime Scene Unit who witness death more frequently than any other NYPD unit. "They are possessed of a strong professional identity, a sense of connection to other unit members, [and] a powerful sense of personal and professional integrity . . ." (Henry, 2004: 201).

When a recruit joins the force, he or she can lose friends. The next person you arrest may be an old friend. The question is, "How are you going to keep your professional integrity and live with yourself?" The answer, more often than not, is to have few civilian friends. This is what it means to be a police officer and part of an isolated vocational subculture in America.

INFORMAL GROUP STRUCTURES IN POLICE ORGANIZATIONS

Every organization has a formal and an **informal structure**. The formal structure involves the organization chart and lines of authority (e.g., police chief, deputy chief, inspectors, captains, lieutenants, sergeants, and police officers). Although official business is conducted by the formal organization, the informal structure often determines which decisions will be made and the manner in which these decisions will be carried out.

In policing, it is not just critical to establish intra-agency informal structure and lines of communication, but inter-agency, as well. Criminals and emergencies do not stay within designated police jurisdictional boundaries, so policing can't either. A good police leader knows that it is important to establish healthy working relationships with other agency personnel and leaders when the sea is calm, so that working together in times of need can be done more effectively. Roberts and Roberts (2006) conducted an extensive study on how police agency personnel interact informally, such as in sharing research on an issue faced by multiple agencies. Agency size and geographical nearness were found to play a significant role in inter-agency contacts.

Effective informal intra- and inter-agency structures are a reality that every manager has to be able to deal with if he or she is going to have a smooth, efficient police organization with high morale. This is the role of the social groups within the informal structure and the effect of these groups on the formal structure and the police manager's ability to manage. Light and Keller (1975: 184) give us a widely accepted definition of social groups: "A number of people who define themselves as members of a group; who expect certain behavior from members that they do not expect from outsiders; and who others (members and nonmembers) define as belonging to the group." Typical social groups that exist in and influence police in a police department include fraternal orders composed of officers; officers who play golf, racquetball, or cards together; and ethnic and extended kinship groups.

The Hawthorne Study

In the early 1920s and 1930s, under the leadership of Elton Mayo, the Harvard Business School conducted a series of research projects at the Hawthorne plant of the Western Electric Company (Roethlisberger and Dickson, 1939). Many observers refer to this as the beginning of the human relations approach to management. The key to this approach was the discovery of the informal organization and its communication system.

Management in one part of the Hawthorne plant tried to speed up the production of parts for telephone switches by placing the workers on a piece-rate system. Production did not change, even though the workers could have easily increased production. Researchers discovered informal work norms within the workers' group that placed social penalties on (1) "rate busters" who exceeded the work norm, (2) "chiselers" who did not fulfill the work norm, and (3) "squealers" who might have informed management of this system. This research on the informal structure has been replicated in many organizations both public and private, with much the same results.

The Work Community

We shall now look at a variety of groups within the police organization, such as informal cliques, ethnic and racial groups, and fraternal societies. All these make up what Drucker (1974: 281–84) calls the *work community*.

> According to Drucker, management is interested in making necessary decisions in relation to the mission of its business. He also states that management should not be making incidental decisions related to the work community and that these decisions can clog the organization's decision-making machinery. Decisions on such items as vacation schedule and cafeteria and recreation facilities should be decentralized and left to the work community. Although these decisions may not be of high priority, they are important and can be a means of fostering leadership opportunities for the worker. This is not a participatory democracy, for management organizes the working teams.

This is an approach that we recommend for modern, reality-based police managers. The officer on the street and his or her immediate supervisor have a great deal of responsibility. Peter Drucker's recommendation enables a police management even today to tie this commitment to discretion and responsibility to quality work. As discussed in Chapters 3 and 8, this concept was reinvented in the 1990s for "quality circles" and work teams for community-oriented and problem-oriented policing. However, this requires a precise knowledge of the law enforcement work community and the informal norms and social groups that govern much of this community.

Social scientists, business psychologists, and personnel managers have been studying this informal group structure for many years. A basic concept that they use is that of the primary group as it operates in the secondary or formal organization. This concept must be understood to use it to analyze police organization and how it really operates on a daily basis.

The Effect of the Primary Group on Police Bureaucracy

In the primary group, communication is normally

Deep and extensive

Face-to-face

Intimate

Relaying a sense of belonging

A response to a whole person rather than to a fragmented social role

In addition, the primary group assumes many of the characteristics of what Max Weber calls a **gemeinschaft** group, where there is a high degree of cohesion and the group is often perceived as an enlarged kinship (e.g., when male officers speak of their partners as if they were talking about their spouses).

As enlarged on in Chapter 4, which examines bureaucracy, secondary organizations are normally

- Impersonal
- Formal

Communications are also impersonal and formal, and relations are based on specialized roles. This is what Max Weber calls **gesellschaft**, and that is the modern corporate bureaucracy that is found at the core of many police structures.

Primary groups include the family, personal friends, neighborhood social groups, and people who play friendly card games on a regular basis. Examples of secondary organizations are civil service, organized religion, local government, and military groups.

These secondary organizations normally operate as classical bureaucracies with hierarchical sets of offices and chains of command. As Niederhoffer (1969: 11) states, "Large urban police departments are bureaucracies. Members of the force lose their bearings in the labyrinth of hierarchy, specialization, competitive examinations, red tape, promotions based on seniority and impersonality."

Members of the public discover that they have encountered a bureaucracy in such instances as obtaining an accident report or attempting to find out the status of a case in which they were a witness or a complainant. They are dealt with courteously but impersonally, and the correct form must always be filled out. Although officers in smaller agencies tend to be generalists, offering the entire range of police services, bureaucracy occurs in the smaller setting for the same reason as in the larger urban department.

It is in this impersonal setting that primary groups grow and have a profound influence on organizational life. To feel that he or she is a total human being, the police officer needs roots in the security of a primary group setting within the organization. Primary groups provide the following for individual members:

- Personal development
- Sense of security
- Sense of well-being
- Sense of being accepted for one's self
- Sense of sustaining one's identity and defining that identity

Primary groups are powerful, supportive mechanisms maintaining a sense of personal identity and security for the individual. They become of major significance for the police manager who recognizes the importance of informal police groups in sustaining morale. The role of primary groups in the police bureaucracy may be to

- Support or undermine the formal police organization
- Form a powerful informal police structure
- Have a mediating function, binding the individual to the larger police organization
- Have a major role in creating social stability in the police organization and in society in general

Generally, these primary groups form around a community of shared experience and proximity. The members of the same police academy class or those who work in the same squad may become members of the same social group. Those who grew up in the same neighborhoods form groups. In larger departments, Irish, Italian, German, Jewish, and African American social groups may pressure management in many subtle and not-so-subtle ways to have their policies promoted or their group protected or enhanced. The NYPD, for example, has the Emerald Society (Irish), the Columbus Society (Italian), and an influential organization of African American police officers.

Besides shared experiences, there is often a core of officers who plan group activities and encourage new officers to join. Finally, there are often family ties within and without the group. In relation to the secondary police organization, we must examine the group's informal ties to top management. Is the chief or deputy chief a former member of the group? Does the chief have a relative or close friend in the group? Answers to these kinds of questions often determine who will get an assignment, who will get a promotion, and whose policy will be adopted by the department. This kind of information is simply not available in an organization chart. These organizations may also determine productivity. Officers do not want their colleagues to be rate busters, chiselers, or squealers to management.

In one case, a state trooper assigned to traffic duty on a major Interstate highway decided to be a rate buster. He issued three times the number of traffic citations that other officers were issuing at that same duty station. Many of the other officers talked to him, but he replied that he would not change and that he thought that his high rate of citations was just part of doing the job. After a few months, most of his fellow officers would not talk to him. His superiors praised him officially for his work but indicated informally that he might have overdone it as a rate buster. Everyone at the station was relieved when he was transferred.

POLICE PEER NORMS

Secrecy, solidarity, and social isolation are the major police norms. They are fiercely strong and have been documented time and again (Niederhoffer, 1969; Westley, 1970; Blumberg and Niederhoffer, 1985; Balkin, 1988; Shernock, 1988; Peak, 1993). Shernock's report on 11 police departments (1988: 185) showed that secrecy "maintained group identity and supports solidarity." He added a curious footnote: When he asked if the police officers would turn in another officer for illegal behavior, "as many respondents pointed out to the researcher, they possibly 'should' but 'would not' take the aforementioned actions against fellow officers" (1988: 193).

Discussing internal police norms in his book *Walking the Beat*, Radano (1968: 13) presented a discussion of the coop, which was a hiding place to rest while on patrol.

What is obvious from the rest of his discussion is that the **coop** is an out-of-sight place for officers shirking their duties and that the officers who know about the coop are under considerable pressure not to inform management of its existence. On coming into the coop, the rookie realizes that he is becoming accepted as a member of the line officer police group.

Savitz (1971) documents Westley's finding of strong interpersonal police loyalty in the face of citizen hostility and as a self-protection society of line officers against the brass.

In his book, *Walking with the Devil: The Police Code of Conduct*, Quinn (2005) makes a good point in that almost all police officers are ethically sound, and wouldn't even contemplate illicit behavior, but for some reason, many would tolerate other officers breaking the rules without reporting them. This is The Code of Silence, which Quinn describes as, "the singularly most powerful influence on police behavior in the world" (p. 4).

Police Corruption and Internal Norms

Another source of information about internal police norms and pressure involves police corruption and police abuses. Some of the classic reports and studies are from the Wickersham Commission (National Commission, 1931); Smith's *The Tarnished Badge* (1965); the report on that famous organized crime town in Pennsylvania, Wincanton (Gardiner, 1965); Chevigny's "ride-around" view of police abuses, *Police Power* (1969); Stark's study based on newspaper clippings, *Police Riots* (1972); the well-known Knapp Commission report (1972), which came about as a result of an NYPD officer courageously breaking the *Code of Silence*, reporting systemic corruption at multiple levels within the agency in the late 1950s and early 1960s. Details of the officer's experiences were later depicted in the movie *Serpico*, starring Al Pacino in the title role (Maas, 1973). The issue of police corruption in four large U.S. cities were further studied by Sherman in the LEAA report, *Controlling Police Corruption* (1978), and his book *Police Corruption* (1978).

A 2013 study thoroughly addressed decades of police corruption in Chicago (Hagedorn et al., 2013). In it, the authors reviewed 50 years' worth of incidents of police corruption in the city, and similar to Quinn in the previous section, found that police officers are reluctant to turn in other officers. The study found that increases in gang violence are related to increased police corruption, and that strong leadership is critical to breaking the *Code of Silence* (2013).

The basic approach of these varied studies is to examine (1) how police officers corrupt other police officers, (2) the sources of temptation, and (3) whether the payoffs are regular (e.g., the pad) or a one-time affair. The studies include advice to management on how to break up internal cliques and bring about more central control. However, there is very little discussion of the effect of primary group cliques on the formal structure. Sherman focuses on breaking the linkages between local politics and police corruption. He proposes various strategies that police managers can use to control their staff. Sherman's conclusions are as follows (1978: 1):

1. Premonitory strategies (aimed at ongoing corruption) for corruption control can reduce the level of organization of police corruption.
2. Postmonitory strategies (aimed at past corruption) for corruption control do not seem to be as effective as premonitory strategies.
3. The same strategies for corruption control can be employed in a police department of any size, although the tactics may differ.

Corruption cannot exist without the active cooperation of top police officials and major figures in the political hierarchy. In the past decade, many major cities have experienced a corruption scandal, the new variable being narcotics. Still, Sherman's model, based on management control of investigations and employee drug testing, remains a viable strategy.

Corruption, Cliques, Meat Eaters, and Grass Eaters

One of the early research articles on police corruption that investigates primary group cliques in the police structure is that of Stoddard's "The Informal 'Code' of Police Deviance: A Group Approach to 'Blue-Coat Crime'" (1968: 246). Stoddard indicated that it was the cliques dominated by older officers that first corrupted the recruits. The Knapp Commission report (1972: 3–4) revealed widespread corruption through the street concept of either "grasseaters" or "meateaters." A grass eater was an officer who accepted gratuities in the form of money or services if it fell his or her way. For example, a tow truck operator might tip the officer a fee for having the company respond to a traffic accident to tow vehicles. On the other hand, a **meat eater** was an officer who went out of his way to make money such as offering protection for gamblers or prostitutes or coming up with schemes to shake down dealers and sell drug taken into evidence.

Positive Police Ethics

In his article on police ethics in Britain and the European Union, Peter Neyroud (2003: 584) states the following principles:

- Police respect citizens' personal rights and autonomy through morally respectable laws.
- Police officers help people without harming others.
- The middle way brings mutual respect between citizens and police.
- There is police trusteeship over police powers and care for the community.
- Honesty is a key value of police integrity.

Although police should always protect the community from those who wish to harm it by stealing and violence, there is another side of policing where police are seen to be a positive force in the community. Virtuous officers helping in police-sponsored youth ball games, police-sponsored youth camping, ride-along programs, and even Officer Friendly (who is truly a friend to the citizen) are examples of positive policing that needs to again be emphasized and honored throughout the land. Officers save lives in car accidents, deliver babies in emergency conditions, and have virtue.

POLICE TYPOLOGIES

Another approach to the study of internal groups has been the "typology of ideal types" study. The theory of ideal types, introduced into social science by Max Weber, says that models of reality can be created as an extreme form of that reality and used to clarify the relationships embodied in that reality.

Wilson's (1968) styles of policing described as watchman, legalistic, and service, are perhaps the most widely known among police administrators. Wilson created these typologies after observing the way law enforcement services were delivered in several cities in New York State, which included Albany, Newburgh, and Nassau County in the Long Island area. Applying these "styles" to a homeless person causing a disturbance, the watchman officer might take the person into custody or simply warn the person to leave town or else. The legalistic officer, on the other hand, would arrest because the law was broken while the service officer would take the person to a shelter.

Has the legalistic style of policing ever existed in reality? The usual answer is no, not as the style of a police agency or the style of an individual officer. However, some agencies prefer this type of policing, even though the other styles may also exist in a legalistic police agency. The same

CASE STUDY

The Wincanton (Reading, PA) Protection System

The following account is taken from the task force report on organized crime (National Advisory Commission, 1976), which is a well-documented government report on how organized crime took over a criminal justice system. Even though the corruption reported here occurred more than 30 years ago, this study is considered to be the classic on corruption and organized crime.

Wincanton, which was a pseudonym for Reading, PA, was an industrial city with a population of about 60,000, located in western Pennsylvania. The primary author of the study, John Gardner, describes the relationship between the police, politicians, and local gangsters, the most notorious being Irv Stern, who controlled the city's gambling activity after World War II.

Two basic principles were involved in the Wincanton protection system: (1) pay top personnel as much as necessary to keep them happy (and quiet) and (2) pay something to as many others as possible to implicate them in the system and to keep them from talking. The range of payoffs thus went from a weekly salary for some public officials to a Christmas turkey for the patrolman on the beat. Records from the numbers bank listed payment totaling $2,400 each week to some local elected officials, state legislators, the police chief, a captain in charge of detectives, and other people mysteriously labeled "county" and "state." While the list of people to be paid remained fairly constant, the amounts paid varied according to the gambling activities in operation at the time; payoff figures dropped sharply when the FBI put the dice game out of

business. When the dice game was running, one official was receiving $750 per week, the chief $100, and a few captains, lieutenants, and detectives lesser amounts.

While the number of officials receiving regular "salary" payoffs was quite restricted (only 15 names were on the payroll found at the number bank), many other officials were paid off in different ways. (Some men were also silenced without charge. Low-ranking policemen, for example, kept quiet after they learned that officers who reported gambling or prostitution were ignored or transferred to the midnight shift; they didn't have to be paid.) Stern was a major (if undisclosed) contributor during political campaigns—sometimes giving money to all candidates, not caring who won, sometimes supporting a "regular" to defeat a possible reformer, sometimes paying a candidate not to oppose a preferred man. Since there were few legitimate sources of large contributions for Democratic candidates, Stern's money was frequently regarded as essential for victory, for the costs of buying radio and television ads and paying poll watchers were high. When popular sentiment was running strongly in favor of reform, however, even Stern's contributions could not guarantee victory. Bob Walasek, later to become as corrupt as any Wincanton mayor, ran as a reform candidate in the Democratic primary and defeated Stern-financed incumbent Gene Donnelly. Never a man to bear grudges, Stern financed Walasek in the general election that year and put him on the "payroll" when he took office.

is true of individual officers. What this and other typologies do is enable the researcher and the student of police management and police culture to use the ideal typology as a tool to analyze police departments and police groups. We will see this tool in use when we look at styles of leadership and management.

Hundreds of typologies have been produced for the study of police management and police culture. There are professional cops, street cops, by-the-book cops, bad cops, good cops, and many others. These studies look at whole departments, styles of leadership and management, and types of police officers. Police managers need to deal with all kinds of police personalities. They would do well to look over some of these typologies to see if any relationship can be found between these social constructs and police behavior.

Consider, for example, a chief with a service orientation who takes over a legalistic-style department. He sends standard operating orders to the officers telling them they should spend time talking to citizens, delivering babies, teaching courses at the local schools, serving as guest speakers, and *also* apprehending criminals. The new chief will find tight-and-fast resistance because the prevailing style gives priority to enforcing the law and apprehending criminals.

Chiefs who do not understand the difference between their style of policing and the one prevailing in the department will fail. Police managers need to understand and consider police styles every day if their orders are to be effective.

The dramaturgical approach of sociologist Erving Goffman creates psychological typologies of **police personality types**, also called over the years, styles of policing or predispositions. These typologies create different social roles in the police subculture that are related to specific attitudes and behaviors. Just as the occupational roles of a teacher or a business manager come with a pattern of predispositions affecting behavior, so do different social roles encompassed by the police officer. In her article concerning styles of policing and police discretionary behavior, Brooks (2005: 94) writes, "Predispositions supply the officer with a repertoire of possible behaviors, and from this collection, the officer selects an appropriate response to a specific situation."

One of the latest of these typologies, called "Attitudinal Dimensions of Police Culture," shows a typology of five personality types (Paoline, 2004: 205–236):

1. *Tough cops.* These are cynical officers who believe that the public is hostile and police supervisors unsupportive. They perform their law enforcement duties aggressively and selectively.
2. *Clean-beat crime fighters.* These officers express cynicism and are upset with supervisors who do not support them. They want to fight all crime, including minor crime, and believe in the individual rights of citizens.
3. *Avoiders.* These officers are of another cynical type and are somewhat hostile, but not while on patrol. They are basically serving time, waiting for retirement.
4. *Problem solvers.* These officers are not aggressive in patrolling tactics and use selective enforcement, avoiding arresting citizens. According to the two authors, problem solvers (unlike the first three types) want to help citizens. The officers are supposed to hold favorable attitudes toward community policing and order maintenance.
5. *Professionals.* These officers hold the most favorable attitudes toward innovation and change, supervisors, citizens, and procedural guidelines. Of all the types, they have the broadest role orientation. They do not support aggressive patrolling and selective enforcement.

Paoline (2004: 208) also states that more minorities, college-educated officers, and female officers, along with community policing, "may have eroded the monolithic police culture."

As long as these different types of officers generally abide by the police culture norms of secrecy, social isolation, and solidarity, there is little or no incompatibility with the pervasive police culture. Also, as Laura Brooks (2005: 98) points out, "While there exists intuitive support for the connection between police attitudes and behavior, little empirical research has been conducted to examine the issue and the few studies that address this have reported disappointing results." She cited Crank (2003) and Worden (1989) for the disappointing results. The most important variables predicting police behavior in the field are lower economic class and race

CASE STUDY

Canal City Police Department

The Canal City Police Department is a traditional, hierarchical department in a small city on the East Coast. The middle-sized department reflects the social and political makeup of the municipality, which is dominated by one ethnic group. The informal relationships that have developed over the years have created a number of strong cliques based on kinship and a variety of interests.

One ethnic group dominates the police hierarchy so much that other officers complain about how these officers stick together. The perception of the other officers is that the officers from this ethnic group do favors for one another, including preferential treatment for promotions, shift assignments, and attendance at special training programs outside the city. This is quite similar to the behavior of the Irish in Boston and the Scandinavians and Germans in parts of the Midwest. Unlike the New York City Police Department, where a number of ethnic groups compete with one another, in Canal City there exists only one ethnic group and the others are unorganized. In Canal City, the "rabbi" who helps officers up the promotion ladder is from this ethnic group. Kinship permeates the ethnic cliques. Favors are performed by uncles, cousins, and godfathers of higher rank for relatives in the lower ranks.

Naturally, in this traditional, autocratic department, the chief and his cronies form the most powerful clique; moreover, the chief retains power and influence, not just through the normal means of command rank, but also through a communication network operated by his clique. Officers who attempt to go against the chief are inevitably discovered by members of this clique, which extends to the lower ranks. When a malcontent officer is identified, the information is conveyed to the chief, and the officer is disciplined.

A unique clause in the union contract allows command officers to participate fully in all union activities. Not surprisingly, the agenda of the Police Benevolent Association's meetings contain few criticisms of the chief or of members

of his clique. Thus, control is exerted downward through the ever-watchful eyes of the chief's clique, even when he cannot be present.

One shift, shift C, has been a thorn in the side of this autocratic chief. The mainly younger, college-educated officers in this shift have been known to pull pranks that make the chief angry. Once, while the chief was trying to transmit a radio message, members of the shift keyed their microphones in to the chief's frequency, causing considerable interruption. The culprits were invited to report to the chief's office. In the tradition of the fierce loyalty that police officers have for each other, no one reported and no one told the chief anything. Every man in the shift was ordered to one tour of foot patrol each month, and patrol partners were changed from day to day.

This was a punishment directly attacking the informal organization of the shift. Over the years, partners come together who like and trust each other. In Canal City, partners are often said to be "married" to each other.

Rotating the tours of duty broke up the partnerships and disrupted much of the informal organization of the shift. In sociological terms, this was probably the worst type of punishment the chief could devise in terms of the morale of his young officers.

Within shift C, the following cliques were identified:

The elite clique. Three experienced and powerful men who are close to the chief and enjoy his protection. One is a patrolman, one is a lieutenant, and one is a captain. All have over 20 years of seniority.

The young ambitious. These six with young families are aggressive officers in terms of making arrests and doing "real" police work. They privately voice their opposition to the chief's dictatorial policies and fervently hope that he retires soon. In addition, they feel that some members of the shift are lazy and corrupt, and they have little use for these officers.

Pistol clubbers. These three married officers belong to the department's pistol club and take part in statewide competitions. The club provides a common meeting place away from the police station for socializing and sharing gossip and criminal information. The pistol club has the blessings of the chief.

Social drinkers. These five officers go drinking together, sharing both police and private gossip. They all have at least seven years of experience and are known to socialize with their families.

The shift also has sportsmen, golfers, and officers attending college. However, these are the main cliques. What makes this shift stand out from the rest is that cliques are formed mainly on the grounds of interests, not ethnic and kinship ties. Every officer knows that when you are dealing with one of these officers, you are also dealing with his clique and the relationship between his clique and your clique.

At times, the entire shift gets together at their favorite police bar to drink and play cards. After the evening shift, 4:00 p.m. to midnight, there are frequent and rather rowdy get-togethers at local bars and in private homes. This has become known in Wambaugh's terminology as "choir practice."

The officers are deeply imbedded in their various social and professional groups, which define power relationships in the department. They also make a fairly large department with strong hierarchical relationships more humane and give the individual officer a sense of personal worth and security.

At present, traditional ethnic cliques dominate the department and support an authoritarian chief. If the young ambitious clique manages to form an alliance with a number of the stronger kinship groups, the chief may have problems, and a new power relationship may be forged in the Canal City Police Department.

This is a real department in which participant observation research has been done. However, considering the explosive nature of the power relationships discussed, the authors have decided not to reveal additional geographic details.

demeanor, as well as whether the victim wishes to have an arrest made. Brooks and many others have pointed out that officer characteristics have little effect on police behavior while situational variables have a stronger effect.

MINORITY GROUP STRUCTURES

The early research on minority law enforcement officers has generally been directed toward the experiences of African Americans and their encounters in predominately white organizations. More recent research has emerged on the experiences of women and other groups.

African American Officers

From December 1964 to October 1965, Nicholas Alex interviewed 41 African American New York City police officers, using a series of open-ended questions. The result was the first book on black police, *Black in Blue* (1969). Alex discovered that black police officers were often accepted as brother police officers but were often excluded from white officers' social activities when off duty (p. 87).

Alex also shows ethnic rivalry in terms of blacks being excluded from the detective division (1969: 111). At the time of this writing, most upper-level management positions were held by Irish bosses. There are some data here, but this is basically a descriptive study with little analysis, except in terms of general racial discrimination.

A 1973 article by Bannon and Wilt on African American police officers based on a number of interviews with Detroit police of various ranks found that African American cops were more often referred to simply as good or bad cops by white police officers. African American police officers did not want to lower the standards to bring more African Americans into the police agency since they felt this would lower their own status in the eyes of their fellow police officers. Here you see a closer identification with the prevailing police culture.

However, many of the same problems persisted. Blacks felt that opportunities for promotion had improved over the years. However, they were still disturbed that "assignment to preferred jobs often occurred on a friendship basis, rather than strictly on a qualification basis" (Bannon and Wilt, 1973: 27). The basis of group friendships and its analysis was not carried forward. The social exclusion of black police officers persisted. As one black Detroit police officer stated, "I have observed a certain amount of discrimination in that white officers tend to keep to themselves and exclude blacks from their groups not only socially but even in everyday relations at station houses" (Bannon and Wilt, 1973: 28). No group activities of blacks were documented.

In a follow-up study to Alex's work, Leinen (1984) discussed racial discrimination in the NYPD from the Civil Rights era to the beginning of the 1980s. Until the 1960s, black officers were assigned only to black neighborhoods and were neither promoted nor assigned to special units. Disciplinary actions against black officers were inequitable when compared to those against white officers. In the past two decades, many improvements have been made in these procedures. Based on a series of interviews with black patrol officers, detectives, and supervisors, Leinen found that institutional discrimination had largely disappeared. He felt this was due to the legal, social, and political events of the civil rights era, along with the efforts of black officer associations like the **Guardians**. Leinen (1984: 255–56) reported that there were some white officers who continued to deny blacks and other nonwhite officers opportunity and mobility in the NYPD. This problem, he maintained, was compounded by the senior positions held by these racist white officers. Although blacks and other minorities have made strides in the department, there was still the obstacle of the racist senior officer to contend with.

A study by McBride (1986) on the recruitment and training process for three medium-sized police departments in New York State found that African Americans were generally accepted by their white colleagues based on the officer's ability to do the job. Based on a series of face-to-face interviews, the study found some instances of discriminatory treatment toward black officers during employment selection and police training.

African American recruits indicated that they had encountered difficulties during field training because of both personality clashes and the treatment of African American citizens by their field training officers. The same recruits indicated they had little difficulty in dealing with the areas to which they were assigned after field training, regardless of the racial makeup of the suspects and victims in the area. They felt that the few cries of "**Uncle Tom**" came from citizens who had a bad attitude toward police in general.

The number of African Americans, Hispanics, and Asians on the force and in officer ranks has continued to grow over the years as a result of affirmative action programs as well as more progressive attitudes. Even as the research becomes more sophisticated, it is still evident that blacks and other minority officers are generally treated equally on the job by white police officers but continue to be generally isolated from the social activities of white officers.

Weitzer (2000) looked at the issue of black versus white officers from a unique perspective—the customer or citizen. He interviewed citizens of Washington, D.C., to assess their opinions on officer behavior, including whether or not they felt that there was a difference in community interaction between black and white officers. Bolton and Feagan, in their book,

Black in Blue: African-American Police Officers (2004), interviewed male and female African American police officers in an effort to determine their experiences. The results of their interviews provide clear indication that as far as law enforcement has progressed over the past half century in terms of a fully integrated multi-racial police force, strong leadership is still needed if we hope to eliminate biases.

Female Officers

The first female officer was appointed in the Los Angeles Police Department in 1911 (Sherman, 1973: 383). As Owings pointed out in *Women Police* (1925), the female officer was normally used in three areas: vice, juvenile work, and the handling of female prisoners (police matron). Sherman (1973) indicated that in the early 1970s, women still constituted only 2 to 3 percent of the national police force and that they still held the traditionally female police jobs in the male-dominated departments around the nation.

In 1968, Chief Winston Churchill of the Indianapolis Police Department assigned two women to car 47 to do regular patrol work. He thus earned the distinction of having the first female officers doing "regular" duty. As Sherman points out, "The crew of car 47 has earned open if grudging acceptance from most Indianapolis policemen." "Grudging acceptance" exemplifies the place of women in policing. Police management decides to assign female police officers to regular duty. Over a number of years, these female officers earn the grudging acceptance of the male police officer.

From the many stories that come from jurisdictions around the country, the following trends are well documented.

Catherine Milton (1972) found that female officers were used as secretaries and dispatchers but were infrequently accorded equality with men. By 1974, there were enough female police executives in Pennsylvania that Barbara Price could publish an article entitled "A Study of Leadership Strength of Female Police Executives." Susan Martin (1979), a police officer in Washington, D.C., interviewed 32 officers on their feelings and concluded that women in policing must deal with isolation from male co-workers and being trapped in the traditional duties assigned to female officers. Weaknesses and mistakes made in the field are often overblown and those individuals who are aggressive are given the labels of "bitch" and "lesbian" (322).

Martin also pointed out a lack of unity among female police officers and noted that they failed to act as a political faction or as a group. Instead, they competed individually and lacked internal political clout.

In 1971, women were only 1.4 percent of sworn police officers (Martin, 1993: 328). In 1990, Martin found that women were 10.5 percent in cities over 50,000 and 11.3 percent in the suburbs. In 1986, nonwhite women were 40 percent of the female officers. Female officers in that year represented 3.3 percent of all supervisors in municipal agencies (Martin, 1993: 328)

In 1993, female police officers made up 9.4 percent of sworn police officers and 63.1 percent of civilian employees of police departments in the United States (Maguire and Flanagan, 1995: 55).

Langton (2010) reported that by 2007 women filled nearly 80,000 law enforcement positions in the United States, with over 55,000 in local agencies, 19,000 in county sheriff's offices, and nearly 4,000 working in a state police agency.

In 1993, there were four female police chiefs in major cities: Elizabeth Watson of Austin, Texas; Elaine S. Hedtke of Tucson, Arizona; Leslie Martinez of Portsmouth, Virginia; and Mary F. Rabadeau of Elizabeth, New Jersey (Schultz, 1995: 372).

The courts have backed women when they have been discriminated against in hiring and promotion. In *Webb* v. *City of Chester, Ill.*, Webb testified that on the day she got her badge, a member of the Board of Fire and Police Commissioners told her, "I don't want you here, you are a woman and a woman has no business being a police officer." Even though she was at the top of her police academy class, two and a half weeks after graduation, she was fired. The jury awarded her $20,250 for embarrassment and humiliation and $9,750 as compensation for lost wages. The judgment held on appeal. Webb sued under Section 703(a) of Title VII of the Civil Rights Act of 1964, which states it is illegal to discriminate because of sex.

In *Thomas* v. *City of Evanston* in 1985 and *Baurney* v. *Pawtucket* in 1983, courts decided that a physical agility test discriminated against women. In *Vanguard Justice Society* v. *Hughes* in 1979 and *U.S.* v. *North Carolina* in 1981, courts decided that certain weight requirements also discriminated against women. Hale and Menniti conclude from these and other cases that "where the success rate of a plaintiff class is less than 80 percent, a finding of a disparate impact is appropriate for the courts" (1993: 181–83). This means that if 80 percent of a certain class flunks, then the test or criteria is suspect.

Balkin did an empirical study in 1988 titled "Why Policemen Don't Like Policewomen." He quoted one respondent: "If you are sleeping with someone you are a slut; if not you are a dyke" (Balkin, 1988: 29). The reasons why female police officers have such a hard time being accepted by the male police force are once again the three *S*'s: secrecy, solidarity, and social isolation. Leslie Kay Lord (1986: 89) found that "male officers still harbor grave reservations about women's suitability to be competent police officers." In a study of stress on the female officer, Wexler and Logan indicated that these types of attitudes put a great deal of stress on the female officer. As one officer in their study said, "The academy said they didn't want women. We stuck together and said we were going to make it." One training officer said, "This is my personal opinion. I don't think you should be in this job. You should go home and have babies" (Wexler and Logan, 1983: 50). The researchers concluded that female officers had a difficult time in being accepted and that they were either "ignored, harassed, watched, and gossiped about and viewed as sexual objects" (p. 52). However, another study showed that when the researcher controlled for age, the younger male officers were more accepting of female officers (Wheisheit, 1987). Yet another study found that women reported higher stress than men but that "improvement in status and income associated with entry into male-dominated employment may ameliorate stress consequences for policewomen in comparison to other employed women" (Pendergrass and Ostrove, 1984: 138).

A final issue that has had a negative impact on female officers and their relationship to their male counterparts, as well as the community is a charge that female officers are cowardly (Homant, 1983). Some male officers also accuse female officers of being emotionally unstable in the face of violence. However, a 1987 study refutes these stereotypes. Sean A. Grennan (1987: 83) in a study of the NYPD found that there was no gender difference in the number of injuries sustained on patrol and the reaction to violent confrontations. He concluded that women officers were "more emotionally stable" in that they did not have to adopt the aggressive "macho image" often used by male officers. He showed that in a male/female team, the male was more likely to discharge his firearm.

WALKING THE THIN BLUE LINE IN THE TWENTY-FIRST CENTURY   Conditions for women are better now than in the past, but they are far from being fair in the areas of promotions and job selection. Many female authors writing about female officers have said that the discrimination still exists but that it is more sophisticated.

Teresa Lynn Wertsch interviewed 16 female officers who were "walking the thin blue line." By this she meant that female officers could not be better than male officers, nor could they be worse. They had to walk this thin blue line if they were to avoid being attacked. Wertsch (1998: 31) described the **role entrapment** of female officers. While male officers are dispatched to major criminal and assault calls, females were assigned to family violence, sexual assaults, and rape and traffic accidents/incidents. She blamed sexist police dispatchers.

Role entrapment has been widespread throughout the United States, as numerous studies have shown. One officer said that when female officers go to DARE or become a Neighborhood Service Officer, male officers say, "Well, she is only doing this because she can't do *real police work*" (Wertsch, 1998: 35). For these male officers, "real police work" is patrol work and crime fighting.

Gossett and Williams (1998: 60) interviewed 27 female police officers concerning perceived discrimination. Female officers were concerned about the covert discrimination of the 1990s. "The officers who perceive discrimination today see it as subtle and inadvertent, 'It is behind the closed door, in one-on-one conversation.'" Another female officer said, "It is not blatant. It is not something that occurs on a daily basis."

What is this covert discrimination? It is the "old boy" system where senior male officers help junior male officers on promotions and job assignments. Male African American and Hispanic police officers complained about this in the 1980s. That was partially solved when enough Hispanic and African American officers got promoted and became police chiefs and administrators. Then they could help the junior minority officers in career advancement and job assignment. It happens that it is taking much longer for the female officer to have her "rabbi" or "book" in the upper ranks, compared to minority officers.

Research has shown conclusively in every study that male and female police officers do equally well on the job in all areas. One three-year study of a large police department in the Southeast showed that the female police officers had somewhat fewer citizen complaints (Lersch, 1998). The study also concluded that there were no differences between male and female officers in the type of complaint, including the use of force.

Hale and Wyland (1993: 4) pointed out early in the 1990s that "it is no longer necessary to debate or discuss the effectiveness of women on patrol. It is time however to address the greater issue of how women can unconditionally be accepted by their peers and supervisors." This is a major issue for policing in the twenty-first century.

Female Police Executives

The number of women in policing has risen slowly over the years. According to the FBI's *Uniform Crime Report* (2011), women accounted for approximately 11.9 percent of the 6,698,460 municipal, county, and state police officers in the United States. In 1993, this number was estimated at 9.4 percent.

The number of female executives today is very small. According to Schultz (2002), only 172 police chiefs in the entire country are female, which amounts to about 1 percent of all departments surveyed. Of this number, 40 lead college or university police departments with full-time police officers and 48 manage municipal departments. Two head state police forces. As in other American industries and professions, the number of female police executives continues to steadily rise as women are promoted and transferred to major command and policy-making levels.

Already, changes are being felt in the national policy-making arena. For example, Chief Mary Ann Viverette of the Gaithersburg, Maryland, Police Department recently served as president of the International Association of Chiefs of Police (IACP). She received degrees from the University of Maryland, graduated from the FBI National Academy, and has served in her department for more than 20 years. Recently, she received national recognition for her work on reducing gun violence and motor vehicle theft. She was also a founding member of the **National Association of Women Law Enforcement Executives (NAWLEE)**.

Like similar associations in other professional occupations, NAWLEE was created primarily as a mentoring organization for rising female executives. The current president, Susan Rockette, is the chief of the Mexico, Missouri, Police Department. At the beginning of her career, she was appointed to the Sikeston, Missouri, Department of Public Safety and cross-trained in police and firefighter duties. She was appointed to leadership positions at Charleston, Missouri, and

CASE STUDY

The Struggle: Paula Meara Becomes the First Female Police Chief in Springfield, Massachusetts, in 1996

The case study of Paula Meara shows how women have to deal with discriminatory treatment that impedes advancement through promotion. This is her story, as summarized from Carolyn Boyes-Watson's *Crime and Justice: A Casebook Approach* (2003: 174–79).

Paula Meara, a single parent, had to win a lawsuit in 1974 to become one of the two female officers in a department of 400 in Springfield, Massachusetts. She was assigned the shift from midnight to 8:00 A.M. and dealt with all calls. In 1983 she scored third out of 143 applicants for police sergeant, but it took her two years to be promoted at age 40; she was still assigned to the midnight shift. In 1987 she made the top score for lieutenant. The 40-min oral interview consisted mostly of questions on her use of sick days to give birth to her three children. After being passed over for promotion in favor of male officers with lower scores for four years, she filed a gender discrimination complaint and won her case with the Massachusetts Civil Service Commission. At her swearing-in ceremony in 1989, her superior officer refused to shake her hand. She continued on the midnight shift. After her promotion, the department asked her to drop her federal Equal Employment Opportunity Commission (EEOC) suit, but she refused. After a federal judge recommended settlement, the department admitted discriminating against Lt. Meara in 1989; in the same year, she scored second on the captain's

exam. Over the strenuous objection of the police chief, the Massachusetts Civil Service Commission appointed her the first female captain in Springfield Police Department's history.

In the 1980s in the Springfield Police Department, there was constant harassment of female officers by male officers, including at least one threat of rape, incidents of tire slashing, sanitary napkins taped to female lockers, sexual cartoons with female officers' names placed on them, and nude photos of females displayed in public places. One female officer committed suicide by "eating her gun." It was a department full of hate for female officers. In 1992 Captain Meara testified before Senator John Glenn's congressional committee on the sexual harassment of women in the workplace. In the 1990s, the first Hispanic mayor, Michael Albano, won election with the help of a growing minority population. In appointing a police chief, Mayor Albano and the police union agreed on a professional outside evaluation organization, and the Massachusetts Municipal Association Consulting Group of Boston was hired. Captain Meara scored first in the competition against nine other candidates, including a former police chief and deputy chief and others from the old boy network. Naturally, there was a lawsuit. The final interview by the police commission was aired on public television. On February 2, 1996, Paula Meara became the first woman police chief in New England.

Calamet Park, Illinois. She is a graduate of Warner University, Lake Wales, Florida, the Anderson Divinity School, and the Northwestern University School of Police Staff and Command.

Female police officers are beginning to emerge as leaders in police departments throughout the United States. The twenty-first century police departments will have proactive police officers and leaders of both sexes. Yet, there are many hurdles to overcome. As discussed in her best selling book, Sheryl Sandberg (2013), the chief operating officer for Facebook, states that although women constitute about 50 percent of all college graduates, they are still in a minority for leadership positions in business and government. She cites many reasons for this including an unwillingness to "step up to the plate" when leadership positions or situations become available. A major issue is that women still place professional careers on hold to raise families. Added to this are cultural norms and organizational policies that do not allow equal distribution of child-rearing tasks to the male partner.

Gay and Lesbian Police Officers

Today there is increasing acceptance of gay, lesbian, bi-sexual, and transgender police officers as many states have legalized same sex marriages and outlawed employment and housing discrimination. In June 2013, the United States Supreme Court ruled that it was unconstitutional for any form of marriage to be discriminated against in any way, including insurance-related issues. As in the military, gays in law enforcement are in a period of transition. Some of the same arguments used against hiring women surface in hiring gay or lesbian police officers. Reflecting the macho trait that occurs in policing, some officers feel that a gay police officer would not be masculine enough to exert authority or to quell a bar fight. Regardless of these attitudes, many states prohibit discrimination in employment based on sexual orientation. A proactive approach, including cultural sensitivity training, can ease the transition to accepting an openly homosexual police officer.

As discussed by Shusta et al. (2005: 55), the general term "gay and lesbian" refers to a number of the following orientations:

- Gay—a male homosexual
- Homosexual—attracted to members of the same sex
- Lesbian—a homosexual woman
- Bisexual—sexually attracted to both men and women
- Transgender—refers to a wide number of individuals who may cross-dress, undergo medical procedures to change gender, or transsexuals, who have doubts about their original birth gender.

The most cited study on gay and lesbian officers took place in San Diego, CA, by Belkin and McNichol (2002). The study concluded that "fully integrating gay and lesbian officers has improved the agency's quality and responsiveness to the community." The authors cited San Diego's 10-year history of integration and noted that "diversification and integration were not expensive to implement financially, but they did require some political capital from the police chief." Some officers resented the promotion of openly gay police officers, and some older male officers were unhappy with the program of integration (Belkin and McNichol, 2002).

The report gave three reasons for the success of San Diego's program:

1. Strong support and leadership from three police chiefs
2. A special training program for all new recruits that covered appropriate rules of conduct
3. The use of openly gay and lesbian police officers as special liaisons with the local gay community

The report also concluded that the acceptance of openly gay and lesbian police officers did not hurt recruitment, and there was no lack of close support for officers in hazardous situations. The police chief marched in gay pride parades in the city, and the department cut off its ties to the Boy Scouts when that organization rejected an openly gay police officer as a teacher in a cadet program.

In 2007, Greg Miraglia, a law enforcement training director at the Napa Valley College in California, published a book of personal stories including his own on being a gay police officer. He became a police officer in 1978 and came out in 2004 and regrets his 25 years of secrecy. The biographies presented included those of police chiefs, supervisors, and officers from across the country. All of the stories had the following theme:

1. A number of years of hiding the officer's sexual orientation
2. Coming out
3. Expecting the very worst
4. Relief that the very worst had not happened
5. Finally a return to normal

It was always difficult but it looks like most departments simply accept gay police officers even though some police officers, family, and friends do not accept the officer's choice. What matters most is that the department continues to support the officer's career. Despite an increase in the adoption of anti-discrimination laws in housing, employment, and social relations on the basis of sexual orientation, and increased presentation of lesbian, gay, bi-sexual, and transgender (LGBT) relationships in the media, LGBT officers in many departments still face have an uphill battle in overcoming covert discrimination in hiring and gaining acceptance by other officers. This is very apparent in smaller departments outside of major metropolitan areas which are dominated by white males. However, as the LGBT population moves into the social and political community limelight, most police departments do not want to get involved in lawsuits and civil rights actions. There is also a supportive network of gay police officer organizations that have events locally, regionally, and nationally. They include Law Enforcement Gays and Lesbians (LEGAL), San Francisco Pride Alliance, Transgendered Police and Sheriffs, and Gay Officers Action League of New England and New York.

COMMUNITY POLICE IMPACT ON THE POLICE SUBCULTURE

There has also been an impact on police culture by community policing , which is discussed in detail in Chapter 8. Wood et al. (2004: 136–61) state that there has been an impact on police culture by this new philosophy of policing. But first one has to examine the changes in technology and demographics in the United States.

In this century, the United States has had the largest influx of immigrants from Asia, Africa, and Latin America, with a large percentage of households speaking English as a second language. Women, Hispanics, and African Americans today are in middle management and the top ranks. Gay and female police organizations are growing. Technology, including Google maps, DNA, GPS technology, wireless digital photographs, and digital video with sound, has made a revolution in locating officers, criminals, and victims, remote communications, recording information, and field investigations. In addition, community policing has brought the community into the station house and administration as part of the decision-making process concerning basic police policies.

Wood et al. (2004: 136–61) say that there has been a fragmentation of police culture. They logged 3,000 hours in ride-alongs and did 200 interviews in a police department in the "Sunbelt" of the western United States.

They describe a number of different police officer subcultures. The traditional subculture consists of dedicated crime fighters who operate mostly independent of the community and their own police supervisors. The paramilitary subculture has a SWAT mentality with a war on crime. The opportunistic subculture consists of cynical officers who are looking for personal advancement with little loyalty to the department as a whole. The expert, community-oriented police (COP) subculture is dedicated to carrying out this model. The authors say the traditional and paramilitary subcultures are hostile to community-oriented policing. These latter subcultures treat community policing as mere public relations. However, these subcultures seem to operate more as social roles and police cliques within a universal police culture.

The community policing model and the other described changes within policing may have an effect on the cultural norms of policing. The police norm of social isolation is weakened by the COP model of involvement with the community. Minority, women, and gay police associations have major ties with groups outside of policing. However, the traditional bureaucratic model and intelligence-led policing can reinforce the social isolation norm.

The weakening of social isolation is a positive change for police officers, management, and the communities they serve. An increasingly diverse community equipped with twenty-first century information technology has made this a necessary change.

The secrecy norm is mixed. Police and government Web sites have made the police more transparent than ever in history. Interactive information technology will continue this trend and become important sources of information for both the community and the police. Secrecy is needed to protect investigation files, reputation of victims, and civilians who are the targets of unfounded investigations and court cases. A famous poster from World War II is "LOOSE LIPS SINK SHIPS!" If you want to talk about shipping, a submarine may sink a ship. In policing, loose lips can destroy investigations, personal legitimate reputations, and court cases and convictions and put lives at risk. Departmental files have to be protected from criminal hackers. A certain level of secrecy protecting departmental security is a serious norm that is worth keeping.

Solidarity can destroy corruption investigations but is also a major support for officers in a high-stress job. The acceptance of women, minority, and gay police officers strengthens solidarity. This means that these officers are not female, Hispanic, or gay; they remain, simply, dedicated, professional police officers.

The conflict and division between supervisors and employees is a traditional refrain in all occupations and even more so in American policing. As discussed by Crank (2004), studies on the police subculture illustrate this state of affairs in most departments in that the police officers are often faced with boredom and routine interspersed with life threatening situations overseen by "the bosses." Supervisors and superior officers are often referred to in derogatory terms and labeled as untrustworthy and "out to get" subordinates. The real reason for many early retirements Crank finds is the inability to put up with the "bullshit" related to the bureaucratic aspects of the police occupation.

The main cause of stress for many officers is not the horrors seen on patrol but rather the arbitrary enforcement of departmental and governmental policies and uneven or illegal command decision making. One of the authors of this text found this out in an early stage of his career when he was given a written reprimand for failing to wear his cover (hat) after evacuating a building that was the scene of a fire.

Crank and the other writers cited in this chapter are good at making observations on the aspects of the police subculture but fail to present potential remedies. Police managers, from chiefs to sergeants, have to realize that most officers like to be treated as professionals and demand that their leaders are respectful, supportive, decisive, and know what they are doing. From the authors' perspective there is a need for fundamental fairness in dealing with both citizens and fellow officers.

Conclusion

This chapter focused on police subculture and informal organizational structure as forces to be dealt with by police managers. We began by defining the concept of subculture and offered examples of how it appears in police argot, esoteric knowledge, internal sanctions, solidarity, social isolation, perception of violence, and psychological distance. The implications for police managers are obvious. Issues and problems based in the notion of subculture have a tendency to become major.

Internal factions based on the primary group organization exist in every police department. It is up to the management to use these groups as positive reinforcement for the basic purpose of the organization. The deep ties of loyalty generated by primary groups operating through the informal social structure can make or break management in any police department. Most books on police management and administration ignore the effect of these groups on the operations of the basic organization and management style.

However, we can no longer afford to ignore the fundamental group dynamics that structure departmental activity on a daily basis. These groups, along with police subculture and unions (described in Chapter 15), operationalize management directives and determine the impact of management decisions on the operation of the organization itself and on the citizens. Primary groups shape and run most organizations in terms of the personal effect on individual officers. Even with the demographic and technological changes in the twenty-first century, no policy can be implemented without taking these groups and their actions into account. The sophisticated police manager knows that there is a long way to go from issuing orders to implementing them in the squad room and on the streets.

Questions for Review

1. List the major characteristics of police departments as vocational subcultures. Give special emphasis to the notions of secrecy, solidarity, and social isolation.
2. Use the concept of police argot to explain some major tenets of the police subculture.
3. How would you, as a police administrator, deal with your department's informal norms and sanctions while trying to introduce a new crime-prevention program?
4. Do police really have a daily perception of violence? How does this relate to the perceived need for psychological distance?
5. Explain the differences between formal organization and informal organization.
6. Analyze the effect of police primary groups on police organization.
7. What is the effect of peer group norms on police corruption? As a police administrator, how would you use these norms to deal with the problem of police corruption?
8. Describe, analyze, and apply the different styles of policing—legalistic, watchman, service—to a local police agency.
9. Based on the conclusions of available research, compare and contrast how Hispanic, African American, LGBT, and female police officers fit into both the formal and the informal police organization.
10. Do informal cliques help or hinder good police management? Why?

Class Project

Compare and contrast the police as a vocational subculture to any other vocational subculture. Interview both a police officer and a member of the other vocation or profession. In your interview, ascertain whether the interviewee feels that his or her occupation is characterized by such things as argot, internal sanctions, solidarity, social isolation, and the like.

Web Works

A wide variety of police officer associations have established Web sites to promote their programs and membership. Nationally, these include the National Association of Women Law Enforcement Executives (nawlee.com), the National Organization of Black Law Enforcement Executives (noblenational.org), National Black Peace Officer Association (blackofficer.org), the National Latino Peace Officer Association (nlpoa.com), and the National Asian Pacific Officers Association (napoaonline.org). Police fraternal associations for various ethnic groups in major metropolitan areas can be found by searching on Google and Yahoo.

References

Alex, Nicholas. *Black in Blue*. New York: Appleton-Century-Crofts, 1969.

Arnold, David O. *The Sociology of Subcultures*. Berkeley, Calif.: Glendessary, 1970.

Balkin, Joseph. "Why Policemen Don't Like Policewomen." *Journal of Police Science and Administration*, 16, no. 1 (March 1988), pp. 29–38.

Bannon, James D., and G. Marie Wilt. "Black Policeman: A Study of Self-Images." *Journal of Police Science and Administration*, 1, no. 1 (March 1973), pp. 21–29.

Banton, Michael. *The Policeman in the Community*. New York: Basic Books, 1964.

Beard, Eugene. "The Black Police in Washington, D.C." *Journal of Police Science and Administration*, 5, no. 1 (March 1977), pp. 48–52.

Belkin, Aaron, and Jason McNichol. "Pink and Blue: Outcomes Associated with the Integration of Open Gay and Lesbian Personnel in the San Diego Police Department." *Police Quarterly*, 5, no. 1 (2002), pp. 46–89.

Berger, Peter L., and Brigitte Berger. *Sociology: A Biographical Approach*. New York: Basic Books, 1972.

Blumberg, Abraham, and Elaine Niederhoffer. *The Ambivalent Force*. Hinsdale, Ill.: Dryden Press, 1985.

Bolton, K., and J. Feagin. *Black in Blue: African-American Police Officers*. New York: Routledge, 2004.

Boyes-Watson, Carolyn. *Crime and Justice: A Casebook Approach*. Boston: Pearson Education, Allyn and Bacon, 2003.

Broderick, J. *Police in a Time of Change* (2nd ed.). Prospect Heights, Ill.: Waveland Press, 1987.

Brooks, Laura Weber. "Police Discretionary Behavior: A Study of Style." In Roger G. Dunham and Geoffrey R. Alpert, eds., *Critical Issues in Policing*. Prospect Heights, Ill.: Waveland Press, 2005, pp. 89–105.

Chevigny, Paul. *Police Power: Abuses in New York*. New York: Pantheon, 1969.

Clark, John P. "Isolation of the Police: A Comparison of British and American Situations." *Journal of Police Science and Administration*, 56, no. 3 (September 1965), pp. 307–331.

Crank, John P. "Legalistic and Order-Maintenance Behavior among Police Patrol Officers: A Survey of Eight Municipal Police Agencies." *American Journal of Policing*, 12 (2003), pp. 103–126.

————. *Understanding Police Culture*. Cincinnati: Anderson/LexisNexis Publishing, 2004.

Drucker, Peter F. *Management: Tasks, Responsibilities, Practices*. New York: Harper and Row, 1974.

Gardiner, John A. "Wincanton: The Politics of Corruption." In President's Commission on Law Enforcement and Administration of Justice, *Task Force Report: Organized Crime*. Washington, D.C.: U.S. Government Printing Office, 1965.

Gossett, Jennifer Lynn, and Joyce E. Williams. "Perceived Discrimination in Law Enforcement." *Women and Criminal Justice*, 10, no. 1 (1998), pp. 23–61.

Grennan, Sean A. "Findings on the Role of Officer Gender in Violent Encounters with Citizens." *Journal of Police Science and Administration*, 15, no. 1 (March 1987), pp. 78–85.

Hagedorn, J., B. Kmiecik, D. Simpson, T. Gradel, M. Mouritsen-Zmuda, and D. Sterrett. *Crime, Corruption, and Coverups in the Chicago Police Department*, 2013. Retrieved from uic.edu/depts/pols/ChicagoPolitics/policecorruption.pdf

Hale, Donna, and Daniel J. Menniti. "Discrimination and Harassment: Litigation by Women in Policing." In Roslyn Muraskin and Ted Alleman, eds., *It's a Crime: Women and Justice*. Upper Saddle River, N.J.: Prentice Hall, 1993, pp. 177–190.

Hale, Donna, and Stacey Wyland. "Dragons and Dinosaurs: The Plight of Patrol Women." *Police Forum*, 3 (April 1993), pp. 1–6.

Henry, Vincent E. *Death Work*. New York: Oxford University Press, 2004.

Homant, Robert J. "The Impact of Policewomen on Community Attitudes Toward the Police." *Journal of Police Science and Administration*, 15, no. 1 (1983), pp. 16–22.

Hughes, Helen MacGill. *Social Organizations*. Boston: Holbrook, 1971.

Hyatt, William D. "Parameter of Police Misconduct." In Michael J. Palmiotto, ed., *Police Misconduct*. Upper Saddle River, NJ: Prentice Hall, 2004.

Kappler, Victor E., Richard D. Sluder, and Geoffrey Alpert. "Breeding Deviant Conformity: The Ideology and Culture of Police." In Roger G. Dunham and Geoffrey R. Alpert, eds., *Critical Issues in Policing*. Prospect Heights, Ill.: Waveland Press, 2005, pp. 231–257.

Knapp Commission. *Police Corruption in New York*. New York: Whitman Knapp, 1972.

Langton, L. *Crime Data Brief: Women in Law Enforcement, 1987-2008*, 2010. Retrieved from bjs.gov/content/pub/pdf/wle8708.pdf

Leinen, S. *Black Police, White Society*. New York: Basic Books, 1984.

Lersch, K.M. "Exploring Gender Differences in Citizen Allegations of Misconduct: An Analysis of a Municipal Police Department." *Women and Criminal Justice* (Summer 1998), pp. 69–80.

Light, Donald, Jr., and Suzanne Keller. *Sociology*. New York: Alfred A. Knopf, 1975.

Lord, Leslie Kay. "A Comparison of Male and Female Police Officers' Stereotypic Perception of Women and Women Police Officers." *Journal of Police Science and Administration*, 14, no. 2 (1986), pp. 83–97.

Lord, Stephen, John Crank, and Ronald Evans. "Goodbye in a Sea of Blue." In John P. Crank, ed. *Understanding Police Culture* (2nd ed.). Cincinnati: Anderson Publishing/LexisNexis, 2004, pp. 353–363.

Maas, P. *Serpico*. New York: Harper Collins, 1973.

Maguire, Kathleen, and Timothy J. Flanagan, eds. *Sourcebook of Criminal Justice Statistics, 1994*. Washington, D.C.: U.S. Department of Justice, Bureau of Justice Statistics, 1995.

Martin, Susan E. "Policewomen and Police Women. Occupational Role Dilemmas and Choices of Female Officers." *Journal of Police Science and Administration*, 7, no. 3 (September 1979), pp. 314–323.

_____. "Female Officers on the Move." In Roger G. Dunham and Geoffrey P. Alpert, eds., *Critical Issues in Policing* (2nd ed.). Prospect Heights, Ill.: Waveland Press, 1993, pp. 327–347.

_____. "Women Officers on the Move: An Update on Women in Policing." In Roger G. Dunham and Geoffrey P. Alpert, eds., *Critical Issues in Policing* (5th ed.). Prospect Heights, Ill.: Waveland Press, 2005, pp. 356–371.

Marx, Gary T. *Undercover: Police Surveillance in America*. Berkeley and Los Angeles: University of California Press, 1988.

McBride, R. Bruce. "Perceptions of Racial Discrimination within Occupation Socialization Process as Held by Newly Appointed Police Officers in Selected New York State Police Departments." Dissertation, SUNY at Albany, 1986.

McCamey, William D., Gene L. Scaramella, and Steven M. Cox. *Contemporary Municipal Policing*. Boston: Pearson Education, 2003.

Miraglia, Greg. *Coming Out from Behind the Badge*. Bloomington, Ind.: Author House, 2007.

Milton, Catherine H. *Women in Policing*. Washington, D.C.: Police Foundation, 1972.

National Advisory Commission on Criminal Justice Standards and Goals. *Report of the Task Force on Organized Crime*. Washington, D.C.: U.S. Government Printing Office, 1976.

National Center for Women and Policing, no date but latest bibliographical citation is the year 2001. *Recruiting & Retaining Women: A Self-Assessment Guide for Law Enforcement*, Los Angeles.

National Commission on Law Observance and Enforcement. George P. Wickersham, chairman, *Wickersham Commission Report 14: Police*. Montclair, N.J.: Patterson Smith, 1931, reprinted 1968.

Neyroud, Peter. "Police and Ethics." In Tim Newburn, ed., *Handbook of Policing*. Cullompton, Devon, UK: Willan, 2003, pp. 578–602.

Niederhoffer, Arthur. *Behind the Shield*. Garden City, N.Y.: Doubleday, 1969.

Owings, Chloe. *Women Police*. Montclair, N.J.: Patterson Smith, 1925, reprinted 1969.

Paoline, Eugene A. "Shedding Light on Police Culture: An Examination of Officers' Occupational Attitudes." *Police Quarterly* (June 2004), pp. 205–236.

Peak, Kenneth. *Policing America*. Upper Saddle River, N.J.: Prentice Hall, 1993.

Pendergrass, Virginia E., and Nancy M. Ostrove. "A Survey of Stress in Women in Policing." *Journal of Police*

Science and Administration, 12, no. 3 (1984), pp. 138–144.

Price, Barbara R. "A Study of Leadership Strength of Female Executives." *Journal of Police Science and Administration*, 2, no. 2 (June 1974), pp. 223–240.

Quinn, M. *Walking with the Devil: The Police Code of Silence*. Minneapolis: Quinn & Associates, 2005.

Radano, Gene. *Walking the Beat*. Cleveland: World, 1968.

Reiser, Martin. "Some Organization Stresses on Policemen." *Journal of Police Science and Administration*, 2, no. 2 (June 1974), pp. 138–144.

Roberts, A., and J. Roberts. *Police Innovations and the Structure of Informal Communication Between Police Agencies: Network and LEMAS Data*, 2006. Retrieved from ncjrs.gov/pdffiles1/nij/grants/216150.pdf

Robertson, Ian. *Sociology* (3rd ed.). New York: Worth, 1987.

Roethlisberger, F.J., and William J. Dickson. *Management and the Worker*. Cambridge, Mass.: Harvard University Press, 1939.

Sandberg, Sheryl. *Lean In: Women, Work, and the Will to Lead*. New York: Knopf, 2013.

Savitz, Leonard D. *Socialization of the Police*. Final report to the Pennsylvania Justice Planning Board. Philadelphia: Temple University, 1971.

Schultz, Dorothy M. *From Social Worker to Crime Fighter: Women in United States Policing*. Westport, Conn.: Praeger, 1995.

Schultz, Dorothy. "Law Enforcement Leaders: A Survey of Women Police Chiefs in the United States." *Police Chief* (March 2002), pp. 25–28.

Sever, M. *Effects of Organizational Culture on Police Decision Making*, 2008. Retrieved from lemitonline.org/publications/telemasp/Pdf/volume%2015/vol15no1.pdf

Sherman, Lawrence. *Controlling Police Corruption: The Effects of Reform Policies—Summary Report*. Washington, D.C.: U.S. Government Printing Office, 1978.

Sherman, Lewis J. "A Psychological View of Women in Policing." *Journal of Police Science and Administration*, 1, no. 4 (December 1973).

Shernock, Stan. "An Empirical Examination of the Relationship Between Police Solidarity and Community Orientation." *Journal of Police Science and Administration*, 16, no. 3 (September 1988), pp. 182–194.

Shusta, Robert M., Deena R. Levine, Herbert Wong, and Philip Harris. *Multicultural Law Enforcement: Strategies for Peacekeeping in a Diverse Society*. Upper Saddle River, N.J.: Pearson, 2005.

Skolnick, Jerome H. *Justice Without Trial: Law Enforcement in a Democratic Society*. New York: Wiley, 1966.

Smith, Ralph Lee. *The Tarnished Badge*. New York: Thomas Y. Crowell, 1965.

Stark, Rodney. *Police Riots*. Belmont, Calif.: Focus, 1972.

Stoddard, Ellwyn R. "The Informal 'Code' of Police Deviance: A Group Approach to 'Blue-Coat Crime.'" *Journal of Criminal Law, Criminology, and Police Science*, 59 (June 1968), pp. 244–250.

Stratton, John G. *Police Passages*. Sandusky, Ohio: Glennon Publishing, 1984.

Tauber, Ronald K. "Danger and the Police: A Theoretical Analysis." *Issues in Criminology* (Summer 1967), pp. 69–81.

Taylor, Edward B. *Primitive Culture*. London: John Murray, 1871.

Van Brocklin, V. *Good Cynicism vs. Bad Cynicism*, 2009. Retrieved from lawofficer.com/article/leadership/good-cynicism-vs-bad-cynicism

Terrill, W., E. Paoline, and P. Manning. "Police Culture and Coercion." *Criminology*, 41, no. 4 (2003). Retrieved from fitting-in.com

Walker, Samuel. "Racial Minority and Female Employment in Policing: The Implications of 'Glacial' Change." *Crime and Delinquency*, 31 (October 1985), pp. 355–372.

————. *The Police in America* (3rd ed.). New York: McGraw-Hill, 1999.

Wambaugh, Joseph. *The New Centurions*. Boston: Little, Brown, 1970.

————. *Hollywood Station*. London: Quercus, 2006.

Wasilewski, M., and A. Olson. *Police Isolation, Part III: Isolated Officers & the Cost to Society*, 2010. Retrieved from lawofficer.com/article/leadership/police-isolation-part-iii

Weitzer, R. White. "Black, or Blue Cops? Race and Citizen Assessments of Police Officers." *Journal of Criminal Justice*, 28 (2000), pp. 313–324.

Wertsch, Teresa Lynn. "Walking the Thin Blue Line: Policewomen and Tokenism Today." *Women and Criminal Justice*, 9, no. 3 (1998), pp. 23–61.

Westley, William A. *Violence and the Police*. Cambridge: Massachusetts Institute of Technology, 1970.

Wexler, Judie Gaffin, and Deana Dorman Logan. "Sources for Stress among Women Police Officers." *Journal of Police Science and Administration*, 11, no. 1 (1983), pp. 46–53.

Wheisheit, Ralph A. "Women in the State Police: Concerns of Male and Female Police Officers." *Journal of Police Science and Administration*, 15, no. 2 (1987), pp. 137–144.

Wilson, James Q. *Varieties of Police Behavior.* Cambridge, Mass.: Harvard University Press, 1968.

Wood, Richard L., Mariah Davis, and Amelia Rouse. "Dining Into Quicks and Program Implementation and Police Subculture." In Westley G. Skogan, ed., *Community Policing, Can It Work.* Belmont, Calif.: Wadsworth/Thompson, 2004, pp. 136–162.

Worden, R.E. "Situational and Attitudinal Explanations of Police Behavior: A Theoretical Reappraisal and Empirical Assessment." *Law and Society Review*, 23, 1989, pp. 667–711.

3 The Art and Style of Proactive Police Leadership

KEY TERMS

benchmarking

chaos

charismatic authority

conceptual skill

dispersed leadership

emotional intelligence

14 points

hierarchy of needs

high touch

human skill

hygiene factor

International Association of Chiefs of Police (IACP)

KITA

leadership

legal authority

management skills

managerial grid

motivators

reengineering

seven habits

technical skill

Theory X

Theory Y

Theory Z

total quality management (TQM)

One of the critical management issues of today is leadership. Too often, the public media discusses the so-called crisis in leadership or why leaders cannot and do not lead. Ethics also remains a major issue. At a recent leadership conference, we rhetorically asked: Who are the most prominent police leaders in the United States today? The class cited prominent police figures, but they had a hard time naming police leaders whom they would want as models for their own careers.

The irony here is that many of the police leaders whom we cited in Chapter 1 were not held in high esteem by their subordinates during their tenure in office. Others were respected by the troops but not by the public. Former Los Angeles Chief of Police Darryl Gates, for example, was damned by the public for insensitivity and errors of judgment for the department's handling of the Rodney King incident.

Reflecting on leadership as described by Amitai Etzioni, Richard Hall (1996: 139–40) points out that leadership is a special form of power closely related to the ability of the leader to elicit the followers' voluntary compliance in a broad range of matters. Leadership is distinguished from the concept of power in that a leader has influence over subjects, while power implies that subjects' preferences are held in abeyance.

Perusing our personal libraries, we came up with over 30 different definitions of leadership. Simply summarized, **leadership** is the ability to get things done under the right circumstances. So much for definitions. The real challenge is to examine and understand the problems and theoretical parameters involved in the characteristics of leadership in American policing. We decided to mix some of the classical leadership theories required of all graduate students for comprehensive exams with those of some current theories being discussed in the business world.

PROACTIVE LEADERSHIP

Proactive leaders anticipate day-to-day events. They do not wait for events to reach them; they plan for events. They form a team that is flexible enough to seek a wide variety of solutions to the everyday problems of police management. This entails a deep commitment to contingency planning so that the eventual crises that do reach their desks do not overwhelm them. Crises, for a proactive police management team, are something to be dealt with and learned from, not simply reacted to.

To exercise this proactive leadership, five essential areas of competence are needed:

- Authority
- Talent
- Experience
- Ethics
- Training and education

While a whole range of competencies is needed for the exercise of leadership, these five areas are significant enough to become prerequisites for other competencies.

Authority

Authority in an organization can be exercised in two ways: through the person of the officeholder or through the office itself. Of course, the reality is that authority is exercised in a synthesis combining both ways. However, the emphasis can go either way.

Max Weber's concept of **charismatic authority** is one of the earliest and clearest conceptions of authority being exercised through the person rather than the office (Weber, 1961: 628). Weber describes the three major bases for legitimate authority:

1. *Rational grounds*, which rest on a belief in the "legality" of patterns of normative rules and the right of those elevated to authority under such rules to issue commands (legal authority)
2. *Traditional grounds*, which rest on an established belief in the sanctity of immemorial traditions and the legitimacy of the status of those exercising authority under them (traditional authority)
3. *Charismatic grounds*, which rest on devotion to the specific and exceptional sanctity, heroism, or exemplary character of an individual person (charismatic authority)

In its purest form, charismatic authority creates the authority of the office in terms of the person holding the office. Modern figures who are supposed to have exercised a great deal of their authority through the charisma of their person include Mahatma Gandhi, John Kennedy, and Eleanor Roosevelt.

Many police chiefs and sheriffs often depend on the strength of their personalities in exercising public office. However, such authority is short-lived. According to Weber (1961: 697), "In its pure form, charismatic authority has a character specifically foreign to everyday routine structures. The social relationships directly involved are strictly personal." To create stability in the organization, charismatic authority needs to be channeled into the mechanics of a routine bureaucracy, thus taking on all the trappings of legitimate authority based on legal and rational grounds. Charismatic authority, with its reliance on personal relationships, creates inconsistent policies based on personal whims and often breaks down.

Over time, the charismatic figure institutes the normal legalistic aspects of a rational bureaucracy, namely (1) a set of written rules that persist over time and that are adhered to, (2) a clearly identified set of administrative officials with their authority specifically defined and limited, and (3) a hierarchical organization with publicly known operational lines of authority.

A chief who has a strong personality and good rapport with the public may be able to operate for a time, depending on charismatic authority, by ignoring the rules of rational bureaucracy. Modern, organized society, however, is basically a bureaucratic society based on rational **legal authority**. Some charismatic sheriffs who are inconsistent administrators are kept in power by political party officials because of their vote-getting power. However, the rational rules of the organization take over the day-to-day business of the police department and even the most powerful sheriffs have to recognize this, especially when they see their power curbed by police union contracts and the courts. However, a certain amount of charismatic authority is valuable and useful in exercising the duties of police leadership.

Talent

A talented police leader is one who also has a high degree of intelligence. He or she must be able to understand theoretical concepts as they relate to the job and be able to create abstract plans and operationalize these plans. This involves a high degree of abstract manipulation of data and the ability to comprehend and make the most use of the computer age.

Talented police leaders must also have what has been called a certain native shrewdness; that is, they have to have a grasp of politics and be pragmatic problem solvers. They must also be goal oriented—that is, individuals who truly want to get the job done. Police leaders have to balance many demands on their time along with conflicting demands that bear on their decisions. Special-interest groups, politicians, fellow police leaders, and their own officers, including the diverse groups within the official police community, all create pressures on their decisions. A leader must have a sense of fair play and balance to get the job done amid conflicting pressures.

Our police leaders must also be excellent communicators. They need to be clear and forceful yet be able to listen and understand other points of view. Their ideas of leadership need to be marketed just as business and industry market ideas. Police leaders have many publics, including their own officers, various community groups, and governmental and criminal justice leaders. Communication ability is crucial. Former New York City Police Commissioner William Bratton was a master at this by appearing at important police events and communicating with the print and electronic media on the progress the department was making in the "crime war." Unfortunately, his media fame and public stature came into conflict with Mayor Rudolph Guiliani's, and Bratton retired in 1996.

After reading these few paragraphs on talent, the reader might begin to wonder if every police leader has to be a comic book superhero. The answer is, not quite. Too often, we have been satisfied in police management with mediocre leadership. The demands of the twenty-first century on police management will no longer allow us this luxury. Today's police leader may not have to be a superhero, but he or she does have to be a supremely talented human being who can bring that talent to bear on the exercise of office.

Experience

An experienced police leader is one who has gained a wide range of leadership talents.

He or she does not simply need operational experience. The chief really does not need to know how to fix a patrol car, how to write a parking ticket, or even how to drive a motorcycle. Management skills are developed through the exercise of management and administrative experience. They may seem obvious, but many departments operate when choosing their leaders as if this fact did not exist. If there were advertisements in the local newspapers for police chiefs, in terms of the history of electing and appointing police leaders, most of them would read like this:

Job Vacancy for Police Chief: No Management Experience Necessary.

Experience is necessary, but it has to be experience of a certain kind and quality. Technically trained, operational administrators need experience in making decisions based on complex, often incomplete facts and the human situation.

Experience in the day-to-day activities of police work is valuable and contributes to being a good police administrator. The operational and technical skills needed for administrators must be superseded by the necessary human relations and conceptual skills needed to manage a police department.

Some of this lack of experience can be made up with a good management training program. Police leaders can be trained in how to draw up and present a budget, in what is necessary in exercising leadership skills in relation to personnel, and in what goes into such items as contingency planning and communication networks. Thus, what is necessary in the exercise of proactive police leadership is a careful blend of ability, experience, ethics, and, finally, training and education.

Ethics

The downfall of major investment companies such as Bear Sterns, Enron, and Adelphia during the past years was based on corporate and executive greed, criminal behavior, and corporate board and state and federal laissez-faire policies. Quite simply, the executives under investigation or in prison were accused of issuing false earnings reports or taking the corporation's money for their personal use. It is no surprise that the issue of ethics is being reviewed in business and management courses around the country. In some cases, they used bad judgment in making decisions, as was done by AIG, which accepted federal bailout funds but gave executives hefty financial bonuses and held meetings in expensive resorts.

Police executives face a number of ethical dilemmas every day when striving to make the right choice from the competing choices. Needless to say, outright criminal behavior, violating department policies and regulations, and engaging in conduct unbecoming of a police officer do not reflect well on one's ability to lead the organization and to exhort line and staff officers to behave in an ethical manner.

Training and Education

Police leaders are promoted, appointed, and elected, in most cases, without any further training in management skills. There is general agreement that police executives need training to both obtain and refine leadership skills especially in such areas as emerging technology, counter-terrorism, budgeting, and planning. This review was updated to include the skills needed to address both community policing and homeland security activities.

Over the years, a number of private and public agencies have developed courses for police officers and managers. Major agencies routinely offer some management courses, as does the Federal Bureau of Investigation, Northwestern University, and various professional and state organizations. However, there still remains the lack of a systematic approach to basic training for all police managers.

The specific **management skills** based on recent deliberations on executive training are as follows:

- Police chief as leader
- Motivation of personnel
- Personnel administration
- Budgeting
- Strategic and short-term planning
- Marketing services to the community through traditional and electronic means
- Emergency command situations
- Legal issues involving operations and personnel administration
- Planning for and upgrading police technology

This list, indeed, makes a fine curriculum for a modern police management academy. When we analyze this list, some skill patterns emerge: organization and administration skills; technical skills, such as fiscal management and knowledge of advanced technology; and, overwhelmingly, communication skills on all levels.

Major metropolitan areas normally maintain their own police academies and offer some management training programs. However, the medium-sized and smaller departments do not have the economies of scale of the larger municipalities and thus have neither the budget nor the continuing demand for such large-scale training. There is a need for systematic leadership/ management courses for newly promoted police executives. These should be readily available on a systematic, recurring, and regional basis. Upon promotion, new administrators should have the opportunity to attend a regionally based or state training academy.

Today, the criteria for police executive selection in progressive departments are similar to those in the selection of a business executive. Community search committees look for candidates who have a combination of education, training, and field experience. In addition to management skills, police chief candidates must also be able to define what the department's organizational vision of the future is. As Garner (1993: 3–4) discusses, this vision includes communicating a clear mission statement that is derived from discussion with employees and community leaders. While there are no formal data available, the number of chief executives with bachelor's and master's degrees in fields ranging from criminal justice to law and public administration is growing.

MANAGEMENT STYLES

Over the years, numerous management profiles have been taken from the areas of public and business administration and applied to police management. There is a great deal of overlap in this area with communication models, since the style of police leadership is directly linked to the communication process within the agency. When communication goes from the top to the bottom, with no feedback system, for example, the management style tends toward the hierarchical and autocratic. When communication is two-way, ongoing, and considered to be effective in deciding policy between equals in an organizational structure, the management style tends toward the democratic team approach.

The following 13 approaches will be examined in terms of their applicability to the art and style of proactive police leadership:

1. Dispersed leadership
2. Leadership and Giving
3. Effective leadership
4. Managing in chaos
5. Digital nervous system
6. Emotional intelligence
7. Total quality management (TQM)
8. Reengineering
9. Katz's three skills approach
10. Maslow's hierarchy of needs
11. Herzberg's hygiene/motivators approach to job satisfaction
12. McGregor's Theory X and Theory Y
13. Theory Z

Dispersed Leadership

The main idea behind **dispersed leadership** is that all members of an organization are leaders. Whether a person is a dispatcher, patrol officer, field supervisor, or chief, operational policing requires all its members to make decisions, take actions, and be held accountable for what occurs. This forms the basis for the Leadership in Police Organizations course that was created by the **International Association of Chiefs of Police (IACP)**.

As discussed at a national summit held in 2005, dispersed leadership is based on the following concepts:

Shared understanding. Common definitions and knowledge are needed to discuss what leadership is all about.

Commitment to shared goals and values. Members of an organization should understand the basic tenets of a department's mission and values.

Recognition of the different styles of leadership. This deals with the reality that people lead in different ways based on rank, job category, and the situation at hand. As discussed, "leaders at different levels of the organization do different things and lead in different ways, ranging from face-to-face leadership to indirect leadership with infrequent personal contact" (IACP, 2005: 2). Thus, leadership training must adapt to various roles and levels in the organization.

Focus on the individual and the organization. This involves developing skills and knowledge that will benefit all members of the organization. What is needed—and is often the main problem in policing—is the need for a formal training and periodic and personal assessment of all organizational members (2005: 2).

What differentiates this program from others is the need for leadership to be taught at all phases of a person's career. For this program, assessment instruments are used to gauge a person's strengths and weaknesses. The training course is presented to a cross section of personnel of about 24–28 persons with assessors assigned to 6 students. Topics in the program offered over a four-week period include motivation, organizational culture, ethics, problem solving, critical skills, and review of assessment results. At this time, the program is a "work in progress" and further efforts and funding must be undertaken to make the program available and accessible to police personnel.

Leadership and Giving

Helping others is a theme that resounds in a recent work by James Grant, an organizational psychologist at the University of Pennsylvania. Grant (2013) points out that as the United States increasingly becomes a service-based economy, those buying and receiving services are concerned about interactions with and trust in the provider. Thus, three business relationship types have developed in many organizations: takers, givers, and matchers.

Takers are very common in many organizational environments. Takers feel that they must win at all costs and only take other people's feelings and predicaments into the equation if it fits their needs. Takers often promote themselves and take all the credit for a job well done. The term—"so and so was thrown under the bus"—is a good way to describe the outcome of dealing with an ultimate taker. On the other hand, there are takers who only act when it is in their self-interest to do so.

Givers, according to Grant, are more concerned with others. They are, he writes, "a rare breed." They view reciprocity in the other direction, preferring to give more than they get. Givers do not work with a balance sheet; they help others and are generous with their time, skills, and business and social networks. In the world of work, givers focus on relationships, such as giving credit to others as a strong measure of success.

Matchers are those who have both the tenets of givers and takers. Think of a friend whom you meet for lunch and keeps tabs in an annoying way on how many times he or she picked up the check. Matchers always keep a balance sheet and will act or do something when requested but they will expect something in return. The most common result is the adage "You owe me."

According to Grant, leaders use all three styles in daily interactions depending on the situation. However, effective leaders tend to have a more dominant style. Based on a number of occupational psychology studies cited in his book in such areas as medicine, sales, software development, and the military, Grant feels that givers are the ones who overall provide effective leadership and benefits to an organization. This is not to say that they are pushovers or what is commonly referred to as "chumps." Givers have self-interests and are motivated to succeed but in a way that benefits the organization and larger social networks.

How does this impact police management? Overall, we feel that the majority of police officers who fall into the giving category want to make a contribution to increase public safety, reduce crime, and improve the community. This was illustrated at a recent police awards ceremony for professional service and valor. What was interesting is the degree to which the award winners were heavily involved in their communities outside of normal work hours.

Police managers who fit the giving mold are those that take extra pains to contribute to the organization perhaps outside of the usual job description and beyond the normal eight hour day. They are willing to accept tough assignments and go out of their way to represent the agency outside of the department, for example at community events or inter-agency professional meetings. Above all they are concerned about the care and welfare of "the troops" under their supervision. For example, at long-term assignments involving emergency situations or security details, the giver will also focus on food, breaks, and lodging for personnel. For day-to-day operations it is the little things that count such as making sure the vehicles are operating properly, equipment is purchased, and assignments are given on a fair basis. Givers also find it important to recognize those personnel who go out of their way to help others through formal department awards programs or simple thank you letters. Above all they are willing to step back and listen. As Grant writes, "If you want other people to be givers, one of the easiest steps is to ask" (p. 268). This creates a situation where people can express ideas and a personal statement on how the organization should operate or how the situation should be handled.

Effective Leadership

A recent trend in management seminars has been the paradigm of "effective habits" of leaders in business or public service. The most popular and successful of this genre is the Stephen Covey series, *The 7 Habits of Highly Effective Leaders*, first published in 1989. Several versions of this work have been published for various professional adaptations by the Covey Leadership Center. Recently, the Covey Leadership Center applied its concepts to law enforcement agencies. One version of the **seven habits** is in use by the Royal Canadian Mounted Police, and some American police agencies have adopted aspects of the program for both command and line officers. Recently, Covey was the featured speaker at the annual conference of the IACP.

According to Covey, leadership is often taught as a skill such as planning for an event or taking command of a situation. He argues that the core of leadership is character, which, in sum, defines the motivations that each individual has in order to make others follow. Leadership differs from management in that management is efficiency in climbing the ladder of success, while leadership determines whether the ladder is leaning against the right wall (Covey, 1989: 101). Leadership development is based on the "Maturity Continuum," which consists of the following seven habits:

1. *Be proactive.* This is defined as the habit of personal vision—that one is responsible for one's behavior and choices in life. In short, each person is responsible for his or her own life through decisions that he or she makes on a daily basis. This means taking the initiative and taking actions in one's circle of influence, which is broadly defined as areas that a person has control over.

2. *Begin with the end in mind.* In this stage the proactive leader is responsible for setting goals, which is done through a mission statement of things that can be accomplished in the circle of influence. Core factors that contribute to a mission statement are wisdom, security, guidance, and power. These in turn are influenced by factors that affect decision making, such as self, religion, and work.

3. *Put first things first.* This deals with taking care of yourself and your schedule. It is no secret that personal and time management is a skill that many people need to learn in terms of getting things accomplished each day. The Covey method uses what is called the "Big Rocks" concept: Each "Rock" is defined, and that is where one should spend most of one's time and attention. What often happens is that police managers spend most of their time on nonurgent activities such as phone calls, trivia, and other items (called time wasters).

4. *Think win-win.* This is a habit that is built on the premise that agreements or solutions can be mutually beneficial to all parties in a negotiation. The alternatives to win-win are

win-lose, lose-lose, lose-win, lose-lose. Then there is the option of no deal, which is simply an acknowledgment that the parties cannot come to terms with an issue at the present time. The key to the win-win and no deal areas is to build on relationships. This all depends on whether the company or agency can support a win-win type of arrangement because most businesses think win-lose.

5. ***Seek first to understand and then to be understood.*** This deals with many of the concepts discussed in Chapter 5 on operating principles. Communication, Covey (1989: 237) writes, is the most important skill in life, but few people have had any training in it. Communication includes not only writing, reading, and speaking but also listening. Listening skills should be based on empathic listening, which is to intentionally take the time to understand or diagnose what the speaker or writer is actually trying to express. This skill includes perceiving the tone, presence, hand gestures, and social context of the communication.

6. ***Synergize.*** This integrates the above habits and results in cooperation and betterment of the group or organization. *Synergy* is a term that is often used in business discussions or motivational speeches. According to Covey, the whole is greater than the sum of its parts when it comes to creative cooperation for problem solving. People working together can achieve many goals.

7. ***Sharpen the saw.*** This habit deals with self-renewal in terms of a person's physical, mental, spiritual, and social-emotional health. As discussed in other chapters, police officers have high rates of divorce, alcohol and prescription drug abuse, and suicide because of their work situations, schedules, and influences of the work subculture (discussed in Chapter 2).

Intertwined with these stages are a number of paradigms that contribute to each habit. For example, the first three habits deal with private victories that people need to achieve in order to get their lives in order. The last four habits, which are built on the first three, are public victories, measures of achievement for an organization. As discussed by Bailey (2005), there is little research to ascertain if the Covey method is successful in bringing about changes in organizations that have adopted the seven habits framework. For example, is there improved productivity, decreased personnel complaints, better morale? The Covey method, however, may have an impact on individual performance.

Managing in Chaos

At a seminar on strategic planning, the presenter used the following excerpt from the *New York Times*, which described the leadership challenges facing several executives in charge of offices in the World Trade Center on September 11, 2001:

> There is no Harvard MBA course, no corporate strategy session, no business celebrity memoir that can prepare a chief executive to lead a corporation, and thousands of employees, when 110 floors fall out from under them. And in the hours that have passed since the collapse of the World Trade Center (WTC), many of the nation's chief executives registered the strange sensation of living in a world that they, always so capable, always so sure, had never encountered. (Wayne and Kaufman, 2001)

Responding police and fire unit supervisors and commanders experienced the same feeling. They faced a terrible situation involving the tallest buildings in the world whose upper floors were engulfed in flames because of two kamikaze crashed airliners. They witnessed people jumping out of the buildings rather than face being burned to death. Forget about fire suppression—their first order of business was to get people evacuated. Within 45 minutes, the buildings collapsed, sending a debris surge of cement, paper, dust, and chemical particles throughout Lower

Manhattan. Added to this **chaos**, the city's high-tech emergency command center was located in Tower 2 of the WTC and was evacuated minutes before the building was destroyed.

At the Pentagon site, the first responding units saw smoke and fire and, eventually, airplane parts scattered about. The first supervisor assessed the overall situation and began charting on a notepad where to put equipment and personnel in what would become the incident command center for the duration of recovery and cleanup. She then started to issue orders and called for additional assistance according to an emergency plan that the Arlington County Police Department had practiced several times before September 11 (Farr, 2002).

The following recommendations for addressing disasters of such outrageous proportions are based on our own experiences and from various police and private-sector after-action reviews of September 11:

1. *Be calm.* In one account after another, the emergency responders and the people in charge of business and operations at the WTC assessed the situation and began making decisions and issuing orders to subordinates based on the information that each had. There were few reports of people in leadership positions going berserk or abandoning their posts unless ordered to do so. Call it leadership under fire, the leaders that day did not lose their cool in front of their subordinates—at least not in public.

2. *Communicate.* One of the things that the public admired about former mayor Rudolph Guiliani in the days that followed the attacks was his sincere, calm, and matter-of-fact public reviews of the situation and of the actions that he and other city leaders were taking to deal with the massive problems caused by the destruction of the WTC and the surrounding neighborhood. Information was reported and clarified in a professional manner each day for the media. The former mayor recently wrote that he immediately began speaking to reporters on the street as he and his staff were retreating to establish a new command post. "I had to communicate with the public, to do whatever I could to calm people down and contribute to an orderly and safe evacuation," he stated (Guiliani, 2002: 36).

3. *Take care of your people.* Firefighters and police officers share an unwritten axiom that you never leave your colleagues behind when retreating from an impossible situation. Many police officers and firefighters were probably lost trying to rescue or locate their comrades. In the chaos that followed, police and fire commanders began to take head counts to determine if their people made it out of the WTC. This was further complicated by the number of off-duty emergency police and fire personnel who went to the scene directly from their homes. With the assistance of New York's construction industry, a massive undertaking was begun to locate survivors who could be trapped under the rubble at Ground Zero. Field managers also had to deal with basic life and operational functions, which included food, equipment replacement, leave arrangements, and rest breaks, which in this case, spanned for months after the event.

   For the police and fire departments, preparations were enacted to deal with survivors of those killed in action or presumed dead. While these procedures are often standard operating procedure (SOP) for police and fire departments, it was a massive, grueling undertaking because of the high number of casualties that occurred on September 11. As discussed in Chapter 12, factors that have to be considered include burial arrangements, return of personal property, and review of insurance and other death benefits with the next of kin. Private-sector managers also had to deal with the same factors for employees killed that day. In New York State, special legislation was enacted to allow affected families to submit insurance claims without obtaining the traditional death notice, which is based on recovery of the actual body.

4. ***Get back to business as soon as possible.*** In the days that followed, the city of New York cordoned off the WTC and affected areas and began resuming regular city services. Thanks to round-the-clock efforts by communications workers, the cable networks that run the New York Stock Exchange were repaired, and trading was resumed that following Monday. Subway service was restored, with the exception of those stations directly under the WTC. The mayor urged people to get back to work and to return to New York. In Washington, the Pentagon resumed business shortly after the destroyed sections had been cordoned off.

   For psychological and operational reasons, businesses have to return to some sense of normalcy. After the WTC bombing of 1993, most WTC tenants had prepared emergency and business-interruption plans. They had already set up satellite locations in New Jersey and upstate New York and simply moved surviving personnel so that they could return to general business operations.

5. ***Maintain critical communications.*** We have been in a number of critical situations, and in each and every case, command communications during the situation were always a problem. A case in point is the separate radio channels that often exist in a region or a county for the police and fire departments. Field units cannot communicate with each other. Although all reviews are not yet completed of the aftermath of the WTC attack, it appears that the fire department lost most of its communications with field units involved in evacuation efforts.

6. ***Have an incident command plan.*** This is a plan in which various agencies come together and address a situation at a central location. To be candid, turf battles are common between the police, fire department, and emergency services units in terms of who is in charge and who makes the critical decisions. They often do not practice the plan together, and the chain of command is not defined. The aftermath studies conducted of the rescue efforts of September 11 in New York noted the absence of an incident command plan and found that the fire and police departments did not work with each other during the initial response.

7. ***Be prepared to retreat.*** Although no one likes to admit it, there are times when it is advisable to retreat to limit casualties and equipment losses and to protect agency heads during a critical incident. As the New York City emergency-management center was destroyed, Mayor Guiliani and his staff moved to several locations until they decided to take up command quarters in the police academy.

8. ***Deal with postevent stress and physical conditions.*** A number of colleagues we know in the police and emergency services areas have nightmares, drink too much, and fight with their friends and family over minor things weeks and months after dealing with a critical incident. Many rescue workers still complain of having the "WTC cough" from breathing in various particles at the site. Agencies have to be prepared to deal not only with the psychological needs that occur after such an incident but also requests for early retirement, claims for worker's compensation, and voluntary resignations. This is why the police department and the people in charge of human resources must have a close working relationship and the expertise to deal with such individual situations.

Digital Nervous System

The most influential leader in the technological revolution is Bill Gates, former CEO of Microsoft, the company that developed the Windows software system. The Microsoft Windows operating system is used by most computers in the world. In his book *Business at the Speed of Thought* (1999), Gates reviewed the operational and organizational changes taking place through "digitizing" in operational practices ranging from paper reports to organizational design. He presented a number of business practices that organizational leaders should consider based on the adoption of digital tools. The major points were that paper transactions can be eliminated and digital tools can assist in the development of intra-organizational communication (e-mail), virtual teams, instant customer service, and increased attention to data collection and analysis.

Today the personal computer, cellphone, and Internet define how organizational decisions and interactions with customers are created and executed. Gates viewed this entire enterprise as a "digital nervous system" involving rapid activity and responses both within and outside the organization.

The leadership factor for managing the digital enterprise is important to determine how information technology can best be obtained, applied, and managed for organizational processes and relations with customers. The most basic tenet here is that the leadership structure must comprehend and understand the technological revolution that is going on and be able to forecast potential applications. There must be a commitment to expend budgetary resources to obtain equipment and training. At the time of publication, Gates declared that information technology is terribly expensive and that too much money goes for administration rather than applications. However, as time has proven, the cost for digital tools continues to decrease.

Then, too, there has to be a review of the organizational structure and a commitment to creating digital teams to share information and to address issues and problems. This sharing of information, according to Gates, is the development of institutional intelligence, or corporate IQ (1999: 239). Companies with high IQ tend to collaborate effectively so that key people on a given project are well informed. Company leaders must also "lead by example" by sharing both good and bad news with all segments of the organization. In summary, leadership becomes defined by knowledge management or the extent to which a company and its employees are capable of using information for planning, customer relations, training, and project coordination.

The impact of all this on police organizations is both immediate and abstract. Most police departments remain based in the traditional organizational structure and often have limited resources for acquiring information technology. The application of the digital revolution around the United States, and the world for that matter, has created a sense of both reality and irony for many police departments:

1. Cyber crime complaints are increasing, but many smaller police departments still do not have the most basic application of computer technology.
2. Collaboration is often difficult between intradepartmental units because of power and turf wars.
3. There appears to be increased sharing of information between departments and districts by the development of localized mobile radio district and crime/suspect networks.
4. The patrol car has become the digital office; the patrol officer can run data checks, match suspect information, complete reports in final form, and process a prisoner, all in the front seat of a patrol car.
5. Through Compstat and other forms of crime and police-service analysis, police managers are being held accountable for crime trends and service calls in their area.

Emotional Intelligence

We all are emotional human beings. Psychologist Daniel Goleman points out that leaders need to understand both their own emotions and those of others. When leaders make judgments, they need to have categories that will help them analyze their own emotional judgments. Leaders also have to know how emotions affect police personnel.

Emotional intelligence is a concept that continues to be embraced by corporate management today. It is an approach that works with today's community policing and personnel policies. Goleman recommends organizing groups, negotiating solutions, personal connections, and social analysis. Social analysis includes "being able to detect and have insight about people's feeling, motives and concerns" (Goleman, 1995: 118). Emotions are more immediate, intense, and different than conceptual and rational decision making. Successful proactive police management has to anticipate and deal with this aspect of human behavior.

Goleman gave these valuable insights for an emotional competence framework and analytic categories:

Self-Awareness	Emotional awareness, accurate self-assessment, self-confidence
Self-Regulation	Self-control, trustworthiness, conscientiousness, adaptability, innovation
Motivation	Achievement, commitment, initiative, optimism
Empathy	Understanding others, developing others, service orientation, leveraging diversity, political awareness
Social Skills	Influence, communication, conflict management, leadership, change catalyst, building bonds, collaboration and cooperation, team capabilities

Too many of the "old guard" of police leaders feel that they are always making rational decisions. They think that public personnel and the public will judge them rationally and logically. This has never been true. Instant communication and community policing demand more emotional intelligence skills on the part of our police leaders.

Emotional intelligence is being adopted by corporate leadership because of the challenges of global business and e-business. Dealing with worldwide cultures means that corporate leaders must adapt, innovate, and have personal initiative based on emotional intelligence. This is also true of our law enforcement leadership.

Modern police managing requires people skills and team building. Our new police leaders need to encourage field supervisors to grow in their job, take credit for success, and become part of the police leadership team. All police leaders, from the chief's office through supervisory field personnel, must be politically aware and work in the community. Community leadership, like democracy, is always a political process. Creating a positive community leadership–police team is a political process.

Total Quality Management

Total quality management (TQM) was a standard agenda item at police management conferences in the early 1990s. While some of the luster has worn off, the tenets of TQM still remain important for customer relations and modern management practices in terms of product quality. The foundations of TQM were written and discussed before and after World War II by W. Edwards Deming, who served as the leading organizational consultant during the rebuilding of Japanese industry. According to Halberstam (1986: 380), Deming is held in the same regard as General MacArthur by the Japanese with regard to his contributions to postwar economic development. In the United States, however, Deming's ideas were never seriously discussed by organizational theorists until serious inquiry was made into Japanese management practices in the 1980s. In fact, the authors of this book came across Deming's theories as an aside during leisure reading on a comparison of auto industries of the United States and Japan.

By itself, TQM is defined as a strategic, integrated management system for achieving customer satisfaction. TQM involves all managers and employees and uses human resources and managerial and quantitative methods to continually improve organizational processes. According to TQM proponents, it provides attentive leaders, trained workers, data and measurement, a guiding vision, and operating values for any organization. Attention to quality becomes the cornerstone for employee training, assessment of customer satisfaction, creation of management teams, and the corporation's recognition and reward system. An important component in TQM is **benchmarking,** which is defined as "the continuous process of measuring our products, services, and practices against our toughest competitor, or those recognized as world leaders and to identify areas that need improvement" (Xerox, 1991).

The basic components of TQM are summarized according to the 14-point philosophy presented by Deming. As discussed by Butterfield (1991: 50–59) on their application to the service industry, the **14 points** are as follows:

1. A consistency of purpose toward improvement of product and service
2. The adoption of the quality philosophy by management, which must begin with corporate leaders
3. An emphasis on improving work processes rather than relying on mass inspections
4. The awarding of contracts and business on the basis of quality rather than price tag
5. Constant improvement in production and service
6. Much attention to training
7. Uncovering barriers to workmanship
8. Driving out fear, such as the fear of asking questions or expressing ideas
9. Breaking down communication barriers between departments
10. Eliminating slogans and targets for zero defects and new levels of productivity (instead, management concentrates on showing people how to do their work more accurately and efficiently)
11. Eliminating work standards that dwell on numerical quotas (instead, use leadership to look for differences in performance)
12. Removing barriers that rob hourly workers of their pride in workmanship (this is often created by communication barriers between management and employees related to job performance or ways to improve services)
13. Instituting a vigorous program of education and self-improvement for workers for new or improved skills
14. Having everyone in the organization working toward the objective of quality

It is important to stress that TQM does not mean any change in the traditional organizational structure postulated by Weber. There is still the hierarchy, and management is still in control. Quality teams, with the approval of management, are brought together to define and solve problems related to their sphere of influence, but they may have little impact on overall company strategy. Comparing TQM to directed teams, Holpp (1992: 72–73) showed that the main difference is that directed teams in theory are given all kinds of flexibility for production and problem solving.

TQM remains an important concept in organizational theory. It should be noted that in the 1950s, Deming used royalties from his books to create the Deming prize for Japanese companies and their quality control initiatives. Ironically, in the United States today, there is a Deming prize and a Baldridge award, both of which are awarded to companies that have outstanding quality-control mechanisms.

As discussed in Chapter 1, an important component of TQM is leadership. For Deming, leadership is important insofar as managers must remove barriers to producing quality goods and services. Organizations committed to TQM are committed to quality. If some process does not work or produce the right result, then the components that lead to the output are analyzed by a work team to find solutions. A midsized police department could use TQM to facilitate the return of recovered stolen property to the rightful owners. A team would be formed to look at the problems inherent in the current system. The team might include an evidence technician, a patrol supervisor, a patrol officer, and a representative from the district attorney's office interested in evidence for criminal cases. The team would then ask some basic questions such as the following: Why do we have to keep certain items? Could some items be immediately returned? How long after a court disposition do we keep items? How are the items properly tagged and inventoried? What do we do with unclaimed items? How do we destroy contraband, such as drugs? Each question would be broken down into various distinct components, and the team would try to provide new thinking and processes to answer these questions. This is not a one-shot deal. The team would look at how other organizations deal with the problem of over-loaded evidence supply systems. New ideas would be tried, and victims (the customers) would be asked by phone or by mail to evaluate the method used to return their property. The idea is to get the property back to their rightful owners as soon as legally possible and to keep the evidence rooms free of junk. The leadership role in this enterprise is for management to permit formation of the team and to allow it to constructively attack the problem without cumbersome red tape or meddling supervision.

Obviously, this quest for quality must begin at the top and filter down to all layers of the organization. Quality controls and innovations are tied to promotions and rewards. For TQM proponents, there must be true commitment and not lip service; otherwise, the program becomes another fad. According to Halberstam (1986: 313), Deming had little use for managers who had not graduated from the factory floor. At that time, the science of management was exerting itself in many organizations, and many managers dealt with abstractions rather than practical experience.

Reengineering

As businesses were adopting TQM as a way to improve the quality of their goods and services, a concept called **reengineering** was being developed by certain companies as a way to review how tasks were being performed. The term was coined by MIT professor Michael Hammer in 1980 as he observed radical reorganizations undertaken by many major companies. In their book *Reengineering the Corporation*, Hammer and Champy (1993: 4) wrote that reengineering is the fundamental rethinking and basic redesign of business processes to achieve dramatic improvement in critical contemporary measures of performance, such as cost, quality, service, and speed. In comparison to TQM, reengineering involves a radical review of the entire organizational structure, while TQM programs exist within the framework of existing organizational structure.

Hammer and Champy (1993: 32–36) present the following questions when a company or an organizational unit is considering reengineering:

1. Why do we do what we do?
2. Can we disregard all existing structure and procedures and invent new ways of accomplishing work?

3. Do we need dramatic improvement? Should we blow up the old and replace it with something new?
4. What is the range of activities that creates output that is of value to the customer?

This concept came about because of competition, cost, and the drive for quality facing American companies from Asia and Europe. According to the authors, companies that have undertaken reengineering have ranged from those that were in deep trouble, such as auto manufacturers, to those that were having no discernible difficulties but were not satisfied with the current performance. Walmart, Hallmark, Kodak, and others are cited as examples of successful companies that used reengineering as a method to keep an upper hand in their markets.

Companies that have undertaken reengineering are not tied to the idea of centralized control. The development of informational technology, which resulted in information being shared throughout the organization, contributes to this concept by tearing down distance. Units that are miles apart can now teleconference, e-mail, fax, video sell, digitize, use the Internet, and so on.

For his work, *Time* magazine hailed Hammer as one of the 25 most influential people in the United States in 1996. Many observers, however, have used the term *reengineering* in connection with "downsizing," "flattening," or "right-sizing" the organization, which in basic terms means reducing the size of the organization, producing less, and creating more profits for shareholders and executives. In most cases, reengineering means that the company will produce more with fewer departments and levels of control, which indeed results in reduced organizational structures.

In a follow-up work, Hammer (1996) wrote that reengineering had not just modified the ways of working; rather it had transformed many organizations into structures that could not be recognizable. What took place is that some organizations lost sight of creating value for their customers. Reengineering operational concepts appear somewhat similar to TQM guidelines. Problem-solving teams are formed to develop new products or processes to achieve results. Managers have to be retrained to think as coaches rather than traditional supervisors. Workers and managers, who share joint responsibilities, are rewarded according to results, not activity. Returning to our TQM discussion on ways of returning property to their rightful owners, a review team undertaking a reengineering of the recovery of stolen property would ask certain questions relating the process to the entire property operation: Why do we have to keep the property in an evidence room? Do we have to have an evidence room? Why can't the district attorney keep the evidence since that office deals with the evidence at trial? Okay, let's say that we keep the evidence room, but what if the property is videotaped and returned to the owner immediately?

In this process, the role of the leader is critical. The leader must have a vision and persuade others that reengineering is important. For policing, the chief must be able to delegate responsibility to the review team to come up with ideas and to make them occur. Depending on the size of the organization, the chief or assigned deputy must run interference for the review team and give active support to team members. He or she must keep those with vested interests at bay and allow the team to have an open discussion. Once a new process is achieved and tested, the management team must make sure that it goes into operation (Hammer and Champy, 1993: 104–5).

The above discussion understates the complexity of reengineering planning and decisions undertaken by major corporations with multinational sites. So far, we have seen few examples of reengineering case studies applied to the public sector, mainly because most public organizations are still the sole providers of services in a given geographic area and work rules are tied to union contracts and civil service procedures. Reengineering for police organizations may become part of the lexicon for managers because many large departments are being decentralized through modern technology and community policing, which together place command, information, and responsibility on local units. Traditional departments are being challenged by community and political groups as expensive, not responsive, and at times not necessary in view of the overlap of competing jurisdictions that occurs in many areas. There is also increasing competition for support and resources between certain public departments and private security organizations. Reengineering as a concept provides a method to review the organizational structure in order to improve police services.

Commissioner William Bratton used reengineering to reorganize the New York City Police Department (NYPD). The hierarchy was flattened. Police focus groups created a better information flow. Decision-making authority was brought down to the precinct commander's level. Precinct commanders were rewarded and punished based on the reduction of crime in their precincts. Crime-mapping techniques (Crimetac) were made available to all levels of the police bureaucracy. Detectives, special street crime units, federal and NYPD drug-enforcing units all shared information with precinct commanders. Quality-of-life neighborhood issues were attacked with city civil lawyers assigned to police precincts using nuisance laws to eliminate centers of illegal drugs and prostitution in specific neighborhoods. Public housing projects were successfully targeted as hot spots of crime and drug dealing with massive and swift police responses. Reengineering, which led to the Compstat approach to management, has been continued. The most important lesson learned is that the reduction of crime depends on good information flow throughout the police department, but especially to middle management (Silverman, 1999).

Katz's Three Skills Approach

Robert Katz (1975: 23) attempts to answer the question, "What observable skills does an effective administrator demonstrate?" He states (1975: 24),

> It is assumed here that an administrator is one who (a) directs the activities of other persons and (b) undertakes the responsibility for achieving certain objectives through these efforts. Within this definition, successful administration appears to rest on three basic skills, which we will call technical, human, and conceptual.

According to Katz, **technical skill** "involves specialized knowledge, analytical ability within that speciality, and facility in the use of the tools and techniques of the specific discipline." This is the skill most easily trained for. It is more operational than managerial. More complex is **human skill**, which Katz describes as "the executive's ability to work effectively as a group member and to build cooperative effort within the team he leads." Human skill means that the police executive is sensitive to other people's feelings and is aware of his or her own feelings.

This human relations skill involves (1) tolerance of ambiguity and (2) empathy. Tolerance of ambiguity means that the manager is able to handle problems for which insufficient information precludes making a totally informed decision. The effective manager must also have a keen sense of appreciation and understanding of widely different viewpoints and cultures and be able to approach problems and people with no preconceptions.

Empathy is the ability to put oneself in another's place. A good police manager is able to put himself or herself in the place of the patrol officers emotionally and intellectually and thus understand the effect of any issued orders on these officers. The manager must be able to look at a situation from the viewpoint of the minority groups in the community and from that of the superior officer. The effective manager must also be willing to act in terms of these perceptions.

Katz's approach to **conceptual skill** is in terms of an organizing and integrating function, "coordinating and integrating all the activities and interests of the organization toward a common objective" (1975: 27). This is not meant to be simply an intellectual process, as Katz considers such skills to include "an ability to translate knowledge into action." Police managers with conceptual skills are able to see their relationship to the rest of the organization of the department and understand how their orders and policy will affect the various structural relationships within the department. For example, an order concerning the use of evidence needs to be examined in terms of how it affects detectives, court cases and evidence flow, the laboratory, the property room, and the work of the line officer. Besides these internal relations, good conceptual managers are also able to understand and operationalize in their daily behavior the relationship their policies have to the place of the police department in the local government, community, and, when necessary, state and nation.

As Katz points out, these skills are divided for analytic reasons. However, in the day-to-day activities of the police manager, all these skills are brought into play with the emphasis changing depending on the problems and the organizational context of the department. Katz also emphasizes that these skills can be taught to current and future executives just as any other skill. Thus, good administrators are not simply born but can be trained in the classroom and by practicing the skill in the field.

Maslow's Hierarchy of Needs

Maslow attempted to understand what motivates human beings. If police managers understand this, they should be able to motivate their personnel and understand their own needs and satisfactions so that they can become more effective. According to Maslow, first there is the basic need to feel secure and to have one's physical needs taken care of. Next is the need to have good social relations. The third need is that of feeling worthwhile in terms of one's work and place in the organization. Many police administrators call this need a need to be respected by one's fellow officers and superiors. Fourth, there is a need to feel that one has enough authority where one's opinions are listened to and that the individual is actually participating in making policy in the organization. Finally, there is the ultimate need that some people will never have satisfied, what Maslow calls the need for self-actualization or self-fulfillment. This combines a feeling of wanting personal growth along with such factors as being a creative self-starter who will be able to grow to his or her potential as a human being in this job. This **hierarchy of needs** is often diagrammed as a triangle going from the basic needs of security to self-actualization at the top (see Figure 3-1).

1. Security needs
   a. The feeling of security in the position
2. Social needs
   a. The opportunity to give help to other people
   b. The opportunity to develop close friendships
3. Importance, self-esteem needs
   a. The feeling of importance from being in the position
   b. The importance of the position inside the agency (i.e., the regard received from others in the police agency)
   c. The importance of the position outside the agency (i.e., the regard and esteem received from others who are not members of the police agency)

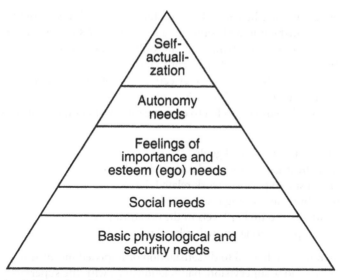

FIGURE 3-1 Maslow's hierarchy of needs. *Source:* Maslow, A., and Frager, R., *Motivation and Personality*, copyright 1987. Adapted by permission of Pearson Education, Inc., Upper Saddle River, N. J.

4. Autonomy needs
   a. The authority connected with the position
   b. The opportunity for independent thought and action
   c. The opportunity for participation in the meeting of agency goals
   d. The opportunity for participation in the determination of methods and procedures
5. Self-actualization needs
   a. The opportunity for personal growth and development in the police management position
   b. The feeling of self-fulfillment (i.e., the feeling of being able to use one's own unique capabilities, realizing one's potentialities)
   c. The feeling of worthwhile accomplishment

To obtain a full range of answers concerning the police executive's feelings about his or her position in terms of fulfilling his or her needs, three rating questions are recommended: (1) How much of the characteristic was connected with your police management position? (2) How much of the characteristic do you think should be connected with your police management position? (3) How important is this characteristic to you? It is obvious that if the manager is to operate successfully, this hierarchy of needs must be satisfied. Maslow warns us that executives vary in terms of how much of each need has to be fulfilled and which needs have priority; however, some attention in any organization has to be given to these needs if managers are going to feel that they are being rewarded for their efforts. Herzberg has tried to operationalize a similar scheme.

Herzberg's Hygiene/Motivators Approach to Job Satisfaction

Frederick Herzberg (1975) feels that the externally generated, traditional kick-in-the-pants approach, which he calls **KITA**, has not worked.

Herzberg looked at what he called **hygiene factors** (pay, fringe benefits, labor relations) contributing to job dissatisfaction and found in a sample of 1,685 employees that these factors contributed 69 percent to job dissatisfaction and only 19 percent to job satisfaction, whereas what he calls **motivators** contributed 81 percent to job satisfaction and 31 percent to job dissatisfaction. Police managers who wish to be effective in motivating their employees and even themselves need to be aware of these dimensions of job satisfaction. Herzberg found that the following "events" reported by employees led to extreme satisfaction on the job and a willingness to increase performance:

- Being able to attain work related goals
- Recognition by the organization for doing a job well
- Having a great desire to perform work related duties
- Having responsibility for getting tasks completed
- Being able to advance to higher levels in the organization
- Having a sense of professional growth related to the job.

In like manner, factors that led to dissatisfaction or impeded motivation were silly or dictatorial company policies, poor supervision, bad relationships with the supervisor, and inadequate work conditions including salary. As can be seen, Herzberg's positive motivators are similar to those of Maslow.

Herzberg's approach is to apply what he calls motivators to management personnel. He does this by relating certain principles to the motivators involved. By removing a certain number of controls but still keeping the principle of accountability, he feels that personnel will retain a sense of responsibility and personal achievement. He emphasizes that by holding individuals increasingly accountable for their work, a sense of responsibility and personal recognition will be achieved. Along this same line, he recommends giving personnel an area of work for which they are responsible, which will result in a sense of achievement, responsibility, and recognition. Decentralizing authority and thus allowing more job freedom should also bring about an increase in these three areas. Internal recognition is obtained by sharing periodic reports with personnel as well as supervisors. Personnel are seen to achieve growth and learning through the handling of new and more difficult tasks. Finally, growth, achievement, and responsibility are increased by allowing personnel to become experts through the handling of specialized tasks.

The whole idea of motivating employees is an important concept begun by Herzberg that continues today through the concept of empowerment. *Empowerment* is defined as allowing employees to actively participate in setting and achieving department or unit objectives. This results in a sense of ownership and pride in the tasks that are performed (Garner, 1993: 4). In the police case studies in which empowerment as a concept was presented, the main motivators were those described by Herzberg that lead to extreme satisfaction. Police managers must also pay attention to hygiene factors because officers and staff may leave for better-paying organizations. As with any participative management scheme, the chief must be able to share and delegate power.

McGregor's Theory X and Theory Y

Douglas Murray McGregor's approach to management is similar to Herzberg's insofar as McGregor's advocates an industrial humanism that would provide a check against the autocracy created by stifling hierarchical discipline (McGregor, 1978).

MacGregor was one of the leading theorists of what became known as the Human Relations School in the early 1960s. His view of management and its relationship with workers was presented in the often cited concepts of Theory X and Y. For **Theory X**, workers are viewed as needing strong leadership in motivating and controlling their actions, and modifying behavior through punishment and rewards. From a Theory X perspective, they are viewed as "lazy and passive" and not willing to accept responsibility.

On the other hand, **Theory Y** speaks to the need for management to provide the means for people to achieve both personal goals, which in turn, would lead to the attainment of organizational goals. Contrary to Theory X, Theory Y posits that employees will, in fact, accept responsibility and often present creativity in addressing organizational issues.

Most theorists and observers of organizational behavior agree that very few organizations are solely Theory X or Theory Y. However, from a leadership perspective, American police management and organizations tend to be labeled as Theory X based on the tradition of "top down" decision making, and the heavy reliance on rules and procedures. There is also the need to have one person in charge in emergency situations. From our own experiences there are police managers who are indeed Theory X when it comes to dealing with their employees. However, managers today can be termed as "situational," based on the seriousness of the problem or the issue at hand. A traffic accident with fatalities requires a Theory X response while planning for an annual staffing schedule provides an opportunity for shared decision making according to Theory Y.

The motivation of employees in non-punitive ways is an important management concern in American policing, for salaries and benefits are, for the most part, fixed according to a schedule created by the sponsoring governmental entity through civil service/employment rules and collective bargaining agreements. Outside of some promotional opportunities, financial raises and bounties are not given for increased productivity. Thus, Theory Y and related theories related to employee motivation and satisfaction provide the theoretical background for a number of recent innovations such as team policing, employee/employer problem solving teams, and individual initiative in addressing community crime problems.

Theory Z

McGregor's management approach talked about a humanistic approach to management. However, we have a corporate culture that involves both **high touch**, that is, the humanistic approach for terms of personnel management skills, and the use of high technology for day-to-day business. John Naisbitt, author of *Megatrends*, in his book *Re-inventing the Corporation*, stated that "the old bureaucratic layers are giving way to the more natural arrangements of the new information society" (Naisbitt and Aburdene, 1985: 36). This is also true of police managers, who have to learn new ways of processing information. However, as Naisbitt and Aburdene state, "Information is no substitute for thinking and thinking is no substitute for information" (1985: 149).

It is not simply information or using a new technology. As Peter F. Drucker states, "The 'new technology' is entrepreneurial management." It is a management that knows how to use the new technology in a context of being able to motivate the workers to be efficient and loyal to the organization (Drucker, 1986: 11). The latter is actually a reformulation of McGregor's humanist approach but in the context of the new technology.

One approach to the use of both high touch and high technology is **Theory Z**, as characterized by the following (Ouchi, 1981: 60–79):

1. There is a guarantee of lifetime career and employment in the agency.
2. One's career develops with different jobs throughout the agency rather than being limited to one specialization.

3. Decisions are developed relying on a high-technology total information system.
4. Management is characterized by the use of modern information and accounting systems, formal planning, management by objectives, and formal means of control of the system by management.
5. Decision making is initially consensual and democratic, where employees take a great deal of time agreeing to changes and talking about it. When a decision is made by top management, everyone is expected to go along with it and carry out the new decision.

The Japanese style of consensus building is foreign to American management philosophy as well as police management, which tends to be autocratic in dealing with individuals. However, some of the principles of the Type Z approach are already characteristic of many police organizations, including a lifelong career and both a formal and an emotional support system for the individual officer. Police management is used to giving orders from the top, and the Japanese group culture may not work in America. On the other hand, American police managers dealing with the new information society may want to look at ways of building a consensus before major decisions are made in a police agency. Some of the mechanisms of decision making and placing of responsibility and authority lower down the chain of command might work for some departments. Access to new technology and information processing all the way down to the line officer may mean that the police management of the twenty-first century may have to look at new ways of making decisions and become more flexible in the granting of authority to first-line supervisors and line officers.

Conclusion

The art and style of proactive leadership is based on talent, experience, and training and formal education. Proactive leaders are goal oriented and have the ability to communicate their vision and the agency's mission to all members of the department and to the community. They have had a variety of learning and leadership experiences on their way to the top of the organization hierarchy. They look on critical situations not as problems but rather as leadership opportunities.

The greatest dilemma facing police managers once they have achieved higher ranking positions is in the area of continuing training and education. The focus of police training courses today remains directed to line and supervisory personnel on operational skills and not to executive development. Many large departments and state training agencies are just beginning to fill this void with management courses for chiefs and their deputies and higher

education degrees in criminal justice management as a formal or informal norm for promotion. To this day, we begin our own management seminars with the question, What is the latest book or article you have read regarding police management? Unfortunately, the question draws much nervous laughter, which forces us to conclude that greater attention must be directed to management training.

The chapter also introduced the leading organizational theories related to proactive police leadership. These range from the traditional concepts found in every management course (Maslow's hierarchy of needs, and Theory X and Theory Y) to newer concepts (giving chaos, TQM, and reengineering). Each concept has an application to a wide variety of department and management problems in police organizations. However, no single concept represents a quick fix for departments with serious problems.

Questions for Review

1. Make a chart comparing styles of leadership along a continuum from totally democratic leadership to totally authoritarian leadership.
2. Create your own theory of leadership, and defend this theory in terms of maximizing employee morale.
3. Is Maslow's hierarchy of needs relevant to police work? Why or why not?
4. Explain why McGregor's Theory X and Theory Y are so popular among textbook writers concerned

with police leadership. Would this theory be useful in a local police department? Why or why not? Would it make sense in terms of a police department of 10 professionals or fewer? Explain.

5. Review the theories concerning leadership, and choose the one that you consider best suited for a midsized police department. Defend your choice.

Class Project

1. The challenges and dilemmas of leadership are often portrayed in popular media. Make a visit to Netflix or your cable provider and select a work that deals with the leadership issues and theories presented in this chapter. Focus also on the issues confronting subordinates who must deal with their supervisors. Some of our favorites include *Band of Brothers, Full Metal Jacket, K19: The Widowmaker, Training Day, Copland, Sum of All Fears, Green Mile*, and *Schindler's List*.
2. Leadership appears as a popular agenda item in police executive training. Go to Google and search

"police executive training courses." Other than the Covey program discussed in this chapter, what are the other programs that are offered for police chiefs? What are the topic areas assigned under the heading of "leadership"?

3. Based on the discussion of Grant's "givers and takers," how do you measure? The author invites readers to go to www.giveandtake.com and take a free assessment. Associates in your professional and social network are also invited to rate your reciprocity style at this website.

References

Bailey, Michael J. Law Enforcement Leadership Training. Unpublished paper, Utica College, 2005.

Blake, Robert R., et al. "Breakthrough in Organization Development." In *Business Classics: Fifteen Key Concepts for Managerial Success*. Cambridge, Mass.: Harvard University Press, 1975, pp. 159–181.

Butterfield, Ronald W. "Deming's 14 Points Applied to Service." *Training*, 28, no. 3 (March 1991), pp. 50–59.

Covey, Stephen. *The 7 Habits of Highly Effective Leaders*. New York: Simon & Schuster, 1989.

Drucker, Peter F. *Innovation and Entrepreneurship*. New York: Harper and Row, 1986.

Farr, Jay. "Review of the Pentagon Attack—9.11." Presentation to WMD Training Workgroup for State and Local Police Academies and Campus Law Enforcement, Louisiana State University, Baton Rouge, La., March 26, 2002.

Garner, Ronnie. "Leadership in the Nineties." *FBI Law Enforcement Bulletin*, 62, no. 12 (December 1993), pp. 3–4.

Gates, Bill. *Business at the Speed of Thought*. New York: Warner, 1999.

Goleman, Daniel. *Emotional Intelligence*. New York: Bantam, 1995.

_____. *Working with Emotional Intelligence*. New York: Bantam, 1998.

Grant, James. *Give and Take*. Viking: New York, 2013.

Guiliani, Rudolph. *Leadership*. New York: Hyperion, 2002.

Halberstam, David. *The Reckoning*. New York: William Morrow, 1986.

Hall, Richard H. *Organizations: Structures, Processes and Outcomes*. Upper Saddle River, N.J.: Prentice Hall, 1996.

Hammer, Michael. *Beyond Reengineering*. New York: Harper Business, 1996.

Hammer, Michael, and James Champy. *Reengineering the Corporation*. New York: Harper Business, 1993.

Herzberg, Frederick. "One More Time: How Do You Motivate Employees?" In *Business Classics: Fifteen Key Concepts for Managerial Success*. Cambridge, Mass.: Harvard University Press, 1975, pp. 13–22.

Holpp, Lawrence. "Making Choices: Self-Directed Teams or Total Quality Management?" *Training*, 29, no. 5 (May 1992), pp. 69–76.

IACP. Report from the Summit: Proceedings and Recommendations of the 2005 National Leadership Summit. International Association of Chiefs of Police, 2005.

Katz, Daniel, and Robert L. Kahn. *The Social Psychology of Organizations*. New York: Wiley, 1966.

Katz, Robert L. "Skills of an Effective Administrator." In *Business Classics: Fifteen Key Concepts for Managerial Success*. Cambridge, Mass.: Harvard University Press, 1975, pp. 23–35.

McGregor, Douglas Murray. "The Human Side of Enterprise." In *Classics of Public Administration*. Oak Park, Ill.: Moore, 1978, pp. 187–193.

Naisbitt, John, and Patricia Aburdene. *Re-inventing the Corporation*. New York: Warner, 1985.

Ouchi, William G. *Theory Z*. New York: Avon, 1981.

Wayne, Leslie, and Leslie Kaufman. "Leading in Turbulent Times." *New York Times*, September 16, 2001.

Weber, Max. "Power and Bureaucracy." In Kenneth Thompson and Jeremy Tunstal, eds., *Sociological Perspectives*. Middlesex, UK: Penguin, 1961.

Xerox. "The Xerox Quest for Quality." Rochester, N.Y.: Xerox, 1991.

4 Purposes and Principles of Police Organizations

KEY TERMS

humanist approach

Kansas City Experiment

line organizations

mechanical approach

omnipresent

performance

preparedness

progressiveness

random patrol

recover

regulate

reinforce

repress

respond

restrain

sting operation

Taser

Uniform Crime Reports

Traditionally, most police agencies tend to be highly reactive **line organizations**; that is, the police wait for citizens to call them and then they react to that phone call for service. In most departments, officers on patrol generally spend their time waiting for that radio dispatch that sends them roaring to the scene of an incident or crime requiring police intervention. Interspersed are attempts to garner sufficient traffic and parking violations and to check on assigned areas.

O. W. Wilson, former superintendent of the Chicago Police Department and author of the classic textbook *Police Administration* (1950), used the term "the **omnipresent** police officer" to characterize the police officer who was everywhere in his random patrol duties, deterring crime by his mere presence. However, a study of the effect of **random patrol** in Kansas City indicated that the mere presence of uniformed police and marked vehicles may not be the deterrent that we once thought (Kelling et al., 1978).

In this much cited study, the **Kansas City Experiment** divided that area's 15 precincts into three groups to study three approaches to patrol: (1) respond to calls only, (2) provide normal random patrol, and (3) provide two to three times the normal level of random patrol. This was the conclusion: "The experiment found that the three experimental patrol conditions appeared not to affect crime, service delivery and citizen feelings of security" (Kelling et al., 1978: 164). The study questioned the deployment of officers without the need for some kind of planning. This kind of research also showed the need for the administrators of an agency to pay attention to patrol and staff management.

LAW ENFORCEMENT AS BIG BUSINESS

According to the Bureau of Justice Statistics (2011), *Census of State and Local Law Enforcement Agencies, 2008*, there were 17,985 state and local law enforcement agencies. The data include sheriffs' offices and special jurisdiction agencies responsible for campus and transportation policing. These agencies reporting in 2008 collectively employed 765,000 full-time and 44,000 part-time sworn personnel with some kind of arrest powers. There were 368,699 nonsworn full-time employees (clerks, communications, and analysts).

According to the census, approximately half (40%) employed fewer than 10 full-time officers. While state and local agencies added approximately 9,500 full-time employees overall, 30 percent of the nation's largest police agencies experienced a decline in personnel. This was the result of fiscal cutbacks in municipal government starting with the 2008 recession.

The most recent survey by the Bureau of Justice Statistics reported in December 2011 (Kyckelhahn, 2011) that federal, state, and local governments across the country spent over $228 billion in fiscal year 2007 for both criminal and civil justice expenditures. Local governments contributed almost one half of these expenditures. As indicated above for employment, there has been a decline of expenditures for police from 57% to 48% of total justice. These figures include not only federal, municipal, state, and county departments but also specialized departments such as campus, transit authority, railroad, housing, and environmental conservation units. Exclusive of school boards, the public agencies that make the greatest demands on the tax dollars of most communities are the big three: police, fire, and public works. The police department often leads the field in using up available tax dollars.

The rational citizen, looking at a major business, would expect the most administratively competent personnel to be selected to lead this corporation, the local police agency. However, this is not so. Most police organizations are headed by former line officers who have worked their way up through the hierarchical, civil service organizational structure. While these individuals were generally excellent operating personnel, many need advanced skills and knowledge necessary to manage a police organization. Moreover, few have had the opportunity to expand their knowledge of modern management techniques, which is necessary to perform their new responsibilities satisfactorily. Unfortunately, some communities even mandate in their municipal charters that the new police chief has to be chosen from existing members of the police force.

CIVIL SERVICE AND PROMOTIONS

In many states, the system of civil service, based on examinations, does much to inhibit management success. Consider taking the civil service examination for captain and having to answer the following vehicle and traffic law questions: "How far must a vehicle be parked from the curb?" "How far from a stop sign?" "What is the stopping distance on wet pavement?" Such information is important for operating personnel. Any officer taking a captain's examination should know this information. However, wouldn't it be more useful to test the candidate's ability and judgments concerning the administration and management of human and physical resources? Continuing to espouse a line-officer management philosophy in a test for upper-level management positions gives official sanction to a continuation of bad management practices.

In addition, administrators' choices must come from among the top three candidates completing these examinations. In business or industry, on the other hand, we would seek out the best candidate possessing the qualification from within or without the corporation. The lack of lateral entry, the parochialism, and the influence of police associations and unions support the concept that the *best* must come through the ranks.

We are not suggesting that civil service exams be abolished; rather, we would like to see them upgraded and made more relevant to the positions. They should not be used as the sole criterion for promotion. There should be some evaluation of the candidates' past performances—an oral interview and perhaps even a battery of psychological and management tests.

It seems that many agencies, especially in western and southern states, have developed alternative methods of promotion with a more progressive approach to the selection of candidates for the respective positions. Namely, the promotion to sergeant, while being based somewhat on a written examination, is strongly influenced by assessment with established criteria. A promotion from sergeant to lieutenant, while being the prerogative of the chief of police, is often based on an assessment evaluation that includes oral interviews, with the final decision being the chief's. In many instances, promotion to captain or a higher rank rests in the hands of the chief and whatever additional criteria he uses to help in his judgment.

While there is no ideal or foolproof way of getting the best candidates, the above suggests that the progressive administrator has the greatest opportunity of getting the people he feels are the most qualified and/or compatible with his goals and the goals of the community. There is always the problem of favoritism or "political" interference in the system of promotion. However, the professionalism of modern police agencies and the expectations of its leaders make this interference more difficult.

The Use of Civilian Employees

According to the United States Department of Justice (2008), civilians constituted approximately 31 percent of the total law enforcement employee force in the United States and represented about 23 percent of the police employees in cities. Women accounted for almost 62 percent of all civilian employees. This number is expected to increase given the movement to use civilians for non-sworn police functions.

Important considerations for the hiring of civilian police personnel are a thorough background check and a psychological assessment and the need for college education. Civilian personnel are now being used in sensitive positions in records, human resources, crime laboratories, communications, and crime analysis, which results in making judgment calls that will affect the department and sworn personnel. This should emphasize the need for more attention by management to proper training necessary to equip these civilians to perform efficiently and effectively.

TRADITIONAL PURPOSES OF POLICE ORGANIZATIONS

The purposes that we have traditionally accepted to be the main thrust of managing a police agency are as follows:

1. Protecting life and property
2. Preserving the peace
3. Preventing criminality
4. Apprehending criminals

Although these are still legitimate purposes for policing, they have a major defect: They have become reactive. The activities used to carry out these purposes include routine patrol to discourage wrongdoers, arrest of criminals, recovery of stolen property, monitoring of sporting events, and such additional items as controlling traffic and pedestrian movements. Little encouragement is given to line officers to act proactively.

It has become increasingly apparent today that the concept of policing has embraced a new dimension that encourages us to add a fifth purpose: enhanced community involvement. While police work begins with law enforcement, it does not necessarily end there. Police have always provided services above and beyond what was often described as "police work," and more and more, these services have been refined and identified as "community relations." An excellent article by Solar (2001) discusses the promise of a higher level of effectiveness by giving officers greater autonomy and by encouraging them to become problem solvers and partnership builders under the rubric of community-oriented policing (COP). Another important function that has emerged is providing information related to crime trends, emergencies, and community events. This has further increased through the use of department managed social networking sites.

TRADITIONAL MEASURES OF POLICE EFFECTIVENESS

Look at the annual report of almost any police department in the country. First, you will see a cover letter from the administrator to his sponsoring institution. This is followed by a brief description of the department, usually accompanied by a standard organization chart. Then comes the bulk of the report, page after page of tabulated statistics—for example, on crimes in the community, cases cleared by arrest, traffic and parking tickets issued, percentage of stolen property recovered, accident rates, and so on.

These tabulations are supposed to show the efficiency of the agency. However, these are indexes of efficiency *after the fact*. At the time of reading, some citizens may have just been killed, injured, robbed, or arrested. The increase or decrease in crime as released to the media through the *Uniform Crime Reports* or state crime reports is taken as an indication of the effectiveness of the police agency. Unfortunately, such reactive measures tend to promote poor management, leading to the issuance of more traffic tickets, the growth of an unofficial quota system, and the "fudging" of crime statistics. For example, it may be that the officer who stops citizens in traffic and advises them concerning their poor driving habits may be more effective than the officer who simply issues tickets. It takes a realistic, superior manager to recognize the difference.

As noted in Chapter 1, the Metropolitan Police Act of 1829 created the first modern police force in London, England. In the force's first duty manual, Sir Charles Rowan stated the primary purpose for having a law enforcement agency (Reith, 1956: 135–36): "It should be understood at the outset, that the principal object to be obtained is the Prevention of Crime." Officers were specifically evaluated and rewarded for the attainment of this goal. This proactive, preventive approach led to better police–community relations.

Citizens are never happy about being the victim of a crime, even if the crime is solved and the goods are returned. From 1829 to the present, this citizen attitude has not changed. In a study of victims of crimes in inner cities outside the South, Block (1970) confirmed this point of view. He found that follow-up and even arrest of criminals who attacked victims had only a slight effect on the victims in terms of their support for police. Victimization itself brought about a significant decrease in support for police.

His conclusion backs up the basic insight of the 1829 manual that "the best way for the police to gain support is to strengthen their efforts in crime prevention" (Block, 1970: 12).

O. W. Wilson, in *Police Administration* (1950), agreed with this statement on how the police carry out their primary purpose in serving the citizens: "The police do this by preserving the peace and protecting life and property against attacks by criminals and from injury by the careless and inadvertent offender." A proactive department is more concerned with protecting the citizens from harm than with tallying up some kind of score of arrests after the citizen has been victimized.

Another modern day issue concerning public support of the police is traffic enforcement. Most citizens were generally pleased to see speed enforcement or sobriety road checks, as examples, but not so much when the cruiser stops behind the driver's own vehicle. Engel (2005) looked at citizen perceptions of police exercising arrest and detention authority by examining citizen–police traffic encounters. To capture data from the study, Engel asked drivers who had been stopped by police if they believed the traffic stop was legitimate, and if the officer acted properly during the stop. Respondents reported a negative perception of the encounter 19.1% of the time, with 14.7% believing the stop was not legitimate, and 9.9% believing the police acted improperly. Thus, it is important for police leaders to remember that it is not only the citizens and visitors to their respective communities that serve as the law enforcement client base, but in many cases, the motoring public, as well.

POLICE RESULTS AND PERFORMANCE MEASURES

Police department funding bodies, such as legislatures, are concerned with what works in policing. They want specific data and performance measures to justify the funding of specific police services. Police researchers and managers have had to develop models that speak to these issues.

While making comments before an audience of private-sector security directors, one of the authors spoke on the issue that if participants did not deal with certain basic administrative issues and concerns such as employee safety and emergency preparedness, they would find themselves out of a job; most members of the audience nodded in agreement. In the public sector, the opposite occurs. Police departments operate every year, hire people, fire people, receive public monies, and deliver services, and often there are no benchmarks by which to measure success or improvement of these efforts. For police chiefs, a measure of success is surviving political battles over the budgets, major scandals, or labor battles with line personnel.

There is a growing movement to request accountability as part of measurement and evaluation for public services (a glimpse of this is offered in the Compstat planning model discussed in Chapter 14). Police commanders who could not perform or respond to issues were replaced or transferred to other divisions. What, then, are the general benchmarks for evaluation?

Addressing General Crime

As any first-year criminal justice student knows, there are many reasons why crime occurs and why crime rates increase and decrease. While deemed "crime fighters" by the media, police in any community are only one part of the overall criminal justice system and deal with the reporting, investigation, and arrest areas in a crime incident. There are certain realities. For example, crimes are concentrated in lower-income neighborhoods that often have more multiple-family dwellings and higher concentrations of people. Thus, there are more requests for calls for police and social services. There are also more reported incidents of domestic violence as well as child abuse and neglect issues; drugs and gang activity can be present. In rural areas, the same is true in those pockets of the rural poor. Despite these realities, a police department should be able to define major community crime issues and their root causes and create overall strategies for addressing these problems, including requests for public support in dealing with specific issues. There is also a need to make public reports on crime issues that go beyond the statistical data presented in annual reports. This is what community policing is all about.

Dealing with Serious Crime Incidents

In any jurisdiction there will always be the "big case," which might be related to an incident involving serial murder, a hostage taking, a school shooting, a kidnapped child, or a major natural disaster such as a hurricane. When such an incident occurs, the police department has to be responsible for providing a professional first response and, when necessary, calling for additional resources from outside the jurisdiction. Officers, supervisors, and senior administrators must be trained and equipped to deal with the incident from the moment the call comes to conducting follow-up investigations and dealing with media queries. When this does not occur, the department is viewed as "dropping the ball" by the media, the crime victims, and the law enforcement and criminal justice community.

Achieving Major Short- and Long-Term Objectives

At executive seminars, we challenge chiefs and their command staff to set long-term goals and objectives. These should be defined in measurable terms such as reducing certain types of crimes, increasing a certain kind of service, or obtaining a resource. As discussed by Long (2003: 634) in reviewing best-value practices for British police departments, these are used to measure how well a service has been operated in order to achieve various objectives and include the usual data of recorded violent and nonviolent crimes, field-generated activities, noncrime services, and persons affected by police interactions.

Analyzing the Costs of Policing

The costs of a police department should be fairly well known, but they are not. Many of our students have a difficult time obtaining general police department budgets submitted to the legislature. The hidden costs, however, are never found in the budget. Consider the following:

- Overtime costs may be funded from external sources that are charged for the costs of officers' services. For example, officers assigned to a block party may be compensated by the municipality, which then charges the coordinators of the event.
- Some personnel positions are generated by grant funding (called "soft money" lines). These positions are intact only for the duration of the grant. This was often the case with community policing personnel hired by community policing grants in the late 1990s. The costs of these officers were then assumed by the local police departments at the end of the grants.
- The number of personnel who are defined in an organizational chart is different from the number of personnel available for and on duty. Often staff are assigned to drug task forces, major training programs, and other areas. In some instances, an officer is out on long-term disability because of an on-the-job injury, and others may be suspended for misconduct.
- As discussed in Chapter 12 on recruitment and selection, some of the budget should cover the cost and time for recruitment and selection, training, health and retirement benefits, and general officer turnover.

Evaluating the Quality of Services

How do people feel about the police services in their community? The private sector goes out of its way to measure quality by asking people, for example, if they are satisfied with their recently purchased vehicle or their overnight stay at a hotel. Few police departments measure customer satisfaction in terms of general call response, courtesy, advice on next steps, and follow-up of criminal complaints.

One might say that this is all fine and dandy, but the reality is that in policing the competition factor is absent. We both agree and disagree. In certain communities, police services are fixed entities because they are established by an entitlement from the state; however, administrations can change if there are complaints. On local levels, there is nothing that says that any police department will stay in existence if the funding is not available or the department is plagued by continual charges of mismanagement, corruption, or absurd legal costs for lawsuits. In several case studies known to the authors, serious community complaints or police misconduct resulted in outright dissolution of the department and a takeover by the state patrol.

The 2008 economic slowdown and the relatively nationwide government hiring freezes that reduced a large percentage of the police agencies by approximately 10% of the pre-2008 numbers have had direct and indirect bearing on police effectiveness. Perhaps no municipality was harder hit than Camden, NJ, which laid off nearly half of its officers in 2011 to meet budget shortfalls. Crime, however, was not obliged to go down 10% over the past five years as the downsizing occurred across the country, meaning that the reduced number of officers not only had to deal with the same amount of, if not more, day-to-day crime with significantly less personnel, but also had to address new public demands for service. The U.S. Department of Justice reports that the effects of the stock market crash on law enforcement may be felt for the next 5 to 10 years, or even permanently (U.S. Department of Justice, 2011). This, when combined with municipalities struggling to balance budgets, as well as the cost for a town or village to operate a police force, could be a turning point toward police consolidation spoken of in Chapter 11.

REALITY-BASED PROACTIVE PURPOSES OF POLICE ORGANIZATIONS

Modern society calls on all police managers to provide satisfaction for the citizens of the community in fulfilling the traditional purposes of policing. However, police managers also need to go beyond the traditional purposes of policing to the following areas of responsibility: (1) performance, (2) preparedness, and (3) progressiveness.

Performance

Specific role definitions of police **performance** and productivity measures need to be created in terms of the daily activity of both the line officer and the police manager. Criteria need to be developed to evaluate effectively and to reward positive, proactive police activity. For example, how do you measure performance in terms of patrol activity? How do you evaluate the effectiveness of response to human service calls and calls that entail referrals to other government and community agencies? Feedback mechanisms must be developed to monitor the performance of line officers and police managers and to evaluate their activities so as to reward appropriate delivery of police services to the community. The focus is on measures of individuals in official positions and measures of organizational effectiveness.

Preparedness

Preparedness speaks to the needs of short-range as well as long-range planning and entails the relation of the police agency to other community and government organizations, such as social welfare and health agencies. Police organizations have normally planned only in terms of police rather than the whole human service group of agencies. Today, all personnel should be trained to handle future problems. Preparedness entails the need for better communication among all agencies. Time and resources need to be developed so that this type of thinking permeates the entire police organization.

Progressiveness

Progressiveness is a basic management-for-change concept in which leaders are flexible and tolerant of ambiguity and are willing to institute new ideas because they may work. Such leaders do not feel threatened by such changes. The opposite of this type is the hierarchically oriented administrator who seeks closure and places limitations on his staff's ideas.

MANAGEMENT PRINCIPLES

To accomplish these purposes, management guidelines are needed. The following six principles allow for both the traditional reactive approach and the aggressive proactive approach: (1) **respond**, (2) **regulate**, (3) **restrain**, (4) **recover**, (5) **repress**, and (6) **reinforce**.

Respond

Most police activities are reactions to calls for service (Cumming et al., 1965; Bayley and Mendelsohn, 1969; Webster, 1970; Reiss, 1971). Even in large cities, the calls are largely service-oriented. Contrary to the television dramas, calls for crimes in progress are few. Thus, police respond after a crime has occurred, and there is a victim. As has been noted, victims are more hostile to the police after having been the target of a crime, even if the criminal is apprehended.

There is also a strong controversy in the field over response time. Most departments are told to aim at two minutes or less when responding to a call. This early response time is significant only in cases of crimes in progress or calls of an emergency nature. Response time becomes important in the securing of crime scenes and the immediate apprehension of criminals. It is irrelevant to the majority of service calls. Too much management and training time is spent on this issue of response time.

Regulate

Consider a long line of cars wending its way through the city streets with a funeral hearse in the front and a police vehicle escort. Also consider events such as field days, ice cream socials, and ball games that require the police for traffic and crowd control. Police are also used as bodyguards and chauffeurs for visiting dignitaries and even some mayors. These are traditionally noncriminal police activities, and regulations are necessary to prevent crises in our communities. This area of policing provides an excellent opportunity to improve relations with community members, countering the police image as a repressive, restrictive force demanding compliance with rules, ordinances, and so on.

Restrain

This represents one of the traditional purposes for police: the apprehension of criminals. It should also include restraint of mentally ill people and the prevention of one citizen from annoying or doing damage to another. For example, a woman who mows her lawn at midnight just to annoy a neighbor with whom she is feuding might have to be restrained by police.

On a more serious level, we find that many police departments today are beginning to use less-than-lethal techniques to apprehend individuals threatening the safety of citizens or arresting officers. New pepper-ball launchers, beanbag shotguns (Moreland, 2000a, 2000b), foam, and M-26 **Tasers** are among the many devices being used to temporarily immobilize combative or violent subjects (*Use of M-26 Advanced Taser*, 2001: 1–5).

With the increased demand on calls for police services today, we find that many agencies prioritize their calls. The San Diego County Sheriff's Department, for example, prioritizes its calls into four categories. Priority 1 and 2 calls get immediate attention as emergency calls. A priority 1 call might be a serious accident, an officer needing help, an airplane crash, a SWAT alert, a fire, or a natural disaster. Priority 2 calls are mainly crimes against people, arson, weapons, explosions, pursuits, and so on. Priority 3 and 4 calls, such as a burglary not in progress, a damaged mailbox, a minor property damage auto accident, do not demand an immediate response. However, the department takes great pride in responding to every complaint and request for service—something not all law enforcement agencies still do (Moreland, 2000a, 2000b).

Recover

A major effort by police is the recovery of stolen property and its return to the citizens. **Sting operations**, in which a police agency sets up a phony fencing business to entice criminals to sell them stolen goods, result in the arrest of the criminals and some of their fences (those who deal in stolen goods). Millions of dollars in stolen goods are given back to the citizens in the course of such operations. This is one area in which the police provide a very useful service to the community and do recover considerable property of value, reducing insurance and personal losses.

Repress

There are two important elements necessary for a crime to take place. First, the individual must have the desire to commit the crime; second, the opportunity must present itself for the satisfaction of this desire. Police have traditionally attempted to prevent crime by reducing the opportunity of the individual to commit the crime. The random patrol concept is justified by many police managers as a means of reaching this end.

In recent years, drug-control and gang interdiction strategies have included targeting "hot spots," such as high-crime street areas, crack houses, and gang handouts. The basic philosophy here is that it is very hard to buy and sell with increased police presence, which includes raids, arrests for minor violations, checks for violations of city housing codes, and legal actions against slum landlords. It also includes the use of intervention techniques such as "stop and frisk," which is stopping someone who has or is about to commit a crime, and then conducting a pat down search if there is probable cause that the suspect has a weapon. At this time, this is a controversial technique in New York and other cities as it is often targets young minority populations.

Reinforce

This activity is designed to reinforce good citizenship and respect for the law and to encourage citizens to aid and assist officers and the agency. Examples of this type of activity are talking to citizens' groups and instituting traffic and bicycle safety programs. There are many programs that reach out to business owners and citizens to burglarproof their premises and to watch their neighbor's property when the neighbor is on vacation, and how not to become a victim of identity theft. School programs are also used, such as the School Resource Officer program in elementary schools and the teaching of criminal justice topics by community relations officers in high schools.

In responding to this traditional purpose, police agencies have tended to create special units and to focus on response activities to the detriment of effective service to the public. Although these are legitimate purposes, these purposes are not broad enough to contain the range of legitimate police activity. Each officer should consider himself or herself a community relations specialist.

Defining the Organization

To carry out these six principles, it is necessary to come to an understanding of what the organization itself is all about. Here, we are looking for a definition of *organization,* which is a group of people organized to do something, and that will fit the requirements of both management and operations. This definition for policing is broad enough to encompass the many tasks concerned with the creation of operational policy as well as the duties of administration.

Although a clear understanding of basic relationships specified by modern organizational structures is necessary, we must never forget that the tasks are carried out by real people with human concerns, needs, and emotions. Thus, any concept of organization from the perspective of current practices and theory is basically people oriented. The reason is that if any police organization is to operate efficiently, people have to be motivated to carry out tasks on the job and to put out that little extra effort that makes organizations work. A good argument has been made that the most desirable learning organization is one that includes rules and procedures, covering a variety of low- and high-level tasks, that are continually reviewed for content and practicality (Solar, 2001). Such an organization is efficient and effective in both routine and nonroutine tasks, with an emphasis on cooperation and innovation guided by broad policies and reinforced through training.

THE CONCEPT OF ORGANIZATION

Mechanical Approach

As discussed by Jones (2004), the mechanistic structure is "designed to induce people to behave in predictable, accountable ways" (115). In these structures, which in theory apply to both the military and police organizations, there is close supervision, much accountability, and information flows up and down the organization. Unity of action is accomplished by specialized work assigned and great coordination. A good example would be your typical organizational chart, which is developed in the form of a triangle with the head of the unit at the top and various layers of management to the lowest level which is composed of workers or soldiers.

This definition emphasizes the mechanics, or the physical aspects, of organization.

The **mechanical approach** uses bodies to fill boxes in an organization chart. Examples are assembly-line tasks and many military jobs. Police managers have been hiring and promoting to fill slots, without concern for the personal qualifications of the individual.

Organic or Humanist Approach

The organic or humanistic theorists view the organization is terms of work groups, delegation of authority to many levels of the organization, and much face-to-face contact. This definition emphasizes the people who make up an organization and through whom all work is done.

This **humanist approach** is used in most professional organizations, where a particular skill must be developed at a particular level with the exact knowledge needed to fill a position. This is often the norm for many technical groups whereby workers are connected via the Internet. Imagine a law firm, for example, that needs a new associate partner in corporate law. The firm's management interviews individuals, looking for specific knowledge, skills, and professional relationships that have developed over the candidate's career. In the same way, modern police organizations should not be limited by a mechanical promotion exam. They should look for talent and professional skills. Just because an officer has been promoted to lieutenant does not make her an expert in personnel, even though the personnel department needs a lieutenant to manage the department.

THE TRADITIONAL CONCEPT OF BUREAUCRACY FROM MAX WEBER

Basic to any modern organization is the concept of bureaucracy. Police organizations, for example, are bureaucracies. Although the term *bureaucracy* has acquired negative overtones, it is the basis for modern civil service and a rational approach to administration and organization. The German sociologist Max Weber (1889–1920) provided the formulation that has become the basis for all modern bureaucracies, including police organization (Gerth and Mills, 1946: 196–244).

A modern bureaucracy depends on having a money economy to pay salaries. The society also must subscribe to the view that success and rewards should be based on merit and hard work rather than on the condition of birth. Moreover, there should be a belief in treating each person equally and providing true equality of opportunity.

The following are, in shortened form, the general rules that Weber felt should govern and define a modern bureaucracy (Gerth and Mills, 1946: 196–204):

1. Regular activities are distributed in a fixed way as official duties.
2. Authority to give commands is distributed in a stable way, and coercive means of sanction are defined by rules in a consistent manner.
3. Only those who have generally regulated qualifications to serve are employed.
4. Fixed jurisdictions are ordered by administrative regulations.
5. An official hierarchical system of superiors and subordinates, monocratically organized, exists.
6. Management is based on written documents, normally called "the files."
7. Specialized officer of management requires thorough, technical, and expert training and knowledge.
8. Generalized rules are
   a. stable,
   b. exhaustive, and
   c. learnable.
9. Knowledge of the rules represents special technical knowledge that officials possess (in modern society, accountants and lawyers are special officials who are rule experts).
10. Office holding is a vocation and a career.
11. Officials have more status than the governed: Insulting officials is proscribed by law with appropriate sanctions.
12. Bureaucratic officials are appointed by a superior authority (civil examination), not elected.
13. Tenure in the job is for life.
14. Employees receive regular pecuniary compensation (a regular and fixed salary).
15. Officials have a career in the hierarchy.

This is the ideal by which many modern public organizations are measured. When first developed and applied, it made capitalism work by providing a structural context for capitalists.

Bureaucracy provides stability in the delivery of governmental services, even though the political machinery may be in turmoil. Politicians can fight all they wish, but while a modern bureaucracy exists in public service, citizens will receive their police and fire protection, have their mail delivered, and have their sewers fixed. This organizational concept will become more important as we examine how to carry out specific police management tasks in the modern police organization.

Conclusion

Managing a police department effectively requires considerable organization. Although humanist concepts and democratic principles are useful in enhancing morale and producing evenhanded personnel policies, they have to be dealt with in the context of a traditional bureaucratic structure.

A police department is a big business with a budget of hundreds of thousands or, in some cases, millions of dollars. The traditions of a nineteenth-century civil service are part and parcel of the organizational style of most police agencies. Part of the reality of modern police administration is the traditional civil service/Weberian bureaucratic structure. To perform the police function, orders have to be written and carried out. Over the years, it has been shown that a traditional hierarchical organization can be an effective medium for fulfilling the major purposes of the police function.

The reality-based proactive approach adds another dimension to the traditional bureaucratic structure: forward planning. The central core of the proactive approach is the need for police management to have the necessary planning skills to anticipate events. This is in good part what is meant by the three *P*s:

1. Performance
2. Preparedness
3. Progressiveness

A reality-based progressive department is flexible enough to adapt to changing events and a changing society. It is prepared with adequate resources to deal effectively with future events and crises. The performance of this department speaks for itself by any reasonable measure of police effectiveness.

Although it is necessary to use the principles of the traditional bureaucratic structure to administer the modern proactive police department, these principles are applied in a flexible manner. One of the problems with reactive police departments is that they become so bound by rigid bureaucratic procedures that they lose sight of the real purpose of policing: providing a service to the community. The flexibility instilled in the traditional police structure allows for the anticipation of events and the ability to deal with an ever-changing society. The ideal police structure is the synthesis of proactive, traditional, democratic, and authoritarian styles. This department may be viewed by the citizens as an effective force in achieving a stable community—a good place in which to live and raise children.

Questions for Review

1. Do you agree with the traditional purposes of police organization? Has the modern police organization fulfilled these purposes? Should it?
2. Distinguish between a proactive and reactive police agency. What major characteristics identify the proactive police agency?
3. Describe the role of planning in terms of (1) performance, (2) preparedness, and (3) progressiveness.
4. Place the following six management principles in order of priority: (a) respond, (b) regulate, (c) restrain, (d) recover, (e) repress, and (f) reinforce. Justify your order.

5. If you were going to create your own police organization, what type of management would you prefer: mechanical or humanist? Explain why. If you have trouble subscribing completely to either view, specify what mix of mechanical and humanist concepts of police organization would perhaps work best.

6. Apply Max Weber's concept of bureaucracy to a local police agency.

Class Project

Select a local law enforcement agency and observe or review its manner of operations in an attempt to determine whether it is a proactive or reactive type of agency. Give your reasons for your determination and your suggestions as to how you might change or improve its mode of providing service to the community.

Web Works

Check the Web site of a major city and see if you can find the performance objectives for the department for the past year. To what extent do they compare to or contrast with the discussion on accountability described in the chapter? If you cannot find it on the Web, then you can request a police department's recent annual report. The fact that it either has or does not have such an item is indicative of this discussion. Based on the report, define the measures of performance presented in the report.

References

Bayley, David H., and Harold Mendelsohn. *Minorities and the Police*. New York: Free Press, 1969.

Block, Richard L. "Support for Civil Liberties and Support for the Police." *American Behavioral Scientist*, 13, no. 5/6 (May/June 1970), pp. 10–16.

Bureau of Justice Statistics. *Census of State and Local Law Enforcement Agencies, 2008*. Washington, D.C.: U.S. Department of Justice, 2011.

Cumming, Elaine, Ian Cumming, and Laura Edell. "Policeman as Philosopher, Guide and Friend." *Social Problems*, 12 (Winter 1965), pp. 276–286.

Engel, Robin S. "Citizens' Perceptions of Distributive and Procedural Injustice During Traffic Stops With Police." *Journal of Research in Crime and Delinquency*, 42, no. 4, November 2005, 445–481. Retrieved from uc.edu/content/dam/uc/ccjr/docs/articles/procedural_injustice_during_trafficstops.pdf

Gerth, H.H., and C. Wright Mills. *From Max Weber: Essays in Sociology*. New York: Oxford University Press, 1946.

Jones, Gareth. *Organizational Theory, Design, and Change* (4th ed.). Upper Saddle River, N.J.: Pearson, 2004.

Kelling, George L., et al. *Patrol Experiment: A Summary Report and a Technical Report*. Washington, D.C.: Police Foundation, 1978.

Kyckelhahn, Tracey. *Justice Expenditures and Employment, FY 1982–2007 – Statistical Tables*. Washington, D.C: United States Department of Justice, 2011.

Long, Matt. "Leadership and Performance Management." In Tim Newbury, ed., *Handbook of Policing*. Cullompton, Devon: William, 2003.

Moreland, Jo. "Changes Might Affect Deputy Response Time." *North County Times*, July 22, 2000a, p. B-2.

———. "Sheriff's Department Shifts Its Crime-Fighting Focus as It Updates." *North County Times*, July 22, 2000b, p. B-2.

Reiss, Albert J. Jr. *The Police and the Public*. New Haven, Conn.: Yale University Press, 1971.

Reith, Charles. *A New Study of Police History*. Edinburgh: Oliver and Boyd, 1956.

Solar, Patrick J. "The Organizational Context of Effective Policing." *Police Chief*, 68, no. 2 (February 2001), pp. 39–47.

United States Department of Justice—Federal Bureau of Investigation. *Crime in the United States 2008*. Web posted at fbi.gov/ucr/cius2008/. Accessed on September 14, 2009.

Use of M-26 Advanced Taser. Escondido, Calif.: Escondido Police Department, August 2, 2001, pp. 1–5.

Webster, John A. "Police Task and Time Study." *Journal of Criminal Law, Criminology and Police Service*, 61 (1970), pp. 94–100.

Whitaker, Gordon, et al. *Basic Issues in Police Performance*. Washington, D.C.: U.S. Department of Justice, 1980.

Wilson, O. W. *Police Administration*. New York: McGraw-Hill, 1950.

CHAPTER

5 Operating Principles

KEY TERMS

auxiliary/service function

budgeting

control

coordinating

directing

ethics

line function

operations

organizing

planning

policy

POSDCORB

RESPECT

reporting

staff/administrative function

staffing

victimless crime

In every organization, there are three major areas of work:

1. Administration
2. Supervision
3. Operations

Administrative functions are performed by top management and the immediate subordinates of the top-management team. They create and set **policy** (a course of action), providing guidance for the organization. *Supervision* is normally performed by the immediate supervisors of line personnel. They help set the tone of the organization and ensure that the policies created by top management are actually carried out by the line personnel. *Operations* are performed by line personnel who normally have direct contact with the public and who carry out the daily police activities.

ADMINISTRATION

POSDCORB is a classic theoretical model that describes the major functions of an organization and how these functions are carried out. The acronym POSDCORB stands for planning, organizing, staffing, directing, coordinating, reporting, and budgeting (Gulick and Urwick, 1937: 1–45).

Planning

This activity includes short- and long-range **planning** that specifies goals and objectives in cooperation with other public agencies. Cooperating with other public agencies is a requisite. More and more urban police departments are seeing that they have to involve themselves with the long-range planning of urban renewal, social service, health, and other agencies. Even smaller departments and those in rural areas are beginning to see how long-range planning can help them deal with the increasing complexity of the police role and rural crime on the urban fringe.

Organizing

Organizing deals with the creation of the formal structure of the police organization, the work of the enterprise. The goal is to coordinate all the organizational units to perform most efficiently to meet the purposes of the organization.

The organization itself becomes the total responsibility of the manager and reflects the organizational ability of the top-management team. Modern business principles are combined with knowledge of public administration and modern police activities. The key to success is to create an organizational structure in which the right person does the right job at the highest efficiency with the correct level of personal and organizational morale.

Staffing

The **staffing** function of management covers such aspects of the organization as hiring, firing, and training, as well as assigning personnel to specific tasks and roles. There is also a concern with establishing satisfactory working conditions, including safe and appropriate physical facilities. For example, patrol car computers should operate to retrieve information in an efficient manner so as not to endanger the life of an officer at a traffic stop. Included also is the need to provide weapons to officers who need to carry out the job and to keep those weapons in functional order.

In theory, staffing includes developing job descriptions. Each job should be clearly defined and filled by a qualified employee. *Qualified* means that the employee has the necessary skills, background, and training to accomplish the tasks that the job description calls for.

Job satisfaction should also be considered. Every attempt should be made to match each employee to a job where he or she is

- Satisfied
- Qualified
- Gratified

Directing

In **directing**, the police manager needs to (1) act as the overall leader of the organization and (2) direct the day-to-day activities of the enterprise. As leader of the police organization, the manager has to make decisions and issue orders. Using modern management principles, this is normally a team process in which the leader receives information and advice from the top-management team. The information that is obtained through this consultative process should lead to a firm decision.

A police manager using this approach should seek advice from local community leaders as well as from top-management staff and experts in law enforcement. Then, once a decision has been made, the team is expected to carry out daily the specified directions and procedures.

Coordinating

The two major activities in this category are (1) **coordinating** police agencies with other private and public agencies in the community and (2) coordinating activities within the police department itself. Coordination is designed to bring about agreement on specific courses of action to solve specific problems.

Typical problems that involve the coordination functions include legal ramifications of policy decisions and deciding who is going to be in charge in cases involving overlapping jurisdictions. For example, a visit from a foreign dignitary might entail coordination among civic organizations and local, state, or federal authorities; it could require long-range planning to prepare for problems or situations that might occur. Coordination is an often overlooked but essential part of police management.

Reporting

Reporting entails keeping the flow of information going up, down, and across the organization. It also includes reporting to the police organization's political superiors: mayors, county executives, and the like. Today many departments use traditional press releases and social networking to get department information to the public.

Communication cannot be just one way if it is to be effective. Communication flows in an organized manner through a three-dimensional matrix to all superiors and subordinates. Increasingly important for modern management is lateral flow to specialists and staff.

Budgeting

Budgeting includes preparing an annual financial plan and operating within the confines of the plan. Budgeting is a form of fiscal planning and requires knowledge of the kinds of budget models available. Most police departments operate on some variation of line-item budgeting. There is increasing pressure on departments for fiscal accountability and expertise in the realm of financial planning and reporting. Running any law enforcement agency is like running a corporation but on the fiscal basis of tax dollars.

SUPERVISION

Police administrators and supervisors in small departments readily admit that they are forced to be generalists simply because they are the only person on duty during certain shifts. Thus, the chief may perform the daily routine of the street officer as well as deal with administrative tasks. On the other hand, there are very tangible benefits in the absence of a complex chain of command, especially in the areas of direct supervision and communication.

Regardless of size, the top administrator requires conceptual skills, the ability to develop long-range goals, and the ability to communicate with all segments of the community. If anything, by the very nature of their presence in the community, the members of a small department indeed practice community policing by knowing virtually everyone in the community and by providing a wide range of services.

The RESPECT Approach to Supervision

POSDCORB has been a useful approach to organizing basic management functions. What is proposed here is a similar approach to the functions of a police supervisor with the rank of sergeant or lieutenant. The acronym **RESPECT** stands for

- Reporting
- Evaluation
- Services
- Planning
- Ethics
- Control
- Teaching

Because the supervisor is the vital organizational link between the street officer and management, the duties and functions of the supervisor must be systematically analyzed. The following functions can be applied by both the small police department and the large urban police department; while the applications will differ, the principles remain the same.

REPORTING   A police organization, among other things, is basically a complex communication network fulfilling its responsibility to keep all members informed so that they can adequately perform their assigned duties. The police chief and other administrators receive reports and review them for information, clarity, and accuracy. This is a vital responsibility since future actions involving citizens are based on these reports.

In the important area of internal communications, management needs to know what the officers are thinking and how they are acting. The line supervisor and the internal department supervisor are in a position to perform this vital communication function by reviewing reports and recording observations.

Orders must be communicated to staff, and it is the supervisor who converts orders to operational activities. Communication is a vital two-way flow for every police organization. Supervisors need a basic knowledge of communication skills and communication links if they are to perform effectively. They must distinguish between statements and feelings. Techniques for achieving effective communication are fully developed in Chapters 10 and 12.

Accurate reports are necessary if a department is to operate effectively. Reports have to convey the maximum amount of information in a minimum amount of space. Time is valuable, and the reading of reports is an expensive way in which to spend time in any organization.

EVALUATION   The supervisor's basic responsibility is to continuously inspect and evaluate the officers in terms of their appearance, use of equipment, habits, and performance. *Habit* refers to behavior, mannerisms, use of language, and professional attitude; *performance* refers to the knowledge of the job and the ability to do the job in terms of professional qualifications. Dress and demeanor are also part of this evaluation and inspection process.

Even "unmeasurables," such as empathy and the ability to deal with people, have to be a solid part of the evaluation and inspection process. The supervisor becomes the enforcer of professional standards while helping the officers conform to these standards through a solid management support system.

SERVICES   Since the police department is a public service organization, one of the supervisor's first responsibilities is to maintain the quality of the delivery of services to the citizens. This is done by making community relations activities part of the evaluation of each officer. The supervisor helps the officer understand that he or she represents law enforcement in the community. With support from supervisors, community policing is not just relegated to a public relations department in the police agency but becomes the responsibility of each officer.

The officer needs training to deal with emergencies and the myriad of other services that constitute police work. Although arrest and apprehension of criminals are the most visible parts of the business of law enforcement, the human service function is just as vital. Top management must thus constantly reward its supervisors for the effective delivery of quality human service. Thus, an effective law enforcement support team can create a department that is deeply concerned with helping each citizen of the community.

PLANNING   This function refers to both long- and short-range planning and implementation. Supervisors are normally involved with daily planning activities such as scheduling the roster and reviewing patrol and detective assignments. Management must involve these supervisors in longer range planning, specifying the needs of the unit(s) for the next month, year, or even decade.

Supervisors are close to the information needed for planning—they generally know the conditions on the street. A major rule in management communication is that the closer you are to your data, the more accurate your knowledge of the data is. As the first line of management, informed and involved supervisors are vitally needed if planning is to be implemented.

Much of what top management has intended in terms of long-range planning has failed because the supervisors closest to essential planning data were neglected. It is the supervisory managers who will be in charge of actually carrying out the detailed implementation of long-range planning. Supervision and planning need to come together before implementation can be accomplished.

Supervisors have to understand the plans and intent of management and have some general agreement as to the implementation of policy. If supervisors adopt a hostile attitude, the line officers will not readily implement the policy. There are many obvious and subtle ways of not implementing policy. The line officer on the street has a great deal of discretion and can use this discretion to support or harass management. Policy can be implemented so slowly, for example, that the impact of the policy decision is diffused and wasted, or it can be implemented so rapidly that there is no thought of the side effects of implementation. The voluntary cooperation of supervisory personnel is necessary in any implementation of policy; policy will work in the field only with the active understanding and cooperation of supervisor personnel.

ETHICS   Professional organizations, including police organizations, have a code of **ethics**, which is defined as standards of conduct and moral judgment applied to everyday operations. Implementation of the profession's code of ethics depends on the individual supervisor and is strongly related to the morale of personnel. Management guided by ethical principles carried out with integrity is more apt to have an organization with high morale.

Morale is also determined by management that has sympathetic knowledge of the problems of line personnel. As stated previously, an effective communication system will provide management with the necessary knowledge of line operating conditions and problems.

Problems arise because of the lack of communication and inaction. Finally, management's own code of ethics must be operational because each supervisor becomes an ethical role model for personnel in the organization.

CONTROL   Effective management must **control** both personnel and material, providing guidance and instilling a sense of responsibility. With increasingly scarce resources available to public agencies, their efficient use will be a paramount measure of management success in the future.

Knowledge and effective use of personnel are critical because 70–90 percent of the average police budget is devoted to personnel. Personnel hours are money. Reactive management wastes human resources by failing to plan aggressively; for example, allowing officers to wait for assignments while on duty is a waste of personnel resources. Management today is being held accountable for employing human resources wisely and efficiently. An aggressive, proactive, reality-based management will develop an efficient and accountable police force.

TEACHING   The supervisor is concerned with personnel reaching their highest potential. By providing good direction and constantly training personnel in the use of proper procedures for meeting the objectives of the police organization, supervisors become teachers. The supervisor selects specific individuals for in-service training and evaluates the training in terms of the enhanced worth of personnel to the organization. As corporate management has learned, regular in-service training is needed to run an efficient organization; training is needed to develop leadership as well as skills. Included in this function is the need to direct personnel, which is also a teaching skill.

The acronym RESPECT symbolizes the need for management to show respect for the basic integrity of the individual and to treat each employee in a professional manner. In the absence of this approach, the organization will be inefficient and autocratic and will experience many morale problems. A positive climate conducive to cooperation is created when basic respect is shown by management for all personnel and by all personnel for management. It is always a two-way street—a two-way street that pays big dividends for the modern reality-based police department.

OPERATIONS

Operations is defined as all the activities necessary to carry out the basic goals of the organization. Controlling crime and providing service are the major goals for law enforcement agencies. Good management carries out these goals without wasting resources on irrelevant activities. Operations include (1) line functions, (2) staff/administrative functions, and (3) auxiliary/service functions. This is the basic way the police organization is structured.

Line Functions

For close to a century, full-service enforcement agencies have organized **line functions** into the following categories: (1) patrol, (2) traffic, (3) investigation (detectives), (4) vice, and (5) juvenile. Recently, some agencies have had to change, consolidate, and even eliminate some of these functions; this will be discussed in Chapters 8 and 9.

PATROL   When modern communities feel the need for a new police organization, the first function they think of is patrol. This function provides a public manifestation of the police through uniformed personnel being visible in marked patrol vehicles.

This leads to home rule pride and the creation of many new, small police departments. A major concern for modern police management is the consolidation of police forces to eliminate overlapping police jurisdictions and to provide more efficient delivery of services. Thus, the patrol function, although central and essential to law enforcement, also creates its own variety of problems that need to be resolved. As we shall see later, the random patrol controversy has become a central management problem in an era of scarce resources.

The patrol function, as used in many departments, treats the patrol officer as a generalist—a professional who can handle anything happening in the streets of the jurisdiction. It also requires the patrol officer to hand over certain activities to police specialists after the immediate street action has been handled. Thus, when treating the patrol function in terms of management, we must always be aware of the generalist—specialist concerns and must target specific solutions for this continuing problem area.

Over the past decade, police departments in large cities or metropolitan areas created special units to address crime problems related to their jurisdiction. Today many departments have full-time special units or part-time personnel assigned to various assignments involving general crime prevention, impaired driving enforcement, drug education in schools, missing children, and gang interdiction.

There is an increasing awareness today of the need of smaller agencies to form alliances with neighboring departments to address mutual problems. Examples of this are task forces devoted to regional auto theft, narcotics, and gangs; rapid response teams; and major felony squads. There is also evidence that agencies across local, state, and federal governments are experiencing closer working relationships, especially since the terrorist attacks of September 11, 2001.

TRAFFIC   This function deals with both the motoring public and pedestrians. Police agencies spend a considerable amount of time on accident investigations and traffic enforcement. When an ever-increasing traffic problem takes too much of an officer's time from normal service and patrol functions, an independent traffic unit may be justified.

INVESTIGATION   Investigation is the function of a nonuniformed follow-up force of detectives. Basically, this specialized unit is established when patrol officers do not have time to do investigations and when a certain level of expertise and experience is needed to deal with crime cases. A vital function of this unit is the preparation of cases for prosecution after arrest.

VICE   The members of this nonuniformed, investigative unit focus on specific crimes, such as prostitution, gambling, and narcotics. Many of these crimes have been called **victimless crimes**, although many law enforcement managers consider this designation to be quite controversial. Vice units also handle organized crime, such as receiving and transporting stolen goods, extortion, and other continuing criminal conspiracies.

JUVENILE   It is estimated that roughly 80 percent of street crimes are committed by youths between the ages of 8 and 18. The crime statistics are showing increasingly younger offenders, however.

Juvenile laws and due process for juveniles differ from adult penal and criminal process statutes. Officers assigned to this function require specialized training so that they can work closely with juveniles, parents, and various juvenile authorities.

Staff/Administrative Functions

The administrative staff directly assists top management. They have no command or patrol duties but are responsible for the everyday activities that concern the management team. The following might be found in a police organization:

Staff/Administrative Units

Personnel	Inspections/Internal Affairs
Training	Intelligence
Legal advisor	Research and planning
Public relations	Budget
Community relations	Crime prevention

The **staff/administrative functions** are necessary to support the line functions, which are directly related to the output services of the agency. Auxiliary functions are important, but the management team normally does not need daily input from these units. In a normal staffing chart, they are delegated down the line from management.

Auxiliary/Service Functions

Auxiliary/service functions are the support and maintenance jobs that need to be performed by every organization. All patrol and investigation units make use of these functions at some time or other. The following services might be included in the police organization:

Auxiliary/Service Units

Records	License section
Data processing	Maintenance section
Identification bureau	Communications
Jail	Crime laboratory
Transport sections	Animal complaints
Property clerk's office	

Over the years, police departments have inherited functions that would normally be serviced by other units of the government. Many of the licensing functions have been relegated to police agencies based on past practice. Some of these functions could be better handled by other governmental agencies. This management problem will be discussed in Chapter 11.

Conclusion

The functions discussed in this chapter are the normal functions that exist in every full-service police agency. Students of management must be aware of how these functions are carried out. They also need to be aware of the kinds of criteria that can be applied to determine the success or failure of police agencies in carrying out these functions.

To do this type of examination, we look at how specific departments are organized and how these structures successfully implement or fail to implement these functions. Of course, in the specific application of these functions, we must also judge the worth of the function to departmental goals and general law enforcement goals. In later chapters, this analysis will be done with case histories. At this point, the student needs an understanding of these functions and how they interrelate before undertaking a more elaborate analysis and application; however, the practical application of principles is vital if management is going to be proactive and reality based.

Questions for Review

1. Rank the following in terms of importance: (a) administration, (b) supervision, and (c) operations. Justify your answer.
2. POSDCORB has been a useful theoretical model since 1937. Why is it so useful? Relate the planning function to the other functions of POSDCORB.
3. Explain the difference between administering a small-town police department and a large-city police department.
4. Rank in order of importance the functions of the supervisor as listed in the RESPECT approach to supervision. Justify your answer.

5. How does the operational job of supervision differ from the overall tasks of management?
6. What management and personnel skills does a supervisor need? Why?
7. What are the major distinctions separating staff/administrative functions from auxiliary/service functions? Explain.

Class Project

On a sheet of paper, list either POSDCORB or RESPECT and give a brief definition for each letter in these terms. Schedule an interview with a police supervisor or administrator, and ask the official to rank those items that he or she performs on a daily basis. From this ranking, report on what each model looks like in terms of importance. From POSDCORB, you might end up with something that looks like CODPOOB!

If it is impractical to conduct an interview, then obtain a job description for the police chief from a local governmental entity and cite those duties that would relate to POSDCORB or RESPECT. Use the appropriate letter for each duty for citation purposes.

Reference

Gulick, Luther, and L. Urwick, eds. *Papers on the Science of Administration.* New York: Institute of Public Administration, Columbia University, 1937.

6 Proactive Communication and Information Management

KEY TERMS

all-channel communication	medium
assumption	memorandum (MEMO)
bypassing	network
chain of command	overgeneralization
decoding	special order (SO)
directive	standard operating procedure (SOP)
duty manual	subscript
feedback	symbol
general order (GO)	temporary operating procedure (TOP)
inference	"Y" communication
Johari window	

Laptop computers, iPads , cell phones, e-mail, the Internet, and the need for encryption have moved communication beyond standing orders and paper forms. The twenty-first century police department is quickly moving to electronic forms of communication while still depending on traditional items such as paper orders, radio communication, and the landline telephone. However, human-to-human communication still needs organization, good grammar, and clarity. Policing is still largely a human enterprise delivering human services to citizens.

This chapter will look at the analysis, organization, and conceptualization of police communication. A persistent issue among all police organizations involves communication between all members of the department and between department members with the external environment. This simple premise has been made more complex with innovations in e-mail, and electronic communication. The communication system in an organizational setting is based on the human element and design; information, statements, views, instructions, and policies are transmitted through various kinds of messages that can often vary in length, form, and content. The purpose of this chapter is to discuss communications theory and the basic forms by which managers operationalize communications.

COMMUNICATION DEFINED

In his chapter on information management for *Local Government Police Management*, Richard A. McDonnel (1977: 406) states, "Communication is essentially a social affair involving the sharing of information." He goes on to add, "The ultimate conclusion was that the most valuable tool that could be made available to the police officer, on whatever specific assignment, was *information*." This broad-based approach to communication encompasses the essentially two-way street of basic human interaction as well as the more narrow approach of technological communication. The emphasis is always on the sharing of information between two communicators. Communication should never be one way. The more the sharing involved, the clearer the message.

In most police departments, communication has traditionally included dispatching public press releases and records. These essentials of good policing must be part of any well-ordered management plan for communication. However, police information management entails more than these technological aspects. Information management also includes, as McDonnel emphasized, communication as a social affair, involving the sharing of information between two or more human beings. The emphasis for proactive management is on the sharing aspect of communication.

In one-way communication, the chief gives orders to his or her subordinates. The subordinates then give orders to the line officers, and some action is expected to take place. Conversely, the social sharing of information is essentially a two-way process. When we talk to anyone, we expect **feedback**. This feedback could be as varied as a nod, a stance, an answer to a question, an agreement to orders, or a recommendation to modify orders. The recognition and feedback that we continually receive keep the communication process clear. Feedback enables the sender to know that the message was sent, received, and understood in some manner by the receiver.

Thomas C. Neil (1980: 17) has summarized the typical model of communications that is in most general use even in this digital age:

> A typical model . . . contains the following parts: the *sender* of the original message; the *receiver* of this message; *encoding*, which is the translation of personal meaning into symbols; *decoding*, which is the reverse of encoding; and *channel*, which is the means by which stimuli are sent and received. [author's emphasis]

The sender could be a police chief, and the receiver could be a line officer. The encoding is normally in the form of an order in writing, such as a standard operating procedure (SOP). **Decoding** takes place when the line officer reads the order and attempts to place it in behavioral terms. The channel in this procedure is the written order that is transmitted through a standard communication process.

The chief might, for example, be worried about the line officers wasting time talking to each other on duty. Let us also assume that the chief happens to be authoritarian. The following is a paraphrase of an actual order in an actual department:

Standard Operating Procedure, Order 538.71

No sworn officer shall converse with another sworn officer while on duty for more than two minutes, unless the conversation shall consist of information concerning official duties.

The chief has encoded his concern into an order. The receiver, the line officer, decodes the message: "I'd better watch the time I spend socializing and having coffee with the other officers. I might have to justify that time in terms of some departmental business. That two-minute limit really doesn't make much sense given the nature of our patrol duties. So I'll ignore the two-minute part of the message, but I'll watch the time I spend socializing." The line officer also took a look at the **medium** of the message: an official order. The officer will take this message more seriously than if the officer had heard a rumor that the chief was worried about officers' socializing too much.

The channel has also been called the "medium by which the message is sent." It can be the difference between a rumor and a written memorandum. Computer messages on inter-agency crime sharing systems are expected to be short, fact-filled pieces of information. An incident described in a teletype message would have different details and content than the same incident reported in a newspaper story. An officer telling a fellow officer at a social affair about the incident might fill out the story with details and colorful words that would never appear in an official report. The incident may be the same, but the messages are decidedly different. The media used to convey the messages—teletype, official report, newspaper story, casual conversation at a social affair—change the messages.

Although we do not agree with McDonnel that the medium is the message, since there is content to every message, we do agree that every police manager has to be aware of how different communication media can affect the interpretation of the content of messages. Thus, police managers have to use both the formal and the informal communication system to send different kinds of messages. By using both media effectively, chiefs will find that they can communicate effectively and receive both informal and formal feedback to their messages. In the two-minute talking-limit example, it is hoped that this chief will receive feedback through informal channels that the memorandum is unrealistic. Then, if the chief has developed any good communication skills, he or she will modify the message to meet the needs of the line officer.

ENCODING AND DECODING: THE MEANING OF MEANING

Whenever we use language, we are taking an incident and encoding it into a prestructured formula. General semantics indicates that the symbol is not the thing and the map is not the terrain. **Symbols**, which include all words, stand for something else. When we pull down a map of the ocean, we do not get wet because the map is a symbol for the wet ocean—the map is not the ocean itself. Therefore, the map and words are something less than an immediate apprehension of the ocean. In short, a map of the ocean is less than the experience we would have standing on a sandy or rocky beach, listening to ocean sounds, smelling the ocean smells, and gazing at the endless horizon. What does this mean when we try to communicate?

We all talk in **subscripts**. Subscript 1 might be what the sender means by a word. The various receivers might be receiving subscripts 2 and 3 and so on. Let's try an illustration.

Officer Smith tells Officers Jones and Brown that he arrested a juvenile in a tough section of town on his duty shift, late at night. Officer Smith is thinking of a blond-haired, middle-class boy who had run away from home and found himself in a tough neighborhood. Smith's juvenile is $JUVENILE_1$. Officer Jones, who knows that neighborhood, might be thinking of a young tough who smokes marijuana, has black hair, and runs with a gang. Jones's juvenile is $JUVENILE_2$. Officer Brown might be thinking of a young girl he had picked up recently in that neighborhood for prostitution. She is a crack user. Brown's juvenile is $JUVENILE_3$. Unless there is some kind of feedback to Smith's message and a clarification from Officer Smith, the symbol *JUVENILE* might lead to some real problems in this communication.

Very simple words—for example, *desk, car,* or *juvenile*—can refer to a number of different actual things or types. Language is actually a form of shorthand. It is hard for every communicator and receiver to have experienced everything that they may want to discuss. The shorthand of language is used where general descriptions of the symbols are accepted until specifics are added. However, in the case of symbols, people normally add their own subscript, thereby shaping the reality of the spoken word into a picture that may or may not be meant by various communicators. It is necessary to add subscripts to the word symbol since the word symbol can never encompass all the empirical referents. The symbol is often used to describe a particular sensory experience, for example, that middle-class juvenile boy with blond hair that Officer Smith picked up while on duty last night.

A perfect process would occur when the encoder and the decoder know exactly what each symbol means and what the relationship of each symbol is to every other symbol. This happens in simple mechanical means of encoding the decoding, such as Morse code. You have a symbol chart, and you simply relate the dots and dashes to the symbol chart and come out with letters. However, encoding and decoding language and orders entails a more complex process prone to error. Continual feedback to the encoder, explaining what the symbols mean to the decoder, keeps messages clear.

FEEDBACK

Two-way communication is always clearer than one-way communication. One-way, hierarchical communication lacks the essential feedback that tells the encoder that his or her message has been decoded in the manner he or she desired. With no feedback mechanism, the encoder/sender will not know if the decoder/receiver will receive the message in terms of (1) JUVENILE$_1$, (2) JUVENILE$_2$, or (3) JUVENILE$_3$.

To have consistency in message communication, the decoder must have the same basic understanding of the encoding language that the transmitter has. The receiver must decode the message and fulfill the intentions of the person doing the transmitting. That is one reason why law enforcement officers often use codes and other shorthand devices. They know that the receiver—that is, another police officer—will understand the message since the decoding content of the message has already been agreed on. Thus, when an officer hears the code for an officer in trouble, he or she knows that this message (1) demands immediate action and (2) has top priority.

Feedback is what makes management aware of problems in the communication process. Orders sent down the line may get lost if there is no feedback. For example, there could be a fairly general order issued concerning checking certain businesses at night. Sergeants would then detail this duty to specific officers in the area during the times specified. However, the police administrator may have no idea of the action being taken unless there is feedback. The administrator needs to know at a minimum (1) if the message was clear and specific enough, (2) what kind of action took place as a result of the message (order), and (3) what modifications should be made to the message as a result of the actions taken or not taken.

Who Communicates to Whom, and How?

When we consider communication in context, we are looking at a situation. Is the situation an emergency, or is it routine? What are the ranks of the message sender and the message receiver? Will citizens be receiving the message? Who communicates with whom, and how are the elements to be considered in communication? Let's look at some examples.

A judge tells a citizen that he is convicted of a crime and will be sent to prison. The context is the court setting. The result is a change of status of the individual from civilian to prisoner. The context is charged with authority, and there is a powerful difference in the status of the judge and the citizen who is about to be sentenced.

It is of vital importance that top police management understand the effects of their communication within the context of authority relations. We also have to consider what audience hears the message (e.g., civilians or uniformed officers). The chief can take an officer aside and reprimand him or her for wearing a sloppy uniform. Or the chief can communicate this at lineup in front of fellow officers. Or the chief can give the officer the same message while the officer is engaged in an investigation in the presence of news reporters. It is the same message but different audiences. It also makes a difference whether it is the chief of the department or some fellow officer making the same statements. In this case, it is the same statement, different message. It is obvious from these examples that managers who wish to communicate clearly have to understand

1. The authority context of any message, giving the relative status of the sender and receiver of messages.
2. The audience receiving the message.
3. The effect of the message on both the person receiving the message and the audience that may also be hearing the message.

The style of delivering messages deserves consideration, too. Messages from police commanders and other management personnel in law enforcement tend to be brusque, unfeeling, and in the form of orders. In a tense street confrontation with immediate potential violence, for example, this might be the correct approach. However, in many situations, this brusque approach will only tend to alienate line officers and citizens.

A commander could tell a line officer, "You are ordered to change your vacation time because the department needs more personnel at that time." Or the commander might say, "I know that you planned this vacation time and that it is important to your family. However, we have a special event and we really need the extra coverage. I would appreciate it if you would change your vacation time or maybe you could trade with another officer who has that time off. Try to work something out. You know if we can't work something out, I'm simply going to have to draft an order. I would rather not do that. Could you see me in a couple of days concerning this matter? I really appreciate your help here. Thanks." What did we accomplish with the second version of the message? The commander told the officer that he knew and felt sorry about inconveniencing the officer's family. He also told the officer that no matter what, the department was going to need the extra officers. He also gave the officer some flexibility in fulfilling the departmental need. Yes, it would have been easier to have simply written the order. However, the second message would make for a department with much higher morale than a department that simply writes orders.

In the second message, the police commander was also telling the officer to use his support **network**. In every police department, over the years, everybody owes somebody for something. It could be simply a cup of coffee after a bad moment. It could be some help with a family affair or backup in a difficult situation. That is the nature of the police business: A supportive network of fellow officers is built up over the years.

What is important for an officer to learn—from the first day on the job—is that one of the officer's strongest psychological and emotional support resources is the existing network of fellow police officers. This means that when messages go out, even though they are hierarchical in form, they are actually going to a network. The network exchanges messages continually with everyone. Given all the messages a police officer receives and sends from his or her fellow officers in one

24-hour day, each officer would be surrounded by so many lines that it would be hard to see the officer in the midst of this concentration of messages. This networking approach to communications is often called **all-channel communication**. All-channel communication is a participatory management style with communication channels open between all parties.

Most departments, although deeply imbedded in the police network style of communication, have an official departmental style of formal communication called *chain communication*. Chain communication is the chain-of-command style where person 1 does not communicate with person 4 except through persons 2 and 3. This means if a line officer wants a message to reach the chief, he or she has to give that message to the sergeant, who in turn gives it to the lieutenant, who gives it to the captain, who finally gives it to the chief or even the deputy chief. It also means that if the chief wants to communicate with that line officer, he or she has to go through the **chain of command**. The communication process is most rigid going from the bottom to the top. A top officer may bypass part of the chain of command.

However, while this formal process is going on, at least two interesting phenomena are occurring. First, the networking effect takes over, and all kinds of people in the uniformed department have either part of the message or one of various versions of the message. The informal communication network in policing is very strong.

Second are the friendships that have been formed that skip a rank. For example, sergeants do not normally become great friends with lieutenants; captains and sergeants are more likely to become friends, as are lieutenants and line officers. This means that the message may, in fact, informally skip some of the chain of command while formally going up or down the chain of command. Except for routine communications that are noncontroversial, the chain of command is a cumbersome communication process. The chain of command becomes especially costly in two important areas: distortion of messages and the time it takes a message to reach the bottom and have the feedback reach the top.

Another style is **"Y" communication**, in which two superiors communicate to the same subordinate. The subsequent communications may go from subordinate to subordinate. An example of this is one secretary with two bosses. Pity the poor secretary when she receives priorities or contradicting messages from each boss. If this style is to work at all, there must be a key communicator at the junction of the "Y." Then, two bosses give messages to the key communicator, who sorts out priorities and eliminates contradictions and sends the messages to the subordinates. In general, "Y" communication systems fail because of the built-in conflicts.

OBSTACLES TO COMMUNICATION

People fail to communicate with each other even when they truly want to reach out and communicate. A major problem is that we communicate through symbols. As mentioned earlier, what one officer means by *juvenile* may incorporate violent actions, whereas another officer may consider a juvenile to be a smart kid who talks back. Police officers rely on penal law definitions, in part, for the official purpose of arresting offenders.

Another problem is **inference**, as when we attach meanings to a message that the message giver never intended to be part of the communication. For example, Officer Brown says, "We need to roust that kid." Officer Smith says, "Yeah, I know. I'll go over to his house tonight, stand him up against the wall, threaten to arrest him, and see if he will agree to let me take a look at his room." Officer Brown says, "No, I didn't mean for you to do that. I think we could just stop by and question him concerning the crime. He has helped us in the past, and there is no reason why he wouldn't help us again." The key is "I didn't mean for you to do that." Officer Smith created a message by inference. He thought that the original message included content that was not actually in the message—by inference.

Officers make **assumptions** about messages that become part of the message but were not meant to be part of the message originally. Assumptions exist when you think that there are specific grounds for the content of a message, but these grounds may not exist. Assumptions may be warranted or unwarranted. For example, Officer Brown may feel that a juvenile who has a record of violent crime and with whom he has dealt personally in violent situations may, in fact, be responsible for a violent crime. Now, if there is evidence that matches the youth's profile, Officer Brown may be correct. He has a warranted assumption concerning the potentiality of that particular youth's behavior. His assumption is based on reasonable evidence.

On the other hand, Officer Brown may have known that another youth comes from a bad family. He may have arrested that particular youth's brother for burglary and known that the youth's sister was a drug addict. Therefore, when there is a burglary in the vicinity and that youth is seen around the burglarized premises, Officer Brown may assume that the youth from the bad family is a likely suspect. Unknown to Officer Brown, this particular youth is an honor student at school and has just been awarded an athletic scholarship to a good college. Officer Brown's assumption is unwarranted because it is not based on good evidence. In fact, by saying that all members of the family are most likely bad, he has unfairly labeled every child in that family.

Bypassing, another obstacle to communication, occurs when two people talk to each other and miss each other with their meanings; that is, the same words can mean different things to different people. Bypassing is a common occurrence in the ordinary life of a line officer. For example, a sergeant asks a line officer to finish up a sick officer's reports. The line officer then stays overtime to finish the reports. The next day, the sergeant tells the line officer that he meant for him to finish the reports during normal duty hours. The line officer says, "I thought you meant immediately!"

Another obstacle to communication, **overgeneralization**, is basically a variation using unwarranted assumptions. A common example is when a police officer refers to someone as "a good guy." The general meaning of a "good guy" is someone who is helpful and will assist anyone recommended by the officer simply by dropping a name; for example, "Hello, Dr. Forest. This is Sergeant Francis over at Riverview Station. I spoke to Detective Williams, and she said you're someone who could assist me on a case I'm working on."

The "good guy" is simply a generalization that is used for network referencing and assists in daily communication within and between complex organizations. However, in situations involving misconduct or corruption, a "good guy" is someone who may assist in a cover-up or turn the other way "to see nothing." A "good guy" can also be one to bend the rules; for example, "Lou, be a good guy and don't report that dent I put in the fender of car 203 last night."

Proactive police managers need to have a basic awareness of these problems and prepare strategies that provide for better communications before miscommunications occur.

THE JOHARI WINDOW

The **Johari window** is a basic exercise in communication flow that monitors how information is passed from the police manager to others and back again according to interpersonal style. It is a basic 2 × 2 table based on (1) information known and not known to yourself about yourself and (2) information known and not known to others about you (see Figure 6-1).

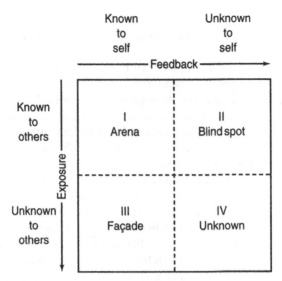

FIGURE 6-1 Johari window.

When you and others share information, this occurs in region I, the *arena*. Mutually held information becomes the most valuable approach to communication. If others know information and you do not know the information, you may suffer a *blind spot*, region II. It is a personal handicap for the manager since he or she cannot understand the behavior of others if he or she lacks essential information concerning why they behave the way they do. This was involved in the example of Officer Brown thinking that a youth from a bad family was a likely crime suspect. Brown lacked information that the youth was an honor student with a good career ahead of him. This was Officer Brown's Johari window blind spot.

When you have information that is unknown to others, it is called region III, the *façade*. The façade is a protective front where information is withheld from others to protect the self. The question is how much defensiveness should be tolerated before the withholding of information interferes with good management communication.

When information is unknown by self and others, it is considered an area of potential creativity, region IV, *unknown*. As management communication becomes more effective, the unknown becomes known, and region IV diminishes in size.

The two basic processes for the creation of information are exposure of self in terms of giving information, including information about emotions and attitudes, and the feedback process, where others expose themselves and give information to self. The model calls for a climate of mutual exposure to achieve maximum communication and thus calls for an open democratic management model. This would normally be in direct contradiction to the strict hierarchical chain of communication model.

The model calls for four types of communication in relation to the two processes of exposure and feedback. Type A is an impersonal style characterized by minimal exposure and feedback: the traditional police chief–dominated department. Type B minimizes exposure of self but attempts to maximize feedback. Management distrusts others but wishes emotional and general information from others. This normally results in a basic management model based on mutual distrust, often reverting back to type A.

Type C is an overuse of exposure to self and a minimal use of feedback from others, a giant ego ride. This is the "cult of personality" police chief with idiosyncratic policies. You generally know what the chief is thinking, and the chief does not care what you think or feel. This style triggers feelings of hostility and resentment from the general officer population, especially the line officer population. The preferred style according to this model of communication is type D, open and frank communication—that is, a mutuality of maximum exposure and feedback. It is hoped that over time a context of trust and creativity will be created in the police department. Given the various demands of police departments, especially for emergency procedures, this is difficult to achieve. Type D communication is most often found in a police department dedicated to a democratic management style. It is often tied in with some variation of team and community policing styles.

The basic exercise is for individuals to answer a number of questions concerning their exposure/feedback styles and then, using standard scores for the model, see where they stand in terms of the four regions. You then examine various strategies that would bring the maximum number of members of the police management team into the open communication model designated as the arena. According to the model, the larger the size of the arena in relation to the other three regions, the more effective will be the management communication model used by the police organization. The secret seems to be to bring employees, colleagues, and supervisors into a feedback/exposure position that will maximize their communication with one another in the arena.

This type of model can be useful up to a point. Everyone in the department is expected to spend some time communicating his or her emotions to everyone else in the department to gain maximum feedback, but there probably is not enough time to fulfill this requirement completely. Also, normal psychological health demands a certain amount of private space for individuals. Exposure and feedback in terms of producing some basic honesty in human relations can be useful for getting the job done, but spending too much time discussing emotional relationships can become counterproductive. After all, the department still has to arrest criminals and deal with myriad social problems.

As with other theoretical models drawn from the social sciences, business, and public administration, the Johari window communication model also needs to be tempered by the reality of managing real police departments with real problems. For a long time, police organizations have been closed and rigid in their authoritarian management style. Conversely, however, reliance on feelings and democratic ideals will not work for police organizations either. The proactive approach is a tempered approach: consultative with enough exposure and feedback to do the job with sensitivity and efficiency. It is a forward-looking communication model where feedback becomes part of the planning process, and the planning process is a consultative process for all members of the police agency. This is an effective use of the Johari window as another analytic tool used to bring about consultative, effective communication.

DIGITAL COMMUNICATIONS

E-mail systems by Google, Yahoo, AOL, and various phone carriers as well as social networking services, such as Facebook, Twitter, Myspace, Instagram, Vine, YouTube, and LinkedIn, allow individuals and organizations to share information such as messages, documents, books, videos, and photographs over the Internet. The first such service was Facebook, created by two students in 2004 as a medium for Harvard and other campuses' students to communicate with each other. It eventually spread to other campuses and to the general public. This was soon followed by Twitter, which offers subscribers the medium to comment on anything in less than 100 words. By 2008, presidential candidates were using these media to get their campaign messages out to the public.

This development of the Internet and social networking sites, as well as the continued development of relatively accessible and cheap communications devices such as cell phones and iPads has revolutionized communication theory. Access to information has turned the world upside down when it comes to the speed and scope of communications theory as messages and information move fast and globally in a few minutes. This was experienced recently by one of the authors who attended a labor management meeting with a police union. Within minutes of the meeting, several commentaries on certain topics were being debated by members of the force before he had returned to the office.

It is estimated that by 2010, there were 2 billion people connected to the Internet. Concurrently, the number of cell phone users has reached approximately 6 billion (Schmidt and Cohen, 2013). Today "going viral" means that the message has gone out to the world in an uncontrolled manner through the Internet. Many examples are reported daily. A good example occurred when a woman broke up with her boyfriend in a message on Twitter. Within hours, there were millions of tweets around the world on whether people thought that it was a good idea. Every patrol officer today knows that every cell phone is a camera that can record and transmit arrests and use of force incidents to the public by way of social media sites.

There is also the issue of personal privacy. From one standpoint, once a message or video goes on the Internet, it belongs to the Internet forever. "Anything you say can be used against you" as the saying goes, which can impact relationships, employment, and personal and institutional reputations (Goel, 2013).

It is no surprise that a majority of police departments in the United States have adopted some form of social networking in order to relay information to the public and to counter misinformation especially after disasters or major crimes. The use of social networking for investigation purposes for traditional and Internet-related crimes, as well as the need for departmental policies on official and personal use by employees, will be discussed in later chapters.

OPERATIONAL COMMUNICATIONS

This type of communication normally takes the form of writing. Written documents have one advantage in that they can be referred to with ease. They are normally more precise than informal and verbal communication. They provide a certain consistency of standard, along with rules and norms for a police organization.

Certain objectives need to be established and met if the organizational goals of the police agency are to be accomplished. These goals are achieved through the six objectives of written communication:

1. To make plans operational
2. To carry on day-to-day operations
3. To relay and interpret policies
4. To provide details for activity completion
5. To complete assignments satisfactorily
6. To provide for evaluation and feedback

Types of Orders

Specific assignments are needed to give managers and line officers direction concerning how to carry out vital activities of the police agency. Traditionally, these written activities have taken the following forms:

SOP	Standard operating procedure
TOP	Temporary operating procedure
GO	General order
SO	Special order
MEMO	Memorandum

There are written **directives**, which are necessary for the daily operations of every police agency. They may be gathered into a volume called the **duty manual**. These directives are expected to operate consistently over time. While duty manuals should be kept up-to-date, they generally change in only minor ways from year to year and from one police administration to another.

STANDARD OPERATING PROCEDURES   A **standard operating procedure (SOP)** is a procedure that will affect the total department on an ongoing basis over time. It has a specific starting date but no ending date. SOPs are changed by the creation of a new SOP that says the old SOP is no longer in effect. They are numbered and dated for filing purposes.

Basically, all new SOPs should be incorporated into a revised duty manual in a timely manner. This way, all the officers in the department will have access to an organized set of rules. When this does not occur, the duty manual becomes dated, and new officers have to resort to file cabinets of SOPs to learn the basic rules of the department. Even experienced officers can become confused when the duty manual consists of hundreds of files.

SOPs include what is and is not acceptable communication under a wide variety of circumstances and authority relationships as they are met in the normal course of police business. The duty manual is simply an organized way of having all of the SOPs in one place.

TEMPORARY OPERATING PROCEDURES   A **temporary operating procedure (TOP)** has all the characteristics of an SOP with one exception: It has a termination date. That means that on the termination date, the TOP is no longer in effect. Of course, TOPs are dated and numbered. Events that are handled by TOPs would be one-time events, such as sporting events, parades, and visits from dignitaries.

GENERAL ORDERS   Like an SOP, a **general order (GO)** is numbered and dated and distributed to all personnel. The GO is created for informational purposes, whereas the SOP and the TOP are operational orders. Legal changes, such as those created by search and seizure cases, would be GOs. New procedures for handling drunken persons according to new state directives would go out as GOs. Relations with mental health or probation agencies might go to all personnel in the form of GOs.

SPECIAL ORDERS   Special orders (SOs) are numbered and dated and refer only to personnel matters. They are very specific and refer to such items as transfers, job assignments, promotions, and disciplinary actions.

MEMORANDUMS Memorandums (MEMOs) are written to communicate information or orders of short duration. These are dated but not numbered. They are generally for very limited distribution. MEMOs are used when a verbal order is adequate but putting the order in writing will eliminate all possible misunderstandings. (They might apply in such mundane matters as having patrol cars fixed by the police mechanic.) MEMOs are especially useful in maintaining continuity of information to a staff that is operating on various shifts over a 24-hour period and a 7-day week.

Basically, these directives are of vital importance for the maintenance of communication in a department. All should be written with care. There should also be a time period when these various types of communications are either destroyed—all copies—or codified in some manner. Operational orders that last over time should be incorporated in the duty manual. Personnel matters become part of permanent personnel files when they are significant enough to affect an officer's performance appraisal. Occasionally, the department may wish to resort to microfilm or microfiche for the storage of some of these materials. However, at the end of a specified period, most of this paperwork should be destroyed. This normally entails a change in some state laws concerning document retention.

The Effectively Organized Directive

Directives can be effective, or they can be jumbled and vague. They should be both precise and concise. Police departments tend to drown in a sea of ill-conceived, badly worded phrases. If the department is to be effective, these general rules for writing directives should be followed:

1. The contents of the directive must be achievable and reasonable. To carry out the order, the recipient must have the means and the ability to act effectively.
2. The instructions concerning the directive should be sufficiently detailed to ensure the completion of the task. An example might be a directive concerning the disassembly of weapons. A directive that simply says that the officer must be able to assemble and disassemble his or her weapon does not contain enough information. Detailed information is needed concerning the variety of weapons at an officer's disposal. The directive might also include specific training procedures for officers needing additional information and skills to disassemble specific weapons.
3. Directives should use normal English language that would be understandable at the tenth-grade reading level. Although all police officers are high school graduates, they may not be able to read at a twelfth-grade level. Many college texts at the freshman level are being written with a tenth-grade vocabulary. It is vital that technical terms be clarified in simple English.
4. Orders that need explanation should be given some justification concerning why the order has been issued. This enhances morale, compliance, understanding, and two-way communication.
5. Orders should be edited. First, drafts should be examined for clarity by a close colleague of the originator. If possible, the directive should be edited by a member of the management team other than the author. After editing for clarity and use of language, you can then decide whether the order actually means what you meant.
6. The directive should be of sufficient importance to the management of the department to justify its being written. Given today's proliferation of paperwork, directives should not be written unless there is a proven need. In general, a directive should
   a. Be an order of some complexity
   b. Extend over a fairly long period of time

c. Go to more than one officer

d. Affect a fairly large number of personnel.

Basically, the more personnel affected by an order, the greater the justification for putting the order in the form of a written directive.

7. A feedback mechanism should be part of every order. Some directives may be followed up automatically, but this does not always happen. A police management team is only as good as the information at its disposal. Management needs to know if the directive (1) was carried out, (2) in what manner, and (3) with what effect.

THE DUTY MANUAL

The codification of the written rules of the police agency is variously called the *operations manual,* the *procedures manual, rules and regulations,* and even *standard operating procedures.* The usual title is *duty manual.*

The duty manual governs many aspects of an officer's private life as well as his or her behavior during a tour of active duty. Most duty manuals are very specific. For example, concerning a part-time job, a duty manual may specify that the officer needs the permission of the department. It may also specify the length of hair, the length of sideburns, and the width of mustaches. Officers are expected to be fit and ready for duty at all times. They are often expected to carry their badges and even their guns while off duty.

The duty manual of the London Metropolitan Police in 1829 specified how the duty manual was expected to be used, including areas where discretion necessarily must come into play, as it would be impossible for any manual to cover every single possible human condition and event.

Duty manuals were rightly expected to contain some flexibility in terms of interpreting the general rules of the department. A professional police agency must leave a great deal to the intelligence and discretion of the individual police officers.

O.W. Wilson (1963: 33) ably stated what is now considered the normal definition of the duty manual:

DUTY MANUAL: Describes procedures and defines the duties of officers assigned to specific posts or positions. . . . Duty manuals and changes in them should be made effective by general order; the changes should be incorporated into the first revision of the duty manual.

The duty manual usually has a chart of the organization and some job descriptions. This is to fulfill the need for consistency and fairness in normal departmental regulations. The manual would begin with the general job description of a sergeant, which would include language as being typical of a duty manual and might describe the general duties of a sergeant as follows:

Police sergeants are sworn members appointed in charge of one or more members and/or employees. In addition to the general and individual responsibilities of all members and employees, sergeants are specifically responsible for the following on their shift.

Besides this general job description, a good duty manual would also outline some of the specifics of the job of a sergeant:

1. Train, direct, supervise, and evaluate members in their assigned duties. Recommend remedial or disciplinary action for inefficient, incompetent, and unsuitable members.

2. Inform his or her relief of all necessary police matters.

3. Report to his or her commanding officer absentees and any deficiencies in personnel and equipment.
4. Ensure that recovered property is handled in accordance with department orders.
5. Without unnecessary delay, visit all officers of the force on duty in the territory subject to supervision. Advise them of all important information or details relating to the efficient operation of the department functions, and inquire as to the conditions of the member's post. Report all matters requiring police action to the desk officer.
6. Visit at least twice during each tour of duty the patrol officer(s) assigned to special posts, hospitals, or other details located within the territory subject to supervision.

Of course, many other duties, both general and specific, could be spelled out. However, this gives some idea of how the duty manual is organized and how specific it should be. The duty manual must provide enough detailed information so that the job can be accomplished with the maximum amount of efficiency and yet not be so detailed as to abolish that necessary use of intelligence and discretion that makes for good police work.

The duty manual is a clear, concise, and logical way in which to order procedure in a police department. It also helps to order normal business by describing the duties of each rank of officer and the way in which the ranks relate to one another. It can and does succinctly incorporate procedures to be used for such emergencies as natural disasters. The general rule is that the operations mandated by the duty manual, along with personnel procedures, must be of a recurrent nature. This is something that the department will have to deal with on an ongoing basis.

Some duty manuals become very specific. This happens when one-time incidents are used to create a general rule. Often, these rules become unrealistic, and good management must always be on the lookout to make sure that the duty manual specifies rules and regulations that are efficient, humane, and, above all, reasonable.

Examples of some very specific rules from an actual duty manual follow:

No smoking on the job. No member of the department shall smoke on post or beat while in uniform or while conducting an investigation of any nature.

No entering places where intoxicants are sold. No member of the department, while on duty, shall enter any place in which intoxicating liquors are sold except in the immediate performance of his or her duties.

No inebriation off duty. No member of the department shall drink intoxicants at any time off duty to the extent that he or she becomes unfit for duty.

Two-minute limit for talking on duty. Conversations of more than two minutes between members of the force on patrol, unless concerned with their immediate performance of duty, are prohibited.

Many regulations that appear in duty manuals are either too specific or too general to be obeyed. Their purpose often derives from the chief's need to exert internal control over his or her officers. With modern civil service legislation, it is difficult to fire a police officer. Therefore, the chief may write down a number of rules simply to pinpoint an officer who is violating the rules. This is not a good way to handle internal police discipline since many of the rules are unfair and cannot be enforced in a just manner.

If the rules of the duty manual are seen as being unreasonable and used to "set up" officers, the agency will have a growing morale problem. The duty manual will not be seen as an effective instrument for the implementation of policy. When the rules are clear and reasonable, the duty manual can legitimately be used for official reprimands and even the firing of an officer. In general, the rules contained in the duty manual should

1. Be kept short so that everyone can read and understand the total manual in a relatively short time.
2. Be consistent
3. Be reasonable
4. Conform to principles of good management
5. Be humane
6. Be enforceable
7. Be stated in an unambiguous manner
8. Be related to the actual operations of police procedures
9. Not deal with the trivial
10. Be written in a good English format with a professional tone to the choice of words.

It is especially important that any words that denote an autocratic, arbitrary manner should be deleted (see principle 10).

An effective and fair duty manual is an essential tool for the efficient operation of a police agency. If an officer is reprimanded or fired because of failure to comply with the rules and regulations of the duty manual, he or she must be able to see some essential honesty and fairness involved in this procedure. At that point, the duty manual becomes an effective management communication tool and legitimately produces general rules for the social control of the civil service police force by the police management team.

CASE STUDY
Rules and Regulations

Are trivial rules enforced so that autocratic and often unprofessional police leadership can exert control and harass professional police officers? The following is adapted from a newspaper account of an actual incident.

A man ran into the station house with a loaded shotgun. After the man was disarmed, the officers saw that he was cut with a knife, and the man was taken to a hospital. Meanwhile, a television camera crew interviewed an officer who had handled the incident. The officer appeared on television . . . hatless! The commissioner gave the officer an official reprimand for appearing hatless on television. The officer said, "In the confusion, I inadvertently left my hat in the station house."

The commissioner decided not to take disciplinary action against the officer but gave out a strongly worded memorandum the next day concerning proper dress. The commissioner stated in his memorandum, "Any violations of the procedures and regulations concerning the wearing of proper and mandated articles of uniform will be dealt with severely. Disciplinary action, which could result in charges against a violator, will positively be taken. The most flagrant violation of the regulations concerning wearing of uniform relates to not wearing the police cap."

This is a good example of the misuse of the duty manual. A normal regulation referring to the wearing of a uniform, neatly, has been used to harass police officers in the performance of their duty. Adverse publicity was generated, and the chief looked like an incompetent and a petty tyrant.

PROACTIVE ORGANIZATIONAL COMMUNICATION MODEL

A proactive communication model must include the following elements:

- Planning
- Organizing
- Operationalizing
- Evaluating

All these elements have to be related to an ongoing feedback system if this communication model is to operate effectively. These elements are naturally related on an ongoing basis to actual operational procedures and the objectives of the police organization.

The proactive communication grid in Figure 6-2 shows how these elements are interrelated. The double-headed arrows show that each element has to be related to every other element of communication and that all the elements need to be related to an effective feedback system.

Planning

1. Identifying needs
2. Forecasting
3. Researching and developing
4. Ensuring conformity to goals and objectives
5. Using staff in developing the planning process
6. Getting input from police personnel
7. Consulting and coordinating with outside sources
8. Making decisions

Organizing

1. Hiring personnel
2. Training

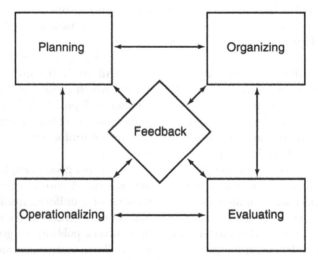

FIGURE 6-2   The proactive communication grid.

3. Creating rules of procedure and directives
4. Developing auxiliary services and infrastructure of support
5. Servicing, capitalizing, and maintaining physical plant and equipment
6. Drawing up implementation orders

Operationalizing

1. Supervising implementation procedures
2. Providing continuing direction and control
3. Coordinating various parts and segments of the police agency
4. Coordinating with outside agencies

Evaluating

1. Developing standards that lead to operationalized evaluations
2. Listing criteria of success
3. Developing evaluation procedures and relating them to empirical standards of success
4. Creating a centralized data file
5. Creating a centralized staff of research analysts
6. Outlining inspection procedures
7. Obtaining feedback with recommendations for planning

Conclusion

The central concern of police communication is mutual unambiguous understanding among all communicators. Communication can and does shape the nature of the police organization. If it is all one-way, from the top to the bottom, and with little or no feedback, the department will be organized in an autocratic manner. The autocratic style, although effective in terms of rapid response, actually fosters inefficiency. Management needs to know which orders are effective in operation and which are not, and this is determined through a solid feedback system. With such a system, ineffective orders can be eliminated or modified until they become effective.

For communication to be understood by all parties involved, orders should be written in a consistent and organized manner. Unambiguous communication is especially important in police work, where the professional officer has to respond time and again to citizens in crisis. The line officer has to be an effective communicator, but this can be achieved only when the officer is supported by an orderly process of departmental communication. With so much time spent on doing paperwork, as well as on giving and receiving orders, all police organizations should develop an ongoing proactive communication system.

Questions for Review

1. Explain the differences between one-way and two-way communication. Give some examples that occurred in your class.
2. Imagine you are a patrol officer on the radio discussing a tense hostage situation with a commanding officer. Identify (1) the sender, (2) the receiver, (3) the encoding, (4) the decoding, and (5) the channel.
3. If you were the supervising officer of a patrol operation, describe the feedback system you would institute. Defend the efficiency of the system in terms of its information flow patterns.

4. Two of the major problems in communications are misunderstanding and misinformation. Explain how you would deal with these two problems if you supervised a small rural police agency. Also identify how you would deal with these problems in terms of communications with other police agencies in nearby jurisdictions.

5. List the major obstacles to good communication in the day-to-day work of a police agency, and detail the major strategies you would use to overcome these obstacles.

6. If you were a police commander, in what part of the Johari window would you locate yourself, and why? Choose another student in class, and state where you would locate him or her in the Johari window. Justify your answer.

7. Imagine that you are a supervising officer. You have noticed that many of your patrol officers are wasting too much time in convenience stores. It is not just a question of gaining information and community support but an inefficient use of the officers' time. Specify the type of order (SOP, TOP, GO, SO, MEMO) you would issue, and justify your choice in the face of a grievance from one of your officers concerning your order.

8. Define *reasonable* in police management terms, and apply this definition to what you would consider a reasonable duty manual.

9. Apply the proactive communication approach to a local police department. How would this communication model work in the field in the midst of the usual practical difficulties?

Class Project

The best illustration that shows the complexities of communication is giving directions to another person. Select a location that is not too well known near your classroom that requires a classmate to make three to four different moves over a period of about 5 min. Go to the location and leave "markers," which for this exercise can be notes, envelopes, or some pieces of paper that you tape to the wall or leave with another person.

Present the directions to your classmate and have that person go to the location, take one marker, and then bring the marker back to you. If this classmate is successful, then have the classmate do the same thing with another person and continue. If he or she is not successful, then select another person and see what happens.

During this time, apply the main concepts of communication theory to your instructions and reactions with your fellow classmate.

References

Goel, Raj. Social Media and Cloud Computing: Threats to Privacy, Security and Liberty. Presenting at New York State Cyber Security Conference, June 4, 2013.

McDonnel, Richard A. "Information Management." In Bernard L. Garmie, ed., *Local Government Police Management*. Washington, D.C.: International City Management Association, 1977.

Neil, Thomas C. *Interpersonal Communications for Criminal Justice Personnel*. Boston: Allyn and Bacon, 1980.

Schmidt, Eric, and Jared Cohen. *The New Digital Age: Reshaping the Future of People, Nations and Business*. New York: Knoph, 2013.

Wilson, O.W. *Police Administration* (2nd ed.). New York: McGraw-Hill, 1963.

CHAPTER

7 Proactive Police Technology for the Twenty-First Century

KEY TERMS

automatic vehicle monitoring (AVM)

Compstat

computer-aided dispatch (CAD)

crime mapping

digitally driven police department

electronic form

global positioning system (GPS)

laptop

National Crime Information
  Center (NCIC)

911 system

regional communication system (RCS)

real time

Welcome to the mid-twenty-first century. The paperless police department has become a reality as all police forms have been digitalized and can be accessed from every police car. Instant communication includes encrypted messages through laptop computers and special police palm computers for individual officers. Each police car and officer can be located through global positioning. Global communications provide individual officers with criminal information locally, nationally, and cross-nationally. Officers can access information on international drug smuggling as easily as they can obtain the report of a stolen car.

Officer Rauke spots a car with an erratic driver. She types in the license plate and is given a stolen car identification. The data screen indicates that the car may contain a dangerous felon. She calls for backup. Officer Rauke accesses the computer chip in the fleeing car, which immobilizes the car. Backup arrives and the driver steps out of the car. With backup standing by, the officer scans the back of the suspect's hand for DNA identification. A warrant for felony drug dealing with positive identification comes up on the officer's handheld computer screen. A secure arrest is made.

Science fiction or reality? Only two pieces of technology cited here are not available at this moment. The electronic auto-stopping chip is on its way. DNA identification needs some work on field sampling devices and a larger data bank. If the problem is a burglary, a computer map would give all incidences of burglary in the past two months in the immediate area, along with a list of suspects who are not in custody and the suspects' addresses. A suspect-sorting program could then be used to create a short list for investigation. Witness descriptions could provide sorts based on gender, race, height, and so on.

A major problem for police managers in the next decades will be controlling and organizing technology. Technology must not drive police decisions. Police decisions need to be controlled by human police managers. A major problem with Internet information is that there is simply too much information for any human being to comprehend. Another problem is identifying information sources that can be trusted. Today, rather than adding features, program developers are learning how to simplify programs to a more useful, human scale. Technology that makes life easier on police managers has to be on a human scale.

When police went from walking a beat to patrolling in cars, the technology drove policy. Police rode around in their patrol cars and were insulated from the public. It took a proactive use of community policing to move beyond the isolated officer in the patrol car. The 911 universal emergency phone number has once again resulted in technology controlling management policy. The enormous growth of service calls from 911 created a reaction-driven department overwhelmed by these service calls, from critical emergencies to trivial issues. The proactive police manager institutes a split force, prioritizes the responses to calls, and takes control of this unique communication system (see Chapter 8 on patrol).

As all institutions become more information driven, linking information access to policy making through computers becomes vital. This information has to be managed through proactive planning, packaging, and accessing. Computer mapping makes good use of crime data and 911 information to pinpoint hot spots and to help decide different levels of service in different neighborhoods at specific times during a day. Linking information from radio, 911, and computer communication to policy decisions concerning deployment and even personnel decisions is a smart use of information.

Laptop and handheld computers in patrol vehicles become useful only when there is a management system in place to take advantage of them. Secure information channels and organized reporting systems have to be in place before any computer is turned on. This means that the computer is only as good as the information put into the system and the intelligent use of the computer information system by human beings. If you put bad information into your computer system, a bad decision will come out of that system. The bottom line is that police managers need to make sure they are in charge of the system. If that is accomplished, the system becomes a valuable tool for every police manager, from a village police chief to the police commissioner of a major city.

COMPUTER APPLICATIONS FOR INFORMATION MANAGEMENT

Before computerization, paper records got lost, created storage problems in terms of bulk, and were hard to handle. In order not to lose information, great redundancy was built into all police information systems. It took considerable time just to find things. Files would occasionally get misfiled or lost, with disastrous results. Accessibility and security were in constant conflict. There was no solution until the computer. Now information can be processed in a rapid manner while access is limited by use of security codes. One captain recalled the not-so-recent past:

> You would get a phone call from an irate citizen that Officer Smith took too long to arrive at a call and did not do anything about the complaint. It would take me about two hours to find out what

had taken place from a record's perspective. I would have to go and find the radio log and then the police report, which hopefully had been filed or was being followed up by the detectives. Often the report would be on someone's desk. Then I would have to track down who the supervisor was for that specific time.

When we started to computerize, things did improve. The report might be in records waiting to be transcribed into our system. Today I can track any incident from my desk in real time. That is what a records management system should be able to do.

Information also has to be available in **real time**; in other words, police managers, supervisors, and line officers must be able to retrieve information from a number of sources in seconds. For example, if a manager has to present a crime-prevention talk to a community group, he or she would need the crime data that are current in order to discuss trends and department planning. In the same light, an officer on the street who is interviewing a crime suspect needs to be able to ascertain identity and see if there are any warrants on the subject.

Reports for the entire shift can be downloaded or transmitted by cell phones to central servers. Police departments can administer incident-based activities as every call and field contact becomes an "incident." Digital imaging has also increased. Departments can now maintain scores of mug shots of arrestees for identification, transfer to other departments, and photo arrays for investigative purposes.

However, the computer is simply a tool, a machine, to process information. The computer does not create solutions, manage problems, or become a panacea for all solutions. Police managers manage and solve problems using the computer. Given this warning concerning the overreliance on computer technology, we also have the opposite end of the spectrum—that is, fear of computers. There are still police managers who cannot operate without hard copy (a piece of paper) and who are fearful of using computers. These managers need to be retooled or retired. This may sound harsh, but the realities of the information age in terms of an efficient means of organizing so much information are overwhelming.

When mainframe computers first came into existence, data were generated with huge amounts of output, overwhelming police managers and administrators. When one of the authors first did a survey run of police attitudes on an old IBM 360, he ran hundreds of tables, creating a paper pile over three feet high. The second thing he did was throw away this three-foot-high stack of tables. The police managers, with their mainframes, also threw out hundreds of feet of output. Why? What happened?

It was so easy to get the data and the data output that police managers asked for everything without thinking through what they wanted. Managers need to use computers as tools and ask for only the output they need to get their jobs done in the most efficient manner. The ability to ask the right question is the basic talent needed for police administration.

The records management system, then, is a compendium of criminal data, crime statistics, and prosecution records, and it is the means by which an authorized department member can access and retrieve information. The following items comprise the management information system, which becomes the lifeblood of the department for accountability and deployment and is the living record in dealing with crime and public safety services:

1. *Payroll.* Periodic payroll records, actual paying of personnel, and analysis of payroll records in relation to time sheets, court time, sick time, and so on, with enhanced fiscal planning ability.
2. *Budget.* Fiscal control of the existing budget with up-to-date record of expenditures; fiscal impact of any emergency/overtime procedures; planning capability in terms of generating

future budgets; the manipulation of fiscal data for mayors, city managers, legislators, police management, and so on.

3. *Purchasing.* Purchase of uniforms, supplies, equipment, and so on. Data processing provides controls for purchasing, especially when correlated with maintenance and depletion schedules, for example. The cost of uniforms provided for personnel by contract in many departments can be a large expenditure that benefits from good control. Also, there is a need for controls in terms of bulk versus retail purchases with the use of a cost/benefit subroutine.

4. *Vehicle maintenance.* Maintenance of patrol cars, boats, bicycles, and so on. Detailed records are needed to get comparative cost per mile and such information as the optimum trade-in mileage.

5. *Annual report.* Gathering of the necessary data to justify department operations to the legislature, administrative officials like mayors and county executives, and the general public.

6. *Inventory.* Adequate control of department assets along with replacement schedules and similar details.

7. *Personnel.* Maintaining of current personnel records, allowing the convenience of updating with a subroutine, that permits selective information to be readily available to the police manager. Software programs today allow investigators to create systematic files on candidates related to employment, residencies, references, criminal history, illegal substance use, and the like.

8. *Training records.* Maintaining of information related to the past, ongoing, and future training of the members of the department. This has become increasingly important in today's litigious society, where training is an issue in relation to liability.

9. *Scheduling of personnel.* Difficult task of scheduling 24-hour, seven-day coverage for patrol officers patrolling a community. The police manager needs to consider a number of variables, such as shift changes, vacation time, rest days, and training time. There is also a need to have enough personnel to cover effectively the different numbers of calls for service at different times. Computer software programs have come a long way in making such scheduling easier.

10. *Community relations.* Maintaining of records on the speaker's bureau, tours of the department, press and media relations, and so on, including the use of desktop publishing for newsletters and news releases.

Productivity can be increased throughout the department by using data processing, at least in the following areas:

Crime reports	Fingerprints
Evidence control	Found property
Modi operandi	Warrant files
Traffic tickets	Court appearances
Vacant house checks	Burglar alarms
Hazardous conditions	Daily bulletins
Mug-shot images	Computer crime mapping

The use of microcomputers, which allow data input into systems, enhances the ability of administrators and officers to have instant and adequate input and output of essential information. Security codes and assurance can protect files while providing access to authorized personnel.

Computer-Aided Dispatch (CAD)

Computer-aided dispatch (CAD) enhances calls for service from the public and the dispatching of police cars and personnel. The CAD system verifies addresses, determines the beat of incidents, and gives a case number and priority number to each call. Some systems even report "dangerous histories." The computer automatically records all calls and can recommend to the dispatcher a choice of units to dispatch to the call. The time of dispatch is recorded as well as time on the scene and time the unit is free. Thus, CAD provides real-time monitoring of vehicle status and a continuously updated incident file; allows supervisors to monitor the incident status; and provides telephone, radio, and digital activity statistics. The system can also generate crime statistics reports, flag deviations and trends, automatically generate required data for resource allocation models, and provide online information for line supervisors, administrators, and officers.

CAD, combined with information laptop technology and computer mapping, can supply a great deal of data and services to officers in their patrol cars. Its uses in technologically smart departments include the following:

1. Victim identification
2. Patrol planning
3. Hot spot identification
4. Notification to emergency fire and medical services
5. Improved officer safety through driver and vehicle identification
6. Crime mapping for service call responses
7. Access to multiple data resources, including stolen cars, outstanding warrants, and other calls to the same location
8. Verification of all data
9. Improved service through the use of information technology
10. Rapid field report writing

As discussed in Chapter 11, police communications may be organized in a center for all fire, police, and emergency medical personnel in a city, region, or county. In other instances, a communications center only provides primary services for a police department while fire and ambulance calls are routed to other agencies. Regardless of its range of services, the communications center is the "front door" of a records management system. It is also the information system for the organization because all informational resources are stored either in hard copy or on computers.

Police incidents are generated either by officers working in the field or by citizens making a complaint. This elicits a response for additional personnel and equipment. Before computerization, communications personnel kept a number of handwritten records in terms of logs and disposition of incidents. CAD offers additional assistance in terms of hardware and software. Ideally, every time a call comes in or an incident is generated by a patrol unit, the event becomes an incident and is monitored by the dispatcher in the following ways:

- Assignment of a record number and incident file
- Monitoring of the time spent on the incident
- Checks of addresses or persons for previous incidents
- Checks for warrants on suspects
- Alerts to responding personnel regarding potential violence or wanted persons

To assist field personnel, CAD systems also contain information on community and auxiliary resources patrol units need such as tow trucks, hazardous materials agencies, court locations and schedules, animal control personnel, and hospital phone numbers. For shift deployment purposes, a well-designed CAD can list employees on or off duty, vehicles in service or out of service (on calls or breaks), or assignment details.

Ideally, CAD offers a number of factors for management purposes in terms of the following types of information:

- Type and date
- Name of complainant, suspect, or witness
- Classification of events according to state crime-reporting categories
- Classification of each event according to department service categories
- Disposition of the incident (arrest, no action taken, under investigation, referred for further investigation/open)
- Preparation of special reports for state and federal agencies

A key feature of CAD is the use of wireless transmissions between the patrol units and the reduction of voice messages between the communications center and police personnel. When the authors first began their careers, we had to talk to dispatchers on one channel for calls and on another for data such as motor vehicle registrations, wants and warrants, and requests for additional resources. Today, CAD allows patrol units to obtain field data or information by wireless communication entries in place of asking a communications person for license plate information, information on a suspect, and so on. The trend in CAD is to reduce the amount of time spent on radio communications. Many departments are moving to the regular dispatch of patrol units via wireless transmissions.

Proactive Dispatch Benchmarks

CAD has been a useful tool for many years. Technologically sophisticated departments have used computer models to "determine the most effective deployment of personnel with respect to call-for-service workload" (Sweeny, 2003: 126). Thomas Sweeny recommends this approach to patrol, along with crime and traffic analysis and beat profiling (beat profiling would include critical neighborhood information, special problems, and resources shared with different tours and shifts through preformatted formats).

Ensuring that a department is a proactive data analysis–driven department rather than a reactive incident-driven department can be done through the development of rules to control and limit incident-driven dispatching. The following is based in part on Sweeny's recommendations (with our additions) on how to stop the "endless incident-driven cycle" (Sweeny, 2003: 127–28):

- Critically reexamine the total calls-for-service workload, abolish low-priority services such as mail runs or errand running, make referrals to other government agencies (such as when a building's heat is off) rather than send a patrol car, and, of course, reduce paperwork. A department Web site with standard forms that can be filled in online would be used for a standard referral, with an online follow-up from central dispatch. This could save a huge number of dispatch calls.
- Make a rigid rule for calls that will not be handled by dispatch; include an immediate referral to a superior officer if there is any dispute.
- Have the department's priority of calls list include categories of calls that are immediately answered and calls that normally won't be answered for a specific period of time.
- Have a follow-up callback system for certain calls such as quality-of-life incidents (complaint of loud noise, larceny from auto).

- Use specially trained civilian employees (e.g., community service officers) to handle routine and low-priority calls such as minor accidents, reports on found property, or a car blocking a driveway for a long period of time.
- Encourage community residents to make more referrals, especially problem solving and youth incidents, to neighborhood and beat officers rather than calling dispatch. Use neighborhood problem solving and community police officers for follow-up to dispatch calls.
- Immediately institute a nonemergency number such as 411 and publicize it widely.
- Let regional supervising field officers override any dispatch and assign it to another (closer) car or community service officer.
- Protect certain officers and classes of officers from answering dispatch calls except for dire emergencies. These protected officers would include officers giving speeches and working with community groups as well as those involved with interagency gun and drug suppression and investigation efforts.
- Have department-wide policies limiting the percentage of the sworn workforce that answers dispatches.
- Provide special training for civilian dispatchers, including a mandatory monthly ride-along program.
- Always have experienced sworn officers in charge of dispatching, with immediate superior officer backup.

Sweeny states, "Field testing of these various call management strategies in three cities by NIJ demonstrated that 47% of all calls for service could be handled by an alternate approach rather than dispatch an officer for nonemergency calls." The overwhelming number of callers had no problem with the use of the alternate approaches.

Sweeny concludes that since 97 percent of alarm calls are false, these calls can be reduced by 50 percent by using the Model Alarm Ordinance developed by the National Burglar and Fire Alarm Association and "proactive alarm oversight." Using directed patrol from the past, intelligence-led policing of the present, and enforced dispatch rules along with CAD, computer models, and spatially designed crime models, literally billions of dollars can be saved on patrol while giving our citizens more satisfying service.

Automatic Vehicle Monitoring/Automatic Vehicle Locater Based on GPS

Automatic vehicle monitoring (AVM) provides the location and status of the vehicle, such as in pursuit, en route to scene, door open, and so on. It is more inclusive than an automatic vehicle location (AVL) system, which simply provides a vehicle's location. Location is provided by four devices: (1) a navigation (hyperbolic) system that uses a radio location technique called Loran C, a system used by ships at sea; (2) a trilateration system that uses radio location from three or more fixed sites; (3) a signpost/proximity system that locates a vehicle through the use of fixed electronic signposts located throughout an area; and (4) a dead-reckoning system that uses computer-assisted instruments to track vehicles on a city map (e.g., utilizing an advanced geocoding system).

The first AVM program, a signpost transmitter system, was installed in Monterey, California, in the early 1970s. Both the St. Louis and the Dallas police departments have installed AVM systems.

The **global positioning system (GPS)**, based on data from 12 satellites, provides the real-time location of every police vehicle and can be monitored on a digital map by management. With the GPS inside the police vehicle, directions to any location in North America are immediately available. This should shorten response time and save on gas. Both AVM and AVL provide digital data on the use of police vehicles for analysis by management and are also used to locate vehicles in case of emergencies and breakdowns.

The GPS provides a legal data-verified location of a vehicle for use in court cases and for internal affairs investigations. Vehicles can also be monitored over the Web, and a number of private agencies have sprung up to do this for companies that have a fleet of vehicles. To find out more, simply use Google and go to "Automatic Vehicle Monitoring." Paulsen and Robinson (2004: 199) point out one criticism from the field, but they also add a caveat of approval: "While some officers have resisted GPS because of its ability to track their every move, overall reviews of its ability to provide assistance in call response has been positive."

The AVM systems are not without their critics. One reason for the controversy becomes very obvious to both management and line officers: There is greater control and supervision of the patrol force. It stands to reason that if supervisors know the condition of all patrol cars and where the cars are at all times, they also have a pretty good idea of where the patrol officers are and what the status of the patrol officer is. This has great potential for increasing police productivity in terms of service to the public.

Cameras in Cars and on Officers

Related to the issues of AVM are video cameras in patrol vehicles. Several years ago, the first cameras used VHS technology and were very cumbersome. Tapes had to be replaced after each shift. Today, digital cameras are commonplace that can "shoot" with sound from the vehicle, the back, and the interior. They have been invaluable for reviewing incidents of major felony stops, driving while intoxicated offenses, high-speed chases, and allegations of officer misconduct. However, there are limits especially outside of a vehicle. What happens if an officer chases someone into the woods or deals with an event on the fourth floor of an apartment building? Thus, the new wave of video devices being field-tested having GPS capabilities is worn by the officer. Such cameras are worn either on helmets, glasses, or with remote microphone clips normally clipped to a lapel. This will allow for recording incidents the same way as an in-car camera does. This capacity may also provide real-time viewing by supervisors.

911

The **911 system** provides one phone number for calling all police agencies in a geographic area with one central dispatch system. The 911 system has achieved a high degree of acceptance from the police and the public. In some communities, phone service is "taken" to fund 911 services. Generally, when this system is not in existence, it is due to interference by local politics rather than technical difficulties, which have been and can be overcome. A basic 911 system also provides a number of useful features: (1) automatic identification and display of the calling number and address of the caller; (2) jurisdiction selective routing, which allows routing of the 911 call to the appropriate jurisdiction; (3) supplementary dispatch/support data, which give the police beat, fire alarm area, and ambulance zone of the location of the call; (4) internal selective routing, which allows routing of calls to the appropriate operator in large law enforcement jurisdictions; and (5) automatic registered name identification, which automatically displays the name of the person who owns the phone used for the call. Although the 911 system should be adopted by every jurisdiction, there are two major problems that need to be dealt with: (1) duplication of street names and (2) mobile cell phones that move through too many locations.

Linked to 911 is the **regional communication system (RCS)**, whereby a number of law enforcement agencies cooperate in the creation of a common communication network. RCS decreases operating costs, especially personnel and total equipment and installation costs. Jurisdictions are able to afford computer-assisted communication systems that would otherwise be out of reach of their budgets. Furthermore, with an RCS, municipalities have also been able to afford technologies such as CAD. This approach can also overcome channel congestion problems, coordinate police actions during emergencies, and provide a regional base for attracting outside funding. As with 911, many efforts at establishing a regional communication system have been blocked by petty politics.

Linked to 911 is reverse 911, which allows police agencies to alert citizens of crimes in progress or impending weather emergencies. Reverse 911 systems today can be programmed for specific areas as part of the 911 program publicly funded through phone charges. Reverse 911 in many regions is a "work in progress" in terms of its accuracy and use during emergencies. Programs in California have been criticized for giving citizens incorrect information on when and where to evacuate during the wildfire season in summer 2007. On the other hand, Reverse 911 has also been praised for saving a number of lives.

The next stage of 911 is called Next Generation 911 or NG911. As discussed by Reyes (2013), NG911 will be a compromise of digital networks that will increase data available to police through the use of mobile devices, text messages, videos, maps, and photos. Digital data will be able to be transmitted from citizens to public safety answering points and then to units in the field. The location of callers will be able to be pinpointed faster and responses for major incidents and disasters will be improved. As discussed by Reyes (2013), NG911 is now at the planning stage for many areas but it will be "state of the art" for the coming decade.

National Crime Information Center (NCIC)

The **National Crime Information Center (NCIC)** maintains a computerized filing system, including such information as wanted persons, stolen property, criminal history, and information on identifiable persons in relation to investigations of reported crimes. The NCIC system is supported by the federal government and has a national advisory board made up of police administrators from all over the United States. This advisory board makes recommendations to the director of the Federal Bureau of Investigation (FBI) in terms of NCIC policy. Since its creation in 1967, the NCIC has accomplished the following goals (U.S. Department of Justice, 1985: Intro-1):

1. Enhancing the development of state, county, and metropolitan computerized criminal justice information systems, thereby making NCIC information more readily available to the officer on the street
2. Establishing uniformity of coding standards for the exchange of criminal justice information
3. Increasing the probability of criminal detection by providing law enforcement with timely and accurate information necessary to combat today's highly mobile criminal
4. Improving the overall crime solution rate

With the number of mobile data terminals and agency users currently at 110,000, the system is currently involved in an upgrading program entitled NCIC 2000. The purposes of the enhancements are the following:

1. Establish national distribution system for data sets stored by states instead of keeping a central database
2. Establish the National Fingerprint File, which will allow electronic transmittal and identification of fingerprints
3. Establish the Alcohol, Tobacco, and Firearms Violent Felon File, which will create files of people who are suspected terrorists or of interest to law enforcement officials

Automated Regional Justice Information System (ARJIS)

The Automated Regional Justice Information System (ARJIS) operates in California and is similar to other state data networks. ARJIS consists of nine components:

1. Arrests and juvenile contacts
2. Automated worthless document index
3. Citations (misdemeanor citations, traffic citations, traffic warnings, traffic accidents)
4. Crime analysis
5. Crime cases
6. Field interviews
7. Master operations index
8. Personnel
9. Property (pawned/wanted property)

Each police agency has one or more terminals that allow online access for either inquiry or update activity. For example, the worthless document index deals with forgeries, while crime analysis allows searches by name, partial name, or nickname; date; pawned, stolen, lost, or found property; addresses; and so on. Crime cases allow for searches by modus operandi, or method of procedure. It is obvious that when these systems are in place, a great deal of sophisticated information sifting can take place. In California, as in most states, additional information is accessible from standardized files, called the Criminal Justice Information System, which contains six systems:

1. Stolen vehicle system
2. Automated boat system
3. Wanted persons system
4. Criminal history system
5. Automated firearms system
6. Automated property system

Despite all these new technologies and data banks, there is still a need to have a system for regional, national, and international data sharing. Each data bank is like a file cabinet—unless you have a key, you do not get in. Intelligence-based policing can help with this, but there needs to be protocols in place for access and sharing. Internal to the organization, there must be protocols—from the chief to the patrol officers to the nonsworn staff persons—in terms of who has access to the information and who can make additions and deletions.

The Digitally Driven Police Department

Related to the new changes in computer technology is the transformation that has occurred in report writing and record keeping. Every police activity or crime incident demands a report of some form. The majority of police patrol reports written before 1975 were handwritten; typewriters were reserved for detectives who needed four carbon copies for depositions and court papers.

As an example of this, one of the authors recalled that upon being promoted to sergeant in the early 1990s and assigned to a new station house, he was shocked to find only manual typewriters in the squad room. He considered it an accomplishment when he managed to replace each of those manual units with 1970s and 1980s electric typewriters. Standardized forms were introduced at this time to assist in data processing for mainframe crime analysis and to reduce the narrative portion of the report. Writing reports and completing forms take time. Booking processes for the average misdemeanor take about two hours. Police administrators continue to look for ways to reduce the paperwork associated with arrests and investigations.

Today, officers write reports on small laptop computers located in the front seat of the patrol units or manual personal devices, such as iPads. Laptop computers with forms-based software and smart keys that conform to the police **electronic forms** can make police more efficient. The paperwork done on an arrest, for example, can be spell-checked and readied for downloading for access by administrators, prosecutors, and defense lawyers. Today traffic tickets in many states are digitally produced from the patrol vehicle via laptop. Once the ticket is issued, an electronic copy is sent to the court where the defendant will appear, then to the police department, and then to the state department of motor vehicles. The driver receives a hard copy of the summons and often a supporting deposition related to the charge generated from a printer housed in the patrol vehicle. Traffic accident investigations can also be handled by these systems. The information on the drivers and accident cause and location is entered into the computer and a report is produced. Many programs also allow the officer to draw digital diagrams of the event.

E-mail can be distributed to administrators and can bring experts online during an ongoing investigation. E-mail can also be transmitted from dispatchers to patrol units on sensitive calls. Legal statutes, community and human service addresses, and personnel can be directly accessed during routine calls. Information and forms can be printed and handed to administrators and citizens as needed. Everything, from warrant checks and stolen vehicles to mug shots and detailed maps, is immediately accessible.

E-mail, and its paper trail, can be a useful management tool. For example, not long ago station sergeants would post a memorandum with a new order or instruction on a squad room bulletin board. Below it would be of a list of officers assigned to the station. Each officer would, upon reading the memorandum, initial next to his or her name, indicating that the memorandum had been read, and was understood. E-mail allows for electronic accountability, as the sergeant can verify that an e-mail has been opened by an officer. It is also imperative that officers be cognizant of the permanence of an e-mail transmission, and that the content of e-mails could be subject to subpoena, possibly leading to embarrassment, or worse.

Digital Information Systems

New police officers have grown up in this digital age and they use various information services such as Google and Yahoo. The **digitally driven police department** is an eternity beyond our first mention of the paperless police department. Police, citizens, and criminals all live in the networked society with their iPods (given free to the freshman class of Duke University), laptops, wireless fidelity (WiFi), camera cell phones, digitized cameras, and video recorders.

Many civilians have satellite phones, satellite radio, and computer mapping (such as Magellan) in their cars. Hospitals and medical doctors are setting up e-mail systems for patients to communicate concerning services, etc. Many police departments today use their Web sites for the receipt of minor crime complaints. Crime topics for the public are now available on police department Web sites. Here are some examples:

- Analysis of gun-related incidents and gang-related shootings in Springfield, Massachusetts
- Evaluation of a drug crackdown in Prince George's County, Maryland
- Evaluation of a Neighborhood Watch program in Spokane, Washington
- Use of maps for police redistricting in Charlotte–Mecklenburg, North Carolina

- Use of crime mapping by the Blue Hills Civic Association in Hartford, Connecticut, to prevent crime
- Geographic display of evidence in a murder trial in St. Petersburg, Florida

If a Chicago resident gives an address on the Chicago police Web site, it will give the citizen a map of crime in his or her area (McEwen, 2003: 396–97). The Largo, Florida, Police Department transmits domestic violence information to the state's attorney general or the local domestic violence center so that evidence is available immediately to the courts for the alleged batterer's bond hearing through a secure Web site (McEwen, 2003: 399).

In this age of man-made terror and disasters, as well as natural disasters, first responders (including the police) should have all the technology they need paid for by national and state governments. Law enforcement can no longer afford to technologically fall behind present-day high school and college students. All police officers need access to police databases and Google, at all times wherever they are, by using national and global wireless and satellite communications. This is simply a minimum standard for all police departments that wish to truly function proactively in the twenty-first century. When first responders are cut off from information technology, as happened in the 2005 New Orleans Hurricane Katrina disaster, innocent people die.

New Technologies for Police Managers

What is possible today? Each officer can have a personal locator transmitter that keeps track of the officer and offers hands-free communication. The Remote Control Information System (RCIS) is portable and has full-color video, two-way audio, and officer location and monitors and transmits vital signs. A smart card with storage capacity that turns itself off with tampering will provide secure identification in the size of a credit card. People can be identified with computerized signatures provided by fingerprints, DNA, and voiceprint.

The Advanced Regional Justice Information System, a user-friendly, client-based, PC system, provides information for an investigation or just for a beat officer. Graphics such as computer mapping and photo lineups will be available in the field, along with form-based software for field reports via the laptop.

Each officer will have access to an immense amount of data, including graphic and photographic interfaces, for identification of suspects. Officers can interview a victim while calling up an identity kit program to focus on victim image and then compare this to suspect profiles and modus operandi. Eastman Kodak has a writable CD that provides 20 file cabinets full of storage, combining image-processing technology with case-management functions for the detective on the street or in the courtroom. Voice-recognition technology is now available, enabling officers to speak their reports into the system.

The Internet provides incredible services but needs organizing. The International Association of Chiefs of Police has its own Web page, as do agencies such as the Drug Enforcement Administration, FBI, Federal Bureau of Prisons, National Institute of Justice, Supreme Court Decisions, Bureau of Justice Statistics, RAND, National Criminal Justice Links, and U.S. Department of Justice. There is also a Criminal Justice e-mail listserv. Online newsletters are available, such as *American Police Beat, Justice Information Distributions List, Journal of CJ*, and *Popular Culture*.

The United Nations Criminal Justice Information Network provides a worldwide automated system used for communicating and exchanging criminal justice information, including a Gopher-based electronic discussion forum. The United Nations Online Justice Clearinghouse will provide access to criminal justice member holdings all over the world, including an e-mail service.

There are sites called Cops, Help Locate a Fugitive, Internet Crime Writing Network, and many others. For example, Justice Technology Information Network (JUSTNET) "provides information on new technologies, equipment and other products and services available to the law enforcement, corrections and criminal justice communities." JUSTNET provides news and information services, a chat line, a topic board, and data and publication services. For registered law enforcement and correction users, there are data links to agencies that have used the products.

One of the major issues is security, including encryption protocols and privacy for address linkages and chat groups. What if you are tracking a serial killer and want to set up a law enforcement board, data link, and some kind of roundtable discussion group? It would be important to *not* transmit this information to the criminal community. Personal encryption, which allows only the receiver to decrypt the message, offers a solution.

Crime Mapping

Crime mapping superimposes computer-generated data on a city street grid or other map. Data sets are taken from various public agencies, such as

- Demographic data from the Census Bureau
- Property tax agencies for location, condition, and paid or unpaid property taxes
- Traffic corridor maps, with number of cars using these corridors
- Local police statistics and *Uniform Crime Reports*
- Local crime and victimization surveys
- Court and community corrections files supplying residence and work addresses of parolees, probationers, and court-processed criminals
- Licensing units and public health data

This is just a sampling. Information detailing the number and location of various crimes, such as rapes, burglaries, family violence, and robberies, has proved useful.

Some data that can be added to a map include location of offenders, police cars, and medical emergency vehicles using the GPS; convicted offenders being tracked by electronic monitoring systems; and hot spot identification based on police calls to specific locations. Maps also can indicate where schools, fire stations, hospitals, drug markets, major shopping malls, and bars are located.

Hypothesis-generating data with a spatial dimension, such as "broken windows," include such items as abandoned cars, vacant buildings, litter, graffiti, and houses with a three-year non-payment of property taxes. These variables are useful for arson investigations when an arson incident map is superimposed over "broken windows" variables. Relationship data can be graphed to show the following (Rich, 1999):

- Distance from an offender's residence to the location of the offender's crime
- Relationship between crime and bars and liquor stores
- Police interventions and spillover to crime in other areas
- Easy access to getaway routes
- Property crimes and muggings

Powerful software helps the viewer make sense of disparate data through the use of symbols and color. The New York City Police Department's Crimetac system has a program that summarizes data on a map by shading in such dimensions as number of burglaries, robberies, or muggings. The higher the number of crimes, the darker the shading. This is also done by graphing—by time, hour, day, week, or month—whichever time dimension is the most useful.

Compstat

A major issue confronting police administrators and policymakers is how to monitor police performance and its impact on crime. As discussed by Cope (2005), Compstat is a process by which crime is analyzed in order for police administrators to identify problem areas and respond accordingly.

Many police administrators and scholars have asked about the origin of Compstat, and now it can be told. **Compstat** was originally a computer file called Compare Stats for the New York City annual report of crime statistics. It became a management program committed to management accountability at the precinct level and to the lowering of real crime rates. Weekly Compstat meetings have become a basis for planning, coordination, and evaluating crime fighting at the precinct level.

In New York City, from 1994 to 1997, the rates of various serious crimes dropped significantly (Silverman, 1996: 10):

- Homicide dropped 50 percent
- Rape, over 8 percent
- Robbery, over 40 percent
- Felonious assault, over 25 percent
- Burglary, 37 percent
- Grand larceny, over 31 percent
- Grand larceny autos, over 45 percent

This real decrease in crime was due to new policies and actions by the New York City Police Department and Commissioner William Bratton. The general contextual and demographic data for New York City changed very little during that time. Hence, the police department can take credit for the successful drop in crime rates.

During Commissioner Bratton's first year in office, two-thirds of the 76 precinct commanders were replaced. Some of the centralized responsibilities for drug enforcement, public morals, and auto theft were transferred to the borough and precinct commands. There was an attempt to integrate detective squads with precinct commands.

Responsibility and decision making were decentralized down to the precinct level, and the precinct commander was held responsible for the level of crime in the precinct. The geography of the precincts was the unit of analysis and control rather than citywide functional units. Specialized domestic violence officers, appointed in each precinct, used a specialized family database to facilitate precinct planning. In the past, centralized databases were difficult or impossible to access. Databases like the Narcotic Investigation Tracking of Recidivist Offenders (NITR), which tracked career felony drug offenders, were made accessible to precinct-level officers and members of the detective and drug units. Access to various intelligence and databases at the precinct level was crucial to the success of the Compstat approach.

At the start of this process, statistical crime data were available only on a six-monthly basis. Pins pushed into a map with acetate overlays were the main graphic device. At the end of this process, data were available on laptop and other computers on a weekly basis with overlays, computer-generated maps, and graphs. Computer mapping became the basis of the weekly Compstat meetings at police headquarters.

At a 7:00 A.M. Compstat meeting, precinct commanders appear before the police brass to view two huge screens showing the latest crime statistics in the precinct. The meeting is devoted to strategies for fighting crime. Precinct commanders have more authority than they have had in years, but they also have more accountability. The key elements are timely and accurate intelligence, rapid deployment of resources, and relentless follow-up and assessment. Precinct commanders are summoned to the meeting randomly.

If the top managers of NYPD did not like the results, the commanders could be transferred immediately, which would result in the loss of experienced precinct commanders. Compstat pressures and accountability have resulted in flexibility and creative problem solving for crimes that affect the quality of life in a neighborhood. The following case history shows how the process encourages creative solutions to preventing crime. Compstat maps charted a large number of daylight burglaries within a few blocks of schools. After discussing this problem with school authorities, neighbors, and line patrol officers, the precinct commander came up with a unique solution. A bus went around the precinct during school hours. When teenagers were found to be on the street, they were asked why they were not in school. The police then put these students who were playing hooky on the bus and brought them back to their schools. Daylight burglaries went down dramatically—a simple but brilliant solution.

A balanced look at Compstat starts with the judgment that it really does work as a crime-fighting strategy. However, as time passes and it becomes more difficult to bring down crime, it might not work as well, as it places too much stress on precinct commanders. The heart of any police organization is its middle management: sergeants, lieutenants, and captains. It is imperative to keep experienced middle management on the job and to keep what has worked with Compstat and to improve on it.

Compstat Lessons Learned: What Worked

1. Instantly accessible information in an easy-to-understand format
2. Accountability and decision making at the level of unit commanders
3. Wide sharing of information
4. Flexibility and creativity in crime fighting
5. Policy decisions based on hard data
6. Quality-of-life enforcement

Compstat Lessons Learned: How to Make It Better

1. Eliminate unreasonable pressure and stress on street-level unit commanders and their line officers.
2. Once Compstat has brought down crime, do not create unreasonable demands to bring crime down even more when it is not possible. Unreasonable demands on street units can produce police brutality. This political interference in police management creates failure out of success.
3. Integrate crime mapping with community policing by sharing information and decision making with community groups.

Compstat is being tried in other major police departments. There has been investment in hardware and software, a willingness to bring decision making down to street-level units, and a major commitment of both resources and management changes.

Compstat and its various variations has become a planning tool for the twenty-first century by combining extensive crime-mapping data accumulation and reengineering. In his *Compstat Paradigm*, Vincent Henry (2002) sees Compstat as a tool that will be used to involve middle management in the proactive crime-control process.

E-policing

Over the years we have presented ideas on what the future of policing might look like, particularly in patrol operations. In some cases, the future is now particularly with the adoption and evolution of technology.

In many cities and high-crime areas, closed-circuit television (CCTV) systems are increasingly being installed. The main idea for CCTV is to deter would-be criminals from committing offenses and to allow playback for identification of information and suspects after a major crime or event has occurred. CCTV is being increasingly used in not only major cities and transportation facilities but also in schools, shopping malls, and retail outlets.

To what extent does CCTV actually reduce crime? Welsh and Farrington (2007) examined the use of CCTV in England and the Unites States. They found that CCTV, when deployed with proper lighting, has an impact on reducing crime. There are some operational realities. It is impossible for one person or a group of persons to monitor a number of cameras for a period of time unless there is some hint that a crime is about to occur. However, CCTV has been extremely useful in follow-up investigations after violent crimes have occurred. For example, in the London bombing in July 2005, the participants were identified after British police combed through hours of recordings near the crime scenes and metropolitan railway stations.

On highways, police patrol vehicles are being equipped with automatic license plate readers that can "read" plates of passing vehicles. Linked via wireless communication technology to motor vehicle and crime information computers, the units can ascertain if the vehicle is stolen, the registration has expired, or if there is an active warrant against the owner. If there is a hit, the laptop computer in the vehicle activates a warning noise and locks in on the plate number. Cameras mounted on the trunk or roof of the patrol unit take snapshots of vehicle plates (Police One, 2008). Plate readers can scan thousands of license plates per minute, which creates a wealth of intelligence. Thus, a patrol unit can cruise through a parking lot to pick up the stolen vehicles or wanted persons. Investigators can also check the unit data file to see if a vehicle of interest was in a certain area of a patrol zone. Costs for the equipment are about $30,000 and it is expected that these costs will decline over time.

To reduce gun violence, many cities have adopted detection systems that "hear" shots being fired from a specific location. Using sensors installed in specific high-crime areas, the devices alert police of the gunshots through links to GPS navigation. Dispatchers are then able to send patrols to the location. According to one company vendor, the technology allows dispatchers to move vehicles toward the location before an emergency telephone call is made. Operational use has found that citizens in high-crime areas do not often report these types of events (ShotSpotter, 2006). The number of cities adopting this technology is on the rise. To date, there has been no systematic evaluation of whether the detection systems reduce the incidents of gun violence.

As discussed in the section on 911, police departments are able to make emergency notifications to citizens and retail outlets in a particular area. After the school shooting at Virginia Commonwealth Institute and State University (Virginia Tech) in 2007, a number of colleges have implemented emergency warning devices and systems that alert faculty and students of an immediate emergency situation or an impending weather condition. Notifications of an emergency situation or weather condition are made to subscriber land and cell phones, social media sites, public address systems, and CCTV public monitor locations. The main management issues are cost and keeping subscriber information updated and testing the system. There is also the issue of who has the authorization to issue an alert.

Internet is being increasingly used by the public and many departments have Web pages that outline the department's organization and services. Citizens can find the following types of information:

- Names and locations of serious sex offenders
- Emergency preparedness alerts
- Traffic conditions on major highways

- File nonviolent crime reports, including regarding minor traffic accidents
- File complaints or commendations regarding services

Defenses Against Cyberterror and Cyberattacks

Going beyond virus detectors and firewalls, police agencies need to have defenses to protect their cyberstructure. Cyberattacks and cyberterror come in the following main forms (Ballard et al., 2002):

1. Altering and destroying the contents of electronic files and computer systems
2. Destroying and disrupting hardware, operating platforms, and programs

Thus, it is important for the information technology system in the department to have up-to-date defenses against attacks.

Law Enforcement at the Speed of Thought

In *Business at the Speed of Thought* (1999), Bill Gates talked about organizations with "digital nervous systems" that include internal and interagency e-mail, public Web sites accessed by the public for government services, electronic forms for all major applications in an organization, and all routine information being handled by computer with a customer service value-added orientation. The last point is the major function of community policing, in which the customers are the citizens.

Gates quotes the ancient Chinese military strategist Sun-Tzu: "Intelligence is of the essence in warfare—it is what the armies depend upon in their every move" (p. 382). This idea is applicable to police departments as well as businesses, as Compstat has shown us. A police department is as good as its intelligence. Reliable and immediately accessible information equals good management. Bad intelligence makes for bad management decisions.

Gates recommends laptop computers for all knowledge workers. Police officers and their supervisors are both knowledge workers and service providers to citizens.

The following example helps make the case for law enforcement use of mobile data access. An officer was running random vehicle inquiries at a local restaurant and received an alert on the system. A vehicle's owner had both a record of a previous homicide and two current warrants for domestic violence. Backup was called, and the suspect was taken into custody without incident. A passenger with active warrants was also arrested.

What Gates envisioned in his book is now available. After a police car has been dispatched to the scene of a crime or emergency, software walks the dispatcher through a series of questions to ask the caller. The dispatcher asks about any hazards at the scene, such as a person with a gun. The dispatcher downloads the information to the police car immediately. Police supervisors at the computer-assisted dispatch center consider needed action and then order backup, fire or medical emergency vehicles, and additional personnel.

A search is done for any previous calls made from the address and any criminal record of the names given by the caller. This information is downloaded. A computer map shows recent calls for service made in the area.

A pen chart laptop system on electronic report forms is filled in by the officers in the car to give immediate information to the supervisor concerning the call for service. Once the forms are completed, they are uploaded by a cell phone to the police information system. All data are automatically encrypted to protect the citizen's privacy and police confidentiality.

Any report that is not filed by the end of a shift is tagged by a supervising police officer and is followed up on. This information will be merged with the police database, and pertinent information will be sent to the courts or jail, when appropriate.

Vehicle maintenance information will also be automatically uploaded and sent to the police fleet supervisor's database. The pertinent parts of the electronic report will be downloaded to booking, if needed.

With these daily reports automatically logged electronically, police managers and supervisors can identify any anomalies and can determine the need to adjust the number of personnel in relation to the number of calls, the time spent on each call, and the identification of hot spots. All police desks will have computer stations, so all this information will be available all the time.

THE ROLE OF THE CHIEF IN TECHNOLOGY

As we stated before, technology is viewed as a tool for helping in operational decision making, planning, and delivering services. Thus, before a new technology is adopted, technology decision making should consider the following:

1. *Review of benchmarks and actual applications.* This involves going to conferences, keeping up-to-date on technology presented in professional journals, and visiting other departments to see what is available and how it works.
2. *Vendor background checks.* There are thousands of vendors who deal with police technology management systems. What is their reputation? How have other departments fared with a particular company? This information can be easily obtained by sending out inquiries on professional and regional listservs. Also, it is important to know how long the vendors have been in business and what their client list is.
3. *Budget costs and value added to services.* This often is the main stumbling block in that there is no analysis of the long-term costs for appropriation, installation, and deployment. In addition, there should be an analysis of what is being gained by adopting the technology for patrol officers, supervisors, and managers.
4. *Service costs and maintenance.* This is an area that is often related to item 3. The technology supply field has many vendors and is very competitive. We also know of many instances where vendors were merged or went out of business and were not able to deliver on service contracts.
5. *Choice of in-house or external vendor.* There are many dedicated and qualified police personnel who are software programmers and can build systems for the department; however, there has to be some kind of backup in personnel skills because major problems arise if the in-house police programmer decides to leave.
6. *Creating in-house review and operations teams.* Every new technology has immediate impact on the police organization. Thus, it is important for administrators to have department review teams review the item and then analyze what impact it will have on the organization in terms of use and cost. This often involves field testing the item and evaluating the positive and negative results.
7. *Related to item 6 is policy creation.* The department needs to prepare a written policy on the use of technology by officers, the need for training, and review by supervisors. For example, simply issuing a laptop to a patrol vehicle without training and written guidelines for proper use can create a whole range of issues. What happens if the unit is not properly functioning? What are the proper use policies related to the unit?
8. *What is the long-term economic impact?* Technology is often adopted through a federal or state grant but little attention is paid to maintenance, replacement, and the long-term economic impacts. Simply stated, will the department be able to afford the system or items after the funding cycle ends?

Conclusion

In this chapter, we reviewed available information systems and previewed the more sophisticated systems of the future. However, all these systems are limited by the programs that sort and label information and by the human beings who use them. Police managers must understand the potential of these systems and be able to use them if they want to manage modern police departments successfully. Just as it would be advantageous if each police commander knew the intricacies of how each unit works in his or her agency, it would likewise be helpful if those leaders kept abreast of each new piece of technology. Such goals would not be realistic, however; there are simply not enough hours in a day for one person to be an expert on everything a police agency does. Rather, the wise police leader stays informed about the capabilities of each unit for maximum overall agency effectiveness.

Technology must be controlled and understood by management. Police technology must be human friendly and easily accessible in emergency situations. Training time is expensive and should be kept to a minimum. Police managers need to have technology that enhances clarity of communication rather than causing information overload. Prioritization must be in place along with an information flow system of command capability.

Digitizing standard forms makes for ease of transmission throughout the criminal justice system. The human element is designing forms for clarity and speed of information flow and deciding who needs the information on the forms. This is good management and today's management needs education and training. The best technology will not save a badly designed information flow form, such as an arrest form that may be needed by supervisors, investigators, and the courts.

When buying a system and software, police management should select a company that has a good track record, has been in business for a number of years, offers good service support, and can change with new technology. Managers need a system that will work for their department today and for the next few years rather than a complex Star Wars system that few understand. "Keep it simple!" is a motto that should hang in big letters in every police communications center.

Buy the latest technology that works for your line officers and for your management team. Technology has been improving and prices have been dropping, but it is still a huge capital investment. Make sure that the system is affordable and that training is available. Place a high priority on reliable, affordable technical assistance from human beings who talk in plain English rather than some obscure technical language.

Most important, listen to your top management, middle management, and line officers and survey their opinions and needs. A system is only as good as its users. Surveys should be done before and after new technology is installed. The NYPD management worked closely with line officers and middle management in reengineering the department and gaining feedback before Compstat went into operation. Police management needs feedback in terms of ease of use, problems encountered, and changes needed. In larger departments, focus groups have worked.

Think proactively, and deal with problems before they grow. With this positive attitude, police managers will have better human- and police-oriented technology that really works for them. Changes and new technology will only be put in place when there is a need and it is shown to be a good decision for the department.

Questions for Review

1. Which three areas listed in the section titled "Computer Applications for Information Management" would you optimize with handheld wireless technology, and which three areas would not be enhanced by this technology? Why?

2. How does computer-aided dispatch contribute to general public safety and the safety of patrol and investigative officers?

3. What problems occur with 911 in terms of misuse by the public?

4. Show how crime mapping can reduce crime in your community. Include an interview with a local police manager in your answer.

5. Present five strong points and three criticisms of Compstat.

6. What technologies will emerge in police field operations in the next five years?

7. What are the main issues that police managers must address before adopting new technology for their departments?

Class Projects

1. Take three of the technological developments presented in this chapter and compare them with the technology that is used by an area police department. To what extent is the department using or planning to acquire the technology described in this section?

2. Taking a sample of police Internet Web sites, determine what services are offered through the Internet.

Web Works

The evolving nature of police informational technology can be reviewed at a number of Web sites. The National Institute of Justice (ojp.usdoj.gov/nij) presents a number of initiatives and evaluations on police information sharing and technology. Operational standards for information systems can be found at the Law Enforcement Information Technology Standards Council (leitsc.org), which consists of representatives from the major police professional groups and technology experts. Evaluations of technology for police are often presented and discussed by the International Association of Chiefs of Police at theiacp.org and in the FBI Law Enforcement Bulletin at fbi.gov/publications. Product vendor Web sites also offer information and updates on these topics and can be accessed via Google or Yahoo under police communications and police information technology.

References

Ballard, James D., Joseph G. Hornick, and Douglas McKenzie. "Technological Facilitation of Terrorism." In Harvey W. Kushner, ed., *Cyberterrorism in the Twenty-First Century*. Thousand Oaks, Calif.: Sage, 2002.

Cope, Nina. "Crime Analysis: Principles and Practice." In Tim Newburn, ed., *Handbook of Policing*. Cullompton, Devon: Willan, 2005, pp. 340–362.

Gates, William. *Business at the Speed of Thought: Using a Digital Nervous System*. New York: Time-Warner, 1999.

Henry, Vincent. *The Compstat Paradigm*. Flushing, N.Y.: Looseleaf Publications, 2002.

McEwen, Tom. "Information Management." In William A. Geller and Darrel W. Stephens, eds., *Local Government Police Management*, 4th ed. Washington, D.C.: International City/County Management Association, 2003, pp. 391–420.

Paulsen, Derek J., and Matthew B. Robinson. *Spatial Aspects of Crime*. Boston: Pearson/Allyn and Bacon, 2004.

PoliceOne.com. MD Police Deploy License Plate Reader, 2008. Web posted at http://www.policeone.com/pc_print.asp?vid=1731021. Accessed June 5, 2009.

———. *The Chicago Police Department Information Collection for Automated Mapping (ICAM)*. Washington, D.C.: National Institute of Justice, 1996.

———. "Mapping the Path to Problem Solving." *National Institute of Justice Journal* (October 1999), pp. 2–9.

Reyes, "What Is NG911 (and Why Should You Care)?" *The Police Chief* (May 2013), pp. 3–5.

ShotSpotter. Case Study—Rochester, New York (2006). Web posted at ShotSpotter.com. Accessed March 18, 2009.

Silverman, Eli B. "Mapping Change." *Law Enforcement News*, 1996, pp. 10–12.

Sweeny, Thomas J. "Patrol." In William A. Geller and Darrel W. Stephens, eds., *Local Government Police Management*. Washington, D.C.: International City/County Management Association, 2003, pp. 89–134.

U.S. Department of Justice. *NCIC Operating Manual*. Washington, D.C.: U.S. Government Printing Office, 1985.

Welsh, Brandon, and David Farrington. "Crime Prevention and Hard Technology: The Case of CCTV and Improved Street Lighting." In James Byrne and Donald Rebovich, eds., *The New Technology of Crime, Law, and Social Control*. Monsey, N.Y.: Criminal Justice Press, 2007.

8 Patrol Operations and Community Policing

KEY TERMS

28 Code of Federal Regulations (CFR) Part 23

community-oriented policing (COP)

community policing

crime analysis

decoy squad

directed patrol

foot patrol

hot spot

intelligence-led policing

Kansas City Study

predictive policing

preventive patrol

problem-oriented policing (POP)

stakeouts

surveillance

tactical debriefing

tactical patrol

team policing

Weed and Seed

The increased use of technology and research has changed the face of patrol operations. Today's police supervisors can be in constant communication with patrol cars and officers. Reports can be dictated into a computer, and police can have access to nationwide information while working the streets. The advent of the 911 systems has drastically changed citizens' access to law enforcement services. A 911-driven department may find itself totally reactive with no time for special programs and citizen interaction approaches such as community policing.

The nation's police forces have moved beyond random patrol. This began with the conclusions from two Kansas City, Missouri, studies that showed the ineffectiveness of random patrol and rapid response. "The results showed that neither crime rates nor citizens' perception of their safety were significantly affected by changes in the amount of random preventive patrol. The study concluded that, for all practical purposes, these operational changes made no discernible difference. Similar experiments with similar results were subsequently conducted in St. Louis, Missouri and Minneapolis, Minnesota." While deemed as important, police response time and making arrests are not by themselves the only factors for positive police–community relations and crime problem solving (Petersilia, 1987, p. 9). The majority of a police officer's time is still spent on patrol and responding to calls for assistance but police managers are increasingly looking for alternative ways of providing services. A major question in police management is how to control certain calls so that they do not overwhelm scarce police resources. The Police Executive Research Forum developed a Differential Police Response System in which trained dispatchers coded all police calls as "critical" or "noncritical." Noncritical calls were "stacked" by order of importance or threat to personal safety and citizens were asked to file reports, and critical calls were answered immediately. Many police departments have adopted these procedures along with other systems of prioritizing police calls. As will be discussed, many departments have adopted Internet reporting programs for those calls involving petty offenses.

Police managers want to be able to choose from various approaches beyond police response to 911. Some approaches are community policing, neighborhood policing, fear-reduction policing, problem-solving and task force approaches, and hot spot targeting. Of note, the Bureau of Justice Statistics (US BJS, Community Policing, 2012) reported that 58 percent of police agencies in the United States deployed full-time community policing officers in 2003.

In our previous edition, we reported that federal funding for these programs was being redirected to homeland security and other programs. It appears that federal funding for community policing activities and personnel may be reinvigorated by the economic recovery funding. In fact, while direct authorized position from Community Oriented Policing Services (COPS) has been stagnant over the past four years, there was a 45.9 percent increase in funding requests from COPS from 2012 to 2013 (US Department of Justice, 2013). The Department of Justice (DOJ)'s COPS 2014 budget request includes an increase of $241 million, for a total budget request of $439.5 million (US DOJ, COPS, 2013).

In this chapter, we will discuss new programs that have emerged as a result of the study and discussion of this issue. We will also review the current managerial issues related to patrol and offer suggestions for improvement.

THE TRADITIONAL MODEL

Until recently, administrative attitudes and practices toward police patrol had changed little since the London Metropolitan Police duty manual, written in 1829. The first police constables assigned to patrol had to walk designated beats within a given time span. Although the automobile replaced many foot patrols in the twentieth century, patrol beats were assigned on the basis of the traditional needs of the community, geographic limitations, and available personnel.

Police patrol continues to consist of the following activities: calls for assistance, patrol officer–initiated activity, preventive patrol, and administrative activities. The jurisdiction of the department is divided into various zones, most commonly with one vehicle assigned to each zone each shift. Certain highly populated zones, such as shopping malls, business districts, and apartment complexes, may be assigned a foot patrol officer or other special services officer, such as bicycle patrol.

In the public's mind, and perhaps reinforced by television, the patrol officer and his or her partner cruise an area, answer a few calls, and occasionally spot a suspicious person or vehicle, leading to a spectacular arrest. The practice of cruising is **preventive patrol**. The rationale behind this is that the deployment of various foot and patrol units can prevent and deter criminal activity. While many officers would like to roam an area in the manner just described, actual preventive patrol depends on numerous variables, such as the number of crimes in a reported area, potential or consistent trouble spots, heavy traffic patterns at certain times, and the whimsy of the officer and his or her supervisor. In large departments, assigned sectors are strictly maintained or jealously guarded by officers and supervisors. Patrol units are not allowed to go beyond their designated sectors except when dispatched or in "hot" pursuit. Preventive patrol time is also spent goofing off, going on personal errands, having coffee, or meeting other patrol units to share gossip. In smaller departments, the same runs true. The great difference is that the patrol unit(s) on duty is supposed to stay within the jurisdiction and not venture outside village or town limits.

Preventive patrol is interrupted by calls for assistance that may be of a criminal or service nature. On receiving a call, the patrol unit is supposed to suspend preventive patrol and respond to a location. Calls for both criminal and noncriminal matters account for 25 to 40 percent of all patrol time, which, of course, depends on the size of the sector, economic conditions (e.g., inner city versus suburban middle-class neighborhood), and the number of units available for the entire jurisdiction during that shift.

Incorporated with preventive patrol are officer-initiated activities. These include questioning suspicious individuals, stopping vehicles, operating radar, laser, or other speed enforcement technology, or conducting informal community service activities (e.g., talking to businesspeople or schoolchildren or making unassigned business checks). Officer-initiated activities account for only 14 percent of patrol time, although this figure may be higher during early morning tours of duty when there are few calls.

The rest of patrol time is designated as administrative. Tasks of this nature include prisoner transport, writing reports, appearance in court, and vehicle maintenance. Administrative tasks consume large blocks of time during all shifts, but especially during regular business hours from 9:00 A.M. to 5:00 P.M., when a majority of non–law enforcement work force is operating.

THE KANSAS CITY STUDY

While many departments continue with traditional patrol in the manner just described, a few major urban departments began experimenting with new patrol tactics around the beginning of 1970. One often-cited study is the so-called **Kansas City Study** conducted by the Kansas City, Missouri, Police Department and the Police Foundation. The general hypotheses of preventive patrol were tested by dividing the southern portion of the city into 15 police beats. These 15 beats were then divided into five groups, each group having three matched beats. For these matched groups, there was one in which patrol was greatly increased, a second beat in which patrol was eliminated altogether except for calls for service, and a control beat in which patrol continued at the same pace as before the experiment. As Wilson (1975: 109) reports,

> After a year, no substantial differences among the three areas were observed in criminal activity, amount of reported crime, rate of victimization as revealed in the followup survey, level of citizen fear, or degree of citizen satisfaction with the police.

In addition, citizen satisfaction was found to have increased in the second and the control beats, whereas it decreased somewhat in the beat where patrol was greatly increased. Today, many researchers and police administrators continue to discuss these conclusions. There have been many criticisms of this experiment because of its faulty experimental design and methodology. Nevertheless, this experiment opened the door for further discussion of the benefits of preventive patrol and the hypothesis that random patrol may be a waste of time.

Further issues were raised by a second experiment conducted in Kansas City in 1977 to study the relationship between response time and crime. The orthodox notion of police patrol maintains that crime will decrease if the police are quick to arrive on the scene. The study found that since citizens generally take too long to report crime, response time has nothing to do with the number of arrests and the rate of crime. Moreover, for nonemergency calls, there were few citizen complaints of the police taking their time to respond to calls as long as the dispatchers advised the complainant of what to expect in terms of estimated time of arrival for the patrol.

RETHINKING THE TRADITIONAL MODEL

Although this model was developed in the 1970s, Table 8-1 conceptualizes some of the current problems that police administrators must deal with when they attempt to improve patrol operations. The general goal for improvement is to (1) reduce administration, preventive patrol, and calls for assistance and (2) add to time spent on directed patrol and crime analysis related to directed patrol. In Reiss' 1971 study of police–citizen interaction, 85 percent of the contact was the result of citizen calls for assistance. With the advent of 911 Centers, staffed by full-time dispatchers rather than patrol officers called in from patrol, and with associated 911 and 311 calls, this number has changed. Thirty years later, a study conducted in Baltimore, Buffalo, Phoenix, and Dallas found that much less of the police–citizen interactions came from calls for assistance. For example, in Baltimore, approximately 20 percent of an officer's shift was spent responding to 911, or emergency, calls, and a minimum of 3 percent was spent on 311, or nonemergency, calls (Mazerolle et al., 2003).

Preventive Patrol

Although preventive patrol takes 40 percent of an officer's time, it is the crux on which modern police practice rests. There are several reasons why patrol units are mobile and do not stay in a garage and respond as needed in the fire-department fashion. These are the objectives of preventive patrol:

- Detecting crime
- Apprehending criminal offenders
- Recovering stolen property
- Maintaining a sense of public security and confidence in the police for the community
- Satisfying public demands for noncriminal services

TABLE 8-1   Patrol Allocation/Improvement

Patrol Activity	Time Used (Percentage per Shift Hour)	General Plan for Improvement
Administration	23	Reduce the amount of time; such tasks detract from patrol
Calls for assistance	23	Manage calls better, especially those of noncriminal nature; create priority system of call returns
Preventive patrol	40	Incorporate specific objectives during this time period; reduce to less than 10 minutes per shift hour
Directed patrol	14	Based on time reduction of other tasks, more time will be available for this activity

Source: W.G. Gay, T.H. Schell, and S. Schack. *Improving Patrol Productivity, Vol. 1: Routine Patrol.* Washington, D.C.: U.S. Government Printing Office, 1977, p. 3.

These objectives raise many questions. For example, preventive patrol may really have nothing to do with detecting crime and apprehending criminal offenders. In reality, most arrests that occur "in progress" within a few minutes after the commission of a crime stem from the police having been at the right place at the right time.

The same may be true of the issue of deterrence. While many administrators assume that police presence suggests a higher probability that criminals will not commit crimes, there is little evidence to suggest that traditional patrol practice leads to this objective. The basis for this objective rests with the assumption that criminals are always on the lookout for police patrols and view these patrols as a serious hindrance to the commission of a crime. In reality, many crimes are spontaneous enterprises that lack long-term planning. In other cases, criminal activity occurs under the eyes of the police in certain areas that are high-crime districts. For example, drug sales on the street in large metropolitan areas may go on uninterrupted even as a police cruiser passes by.

Arrest data are often used to back up this assumption by way of crime clearance rates. Patrol is then deemed effective or ineffective on the basis of apprehensions in a certain area. However, even the freshman criminal justice student knows that crime rates are affected by a number of factors that have nothing to do with police presence (e.g., family situation, economics, and immigration). In short, we do not have satisfactory means for evaluating the effect of patrol tactics.

While recovery of stolen property is cited as an objective of patrol, the fact is that stolen property is usually recovered by investigators following up on a case rather than by the uniformed patrol presence. The only exception to this might be stolen automobiles. But even with a stolen auto, the recovery most often occurs because of the careless driving habits of the offender. It is rare for an officer to recover a stolen vehicle as a result of spotting the license plates or vehicle description, although license plate readers mounted on patrol cars are increasing success rates. Many experienced officers know of vehicles that were parked for weeks in shopping malls, airports, or apartment complexes before being discovered as stolen because of an abandoned-vehicle complaint filed by the owner of the property or a security guard.

If anything, patrol often is a public relations exercise. In essence, the citizen sees the patrol vehicle cruise by and may therefore perceive that the police are "out there" doing their jobs. Research, however, has shown that other factors have to be taken into consideration before one can conclude that the public is satisfied with the police. Such factors are overall crime rates, officer treatment of the public, the level of police corruption, and other community issues.

If anything, traditional police patrol does indeed provide a number of services to the community that are dependent on community norms. Historically, all police agencies respond to domestic disputes, lost-person reports, traffic accidents, loud-party complaints, and so on. In many areas, the community dictates what services the police provide above and beyond the traditional crime-related tasks (e.g., escorting funeral processions, directing traffic near churches on Sunday, providing oxygen to individuals having difficulty breathing, and transporting blood from a blood bank to a hospital). While important, these services may contribute nothing to public satisfaction with the police simply because the amount of time spent on these activities cannot be measured in terms of citizen satisfaction. Still, as one administrator remarked, "I agree with you, but you should hear the complaints that come in once it is found that we are not providing funeral escorts, blood runs, or other such goodies!"

Calls for Service

A common assumption made by the American public is that when you call the police, they will immediately respond—no matter how serious the incident may be. Many observers of patrol believe that there may be a need to dispel the tradition that all calls merit immediate response. In fact, perhaps 40 percent of all calls could be handled by communications personnel. This would save a great deal of time from dispatch to completion of a written report.

Many departments are starting to use various methodologies to handle complaints other than sending a patrol unit to the scene. Some departments are experimenting with mailed-out forms to collect information on traffic accidents of a minor nature and petty larcenies. Other agencies advise the complainant to come down to the station at his or her convenience to complete a report. In addition, many agencies are developing community referral systems to refer complaints to other public or private agencies that might be of greater assistance in handling certain problems.

One immediate benefit of utilizing these methods involves improving officer morale. It is no secret that many officers dislike wasting time on so-called "junk calls" in which there are no suspects and the complainant really wants the police investigation report for insurance purposes. Nevertheless, when compared with procedures of policing, these are radical changes, especially for citizens who may feel that they are being given the runaround. Any new method for reducing patrol responses requires a period of public education by way of media campaigns, civic meetings, and coffee hours. It will also require the dispatcher or a supervisor of the officer on the street to explain the new procedures to citizens and callers.

Another controversial method for reducing the time spent on nonessential calls for assistance by patrol units is called *stacking*. Stacking simply involves classifying calls in terms of priority, thereby increasing the amount of time that can be allocated for uninterrupted patrol for certain units.

Another method to reduce time on minor calls for service involves the use of nonsworn personnel or parapolice officers, such as community service officers. In many departments, these nonsworn personnel are assigned to a variety of duties, including desk duty, writing parking tickets, directing traffic, conducting crime-prevention campaigns, and other similar assignments.

Administrative Tasks

In this age of high technology, many police departments are experimenting with new devices and procedures to cut down on the amount of time uniformed and plainclothes officers spend on administrative tasks. With regard to police procedures ranging from arrests to prisoner transports, many departments are asking the question: How can we improve the amount of time an officer can spend on crucial tasks? In many cases, the answer requires a revision of existing laws, such as those mandating that the arresting officer must appear at arraignment with a defendant in court the next day. In other instances, the duty manual is subject to review and update to cut out unnecessary tasks.

While these issues are often resolved by in-house review, a basic problem that continues to plague all police officers is paperwork. On average, police agencies use over 50 different forms, ranging from arrest reports to motor vehicle accident reports. In fact, the average arrest requires that more than 10 different forms be completed. Computerization has helped and dropdown box report writing software programs have reduced time spent in actual writing. Nevertheless, police departments run on paper reports.

Directed Patrol

When administrative tasks, calls for service, and preventive patrol are reanalyzed, the final objective will be the allocation of greater time for directed patrol. For our purposes, **directed patrol** can be defined as the allocation of patrol services in a planned and rational manner. Departments have applied directed patrol in a variety of ways that will be discussed. In addition, directed patrol depends on two other variables: crime analysis and shift design.

CRIME ANALYSIS Too frequently, patrol deployment is made without referral to when and where the crimes are occurring. Many police personnel prefer to operate by tradition or rule-of-thumb methods rather than rely on **crime analysis**. A minority of police departments in the United States, however, delve into crime analysis with the assistance of federal grants. At present, crime analysis in the United States ranges from sophisticated crime mapping programs to pin mapping.

After pertinent data have been obtained from field reports, arrest sheets, or dispatch logs, the information is collated, analyzed, and then communicated to line supervisors and field personnel. With this information, the patrol supervisor can make rational decisions for deploying staff or devising specialized patrol techniques. Crime mapping has a solid future in crime analysis.

SHIFT DESIGN Crime analysis can be very useful in analyzing workloads by shift or season. At present, police departments often allocate an equal number of officers to each shift, usually three shifts in a 24-hour period. Despite this allocation, all departments realize that criminal activity increases between the hours of 4 P.M. and 2 A.M., which can present some problems with regard to police operations since officers are unable to perform directed patrol when they have to rush from call to call. In recognition of this dilemma, many departments have redeployed their patrol personnel based on need rather than on equalization. For example, many agencies have designed the following programs:

9–40   In this program, the officer works nine hours a day, four days a week, for a total of 36 hours; another four hours are taken up with physical fitness, in-service training, and roll call.

4–10   In this very common program, the workweek consists of 10 hours a day, four days a week.

3–12   Another shift design consists of officers working 12 hours for three days and then having two to three days off. The required number of work days has to be completed within a specific time period of usually 30 working days.

In addition to these and other proposed designs, deployment extends beyond the traditional equal shift allocation in that the shifts are redesigned to provide increased coverage between the hours of 7 P.M. and 1 A.M. Agencies on a five-day 40-hour workweek would be able to do the same thing, provided that there were permanent shifts with more personnel being assigned to high-crime hours. The main problem with shift redesign in traditional agencies stems from union or personnel opposition since most officers prefer to have as many weekends off as possible. Proponents of 9–40, 4–10, and 3–12 point out that accommodations can be made with weekends off by way of rotation.

SPECIALIZED PATROL In some departments, directed patrol comes under the heading of specialized patrol, where specific units are assigned to a special area (e.g., burglary squad and undercover squads for inner-city street crime). The following tactics are commonly employed by these units:

1. *Decoys.* In **decoy squads**, an officer disguised as a "victim" is assisted by several backup officers. This tactic is used for such crimes as muggings, purse snatchings, and assaults.
2. *Stakeouts.* In **stakeouts**, officers—either physically or by use of electronic equipment—are assigned to a likely target area. Crimes in progress are frequently interrupted.
3. *Suspect surveillance.* In suspect **surveillance**, police personnel watch and follow individuals who are suspected of committing offenses with frequency (e.g., burglary, robbery, drugs, and organized crime).

4. *General area surveillance.* As with stakeouts, general area surveillance is used either against specific criminals or in a wide area with a variety of targets. Some jurisdictions even go so far as to station video cameras on certain high-crime street corners.

The assignment of a specialized patrol unit to a problem is based on the analysis of crime data. Specialized patrol is an example of a proactive system that operates according to a rational plan of crime detection rather than randomly stumbling about waiting for something to happen. Some of the advantages of specialized patrol are as follows:

1. Specific units are assigned to a specific problem so that management knows exactly who is responsible for solving that crime problem.
2. The unit normally exhibits a high degree of teamwork and high morale.
3. There is improved skill development in the specialized area over a period of time, with officers being called on by all members of the department in their area of expertise.
4. A great deal of positive public interest might be generated by media attention.

On the other hand, there are problems with specialized units that affect the whole department. There is always the problem of communication (e.g., deciding who is responsible for what problems, like having a burglary unit that may not respond to other street crimes). Officers in regular squads resent the "hot shot" specialists who attain glory and prestige while regular patrol has to take care of more mundane matters. This is especially acute in departments where factions operate in a negative fashion. Departmental morale can be destroyed by resentment over specialized units.

The use of aggressive enforcement tactics also produces negative public attention. People get upset when stakeout squads use heavy-caliber weapons to kill robbers. Citizens also complain about area surveillance, particularly the use of video cameras in high-crime areas. While the outlook toward professional law enforcement services is generally positive, serious questions are raised on the use of heavy-handed tactics and technology.

Foot Patrol

Some police managers feel that automobile patrolling has led to police alienation from neighborhoods and loss of a feeling of security that was generated by **foot patrol**. Foot patrol can have a positive benefit in high-density neighborhoods. When Newark, New Jersey, and Flint, Michigan, reinstituted foot patrol, these were the results (Kelling, 1987):

1. When foot patrol is added in neighborhoods, levels of fear decrease significantly.
2. When foot patrol is withdrawn from neighborhoods, levels of fear increase significantly.
3. Citizen satisfaction with police increases when foot patrol is added in neighborhoods.
4. Police who patrol on foot have a greater appreciation for the values of the neighborhood residents than do police who patrol the same area in automobiles.
5. Police who patrol on foot have greater job satisfaction, less fear, and higher morale than officers who patrol in automobiles.

Personal-contact patrol also brought about fear reduction in Houston. The police started "to drive through the neighborhoods, knock on doors and chat with pedestrians, thus creating a visible presence" (Sherman, 1987). The major object of these programs is not crime reduction, although this has happened in some cases. Foot patrol and personal-contact patrol do increase a feeling of security by citizens and lower the fear of crime.

Bicycle Patrol

Police officers around the world have used bicycles for patrol purposes since the nineteenth century. With the advent of modern mountain bikes, police bike patrols have been established. The Seattle Police Department and other West Coast departments in the United States use bikes for patrol operations all year. The idea has become popular with university and college police departments. Other applications are found in airport parking lots, resort and recreation areas, and locations that impede motorized patrol units. In these locations, bike patrol personnel can respond quicker than vehicles to emergencies.

As with any other function, bike patrols require a great deal of planning with regard to equipment, training, personnel needs, and supervision. Equipment includes mountain bikes, seasonal uniforms, helmets, and foul-weather gear. Equipment or contract services have to be purchased for parts and repairs. Personnel selected for this assignment have to be physically fit. Training programs include topics such as bike nomenclature, proper riding and equipment, emergency response, tactical pursuit, and safety in such areas as woods, stairways, and shopping malls.

The bicycle patrols used by public safety agencies today provide the following benefits:

1. Increased interaction between officers and the community
2. Access to remote or vehicle-inaccessible locations
3. Improved physical fitness for participants

Bicycle patrols should not be viewed as a specialized function but rather as a part of normal assignment dependent on weather and climate considerations.

TEAM POLICING

In the 1960s, the concept of team policing received considerable attention by criminal justice educators, planners, and practitioners. It was seen as a possible solution to the major problems faced by many American police departments: (1) poor police–community relations, (2) duplication of effort, (3) the rise of crime, and (4) the increasing costs of police budgets. **Team policing** involves decentralizing the existing police organizational structure and reorganizing services into specific subunits. These subunits are usually based on geographic, ethnic, and other socioeconomic boundaries found in particular communities. In each subunit, the team is charged with the allocation of patrol, investigation, and other police services and programs, according to the needs of the community. Some vestiges of team policing remain in community policing, which will be discussed later in this chapter.

History of Team Policing

The concept of team policing originated in Aberdeen, Scotland, in the late 1940s as an experiment to counteract low morale and boredom experienced by single officers patrolling quiet areas. A change was made from the one-unit, one-beat method of patrol to teams of 5 or 10 patrolling an area divided according to the concentration of crime and calls for service (Sherman, 1976: xiii). In 1966, because of personnel shortage, the Coventry constabulary in England began a form of team policing called unit beat policing, whereby constables were formed into teams, and each team was assigned to a specific area. Information from the team was fed to a central collator who passed on the information to other teams. Although the Aberdeen patrol method was abandoned in 1963, other British constabularies and a few American police forces have adopted similar plans.

In the United States, the urban and campus unrest of the 1960s brought forth renewed interest in police patrol tactics and police–community relations. It was generally concluded that a gap had developed between the police and the public. This was due to the decline of the neighborhood foot patrol officer and the abandonment of many precinct stations in favor of centralization. The 1967 Presidential Commission on Law Enforcement and the Administration of Justice recommended that agencies introduce team policing as a means to lessen this gap. Team policing was also expected to increase community involvement in crime prevention and detection.

Positive Aspects of Team Policing

The positive aspects of team policing are as follows:

1. The police services rendered by the team become more personal to the community, and in return the relations between the police and the community are improved.
2. Team policing provides a flexible structure for its members in that innovation is made possible and professionalism is increased through the development of shared knowledge and peer review.
3. Patrol and investigatory functions are merged into one task, thus eliminating the social barriers of communication and status conflict between uniformed and plainclothes personnel.
4. A reduction is attained in the chain of command in that decision making is done by supervisors and operating personnel.
5. Each member of the team is given a chance to utilize discretion and enhance personal skills. As a result, greater work satisfaction is expected.

Team Policing and Tactical Patrol

Team policing is often confused with **tactical patrol** techniques. Tactical patrol deals with selective law enforcement for a specific problem in the area. Examples of this type of enforcement are robberies, murders, muggings, and purse snatchings occurring in a routine manner, in a specific geographic area. With team policing, emphasis is placed on territorial exclusivity, maintaining stable and close ties with the citizens of the neighborhood, participation in planning and management, and an orientation toward results in presenting the police mission (Edgar et al., 1976: v).

Between 1970 and 1974, a number of municipalities introduced team policing into their areas, with and without assistance from federal and private funding sources. Evaluation of these programs brought mixed reviews. The Rochester, New York, investigative-team program was deemed successful for improving clearance rates and reducing crime. The community investigative-team programs in New York City and Albuquerque, New Mexico, were assessed as failures, generally because of overall departmental problems. In New York City, the teams failed to change the role of the patrol officer or to increase his or her job satisfaction. In Albuquerque, the teams were unable to deliver a higher level of community service. San Diego, California, had greater success with its program. The officers adapted to their new role, delivered community services, and improved their attitudes toward the community. The full-service teams in Albany (Arbor Hill), Cincinnati, and Los Angeles were extensively evaluated, and the results were somewhat mixed (Gay et al., 1977b: 41):

> While indicators of workload management, investigative effectiveness and police attitudes towards the community have improved, there has been no change in officer job satisfaction and community attitudes.

PROBLEM-ORIENTED POLICING

In 1979, Herman Goldstein proposed what he described as a problem-oriented approach to law enforcement (Goldstein, 1979). In the late 1970s and throughout the 1980s, police managers, faced with more and more personnel with college degrees, attempted a number of approaches at improving job satisfaction, task forces, quality circles, and management by objectives. **Problem-oriented policing (POP)** is another one of these approaches that utilize the educated police force in a more proactive manner. According to the authors, traditional police patrol is a reactive system where police departments deliver services by "reacting to individual events reported by citizens gathering information from victims, witnesses, and offenders; involving the criminal justice process and using aggregate crime statistics to evaluate performance" (Spelman and Eck, 1987a: 3).

In Newport News, Virginia, police were trained in a four-stage approach:

1. *Scanning.* Identify major problems (e.g., burglaries in an apartment complex, thefts from autos downtown, and prostitution-related robberies).
2. *Analysis.* Collect and analyze information from a variety of public and private resources, not just from police data.
3. *Response.* Work with other agencies and the public to tailor actions suitable to the problem.
4. *Assessment.* Evaluate the effectiveness of the actions to see whether the problem was alleviated or solved.

As a result of this approach, downtown robberies were reduced by 39 percent, burglaries in that apartment complex were reduced by 35 percent, and thefts from parked vehicles outside a manufacturing plant dropped by 53 percent. Table 8-2 shows the problem-analysis model, which worked well for the Newport News police agency's problem-oriented policing.

To find out what were important problems for the citizens, a number of citywide and neighborhood surveys were conducted. Citywide problems included domestic homicides, gas station drive-offs, assaults on police officers, runaway youths, drunk driving, and disturbances at convenience stores. Specific neighborhood problems included drug dealing, robberies, vacant buildings, burglaries, larcenies, thefts from autos, and rowdy youths. In one apartment complex, the police successfully organized a building association and had the city intervene in the maintenance of the complex, which resulted in better living conditions and a 35 percent drop in the burglary rate.

What is important is that the community is involved in solving problems, whether these are drug deals, stolen bicycles, or loud-noise complaints. The basic tenets of Goldstein's article were later incorporated into a full discussion in his book *Problem-Oriented Policing* (1990). The term is often used interchangeably with **community-oriented policing (COP)**, but there are some basic theoretical differences between the two. What problem-oriented policing does is provide a planning model for dealing with specific issues in the wider view of community policing. Today, POP is a component part of what community policing has become, in that the police and communities work together to identify problem areas, considering effective ways to address them, and then assess results. The US Department of Justice, COPS, provides funding support to POP initiatives, including the Center for Problem-Oriented Policing, as well as related publications and literature (Center for Problem-Oriented Policing, 2013).

TABLE 8-2	Problem Analysis Model	
Actors	**Incidents**	**Responses**
Victims	Sequence of events	Community
Lifestyle	Events preceding	Neighborhood affected
Security measures taken	criminal act	by problem
Victimization history	Event itself	City as a whole
	Events following act	People outside the city
Offenders	Physical contact	Institutional
Identity and physical	Time	Criminal justice agencies
description	Location	Other public agencies
Lifestyle, education,	Access control and	Mass media
employment history	surveillance	Business sector
Criminal history		
Third parties	Social context	
Personal data	Likelihood and probable	
Connection to	actions of witnesses	
victimization	Apparent attitude	
	of residents toward	
	neighborhood	

Source: Spelman, William and John E. Eck. "Newport News Tests Problem-Oriented Policing." *National Institute of Justice Reports* (January/February 1987a), pp. 2–8.

COMMUNITY POLICING

James Q. Wilson and George L. Keating (1982) published an article titled "Broken Windows," which captured the attention of police administrators. They described how Philip Zimbardo, a noted sociologist at Stanford University, placed an abandoned car in a tough Bronx neighborhood and another abandoned vehicle in a wealthy area in Palo Alto, California. The vehicle in the Bronx was immediately vandalized and became a stripped hulk within a week. The car in Palo Alto remained untouched until Professor Zimbardo intentionally broke its window. The vehicle was then stripped of usable parts by vandals. Kelling and Wilson used this field experiment to present the idea that run-down neighborhoods attract crime and fear.

They recommended foot patrol in tough neighborhoods. The idea was not to simply reduce crime but to have a police presence to make people feel safer. Technology had allowed the police to abandon the streets of the city. Police officers, with their fancy computers and communication systems, rode around in police cars and simply did not communicate with citizens. Foot patrol, with the goal of giving citizens a feeling of safety, was tried around the United States, beginning with Newark, New Jersey, in 1981. Other sites followed: Oakland in 1984, a second Newark program in 1985, Houston in 1987, and Boston in 1986. Although the crime rate usually did not go down, the general conclusion was that the citizens "felt safer and less worried about personal property victimization" (Greene, 1989: 361). This evolved over a number of years into fear reduction programs and finally into **community policing**—all of which have their original roots in the team policing of the 1970s.

One of the major differences between the reactive patrolling of the 911 police force and community-oriented policing is that community-oriented policing can become proactive.

By working closely with citizens, police can anticipate and prevent crime. Community policing, when done right, is one of the most proactive programs that a professional police department can adopt.

Traditional Policing and Community Policing Compared

One of the questions asked time and time again is: What makes community-oriented policing so different from traditional policing? In the past, when an officer walked a beat visiting neighbors and businesses daily, we had a form of community policing. Now that police are barricaded inside their police vehicles, reacting to citizen calls only after a crime has taken place, we have the opposite of community policing.

Giving out traffic tickets is also reactive since it takes place after the fact. Police do not station themselves outside of bars where citizens are known to get drunk and then drive. Instead, police wait for those drunk drivers to drive many miles, possibly injuring or killing someone, before they give out their tickets—much, much too late. Working with the community outside such bars to stop drunken people from driving would be both community-oriented policing and proactive policing.

The comparison of traditional policing with community-oriented policing, provided in Table 8-3, was published by the National Institute of Justice (Sparrow, 1988: 8–9). To summarize Table 8-3, community police consider themselves part of the public they serve. They work proactively by taking steps to eliminate crime and disorder. Community policing focuses on the citizens' problems and concerns.

The Implementation of Community Policing

According to *Implementing Community Policing: The Administrative Problem* by Kelling and Bratton (1993: 4), the police reformers who are carrying out community policing are using middle managers, such as the leadership of line operating units and staff units (e.g., planning and training):

> Thus, the solution to the administrative problem in police departments was the establishment of a powerful mid-management group that: 1) extended the reach of chiefs throughout police departments and 2) became the locus of the practice and skill base of the occupation. As such, mid-managers became the leading edge in the establishment of centralized control over police departments' internal environment and organizational operations.

To establish useful and sustained change in any police department, police managers must overcome the overwhelming resistance of the established police culture. This is especially true in the case of community policing, which attempts to reach outside the police department to involve civilians in police matters. The research on police culture, from Westley's (1970) dissertation on the Gary, Indiana, Police Department in 1950 to Thibault's article "The Blue Milieu," indicates that police have been socially isolated from the public (minority groups in particular), hostile to the public, threatened by any type of change, and very secretive (Thibault, 1992).

The only way a police chief can implement community policing is to have middle management convince the patrol officer that community policing

- Does not threaten his or her sense of identity as a police officer
- Does not lower the professional status or authority of a police officer
- Rewards police officers in terms of postings and promotions for implementing community policing
- Will remain a permanent part of departmental police procedures

TABLE 8-3	Traditional Versus Community Policing: Questions and Answers	
	Answers	
Questions	**Traditional Policing**	**Community Policing**
Who are the police?	A government agency principally responsible for law enforcement	Police are the public, and the public are the police. Police officers are those who are paid to give full-time attention to the duties of every citizen
What is the relationship of the police force to other public service departments?	Priorities often conflict	The police is one department among many responsible for improving the quality of life
What is the role of the police?	Focusing on solving crimes	A broader problem-solving approach
How is police efficiency measured?	By detection and arrest rates	By the absence of crime and disorder
What are the highest priorities?	Crimes that are high value (e.g., bank robberies) and those involving violence	Whatever problems disturb the community most
What specifically do police deal with?	Incidents	Citizens' problems and concerns
What determines the effectiveness of police?	Response times	Public cooperation
What view do police take of service calls?	Deal with them only if there is no real police work to do	Vital function and great opportunity
What is police professionalism?	Swift, effective response to serious crime	Keeping close to the community
What kind of intelligence is most important?	Crime intelligence (study of particular crimes or series of crimes)	Criminal intelligence (information about the activities of individuals or groups)
What is the essential nature of police accountability?	Highly centralized; governed by rules, regulations, and policy directives; accountable to the law	Emphasis on local accountability to community needs
What is the role of headquarters?	To provide the necessary rules and policy directives	To preach organizational values
What is the role of the press liaison department?	To keep the "heat" off operational officers so they can get on with the job	To coordinate an essential channel of communication with the community
How do the police regard prosecutions?	As an important goal	As one tool among many

The old-timers will say, "I remember that team policing crap. We worked with the community and formed what they would call today quality teams. Well, the chief felt that his power was threatened, and *boom!* That was the end of team policing." Only middle management has the staying power to convince these officers, who have heard it all, that community policing is a permanent part of law enforcement.

In Dallas, the lieutenants (middle management) opposed community policing. As Kelling and Bratton report (1993: 5), "Before a single operational element of the strategy was in place [the police chief] was fired . . . and the planning unit . . . was renounced and liquidated." That was the end of community policing for Dallas.

In Cincinnati in the 1970s, decentralized team policing was instituted by the chief and his managers without involving middle management. They jazzed it up with the behavioral jargon of management by objectives, further alienating the middle managers. The result was predictable (Kelling and Bratton, 1993: 6): "By the end of 1975 . . . . while some forms of team policing still existed, little of substance remained."

Recommendations for Implementation

How can a police manager decide if community policing is really taking place? The following seven criteria have to be in place:

1. *The agenda for police activities must be set by citizens, not by the police administrators.* This means there must be formal ways of finding out what the citizens want, such as surveys and the formal involvement of citizen associations.
2. *Middle management must be trained and directly involved in the implementation of community policing, from inception to final performance.* This includes captains, lieutenants, and sergeants.
3. *There must be a split force.* Community policing has to be protected from 911 service calls so officers have time to interact with citizen associations and to plan mutual problem solving with these citizens.
4. *Community policing must be a permanent policy of the department, not dependent on grant money, which comes and goes.* The policies and philosophy of community policing must be part of standard operating procedures. There must be a permanent reward structure for the implementation of community policing by line officers.
5. *Community problem-solving groups are created to identify problems and explore solutions with police managers.*
6. *The prevention of crime must be the major police goal.* This policy is intended to stop crime before it happens rather than arrest criminals after citizens have been victimized.
7. *Officers must strive to improve the quality of life in a community.* This is accomplished by preventing crime, fixing broken windows, repairing or tearing down empty buildings, reducing fear in the community, and cleaning up vacant lots.

If police programs measure up to these seven criteria, they will be judged community policing programs. If the policing programs are missing one or more of the seven criteria, they will be considered public relations programs or something other than community policing.

Community Policing Reduces Serious Crime

Does community policing work? Evaluation studies are often based on time, place, manner, and maintenance of efforts. A study conducted by Connel et al. (2008) reviewed an officer-initiated program in a suburban area. Officers in the department were interviewed and crime data from two comparable beats were evaluated over eight years. There was a significant reduction in property and violent crimes using time series analysis compared to two other areas in the county without community policing.

The article reviewed past evaluations around the country with the following conclusion: The three major outcomes of community policing are positive attitudes of the community toward policing and positive attitudes of police officers toward their jobs, and mixed results concerning crime reduction over the years (Connel et al., 2008: 127–50).

In the Connel study, officers were responsible for crime in their geographical district and were also evaluated in terms of problem solving, teamwork, and community interaction. The major elements also included accountability, decentralization, and collaboration. Collaboration included business and public institutions representing schools, parole, and probation. Decentralization meant that along with the sergeant-in-charge, officers were responsible for the crime in their targeted area. The officers also devised permanent solutions to recurring problems. The district included roughly 60 percent whites and 40 percent African American, Hispanic, and Asian minorities. The police department was composed of 1,000 officers policing about 500 square miles with a population just over 850,000.

The data for the drug crimes showed a decline in both the community policing targeted area and a comparable area that did not use the community policing model. However, the data for violent crimes and property crimes did show a clear-cut positive link between the community policing model used in the target area and the comparable areas without community policing.

The statistics are sophisticated and the study is a strong endorsement of officer-initiated community policing: "The findings suggest that community policing does have the capacity to effect serious crime rates. . . . " According to the time series analysis, the intervention resulted in an abrupt and permanent decline in violent and property crimes in the targeted area (Connel et al., 2008: 150). Community policing increases a positive community attitude to the police department and officer morale. What this article adds is a rigorous evaluation over eight years of serious violent and property crime reduction produced by the community policing model.

The study above shows some parallels with previous case studies reviewed by the author for St. Petersburg, Florida, Seattle, Washington, and Chicago, Illinois.

1. There is a need for police training in human relations skills.
2. Community policing efforts must focus on problems that the community has identified.
3. The impact of community policing is positive on both the police and the citizens.
4. Police get the benefit of civilian support in neighborhoods and businesses and support for the police budget.
5. The citizens get to know the police as human beings and as professionals.
6. The citizens see police in a positive light because the police are helping to solve the problems in their neighborhoods.

Impact of Community Policing

The twenty-first-century police departments throughout the United States have accepted community policing. In 2000, the federal government published a nationwide survey of community policing activities that impacted patrol, crime prevention, and problem solving (Miller and Hess, 2005: 472)

- Gave geographic responsibility to patrol
- Have a citizen police academy

- Conduct beat/neighborhood meeting open to the public
- Opened neighborhood substations
- Adopted problem-solving techniques
- Developed information systems to support problem solving
- Conduct citizen surveys on a regular basis
- Decision making occurs in lower ranks
- Developed evaluation for evaluating success of community policing
- Decentralized detectives
- Changed communication center on how citizen calls are handled
- Eliminated one or more ranks

This provides a behavioral definition of community policing. Although not every department has accepted all these activities, enough have adopted many of these approaches to make a nationwide impact. When students, citizens, or police officers ask what makes community policing different, hand them this list.

Further, the mission statements of police departments around the country have evolved to include community policing values and policies. Success has been reasonably assured because of the national acceptance of the specific policies and values of the community-policing model by a wide variety of departments and communities throughout the United States.

Conclusion: Community Policing

Community policing cannot be implemented overnight. It takes time, training, a restructuring of departmental resources, and daily work with community groups, but it can be done successfully, as the Seattle experience has demonstrated. Middle management must become involved if the social isolation of the established police culture and the cynicism of the public are to be overcome. Line officers and middle managers must be able to see the benefits of community policing, or it will not work. We recommend that any agency that truly wants to implement community policing ask middle managers from a successful program to work with their middle managers.

Without some additional resources in terms of new civilian and sworn-officer positions, it is very difficult for a reactive police department to implement community-oriented policing. But if you start small, say in one or two neighborhoods, and the people and politicians see that it is actually working, new positions and resources may become available. In the fight for additional resources in these tight-budget times, the best allies of the police are involved citizens who have seen community police programs work. It is not easy, but the benefits to both the police and the community are worth the effort. The federal funding of community policing has made community policing efforts successful as permanent institutions in major police departments.

The big question is to what extent will community policing continue if federal funding support ends completely? While we do not claim to have a crystal ball on this, we feel that since this program has made great inroads in American policing, certain community-specific programs will continue for some time. Overall, it has had a positive impact on police–community relations, which will be important for antiterrorism investigations and community-security enhancement in the next few years. Indications are that the economic recovery plans of the current administration include approximately $4 billion for state and local law enforcement, which includes programs in community-related crime reduction efforts (U.S. Department of Justice, 2009).

INTELLIGENCE-LED POLICING

Intelligence to deal with terrorism and major crimes has emerged as an important component of policing. Internationally, intelligence on terrorist activities and military threats is gathered by various agencies, which include the Federal Bureau of Investigation (FBI), the Central Intelligence Agency (CIA), the Drug Enforcement Administration (DEA), the Bureau of Alcohol, Tobacco, and Firearms (ATF), and the National Security Agency. Since September 11, 2001, agencies dealing with terrorism include the Terrorism Threat Integration Center and the Terrorist Screening Center operated by the FBI. In addition, the New York City Police Department maintains an active counterterrorist unit, with representatives assigned to major cities all over the world. The commission that looked into the events of 9/11 felt that although much information was known about the terrorists, there was a failure of intelligence sharing. This finding has led to the creation of a new national intelligence coordinator to eliminate the bureaucratic rivalries among various federal agencies. According to David Carter (2004), the events after September 11 have also led to the creation of regional, state, and national task forces to deal with potential terrorist activities. Today representatives of state and local agencies sit on regional joint terrorism task forces to review potential terrorist threats and trends. Chief Raymond Philo states that intelligence-based policing has currently shifted toward dealing with major street crimes and gang activity (personal communication, 2009).

To date, a national intelligence gathering mechanism has been created by the Department of Justice for American policing. Each state and major region has fusion centers that bring together field- and data-based usable information. A fusion center is staffed by representatives of major agencies in the region and has access to a number of databases related to public and legal publications, vendor white pages, sex offender registration, criminal history files, bias crimes, child abduction attempts, medical and research laboratories, police and security registration, school violence events, and motor vehicle information.

Based on the importance of intelligence gathering, every law enforcement agency must become involved in national and global intelligence initiatives. **Intelligence-led policing** illustrates this by its use of community policing as well as crime-planning and crime-analysis programs such as Compstat, crime mapping, and other analytical tools.

What is intelligence? Intelligence is the shifting of raw information into something that can be used to predict an event, track a target, or look at a new development in criminal activity. According to Carter (2004: 9), "Intelligence is the product of an analytic process that provides an integrated perspective to disparate information about crime, crime trends, crime and security and threats, and conditions associated with criminality." Based on this analysis, police managers can make decisions for tactical and strategic planning. For law enforcement purposes, information is gathered in a number of ways: street encounters, informants and undercover operatives, data banks, media accounts of events, meetings, closed circuit television records, bank records, wiretaps, forensic evidence, and different types of personal records.

How does community policing apply here? Based on relationships between the police and community members, information on crime is gathered from contacts established by individual officers or squads. The question then is how this information is analyzed and presented as intelligence to address crime and terrorism issues.

Historical Issues

There has been a great deal of civilian mistrust of domestic intelligence gathering by law enforcement. During the 1960s, federal and state agencies created domestic intelligence files on antiwar protesters, civil rights activists, peace advocates, and others through the creation of dossiers or files based on people's names and their associates under the premise that someone might commit a crime. Based on the misuse of these files for political purposes, a number of laws and policies were created to protect individual civil rights from infringement by unauthorized police investigations. Lawsuits against police also included civil tort actions against intelligence units by persons who had not committed any crimes. Public hearings on the use of dossiers led to a separation of national and international intelligence sharing between the FBI and CIA and the prohibition of domestic intelligence operations by the CIA.

The use of intelligence on career criminals, crime suspects, and crime trends did not receive a great deal of serious police attention until the rise of organized crime and street gang operations in urban areas in the 1980s. The events of September 11, 2001, led to the creation of a National Criminal Intelligence Sharing Plan, which found that there was a natural link between community policing and intelligence-led policing. According to the Office of Community Policing, both community policing and intelligence-led policing rely on information management, two-way communication with the public, data analysis, and problem solving (Carter, 2004).

Community Policing and Intelligence

The relationships built by COPS officers lead to a number of informational sources that can be used to prevent terrorism and all other related crimes. Also, crime prevention and educational programs, such as the citizen's police academy, can focus attention on terrorism issues, emergency preparedness, and volunteer efforts. There is also a need to direct attention to what is called commodity flows, which include drugs, stolen goods, false identity papers, and money transactions.

As described by Carter (2004: 161–70), the model intelligence process used by the FBI includes the following:

1. *Identification of problem areas.* As with problem-oriented policing, information is collected about offenders, victims/commodities, and locations to begin targeting suspected operations.
2. *Collection of information.* This is accomplished through interviews, informants, information gathered as a by-product of other investigations, review of data banks, surveillances, and liaison relationships with other law enforcement agencies.
3. *Processing and exploitation.* Taking all the raw information, the intelligence personnel try to make some sense of the data through data reduction, translation, and decryption. Both open-source and closed-source information are used. Open-source information is any item available to the general public, such as information on the Internet and in 24-hour news programs. Closed-source data banks and sources are those open only to law enforcement based on clearance classifications. Both kinds of information have to be evaluated for trustworthiness and reliability before using them to understand a crime pattern.
4. *Analysis and production.* This is the process of converting the information into intelligence for law enforcement purposes. Analysis includes the review of data sets and the use of spreadsheets, mapping programs, statistical programs, and investigative analysis software. Link analysis provides a method of matching patterns and relationships between individuals and groups.
5. *Dissemination.* This is the distribution of finished intelligence to the consumers, who can be agency policy makers and other interested parties. Finished intelligence might result in an assessment of a threat, a bulletin that describes a trend, or general information based on raw information.

A key element in Part 2 of the process is called **tactical debriefing**. Tactical debriefing simply means that street officers, detectives, and others proactively question suspects or engage informants on information related to current or future planned criminal activity such as illegal drugs, guns, homicides, missing persons, stolen property, burglaries, larcenies, or any other criminal activity. For suspects, the questions would be directed to events and persons other than for the offense for which they are in custody. Once a lead is developed, the information is recorded on an intelligence gathering worksheet and forwarded to the intelligence office. It is then up to the intelligence officer to make evaluation, analysis, and future dissemination. Information that can be used immediately, termed tactical intelligence, would be applied to an investigation.

Managerial Concerns

The first concern pertains to the intelligence gathering function and who and what groups are to be targeted. The guidelines for this are found in **28 Code of Federal Regulations (CFR) Part 23**, which contains the standards for intelligence gathering for both individual and multiagency units.

Intelligence gathering must be initiated only to obtain information related to criminal conduct and activities that present a threat to the community. The guidelines include the need for reasonable suspicion to show that criminal activity is possible by the individual or group. Information about political, religious, or social views of associations is prohibited unless the group is involved in criminal conduct. The intelligence unit cannot gather information acquired in violation of federal, state, or local laws. 28 CFR 23 requires careful record keeping and administrative and physical safeguards to protect intelligence information. All files are subject to audit.

What happens if the information is eventually found to be of no use or untrue? Department intelligence policies also call for closing files where all leads have been exhausted, or where no legitimate law enforcement is served.

How much and what can be shared is always a topic of continuing controversy in that all agencies have a series of mechanisms that classify information and intelligence based on how sensitive the information is or what damage it could do if obtained by adversaries. These classifications include top secret, secret, and confidential. In certain cases, individuals in other agencies who desire information must obtain a security clearance from the Department of Justice, which is not feasible for all police personnel. The types of security clearances and the processes for obtaining security clearances can be obtained from the FBI Web page and other related publications. The purpose of the clearance is to establish a law enforcement agent's potential for trustworthiness; this clearance process involves going through another background check for any criminal record, a credit history check, and interviews with associates. For general law enforcement use, information can be released according to the following two categories:

1. *Sensitive but unclassified.* This information has been declassified by removing the sources or methods by which the information was obtained. The information is not available to the public.
2. *For official use only (FOUO).* The FOUO designation is used by the Department of Homeland Security to identify unclassified information that has an impact on community safety or a person's privacy.

Local police departments often have classifications that are restricted, confidential, or unclassified. Restricted files include those that contain information that could adversely affect an ongoing investigation or create safety hazards for officers or compromise the identity of confidential informants. Confidential intelligence is less sensitive and may be released to agency personnel. For both restricted and confidential, the intelligence officer would be responsible for releasing the information after consultation with executive personnel.

Unclassified intelligence is information from news media, public records, and other public sources. The intelligence officer would release the relevant information to officers conducting authorized investigations (New Hartford Police Department, 2007).

Additional steps must be taken to ensure the security of physical and computer records; for example, one senior administrator of the department could be responsible for records security. Again, it must be emphasized that sharing information with those with proper clearances is a two-way street. We know of numerous instances of distrust and rivalries that occurred among federal, state, and local police agencies. The challenge faced by police managers is to create an intelligence function that matches the size, geography, and complexity of their unit or municipality. For example, a village police department would not need a full-time intelligence officer; an administrative supervisor could take on this function along with his or her other duties. On the other hand, large metropolitan police departments may have a formal intelligence unit that deals with a wide range of criminal conspiracies and terrorism.

PREDICTIVE POLICING

With the advent of cloud computing and vast amounts of data that are created from crime reports, traffic stops, license plate readers, intelligence reports, and social media sites, crime analysis has moved into an entirely new dimension. Crime and intelligence information can now be used to predict where crimes might occur which can generate a police response, which has developed into the concept of **predictive policing**.

The way it works is that information is obtained from various sources including informants, social media, online videos, Wikipedia, crime data trends, and tactical debriefings. Using mathematical algorithms, analysts then "churn" what is called "Big Data" through data mining processes to look at crime that could occur in a specific area. Based on this information, police resources and tactics can be deployed to address specific issues and problems.

As discussed by Beck and McCue (2009), major corporations such as Walmart and Amazon use advanced analytics to stock shelves and address customer trends based on seasonal needs, major events such as storms, and personal buying habits. They report that the same technologies can be applied to policing to address future violent crimes through risk-based deployment. They cite successful efforts to reduce random gunfire complaints and burglary in Los Angeles. In 2011, *Time Magazine* called predictive policing one of the major inventions for that year. The award focused on the Santa Cruz Police Department that used this method and a concept of after-shock (when one crime occurs others will also follow) to reduce burglary (Friend, 2013). Crime analysts in the department used data and crime mapping to focus on the most likely areas for burglary and related offenses, and had sector patrols focus in these areas during preventive patrol time.

Not everyone is enthralled with predictive policing. Civil libertarians argue that this only brings increased police presence in low-income or minority neighborhoods where violent and property crimes are apt to occur (What's Predictive Policing?, n.d.). As the model is also based on reported crimes, not all offenses become police data such as sex crimes and drug use among the affluent. From a management perspective, there is also the need to have a full-fledged crime analysis unit perhaps on a regional basis that can take various forms of data into use beyond municipal and regional jurisdictional limits.

WEED AND SEED

In response to a rise in drug trafficking and the decline of certain inner-city neighborhoods, the Department of Justice initiated a program in 1991 called **Weed and Seed**. The goals of the program are to address violent crime and problems associated with drug sales in high-risk neighborhoods and to provide a safe environment for residents. According to the U.S. Department of Justice (n.d.), the key to Weed and Seed is bringing together a host of law enforcement and community agencies to "weed out" criminals in the neighborhood and to bring revitalization services (seeding) to the area.

The program uses a problem-solving collaborative strategy in forming alliances between law enforcement and social service groups. The key element is obtaining resident support and participation in program follow-through. As with other aspects of community policing, a primary goal is to improve the quality of life for neighborhood residents. In addition to addressing the crime problem, residents and officials strive to work together to deal with such issues as graffiti and abandoned buildings. Weed and Seed programs are found in a wide variety of urban areas throughout the United States including medium and small cities.

The overall organization of this program is fairly straightforward. Communities with a serious crime problem in a specific neighborhood file an application through the U.S. Attorney's office. If the application is approved, funding is then given to the city or town executive that filed for the grant. The daily operations of the program are directed by local authorities, who then create and work with a neighborhood steering committee. The steering group consists of local stakeholders, including state and federal law enforcement, social services, city services, housing authority personnel, neighborhood block associations, and so on. Also important are the collection of data and an audit of neighborhood problems and the resources available to deal with those problems. Each Weed and Seed program is limited to receiving federal funds for five years (Vandecovering, 2006). Federal funds are then used for additional equipment and resources for a wide number of operations, which can include

- Saturation patrols in high-crime neighborhoods
- Creation of operational Safe Haven for children
- Saturation patrols coupled with an anti-gun violence educational program to deal with firearms on school grounds
- Hiring additional off-duty police officers to run youth programs
- Increasing treatment services for neighborhood drug addicts
- Community beautification programs, including the removal of graffiti and vacant buildings in rundown areas
- Classes for first-time homeowners in obtaining a mortgage

The key to the success or failure of a Weed and Seed program is the extent to which the steering committee is able to function and achieve measurable results over time. An early evaluation of eight urban sites (Dunsworth and Mills, 1999) showed that serious Part I offenses declined (weeding), especially in those areas where neighborhoods were targeted. The evaluation found that it was too soon to measure the efforts on community development and relationship building (seeding). Award recipients today must have an evaluation plan that measures program impact in their community based on community factors.

HOT SPOTS

All the various proactive patrol strategies as well as community policing work only when a police department has a split force. Patrol forces are split into a number of forces. The parts of the patrol force that are held back from servicing the reactive 911 calls are used for other purposes.

Lawrence Sherman found something very special while analyzing domestic violence calls to the police. He found that "chronically violent couples can be identified and predicted [and] chronic locations of domestic calls can be predicted" (Sherman, 1992: 214). He found that "over half (53%) of all domestic calls in Minneapolis occurred at buildings with four or more calls in

1986" (1992: 227). A few years after this research, Sherman cites a case in the same city where 13 patrol cars responded to seven domestic calls in 48 hours for the same apartment. In Milwaukee, he found that two-thirds of domestic calls "involved couples with two or more incidents in a 33-month period" (1992: 214).

This analysis can be applied to street crimes. In "Repeat Calls for Service: Policing Hot Spots," Sherman noted, "Three percent of the 115,000 addresses and intersections in Minneapolis were the subject of 50 percent of the 321,174 calls to police" (1989: 150). He noted under what he calls "dial-a-cop," his name for the 911 reactive system of policing: "The chronic locations are not given extra attention to try to reduce their heavy demands on police."

With a good data-analysis management system tied into the 911 system, a proactive plan for policing **hot spots** can be created. There are a number of issues:

1. *Specific names are needed for specific locations.* For example, a bar can be known as Teddy's Twilight Bar at 110 Main Street. It can be known as (1) Twilight, (2) Teddy's, (3) 110 Main Street, (4) Twilight Bar, and so on. You might need a computer program to sort this out so that management knows that all calls came from one location.
2. *A criterion must be created for the definition of a "chronic location."* An example would be setting a threshold for the number of calls for police service to an address in a certain time period, such as "over 25 calls to one address in a 12 month period." In this case, the twenty-sixth call would trigger the *chronic location* designation. The policy could also state how long an address has to go without a call for police service before it could have the designation removed. The size of the population would determine the criterion.
3. *The calls have to be categorized.* False alarm calls and lockouts would have policy implications in some jurisdictions, while domestic violence and burglary would be important in other jurisdictions. Discount stores, 24-hour convenience stores, various public and private apartments, and medium- and low-priced hotels and bars are common hot spots.
4. *An action plan must be formulated and implemented.* The action plan reduces the number of calls while dealing with the crime and problems generating the calls.
5. *An evaluation must be implemented.* A useful evaluation combines statistics related to charges in the number of calls per location and a questionnaire given to people at the hot spots. The evaluation should also take into account any new hot spots created by the displacement of crimes.

Can focusing on hot spots work? Yes, if there is good analysis with a good police team involved in the planning and implementation efforts. It is better to focus on a few hot spots with an experienced team than to spread the police resources too thin. It will also work with the help of other public and private agencies, including liquor licensing authorities, the telephone company, department of health, and public housing agencies.

POLICE PURSUIT POLICIES

A controversial issue in patrol operations is vehicle pursuit for the simple reasons that both officers and citizens get killed and injured and homes and businesses are destroyed by vehicles in the chase. Often most chases start for relatively minor traffic offenses and then increase in intensity with a number of pursuing police vehicles at high speeds. As a result of public and civil lawsuits, most departments have restrictive pursuit polices that center on the seriousness of the offense and the ability of a supervisor to call off the pursuit. In some cases involving multiple jurisdictions, one department may call off the pursuit only to have it taken up by another agency.

High-speed pursuits remain a source of public fascination on television and YouTube. One of the best selling video games is Grand Theft Auto; every new version has better graphics and crashes. Television news channels, particularly in the West Coast where the weather is clear, will provide optimum coverage of chases to the conclusion of the event. Let us now look at proactive police management policies that will protect citizens and municipal liability while balancing the need to arrest high-risk and dangerous offenders who can harm the public. Given the high property and personal damages in pursuit driving, proactive police managers should create the most restrictive written pursuit policies in situations involving serious felonies. If officers' and citizens' lives and property are put at risk, the pursuit reason should be more serious than a routine traffic violation. Liability is simply too high a consideration. Although not all related to police pursuits, the City of Los Angeles paid out approximately $24 million in settlements or judgments in a recent nine-year period in automobile crashes alone (Rubin, 2012). Post-2008, municipal budgets cannot afford a mistake.

The Pursuit Management Task Force (National Institute of Justice, 1998a: 1) recommended the development of "vehicle-stopping technologies currently available, under development, and potentially available." The vehicle-stopping device that is available now is an inflatable device that is placed in front of fleeing vehicles to pierce their tires. In development are future devices to shut down a vehicle's electrical system.

Helicopters allow for safer pursuits. Police vehicles can slow down and still know where the pursued vehicle is by talking to the helicopter crew. Helicopters can also illuminate the fleeing vehicle and surroundings. With the advent of computer-controlled vehicle systems, an electronic solution to vehicle pursuit should be in our immediate future and would change vehicle-pursuit policies to vehicle-stopping policies. Vehicle-stopping policies are preferable to the present pursuit policies with their high risk for personal injury and property damage.

Pursuit Policy Recommendations

Police pursuit policies have been crafted to reflect the following recommendations because of the high risk for traffic accidents and possible injury and death to suspects and bystanders:

1. The most restrictive written pursuit policy should be in place as a general order.
2. Police pursuit training needs to be universal and continual for all patrol officers.
3. Police pursuit training needs to include the discussion of the criteria used by a police officer to pursue a fleeing vehicle and how to operationalize these criteria.
4. Low-risk, low-speed pursuits are preferable to high-risk, high-speed pursuits.
5. Alternative vehicle-stopping devices are preferable to police pursuit.
6. Vehicle-stopping policies, such as stopsticks and newer technology being tested to automatically shut off engines of fleeing perpetrator vehicles, should eventually be substituted for the present high-risk pursuit policies.

Conclusion

Patrol is the most visible function in police operations. The concept of preventive patrol has come under great scrutiny based on the cost of vehicles and personnel and the seeming noneffect it has on crime incidents. Various studies and experimental programs have concluded that patrol should be directed to certain areas based on criminal activity and that all citizen calls do not merit a two-minute response time. The strategy is to cut down on patrol costs and to create the optimum use of a professional police officer's time. However, political policy for many communities dictates the need for a police presence to reduce fear despite these fiscal and operational considerations.

The need for increased police presence and for new ways to address fundamental crime problems forms the basis for community- and problem-oriented policing. In this chapter, we examined the theoretical differences between these two concepts, which are often used interchangeably. Some writers on community policing refer to community policing as the philosophy and to problem-oriented policing as an analytic tool for dealing with the causes of crime.

Community policing continues to attract much attention at professional conferences and seminars—especially as it relates to homeland security. The concept, however, cannot be perceived as a panacea for a community's crime problem, and it involves a long-term political and fiscal commitment. Recall that team police programs were shelved once federal or state grant support ended. The key players for any change are line and middle-management personnel in the department, which can be a difficult process in view of our discussion on police subculture. As discussed in the chapter, community policing personnel and programs are being directed to address homeland security issues under the aegis of intelligence-led policing.

Questions for Review

1. What is meant by traditional police patrol? What activities are the usual components of traditional police patrol?
2. What is the significance of the Kansas City Study?
3. What variables might lead one to conclude that traditional police patrol is a waste of time?
4. How are many agencies rethinking traditional police patrol in terms of administrative tasks and nonessential calls?
5. Why is crime analysis an important component of directed patrol?
6. What is the track record of cities that have experimented with POP and COP?
7. How does directed patrol differ from specialized patrol? What are some examples of specialized patrol?
8. Why might proactive patrol be an important police methodology in the future?
9. Discuss the positive and negative attributes of community policing.
10. Explain the differences between tactical patrol and team policing.
11. Present the various components needed for community policing implementation.
12. Why is intelligence-led policing an important concept?
13. What is predictive policing and how may this be a useful future way to deal with crime?

Class Project

Select three major police departments in three different states, and locate them on the Internet. From their homepage, go to those sites that publicize community policing programs. Write a brief description of each program, and compare them with your selections and those of your classmates. See if any of the programs are related to homeland security concerns. What methods are used to inform the public about crime and emergency situations?

From the information gathered, analyze whether the programs fit the formal definition of community policing or community relations.

Web Works

The main source of national trends and training programs on community policing can be found at the Office of Community-Oriented Policing Services (COPS) at cops.usdoj.gov/. Related national and regional community policing efforts can be obtained through Google and Yahoo by typing "community policing in the United States."

Information on police mountain bike programs can be reviewed at the International Police Mountain Bike Association Web site at ipmba.org.

Patrol issues presented in this chapter are further discussed by Police Executive Research Forum (policeforum.org) and the International Association of Chiefs of Police (theiacp.org).

References

ACLU of Massachusetts. "What's Predictive Policing?" (n.d.). Accessed at privacysos.org/predictive on December 10, 2013.

Alpert, Geoffrey P. "Pursuit Driving: Planning Policies and Action from Agency, Offer and Public Information." *Police Forum* (January 1997b), pp. 1–12.

_____. *Helicopter in Pursuit Operations.* Washington, D.C.: National Institute of Justice, 1998.

Alpert, Geoffrey P., and Andrew Clarke. "*County of Sacramento* v. *Lewis:* Its Impact and Unresolved Issues." *Police Forum* (October 1998), pp. 1–9.

Beck, Charlie, and Colleen McCue. "Predictive Policing: What Can We Learn From Wal-Mart and Amazon About Fighting Crime in a Recession." *The Police Chief.* Accessed on December 10, 2013 at police chiefmagazine.or/magazine/index.cfm?fuseaction

Carter, David. *Law Enforcement Intelligence: A Guide for State, Local and Tribal Law Enforcement Agencies.* Washington, D.C.: U.S. Department of Justice, Office of Community Oriented Policing Services, 2004.

Center for Problem-Oriented Policing, 2013. Retrieved from popcenter.org/about/CenterforProblem-OrientedPolicing

Connel, Nadine M., Kristen Miggan, and Jean M. McGlen. "Can a Community Policing Initiative Reduce Serious Crime." *Police Quarterly*, 11, no. 2 (June 2008), pp. 127–150.

Dunsworth, Terrence, and Gregory Mills. *National Evaluation of Weed and Seed.* Washington, D.C.: U.S. Department of Justice, 1999.

Edgar, James M., et al. *Team Policing: A Selected Bibliography.* Washington, D.C.: U.S. Government Printing Office, 1976.

Friend, Zach. "Predictive Policing: Using Technology to Reduce Crime (April 2013)." FBI Law Enforcement Bulletin. Accessed on December 10, 2013 at fbi/gov/stats-services/publications/law

Goldstein, Herman. "Improving Policing: A Problem-Oriented Approach." *Crime and Delinquency*, 25 (1979), pp. 236–258.

_____. *Problem-Oriented Policing.* New York: McGraw-Hill, 1990.

Greene, Jack R. "Police and Community Relations: Where Have We Been and Where Are We Going?" In *Critical Issues in Policing.* Prospect Heights, Ill.: Waveland Press, 1989, pp. 349–368.

Kelling, George. *Foot Patrol.* Washington, D.C.: National Institute of Justice, 1987.

Kelling, George, and William J. Bratton. *Implementing Community Policing: The Administrative Problem.* Washington, D.C.: U.S. Department of Justice, 1993.

Mazerolle, L., D. Rogan, J. Frank, C. Famega, and J. Eck. *Managing Citizen Calls to the Police: An Assessment of Non-emergency Call Systems*, 2003. Retrieved from ncjrs.gov/pdffiles1/nij/grants/199060.pdf

Miller, Linda S., and Karen M. Hess. *Community Policing: Partnership for Problem Solving* (4th ed.). Belmont, Calif.: Wadsworth/Thompson, 2005.

New Hartford Police Department. *General Order Criminal Intelligence.* New Hartford, N.Y.: 2007.

Petersilia, Joan. *The Influence of Research on Policing.* Santa Monica, CA: Rand Corporation, 1987.

Reiss, Albert J., Jr. *The Police and the Public.* New Haven, Conn.: Yale University Press, 1971.

Rubin, J. "LAPD Tries New Policies To Cut Costly, Dangerous Traffic Crashes." *Los Angeles Times*, 2012. Retrieved from articles.latimes.com/2012/jan/22/local/la-me-lapd-traffic-20120123

Sherman, L.W. *Team Policing: Seven Case Studies.* Washington, D.C.: University City Science Center, 1976.

_____. *Neighborhood Safety.* Washington, D.C.: National Institute of Justice, 1987.

_____. *Policing Domestic Violence.* New York: The Free Press, 1992.

Skogan, Wesley G. "The Community Role in Community Policing." *National Institute of Justice Journal* (August 1996), pp. 31–32.

Sparrow, Malcolm K. *Implementing Community Policing.* Washington, D.C.: National Institute of Justice, 1988.

Spelman, William, and John E. Eck. "Newport News Tests Problem-Oriented Policing." *National Institute of Justice Reports* (January/February 1987a), pp. 2–8.

Thibault, Edward. "The Blue Milieu: Police as a Vocational Subculture." In John W. Bizzack, ed., *New Perspectives: Issues in Policing.* Lexington, Ky.: Autumn House, 1992.

United States Bureau of Justice Statistics. *Community Policing.* 2012. Retrieved from bjs.gov/index.cfm?ty=tp&tid=81

United States Department of Justice. *FY 2014 Budget Request.* Retrieved from justice.gov/jmd/2014factsheets/state-local.pdf

U.S. Department of Justice. *28 Code of Federal Regulations Part 23.* Washington, D.C.: Federal Register, December 30, 1998.

United States Department of Justice, Community Oriented Policing Services, 2013.

U.S. Department of Justice, Office of Justice Programs. Recovery Act. Web posted at ojp.gov/recovery/. Accessed on June 5, 2009.

U.S. Department of Justice. *Executive Office for Weed and Seed: Implementation Manual.* Washington, D.C.: Office of Justice Programs (n.d.).

Vandecovering, Crystal. *Weed and Seed Program: Rome, New York.* Unpublished report, Utica College, 2006.

Westley, William. *Violence and the Police.* Cambridge, Mass.: MIT Press, 1970.

Wilson, James Q. *Thinking About Crime.* New York: Basic Books, 1975.

Wilson, James Q., and George L. Keating. "Broken Windows." *The Atlantic Monthly,* March 1982, pp. 29–38.

9   Basic Line Functions

KEY TERMS

Amber Alert

Boston Gun Project

career criminals

case screening

doli incapax

Drug Abuse Resistance Education (DARE)

informant

In re Gault

neutral zone

parens patriae

PRELIMINARY

racial profiling

station-house probation

status offenses

vice

Although patrol is a major line function, policing encompasses a variety of other functions designed to provide an entire range of law enforcement services to the community. These services can be classified as

- Traffic
- Vice
- Juvenile
- Investigations

Other specialized line functions include hostage and negotiating teams, arson and narcotics task forces, and emergency services.

In larger departments, these functions—as well as patrol—are organized as separate entities and are assigned specific responsibilities; in smaller departments, each officer may provide the entire range of services. During one tour of duty, it would not be unusual for a village police officer to investigate a car accident, follow through on a continuing burglary investigation, and arrest a juvenile suspect. In larger departments, these tasks would be handled separately by the traffic division, the investigation unit, and the juvenile unit.

The number of divisions that exist in a department depends on the size and history of both the community and the law enforcement agency. Specific problems may warrant the creation of new organizational units. A city with a large financial community may have a computer/financial fraud unit. In one department of 140 sworn officers, the traffic division handled all matters related to traffic enforcement: accident investigations/reconstruction), issuing parking tickets, processing drunk-driving arrests, and even supervising the installation of traffic signs. In another department of similar size, these tasks were delegated as general patrol work.

In discussing this matter of police line functions, it must be stressed that although similar tasks need to be carried out and thus the general descriptions are useful, specific organizational structures will vary. The variables of agency size, community need, and history are of great importance when making realistic comparisons of police organizational structure.

GENERALIST–SPECIALIST CONTROVERSY

A question that normally arises at this point is: Why not simply have the patrol officer handle every type of complaint and situation? This is the standard generalist-versus-specialist argument that police have been engaged in for decades. Realizing that all police officers have to be generalists to some extent, there are good arguments for specialization and the organization of departments into specific divisions.

The first major argument is that of control. Especially in larger departments with hundreds of personnel, organization into divisions is a mechanism with which to direct the overall activities of the agency. Thus, personnel are allocated according to bureau or division to address specifics in a certain category of police problems.

Second, priorities have to be set, and work has to get done in an organized manner. Given the wide range of tasks that police agencies confront, the commander of a division and the chief in charge of all divisions can set up priorities. The delegation of duties by division or squad is traditionally taken to remedy the delivery of specific police services. For example, there may be an outcry in the community concerning juvenile crime. The resources of the juvenile division can be expanded, and the commander in charge of that division can set priorities, depending on community demand.

Finally, there is the traditional argument—namely, that specialization leads to expertise and that the police agency receives the benefit of efficient, knowledgeable experts by organizing according to divisions. Over time, the delegation of the same type of responsibilities to the same officers means that these officers are continually gathering current information concerning these specialized problems. It means that the department can allocate its in-service training resources to send a few specialists to high-powered training sessions in their fields of expertise. These expert professional law enforcement officers can then apply this specialized knowledge in their divisions. As a consequence, the department does not need to send every officer to every specialized training session to have their offices informed and up-to-date.

An example might help to clarify this issue. An officer assigned to the traffic division dealing with traffic and accident investigation will be expected to be familiar with a wide variety of traffic topics. Subspecialties might be developed in traffic-flow planning, community education, accident reconstruction, vehicle and traffic law, and drunk driving. Another officer might develop expertise in disaster planning (e.g., blizzards, hurricanes, and floods and their relationship to traffic flow and accidents).

Looking at the other side of the generalist–specialist controversy, what occurs when specialization goes too far? The answer is often that communication breaks down among divisions and individual commanders begin to build bureaucratic empires, where one bureau tries to outdo another in competition for perceived glory and resources.

This happens too often in the competition between the patrol and detective divisions. Patrol officers are tightly supervised and are expected to control the crime scene and to report the crime to the detective division. Detectives are expected to give the reporting officers credit for their work and to follow up the crime with analysis and investigation. Patrol officers are often jealous of the status that an officer in the detective division enjoys. They also feel that patrol officers may be the first on the scene but the last to receive credit and praise. Often, detectives do feel they are superior and neglect the patrol officers. Over time this can result in patrol officers rationalizing, "Why go out of our way for those guys?" or "Let the detectives do it; it's not our job." Management has to be aware of these tendencies in all divisions and take steps to improve communication continually.

In discussing the duties and responsibilities of line functions, we will also be looking at certain general principles that can lead to managerial improvements:

1. Assignments for all personnel should be based on the assumption that the job should present new challenges and lead to the acquisition and development of professional skills.
2. The best person should be selected for the job based on ability, credentials, and track record.
3. Police agencies should accept that there is a need for certain specialists but should keep the number of specialists and their areas of specialization within reason.
4. Periodically, each agency should review the number of subgroups that exist in the formal organization and the need for their existence. This evaluation should take place in terms of each bureau's contribution to the police mission and whether its functions should be merged or returned to another bureau or division (e.g., patrol).

In agencies where the patrol officer is a generalist, performance improvement is best reviewed by tasks rather than by bureaucratic function. This topic is discussed in Chapter 8.

TRAFFIC

As the United States continues to rely on automobile transportation, traffic patterns and enforcement remain very important. Throughout the country, suburbs continue to proliferate outside central cities, resulting in traffic congestion and flow problems. The new problems faced by highway police units include major traffic tie-ups from even the most minor accidents, aggressive driving on freeways, and assaults with vehicles and weapons between drivers engaged in aggressive traffic behaviors, often referred to as *road rage*. In many states, there has been an increase in new traffic safety laws, such as mandatory seat-belt and child-restraint use, and an aggressive stance toward driving while under the influence of alcohol or drugs. A major issue in traffic safety today is the increase in distracted driving accidents from the use of cell phones especially while texting messages. Traffic enforcement can often yield other benefits, such as the solving of major cases. Recall that a traffic stop for a minor violation resulted in the arrest of Oklahoma City bomber Timothy McVeigh.

Against this background, the role of the police in this function is varied, involving the following:

- Elimination of accident causes and congestion
- Identification of potential traffic problems and hazards and hazardous driving trends
- Regulation of parking on the street and at municipal facilities

- Investigation of property damage and personal injury automobile accidents
- Direction of public awareness toward the proper use of motor vehicles and bicycles
- Arrest of offenders

Effective Management in Traffic Matters

The amount of resources and the number of personnel devoted to traffic enforcement depend, of course, on the needs of the community. We do, however, offer the following guidelines:

1. Parking enforcement should be the responsibility of civilians or traffic wardens. There is little need for trained police officers to be solely involved with issuing parking tickets or directing traffic. These functions are, for the most part, mechanical and do not require a high level of expertise.
2. Patrol officers should be trained in all areas of traffic enforcement, including preliminary accident investigations, use of speed- and alcohol-detection devices, and knowledge of vehicle and traffic laws. This aspect of police training is especially important because of the high number of traffic cases that make their way into civil and criminal courts and require review of the actions of the investigating officers and the policies of the department.
3. Certain officers, according to their interests, should be trained in specialized topics, such as traffic planning, fatality investigation, and community-awareness programs. A number of excellent programs, funded by state and federal highway safety grants, are available for such training. One example is the course offered by the Traffic Institute sponsored by Northwestern University.
4. Greater attention needs to be paid to driving while ability impaired because of the use of either illegal or prescription drugs. While great attention and training is spent on drunk driving based on the consumption of alcohol, there is a need for drug recognition experts to deal with impaired driving after using drugs with or without a prescription. At this time many smaller departments lack trained drug recognition experts to deal with this emerging traffic safety hazard.

Highways remain the primary means of inter- and intrastate commerce for goods and services. As a result, many state police agencies have highway units devoted to the enforcement of commercial trucking and bus regulations related to trailer weight, hazardous cargo, and driver records.

The use of vehicles as the primary means of drug transportation results in aggressive enforcement of state drug statutes based on traffic enforcement stops. This has resulted in increased high-speed chases and high-risk traffic stops between officers and narcotics traffickers. It has also raised the issue of allegedly biased traffic stops by police in which African American or Hispanic drivers are stopped with greater frequency than white drivers.

Technology continues to change the face of traffic enforcement. While pullovers by a single patrol unit via radar remain the mainstay of enforcement, new strategies involve targeting traffic problem areas with multijurisdictional units. In certain municipalities, digital cameras mounted on light poles activate when a driver goes through a red light. The summons is then mailed to the owner of the vehicle. There is some controversy on this practice as to whether this enforcement reduces accidents or is just another way to raise money for the municipality. In one state, state patrol officers use cameras mounted in a van to capture speeders on major expressways, eliminating pullovers in densely driven areas. License readers installed in patrol vehicles yield a number of quick reads for stolen vehicles, suspended licenses, and revoked registration information, as was discussed in Chapter 8.

Racial Profiling

Major incidents in New Jersey, Maryland, and Colorado made **racial profiling** a police management problem in the late 1990s. By September 2002, 21 states had adopted legislation or policies to prevent racial profiling or racial stereotyping. In many departments, traffic officers are expected to check off the race of the citizen involved in a traffic stop on a traffic form. In basic form, racial profiling means that the person is stopped or questioned on the basis of race alone without any probable cause.

Racial profiling in traffic enforcement can be traced to 1984 with the Drug Enforcement Administration's (DEA) Operation Pipeline. For this program, the DEA created a profile of major drug "mule" drivers in Florida driving north: two black or Hispanic males in a fast rented car or a junker, one ignition key, driving above the posted speed limit in shifts with fast-food wrappers in the car, pillows and blankets for sleeping, and air fresheners to conceal the smell of drugs. This became the rationale for racial profiling and the basis for a number of major lawsuits, which include the following:

> *State of New Jersey* v. *Pedro et al.* (1996). Seventeen drug charges based on vehicle stops made by the southern New Jersey drug intervention unit were rejected because of racial profiling. While 15 percent of motorists violating traffic laws were black, as determined by a rolling survey by John Lambreth of Temple University, 46 percent of violators pulled over in a 40-month period on the New Jersey Turnpike were black. Lambreth said black drivers were pulled over 4.85 times more often than white drivers. The court concluded that the "de facto policy of targeting Blacks for investigation and arrest" violated equal protection and due process. The evidence was dismissed. (Buerger and Farrell, 2002: 277–79)
>
> *Wilkins* v. *Maryland State Police* (1992). Police patrols stopped Robert Wilkins and his family and made them stand by the side of the road in the dark and the rain while a drug-sniffing dog was brought to the scene. No drugs were found, and the driver was issued a ticket and let go. Professor Lambreth did another rolling survey. Of the 823 searches done by Maryland State Troopers on the I–95 corridor, 661 were of minority motorists. Contraband was found in 29.9 percent of the stops, which was comparable to statewide stops. The case was settled and sealed before trial.
>
> *Whitefield* v. *Board of Commissioners of Eagle County, Colorado* (1993). The High County Drug Task Force used the Operation Pipeline profile to stop cars. The court ruled that the profile did not constitute probable cause for stopping cars and suppressed 23 pounds of cocaine as evidence. The court stated, "An equation of race with suspicious criminal activity would be nothing more than a racist assumption." It was unconstitutional to stop cars based solely on "race, ethnicity or state of residence." (Buerger and Farrell, 2002: 283–84)

A major case that attracted national attention occurred on the New Jersey Turnpike. On April 23, 1998, at 11:00 P.M., two New Jersey state troopers stopped three Hispanic males and one black male. Their Dodge Caravan rolled slowly backward at one point, and the troopers fired 11 shots into the vehicle, wounding three occupants. A search found no drugs or contraband. A reenactment a year later by a team of experts showed that the whole incident took 10 seconds. Lawyers asserted a pattern of discriminatory stops by troopers. A grand jury indicted the officers for attempted murder.

The Department of Justice threatened to file a suit based on a pattern and practice of racial discrimination on traffic stops by the New Jersey State Police. In 2000, the state of New Jersey settled the civil lawsuit for $12.95 million. The two troopers pleaded guilty to obstructing the investigation by lying about the race of the drivers they had stopped on other occasions to conceal that they were singling out blacks and Hispanics, and they paid a fine of $280 each. Based on 91,000 pages of documents, the New Jersey Attorney General said that 8 out of 10 automobile searches by state troopers were done on vehicles driven by Hispanics or blacks. A consent decree signed with the Justice Department "included a prohibition against relying on race or national or ethnic origin of motorist in selecting vehicles for stops and . . . post-stop actions" (Buerger and Farrell, 2002: 280–91).

Racial profiling is also an issue in the fight against terrorism. However, specific information on members of a group or organization wanted for crimes or acts of terror that includes race as a descriptor may be used as a probable cause for stopping a citizen. A member of California's Diversity Advisory Council for Police Officers, Rabbi David Lapin (2002: 9) states that this would be termed as "descriptive profile" based on intelligence or probable cause if the group has decreed that it will use weapons and bombs to kill people to advance their cause (Lapin, 2002).

VICE

Vice crimes are generally considered to be crimes against public morals. Examples of vice offenses are

- Pornography
- Prostitution
- Gambling
- Illegal drugs (controlled substances)
- Illegal sale and manufacture of alcohol

These have historically been the province of the police because of public clamor for enforcement of laws created to eliminate these activities.

In theory, these offenses are considered victimless, or nonpredatory, crimes. The offender is normally offering a service or buying a service. If there were no customers for vice crimes, there would be no vice. In the area of drug addiction, however, there are secondary victims, as the drug addict attempts to "feed his habit" through street crimes. Also, there are cases of pimps placing young women on habit-forming drugs to enslave them in a life of prostitution. However, because these crimes are perceived as victimless by much of the public, vice laws are especially hard to enforce. In some communities, there is political pressure not to enforce certain vice laws. In other locales, what is a crime in one community may be legal a few feet across the county or state line. This is especially true in states that have legalized gambling.

The term *organized crime* often comes up when discussing organizational dimensions of vice activity. Based on our experience, organized crime occurs when there is a continuing criminal economic enterprise with a succession of leadership. From a media perspective, there is the Italian mafia, the Russian mafia, the Colombian mafia, and so on. However, organized criminal enterprises and groups have to be studied from local, regional, national, and international perspectives in terms of activities, leadership succession, and their involvement in legal and illegal activities.

Drugs

In *The War on Drugs*, James Inciardi (1986: 131–32) concluded that "drug related crime is out of control." In 1992, he reported a decline in drug use but noted, "The drug trafficking/terrorism connection is important primarily because one tends to facilitate the other" (Inciardi, 1991: 227). Drugs, although a major vice problem, had moved beyond the streets to fund terrorism. In *The American Drug Scene*, Inciardi (1995: ix) says, "If anything has been learned about drug use in the United States, it is an awareness that the problem is dynamic and continuous."

Drug epidemics come and go. Heroin was popular for a few years, then crack/cocaine raged across the nation, and at the beginning of the twenty-first century, designer drugs and ecstasy became popular. Marijuana is always popular, and cross-addicted alcoholics are common at "hot spot" bars. Meanwhile, we constantly hear from prison authorities that well over 80 percent of incarcerated felons are in prison because of crimes related to drugs and alcohol abuse. The felons feed their drug habits, selling and using drugs, and are usually high while they commit property and violent crimes. At this time, there is a movement by many states to legalize marijuana for medical uses and to decriminalize offenders found with small quantities, which will require law enforcement to adjust current drug investigation/arrest procedures.

Today from an abuse perspective, prescription drugs for pain control have entered the high abuse category as they are either stolen, resold, overprescribed, or acquired by forays into medicine cabinets especially by teenagers. In the mean time, newer chemical substances called "bath salts" have entered the scene.

In *Criminology Today*, Schmalleger (2002: 412) concluded: "Drug abuse has a long and varied history in American society. . . . Although recent statistics show some declines, a hard-core population of illicit drug users remains." Larry Siegel (2003: 432) summarizes the current situation in *Criminology*:

> The problem of drug abuse stretches across the United States. Large urban areas are beset by drug-dealing gangs, drug users who engage in crime to support their habits and alcohol related violence. Rural areas are important staging centers for the shipment of drugs across the country and are often the production sites for synthetic drugs and marijuana farming.

Some are advocating the legalization of drugs out of frustration, while others want to turn the interdiction of drugs into the country over to the military. The "war on drugs" has largely failed, and most therapeutic intervention programs also have overwhelming failure rates. Police efforts have had some limited success in displacing drugs from one neighborhood to another, with some suppression of drug use and drug-related crime. At the same time, rogue countries like Jamaica, Mexico, and the Dominican Republic protect illicit trade traffickers who flood the United States with a wide variety of illegal drugs.

Suppressing the drug trade comes at enormous costs to local police departments. The federal law agencies have been largely ineffective. Regional police efforts combined with government support of drug intervention therapy have shown some promise, but current local approaches are largely futile. The problem is not going away, and there is a great need for proactive regional and federal cooperation.

Prostitution

Prostitution continues to flourish in most heavily populated metropolitan areas (Lyman and Potter, 2000). The red-light district and brothels, which operated under the protection of gangsters, politicians, and the police, have been replaced by streetwalkers, massage parlors, dating services, and "weekend warriors." The range of organization and the need for protection vary based on the number of employees and the need for payoffs to local officials.

Regardless of any controversy over the organizational structure of syndicated crime, vice street offenses present police agencies with an immediate host of problems, especially if they cluster in a specific area. Beyond the commission of the offense, a variety of secondary effects can occur: Customers may be "rolled," other crimes may be committed, and the area may undergo an economic decline. Vice activity that operates without interference by the police, either in a concentrated or a nonconcentrated area (citywide), is perceived by the public to mean that the police are being paid to look the other way.

The enforcement of vice laws is equally frustrating to police officers. With the length of time it takes to process arrest paperwork, and other administrative tasks following an arrest, it is feasible that the offender could be free to leave the station before the arresting officer. Obviously, that's a problem.

This is due to the relative ease with which offenders raise bail or pay the fines that are meted out by the courts. Police officers often agree with a common public attitude that vice offenses are less harmful than violent crimes. This view can be reflected in organizational policy in terms of low priority for vice enforcement.

Gambling enforcement can be a double-edged sword for law enforcement. Certainly, if gambling is illegal in a jurisdiction, enforcing gambling laws falls under the obligation of law enforcement. However, there are many negative consequences attached to a gambling investigation for a police agency, not the least of which is the lack of widespread community support. Many people enjoy low-scale gambling, such as during college basketball's March Madness, and feel that if they want to pay to join a local bar's tournament bracket, then that is their business. In addition, the personnel hours that must be committed to develop probable cause to intercept phone conversations, and then "sit on a wire" to record bets can be extremely costly to the police department, both in terms of budget and in the loss of personnel available for other assignments. One of the authors recalled his experience heading a detective unit for one of the larger police agencies in the country. He often dreaded the approach of the Super Bowl and March Madness, as both very often brought a call from a District Attorney asking for personnel to work a gambling investigation. It was always a balancing act between maintaining good inter-agency relations, enforcing existing laws, and retaining a fully operational investigative unit. Other crime didn't yield until the gambling season ended.

Vice Units

While some personnel should be given a long-term assignment to vice investigation to establish continuity, vice assignments should generally be of short duration. Continuity is needed to understand the scope of the problem and the nature of investigation methodology, to establish solid interjurisdictional working arrangements, and to train new officers. Short duration is needed for most vice assignments because faces soon become known, especially in undercover work, and officers lose much of their investigative value. Vice investigation is demoralizing, frustrating, and dangerous and often without the kind of backup officers would like to have. It takes a special kind of individual to work undercover, and vice assignments create definite morale and personnel problems for police management.

Units to investigate organized crime are usually found in federal law enforcement agencies and in large city and state police departments because of the multijurisdictional and international nature of cases. Investigations are very expensive in terms of personnel and equipment requirements. Organized crime units investigate the following activities (Albanese et al., 2003):

1. The distribution and manufacturing of narcotics
2. Unlawful gambling enterprises
3. Professional theft and fencing networks
4. The lending of money at high rates of interest to be collected by force or financial takeover
5. Bribery, extortion, embezzlement, and fraud in unions and businesses

6. Corruption of public officials
7. Economic crimes involving financial offenses against businesses, investors, and consumers
8. Money laundering
9. Alien smuggling
10. Technology theft
11. Internet crimes, such as child pornography and identity theft

Since prosecution is so important in ongoing organized crime investigations, the most effective units are those that include representatives from county or federal district attorney's offices who can construct and manage cases involving economic criminal conspiracies, such as Racketeer Influenced Corrupt Organizations (RICO). They often involve grand jury investigations and the need for subpoena powers. There is also a need for additional funding for informants, equipment, and overtime for physical and electronic surveillance.

The organized crime unit needs state and federal and, at times, local representatives along with intelligence analysts and other experts. Areas of expertise include those that involve technical skills in the areas of photography, electronic surveillance, polished detective skills, and content expertise in the various areas of organized crime, such as narcotics and fraud. There is a need to include special security controls, including location and protection for informants and witnesses. Since much of this type of investigation, along with a spillover into white-collar crime investigation, means having to follow a line of money to discover the criminals and to convict them, an investigative accountant is essential to the work.

To be successful, there must be a major investment in skilled personnel and equipment accompanied by a great deal of multijurisdictional cooperation. With ongoing investigations, a screened representative from the local vice squad may prove useful. (*Screened* means that the individual has been carefully investigated in terms of the need for security for the entire investigation.)

Added to this area of crime investigation is computer crime. Computer crimes include a number of offenses, such as invading systems to scan information, change of data, transfer funds and steal money, or place a "bomb" in a program that will "zap" data. This category also includes the commission of crimes with the aid of a computer, such as a financial fraud. Because of increased reliance on computers for daily transactions in all areas of life, individual consumers and computer systems are subject to criminal use and invasion and destruction. Examples of computer crime in the daily news are common. However, computer crime investigation units on the state and local level are a rarity. Obviously, personnel involved in computer crime units must have advanced training in computer science and programming and Internet applications. Computer cases are difficult to investigate and to prosecute, mainly because most judges and juries have a difficult time understanding case evidence.

YOUTH SERVICES AND JUVENILE AID UNITS

The police are one of the main components in the criminal justice system with whom juvenile offenders come into contact, and the police confrontation is highly significant in determining the number and types of cases that eventually proceed to juvenile court. Many jurisdictions agree with the *least coercive* recommendation originally stated in the task force report *Juvenile Justice and Delinquency Prevention* (National Advisory Commission, 1976: 186): "To respect family autonomy and minimize coercive State intervention, law enforcement officers dealing with juveniles should be authorized and encouraged to use the least coercive among reasonable alternatives, consistent with preserving public safety, order and individual liberty."

Thus, in most jurisdictions, almost all police–juvenile interactions and confrontations result in informal action or are settled with warnings of future severe action. Most jurisdictions continue to follow the task force recommendations on when counseling and releasing should take place rather than court action. They instruct police officers to consider (National Advisory Commission, 1976: 210):

1. *The nature of the alleged delinquent act.* In cases of minor delinquent acts, such as disorderly conduct where there are no other serious negative factors, police should consider releasing the youth.
2. *The juvenile's previous behavioral history.* The presence or absence of a prior history of serious law violations should be given substantial weight in making a release decision.
3. *Circumstances possibly contributing to the alleged delinquent act.* Investigation may turn up important information about the youth's neighborhood or associates, which may be influencing negative behavior.
4. *The juvenile's willingness to change behavior.* The juvenile should demonstrate a cooperative attitude; assurance of good conduct is an important factor.
5. *Parental supervision.* The interest and attitude of the parents or guardians toward the juvenile and the alleged law violation, as well as their ability to provide the necessary supervision and guidance, are important considerations.

The task force also recommended interviewing the parents at home. Judgments can be best made by the police officer concerning the youth's living conditions and the ability of the parents to supervise the youth in the youth's home environment.

In cases that are more serious or that involve repeat offenders or suspects who have attitude problems, the result may be official action followed by an appearance in family court. This also happens when the complainant presses for some official action. In large departments, this action might take place at a juvenile bureau that is part of the investigation division; in medium-sized departments, this action might take place in a juvenile unit that is part of the patrol division; in smaller departments, most likely a juvenile officer who reports directly to the chief would handle this matter.

Background

Juvenile aid divisions were formed in the early part of the twentieth century in response to urban crime and related social problems involving children, many of whom were newly arrived immigrants. The legal and social reforms that gave certain protections and services to children were based, in part, on two theories developed in the common law: (1) *doli incapax* (a child under a certain age is incapable of wrongdoing) and (2) *parens patriae* (the state must assume the role of the parents if the parents cannot live up to their responsibilities in the care of the child). In all states, children under a certain age, usually 16, are accorded the title of *juvenile* for criminal and civil matters.

Until the 1960s, the rules of criminal prosecution for children regarding their legal rights under due process were ill defined. In 1967, in a case titled *In re Gault*, the U.S. Supreme Court ruled that children must be afforded the same legal protections as adults. In many localities, the investigation and prosecution of juvenile cases is strictly defined by state statute and is reinforced by rules and procedures of juvenile court. In most states, a juvenile suspect cannot be questioned unless accompanied by a parent. The place where the interrogation occurs has to have a nonpolice atmosphere, which is defined as being a room or office away from the mainstream of police activity. Juveniles cannot be confined in adult jail lockups but must be transported and held in special juvenile facilities.

The range of juvenile offenses, however, also incorporates offenses that would not be considered offenses if the act or activity were committed by an adult. We are referring here to **status offenses**. These include running away from home, truancy, and not behaving according to parental rules in the home.

Many officials and the general public remain concerned about the rise of juvenile crime versus the "revolving door" system of justice that appears to let juvenile suspects go free with no punishment. In his review of the criminal justice system, Charles E. Silberman (1980: 355) found that most juveniles did not receive any type of sentence in juvenile court until they had been before a judge four or five times.

As a result, many states lowered the age at which a juvenile would be treated as an adult if he or she committed a felony, which means criminal court and adult arrest procedures and incarceration. Thus, rape, robbery, arson, and murder became adult offenses if they occurred within a certain age bracket and under certain circumstances. The trend was to "get tough," a posture that will have a significant effect on how police behave with juvenile offenders. Today the pendulum is swinging in a different direction. In general a juvenile delinquent status occurs between the ages of 7 and 18 years; only two states including New York have designated 16 years of age for adult prosecution.

The Role of Juvenile Aid

The police juvenile aid operation or division performs a variety of activities. First, it acts as a protector of children's rights, seeing that the rules of criminal prosecution for criminal and status offenses are maintained. Second, it sees that the security of the community is maintained: The public has the right to be safe from youth crimes. Third, it must deal with children who are victims of parental abuse or neglect.

In summary, the juvenile aid division has the following responsibilities:

1. *Investigation of juvenile cases.* This involves not only criminal cases where the suspects may be juveniles but also cases where juveniles are victims. Generally, cases involving adult crimes committed by juveniles are handled by regular investigative and patrol personnel. When an arrest is made or a suspect is brought in for questioning, juvenile aid personnel should be notified. Those cases involving status offenses or child victims should be handled by the juvenile aid personnel. In many situations, cases of this nature do not involve a typical police response but demand patience, knowledge of referral agencies, family crisis intervention skills, and counseling techniques. The officer may need to handle child abuse. Or there may be cases of simple neglect. In one case, an officer walked into a home and saw a child being bathed in a tub with feces. It takes a strong stomach to handle these cases. Normally, social agencies are available to work with these parents, but in the long night hours, immediate police action may be necessary.

2. *Screening of cases.* Cases forwarded to the juvenile aid division must be screened for a future course of action. The recommendations of the investigator or the patrol officer should be taken into consideration in view of their familiarity with the circumstances surrounding the case. It is at this stage that the juvenile aid officer may wish to divert the case from the normal progression found in the criminal justice system to either a formal or an informal mode of treatment. Such options include referral to a community agency, police counseling, or **station-house probation**, where the offender reports to the juvenile aid

division on a regular basis to account for his or her actions during the week. The case may be disposed of if the situation warrants restitution and it is made, or if there are no grounds for future action.

3. *Preparation of cases for juvenile or family court.* The necessary paperwork and evidence must be gathered by the officer if the case is forwarded to the juvenile court. The experienced juvenile aid officer knows how to present the documentation needed for the court and is able to keep track of when the case will be called. The officer should follow the ultimate disposition of the case and advise the arresting officers of the results.

4. *Community liaison.* This is an important aspect of the juvenile aid function. The police should be viewed as the experts in all areas of crime in the community, especially that related to youth. This is important for the planning and funding of special programs undertaken by community groups for juveniles. At the same time, the police should maintain an active liaison with community groups that are involved in problems with juveniles, such as the YMCA/YWCA, Catholic Charities, substance abuse programs, and the school district.

   Another aspect of community liaison involves keeping abreast of community programs where children may be referred if special treatment is needed. These might include programs involving youth employment, professional counseling, vocational training, and recreational activities.

5. *Grant preparation.* Federal and state governments offer special funding to police and social service agencies and community consortiums for programs that address youth crime. Such programs might offer drug education, involve gang interdiction, or deal with at-risk youths. Thus, the juvenile aid division becomes an active stakeholder in these grant programs, either as a prime sponsor or as a source of data for the grant application.

6. *Investigation of missing children.* In response to a number of well-publicized child abductions, Congress created funding that gives states assistance in setting up **Amber Alert** systems. Named after Amber Hagerman, a nine-year-old girl kidnapped and murdered in Arlington, Texas, in 1996, the Amber Alert is activated when a child is reported abducted and in grave danger. Information on the victim, the suspect, and his or her vehicle and direction of travel would be distributed to area police departments, public broadcasts would be made by television and radio stations, and a message would be posted on reader boards at toll booths and along major highways. The concept here is to employ a major public alert to find the victim and suspect before too much time passes. At this time, the merits of this program are still debated; many child abductions are custodial situations in which one parent has taken the child from the other. Supporters of the program refer to various success stories in which abductions were thwarted, and the victims were rescued. To prevent these programs from becoming overused and ineffective, many police departments have strict guidelines before an alert can be activated.

7. *Sex offender monitoring.* National public policy today calls for the registration of sex offenders and the release of information to the public on where they reside. In addition, notification can be made to schools if a sex offender moves into a neighborhood. Further, in some communities, sex offenders are not allowed to live near school grounds, playgrounds, or any areas where children may converge. The main purpose of these efforts is to deter sex offenders from committing future acts, to assist the police in investigations, and to give public information on the whereabouts of sex offenders residing in the community. According to Rebovich and Martino (2007), sex offenders monitoring became an important public policy issue when a Bureau of Justice Statistics study indicated that

approximately 40 percent of offenders tended to repeat similar offenses. In addition, there had already been a number of major child abductions and murders resulting in public outcry, and state and national legislation for sex offender registration and notification. Previous federal laws enacted as a result of these major cases included the Jacob Wetterling Crimes Against Children and Sexually Violent Offender Registration Program of 1990 and Megan's Law of 1996, which together required states to create state database and to make the personal information on sex offenders available to the public. The definition of a sex offender includes persons who commit a wide range of sex crimes against both children and adults. Most states today have public notification processes that are available upon request or on the Internet to identify registered sex offenders with their description, address, and photograph.

On July 27, 2006, the Adam Walsh Act was signed into law, which created, among other provisions, the Sex Offender Registration and Notification Act. Walsh was a seven-year-old boy who was abducted and murdered in Florida in 1981. His father, John Walsh, founded the National Center for Missing and Exploited Children (NCMEC), which advocates for child victims' rights. He also hosted the TV show *America's Most Wanted* (Johnson, 2009). The Act requires each state to set minimum guidelines for sex offender registration and public notification. The Act created the National Sex Offender Registry, which is a national database for both adult and child sex offenders. Once registered with the state upon completion of a sentence, sex offenders are required to notify their registration collection agency of any address changes and to update their information on an annual basis including a photograph, with serious criminal consequences for failing to do so. Nevertheless, there are many offenders who do not keep their registration updated or fail to notify authorities if they move from one state to another.

In many departments, the juvenile office or a special unit for sex offender monitoring is responsible for monitoring the whereabouts of sex offenders in their jurisdiction. They also play an important role in using their information and databases in the event of a child kidnapping or any sex crime involving an unknown suspect.

Juvenile Record Keeping

Information regarding youth crime must be stored in an area that is maintained separately from adult files. In most cases, the case folder is confidential and not subject to any review except by youth-division personnel. At the same time, information on youth crime, projected trends, and gang activity must be available and disseminated to the department and, at times, to the community.

While all officers should have the training to deal in all aspects of juvenile crime, specialization in this area is needed because of the ever-changing rules and statutes on juvenile prosecution as well as the development of new skills and knowledge. In short, personnel assigned to juvenile duties should be trained for and considered experts on all matters of juvenile crime and procedure. They should be consulted by members of the department for their expertise and continually called on for juvenile interactions, especially by the patrol section.

Personnel Selection for Juvenile Aid

In the past, the juvenile aid units were staffed by female officers and older male "father figure" officers. This was unfair to these officers since it stereotyped their professional roles. Personnel in juvenile departments should be highly trained individuals who are picked or volunteer because they have characteristics unique for the assignment of working with the juvenile offender.

In addition, it is recommended that qualified officers be able to pursue a career as police juvenile specialists and have the same opportunities for advancement and promotion as other officers in the department. Very little has changed in personnel selection since 1976.

Organization of Juvenile Aid Operations

As discussed earlier in this section, depending on the department, a specialized juvenile unit should be organized. In the smaller departments, at least one officer should have the specialized knowledge needed to deal with juvenile offenders.

A juvenile specialist provides the department with expertise in juvenile court procedures and juvenile offenses, which are normally handled differently from adult offenses. This officer can also develop useful ongoing relationships with whatever youth-service agencies exist in the area. He or she can even provide useful information to help the detective division solve cases. Many a case has been solved through information that juvenile offenders have mentioned casually to the juvenile police specialist.

Some departments have initiated a family service bureau. Most problems with juvenile offenders start and end in the home. Police officers have found time and again that the troubled youth of the community come from a disrupted family. To deal with this situation, some departments have combined juvenile services and domestic crisis intervention so that a total approach to potential offenders can be developed. Also, with the family service bureau approach, it may be more likely that the agency can provide proper referral service for the whole family. For example, the father might be an alcoholic, the mother might be out working, and there is no adult babysitter in the home. The older boy becomes a juvenile delinquent, while the younger children wander the streets. This family needs help, but it might not be provided if only one family member at a time is seen by police officers.

Officers in this juvenile unit could also specialize. One officer might learn the juvenile law and keep abreast of late-breaking legal developments. Another might specialize as a liaison officer with various juvenile agencies in the community. Another might develop relationships with local merchants to help solve and prevent juvenile crime against businesses and commercial establishments (shoplifting, burglary).

However the unit is organized, it can be of great value to the total department. The department will have its own team of experts on juvenile offenders to call on for their knowledge and training.

Gangs

Related to traditional juvenile aid responsibilities are gang monitoring and suppression. Juvenile gangs are defined as groups composed of youths between the ages of 11 and 18 who commit crimes over a long period of time. These groups have a succession of leadership, are clearly identifiable by various types of dress, and are held together by race, ethnicity, or common geographic area.

Dealing with youth gangs involves monitoring members, training parents and groups dealing with juveniles on gang trends, intercepting and investigating criminal activities, and counseling members when they decide to leave the gang. The activities of gang-intervention personnel also become pivotal when city or area resources are directed to gang suppression, whereby leading members are arrested and prosecuted.

Other gang and juvenile crime-suppression tactics used nationwide involve the following:

1. Active enforcement of school truancy statutes during school hours that could result in fines for students and parents.
2. Use of police patrol officers to conduct "spot checks" to review family court mandates involving curfews and association with gang members.
3. Use of court-mandated injunctions against juveniles wearing gang colors and apparel gathering in certain areas.
4. Active enforcement of state alcohol regulations that might result in revocation of driving privileges.
5. The use of organized crime intelligence and suppression tactics that include targeting gang leaders, their hangouts, and specific illegal activities that may fall under federal or state conspiracy statutes such as Racketeer Influenced Corrupt Organizations (RICO).

Model Youth Programs

The following descriptions are taken from a variety of police youth programs found in a variety of police agencies throughout the United States. Not every agency may wish to promote every item in this program. This model can, however, serve as a source of ideas when youth programs are developed for specific agencies. Let us examine some general guidelines for these programs:

1. The program should be open to all youths in the community regardless of gender or background. Although delinquent youths may be the target population, it would be unfortunate to have all program participants labeled "bad." This outcome would most likely further rather than prevent delinquency.
2. The program should not be expensive to join. Unless they steal or burglarize, most delinquent youths cannot afford expensive equipment. Thus, most programs have to be subsidized or not need expensive equipment. Once again, the program must be open to all the youths in the community.
3. The objectives of the program are to prevent delinquency and to enhance the image of police officers among youth of the community. Another objective is to develop informants and information concerning juvenile activity. Thus, many programs that may seem, on the surface, unrelated to police activities, such as baseball games or canoe trips, become valuable as part of the work of a police juvenile specialist.

Following is a discussion of a variety of programs that have been tried—some with more success than others. All programs must, of course, be adapted to local conditions.

MOBILE NEIGHBORHOOD WATCH   This program is patterned after traditional Neighborhood Watch programs. Participants use their own vehicles and are equipped with mobile phones to call in for police assistance with juvenile gang activity. Other activities may include graffiti removal, cleanup programs, and youth athletic programs.

NEUTRAL ZONES   Activities for area youth are provided in a designated area, known as a **neutral zone**, during high-crime hours or weekends. In Mountlake Terrace, Washington, the police department and volunteers run such a program in the local high school and provide meals, athletic opportunities, tutoring, and a food and clothing bank. According to the Crime Prevention Coalition (1996), a key concern is safety for the participants; thus, gang affiliation clothing is prohibited, and a pat-down search is required for entry into the area.

PARENT NETWORKS   Through this program, parents are urged to get to know their children's friends and to share ideas and concerns about behavior and activities. Juvenile units provide brochures and speakers to talk about networking and responsible hosting of parties and sleepovers.

EXPLORER POSTS   Many departments have established police explorer posts to work with youths who have indicated an interest in law enforcement. The Boy Scout model of exploring involves the formation of a post, sponsored by a host agency that will involve youths between the ages of 14 and 21 in a vocational or educational field.

The explorer concept is designed to allow youths to gain firsthand information on law enforcement operations and career possibilities. Explorers are assigned various station house tasks in addition to formal classroom learning. Many agencies even allow their explorers to ride along with regular officers on patrol. Explorer post members can also be of great assistance at parades, field days, and other large public gatherings requiring personnel for traffic and crowd control. Many departments issue their explorers a distinctive uniform for this purpose.

While the explorer concept offers unending possibilities for police–youth interaction, some drawbacks must be pointed out. Agencies that invest their total youth resources into exploring soon learn that not all youths are attracted to this type of program, especially those who would be termed "delinquent." On the other hand, some youths are attracted to police explorer or other volunteer groups since they provide an opportunity to act out authoritarian tendencies or to capture the excitement of police work. Members of explorer posts can be subject to ridicule and abuse in the school setting, since peers view them as police informants. Therefore, the continuance of such a program by the police agency can, at times, be a trying experience. The role of the police advisor will vary from personnel and recruitment manager to counselor and general troubleshooter.

SCHOOL LIAISON PROGRAMS   At one time, the presence of police patrol cars in the school parking lot signified that there was trouble of one form or another since school officials generally called for the police only as a last resort. Today, the police presence at school has become commonplace in many cities and communities because of the rise in weapons possessions, assaults, drug use, and property crime occurring during regular school hours. In many cities, police units patrol the school grounds and buildings as a normal assignment.

Shootings and murders of school pupils and teachers at various locations, including Columbine, Colorado, in 1999, and the more recent 2012 attack at the Sandy Hook Elementary School in Newtown, Connecticut, have prompted national debate on school violence. As a result, many schools and police agencies have initiated formal and informal relationships in dealing with school crime. Sitting down and discussing mutual concerns can be an important first step for many communities whose citizens may perceive the school and immediate grounds as "out of bounds" for regular police operations. An important part of this relationship is an agreement as to how and when police officers will be summoned for school-related situations, including arrests on campus or during school hours, the types of incidents that result in immediate dispatch of officers, the interception of nonstudent trespassers on school property, and crowd control at school events.

Other operational issues include random searches of lockers, patrol activity in parking lots, the use of non-lethal weapons against students, non-student access to facilities, and training for administrators and teachers on crisis management. As one solution, the school liaison officer or school resource officer program, a police officer is assigned to a school on a continuous basis. The officer's presence in the school is not so much for law enforcement or intelligence purposes as it is a learning and community resource for school administrators, teachers, and students. Here the officer might teach a course on crime problems or police operations, assist teachers in the preparation of course materials related to law enforcement and criminal justice, or meet informally with students to discuss issues that are of concern to them. Nationally, the National Association of School Resource Officers has been organized to discuss and advocate for policy changes related to shootings, bullying, truancy, drug use, and emergency planning. A list of topics being addressed by this group can be accessed at nasro.org.

EMERGENCY-RESPONSE PLANS   In addition to these programs, elementary, middle, and high schools have by state laws been required to develop emergency-response plans to deal with varied issues such as bomb threats and reports (a favorite during exams), armed intruders, evacuation protocols, and serious situations involving weather and hazardous materials. The school plan also includes a first-response protocol with the local police department for dealing with critical events. A first-response protocol may include communication between responding officers and school officials, staging areas, and most importantly, guidelines on when police are to be summoned to school grounds by school administrators or staff.

If anything, events involving armed student intruders have forced schools to engage in planning activities with local and regional police departments. Many school districts have encouraged departments to assign patrol officers to spend time in parking lots, cafeterias, and athletic fields as a means of increasing police presence.

Police departments have been forced to review patrol and operations tactics involving schools. Situations involving armed intruders are a case in point. Before 2000, most tactical responses called for the creation of a perimeter to contain the shooter and having a tactical team enter the building to stop the intruder. The main problem with this is that most areas do not have emergency-response teams. What is usual is that police officers from a number of agencies respond to the scene. The police response at Columbine, Colorado, was particularly criticized because the two shooters continued to kill and terrorize students and staff while police waited for a tactical team to assemble. The model that evolved from the Columbine experience became known as "Active Shooter," which involves the creation of quick-response groups of three to four officers to immediately enter the building and neutralize the shooter. This, of course, requires both training and practice between area police departments and school district officials.

Policing must always adapt to new events and conditions, however; and incidents such as the Newtown, CT, attack have led to a more engaged debate on the now generally accepted "Active Shooter" small-team response. Instead, since in many cases active shooters surrender or commit suicide upon first pressure from law enforcement, new models are calling for the first officer to engage the shooter immediately to reduce the likelihood of increased injuries and death. Even before Newtown, a strong argument was being made against the staging-for-a-team model, and for the first responding officer to attempt to engage the shooter. Haggard (2008) makes an excellent case for just such an argument, noting that, at the least, the shooter having to account for the single police officer necessarily alters the shooter's initial plans, and buys time for the innocent people in harm's way.

Drug Abuse Resistance Education (DARE)

Drug Abuse Resistance Education (DARE) is presented by specially trained officers to reduce drug, alcohol, and tobacco use by children. Instead of using scare tactics, the program teaches life skills, such as making choices and dealing with peer pressure. Program topics include drug information, assertiveness, stress, personal safety, how to say no, and the consequences of behavior. The 17-week elementary school curriculum for fifth and sixth graders is taught in classrooms during the regular school day. Many states adopted this program for implementation in all schools. Posters, T-shirts, DARE patrol vehicles, and other visual aids are provided through private contributions.

At one time, DARE was the most popular school-based police program in America with about 10,000 courses offered in the 1990s. In the late 1990s, researchers began to review the benefits of the DARE program. Sherman et al. (1998: 8) found that DARE "fails to reduce drug abuse when the original DARE curriculum is used (pre-1993)." Because of the criticism of criminal justice scholars, DARE administrators made some curriculum changes. Subsequent research found that the revised program had little impact on future drug and alcohol use. Thus, as it stands today, DARE seems to be a fine public-relations program for both police and schools, but it has little or no effect on changing behavior.

Other Police Youth Programs

One program that always generates local controversy is the juvenile curfew program. Curfew programs are becoming increasingly popular in high-crime neighborhoods around the country.

Teen curfew programs have been initiated in suburban or rural communities whereby teenagers under age 18 must be home by 10 P.M. Offenders who are found out on the streets can be escorted home and, along with their parents or guardians, summoned to court after repeat offenses. These programs are only effective if there is consistent enforcement by police and cooperation by schools and parents.

Similar to teen curfews, tried by many communities, major shopping malls have initiated programs whereby persons under 18 years of age cannot enter a mall unless accompanied by an adult over 21 years old. The purpose of the program is to reduce loitering and fights. There are variations of this program based on local economic realities. For example, some malls allow persons under age 18 to attend movie theaters after curfew hours.

Internet safety has become an often-requested program at schools at all levels because of the increase of stalking and identity theft. Topics include identity protection, ways stalkers operate, child porn methods, and ways to monitor computer use at home or in school libraries and laboratories.

In 1997, police departments began trying the DARE approach to decrease adolescent involvement in gangs. They call this program Gang Resistance and Education Training (GREAT). Uniformed police officers teach a nine-week course covering drug resistance; crime's impact on the school, the neighborhood, and victims; cultural sensitivity; conflict resolution; goal setting; and ways to fulfill personal needs without joining a gang. In one study, students who completed the program were compared to a nonstandardized group that did not complete the program. The study's authors say the program was successful based on self-reports, but they give no data. For example, they claim that the GREAT students "reported lower levels of gang affiliation and self-reported delinquency" than the control group (Howell and Hawkins, 1998: 296–97). The program had an after-school component.

Police liaison officers stationed inside schools counsel students, teach drug and alcohol classes, train school personnel and students in security precautions and crime-prevention techniques, and work to improve the safety of the school (Lawrence, 1998: 175). Small police departments also have special youth officers who work with individual youth as well as school administrators. Juvenile units in larger departments perform all of these tasks and become familiar with juvenile court and probation personnel and procedures. Gang units also include units that specialize in adolescent gang activity.

Ever since Big Brother and Big Sister programs, youth mentoring has been extremely popular throughout the United States. The federal government has spent millions of dollars on mentoring, with little or no scientific evaluation. However, mentoring programs do report positive results: Mentored youth are less likely to drop out of school, start using drugs, and engage in violent behavior.

ATHLETIC PROGRAMS   In the early part of the twentieth century, many urban police departments formed athletic programs to offer underprivileged youths a chance to participate in organized sports. Today, these Police Athletic Leagues still exist, but in name only. Private charities have taken over the entire responsibility for the programs. The police connection exists only for fund-raising purposes.

Sports and athletic programs provide a good environment and opportunity for police–youth interaction. In most communities, officer volunteers provide the staffing support. Frequently, the department or the police union may sponsor a team in an organized athletic program like Little League or youth hockey, with police officers acting as coaches or trainers.

OUTDOOR ADVENTURE PROGRAMS   These programs, variations of Outward Bound, offer youths a series of wilderness challenges. Programs of this nature cannot always be operated within a traditional shift and may run into political and union opposition, as the following case study illustrates.

In the absence of opposition, many programs operate successfully for many years. It is hard to feel hostile toward the police officer who guided you on an overnight camping trip, as many a potential delinquent and many an officer have found out to their mutual satisfaction.

CASE STUDY

One summer, the Oakdale Police Department embarked on an ambitious program for youths in the community: a 10-day canoe trip to the nearby Allegheny Mountains. Youths who had been in trouble with the police during the year were selected as participants. The objective was to give these youngsters a chance to spend time in the outdoors, learn camping skills, and meet the police in a nonconfrontational atmosphere.

One of the two officers assigned to the group was a state-certified guide. Various civilian volunteers also accompanied the group. The officers were paid their normal salaries.

The trip was successful, and plans were made for another trip the following year. Opposition to the idea arose from certain members of the city council, however, who argued that police officers should be paid to patrol city streets, not to conduct camping expeditions. As the controversy mounted, the officers argued that they could only accompany the group if they were paid overtime along with their normal salary, which, since they were away from home for 10 days, amounted to some 200 hours per officer.

Opposition to the program was stifled when community leaders and the local newspaper came out in total support of the program.

In the final compromise, it was decided that only youths who lived in the municipality and one police officer would be allowed to go. The trip, moreover, was reduced from 10 days to 7 days.

CASE STUDY

Deterring Youth Homicide: The Boston Gun Project

Cesare Beccaria (1738–1794) said that if deterrence is to work, justice must be swift and sure and that an increase in the severity of the punishment alone would not work. For more than 200 years, criminologists and criminal justice researchers have agreed with Beccaria's conclusion. In the ordinary workings of our justice system, with plea bargainings, lenient probation sentences for violent young offenders, and months and months of court delay, justice is not swift, certain, or even severe. For example, in Massachusetts, "the average number of days between arrest and conviction for felony cases disposed by state courts was 173" in 1992 (Kennedy, 1998: 4). That's almost six months! The **Boston Gun Project** aimed to turn this dismal state of affairs around, and it worked.

The Boston statistics were horrifying; 155 youthful victims had been killed by a gun or knife over a five-year period, and there were 125 youthful killers. The target group of teenage killers and victims were chronic offenders who had intense involvement with the criminal justice system with little or no effect on their behavior. The statistics showed the ineffectiveness of the case system to do anything about these homicides. Victims and killers averaged more than nine arraignments per youth, with 41 percent having more than 10 arraignments. There were a total of 1,009 arraignments for the 125 youthful killers. Twenty-six percent of the killers were on probation when they killed, with 54 percent having served time in a facility. The secret of success in Boston was immediate and massive action on the target group, using an interagency task force.

The Boston police targeted the illicit firearms market, while the interagency group targeted violent gang members using all the legal weapons available. They called it "pulling levers." They used federal prosecution rather than state prosecution because of the more severe punishment of a 10-year minimum sentence. There was also less delay in prosecution. The traditional "clunky" approach of the normal case process was rejected because there was no clear-cut message to the violent youth concerning swift and sure punishment.

The Ceasefire Working Group in Boston included the following:

- Boston police
- School police
- Parole officers
- Federal prosecutors
- Local prosecutors
- Clergy
- Youth connections
- Gang outreach workers
- Probation officers
- Neighborhood groups
- U.S. Drug Enforcement Agency
- U.S. Bureau of Alcohol, Tobacco, and Firearms
- U.S. Immigration and Naturalization Service

This group met every two weeks in addition to informal meetings.

The police met with violent gang members and told them they would use every legal tool they had to stop youth violence in Boston. They sent fliers to people involved in the drug and illicit gun markets. They made sure their target group knew exactly what was happening and repeatedly raided the violent gangs, with swift prosecution. When violent youth were on parole or probation, the police and the community correction professionals used close supervision and scrutiny. They made it clear to the gangs that violence would draw their attention and that this attention meant immediate action.

The cost of a gang homicide to the gang was immediate (Kennedy, 1998: 5–6):

[C]ash-flow problems caused by street drug market disruption, arrests for outstanding warrants, the humiliation of strict probation enforcement, even the possibility of severe sanctions brought by Federal involvement. Those costs were borne by the whole gang, not just the shooter.

The working group talked to the gangs continually and told them that violence would bring an immediate and strong response. They said to the gangs, "We're ready, we're watching. Who wants to be next?" (Kennedy, 1998: 6).

The Boston Gun Project worked. Boston's Ceasefire Working Group brought the city's youth homicide figures down by two-thirds.

This approach was also tried in Lowell, Massachusetts, and Minneapolis, Minnesota. In 1997, in Lowell, representatives from seven city and state agencies met 20 chronic offenders, 35 less chronic offenders, and 16 members of a street gang. Their message was as follows (Kennedy, 1998: 3):

"We just wanted to tell you that we know who you are," says assistant district attorney Michael Oritz. "If you continue to get into trouble you're going to end up in jail, or hurt, or even dead. But if you want to get out of a gang or back into school, or you want a job or counseling we're here to help."

Youth assaults declined, and there was an immediate quieting effect on a troubled school.

In Minneapolis, the police department arrested 12 members of a violent street gang, the Bogus Boyz, on federal weapons charges. Police and probation officers immediately visited 250 members of the most chronic gang offenders. Once again, the message was made clear to the target group (Kennedy, 1998: 3):

The Bogus Boyz's arrests were no accident. The Bogus Boyz were violent and their violence won them this treatment. This is how the city is

doing things from now on. We've got a dozen agencies from probation to the Feds, meeting regularly and focusing on gang violence. When we find it we're going to act.

"Patrol and gang unit police officers, together with ATF agents, also conducted saturation patrols 2 nights per week in targeted areas" (OJJDP, 1999: 59). This rapid response immediately reacted to shootings that might provoke gang revenge based on Boston's Operation.

They visited injured gang members in the hospitals and gave them a message: "Retaliation will not be tolerated. Remember the Bogus Boyz." Police and probation officers made unannounced visits to gang members' homes. The Law Enforcement Task Force met continually with neighborhood groups.

Homicides fell by 30 percent from 1996 to 1997. From 1997 to 1998, gang-related homicides as a percentage of all homicides fell from 52 to 23 percent (OJJDP, 1999: 60). A community survey showed a favorable response to safer neighborhoods. Crime was deterred, and crime rates came down.

This proactive approach worked because of immediate action that was swift and sure and because of intense interagency cooperation. One of the secrets of success was clear communication to the target group. The message was that the city would not put up with this violence and that all the authorities would act immediately. Credibility was created by continual and direct action.

INVESTIGATION

Investigation is the police activity concerned with the apprehension of criminals by the gathering of evidence leading to their arrest and the collection and presentation of evidence and testimony for the purpose of obtaining convictions. Investigation is normally divided into two major areas of activity: (1) the preliminary investigation normally carried out by officers in the uniform patrol division and (2) the follow-up investigation normally carried out by officers formally trained in investigative techniques and often part of a detective bureau.

In larger departments, a division or bureau is responsible for follow-up investigations; special investigations are assigned by the chief of police. In addition, this function also covers the recovery of stolen property, the gathering of criminal intelligence, and the preparation of cases for trial. Organizationally, this division may be called the *Detective, Central Investigation*, or *Criminal Investigation Division*. For our purposes, we will use the simple title of *Investigations*.

The role of the investigator is probably the most glamorous one in the police department. This modern Sherlock Holmes is portrayed in movies, television, and novels as a meticulous and tireless gatherer of evidence that miraculously leads to the arrest and conviction of criminals. As shown on the television series *Law and Order*, this super police officer is a bit unorthodox, normally at odds with his superiors, and normally willing to bend the rules, especially if this involves a deliberate violation of departmental directives. Embedded in a web of unsavory informers, the heroic investigator maintains his integrity in his unrelenting pursuit of crime and the master criminal.

The public, and to some extent the patrol officer, maintains this glorified notion of what an investigator is all about. Reality, as usual, is a mixture of fact and fiction. In some cases, detective work is all that the media says it is, but in most investigative jobs, it is a series of monotonous tasks that may or may not lead to a break in the case. Long, hard hours are put in interviewing neighbors after a major crime has taken place.

The use of forensic specialists at crime scenes and in laboratories is another recent theme on television and in movies. The reality is that many departments do not have access to this technology unless state or federal police agencies are summoned. Forensic personnel are usually not deployed except for major felony cases. All police investigators must be trained in the general scope of forensic science to understand the capabilities and limitations of such specialties as DNA testing, ballistics, microscopy, glass and paint analysis, and arson and explosives testing.

Many investigations are solved step by laborious step. Unlike the outcomes on television and in the movies, clearance on crimes investigated against property is less than 20 percent. This means that more than 80 percent of these types of crimes are never solved.

Preliminary Investigation

Cases would not be solved and offenders would not be arrested unless patrol officers were willing and able to use some preliminary investigation skills. The patrol officer's tasks in crime incidents normally entail both investigative and noninvestigative action. O. W. Wilson (1963: 282) gives us an excellent listing of these duties, under the heading **PRELIMINARY**:

P		Proceed to the scene with safety and dispatch.
R		Render assistance to the injured.
E		Effect arrest of perpetrator.
L		Locate and identify witnesses.
I		Interview complainant and witnesses.
M		Maintain scene and protect evidence.
I		Interrogate suspects.
N		Note all conditions, events, and remarks.
A		Arrange for collection of evidence.
R		Report incident fully and accurately.
Y		Yield responsibility to detectives.

One of the most important duties of the police officer responding to a crime call is to secure the crime scene. Cases are often lost because reporters, higher administrative officials, and various other personnel were allowed to indiscriminately contaminate a scene by handling evidence or walking through the area. There have even been cases of patrol officers taking weapons from a crime scene and turning them in two or three days later.

To win a case, there must be continuity of the evidence from the scene of the crime, to the vaults of the police laboratory or property room, to the hands of the prosecuting district attorney. Documentation must be made of any person who handled any piece of evidence and the circumstances under which the evidence was handled. Otherwise, alert defense lawyers can point to the discrepancies and win cases on technicalities.

It is a cardinal rule in most agencies that there should be only one person in charge at any crime scene. Once the scene is secured by the first officer at the scene, those assigned to evidence collection should be in charge. In some instances, this is the responding officer who is also a trained evidence technician, or it may necessitate summoning others with the necessary expertise and equipment. In any event, no one else—victims, witnesses, higher police officials, other police officers not assigned to the case, reporters, TV crew—should be permitted access to the crime scene area until a thorough examination has been completed and all photographs taken and evidence collected.

Evidence should be photographed in place, marked properly by the person discovering it, or by the officer so designated, placed in a sealed or appropriate container to prevent contamination, and prepared for transportation in a manner designed to maintain continuity.

The use of patrol officers for preliminary investigations, as O. W. Wilson points out, helps to relieve the detective force of many time-consuming tasks. This practice enables the detectives to concentrate their specialized skills on the tasks for which they have been trained. This use of the patrol officer is also important for the morale of the total agency.

Since a vast majority of positions in a police agency are for uniformed officers, the average officer will never have an opportunity to become an investigator. Expanding the uniformed officer's role, however, helps to (1) make the officer more aware of his or her basic responsibilities in protecting the scene, (2) promote the feeling of belonging to a team rather than being only a reporter called to contain the scene until the specialists arrive, and (3) enable the officer and the department to evaluate future assignments in the investigative areas.

Management should publicly acknowledge the positive contributions of the uniformed police officer as well as his or her detective counterpart to the successful conclusion of cases. When an officer can see that a positive contribution has been made and that he or she will receive recognition for that contribution, the officer will become a more positive and effective employee. However, patrol officers have limited training in investigative skills and have little time to give to any investigation if the municipality is to have effective police coverage. As a result, the time-consuming process of follow-up investigation is often assigned to specialists.

Follow-Up Investigation

The follow-up investigation of a criminal case involves a number of steps:

1. Reviewing all reports and statements relative to the offense and relating physical evidence gathered at the crime scene
2. If necessary, reinterviewing everyone identified by preliminary investigators as having information
3. Communicating necessary crime information to local and national crime-information networks

In most criminal cases, follow-up investigation involves looking for new witnesses with information or other evidence related to the crime and targeting potential suspects. This often occurs as a result of step 2 or canvassing the neighborhood for information. In major felony cases, investigators may reach out to the general public for information or the location of possible suspects through local and national crime programs like Crimestoppers.

For successful criminal investigations, a suspect is identified and questioned. Obtaining a confession from a suspect is an art in which the investigator must play a variety of human roles without having the suspect invoke his or her Fifth Amendment rights to counsel, at which time all questioning must cease. There are a number of criminal investigation courses sponsored by agencies and private concerns that focus on this one aspect. Then again, in some cases, the suspect voluntarily surrenders to clear his or her conscience or to "get it over with" in dealing with the criminal justice system.

An important and often overlooked part of the criminal investigation process involves filing appropriate criminal charges against the suspect, locating additional evidence, and obtaining information for later testimony. For major cases, this step involves working with county or state prosecutorial offices and provides the structure for future testimony in hearings and at trial.

As discussed in Chapter 7, one cannot underestimate the use of technology for evidence gathering, processing, and recording. Police investigators today have the luxury of comparing their information with various databases for suspects and modi operandi. At present, it is possible to do a computer search by alias, modus operandi, and thousands of other set sorts. Currently, systems are being interlocked so that a search can take in a local area, a county, a state, and in some instances the entire nation. However, no matter how good the tools, cases are ultimately solved by a well-trained investigator with an instinct for human nature and tendencies.

Traditional Structure

Historically, the investigations divisions of large urban police departments have been removed from the mainstream of police operations in the station houses. In general, a person enters a detective or investigative squad room by invitation only.

In the early days of policing in the United States, it was the prime task of the police investigator to cultivate informers. This was relatively easy at the time, as both the criminals and the police often grew up in the same neighborhoods. Related to the cultivation of informers was another task: the regulation of vice activity. The combination of these two tasks, with few records being made of payoffs for information and the considerable amounts of unrecorded money surrounding vice activity, led to police corruption, a problem that has persisted to some degree to the present.

However, as any competent detective today will tell you, informers are stock-in-trade. Detectives could not stay in business without their informers. In one crucial area, drug investigation, it has been well documented that these investigators could not operate without informants.

In police departments that have a traditional organizational structure, the detective or investigative division still retains an elite position. According to Niederhoffer (1969: 82), many patrol officers aspired to be detectives or investigators in the late 1960s—not only for new challenges but also to be able to wear street clothes and enjoy relative freedom from constant supervision. Given the present structure of most police departments, even decades later the same held true (Baley, 1994).

In some cases, appointment to investigator does not entail an increase in rank or pay. What does occur is a raise in status as defined by the police subculture. A major way to gain status in the uniformed culture of the police agency is to get out of uniform. This signifies that the officer is reaching a more professional, executive status where he or she is able to take command of important departmental matters.

Managing Criminal Investigations

The value of the traditional investigative division in terms of crime solving and contributions to the overall role of the police agency was questioned in a study conducted by Rand Corporation in the mid-1970s (Greenwood et al., 1976). In reviewing the operations of 23 police departments, the researchers found the following:

1. Clearance rates by investigation divisions are unreliable. Most crimes are cleared (an arrest made) during the initial investigation by patrol officers.
2. Many reported felonies receive no more than superficial attention. In reality, minor property crimes are not even investigated.
3. Too much physical evidence is collected. Most items of evidentiary nature cannot be processed in the crime laboratory.
4. For many cases, there is a serious gap between the prosecutor and the investigator. Key evidentiary facts that could help the prosecutor obtain a conviction are not documented by the investigator.
5. Too much time is spent locating witnesses and reviewing reports on cases that will never be solved. There is also considerable time that cannot be accounted for in the daily tour of duty, which leads to suspicion that too much time is spent on personal errands.

The conclusions raised point out that perhaps investigators, in the traditional sense, may not really be all that effective in solving crimes. Is this to say that all investigation units should be disbanded? Not really, but the Rand study shows the need for reappraising the tasks performed by investigative divisions.

Discussions and reviews on criminal investigation management by the Police Foundation, the American Management Association, and others concluded the following:

1. *The investigative role of police patrol officers must be enhanced.* As stated before, in many departments, the patrol officer is merely a reporter of crimes that come to the attention of the police; the important follow-up work is conducted by investigators. In many cases, when the investigation division is called to the crime scene, the same questions are asked over and over again to witnesses and victims. For minor felony property crimes, there is often a time lag of hours and perhaps days before the investigator actually arrives at the scene to ask questions, process the crime scene for evidence, and do neighborhood canvassing. At a minimum, patrol officers should be trained and equipped to secure evidence, take photographs, conduct neighborhood canvasses, and interrogate suspects. Accordingly, patrol-deployment plans must include ways to allow officers the time and latitude to follow up on their own cases.
2. *The issues involved in case screening must be decided.* How does one decide to continue further investigation of an incident? Typically, there is no set answer. By rule of thumb, a seasoned officer working a case can predict whether the incident has any chance of being solved based on the variety and amount of information gathered within a given period of time. One might ask: What types of information, what variety, and how much time? Experience might be the only answer. In an effort to quantify this process, researchers at Stanford University developed a screening instrument to predict the chance for future success of any given criminal investigation.

    An important aspect of **case screening**, and overall investigative processes, is the advisement of witnesses and crime victims on case progress. Too often, the victim who made a complaint to the police is kept in the dark as to what efforts were made to solve the case.

With case screening, the person making the complaint is advised when the case is suspended based on lack of leads, or variables, related to the case.

3. *The overall caseload must be managed.* Very often, the follow-up portion of an investigation lacks any sense of management. Investigative management programs developed in the 1980s address the following factors in determining what resources ought to be given to follow-up: the seriousness of the act, its solvability, and the availability of personnel. In reality, public outrage is another factor that comes into play. A basic investigative management plan includes the following:

a. *Centralized filing of all investigative folders.* This ends a tradition of officers keeping their own case folders in their desks and allows all investigative personnel and supervisors to review the folders and obtain information when necessary.

b. *Allocation of review dates by a supervisor.* Here, a date is assigned for all paperwork on the case to be brought up to date.

c. *Use of investigative checklists of standard operating procedures.* The officer investigator can present the steps he or she took in the investigation in checklist form, with further explanation, if needed, recorded in the narrative summary. The following is a listing of items to include on the checklist:

Investigators' Checklist
- Victim interviewed in person
- Victim interviewed by phone
- Victim interviewed at home (if not, explain)
- Witnesses interviewed in person
- Witnesses interviewed by phone
- Residential/commercial neighbors interviewed in person
- Residential/commercial neighbors interviewed by phone
- Officer on scene interviewed in person
- Crime scene visited
- Crime scene searched
- Area of crime canvassed
- Fingerprint search conducted
- Photos taken at scene
- Other forensic support provided
- Physical evidence search that produced leads
- Modus operandi files searched
- Photos of known criminals viewed by victim
- Major offenders' files accessed
- Local hospital record search (if appropriate)
- Prison records on recent releases checked
- Parole file checked
- Local police departments checked
- Checked recent aliases
- Informant file checked
- Unit members checked for information sources

Administrative attention must also focus on assigning cases, according to the resources of the department or the nature of the case at hand.

4. *It is critical for the police and prosecutors to maintain a professional relationship.* Both the police and prosecutors have the same goal—justice. Where problems develop is when objectives, policies, and procedures to reach that goal collide between agencies. In that regard, the police and prosecutor dramas on television can be quite accurate. However, it is mandatory for successful investigations and subsequent prosecutions that the leaders from the respective agencies, in this case, perhaps the commander of the police detective's unit and the chief assistant district attorney, maintain continuous contact and build a strong professional relationship. Further, it is paramount that both leaders not tolerate hints of derogatory comments from their personnel against the other agency personnel. Instead, the respective leaders must be cognizant of problems and mitigate them immediately to avoid the start of animosity between the two groups. A strong relationship built during non-stressful times will allow the relationship to remain solid.

Police training courses and various textbooks on criminal investigations recommend that prosecutors and investigators start communicating more frequently before the disposition of the case. This communication can be formal or informal. Participants often have initiated weekly meetings, with representatives of both sides talking about issues or procedures related to criminal investigation and prosecution. The MCI program advocates delegating one officer as liaison between the police's and the prosecutor's offices. The liaison officer's duties include mediating investigator and prosecutor grievances, providing advice on legal procedures and changes, and communicating day-to-day problems that arise between agencies. In Washington, D.C., the office of the general counsel plays an important role as liaison between the police and the prosecutor. This office reviews all cases that may be disposed of by plea bargaining or trial.

Investigative Issues and Concerns

The following issues and concerns regarding investigations confront police managers today.

CAREER CRIMINALS   **Career criminals** are offenders who actively pursue a life of crime. With help from the funding programs of the 1980s, many state and major municipal police agencies established programs to deal with these offenders. After identifying someone as a career criminal, police investigators use such methods as aggressive warrant enforcement, "most-wanted" fugitive advertisements in traditional and electronic media, prearrest surveillance, and working with the state's attorney for timely prosecution and maximum jail sentences. In other words, the offender becomes "targeted," and the objective is to prevent him or her from committing future offenses (Gay and Bowers, 1985).

INFORMANTS   **Informants** are usually divided into three categories: (1) offenders who have agreed to work with the state's attorney and investigators to prosecute associates or higher-level criminals in a crime organization; (2) offenders who have been let off from prosecution or given cash by an investigator in exchange for information; (3) citizens in a variety of occupations and situations who like working with the police and are willing to give information.

Informants in the first category are usually under some negotiated plea agreement arranged between their attorney and the state's attorney. The major issue always at hand is the extent to which the informant is given immunity for past offenses. Category 2 offenders—often called confidential informants (CIs)—present a special challenge in that the department or agency may have formal rules for the informants in terms of cash allocations and immunity from prosecution. Many seasoned investigators, however, like to have these people under their own control. This comes at a great risk when questions arise regarding who is working for whom. As shown in many movies and on television, information is given to informants that actually helps their criminal activities.

TERRORISM   Since the September 11, 2001, terrorist attacks on the United States, state and local law enforcement has been an active participant in the nation's overall homeland security posture and configuration (Davis et al., 2004; Howard and Riebling, 2005; Kelling and Bratton, 2006; Ortiz et al, 2007). At the time of the attacks, however, only a small fraction of state and local law enforcement agencies in the United States, made up primarily of state troopers, county sheriff deputies, and police officers, had personnel trained and committed to counter-terrorism responsibilities (Reaves & Hickman, 2002).

Prior to the attacks, the responsibility for investigating, detecting, and deterring international counter-terrorism fell almost exclusively upon federal law enforcement, while state and local law enforcement agencies focused their efforts and resources on law enforcement issues and concerns that were germane to their respective jurisdictions (Carafano et al., 2005; Deflam, 2002; Henry, 2002; Ickner, 2004; National Commission on Terrorist Attacks Upon the United States, 2004).

That the terrorist attacks altered the nation's perception of safety within the confines of U.S. borders is unquestioned. In response, all levels of law enforcement began to diversify their efforts to account for the international terrorist threat. The federal government restructured its law enforcement agencies under an overall homeland security umbrella, the U.S. Department of Homeland Security (DHS), making anti-terrorism the highest of priorities (US DHS). State governments followed suit, creating their own variations of the federal homeland security model, such as Alabama's Department of Homeland Security, Wyoming's Office of Homeland Security (OHS), and New Jersey's Office of Homeland Security and Preparedness (Alabama DHS, 2010; New Jersey Office of Homeland Security and Preparedness, 2010; Wyoming OHS, 2010).

Indeed, soon after *9/11*, the United States' overall law enforcement posture on anti-terrorism came under the scrutiny of congressional and commission reviews, such as the National Commission on Terrorist Attacks Upon the United States (The Commission). Generally, the focus of The Commission and the other panels that were convened, whether nationally or regionally, was to determine if more effective or efficient procedures could be put in place to make the country safer from international terrorist attack. In addition to calling for the significant restructuring of federal law enforcement coordination and procedures that was taking place, the various commission reviews generally pointed to the need for state and local law enforcement, with their large personnel numbers and more specific local knowledge, to assist and interface with the federal agencies already involved in anti-terrorism efforts (The Commission).

In partial response, FBI Director Robert Mueller began the process to more than double the FBI's pre-*9/11* Joint Terrorism Task Force (JTTF) operations, with 65 new units having been created, and nearly four times the pre-attack personnel level added since 2001 (D'Amuro, 2003; US DOJ, FBI, 2010; US DOJ, FBI, 2004a; Jarboe, 2002; Mueller, 2004; US DOJ, 2004). JTTFs are tasked with bringing together federal, state, and local law enforcement investigators for national counter-terrorism initiatives and investigations in an effort to encourage the inter-agency sharing of information for fusion and possible intervention (D'Amuro, 2003; National Commission on Terrorist Attacks Upon the United States, 2004; US DOJ, FBI 2004a). New JTTF units continue to be created as needs dictate.

To further demonstrate his agency's commitment to inter-agency efforts, Director Mueller also ordered the creation of Field Intelligence Groups (FIGs) across the country in each of its 56 field offices (US DOJ, FBI, 2010; US DOJ, FBI, 2004b; Mueller, 2004). Similar in design to the

Joint Terrorism Task Force model, but holding the specific responsibility of gathering, analyzing, and interpreting intelligence so that it may be shared with federal, state and local law enforcement partners, these FIGs, overseen by the Directorate of Intelligence, serve as an instrument to ensure that, while retaining classified information, federal agencies can still get emergency information down to the state and local level within a time frame of usefulness to allow the information to be acted upon, should it become necessary (Baginski, 2004). FIGs are also specifically tasked with a training function, providing avenues for training and preparedness opportunities for state and local police officers (Spiller, 2006).

Still another example of the federal agencies reaching out to work side by side with state and local law enforcement occurred in 2001 when U.S. Attorney General John Ashcroft issued orders for U.S. Attorneys across the country to create regional Anti-Terrorism Task Forces (ATTFs), which, as one of their benefits, offered the opportunity for senior state and local law enforcement personnel to obtain intelligence briefings on anti-terrorism efforts across the country, and beyond, from federal officials (Casey, 2004; US DOJ, OIG, 2003). ATTFs were later renamed Anti-terrorism Advisory Councils (ATACs) to better reflect their mission (Ashcroft, 2003). Task forces, such as the JTTFs, FIGs, and ATACs, have been found to be the most effective and successful avenues available to address the sharing of terrorism intelligence operations and investigations among law enforcement agencies in the country (Alexander, 2005; US DOJ, FBI 2004).

Cyber and Financial Crimes

With the advances in technology, two interrelated offenses—cybercrimes and financial crimes—are also increasing. *Cybercrime* is a broad term to describe many different forms of criminal activity perpetrated with computers and wireless mobile devices through networks and/or the Internet. The most cited offenses include data theft, misuse of devices, denial of services, child pornography, unauthorized access, and a wide range of financial frauds (Ricke, 2009). Financial or economic crimes include a broad range of offenses where victims are deprived of property, reputation, or money through embezzlement, theft, money laundering, and credit card theft. In many cases, the Internet is used as the communications corridor to facilitate these offenses. Another variation of the two is identity theft, which is the misuse of an identity to commit an offense (Gordon et al., 2007). No doubt, all readers of this text with Internet access have been phishing targets where criminals impersonate a bank or other financial entity using fake Web sites. The individual or group makes thousands of online attempts to obtain personal information and debit/credit card information in order to access and steal money from the victim's account. The above offenses continue to increase and capture media attention.

Cybercrime occurs very easily because of access, affordability, and anonymity. As Huang et al. (2009) state, crimes of this nature are instant and can be committed from anywhere in the world using access to a computer and the Internet. For affordability, many sites across the world, such as Starbucks and McDonalds, have free or inexpensive wireless access. Cyber crooks are anonymous and change names and addresses at the flick of a key stroke.

To date, many police departments have been unable to handle these investigations or the number of personnel assigned to cybercrime or financial investigations is small. Cyber and economic crime require specialized training, equipment, forensic laboratories, and great fortitude. These resources are available only through major departments or regional crime task forces and are operated in conjunction with prosecutors' offices, which have criminal subpoena powers. Thus, responding officers need to be trained to secure hard drives or other electronic evidence from both victims and suspects. Investigators still need to use professional interrogation techniques to interview victims, suspects, and administrators of computer systems and Internet providers. As with any criminal case, investigators have to establish probable cause, apply and obtain search warrants, and secure evidence from hard drives and storage areas from computers, cell phones, or any other wireless device used in the commission of a crime. This continues to be a growing area for investigations and there is a need for more training and regional forensic laboratories to deal with these offenses.

Conclusion

Line functions are complementary to the patrol function and form the core of the time spent on activities in the department. However, a major distinction needs to be made between the traffic function covered in this chapter and the other line functions: vice, youth services, and investigations. Officers assigned to the traffic function, for example, should receive specialized accident investigation training. Well-developed human relations skills are important for these officers because they provide direct service to the public. For many small departments and for some state police forces, much of the uniformed officer's time is spent on traffic. Traffic management should combine the knowledge and skills of a good traffic-flow engineer with computer skills that can be used to pinpoint crucial accident areas.

Vice, youth services, and investigations often involve considerable plainclothes work along with a somewhat different set of skills compared with those used by the uniformed traffic officer. The youth service bureau operates in two major areas: prevention and ongoing investigations. The prevention programs are important to the department in terms of both public relations and the goal of having youth and police on good terms with each other. As most officers who deal with youth have discovered, youths are some of the best informants available. They are everywhere in the community, and they are often willing to volunteer information to police officers they trust. The bulk of the nation's street crime is still committed by youths between the ages of 17 and 25. Thus, it is mandatory that every police department, no matter how large or small, have police officers who specialize in youth work.

Vice and organized-crime units are areas of police work that demand special knowledge and skills. It is well known that the only real way to control this type of crime is to be able to deal with the organizers near the top of the crime hierarchy. This means that the department will be involved in lengthy investigations, often with no immediate payoffs. Vice and organized crime are multijurisdictional and international in scope. This means that a department needs experienced officers and the commitment of specialized resources.

Investigations have come a long way since the days of Sherlock Holmes and Dr. Watson. They are no longer the purview of one person; today they have to be managed in terms of a reasonable return on the commitment of professional personnel.

A theme throughout this chapter is the generalist–specialist controversy. The answer to this controversy is related to the line function, the community that the department is policing, and the size of the department. The entire focus of community policing is to provide a wide array of services. In cities, a specific geographic area becomes defined as the community and line officers are charged to deal with community expectations and needs. For smaller departments, say a village department of 10 sworn officers, personnel must be able to perform a wide variety of tasks, from traffic through drug investigations. This means that each officer is expected to do a variety of generalist functions while certain individual officers also have specialties. One officer may be good at giving speeches, another may be a forensic expert, while another may have special knowledge of the youth community. The way you organize will depend on your department. What is important is that a major focus of police management skills be devoted to the effective administration of the basic line functions.

Questions for Review

1. How are the main line functions classified? Explain how an agency's size affects the organization of these functions.
2. What is the controversy surrounding the generalist versus the specialist with regard to delivering basic line functions to the community?
3. What are the main objectives of traffic enforcement?
4. How might management improve traffic enforcement?
5. How does racial profiling relate to traffic enforcement?
6. Why is vice enforcement truly a managerial dilemma?
7. Should vice enforcement be taken over by state and federal agencies? Why or why not?
8. Explain the historical development of juvenile aid divisions.
9. List the main objectives of juvenile aid divisions.
10. Explain how the following programs assist in the juvenile aid function: explorer posts, school liaison programs, outdoor adventures.
11. Why are cybercrime investigations important for police departments to address?
12. What is the main role of police investigators?
13. What has been the historical basis of detective divisions? How does this affect the investigative function today?
14. Explain the significance of the Rand study and traditional investigations.
15. List and discuss three major issues related to police investigations.

Class Projects

1. You have been appointed chief of police of the mythical town of Loomis, North Dakota. A process known as hydraulic fracturing has been able to extract oil from what is known as the Bakken field. Within one year, the town has grown from 5,000 to 25,000 in population.

   Policing before the oil rush was done by the county sheriff's department, assisted by the highway patrol. With the rapid population increase and increases in crime, the town now needs a municipal police department. The town council has told you to create a police force regardless of cost.

   Your first task is to create an organizational chart showing the police functions. Your instructor will show you how to prepare a basic chart. Include in your chart all those functions that will need to be staffed in the next three years. Write a brief rationale for each position or function you have created in your organization.

2. Review juvenile justice procedures in your state by outlining the steps that must be taken by police if a juvenile is arrested or removed from a family abuse or neglect situation. What are the age classifications for offenders? What programs exist to deter first time or minor offenders from the criminal justice system?

3. Determine if your community participates in the following programs: DARE, Amber Alert, safe school initiatives. To accomplish this you will have to consult with area police departments, police Web sites, school districts, and your instructor.

4. To what extent does your local police department take on cases involving cybercrime, identity theft, and financial fraud? If the department does not handle these cases, to which agency are they referred? As the text discusses, are these cases becoming more commonplace for the department?

Web Works

The vast array of juvenile justice research and training programs are presented by the Office of Juvenile Justice and Delinquency Prevention at ncjrs.gov/pdffiles1/ojjdp/223612.pdf. State criminal justice Web sites also provide trends in juvenile justice crime and programs. Crime trends and data on offenders, such as alcohol and drug use by students, are presented in the Sourcebook of Criminal Justice Statistics at albany.edu/sourcebook.

Related information on school security can be obtained at the U.S. Secret Service Web site at http://www.secretservice.gov/. State and local initiatives on school safety are often presented at Web sites maintained by state police or state criminal justice services agencies.

National programs, such as DARE, maintain Web sites that can be accessed via Google or by title, for example, dare.com.

Programs and discussion issues undertaken by the National Association of School Resource Officers can be obtained at nasro.org.

The latest in identity theft research and other related topics are available at utica.edu/academic/institutes/cimip.

References

Alabama Department of Homeland Security, 2010. Retrieved from le.alabama.gov/

Albanese, Jay S., Dilip K. Das, and Arvind Verma. *Organized Crime: World Perspectives*. Upper Saddle River, N.J.: Prentice Hall, 2003.

Alexander, B. *Strategies to Integrate America's Local Police Agencies into Domestic Counterterrorism*. [Electronic version]. (Master's Thesis, United States Army War College, Carlisle Barrack)

Ashcroft, J. *Attorney General Announces Changes to Anti-Terrorism Task Forces*, September 25, 2003. Retrieved from www.justice.gov/opa/pr/2003/September/03_ag_528.htm.), pp. 54–57.

Baginski, M. Statement before the Senate Committee on the Judiciary, August 19, 2004. Retrieved from mostwanted.org.uk/congress/congress04/baginski081904.htm

Baley, D. *Police for the Future*. New York: Oxford University Press, 1994.

Buerger, Michael E., and Amy Farrell. "The Evidence of Racial Profiling: Interpreting Documented and Unofficial Resources." *Police Quarterly*, 5, no. 3 (September 2002), pp. 272–305.

Carafano, J., P. Rosenzweig, and A. Kochems. "An Agenda for Increasing State and Local Government Efforts to Combat Terrorism." *Backgrounder*, no. 1826 (2005) pp. 1–2. [Electronic version].

Casey, J. "Managing Joint Terrorism Task Force Resources." *FBI Law Enforcement Bulletin, 73*, no. 11 (2004), p. 1.

D'Amuro, P. *Consolidating Intelligence Analysis: A Review of the President's Proposal to Create a Terrorist Threat Integration Center*. Congressional Testimony before the Senate Government Affairs Committee, United States Senate on February 26, 2003. Retrieved from fbi.gov/congress/congress03/damuro022603.htm

Davis, L., et al. *When Terrorism Hits Home: How Prepared Are State and Local Law Enforcement?* Santa Monica, CA: Rand Corporation, 2004, pp. i, xvi, 49–52.

Deflam, M. "Law Enforcement 9-11: Questioning the Policing of International Terrorism." *Newsletter of the SSSP Law & Society Division*, 9, no. 1 (2002), pp. 5–9. Retrieved from cas.sc.edu/socy/faculty/deflem/zssspintterror.html

Gay, William G., and Robert A. Bowers. *Targeting Law Enforcement Resources: The Career Criminal Focus*. Washington, D.C.: National Institute of Justice, 1985.

Gordon, Gary, Donald Rebovich, Kyung Seok Choo, and Judith Gordon. *Identity Fraud Trends and Patterns: Building a Data-Based Foundation for Proactive Enforcement*. Center for Identity Management and Information Protection, October 2007. Web posted at utica.edu/academic/institutes/cimip. Accessed January 20, 2009.

Greenwood, Peter, et al. *The Criminal Investigation*. Santa Monica, Calif.: Rand Corporation, 1976.

Haggard, C. "Single Officer Response in Active Shooter Events." *The Tactical Wire*, 2008. Retrieved from thetacticalwire.com/feature.html?featureID=3593

Henry, V. "The Need for a Coordinated and Strategic Local Police Approach to Terrorism: A Practitioner's Perspective." *Police Practice and Research*, 3, no. 4 (2002).

Howard, P., and M. Riebling, eds. *Hard Won Lessons: Problem-solving Principles for Local Police*. Manhattan Institute for Policy Making, Safe Cities Project. New York: Police Institute, 2005, p. 1 [Electronic version].

Howell, James C., and J. David Hawkins. "Prevention of Youth Violence." In Michael Tonry and Mark H. Moore, eds., *Youth Violence*. Chicago: University of Chicago Press, 1998, pp. 263–316.

Huang, Wilson, Matthew Leopard, and Andrea Brockman. "Internet Child Sexual Exploitation Offenses, Offenders, and Victims." In Frank Schmallenger and Michael Pitard, eds., *Crimes of the Internet*. Upper Saddle River, N.J.: Pearson/Prentice-Hall, 2009, pp. 43–65.

Ianni, Francis A.J. *Black Mafia: Ethnic Succession in Organized Crime*. New York: Simon and Schuster, 1974.

Ickner, W. "Terrorist Indicators: Is Your Jurisdiction Being Targeted?" *Sheriff*, 56, no. 5 (2004).

Inciardi, James A. *The War on Drugs*. Palo Alto, Calif.: Mayfield, 1986.

———. *War on Drugs II*. Mountain View, Calif.: Mayfield, 1991.

Inciardi, James A., and Karen MCElrath. *The American Drug Scene*. Los Angeles, Calif.: Roxbury, 1995.

Jarboe, J. *The Threat of Eco-terrorism*. Testimony before the United States House of Representatives, Resources Committee, Subcommittee on Forests and Forest Health, February 12, 2002. Washington, D.C. Retrieved from gpo.gov/fdsys/pkg/CHRG-107hhrg77615/html/CHRG-107hhrg77615.htm

Johnson, Ashley. *Adam Walsh Act: Factors of Implementation in New York State.* Unpublished report, Utica College, 2009.

Kelling, G., and W. Bratton. "Policing Terrorism." *Manhattan Institute Civil Bulletin,* 43, 2006.

Kennedy, David. "Pulling Levers: Getting Deterrence Right." *National Institute of Justice Journal* (July 1998), pp. 5–8.

Lapin, David. "Racial Profiling in Anti-terrorism Strategies." *Law Enforcement News,* April 30, 2002, pp. 8–9.

Lawrence, Richard. *School Crime and Juvenile Justice.* New York: Oxford University Press, 1998.

Lyman, Michael D., and Gary Potter. *Organized Crime* (2nd ed.). Upper Saddle River, N.J.: Prentice Hall, 2000.

Meehan, Albert, and Michael C. Ponder. "Race and Place: The Ecology of Racial Profiling African American Motorists." *Justice Quarterly,* 19, no. 3 (September 2002), pp. 306–333.

Mueller, R. Testimony before the Select Committee on Intelligence of the United States Senate, February 24, 2004. Washington D.C. Retrieved from au.af.mil/au/awc/awcgate/fbi/mueller022404.htm

National Advisory Commission on Criminal Justice Standards and Goals. *Juvenile Justice and Delinquency Prevention.* Washington, D.C.: U.S. Government Printing Office, 1976.

National Commission on Terrorist Attacks Upon the United States. *The 9/11 Commission Report.* New York: W. W. Norton & Company, Inc., 2004.

New Jersey Office of Homeland Security and Preparedness, 2010. Retrieved from state.nj.us/njhomeland-security/index.html

Niederhoffer, Arthur. *Behind the Shield: The Police in Urban Society.* Garden City, N.Y.: Doubleday, 1969.

OJJDP (Office of Juvenile Justice and Delinquency Prevention). *Promising Strategies to Reduce Gun Violence.* Washington, D.C.: Office of Juvenile Justice and Delinquency Prevention, 1999.

Ortiz, C., N. Hendricks, and N. Sugie. "Policing Terrorism: The Response of Local Police Agencies to Homeland Security Concerns." *Criminal Justice Studies,* 20(2).

Reaves, B. A., and M. J. Hickman. "Census of State and Local Law Enforcement Agencies." *Bureau of Justice Statistics Bulletin,* October (2000), p. 1.

Rebovich, Donald, and Anthony Martino. "Technology, Crime Control and the Private Sector in the 21st Century." In James M. Byrne and Donald J. Rebovich (eds.), *The New Technology of Crime, Law and Social Control.* Monsey, NY: Criminal Justice Press, Willow Tree Press, 2007.

Ricke, John. *A Study of Cybercrime Investigations by Virginia Law Enforcement Agencies.* Utica, N.Y.: Utica College, 2009.

Sanchez, Tom. "Cops Mentoring Kids." *Police Chief,* 69, no. 6 (June 2002), p. 60.

Schmalleger, Frank. *Criminology Today* (7th ed.). Upper Saddle River, N.J.: Prentice Hall, 2002.

Siegel, Larry J. *Criminology.* Belmont, Calif.: Wadsworth, 2003.

Sherman, Lawrence, et al. *Preventing Crime: What Works, What Doesn't, What's Promising.* Washington, D.C.: National Institute of Justice, 1998.

Silberman, Charles E. *Criminal Violence, Criminal Justice.* New York: Vintage, 1980.

Spiller, S. "The FBI's Field Intelligence Groups and Police." *FBI Law Enforcement Bulletin,* May (2006), pp. 1, 4.

State of New Jersey v. *Pedro et al.,* 324 Super. 66, 734, A. 2d 350 (1996).

United States Department of Justice, Federal Bureau of Investigation, Directorate of Intelligence. *Field Intelligence Groups* (2010). Retrieved from fbi.gov/intelligence/di_fig.htm

United States Department of Justice, Federal Bureau of Investigation. *Protecting America against Terrorist Attack: A Closer Look at the FBI's Joint Terrorism Task Force,* 2004a. Retrieved from fbi.gov/page2/dec04/jttf120114.htm

United States Department of Justice, Federal Bureau of Investigation. *Focus on FIGs: Networking Intelligence Across the U.S. to Prevent Crimes and Terror,* 2004b. Retrieved from fbi.gov/news/stories/2005/april/figs_042705

United States Department of Justice, Office of the Inspector General. *Review of the Critical Incident Response Plans of the United States Attorneys' Offices, Report Number I-2004-001, December,* 2003. Retrieved from justice.gov/oig/reports/EOUSA/e0401/final.pdf

U.S. v. *New Jersey and Division of State Police Department of Law and Public Safety,* Civil No. 99-5970 (MIC), December 31, 1999, consent decree.

Whitefield v. *Board of Commissioners of Eagle County, Colorado,* 837 F. Supp. 338 (ID. Colo. 1993).

Wilkins v. *Maryland State Police,* C.A. No. MJG-93-468 (D. Md. 1992).

Wilson, O.W. *Police Administration* (2nd ed.). New York: McGraw-Hill, 1963.

Wyoming Office of Homeland Security, 2010. Retrieved on August 7, 2010 from wyohomelandsecurity.state.wy.us/main.aspx

10 Administrative/Staff Functions

KEY TERMS

audit

community relations

corruption

deviance

early warning (EW) system

electronic newletters/weblinks

internal affairs

legal adviser

line/staff conflict

misconduct

Neighborhood Watch

police violence

professional standards

ride-along

student intern

The term *administrative/staff functions* is used in the title of this chapter because many departments use either *administrative function* or *staff function* to describe the same set of services. We will use the term *staff functions* for the purpose of simplicity and clarity.

The police administrator must seek advice and counsel from people who have various areas of expertise. The chief of police, while directing the overall police organization, cannot manage the daily operations of all units or functions as they do their daily tasks. Those areas of the police organization that assist in performing an advisory role are commonly termed *administrative* or *staff services*. In American policing, many of the following functions or divisions are usually included under this title: personnel and training, planning and research, legal adviser, public relations, inspections and internal affairs, and budget and community relations.

In reality, staff personnel actually command directly or indirectly, in that "advice" often constitutes a decision that is binding on the chief administrator. For example, in personnel selection, the personnel supervisor presents a list of candidates who have successfully completed all requirements—civil service, state or county, and departmental—for the position of police officer. Much time and energy on the part of the personnel staff has gone into the preparation of this final list. With all these variables in mind, it would be difficult for the chief administrator to oppose these candidates. A tacit agreement or realization exists in organizational thinking, in which the chief acknowledges that the personnel supervisor is an expert in his or her field, having mastered all affirmative action and civil service regulations affecting this group of police recruits. The chief will review the list of candidates with the personnel supervisor.

The personnel supervisor will have to answer any questions if problems arise in the future; for example, a lawsuit based on alleged discrimination or an action grant being delayed because the department did not conform to civil service guidelines.

LINE/STAFF CONFLICT AND COOPERATION

In the police subculture, individuals assigned to staff services are often looked on with disdain simply because they are considered to be "desk jockeys," engaged in "Monday morning quarterbacking," and far removed from the everyday realities of police work being done on the street. The cause for this **line/staff conflict** is that, as Nigro and Nigro (1977: 165) point out, "The line frequently resents the controls exercised by staff officials." The reason for this is that the staff officers, no matter how tactful they are, "exercise a veto over the line." Resentment can build up as the experts on the staff use their best judgment concerning line officers' activities. This judgment should and will entail denying line officers' requests. Although this conflict normally occurs between the line and staff officers, regardless of rank, the situation may get intensified when staff functions are operated and supervised by civilians.

Modern management principles applied to police functions normally result in a general recommendation for the hiring of civilians for many staff functions. The major reason given is that civilians may be less costly to hire than sworn personnel for some functions, and they can also be hired with prior training/education for specialized staff functions. The role of the manager is to be aware of the potential conflict between staff and line personnel and to create a system that can accommodate these potential problems. One recommendation is to make sure that the civilian personnel on staff have enough authority in the department to carry out their functions. At the same time, there should be a process for line officers and staff personnel to appeal to upper management for conflict resolution.

This authority has to be clearly defined. Authority in the department goes from top management to middle management and then to the line officers and sergeants operating in the field. The staff officer and staff civilian personnel have authority concerning their internal functions and units. However, their authority does not extend to issuing orders to managers or line officers. Lines of authority need to be clear in any department if the department is to operate efficiently with a minimum of conflict. In this case, staff may recommend to management and line officers, but staff is not in the line of authority in operating the department.

On the other hand, as Nigro and Nigro relate (1977: 166), staff officers and civilians frequently look down on line officers. Such terms as *medieval, slow to change,* and *ignorant* are frequently heard in discussions on this topic. It is easy to see how this attitude develops, for in reality, the staff personnel do have a major influence in the long-range and short-range policy making for the police organization, regardless of what the line officers feel. A good example of this type of situation is shown in the case study on page 193.

In this incident, management has obviously missed the mark in the positive utilization of staff officer Clement. It has also missed the mark in the effective utilization of staff information and recommendations by line officers. However, these problems can be dealt with in a positive manner.

This type of conflict is generally dysfunctional for the police organization and its personnel. Recommendations for counteracting this state of affairs include the following:

1. *Get out of the office.* A common complaint is that staff personnel always stay in their office or the station house, thereby having little idea about what is going on outside. It is healthy for staff personnel, sworn and civilian, to ride along on patrol or be temporarily assigned to a line function, so as to keep in touch with the concerns of the line personnel.

2. *Rotate assignments.* Sworn personnel should occasionally be assigned to staff functions. Sworn police officers should be doing police work in the field. On the other hand, assigning line personnel to staff units from time to time can enlarge the former's perspective on the overall nature of police administration so that they can better utilize staff work when they go back out on the streets. It also allows police administrators to review those individuals who have useful technical expertise or who are aspiring to become police administrators. Basically, this can be an excellent training ground for future executives.

3. *Implement line/staff intervention.* In addition to ride-along or staff assignments, further interaction should be encouraged through meetings and seminars. For example, staff research on the right type of vehicle to be used for patrol should include patrol officers since they will eventually be affected by the decision. This is an often overlooked area of expertise. There are many personnel in agencies who, by virtue of their time on the job and experience, can contribute to the body of knowledge being gathered by staff as input to management decisions.

CASE STUDY

Ron Clement

Although Ron Clement deeply enjoyed police work, he felt that something was lacking in his life, and so he decided to go to college. He left police work as a patrol officer and applied his veterans' benefits toward a bachelor's degree and majored in criminal justice planning. Four years later, he walked through the front door of his old police station, only this time as a criminal justice planner.

Ron's responsibilities included preparing a daily summary of crime trends and analyzing different pieces of information that were gleaned from police reports. These daily summaries were copied and presented to patrol officers at the beginning of their shifts. He also assisted the chief of police and his deputies in overall departmental planning and soon became a part of the regular Monday morning administrative conferences.

"I didn't realize that there would be jealousy or animosity toward me. I mean, it was not too long ago that I was a patrol officer. But I suddenly realized that I had lost my connection with the street cops when I began to see my summaries in the roll-call-room wastepaper basket. I actually had to do a sales job with the cops, showing them how the crime summaries would be useful to their patrol work. The younger guys cooperated, but some of the veterans still shrugged me off.

"It really hurt me when I overheard a conversation in the patrol locker room about me. One guy said, 'Clement has become a real jerk. He works inside and now he thinks he knows everything there is to know about running patrol. Why is it when a good cop, a brother patrol officer, goes inside, he becomes an arrogant jerk?'"

Although a great variety of staff functions exist, certain staff functions are either used in most police departments or considered more vital to effective administration than others. In a text on police management like this one, which is also concerned with certain aspects of police operations as they affect the management of the department, only a limited number of specific operational functions and units can be examined.

COMMUNITY RELATIONS

Many police agencies have established public relations, or **community relations**, units as a formal means of recapturing or establishing rapport with certain segments of the community. Program objectives of such units are aimed at target populations who either are prone to have violent confrontations with the police or have questions about police activities. The concept of community relations grew from the tensions of the 1960s, when many police and public officials realized that there was a gap in communication between the enforcers of the law and those they policed.

However, community relations are not just the responsibility of an organization unit in a police department; they must also become the personal responsibility of each and every professional police officer. Each officer presents the image of policing and his or her police department to the citizens. How each officer deals with citizens in his or her daily work reflects on the department as a whole. Thus, you cannot have officers who shrug their shoulders and respond to a request by a citizen, "Oh, that's the responsibility of a public relations unit. The officers out on patrol do not have anything to do with that community relations stuff." Instead, the officer should consider him or herself a minicommunity relations unit.

This communication gap has derived from a number of factors. At an earlier time, police patrol officers generally had an intimate knowledge of the neighborhoods they patrolled. Even in immigrant neighborhoods, foot patrol officers were accessible and generally visible as they made their rounds through the area. The decline of police–citizen contact occurred for a number of reasons. By the end of World War II, police patrol work was done by car, placing glass and steel barriers between officers and the public. Neighborhood precinct houses, which were community centers of information and problem solving, were eventually closed down and centralized into a few station houses or a centralized police station, thereby becoming more inaccessible for the general public. Furthermore, traditional urban boundaries, shaped by ethnicity and geography, were broken down by politics and urban renewal. In many cities, these "old" neighborhoods were eventually populated by black, Hispanic, and other new immigrants, generally poor and unemployed, who sometimes looked on the police as an army of occupation.

This situation is not found only in the inner city. In many suburban areas, whose municipal boundaries are geographically far-flung, citizens may have difficulty identifying the community police since there are often too few officers to serve the population effectively. Or policing may also be carried out by a number of competing agencies that together may have conflict in providing the entire range of police services.

In discussing some popular programs and services that are offered by community affairs units, it will become apparent that each officer should in actuality be a community affairs specialist. In the end, the daily actions of the community police are the only one true variable that increases or decreases tensions within the community. Community relations, whether done by one division or by a single officer, provides a conduit for individuals and community groups to talk to the police. It also provides the department with a mechanism to undo or address perceived or real wrongs committed by officers in the course of their duties.

Public relations units are often responsible for providing the media with information concerning the department and official police activity. Officers who have been involved in a newsworthy story often do not recognize the incident when it is later written up in the newspaper. Newspaper stories are written to sell newspapers. If the department wants accurate reporting, it must have personnel who deal with the media and are familiar with journalism. These individuals have to establish a rapport with the media so that the latter are treated with respect and are given accurate information concerning police activity. Press police officers need to establish good relationships with professionals in journalism in order to correct any misinformation that may have been published. The key word here is *credibility*. If the department is to have a positive relationship with the press, it must have a credible relationship. This kind of relationship takes time to develop and maintain, but it is vital to the image of the police department in any community.

Personnel for Community Relations

Ideally, we see the specialized community relations assignment as short term and assigned to all officers. Realistically, this is not possible since the very nature of the community relations assignment requires the officer to develop good relationships over a period of time. Moreover, some departments have a few officers that the police managers would prefer "kept under wraps" since their actions and attitudes would do nothing to improve police–community relations. Community relations should not be a "dropping ground" for officers who, for some reason or another, are not able to perform street duties or have been placed inside for disciplinary reasons.

Functions of the Community Relations Unit

The community relations unit functions in two major areas: crime prevention and public relations. However, it must again be stressed that the successful, effective police department is one that is closely identified with the community and one in which the officers do not leave community involvement to a unit of the department. Actually, even though it is not tradition, a better name for this unit would be the "community involvement unit," thus showing the close ties of the professional officer to the community. Following are some of the major functions of the community relations unit.

PUBLIC SPEAKERS'/EXPERTS BUREAUS Through public speakers' bureaus, officers or administrators make presentations on various aspects of police operations to community and school groups. They also maintain a list of department experts who will speak on specific topics such as drug abuse, traffic safety, cyber crime, and child abuse. As a rule, engagements should be planned days in advance and should employ the use of modern audiovisual techniques. The officer in charge of the community relations unit should review any topic that is to be presented with the department speaker so that there is a consistent departmental policy running through all presentations. The community relations department head should actively seek out those officers in the department who have an interesting topic to present and who have some public-speaking talent, experience, or training. A list of these officers and their topics should be on hand when any community group requests a speaker. In the area of issues involving race, ethnicity, gender, and sexual orientation, special care should be taken to assign only those individuals who are knowledgeable and able to keep their heads in the midst of often heated and sometimes rather "sharp" discussions.

TOURS AND DEMONSTRATIONS These programs provide an excellent opportunity to educate the public by reviewing specific police techniques and operations in a realistic setting. Tours should be scheduled in advance, and care and consideration should be given to the nature of the audience so that the operations can be shown and explained in the proper perspective. Care should be exercised so that the tour group does not interfere with police operations going on at the time. Demonstrations in and outside the police station that have sparked community interest include radar use, dusting for fingerprints, use of police dogs, alcohol and drug detection, and computer capabilities.

DEPARTMENT HOMEPAGES AND ELECTRONIC NEWSLETTERS   The Internet has allowed citizens access to the so-called information superhighway, which allows users to communicate, browse, and obtain information from millions of sites around the world. Proactive departments have created Web sites that allow users to obtain general information about the department, crime prevention tips, employment opportunities, and up-to-date information on crime incidents.

A well-designed Web site will generate thousands of hits each month. The greatest challenge facing most departments is keeping the homepage up-to-date. A review of several Web sites in one area found that half of the pages were at least a year or more old. Thus, it is important that a Web master be assigned to oversee this key function.

Beyond homepages, many departments are now offering **electronic newsletters and web links** to inform residents about crime trends, serious incidents, and department activities. A spin-off to these is e-mail alerts to businesses, neighborhoods, and government units regarding criminal or emergency incidents.

As discussed in Chapter 5, many departments have instituted accounts with Facebook, Twitter, and other social media outlets. This allows departments to present their point of view and to accept questions about crime and safety matters and the status of major community events.

RIDE-ALONGS   Scheduled in advance by the community relations unit, a **ride-along** program provides members of the public with a chance to see their community from inside a police car. Departments with such programs have formulated strict procedures on the issues of liability and safety. Basically, we recommend that these programs take place only with officers who volunteer, without coercion, official or otherwise, to have ride-alongs in their patrol cars during their regular shifts.

Officers should be able to explain to the citizen the role of patrol in the total functioning of the department.

Civilians need to be instructed in terms of what to do and what not to do. At a minimum, the following should be considered when preparing agency policy:

1. Civilians should never be armed, even if they have a gun permit.
2. In case of a violent incident, civilians should not leave the patrol car and should leave any confrontation to the professionally trained police officer.
3. The department should define whether civilians should be allowed to use video.
4. Civilians should be aware that this is a working police officer who has a duty to perform and that they should not, in any way, interfere with the carrying out of that duty.

Some officers do not work well with civilian observers. Thus, for these and a variety of other reasons, officers need to be screened before they can participate in the program. If the department management wishes a ride-along program as a public relations tool, controls must be placed on it in order for it to be a positive force in the community and the department. As a final note, it is strongly recommended that any ride-along policy include in it a signed waiver by the civilians, which includes their awareness that they will be checked for criminal history, outstanding warrants, etc.

COLLEGE INTERNSHIPS Many colleges offering criminal justice degrees have established **student intern** programs in which students are allowed to study the activities of a criminal justice agency for a certain period of time. In doing so, they are expected not only to observe the operations of the agency but to perform an academic project that would assist the agency and also earn college credits. Mutually agreed-to guidelines should be drawn up between the institution and the police agency regarding the number of hours and the activities that the student will be assigned (Gordon and McBride, 2012). One officer should be assigned to be a mentor for the student. While the student is able to combine theory and practice in a criminal justice setting, agency personnel act in the capacity of field teachers by showing the student how police operations are carried out. In many cases, former interns have been appointed to departments since the internship has given the agency and the student the opportunity to decide whether policing is a suitable career for the student.

Departments with a well-established intern program use the following guidelines for intern selection and participation. In these cases the student must submit the following:

1. An application or resume with a cover letter stating the duration of the program and the name of the school supervisor
2. A recent writing sample
3. A statement of learning goals that correspond to the student's career plans and the department's operations
4. The criteria from the educational institution for final evaluation
5. A memorandum of understanding between the school and the department regarding the goals of the program and the responsibilities of both the agency and the college
6. Evidence of insurance by the institution for liability in the event of a civil lawsuit for an action taken by the student intern
7. A health insurance policy for the student in case there is an internship-related injury

Many departments will conduct background checks to ascertain if the candidate is of good character and can deal with confidential materials. There is often an oral interview with the student intern supervisor or a review committee.

If the student is accepted, then the department prepares a schedule that includes both field work and observation and assignment to a major project. Examples of student projects are writing and research for major policies, annual reports, emergency management plans, budgets, training procedures, accreditation-related materials, updating the department's Web site, or a unique issue facing the department.

CRIME PREVENTION PROGRAMS Many larger departments have separate units that deal with the issue of crime prevention. As noted previously, one major role of the police lies in the prevention of crime. To further this objective, many departments instituted crime prevention programs in the 1970s as a means to reduce crime. The target populations for these programs were community and special interest groups that wanted to know how they could help in the fight against crime and at the same time reduce the likelihood that they would be crime victims. Here are two examples of crime prevention programs:

1. *Operation Identification.* In this program, the police department allows citizens to borrow an engraver and etch an identification number on certain valuable items. The item of property and its identification number are then recorded in a police log. This process is useful if the engraved item is stolen and later recovered.

2. *Neighborhood Watch.* The **Neighborhood Watch** program, devised by the National Sheriffs' Association, incorporates the ancient notion of frankpledge. Each person on a street block is responsible for watching out for suspicious individuals and incidents, especially those related to burglaries. The role of the community relations units for this program is to foster the need for collective security in the neighborhood and to instruct citizens under what circumstances to call for the police. Residents are issued decals that are posted in windows and doors indicating that the residence participates in the program, thereby attempting to foster some sort of deterrence.

Many crime prevention programs have been half-hearted attempts to improve police–community relations. Often a program is conceived and massive media publicity is generated, but after a few months the program dies. The main problem is that most crime prevention programs are never evaluated in terms of one question: Does the program have any impact on crime? After instituting the program, the police agency must encourage continuing citizen participation in the program. The truth is that most equipment for Neighborhood Watch, Operation ID, and other similar ventures eventually does nothing but collect dust in police property areas. Thus, each program needs to be evaluated in terms of its permanent value to citizens and to the department.

CITIZEN VOLUNTEER PROGRAMS   Citizens can participate in a variety of volunteer programs for crime prevention and emergency response:

- Community emergency-response teams (CERT)
- Neighborhood Watch
- Volunteer in Police Service (VIPS)
- Terrorism Information and Prevention System (TIPS)
- Medical Reserve Corps

These popular programs involve citizen volunteers in auxiliary police activities. These programs, which are often sponsored by the federal government, involve citizens with their local police in a variety of positive ways and are currently being brought into many homeland security efforts. Further information can be obtained from the FEMA Web site (fema.gov). Descriptive and training materials as well as videotapes are available through this Web site.

The Community Relations Officer

The community relations officer (CRO) acts as a liaison between the department, the media, and public-interest groups. In many departments, this specialist might be assigned to a community relations unit or, in some cases, report directly to the police administrator. In smaller departments, the chief of police often acts as his or her own community relations officer.

In addition to acting as a liaison with the media, the role of the CRO includes the following:

1. Preparing releases on police-related news. Such news includes a daily police log, the status of investigations, crime trends, and other information deemed necessary for public knowledge.
2. Coordinating the scheduling of press conferences and updating web and social media pages.
3. Preparing or coordinating special audiovisual materials or pamphlets, such as PowerPoint presentations, handouts, or videotape presentations that portray department operations.
4. Coordinating the creation of Internet homepages or electronic newsletters.

In this role, the CRO must have access to all divisions and personnel in the department. Importantly, his or her viewpoint must relate to the policies of the police administrator and the department.

As has been mentioned, the CRO needs some journalistic training and the ability to have a credible relationship with the press. One problem often encountered is the reporter with a "police blotter" mentality—that is, a reporter, looking for copy for the next day's paper, who simply wants to know what dramatic event happened that evening. The press officer should be trained to handle this kind of mentality and, maybe, guide it to a more positive attitude for the good of both the media and the department.

The CRO should also be trained to speak effectively before the cameras. He or she needs to dress the part of a professional police officer and be articulate. With the new technology of the news (instant replay, portable TV cameras, webinars, and mobile units), an incident could happen and an on-the-scene report could be broadcast within minutes. A well-trained, responsible press officer who can handle tough questions in tense situations is needed for the job. This person should be recognized as a high-priority factor in any police budget and should have higher status and rank than he or she does in most departments. This position is vital for the creation of a positive image for the professional police department.

One last note on the CRO's training and rank. He or she must command enough rank so that he or she has the respect of fellow officers and enough authority to be seen to speak for the department. These officers should have enough time on the road and in rank so that they can be respected for their past police experience and knowledge of the department. Finally, they should have solid training in criminalistics and crime scene control so that they can educate the public and the press and yet protect the confidentiality of an investigation. They must be able to relate to investigators and know what can be said and what should not be said. Since they are also on that television set, the department and their demeanor, training, and knowledge should reflect their professionalism. Since the CRO represents the department to the public, the officer's behavior and language must at all times be professional.

In the Internet age, CROs must be web savvy and monitor any activity that reflects on the department. In some cases, they will be preparing and at times overseeing releases that will appear on the department's Web page. Thus, a number of stories will appear on blogs, Web sites, YouTube, and other outlets that go beyond the traditional print and electronic media. Police departments also must to be able to respond to e-events. How does the department react when the video clip of an officer using unnecessary physical or deadly physical force appears on an Internet location?

THE LEGAL ADVISER

The daily actions of any police officer are subject to legal review according to the parameters set forth by the courts; so too are the operations of the police organization. Traditionally, on criminal matters, police may consult with the local district attorney for advice and assistance in the coordination of criminal procedures and investigations. While this criminal aspect remains important, the police organization and its personnel have recently been the targets of civil suits from individuals or organizations. At one time, the police, as agents of the state, could not be subject to civil suit. Citizens can now sue public officials through various civil rights acts, particularly in the areas of false arrest, employment discrimination, and brutality. The rise of civil suits for money damages necessitates the use of attorneys who specialize in these matters. The role of the police **legal adviser**, then, is to oversee the disposition of civil cases against the department. In addition, his or her duties include keeping the organization updated on changes in criminal and civil laws and procedures as well as advising the chief and staff administrators on methods to decrease the likelihood of successful civil suits against the department. The legal adviser would also be a good resource for the continual problem of search-and-seizure procedures.

The role of the police legal adviser in the future appears most likely to increase with stature in that a civil suit, whether successful or unsuccessful, incorporates procedures that are expensive in terms of legal costs. In many situations, the department or its counsel settles out of court for a lesser sum demanded by the plaintiff simply because of these costs. Successful suits, however, have an effect on the financial and policy operations of the department.

In the 1970s, civil suits against individual police officers became an increasingly important factor when deciding certain departmental policy and individual police behavior (President's Commission, 1967: 30–35; see also Broadway, 1974). Police benevolent associations also became concerned with the threats of such civil action and were involved, through their counsel, in a number of such suits.

Lawsuits against police agencies are on the rise, along with expenses associated with those litigations. A Cato Institute study found $225,000 was the median award for a successful suit regarding police misconduct (Packman, 2010). As important to the bottom line, the study also found that the costs involved in simply the defense of a lawsuit against an agency often was more that the award, itself, which can reach millions of dollars. Almost half (49 percent) of state and local police agencies in the United States have fewer than 10 officers, with nearly two-thirds of all officers employed by the largest 7 percent of the agencies (Reaves, 2011). With a majority of police agencies, then, supported by municipalities with relatively smaller tax bases than the largest agencies, one substantiated lawsuit against a police officer from one of those many small departments could have a dramatic budget impact on a municipality's budget for years to come.

Even though the Cato Institute's findings were that the average award was under $250,000, awards are frequently for millions of dollars. Between 2002 and 2011, 24 settlements or rewards were in excess on $1 million. New York City experienced a 46 percent increase in settlements and judgments involving police lawsuits between 2006 and 2011 (Goldman, 2012), and paid out $119 million in 2011 alone. A $15 million settlement was made in 2012 (2012).

Police departments in small municipalities and counties rely on private attorneys or corporation counsels for legal assistance. However, a part-time counsel on retainer with the local department, however small, would be of more benefit since such legal help would be experienced and knowledgeable concerning the special problems of police departments.

Another useful function for counsel hired by police departments is that of the screening of arrest charges. Because of the use of plea bargaining in reducing charges, police officers may tend to overcharge or undercharge in making an arrest. A good police department counsel or, in larger departments, legal staff would make for better arrest charges and create better cooperation with a district attorney staff. The prosecutors would know that there was a screened legal basis for the charges that were handed to the district attorney's office. Fewer errors and fewer citizens awaiting trial for charges that are going to be reduced or dropped also makes for good management, along with positive community relations. In the long run, there should be more and cleaner convictions for crimes committed.

Police attorneys may also find patterns of errors that officers are making. Over time, through internal training sessions and memorandums to management and staff, such errors can be eliminated. Over the long run, again, we should have a better conviction rate.

Police legal advisers can be the interface between the police department and the courts. They can deal with the courts and bring policies and opinions back into the department so that arrests are consistent with the prosecutor's policies. They can also explain to the prosecutor's office how difficult it may be for officers in the street to carry out these policies. In the long run, this individual or office can bring about consistent policies in a police/court system, even when the chief administrators for police and prosecutor's offices change. Thus, they are a help in transition periods as well as in the day-to-day work of the department, the courts, and the arresting discretion of the individual police officer in the street.

Another area that is often overlooked for department attorneys is that of labor relations. As will be discussed in Chapter 14, the collective bargaining agreement is a legal contract between the municipality, department, and labor union for a specific period of time on wages, benefits, and conditions of employment. The department attorney or legal unit is responsible for contract administration in terms of dealing with the application of the contract to working conditions. In many cases, the department attorney would represent the department in matters related to grievances, improper practices, and disciplinary proceedings arising from the contract.

PROFESSIONAL STANDARDS

From colonial times, officials who enforced the law always had a great deal of latitude in committing crimes during the course of their duties. The histories of many major police departments are replete with accounts of brutality, nonfeasance, bribery, and abetting the activities of gangsters. Although there were periods of reform, corruption generally returned after the ruckus died down (Smith, 1965).

After World War II, many citizens, state and local governments, and interest groups addressed the issue of police corruption in their communities. Spurred by the media, many major police departments in the United States between 1950 and 1974 (and many smaller agencies as well) experienced corruption scandals (Sherman, 1974). This raised issues that still remain unsolved: Who polices the police? How do we stamp out corruption or deal with misconduct?

These Internal Affairs Units became the norm in policing as a result of the large-scale police corruption investigation in the 1970s that spawned the numerous commissions discussed in Chapter 2.

There were a number of noticeable undertakings that occurred just before 2000. New York City created the Commission to Combat Police Corruption in 1995 to more uniformly monitor police corruption issues in the city. The US Department of Justice sponsored a national symposium of police leaders from across the country to examine police corruption. This symposium culminated in a wide-ranging list of recommendations for policy implementations in the form of a publication titled, *Police Integrity: Public Service with Honor* (US Department of Justice, 1997). Through the second half of the 1990s, the Los Angeles Police Department suffered through its most notable corruption scandal, which became known as the Rampart Scandal, which involved an organized rogue street unit. In response, the then chief Bernard Parks ordered an inquiry board, leading to the Rampart Area Corruption Incident (Parks, 2000). A notable focus in the recommendations section of the report dealt with hiring standards, but a thorough review of its citizen complaint handling procedures was conducted, including the recommendation for an expanded Internal Affairs Group (Unit).

These specialized units were designed to keep a watch on the activities of departmental personnel and investigate alleged acts of corruption or misconduct. The title **professional standards** is also being used for a unit or department of this nature. This reflects new thinking on the part of college-educated police administrators and officers. It represents more than just a label change. It reflects how professional police administrators view their ethical and moral responsibility to the public and their wish to be self-governing, using their own professional standards. Today, every police department, large and small, has either a division or a person who handles the internal affairs functions, which, in addition to corruption, include investigating offenses defined by police duty manuals as "misconduct."

Departments that have professional internal affairs operations are often hampered in their effectiveness by opposition from the rank and file, which is then formally expressed in the union contract. Union rules may include the following for the investigation of police officers:

1. A ban against the use of polygraphs or alcohol-detection devices.
2. Defined hours when an interrogation may occur between a suspected officer and investigators.
3. Advance notice advising an officer that he or she is subject to an investigation. Such notice may include the name and address of the complainant and the alleged act.
4. Complex procedures that make it virtually impossible to dismiss or discipline an officer.
5. The right of an officer to pick certain members of the review panel that will hear his or her case.

While such tactics may appear to be self-defeating for addressing the issue of police misconduct and corruption, it must be pointed out that these "safeguards" emerged to combat certain investigatory techniques, including interrogation during the early morning hours, not being informed of the nature of the complaint before being questioned by internal affairs, the use of decoys and entrapment tactics, and disciplinary action being taken against officers without due process. The review of an agency's union contract on this issue often reveals either real or perceived abuses of the internal affairs function on the part of the rank and file.

Management of the Professional Standards/Internal Affairs Unit

Professional standards/**internal affairs** is that section of the police agency that handles citizen complaints or initiates investigations of officers committing crimes or misusing their authority. In larger departments, internal affairs is a separate division that receives complaints and conducts investigations. In smaller departments, the chief of police or a delegate may comprise the entire unit. It is important to note that professional standards/internal affairs is not the only section that handles complaints against police. Petty transgressions are handled on an informal basis by midline supervisors or the peer group. Serious complaints, or those initiated by a citizen directly to the police department, usually become the province of internal affairs.

Professional standards/internal affairs is viewed with suspicion from two fronts. For citizens, suspicions are often raised as to whether making complaints will make any difference since they believe that the police will "whitewash" the incident. For police officers, it poses a threat in that it abrogates the entire notion of fraternity found in the police subculture—the inconceivable idea that fellow officers will prosecute another, resulting in fines, suspension, forced retirement, or jail.

Outside input deals with most of these misgivings. In many cities, citizens have been added to committees to review police misconduct. A nice balance is shown when police management has a major role in choosing the citizens to be added to these committees, thus protecting internal morale while having an outside check on police misconduct.

Essentially, all complaints should be reviewed and investigated, no matter how minor or serious. It is the responsibility of the police agency to publicize the procedure for filing a complaint against a member of the police force. To prevent false reporting, it should also be publicized that a false complaint may result in prosecution. To prevent charges of "whitewashing," the professional standards/internal affairs unit should notify the complainant of the results of the investigation and the disciplinary action taken against the alleged offender. For complaints found to be "unsubstantiated" or when no action is taken, the complainant should still be notified and told the reasons why. If he or she is not satisfied, the complainant should be directed to the district attorney or the U.S. Justice Department, especially in instances of alleged civil rights violations.

Disciplinary Actions

A number of disciplinary actions can be taken against a police officer who has been found to have committed crimes or to have abused his or her authority. If the officer is accused of having committed a crime, the district attorney's office would naturally prosecute. However, while that prosecution takes place, possibly over a period of months, the officer may be kept on the force (presumed innocent until convicted) or may be suspended with or without pay. If the officer is not convicted and has been suspended without pay, he or she is normally reinstated and given back pay. In some cases, the officer may have to bring civil suit to obtain that back pay.

Disciplinary action can be brought against an officer for violation of department rules that legally may not be defined as a criminal offense. Examples of such violations include failure to wear proper uniform or use proper equipment, having long hair or dirty shoes, failure to make proper entries in log books, and being late for duty. More serious departmental offenses that would still not be considered criminal offenses might include discourtesy to a citizen during the performance of a duty, an accident with a patrol vehicle, or drinking on duty.

In these cases, there are a range of sanctions that can normally be employed:

1. Field counseling or verbal reprimand
2. Written reprimand/formal counseling
3. Loss of vacation days or fine
4. Suspension with or without pay
5. Reduction in rank or change of assignment
6. Dismissal
7. Criminal prosecution

In cases involving minor deviation from department rules, supervisors usually resort to verbal reprimands. However, when the deviation becomes consistent behavior, such as being late for work, more formal means of discipline are employed.

The philosophy of discipline that we advocate is termed *progressive discipline*. The three elements of progressive discipline are as follows:

1. *Documentation.* It is the duty of the supervisor to document infractions and bring them to the attention of the officer. In case of tardiness, some kind of official action must take place the first time the officer is late.
2. *Sanctions.* The sanction to be imposed, again ranging from verbal reprimand to a more serious punishment, must be related to the seriousness of the offense. For example, termination from the job is not a proper sanction for an officer who is late for duty for the first time. Termination, however, may be appropriate if the officer has been documented late on 30 occasions over a two-month period.
3. *Administration.* The sanctions must be equally administered to all portions of the department. It is not correct practice if discipline is meted out to one shift or sector but not to another. There must be consistency—which is difficult because of the range of situations and personalities involved in supervision.

Department Rules and Collective Bargaining Agreements

Department rules or collective bargaining agreements related to disciplinary actions must be strictly followed. In collective bargaining agreements, disciplinary procedures follow a grievance-like procedure in terms of a written notice to the offender and in some cases stepwise review by a state labor relations board.

For example, for the officer who is tardy, the supervisor may wish to have a formal counseling session. A counseling session should be done in private and on a one-on-one basis between the officer and the supervisor. A written memorandum should follow, outlining the basis for the problem, the reason the problem occurred, and the actions that will be taken to correct the problem. The written memorandum should be signed by both the officer and the supervisor.

Department review boards and state arbitrators become very concerned if the procedure is not followed in disciplinary matters, no matter how slight the occurrence may seem. For example, in one case, a labor relations arbitrator dismissed the department's request for loss of six days' pay for an officer who was consistently tardy because supervisors had not formally counseled the officer in 10 previous but similar situations over the year. The rule in disciplinary matters is that if the allegation is not in writing and in the officer's personnel file, then it never officially happened!

In cases involving a serious complaint or a criminal allegation, more formal measures are employed. Based on our review of collective bargaining agreements, the rights of a police officer suspected of wrongdoing involve the following:

1. Notice of the nature of the investigation and the name of the complainant, if known
2. Time and place of interrogation or hearing
3. Right to legal counsel at interrogation or hearing
4. The recording of interrogations and hearings
5. Written notification of determination and disposition of the complaint, with reasons presented for the disposition

Immediate suspension with or without pay before the commencement of a criminal proceeding or departmental review process occurs only if the officer is deemed to be a threat to the public and coworkers or has committed a crime. Consider the following examples based on rulings by state arbitrators and police department review boards:

- Suspension without pay was an appropriate measure when an officer was caught shoplifting in uniform during an unauthorized meal break.
- Request for termination for an officer arrested off duty in early morning hours wearing only sneakers was inappropriate since the employee was not officially on duty.
- An officer was terminated after having consensual sex with a woman in a patrol vehicle while on duty. Before entering into a final hearing, the officer agreed to resign in lieu of losing six months' back pay. The attorney for the department agreed to this plea based on the poor investigation that went into the incident, which could have resulted in a not-guilty verdict and reinstatement of this officer.
- Although criminal charges were dismissed based on the lack of probable cause, the termination of a police lieutenant was upheld based on the defendant's service record and complaints involving sexual harassment and the seriousness of the disciplinary complaint—striking a female officer.

If there are three recommendations that can be provided police management in terms of dealing with equity and protecting department morale, they would be

- Consistency
- Consistency
- Consistency

This means that written procedures must be followed and that punishment must fit the offense.

CONTROL OF POLICE VIOLENCE

Police violence is usually dealt with reactively. For example, many major cases have occurred where a citizen is beat up, killed, or ends up in the hospital, and there is a police investigation and sometimes a political investigation. After the investigation, a politically inspired committee devises some remedies that might or might not work, then tells the media. This is not a good way of doing business.

In a proactive approach to police violence, a system of prevention is in place before violence happens. Police violence can be prevented, but when it occurs it can be dealt with immediately only if programs are in place. Violence by police officers takes place within the norms of secrecy, solidarity, and social isolation of police culture. To understand police violence requires understanding how these police norms have encouraged police violence and cover-ups. Prevention strategies, investigation techniques, and specific intervention approaches will be examined. Well thought out professional intervention approaches can protect the rights of both civilians and police officers while ensuring that cover-ups do not take place.

Obstacles to Decreasing Police Violence

Secrecy, solidarity, and social isolation were described in Chapter 2 as the basic norms of police culture. They are neither good nor bad in terms of how police operate. Applying these norms to police deviance and brutality can create great harm for both the public and the police organization.

THE NORM OF SECRECY Police deal with the reputations of people, which can be destroyed through routine investigations. For example, a school official may be the target of an investigation where young women were raped in a van. Any public knowledge of the investigation can destroy the official's reputation, even if the investigation is proved to be unfounded. A drug investigation may take many months to complete. Talking about the investigation, even to a spouse, means that lives can be jeopardized. On the other hand, this norm of secrecy is also used to protect deviant and violent police officers by creating a "blue curtain" between the police and the public.

THE NORM OF SOLIDARITY The officer is part of a police family. His or her children are police children. The spouse is a police wife or a police husband. Police officers stick together. They protect their brother and sister officers from a hostile public and their own brass. The operating norm is "You are never alone."

This solidarity can go too far in treating all nonpolice, including ordinary citizens, as the enemy. Solidarity strengthens the blue curtain that covers up deviant and violent acts by police officers. Solidarity allows each police officer, administrator, and manager to protect violent and deviant cops in order to make the police department look good.

THE NORM OF SOCIAL ISOLATION   The perception of a hostile public creates a police attitude that is hostile to the community. Officers carry a gun, do traffic stops, and arrest people, and this isolates them from the community. Police officers know that they can trust a cop but never an outsider. Every day, officers deal with the underclass in society: people who steal, drunks, drug dealers who sell dope to children, and child molesters who prey on the weak and innocent.

Police officers are doing dirty work. This is work that deals with an undesirable population. Officers, in the public eye, can take on the stigma of that population. Under the socially isolated military model, the public becomes the enemy. As Van Maanen (1978: 221) stated, "I guess what our job really boils down to is not letting the assholes take over the city. . . . They're the ones that make it tough. You take the majority of what we do and it's nothing more than asshole control." Police officers' friends become limited to other cops and people in the criminal justice "business." Police protect their own, including dirty cops.

TURNING PEOPLE INTO THINGS   This is especially damaging to the police officers since it turns citizens into things. It starts with using obscenities aimed at citizens and criminals. If a citizen is an "asshole," a thing, that citizen is not a human being. By being a thing, the citizen cannot have any feelings or any humanity and is simply the enemy. Once a person becomes a thing, you can do anything. Things do not feel, do not have families, and do not have children. Things can be hurt without guilt. This can lead to violent behavior by the police against individuals.

THE MILITARY MODEL   Although a professional police department has a civilian focus, there is at times an aggressive military atmosphere. The military mission is different than the police mission. The military's mission is to use the violence necessary to complete the mission. The police mission is to limit violence and to protect citizens from violence. The use of military training and tactics changes the mission of the police and separates the police from the public. Without the military agenda, the members of the community become valuable allies in the fight against criminal activity. Military personnel do a fine professional job fighting a war, but they are not police, nor does the military have a civilian police agenda. In emergencies, the use of military tactics is, of course, justified and necessary.

INTERNAL AFFAIRS   Secret hearings and investigations by an internal affairs structure create suspicion among the public and the press. Due process police proceedings need to be public affairs that are transparent to citizens and to the press and need to bring serious penalties for police violence and deviance and serious penalties for citizens who bring false charges. Internal affairs, as it works today, can be unfair and dysfunctional for both the individual police officer and the public.

STRATEGIC INTERVENTIONS FOR POLICE DEVIANCE   The best source of professional readings on police **deviance** is Barker and Carter's *Police Deviance* (3rd ed., 1994b). Barker and Carter cite the need for clear, specific directives in a department to control deviance. The directives would include expected standards of behavior to inform both the officer and the community. There would be grounds for discipline and counseling for individual officers, guidelines for officer supervision, and directions for training.

These directives have to be very specific, for example, "Acceptance of any gratuity will be subject to disciplinary action. This includes services, restaurant and fast food meals, and presents of all kinds, including bottles of alcoholic beverages given during holidays. Minimum punishment is suspension without pay for two days."

POLICE USE OF OBSCENITY   The use of obscenity on citizens can be considered psychological and emotional violence because it demeans citizens, treats them with no respect, and dehumanizes encounters with the public. White et al. (1994) give four situational reasons why police officers use obscenity in interactions with citizens:

- To gain the attention of the citizen
- To establish social distance
- To label and degrade citizens
- To dominate and control citizens

Once again we have the "asshole" syndrome. Citizens are stigmatized and treated as things. Once the social distance and stigma are established, further acceptance of these slurs establishes the citizen as a nonperson.

White and colleagues also noted that the use of obscenity can lead to aggression. When a police officer labels a citizen as an obscene thing, then these citizens are no longer human beings. Once the citizen is socially constructed as a thing, the police officer can do anything he or she wants without guilt or thought. There need to be strong, enforced departmental policies concerning the use of obscenity because obscenity against citizens can lead to police violence against citizens.

POLICE USE OF DEADLY FORCE   Since the U.S. Supreme Court case of *Tennessee v. Garner* (1985), it has been illegal to use deadly physical force to apprehend nondangerous fleeing felon suspects. With appropriate departmental policies installed, the shooting of fleeing suspects has been reduced (Blumberg, 1997: 518).

As a result of this case and the appropriate departmental regulations, Blumberg also noted that the police use of guns often changed from aggressive use to defensive use. One problem is the lack of accurate data. Nobody knows how many times police have shot at citizens, justifiably or unjustifiably. From the available research, the evidence is overwhelming that a restrictive firearms policy that is tightly enforced can be effective in reducing the number of police shootings.

POLICE USE OF EXCESSIVE FORCE   The use of excessive force by police officers is a major problem, and it seems that a small minority of officers have the most complaints. For example, of the 3,440 complaints against police officers in Boston in the 1980s, 61.5 percent were lodged against 11 percent of the officers (Barker and Carter, 1994a: 267). The Report of the Independent Commission of the Los Angeles Police Department (Christopher Commission, 1994: 291–306) on why the beating of Rodney King took place showed some major problems. The commission found that there was a group of police officers who repeatedly used excessive force, that they were known to police supervisors, and that no action was taken. From January 1987 to March 1991, of the 6,000 officers who were implicated in use-of-force reports, 4,000 had 1 report, and 63 had 20 or more reports, which accounted for 20 percent of all the reports.

The commission found that performance evaluations of officers who used excessive force were generally positive. Analyses of tape-recorded messages from patrol cars showed that officers had admitted to beatings. The tapes were not audited by any supervisor. The commission also found that the complaint system was skewed against the complainant and that internal affairs investigated only a few complaints. It was also documented that the department treated excessive force offenses more leniently than other types of misconduct.

The blue curtain of police secrecy, solidarity, and social isolation needs to be raised so that the brutal police officer is forced out of the department. The Los Angeles Police Department

(LAPD) was described as "an aggressive police organization that had rapidly distanced itself from the public. While developing as many specialized units as possible and securing as many military gadgets and tactics as the city would allow, Gates instilled a sense of division between police and the public" (Kappler et al., 1994: 135).

Racism, mixed with violence and aggression, also created social isolation of the officers in the LAPD. As LAPD police officers have stated, "I would love to drive down Slausen [an African American neighborhood] with a flame thrower. . . . We would have a barbecue. I almost got me a Mexican last night but he dropped the gun too quick" (Kappler et al., 1994: 140).

Early Warning Systems to Identify Problem Officers

It is possible to manage the risk of police officers being involved in **corruption** or brutalizing behavior by developing an **early warning (EW) system** to identify officers who are at risk. This early warning system works best in departments that are committed to uncovering and working with problem officers. It stops hidden problems from growing and becoming major police scandals, and it makes it hard for the department to ignore and cover up the behavior of problem officers.

The Miami Police Department uses the following criteria to identify problem officers (Walker et al., 2001):

1. Complaints—officers with five or more complaints with a finding of sustained or inconclusive during the past two years
2. Control of persons (use of force)—officers involved as principals in five or more use-of-force incidents during the past two years
3. Reprimands—employees with five or more reprimands during the past five years
4. Discharge of firearms—officers who discharged their firearms on three or more occasions during the past five years

The supervisors notify officers who meet any of these criteria that they are being placed in the early warning system and will be investigated. In Miami, the system affects very few officers, but it is nevertheless a good, proactive management tool.

Also needed are programs to work with problem officers. Miami has six different ways to handle these officers (Walker et al., 2001):

1. Reassignment
2. Retraining
3. Transfer
4. Referral to an employee-assistance program
5. Fitness-for-duty evaluation
6. Dismissal pursuant to civil rules and regulations

Intervention efforts must involve more than the immediate supervisor. There is hope that the early warning system will deter problem officers and that intervention will help problem officers become good police officers. This system might also be used to identify problem supervisors.

THE POLICE MISCONDUCT MODEL

Police **misconduct** has been a persistent problem for police administrators, civilian policy makers, and citizen groups. It remains an important public policy issue because police officers have a wide range of powers affecting liberty and life. They can also take actions under the color of law that would be designated as crimes for ordinary citizens, such as the use of deadly physical force.

Exactly what constitutes misconduct and the reasons for this problem remain a continuing topic of academic debate. Before 1990, most inquiries and studies into police wrongdoing focused on corruption, which took the form of bribes and payoffs from gangsters, protection schemes promoted by officers, and a variety of felony crimes committed by officers while on duty. The most famous study was the Knapp Commission inquiry into police corruption (1972), which among other ideas, presented the concept of "meat eaters" and "grass eaters." A meat eater was defined as an officer who actively sought out graft and money, while a grass eater was one who participated in lesser forms of corruption, such as accepting free meals, discounts on services, and gifts and money that fell their way. The "rotten apple theory" was also presented by administrators to explain that corruption was just limited to a few officers and did not involve the entire department. In some cases, academic studies, grand juries, or official commissions found that the entire barrel, the whole community criminal justice system, was indeed corrupt.

After a number of cases involving the use of deadly force, including the Rodney King beating in Los Angeles, academic and professional police inquiry expanded into other areas of police deviance and misconduct. Most administrators use the term *police misconduct* when a supervisor or an officer is in violation of the state or federal law, department policies, or administrative rules. These violations might range from the most mundane—failing to gas up the patrol vehicle at the end of a shift—to the more serious, such as executing a drug dealer. As will be discussed, the current inquiry into police misconduct focuses on serious behaviors that can be criminal or civilly liable.

From the police misconduct model, a departmental systems approach was also being reviewed as a way to explain and control police misconduct. The Mollen investigation in New York City (1994) and the Ramparts investigation in Los Angeles (2000) found, in those precincts, serious problems based on officer quality, lack of supervision, lack of management audit and oversight, and poor working conditions. In both cases, most of the issues were tied to drug enforcement and related schemes to sell evidence and to punish drug dealers who did not pay for protection (Lersch, 2002).

Based on works by Barker and Carter (1994b), Crank and Caldero (2000), and Lersch (2002), police misconduct activities can be said to include the following:

- Felony and misdemeanor crimes committed by officers on and off duty
- Payoffs for not performing a duty
- Nonfeasance (failure to perform an official duty) or performing a duty incorrectly
- Gratuities
- Sexual abuse and sexual favors
- Free services and goods
- Abuse of deadly and physical force
- "Noble-cause reasons," which deal with bypassing department procedures, lying under oath, or violating a suspect's constitutional rights to enforce the law

Under the heading of "noble cause" are a range of activities that are related to drug offenses. These include planting evidence, lying under oath, stealing money and drugs from raids or evidence lockers, supplying informants with drugs, and killing suspects.

Sexual abuse has received attention recently; media-publicized incidents have involved rape, sexual harassment, and stalking. In one case, an officer ordered female traffic violators suspected of driving while intoxicated to undress or face arrest and immediate imprisonment. These incidents have prompted a number of academic studies, such as McGurrin and Kappler's (2002) review of media accounts of police sexual violence.

THE INTERNAL AUDIT

Police departments should routinely conduct internal **audits** of their operations to ascertain whether they meet department and applicable state standards and expectations. An audit for this purpose is simply a test or review of a department practice or policy as it relates to the delivery of a specific police service. Unlike accreditation, where the department presents its written policies and operations for external review, the internal audit deals with how well the policy or practice is working. The audit can serve as an important planning tool for improving services and identifying potential problems.

The audit is closely related to what is often called *inspections*. In large departments, the inspections unit is often related to internal affairs. Inspectors deal with citizen complaints and audit typical criminal investigation functions, such as evidence processing, case disposition, and personnel complaints.

The audit concept can apply to a number of operational areas that include not only basic line operations, but also training, records, communications, recruitment and selection, promotions, equipment, crime prevention, and community relations. The auditor, who should be a command-level person, prepares questions to "test" the operational item or practice in terms of overall benefit to the department or any administrative concerns and issues. For example, an audit of the police vehicle fleet would include a review of the number of vehicles, their age and condition, the cost for gas and maintenance, accident records, and "likes and dislikes" of drivers. While such an exercise would be important for budgetary reasons, the audit should review not only overall vehicle cost but also the use of vehicles as they relate to services. In one case, an audit found the possibility that gasoline was being stolen. Further review found that certain investigators were not filling out gas tickets when taking assigned vehicles home.

Another audit might involve the use of police overtime. Again, while most departments have overall budget numbers, they may not keep records as to the allocation of overtime for each department member, shift, and intended purpose. An audit test in a suburban department found that most overtime costs were driven by external requests for security at professional sports and social events and that the sponsors were not compensating the department.

Audits of citizens can also be undertaken. For quality assurance, one police department polls a sample of crime and accident victims to see if the responding officers were courteous and knowledgeable in dealing with their cases. They also want to know if the officers returned phone calls to address victim concerns.

The Misconduct Review

Police administrators have to sit down and seriously review the department or divisional areas that are prone to misconduct (McCarthy, 2000; Close, 2001). This misconduct risk assessment is a review of behavior in operational areas that could result in criminal prosecution, civil legal action, internal discipline, or media attention. Misconduct assessment is based on three major premises:

1. Prohibited conduct is defined in the department rules manual, and the department manual is a "living" document that is kept updated and is constantly used for reference.
2. Citizens can make a complaint in person, by letter, by phone, or anonymously. Complaint procedures are well publicized.
3. The steps for complaint investigation, follow-up, and resolution are known not only to department members but also to the community at large. This includes officer protections provided in state civil service rules or the collective bargaining agreement.

When conducting a misconduct assessment, the first step is the internal review. The following questions should be asked during an annual review:

1. How many civil lawsuits are we facing? How much have we paid in legal fees and judgments?
2. How many civilian complaints did we receive? What was the breakdown of these complaints: discourteous behavior, poor driving habits, use of force, drug use, spousal abuse, and so on? How were these complaints resolved? Were they found to be justified? If so, what disciplinary action was taken?
3. How many disciplinary actions were initiated by the department based on supervisory referrals? What were the categories? How were they resolved? How many officers were punished?
4. How many use-of-force actions were taken by department members? Were they justified, based on internal or external (e.g., grand jury) review?
5. Do the civilian or departmental disciplinary actions seem to be directed toward a certain group of officers?
6. What is the relationship between performance evaluations and disciplinary actions for officers and supervisors?
7. Based on after-action reports, polls, and media articles, how does the public perceive us?
8. To what extent is ethics training conducted at all department levels?
9. How are department policies and regulations updated to reflect legal changes or new case law?
10. What new training programs may be needed to address specific legal issues?

When the information is being gathered, certain key operational areas always seem to emerge as problem areas. These include evidence room procedures and review for money and narcotics cases, selection and training of personnel assigned to special vice and narcotics units, and the overall conduct of narcotics investigations, including the use of informants.

Once these and other questions have been answered, the department can prioritize the areas that need attention. Basic to this would be a standard operations policy that deals with the steps to address complaints. As prepared by the International Association of Chiefs of Police (2000), a policy of this nature addresses the following:

1. Procedures that are undertaken to discipline based on violations of law, agency policy, rules, or regulations
2. The acceptance and filing of complaints (this addresses the forms that are used and what office or supervisor receives the complaint)
3. Investigation procedures by either the supervisor or another administrator
4. Interview procedures of employees and witnesses
5. Rules for drug or blood tests of employees
6. The right of employees to have union representation or counsel
7. The filing of charges if necessary
8. The resolution of the charges

Many misconduct policies also have language regarding the confidentiality of records and the prevention of employee misconduct. The former means that the department, as a general rule, is guided by the values of fairness, justice, and accountability to agency standards.

Use of Proactive Community Policing to Decrease Police Deviance

An alternative to the military model, with its adversarial aggressive stance, is the community policing model, by which the community sets the police agenda. Police middle management and line officers become empowered by working closely with community groups on the community's agenda.

For example, police management might be concerned with a rise in burglaries, while the community might be concerned with the growing power of drug dealers. In a world of scarce police resources, choices must be made. With the military command structure model, the pursuit of burglaries would be the police policy agenda. With the proactive community policing model, efforts would be made, with interagency cooperation, to curb the use of illegal drugs in the community and to arrest as many drug dealers as possible. This would be combined with drug education in schools, preaching against drugs in local churches, using government agencies to condemn crack houses, and providing reports to community groups on the success of these efforts.

This approach also curbs the effects of the police norms of solidarity, secrecy, and social isolation. The military model encourages secret decisions made by police management in the interest of security and isolates the police from the community by creating a feeling of police being different from and superior to the public. It encourages many of the bad aspects of solidarity by using such terms as "unity of command" and creating a warrior mystique (Jetmore, 1997). The proactive community model encourages more transparency for decision making by helping the community understand decision making as it exists in a police organization and having the community help set police policy concerning the goals of law enforcement in their community. It is much harder to have an aggressive, unchecked violent police effort when officers work closely with the community to lower crime. Without a military agenda, the members of the community become valuable allies in the fight against criminal activity.

Police culture is a given for police organizations, but it can be modified if the police managers want to do so and if they involve police middle management and the community in the effort. Keeping the best aspects of police cultural norms while curbing their negative aspects is a constant struggle for proactive police management, but it is worth the effort.

DUE PROCESS FOR THE POLICE AND THE PUBLIC   Police managers need to establish a procedure that treats officers accused of misconduct with respect; otherwise, the internal process of justice within the department begins to degrade officers and treat them as things. Officers need to have self-respect if they are to respect citizens. Managers need to establish "self-respect criteria" in all police hearings to protect both the public and the police officer.

Due process rights for police officers during a police hearing were established in *Morrisey* v. *Brewer* in 1972 by the U.S. Supreme Court (More, 1998). These procedural due process rights are as follows:

1. Written notice of the claimed violation
2. Disclosure of evidence
3. Opportunity to be heard in person and to present witnesses and documentary evidence
4. Right to confront and cross-examine witnesses
5. Neutral and detached hearing body
6. Written statement by the fact finders as to the evidence relied on and the reasons for the actions taken

A basically honest due process along with a sense of fair play for all parties concerned may seem to be an unrealizable and idealistic set of goals. However, without the implementation of these goals, the police officers and the public can be brutalized. Civic standards must be enforced daily.

Police departments experiencing problems, including both excessive force and other police deviance cases, need to institute new policies. Some combination of the following intervention policies needs to be analyzed in relation to the specific problems and the size and nature of the police department.

Intervention Policies

1. Identification of officers who consistently use excessive force or other police deviance with active intervention through a combination of counseling, sanctions, and removal from the police force, if necessary, should be done. The use of excessive force and obscenities should be reflected in the officer's performance evaluations.
2. Analysis and random monitoring of tape-recorded patrol car messages, with special emphasis on officers who are part of a targeted excessive-force group or who use a consistent pattern of obscenities and racist remarks. This policy may be thwarted by the use of cell phones.
3. Special investigation and intervention by a team of departmental investigators, lawyers, and counselors should be carried out. This office needs resources and support by the chief of police.
4. Written procedures for all investigations of police misconduct, including rules for witnesses and other rules of evidence, to be published and made available to all police officers and the public. Resources and policies are needed to resolve these complaints, including the use of mediators and the availability of a legal staff. This will protect the rights of both police officers and the public.
5. Specific departmental rules outlining the limits of force used by police officers, to be published and made available to both police officers and the public. This should include both legal guidelines and departmental rules.
6. Ongoing analysis of excessive use of force as part of the schedule of analysis and written reports by departmental research staff or, if the department lacks expertise and staff time, outside consultants.
7. Swift prosecution of any illegal acts by police officers and any false accusations by citizens.
8. Ongoing training for dealing with stress and anger control. Officers should have access to counseling for these and other problems.
9. Procedures for informing citizens and officers of the outcome of any complaint, in writing, with documentation, and in a timely manner.
10. Transparent internal affairs proceedings that include the public and the press in the process. Secret internal affairs proceedings create distrust. Police officers who feel that internal affairs treated them unfairly in secret proceedings support public proceedings.
11. Appeal for unsatisfied complaints by both the officers and citizens to an authority outside the department. Possibilities include a civil service board, an ombudsman, a judicial panel, binding arbitration, and the use of courts and torts.

The secret of success is to deal with every problem in a swift and fair manner without any cover-up. This means that all written rules and procedures should be written in clear English and should be concise and to the point. They should be made available in sufficient quantity for everyone. The rules then need to be followed in a fair and consistent manner by both the police officers and any complaining civilians. Once a reputation for fairness is established, both officer morale and citizen respect will increase.

Writing about the "split-second syndrome" of police violence, James J. Fyfe (1997: 539) states, "The urgent, involuntary and public relationship between police and client creates a high potential for violence. To avert it, police must apply considerable diagnostic skills." A proactive police department will have the following skills:

1. Strict and enforced departmental rules in place concerning the use of police violence
2. A stress-management and anger-control system that actively engages officers on an ongoing basis
3. A fair and public due process system for both the police and the public
4. A civilian rather than a military police management subculture
5. A professional follow-up team that deals with the use of all police violence—reasonable, excessive, justifiable, and unjustifiable.

Proactive management teams and professional police officers plan ahead by creating and following programs and policies that are in place and part of the everyday life of every officer in the department.

Conclusion

Central administrative functions structure the day-to-day activities of the police agency. These functions are part of management prerogatives and are central to the major administrative authority in the department. When management talks about the internal staff of the agency, it is referring to the support personnel that cater to the needs of the line operations.

There is a natural antipathy between line officers and the administrative staff. The administrative staff structures and carries out the basic policies of the department and delivers these policies to the management. Supervisory staff are expected to exercise authority over the line officers in carrying out these tasks. Full communication between line and staff is essential if the cooperation that is needed to have a well-run department is to be achieved.

Three major staff functions are community relations, legal advice, and internal affairs. Community relations can be as simple as an individual officer in a small department or as complicated as a separate unit in a larger department. Traditionally, community relations officers have given speeches and have participated in a wide range of community programs. However, the proactive management approach advocates a more active role for the police officers in the community. This means that all officers are trained in community relations and are expected to make

community relations a part of their duties as police officers, taking part, for example, in such activities as teaching a minicourse in criminal justice at the local high school and organizing sports teams for teenagers.

The legal adviser is usually a full-time attorney employed by the department who can provide up-to-date training in changes in the law and screen cases so that the department has a better conviction record. This is a cost-efficient position. Smaller departments rely on the services of the village or town attorney.

Professional standards/internal affairs is one of the most difficult units to organize. To be effective, it must be evenhanded and represent the rights of both the citizens who are being policed and the officers who are doing the policing. It must be proactive in the sense of having an ongoing anticorruption program. This means that the rules and regulations concerning discipline and corruption are in place and operational before there is any hint of a problem. Too many times, these internal rules and regulations are written and organized in reaction to specific instances of discipline problems and corruption. These reactive rules are often inconsistent since they relate to specific instances rather than to general behavior. Consistency and fairness have to be the major goals of any professional standards/internal affairs unit.

These administrative functions, although closely tied to management, are essential to the operation of the total department. They affect all the personnel and, in the instances of community relations and internal affairs, can have a major impact on the department's image in the community. If the department is to be considered a professional police agency by the citizens of the community, these administrative functions have to be managed with a great deal of skill, knowledge, and consistency.

Police deviance and use of excessive force have become major concerns for police management in the United States today. Immediate and systematic attention has to be paid to these issues. Some departments are taking a proactive and honest approach, while other departments are still in the covering-up and making-excuses stages. Police management in the twenty-first century of global information, Web sites, and press and citizen scrutiny has to have policies and an openness that make sense under existing conditions. The proactive approach to controlling police deviance and violence can and will work, but it will take a great deal of change and personal courage.

Questions for Review

1. In your community, what recourse is available to a person who complains of police misconduct or corruption? To what agencies may he or she submit the complaint?

2. What are the causes of line/staff tension in police organizations? How can these problems be addressed?

3. It would appear that every police officer is a community relations person. Why, then, is it necessary to have specific personnel assigned to this task?

4. Explain the strengths and weaknesses of the following community relations programs: tours and demonstrations, ride-alongs, college internships, and crime-prevention programs.

5. In general, what are the duties of a community relations officer?

6. List the main points of the anticorruption program presented in this chapter.

7. Why have police corruption and misconduct been a persistent problem in the United States?

Class Projects

1. Select a police department in your community and through a phone call or via a Web site ascertain if the department has a reporting form that citizens may use to report an incident of police misconduct. If the person reports that it does not, ask how citizens can make complaints. Also see if there are forms available on the Internet.

2. In a similar vein, review the various crime prevention and informational services presented by a specific department. To what extent has the department adopted various Internet-based services to inform the public about crime and emergency situations?

Web Works

Conduct a review of department Web sites in an assigned state or area to see if the organizational functions presented in this book come under the heading of administrative or staff functions. Also check to see when the Web page was last updated. For your own career use, see if the Web page includes employment listings and procedures for hiring. Finally, see if the site will accept or review how a citizen may file a complaint against the department or a department member.

References

Barker, Thomas, and David L. Carter. "A Typology of Police Deviance." In Thomas Barker and David L. Carter, eds., *Police Deviance* (3rd ed.). Cincinnati: Anderson, 1994a, pp. 3–30.

———. *Police Deviance* (3rd ed.). Cincinnati: Anderson, 1994b.

Blumberg, Mark. "Controlling Police Use of Deadly Force: Assessing Two Decades of Progress." In Roger G. Dunham and Godfrey P. Alpert, eds., *Critical Issues in Policing*. Prospect Heights, Ill.: Waveland Press, 1997, pp. 507–530.

Broadway, Fred. "Police Misconduct: Positive Alternatives." *Journal of Police Science and Administration*, 2, no. 2 (1974), pp. 224–232.

Christopher Commission. "Report of the Independent Commission of the Los Angeles Police Department." In Thomas Barker and David L. Carter, eds., *Police Deviance* (3rd ed.). Cincinnati: Anderson, 1994, pp. 291–306.

Close, Dale H. "How Chiefs Should Prepare for Nine Liability Risks." *Police Chief* (June 2001), pp. 16–27.

Crank, John P., and Michael Caldero. *Police Ethics: The Corruption of Noble Cause*. Cincinnati: Anderson, 2000.

Fyfe, James J. "The Split Second Syndrome and Other Determinates of Police Violence." In Roger G. Dunham and Godfrey P. Alpert, eds., *Critical Issues in Policing*. Prospect Heights, Ill.: Waveland Press, 1997, pp. 531–546.

Goldman, H. "Legal Claims Add to New York City's Budget Woes." *Bloomberg Businessweek*, 2012. Retrieved from businessweek.com/articles/2012-09-13/legal-claims-add-to-new-york-citys-budget-woes

Gordon, Gary, and Bruce McBride. *Criminal Justice Internships: Theory into Practice* (7th ed.). Cincinnati: Anderson/Lexis Nexis, 2012.

International Association of Chiefs of Police. "Model Policy Offers Guidance on Investigating Officer Misconduct." *Police Chief* (October 2000), pp. 44–47.

Jetmore, Larry F. *The Path of the Warrior*. Flushing, N.Y.: Looseleaf Law Publications, 1997.

Kappler, Victor E., Richard D. Sluder, and Geoffrey P. Alpert. *Forces of Deviance: Understanding the Dark Side of Policing* (2nd ed.). Prospect Heights, Ill.: Waveland Press, 1994.

Knapp Commission. *Police Corruption in New York*. New York: Whitman Knapp, 1972.

Lersch, Kim M. *Policing and Misconduct*. Upper Saddle River, N.J.: Prentice Hall, 2002.

McCarthy, Robert. "Steps Chiefs Can Take to Prevent Unethical Behavior." *Police Chief* (October 2000), pp. 36–40.

McGurrin, Danielle, and Victor Kappler. "Media Accounts of Police Sexual Violence: Rotten Apples or State-Supported Violence." In Kim M. Lersch, ed., *Policing and Misconduct*. Upper Saddle River, N.J.: Prentice Hall, 2002.

More, H.W. *Special Topics in Policing* (2nd ed.). Cincinnati: Anderson, 1998.

Nigro, Felix A., and Lloyd G. Nigro. *Modern Public Administration* (4th ed.). New York: Harper and Row, 1977.

Packman, D. *The Truth about Police Misconduct Litigation*. CATO Institute, 2010. Retrieved from policemisconduct.net/the-truth-about-police-misconduct-litigation/

Parks, B. *Rampart Area Corruption Incident*, 2000. Retrieved from lapdonline.org/assets/pdf/boi_pub.pdf

President's Commission On Law Enforcement and the Administration of Justice. *The Police*. Washington, D.C.: U.S. Government Printing Office, 1967.

Reaves, B. *Census for State and Local Law Enforcement Agencies, 2008*. US Department of Justice, Office of Justice Programs, Bureau of Justice Statistics, 2011.

Sherman, Lawrence. "The Sociology and Social Reform of American Police, 1950–1973." *Journal of Police Science and Administration* (September 1974), pp. 255–262.

Smith, Ralph Lee. *The Tarnished Badge*. New York: Crowley Press, 1965.

United States Department of Justice. *Police Integrity: Public Service With Honor*, National Institute of Justice, Office of Justice Programs, 1997. Retrieved from nij.gov/pubs-sum/163811.htm

Van Maanen, John. "The Asshole." In Peter K. Manning and John Van Maanen, eds., *Policing: A View from the Street*. Santa Monica, Calif.: Goodyear, 1978, pp. 221–238.

Walker, Samuel, Geoffrey P. Alpert, and Dennis J. Kenny. *Early Warning System: Responding to the Problem Police Officer*. Washington, D.C.: National Institute of Justice, 2001.

White, Mervin F., Terry C. Cox, and Jack Basehart. "Theoretical Considerations of Officer Profanity and Obscenity in Formal Contacts with Citizens." In Thomas Barker and David L. Carter, eds., *Police Deviance* (3rd ed.), Cincinnati: Anderson, 1994, pp. 223–246.

11 Auxiliary Functions

KEY TERMS

criminalistics

deoxyribonucleic acid (DNA)

emergency plan

forensic science

Freedom of Information Act

Integrated Automatic Fingerprint
 Identification System (IAFIS)

mobile radio district (MRD)

purging

records

sealing

temporary detention facility

P olice organizations, no matter what the size, need personnel to obtain and supply resources to line and administrative units or individuals. Portions of the organization that fulfill this function are called *auxiliary services*. Auxiliary services provide the "behind-the-scenes" support for the police organization. They could also be titled *supporting services* since these services are necessary, normally, to support the daily business of the police agency.

The discussion in this chapter concerns the major auxiliary functions that appear in most departments. Depending on local conditions, other supporting services may be necessary. The auxiliary functions used by most police agencies include (1) communications, encompassing case records, criminal records, and identification; (2) records; (3) property control; (4) vehicle maintenance; (5) building maintenance; (6) licensing; (7) the crime laboratory, including photographic, chemical, and physical evidence laboratories; and (8) ancillary public safety services, including emergency mobilization, animal control, and emergency medical services.

COMMUNICATIONS

Some agencies assign communications to the patrol division since a great deal of communications is related to the patrol function. However, communications serves the whole department. Traffic officers, detectives, laboratory specialists, and experts from other special units all need access to communications. In a modern department, a centralized communications and records unit is considered the most efficient way to organize this major auxiliary section.

The efficiency and effectiveness of daily police operations depend on the nature of the communications unit maintained by the department. This unit must be able to provide the following:

1. Landline, cellular telephone, and other electronic reception for emergency, nonemergency, and inquiry calls
2. Base-to-field communications and return by wireless radio and computers
3. Retrieval of police information related to wanted individuals, lost property, vehicle ownership, and motorist information (commonly referred to as the DATA function)
4. Interface with or scanning of area and statewide police agencies
5. Interface with or scanning of area fire and ambulance, and other emergency services

The degree to which these services are provided depends not only on the size and jurisdiction of the police agency but also on the degree of economic investment that the municipality wishes to make for computerized communications equipment. At present, the advances made in communications and computer technology provide the opportunity for every police department in the United States to offer these services to personnel and the community.

The case study that follows illustrates some of the capabilities of modern communications systems. The nearest cars from the jurisdiction were dispatched since this was a regional communications system. In addition, the dispatched officers had instant access to all records—local, state, and national. In terms of providing the maximum amount of information in a very short time, the system had lived up to expectations.

Consolidation

In an effort to solve communications inferiority, some police agencies have pooled their resources and have formed a **mobile radio district (MRD)**, making a centralized communications center the main reception center for telephone calls for police assistance. Member agencies in the MRD are dispatched according to their jurisdiction. If an officer is in trouble or if a serious emergency occurs requiring the presence of many patrol units from the member agencies, the communications center will be able to act as the focal point for activity coordination. Computers for local and national police information are maintained and operated at the center, and member agencies are provided with a terminal to be used in their own station houses. Mobile, portable, and base-station radio equipment is procured and maintained under the coordination of the MRD. To address issues that arise on procedures or other situations, the MRD has a representative committee of member agencies that meets frequently to iron out any problems.

Consolidated communications centers and 911 Centers using the MRD model have been established all over the United States in heavily populated metropolitan areas or through geographical necessity. One problem that arises in MRD formation is the influence that the political faction or agency that controls the communications center may have on all police operations for that area. This is a common problem when an agency, such as the state police, the sheriff's department, or a town police department, has concurrent jurisdiction with city, village, or town agencies. The question that always comes up is: Who will receive the "glory" calls? This is usually solved by de facto arrangements and formal guidelines ensuring that city units will respond to

CASE STUDY

Communications

On April 12, 2013, Mrs. Stephen Jones telephoned the Riverside Police Department, stating that her husband was threatening to kill her and that she had locked herself in a bedroom. She stayed on the phone and gave the dispatcher a continuous update as her husband tried to break down the door. Her call was recorded on a digital recorder unit. Units 303 and 410 were dispatched to the residence. While en route, the communicator replayed the conversation to the officers on channel 1 of their multichannel mobile radio. The officers responding to the scene therefore had a general picture of the situation as related by Mrs. Jones. At the conclusion of the playback, Unit 303 "punched" the husband's name into the mobile data terminal and found that a man of the same name and address had been arrested by the department four years ago for assault with a deadly weapon. His picture was also brought up on the computer screen. On arrival at the scene, one officer noted that a black BMW sports car was parked in the driveway.

Using the mobile data terminal, the officer looked up the license plate and found that it belonged to a subject by the name of Stephen Jones, who had three outstanding warrants for burglary and assault. A detective unit also arrived at the scene. Using a cellular telephone, the detective called the residence and asked for Mr. Jones. Using his powers of persuasion, the detective asked Mr. Jones to come outside to talk to him about the outstanding parking tickets issued to his valuable sports car.

calls in their jurisdiction and that other units will respond only in emergencies or at the request of the agency. The solution of this problem has been crucial in the formation of consolidated police communications networks.

Communications Personnel

The police subculture at one time viewed those personnel who work inside communications as second-class citizens since they are not out on the streets doing "real" police work. As a result, officers assigned to communications were looked on with some measure of disdain. In some agencies, the communications assignment is viewed as being for those who have physical ailments or have "screwed up" in some way; yet there is nothing second-class about police communications.

These attitudes have changed because of the importance of the communications function and the amount of technological expertise needed. It is not uncommon for police communications supervisors in large agencies to have formal degrees in electronics, computers, or communications and to be able to write grants and computer programs for elaborate police information-communications systems. Because personnel with this type of background are difficult to recruit for general police work, many agencies have relied on civilians with relevant work and educational backgrounds to manage their communications systems.

The communications person is the "ambassador" of the department to the outside world. His or her tone and manner of dealing with questions and situations has immediate impact for many clients, ranging from first responders to community leaders. Communications personnel have to think like police officers when they speak to callers. They often have to go beyond the simple question-and-answer scenarios. For example, a woman calling about being locked out of her car was asked, "Is there anyone locked inside your car?" As it turned out, her five-month-old son was in his car seat, and the temperature was 92 degrees. Her simple request now required an emergency response.

Police departments and regional dispatch centers increasingly use civilians as communicators. In addition to classroom training, the civilian communicator should be assigned to observe patrol operations so as to get a feel for the geography and personalities of the sworn officers with whom he or she will be working. In the same vein, rookie police officers should be assigned to the communications sector for the same reasons. Supervision of a shift in the communications section should be by an experienced sworn officer who, in addition to normal administrative tasks, will act as commander for emergency situations.

In small police departments, the communications function is handled by one person who, in addition to police responsibilities, also has to act as desk clerk and fire dispatcher. Again, there is no clear-cut formula for the number of people assigned to this function. It depends on the size of the agency and jurisdiction as well as on the amount of activity and technology that the agency has to handle.

Personal Attributes

Police communicators should be familiar with all aspects of police operations and agency procedures. A good communicator, in practice, will have the ability to screen calls and solve those situations on the phone that do not require police presence at the scene. As most police communications personnel relate, working on the police telephones and radios is a stressful job. It requires a number of personal qualities—tact, politeness, coolness, rational decision making—and the ability to perform seven different tasks at once. For the police subculture, the chief client of the communicator is the officer on the street, as he or she is responsible for the safety and informational updating of each and every one of the officers. Experienced communicators know when an officer is in trouble simply by a nuance or failure to call back while doing a task (e.g., a vehicle and traffic stop) in a reasonable length of time. Officers assigned to street duty realize this. One of the first inquiries made at the beginning of the shift is "Who's on the radio?"

Today in police training, communications procedures are a standard part of the basic police curriculum. Academies with modern facilities may have a mock communications area where recruits respond to mock telephone calls and requests for information, dispatch patrols, and calm irate citizens—all at the same time! Civilian personnel must be trained according to the same procedures and methods as regular police officers. For example, many states require that all dispatchers complete a one-week training program in police communications. In addition to mock calls, dispatchers learn basic first aid, crisis management, and communications theory.

RECORDS MANAGEMENT SYSTEM

As in all bureaucracies and complex organizations, the efficient recording and flow of paperwork are essential to the successful operation of the police agency. The records division is often considered part of the communications division or at least it works closely with the communications division.

Although often downgraded in terms of funding and personnel, the records division is an important tool for management. To allocate resources, personnel, and budgeted funds, an accessible information system is needed. This means that the information has to be available in more than raw form. Thus, the chief task of records personnel involves classifying, filing, and indexing police paperwork by numerical, alphabetical, and numerous other classification systems, so that this information is accessible for later convenient retrieval. Information is also needed for informing the public and other private and public agencies, such as defense attorneys, prosecutors, and insurance companies.

For police operations, **records** may be divided into the following categories:

Category	Tasks/Operations
People	Arrestees, complainants, victims, missing persons, wanted persons (for questioning or by warrant), and fingerprints
Motor vehicles	Accidents, inquiries, fatalities, moving violations, and parking tickets
Administration	Personnel, payroll, scheduling, budget, purchases, inventories, and fleet and building maintenance
Crime statistics	Arrests and crime reports by legal statute, area, age, race, and so on
Property	Lost, found, stolen
Other	Jail, operations, court dispositions, bail monies, and referral services

These six categories may or may not be centralized, depending on the management philosophy or operational history of the department. Each line, staff, or auxiliary division might maintain its own records system in addition to a centralized system. Investigative divisions, for example, often maintain a file of suspicious people or incidents via modus operandi. Be it a centralized or a decentralized records system, the overall records function is a mainstay of police operations—providing data for investigative leads, allocating resources for certain types of cases, or preparing state or national crime reports.

One of the main goals of the records section is to present a total reporting picture that is critical for management decision making in such areas as workload, types of incidents, and assessment of hazards. The types of crimes encountered or reported are important for participation in the *Uniform Crime Reports* or the National Incident Based Reporting System (NIBRS) program. Disposition information is also critical, as indicated by the following disposition descriptors:

1. Arrest made (refer to original offense report)
2. Assistance rendered
3. Canceled by radio
4. Citation issued
5. Civil matter
6. False alarm
7. Follow-up (supplemental report made)
8. No police action possible/necessary
9. Peace restored without incident
10. Referred to agency other than police department
11. Referred to other police department division

Computerization

Police organizations began to use computers in the early 1960s. Not only was the computer, by this time, an important tool for information transmission and storage, but it was also beginning to be used for managerial decision making. As shown in other chapters, computers have been experimented with in determining patrol allocation and operations in many American cities.

Plentiful funding for computer acquisition was available throughout the 1960s and early 1970s, which made it possible for many police departments in large metropolitan areas to establish computerized data and communications systems.

At present, computer utilization and software programs have been applied to the records function for most police departments. The positive attributes of computer utilization for data retrieval are as follows:

1. Lower routine operating costs of data processing
2. Faster availability of information
3. Possibility of an audit of the system
4. Greater consistency of reporting data
5. Reduced data distortion as the data move from line operations to staff
6. Development of a giant data inventory
7. Greater freedom from mundane, routine record keeping

Entering, storing, and sharing this extensive volume of information continues to get easier due to electronic enhancement elements. What 10 years ago required an entire room of filing cabinets for storage may now fit into a pocket full of flashdrives—or maybe even one the size of a piece of gum.

Computer and Communications Administrator

A new job title that has emerged in this new millennium is that of information technology (IT) director to administer a department's communications and computer system. Technology has become very important in daily operations. However, there needs to be personnel who are educated and trained to administer this phase of the operation. Administrative tasks overseen by such a person or unit include the following:

- Planning and design
- Purchasing
- Installation
- Troubleshooting
- Evaluation
- Renovation
- Staff training

With the expansion of technology in policing, the most somber task facing many police executives is information systems procurement. As anyone who has attended the annual conference of the International Association of Chiefs of Police can attest, the available equipment and software is endless. It seems that information technology equipment changes almost overnight. The most important issue is the expected life cycle and life cycle cost for the system.

The key to this, lies in carefully planning and presenting a procurement proposal to various vendors. The core question involves having an expert on your staff who can devote himself or herself to this task and analyze department needs and available equipment. What often happens is that department heads use certain vendors to act as their information technology staff. For small departments, obtaining the services of a consultant is advisable.

Storage of Records

Historians bemoan the loss or damage of the nineteenth- and twentieth-century records of many American police departments, especially by fire or paper decomposition. This continues to be a special problem since paper processing requires the use of acids that break down the paper.

Also, it is not uncommon to see stacks of police files stored in cardboard boxes gathering dust and moisture in the dark recesses of the station house. This situation has been caused by the lack of storage space for the tons of paperwork created annually and is an unprofessional approach to storage and record retention. The old adage, "One man's garbage is another man's treasure," can come into play. For example, one young sergeant having been recently assigned to a new station house took it upon himself to clear the squad room of clutter. Any document he hadn't seen used in his career was tossed as useless. A veteran patrol officer came into the squad room and saw the piles of papers and old documents in the trash. The officer immediately pulled out one binder of papers from the pile, and complained that that binder couldn't be thrown out, as it contained copies of station personnel schedules going back 20 years. The young sergeant agreed, stating that that was why the binder was in the garbage. What the sergeant saw as useless, space consuming clutter, the veteran patrol officer recognized as valued station history. The ultimate decision can be a fine line. The solution today is to have all the paper record items scanned so that they can be digitally saved for future generations.

Except for those records that, by law, need to be kept in the original, all storage should be microprocessed or scanned. This means that all records are reduced by the various processes available to modern library systems through electronic retention in computer-generated files. There also needs to be a specific retention period for all records. There are problems with this cost-efficient approach to record retention and retrieval: (1) the laws need to be changed, (2) the expense of processing records into microform has to be reduced, and (3) the cost of a retrieval system, including readers and machines to produce hard copy from microcopy, has to come down. The costs of such a system are declining as more and more research libraries create systems using microprocessing of research materials. The U.S. government has encouraged and sponsored numerous research projects to bring down the cost of processing and using micromaterials.

Security, Sealing, Purging, and Public Access to Records

Police departments generally desire that police records be kept confidential to maintain the effectiveness of law enforcement operations. This is especially important since a large percentage of police information involves the criminal history of suspects and arrestees. It is therefore imperative that the police agency ensures the confidentiality and integrity of criminal history information through administrative, computer, and physical security requirements. Based on the Department of Justice regulations with regard to security of federally funded information systems, the following guidelines apply to all police agencies (New York State Department of Criminal Justice Services, 2013).

1. Access to criminal history information—namely, records, computer files, or the operating environments where police information is stored—should be restricted to authorized personnel.
2. Police personnel that have access to criminal history information are responsible for protecting this information from unauthorized access, disclosure, or dissemination.
3. The supervisors assigned to oversee the records function are ultimately responsible for all records.
4. Through written directives, standard operating procedures, and updated procedures, each member of the police organization should be familiar with the substance and intent of record security regulations.

While police organizations are intent on protecting the confidentiality of their records, citizens must have access to police information, especially when that information is related to the individual. In the 1970s, a number of acts were passed by Congress as reforms to the abuses of federal and state domestic spying and increased classification of government operations. The **Freedom of Information Act** of 1974 allowed citizens to request public records and to attend meetings of a nonconfidential nature. The Privacy Act, passed in the same year, gave individuals access to personal records and restricted the collection, maintenance, and distribution of personal information in both private and public agencies. In general, an individual requesting a federal document must go through a formalized process to obtain a copy of the record.

Federal and state regulations give every person who is the subject of a criminal history record the right to do the following:

- Request to be shown a copy of the record at a reasonably convenient location and time
- Review the record (with assistance of a reader/translator, if needed)
- Receive a copy of the record for purpose of challenge
- Request that a record be corrected on a showing of inaccuracy or incompleteness
- Obtain administrative review of record-correction denial
- Request, for purpose of correction, a list of noncriminal justice recipients of inaccurate information (criminal justice recipients to be notified directly by criminal justice agency)

The regulations do not provide a right to review the following:

- Any information other than "criminal history information"
- Any information contained in intelligence or investigatory files

State and/or local criminal justice agencies are required to establish procedures for the following:

- Review of criminal history information by the record subject
- Challenge by the record subject of information that is believed to be inaccurate or incomplete
- Review of source documents by the criminal justice agency to determine accuracy/completeness of challenged information
- Administrative appeal by the record subject of an agency's refusal to correct a record
- Correction of information that has been disseminated that is shown to be incorrect

Citizens and their authorized attorneys are allowed to access and obtain a copy of their own criminal history record. The criminal history report will contain employment or license history where fingerprints are required, a "no record" response, or a chronology of criminal charges. Citizens may also modify their criminal history by contacting the arresting agency or, in cases of disposition data, the court of adjudication. In the case of the FBI record, on payment of a fee or proof of indigency, a citizen may receive a copy of his or her record. However, the FBI will accept corrections to the record only from the agency that sent the FBI the original data.

For police operations, the right to privacy may come into conflict with the need for accurate data on criminal suspects. Yet much police data contain information of little value or are outdated. For example, many people are arrested whose cases result in dismissal or acquittal. When police information systems keep a record of wanted or arrested individuals by street address, it is often the case that the information is outdated. The suggestion that a suspect may still be living on the premises indeed affects the officer's perceptions as he or she responds to a call to the location in question. Both hand-recorded and computerized police information systems, therefore, should have policies that allow the removal of outdated or incorrect information. Two methods that apply to this procedure are (1) **purging**, as when the record is either destroyed or returned to the individual (this often occurs for the arrest records and fingerprint cards of individuals who have been acquitted or found not guilty), and (2) **sealing**, as when general access to the information is strictly limited except for certain instances or individuals. Sealing is generally done for juvenile offenders; only youth officers or officials of the juvenile court can officially have access to the information.

Purging and sealing are used for outdated or declassified information or when legal changes are made, for example, the decriminalization of alcohol or drug offenses.

PROPERTY CONTROL

The property clerk, who may be a sworn officer or a civilian, is the person in charge of the property section. Property is divided into (1) inventory control of physical property, (2) evidence control for court cases, and (3) found property, such as bicycles that have been abandoned in the street. Some police agencies that provide uniforms also have the property clerk serve as quartermaster, issuing and taking care of uniforms.

Inventory Control

Inventory control of physical property can have a major impact on the budget in that this property is being used 24 hours a day, as opposed to the more normal 8-hour or 12-hour day. Planning—including regular maintenance and replacement control—becomes significant to day-to-day operations. Thus, to control inventory, the property clerk has to be on top of what is happening to the physical property. Examples of physical property are desks, chairs, file cabinets, the buildings themselves, heating and cooling units, and so on. Desktop computers may cost over a thousand dollars each and have to be maintained and replaced regularly so the department will be able to recoup residual values by selling these items as secondhand equipment. All this takes strict auditing as well as inventory control. Businesslike procedures created by a full-time property clerk are necessary if the department is to justify this part of the budget to legislative authorities. Estimates must be made of the life use of each item in a police setting, and periodic physical inspections must be conducted to confirm this life use.

In some cases, inventory purchases may be out of the jurisdiction of the property section because of a state or county purchase plan. However, the same principles apply. Also, any civilian agency has to be made aware of the special problems of servicing a 24-hour police department.

Evidence Control

Evidence control will be treated more fully when we examine the basic management of the police laboratory. However, two major principles apply here: continuity and security. A record must be kept of anyone handling any police evidence, and detailed records must be maintained concerning what happens to a piece of evidence whenever it leaves the property room. The second principle of security is paramount in any police agency. However, in the use of civilian personnel, special background checks should be made, and in-and-out security measures need to be strictly observed. One of the major problems relates to keeping drugs in the property room. Small amounts of certain drugs are worth so much money in the street that the temptation of civilians and officers to make a quick dollar is always there. Evidence areas must be audited on a regular basis.

CONTINUITY OF EVIDENCE Continuity of evidence means that there is a clearly documented record of where a piece of evidence has been, along with a record of who handled the evidence and why, from the time the evidence is picked up at the crime scene until it appears in a court case.

Any break in the continuity of evidence is an opportunity for a sharp defense lawyer to break a case. The property clerk, or designee, maintains the security of evidence as it is delivered from the crime scene and documents continuity in the following steps:

1. Evidence is collected by evidence technicians at the crime scene and is sealed in plastic bags or appropriate containers to prevent contamination. It is also marked for future identification, giving date and circumstance of obtaining the evidence on the package or article. On this container or article will be a form that everyone who handles the evidence will sign and date; they will also give a reason for handling the evidence.
2. Evidence goes to the lab if necessary or to the property clerk. Any detective or police officer who handles any evidence during investigation signs in and out for the evidence. All evidence is to be returned to the property clerk for safeguarding when not needed.
3. At the end of the investigation, evidence is often transferred to the district attorney's office, where continuity of evidence must be maintained in case of appeal. The evidence is considered to be the prosecutor's responsibility until he or she returns it to the property clerk.
4. In addition, there must be security and oversight measures for high-risk evidence (narcotics, money, jewels, and firearms). These items must be inventoried on a routine basis, and only certain personnel may have clearance to enter the evidence area. There must also be a process by which old evidence is either returned to owners, auctioned off, or destroyed. It is no secret that many property rooms are full of items gathering dust.

Found Property

Found property is something of a nuisance for the department to handle, but it can be a real service if returned to a citizen. At periodic intervals, after the property has been kept for a reasonable period of time, a public auction is held to sell remaining property. The money from the auction goes into the general coffers.

VEHICLE MAINTENANCE

Next to personnel, police vehicle acquisition, operation, and maintenance represent a major portion of budgetary expenditures whether the department has a fleet numbering 3 or 300 vehicles. A fully equipped police vehicle today includes emergency marking, lights, and computer equipment. Police vehicles that are purchased on contract contain additional items such as enhanced cooling and electrical systems, antitheft ignition, and other items. The average price for a marked sedan with all of the above is approximately $40,000.

Because of the high cost of gasoline, police departments are seeking ways to reduce vehicle operating costs by redefining patrol objectives, increasing foot patrols, redesigning patrol sectors, or experimenting with smaller, more fuel-efficient vehicles. Departments are also using bicycle patrols in certain areas.

Police vehicles are on the road a good part of the 24-hour day. They normally clock between 80,000 and 100,000 miles before they are retired, depending on increased maintenance costs and downtime records. Police vehicles are purchased in large numbers, often with a state or municipal contract.

With these variables in mind, patrol vehicle selection is an important decision. The chief criterion is the environment. Rural and suburban departments generally need vehicles that have space for equipment as well as passengers since the patrol car serves as an office. Municipal departments that operate comparatively close to the police station may be better served by more fuel-efficient vehicles. Terrain and weather are also important considerations for the selection of four-wheel-drive vehicles that can operate in the snow, on hillsides, or in beach areas to supplement the fleet.

One problem affecting many departments is that exact specifications need to be drawn for specific job requirements. However, if the police vehicle cannot accelerate or corner better than the normal stock vehicle, then, especially on highway patrol jobs, the police job simply cannot be done.

Each department should have a preventive maintenance program to detect problems before actual breakdowns occur. With the exception of patrol operations on interstate highways and rural areas, most patrol cars operate on "idle" or stop-and-start situations and then suddenly must increase speed from 0 to 60 miles per hour in emergency situations. Considering the potholed streets, bumpy parking lots, and fields they travel, it is no wonder that most patrol vehicles are functionally dead by 100,000 miles. Moreover, because of the lack of spare vehicles, many departments actually keep their cars running 24 hours a day with "time off" only for maintenance or shift changes.

Preventive and actual maintenance for vehicles is handled by police or municipally operated central garages or, in smaller communities, by private contractors. In any case, each administrator will have to decide which method is desirable based on cost-effectiveness and availability of service and facilities offered by the municipal government. Mechanics who work on the police vehicles and maintenance records should be considered important resources for data on vehicle effectiveness, operating costs, and systems that are prone to break down (e.g., electrical system, cooling system, and tires).

Preventive maintenance is also important because of the variety of drivers for each vehicle, the heavy use, and the use of the vehicles in life-and-death situations. Management needs to be aware of the driving habits of its personnel, including the need for review classes on driving habits and continual testing. Part of this process is the creation of an accident review board where all accidents are strictly analyzed. The result of such a review may mean disciplinary action against sworn personnel and vehicle maintenance staff. It can also mean that management will have to review when a vehicle should no longer be in use. Some models of cars last longer than others, and safety can be maintained only through the use of continual review. Many departments prefer to purchase half their fleet every year, whereas smaller departments may wait for two or perhaps three years to update. Many factors enter into this decision, including the rotation of vehicles into other units of the agency requiring less demanding vehicle usage.

The most important aspect of this discussion lies with the individual officer assigned to the vehicle. He or she is responsible not only for operating the vehicle in a safe manner but also for reporting all minor and major defects that come to his or her attention. Preventive maintenance includes checking oil levels, tire pressure, and emergency equipment before each shift. Cleanliness of interiors is important for public appearance and morale. Some officers would agree that their patrol units look like the devil because of exterior dirt, and waste paper, and candy wrappers and dirt strewn about the interior. Just as many agencies pride themselves on the appearance of their uniforms, so too do many on the appearance of their patrol vehicles, as they are such a visual representation of the agency—and in most cases, the only image many observers ever see. For this reason, police supervisors should hold accountable officers who return their vehicles to the station unkempt.

In Chapter 8 we reviewed the strengths and weaknesses of police bikes, which are an asset for areas with small roadways or large numbers of people. Most departments use several brands of mountain bikes that have become industry standards. There have been a number of departments that have adopted all-terrain vehicles (ATVs) for beach and woodland patrol that allow access to remote areas. ATVs play an important role in the patrol function for the Nantucket Police Department. Nantucket, an island of approximately 6,000 year-round residents and 15,000 summer visitors, is located 30 miles off Cape Cod, Massachusetts. There are several major beaches, and two or three units patrol during the morning and late-afternoon shifts. Patrol officers usually look for parking violations and disruptive persons and offer assistance for water rescues and medical emergencies. As motor vehicles can be driven on certain beaches, they are also used to enforce permits regulations, which can carry stiff fines. Safety is very important. Patrol officers must wear a helmet with goggles at all times. A great deal of time is spent on maintenance as there is a 30-point checklist that ranges from fluid check to police light connections. After each shift, the unit must be washed down to get rid of the sand and salt. While this type of patrol may sound inviting, there are downsides. On particularly hot, humid days when there is no offshore wind, beach patrol can be hot, sweaty, and dusty work.

Perhaps the most unusual vehicle is the Segway, a battery-powered unit that looks like a Roman chariot, which has been adapted for shopping mall, campus, airport, and parking lot patrol. In all applications, training and maintenance of the patrol unit are very important.

At this time, a great deal of attention is focused on hybrid vehicles, which operate on both gas and electric power. The main objective in developing these vehicles for general use is to reduce gas consumption. The following are issues for police applications:

- The comparatively higher cost of hybrid vehicles in comparison to gas-powered conventional vehicles
- Greater maintenance costs for hybrid vehicles
- Safety concerns related to electrical fires in the event of an accident
- Support for police technology by the vehicle's electrical system
- Lack of space for equipment

The efforts by departments to adopt hybrid vehicles are captured by a Web site entitled hybridcars.com. As reported on the site, a number of police departments are moving to hybrid units to save money on gasoline especially those classified as SUVs.

At some point there will be greater use of these hybrid vehicles. Perhaps all-electric vehicles will also be an option once fuel-cell technology is mastered. The use of all-electric vehicles at this time is very limited because of the time that is needed to recharge batteries.

Personal Patrol Car

The use of the personal patrol car has been a controversial topic. In the most common program model, the officer is assigned a marked patrol unit and drives it home at the conclusion of the shift. Variations of the program include one vehicle being assigned to a group of officers who live near one another. Proponents view the program as a way of increasing police presence in neighborhoods and improving emergency response time to critical situations. In theory, the officer assigned to a car would take better care of it and would make sure that scheduled routine maintenance is completed.

A study of personal patrol vehicles for a sheriff's department in a rural area by Fitzgerald (2002) found that the capital costs in purchasing vehicles and equipment was substantially higher when compared to purchasing a centralized fleet of vehicles. However, the operating costs were lower, and the vehicles were able to stay in service years beyond the normal range for fleet vehicles.

There are a number of management issues with personal patrol vehicles. Although changing shifts in the field may save some time and gas in going to a central office, management loses control over the officer and direct communication. Supervisory problems are created in that traditionally an officer would be subject to inspection of his or her person and equipment at a station roll call. Lack of regular inspections can lead to potential abuses of personal hygiene or equipment violations. Also, the lines of communication become more critical, and careful checks must be maintained to avoid miscommunicating the routine daily orders and directives.

In a few cases, there may be some justification for this approach, as when (1) the canine corps needs special vehicles, (2) undercover cars are needed for surveillance, and (3) large rural areas are involved. In the case of rural areas, regional garages may help to modify the distance problems.

One last problem of personal use police cars is that police officers, while off duty, may involve civilian friends and their families in police business where there is potential violence. This means increased insurance concerning potential harm of these civilians. It could also mean an increase in damage suits by civilians against the police agency. When the officer is off duty and wearing old clothes (e.g., cleaning out a basement and then going to a hardware store), he or she does not evoke a professional image in a personal patrol car. Although the increased presence of police cars has had an effect, there is a question whether this has a positive or a negative effect. In summary, departments embarking on this program must have very direct guidelines on when the vehicle may be used and under what conditions.

Around the country it is common for the chief and senior police administrators to be assigned a department vehicle both as a benefit and that the administrator is one call away 24 hours a day. Because of reported abuses of this privilege, many departments have had to create policies for "take home" vehicles. In general, the policy should include appropriate use of the car for personal errands, the extent to which non-department personnel may ride in the car, and keeping records on gas and vehicle maintenance. Questions have arisen as to whether the vehicle is a taxable benefit; the Internal Revenue Service has issued guidelines on this issue and has generally determined that if the vehicle sports a "police package" with lights and other emergency equipment and if the driver is on-call then the benefit is nontaxable.

BUILDING MAINTENANCE

Police stations in many cities in the United States are often outdated facilities that retain most of the attributes of nineteenth-century architecture. In some cities, the police station was built like a medieval castle to protect the police from mob attacks. In smaller cities, towns, and villages, police facilities are tucked away in some remote recesses of the municipal building or fire station, generally as an afterthought to the original plans. Overall, it appears that all police stations, whether old or modern, share a common problem of maintenance and upkeep since they are 24-hour operations.

As the police station is a place where men and women must work and citizens must visit, we feel that it should be properly maintained and provide a sense of pride for the community. Sometimes officers loathe having tour groups come through their station houses because of the deplorable conditions.

With many departments contemplating new police stations, a number of architectural designs exist that can be adapted to fit the community environment. We offer the following planning suggestions:

1. *Security.* Most police stations in the United States are easy targets for terrorist or gang attacks. Although we do not advocate that police station architecture return to medieval design, public access to the various areas of operations should be strictly controlled. While a main desk should be available for the public for information and complaints, the rest of the

police operations should be sealed off by remote-controlled or keyed doors. Further security should be incorporated for communications centers, power plants, and lockup areas. Distinctive identification cards should be worn by personnel and visitors, and anyone who does not display such a card should be immediately stopped and questioned as a matter of course by any in-house personnel. Security considerations must also be extended to parking facilities and grounds near the police station. Ironically, many property crimes occur adjacent to police facilities, especially to patrol and privately owned vehicles.

2. *Personnel facilities.* The police station should have separate locker rooms and shower and bathroom facilities for male and female personnel. A trend is occurring in some departments where a country club atmosphere prevails in terms of a television room being located within the confines of the police locker room. Although additions of this nature are paid for by volunteer contributions or funds from the police union, a negative image can result in that certain segments of the public may feel that such equipment was purchased with public monies. If any "fringes" are to be included in the police personnel facilities, we would advocate adding wellness equipment.

3. *Location to public.* The community police station should be accessible to the general public; this means building in a populated, central area of the community with ample parking facilities and measures to accommodate the disabled. In many suburban areas, state and other municipal police departments have been experimenting with ministations or substations in areas of high public or business traffic, such as in shopping malls, on a full- or part-time basis, to provide this aspect of accessibility. Some college campuses are placing stations in the student unions.

4. *Backup power system.* We know of many cases of chaos that occurred once electricity was disrupted by weather or unexpected emergencies. Each police administrator should ask this question: Can my station function if regular electric power is withdrawn? The solution to this dilemma, of course, lies with backup power generators or battery systems.

5. *Compliance with state and local codes.* Like any other public facility, police stations must be in compliance with a host of rules, laws, and regulations that include building codes, fire codes, state regulations regarding access for the disabled, regulations for interviewing juvenile suspects, and state regulations for temporary holding facilities.

Temporary Detention Facility

Certain states allow municipal and police agencies to maintain a **temporary detention facility**—often called a *lockup*—for prisoners awaiting arraignment, release on bail, or transport. It is here, however, where many serious problems occur. Jail suicide is a common occurrence in temporary detention areas since it is here that the offender finally realizes the various effects that arrest will have on his or her personal life. In other cases, prisoners begin to plot an escape while they wait for the next stage of processing. In still other instances, prisoners have died because of complications arising from being intoxicated, drugged, or beaten by police or other suspects during and after the course of arrest or from an injury sustained prior to being taken into custody.

It is important that detention facilities in the police station be tightly supervised, that rigorous procedures be maintained for searching inmates, and that careful inventory of property and contraband be maintained. We suggest closed circuit television cameras with audio recording units be used to monitor prisoners in the booking area and in cells. This protects the agency from civil suits arising from charges of brutality, theft of prisoner property, and negligence.

It cannot be stressed too highly that for the purposes of police management, this is a temporary holding facility (jail) and is not meant to be a permanent correctional setting. This is basically a lockup pending court appearance for those awaiting bail or for those unable to make bail. For stays of more than a few days, prisoners should be transferred to a permanent correctional facility.

There are also the normal problems of state and federal regulations concerning the separation of adults from juveniles and females from males, plus the security problem of smuggling in and using drugs. This is a crisis period for many detainees, and there is a strong potential toward self-destruction. Thus, constant security must be maintained in the cell area. In the case of separation of adults and juveniles, this may not always be possible in smaller facilities. When it comes to these standard issues of corrections, including that of contact visits, there is a need, at that point, to transfer prisoners to a more permanent location where correctional professionals are in charge.

LICENSING

Based on historical precedent, many police departments serve as the licensing bureau for various public-related activities. These may include issuing permits for parades, use of municipally owned facilities, bike registrations, and business licenses for bars and related entertainment activities.

There is some feeling among professional law enforcement managers that licensing should be placed in the hands of civilians and possibly another government agency. However, there is also some disagreement because of the historical context of the licensing function. Licensing traditionally grew around three police problems:

1. *Vice control.* Licensing of taverns, taxies, and bingo games
2. *Crowd control.* Parade permits, sports events, and rallies
3. *Organized crime.* Overlap on vice on such things as the licensing of jukeboxes

Although it may not be necessary for the police department to have direct control over the licensing functions of municipal government, some control and good communication are needed. Police agencies need to be informed concerning activities taking place in the community so that they may take the necessary steps to provide the services needed to control the situation.

THE CRIME LABORATORY

Crime laboratory management has become a specialized function based on the advances in **forensic science** and crime technology and the increased use of **criminalistics** in major cases. In addition, the general public, through a number of popular TV shows such as the *CSI* series, has a perception that various forms of identifying evidence or cause of death can be automatically obtained from autopsies or minute samples of blood, semen, hair, and foot and tire prints. This has been often termed the "CSI effect." Then, too, there have been a number of major scandals where forensic evidence was incorrectly processed or analyzed, resulting in the dismissal of criminal cases or false imprisonment of innocent defendants.

Thus, every police department needs access to a laboratory. There are four main ways of identifying criminals:

1. Eyewitness testimony, which can be unreliable
2. Confessions

3. Circumstantial evidence
4. Physical evidence

Crime laboratories need full-time directors who work closely with detectives, evidence technicians, the courts, and the training unit. The following are the range of services offered by a forensic laboratory:

- Biological screening
- Controlled substances
- Crime scene
- Computer crimes
- Documents
- DNA analysis
- Firearms/toolmarks
- Impressions
- Toxicology
- Trace evidence

Note that not all laboratories offer every service. According to a census by the Bureau of Justice Statistics (2008), roughly 89 percent of publicly funded laboratories provided analysis of controlled substances. On the other hand, only 12 percent addressed computer or cybercrime evidence. As discussed in previous chapters, this is an area that needs additional attention especially with the rise of cyber-related offenses. As discussed by Martino (personal communication, 2009), every major offense involves some type of digital evidence such as a cell phone or a laptop that often needs some kind of analysis.

As reported in the census, a major issue facing all laboratories is backlogging of cases, which is defined as a case not being processed within 30 days. In 2005, it was reported that each crime laboratory had about 400 cases listed as backlogged from a total of 4,100 overall cases processed.

Crime Laboratory Management

The laboratory supervisor would be in charge of quality control, distribution of cases, and coordination of laboratory services. The civilian manager in charge of this evidence flow, the director of the crime laboratory, should report directly to top command personnel when the laboratory is located in one police department. The crime laboratory should be equipped with sufficient technology and qualified personnel to do both dry and wet chemistry and micro- and macroexaminations with crime scene reproduction capabilities. Most laboratories located in police agencies consist of photography laboratories along with physical evidence examination capability and field narcotics testing. Any operation that is more complicated and that will stand up to courtroom cross-examination entails a major capital and personnel investment. It is important that forensic laboratories undergo accreditation to ensure that equipment, procedures, and actual case samples conform to scientific controls and quality assurance. Accreditation for crime laboratories is conducted by the American Society of Crime Laboratory Directors Lab Accreditation Board. In addition, each state generally has an advisory or oversight commission on state standards.

DNA ANALYSIS   The most innovative area in forensic science is DNA testing. **Deoxyribonucleic acid (DNA)** is a molecule that is found in all life-forms and defines their genetically inherited characteristics. According to Bashinski and Peterson (1991: 512), the genetic code found in a specimen is unique for every individual. Thus, the genetic code found in a specimen of blood, semen, or hair can be directed to one individual. In the early 1990s, DNA testing was done only in a handful of private laboratories and by the Federal Bureau of Investigation. Today, it has been expanded to regional and state police laboratories and to private laboratories under state contract. Approximately one half of all police laboratories today conduct DNA analysis. Concurrently, all states have created DNA databases of individuals convicted of violent felony offenses and of persons arrested for a wide range of offenses, including immigration violations. These profiles are held in the FBI's Combined DNA Index System (CODIS), which allows submission of new profiles for comparison. These databases have been used to identify suspects in previously unsolved cases or to exonerate people in jail. DNA was also an invaluable tool in identifying those who died at the World Trade Center bombing on September 11, 2001. According to the Bureau of Justice Statistics (2008), in 2005 there were about 8,700 matches or hits using CODIS. According to Moore (2009), the FBI was able to process only 5,000 DNA samples each year. With the increase of samples taken from persons convicted or arrested, the FBI will install a robotic system that will have the capacity to analyze 90,000 samples a month.

Evidence Technicians

Evidence technicians are sworn police officers who have been specially trained in the handling and gathering of evidence. Evidence technicians are normally not responsible for protecting the crime scene. Instead, they photograph and diagram the crime scene; identify, collect, and transport evidence; complete reports; and give testimony. The list of activities includes the following (Lyman, 2002):

1. Determining items of evidentiary value
2. Being proficient in the use of several pieces of camera equipment, including close-up equipment; using various collection techniques for blood and fluids; and using silicone or plaster techniques on tire and shoe impressions
3. Collecting minute items of trace evidence, such as hair, fiber, and thread
4. Marking and recovering various types of firearm evidence
5. Collecting and packaging evidence to protect it from contamination
6. Lifting latent fingerprints
7. Examining deceased individuals, charting and photographing wounds, and lifting finger-prints from partially decomposed or mutilated bodies
8. Examining bodies of living people to collect foreign material, fingernail scrapings, and so on
9. Preparing a crime scene sketch
10. Preparing detailed reports to maintain a chain of custody
11. Giving expert court testimony

Every police agency should have at least one well-trained evidence technician available for every shift of patrol duty; larger departments have teams of evidence technicians. This is an efficient use of personnel and saves the use of expensive laboratory time while winning cases because of good evidence and good continuity. With a modest but realistic investment in training and additional equipment, police managers can gain a great deal of respect from the legislature and community because of their efficient use of evidence technicians.

Computers and Fingerprints

Computerized fingerprint identification systems such as the **Integrated Automatic Fingerprint Identification System (IAFIS)** have made it possible for latent fingerprints to be matched with a suspect's prints in minutes. Until this development, a latent fingerprint (a print lifted from a person or object at a crime scene) had to be matched visually with a 10-print or an inked sample of prints taken from the suspect. This old process often took days and detectives needed a suspect. Now fingerprint identification can be done on cold searches.

Computer equipment today can scan impressions and automatically extract and digitize identifying characteristics in detail, enabling the computer to distinguish a single fingerprint from millions of file prints that have been similarly scanned and stored.

Even the taking of fingerprints is changing. "Live scan" is a relatively new technology that eliminates the need for rolling ink onto a pad. Instead, the subject's unlinked fingers are rolled onto a scanning pad attached to a live scan device that captures a digital image of the prints. If the quality of the prints is good, then copies can be electronically transmitted to state repositories and other agencies for storage or analysis via "card scan" technology. IAFIS software programs are expensive; a scan unit can cost about $30,000, depending on the complexity of the system. However, IAFIS programs have led to the greater use of prints and increased identification of suspects, and immediate transmission of criminal information to departments.

ANCILLARY PUBLIC SAFETY SERVICES

Many services provided by American police departments fall under the heading of public safety. These include the following:

1. *Emergency mobilization.* A response plan is required in times of natural disaster or special community needs. These situations can range from a parade that shuts down traffic for five hours to a riot or earthquake that immobilizes the community for days. An **emergency plan** includes resources that can be used for events as well as procedures that define chain-of-command and coordination responsibilities. The critical piece of this plan for police operations is calling in internal personnel and acquiring radios, vehicles, and other equipment. A police department's emergency mobilization plan may be just one part of a countrywide or statewide emergency action plan. Many plans include the use of civilians or auxiliary police who can do the following:
   a. Assist regular forces at crowd control scenes (such as sports events, parades, concerts, and fires)
   b. Assume routine or inside jobs to free up regular officers for street duty for riot control, concentrated investigation activities, or hostage situations needing additional personnel
   c. Augment the regular forces by supplying a second person in a car on patrol or working with the Neighborhood Watch programs
   The importance of emergency mobilizations has intensified since September 11, and further discussion of these plans is presented in Chapter 14, such as National Incident Management System (NIMS) compliance considerations.
2. *Animal control.* A Bureau of Justice Statistics survey on local police departments (1996) found that almost one-half of the departments in its sample were responsible for animal control. This includes enforcing local ordinances related to pets and capturing or destroying wild animals that are a nuisance.
3. *Emergency medical services.* The same survey reported that 20 percent of local police departments in the sample were the primary provider of emergency medical services. This means that officers are trained and equipped not only for police situations but also for emergency first-response procedures, such as heart attacks, accidents, and broken limbs.

Conclusion

The major auxiliary functions of police organizations were analyzed in this chapter. As we noted, auxiliary services direct and supply resources to those units or individuals who provide police services to the community. Central to auxiliary services is communications, insofar as all units or divisions of the police organization must have access to this service. Reviewing main needs and capabilities, we pointed out that technology is rapidly advancing in this area. Many departments, however, have difficulty purchasing updated equipment simply because of their limited size and resources. We emphasized the pooling of resources through the formation of a mobile radio district (MRD). Interagency competition and political considerations, however, are main stumbling blocks in adopting such a program. Our discussion in the communications area also included personnel. Of all the services provided by the police organization, communications is one in which personnel competence is a crucial factor.

Police organizations, like many others, seem to operate by paper; therefore, the efficient recording and flow of paperwork are essential. As with communications, computerized technology for record keeping and word processing continues to advance. The silicon chip revolution is bringing down the cost of small computer systems, making these advances accessible to all departments.

In this chapter, we included a discussion on security, sealing, purging, and public access to police records. Current procedures related to the Freedom of Information Act (1974) and updated regulations pertaining to records were presented. An issue that will continue to be addressed in the future is the citizen's right to privacy and access to personal information versus the police's need for accurate data on criminal suspects.

Although often overlooked, the property section has responsibilities involving inventory control of physical property, evidence, and found property.

Maintaining the security of evidence as it is delivered from the crime scene may appear to be a mundane task, but it is of crucial importance to the investigative process.

The acquisition and equipping of patrol vehicles remain important administrative tasks for all police departments. The type and size of patrol vehicle depend on the environment where patrol is conducted. As patrol vehicles are used virtually 24 hours a day and driven by varied types of drivers, routine vehicle maintenance is a must.

Physical plant considerations were also presented in this chapter. Our discussion included issues related to security, facilities, morale, location, and emergency power needs. The temporary detention facility, or lockup, was discussed in some detail because of the general concern over jail suicides and other incidents.

We briefly touched on the licensing section, which may or may not be under the control of the municipal police in many communities.

The role of the crime laboratory continues to increase in the processing and prosecution of cases. As with other technology, smaller agencies have difficulty both in procuring and in fiscally defending the need for a crime laboratory of any meaningful size. Crime laboratories are, therefore, found mostly in larger municipal and state police agencies and serve many departments on a regional basis. The main operations of a crime laboratory were reviewed, including the rise of DNA technology. The capabilities of laboratory personnel were also discussed in terms of applying scientific know-how to law enforcement operations.

Computerization has streamlined crime laboratory services, ranging from routine record keeping to management systems for death cases, accident reconstruction, criminal profiling, and photography reconstruction and storage.

We concluded the chapter with a review of various ancillary services that relate to the public safety function.

Questions for Review

1. What functions usually come under the organizational heading of auxiliary services?
2. What capabilities must communications units provide? What limitations are placed on many agencies in obtaining updated technology for communications?
3. The authors proposed consolidation as a means of solving police communications inferiority. What are some hindrances to this solution?
4. Why are communications personnel often referred to as "key people" in police operations?
5. List the main categories of police records. How is the computer proving to be a useful tool for record-keeping tasks?
6. Name some general guidelines related to public access of police records. What types of records are not governed by public access regulations (e.g., the Freedom of Information Act)?
7. What kinds of data may be released about an individual who was not convicted of a crime?
8. What are the main duties of the property section? How does this section assist in the continuity of evidence?
9. Why is it said that police vehicles are exposed to the worst road and driving conditions? Why is preventive maintenance important?
10. What general items must be considered in designing or maintaining a police station?
11. List the main functions of a crime laboratory.
12. Outline the flow of evidence from crime scene to crime laboratory. Why is case screening an important procedure?
13. What are the five duties of crime-scene technicians?

Class Projects

There are a number of activities that can be undertaken in the auxiliary function areas:

1. Review the Web site of a police department and see if there are other auxiliary functions that go beyond the discussion in this chapter.
2. Review the services provided by the state office of criminal justice services or public safety and ascertain if there is administrative oversight of crime laboratories in the state.
3. If possible (through your instructor), spend a period of time in the communications area of a police or public safety department. In addition to following the flow of communications traffic, interview the communications supervisor as to the types of skills communications personnel must have.
4. During the tour of a police facility, request to review the components of a police patrol vehicle. What kinds of equipment are carried in the vehicle (e.g., emergency items, radio/computer equipment)? Inquire as to when vehicles are "turned over" from patrol, based on years or mileage, and how they are serviced by the department. Does the department have any kind of special patrol units such as ATVs?

References

Bashinski, Jan S., and Joseph L. Peterson. "Forensic Science." In *Local Government Police Management* (3rd ed.). Washington, D.C.: International Management Association, 1991.

Fitzgerald, Chris. "Take Home Patrol Cars for Police Officers." Utica College of Syracuse University, unpublished paper, 2002.

Lyman, Michael D. *Criminal Investigation: The Art and the Science.* Upper Saddle River, N.J.: Prentice Hall, 2002.

Meyer, Jon'a F., and Matt Joyce. "Investigating Computer Crime." *Police Chief*, 15, no. 5 (May 1998), pp. 28–35.

Moore, Soloman. "In a Lab, an Ever Growing Database of DNA Profiles." *New York Times*, May 12, 2009, p. D3.

New York State Department of Criminal Justice Services. *The Criminal History Record.* Accessed on August 1, 2013, at criminaljustice.ny.gov/ojis/recordreview.htm

12 Human Resources Management

KEY TERMS

affirmative action	lateral entry
Americans with Disabilities Act (ADA)	overtime
assessment center	Pendleton Act
dipping	polygraph
disparate impact theory	rule of three
drug testing	sexual harassment
Equal Employment Opportunity Commission (EEOC)	spoils system
	stress
fatigue	Title VII
hostile work environment	

The objective of police recruitment and selection is to find qualified candidates for law enforcement positions in terms of their talents, ethics, drive, and emotional stability. In the modern police department, computer and human relations skills and the ability to deal with diverse cultures and perhaps speak a foreign language have become important. In addition, "with the advent of community and problem-oriented policing, personnel management issues have become increasingly complex as earlier homogeneous departments have given way to more modern departments reflective of the community population" (Kenney, 1996: v).

There is also the need to have officers and managers who possess emotional intelligence and stability to perform a variety of often difficult and taxing duties. The challenge to recruitment is to keep the highest standards in order to recruit a talented professional police officer while bringing in the skills and backgrounds that are needed in the twenty-first-century police department. Matching police personnel with the appropriate jobs will be discussed throughout this chapter.

PERSONNEL: THE MAJOR COST

Law enforcement is a labor-intensive service industry; 80–90 percent of police agency budgets are devoted to personnel costs. Paradoxically, most managers do not realize the investment they have in terms of their human capital: police officers. Just a few of the expenses involve testing, oral interviews, background checks, uniforms and equipment, and the police academy program. As a rule, it takes about a year and a half before the police recruit becomes a police officer, who then makes a working contribution to the agency and community.

For many communities, the recruitment and retention of police officers is a major issue. To compete with other occupational titles, many departments in the south and west have instituted recruitment bonuses, housing allowances, and educational benefits. They have also relaxed hiring standards related to minor criminal history and past drug use.

POLICE CIVIL SERVICE SELECTION: HISTORICAL BACKGROUND

Figure 12-1 illustrates the police personnel selection process used in many states. The chief criteria in this selection process are the portions overseen by state civil service or the individual department—written test, physical agility examinations, and physical requirements. Candidates who complete a written examination and physical agility test and measure up to the physical requirements are then placed in either a pool or a rank-order certification list prepared by the civil service commission. Many states with a rank-order process continue to follow the **rule of three**, whereby one of the first three candidates on the list is chosen while the other two candidates are returned to the pool for the next ranking of three. This method of selection may seem outmoded, but it is still viewed by many as a reform measure when compared with practices that existed in the nineteenth century.

PUBLIC SERVICE EMPLOYMENT

In the early days of the republic, government service was looked on as a duty reserved for those with aristocratic background. The change of presidential administrations, however, heralded a new break from tradition in that all presidential appointees were replaced by those of the new victor. This was the beginning of the **spoils system** (doling out positions for political support), which became firmly entrenched by 1830. The practice soon spread to all municipalities on the state and local levels. This process affected early police organizations, which often underwent a complete personnel turnover after the victory of the out-of-office party.

In the early days of American policing, there were no requirements for becoming a police officer except having the right connections and being willing to fight to protect oneself. Sadly enough, most police officers were no more than political hacks who received their positions in exchange for a payment to a public official. Many times in urban areas, a local gangster chieftain might have some say as to who would enforce the law in the community. A career in policing, moreover, was seen as an avenue of economic improvement by each wave of immigrants to the United States in the early nineteenth century. Police jobs, which were not often sought after by the native middle-class population, were readily dispensed by the political machine to immigrants in return for votes and support.

Because of the negative effects of the spoils system, such as mismanagement and bribery, a reform movement for personnel selection was under way by the beginning of the 1880s. In 1883, Congress passed the **Pendleton Act**, which covered a majority of federal positions. This law

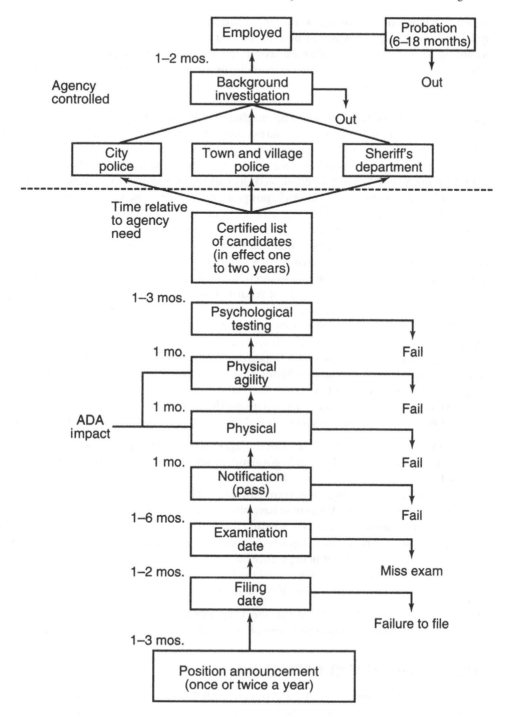

FIGURE 12-1 Personnel selection process.

sought to ban political patronage as the sole criterion for personnel selection, replacing it with a system whereby employees would be selected and retained on the basis of open competition according to experience and ability. Moreover, the new law sought to protect employees against arbitrary discharge or discrimination, especially discrimination based on political influences. In the same year, New York and other states enacted similar laws. The assassination of President Garfield in 1881 by a disgruntled office seeker had focused public attention on problems with the spoils system and had helped to speed up enactment of Pendleton-style legislation in other states.

The passage of civil service statutes did not result in overnight reform. In his history of American policing, Robert Fogelson (1977) showed that civil service reform was stymied by the political machines that existed in most urban communities. He states, "The machine politicians proved to be formidable opponents. When they dominated city hall, which was most of the time, they could usually prevail on the authorities to sidetrack, postpone, or vote down the reform schemes. Even when the reformers took over, the politicians generally counted on their cronies in the police forces, prosecutor's offices, local courts and other agencies to undo any inopportune changes" (p. 110).

Since the nineteenth century, political interference in American policing has not disappeared, even in states that have civil service requirements. Moreover, many municipalities and states still do not provide civil service protection to police officers. For example, county sheriff's departments in many states are often not regulated by any civil service guidelines; often, police selection is strictly a matter of political patronage.

Police employment in civil service-regulated states does not necessarily bring great monetary benefits, but it does provide (1) job security, (2) a pension, and (3) a generous number of vacation and personal days. The Great Depression from 1929 through the 1930s underscored the security of public employment as millions of workers were laid off by private industry. As the range of government services has grown since World War II, the number of workers has likewise risen, making government on the federal, state, and local levels this nation's number one employer.

However, some new factors have altered the traditional notion of government service:

1. In many states and on the federal level, wages and benefits have matched those provided by private industry. This has made government service even more attractive when coupled with pensions, retirements, and time off.
2. As the number and range of government services have increased, taxes have also risen. The taxpayer revolts in the 1990s may have affected the number of workers in public service.
3. Researchers are undecided as to whether this will affect the number of government services since budget surpluses were obtained in previous years, thus stalling layoffs. The notion of government employment being secure has been altered by the financial dilemmas faced by many municipalities. This has forced the laying off of police, firefighters, and other public service workers, as well as post-2008 multi-year hiring freezes and slow-downs.

While these general trends have all affected police administration, one other movement has had a striking effect on selection and promotion: equal employment opportunity legislation.

EQUAL EMPLOYMENT OPPORTUNITY

Although the Fifth, Thirteenth, and Fourteenth Amendments to the U.S. Constitution provide the basis for due process, government was slow to adopt a strict interpretation of these amendments, especially with regard to employment of blacks, Hispanics, and women. Both the Thirteenth and the Fourteenth Amendments gave Congress the right to enact legislation to enforce the provision of law, which resulted in civil rights legislation in 1866 and 1871 on the issue of employment discrimination. Presidents Franklin D. Roosevelt (1941) and John F. Kennedy (1961) issued presidential executive orders for fair employment of minority groups, which have had an impact in industries on government-related contracts. The 1961 order by Kennedy was significant in that it imposed the first requirement for affirmative action in government employment—mainly that each agency had to plan and implement a program to ensure that employment practices were nondiscriminatory in application and had to set out methods by which the effects of past discriminatory employment practices could be corrected. This executive order was updated by Presidents Lyndon B. Johnson (1965) and Richard M. Nixon (1971), who made affirmative action an important area for all government service (Territo et al., 1977: 21–22).

But the real boon to affirmative action resided not with executive orders, but with the passage of the Civil Rights Act of 1964, which had a number of titles dealing with various facets of discrimination. The significant legislation for personnel practices was found in **Title VII**, which provided the following:

> It shall be unlawful employment practice for an employer (1) to fail or refuse to hire, or discharge any individual or otherwise to discriminate against any individual with respect to his compensation, terms, conditions, or privileges of employment, because of such individual's race, color, religion, sex, or national origin; (2) to limit, segregate, or classify his employees or applicants for employment in any way which would deprive or tend to deprive any individual of employment opportunity or otherwise adversely affect his status as an employee because of such individual's race, color, religion, sex, or national origin. (Public Law 92–261, Section 703[a])

Title VII was directed at employers with more than 25 employees, labor organizations with more than 25 members, and private employment agencies. Title VII was further upgraded two years later to include coverage of both private and public employment agencies, including those on the state and local levels employing 15 or more people. The amendment to Title VII also established the **Equal Employment Opportunity Commission (EEOC)** as a regulatory agency to oversee compliance with Title VII. It is the EEOC to which many complaints on police hiring practices are directed. Complaints handled by the EEOC or, in some cases, in the federal court system under Title VII include discrimination in hiring or promotions and a "hostile work environment." Title VII forms the basis for complaints of sexual harassment, which will be discussed later in this chapter. On the state level, there are various corresponding agencies that also deal with complaints of employment discrimination.

AFFIRMATIVE ACTION

Affirmative action is a concept applied to personnel administration in which an employer takes positive steps to expand employment opportunities for nonwhite people and women. These steps include addressing and abolishing past discriminatory employment practices, soliciting more minority and female applicants from different hiring pools, and setting goals for the hiring or promotion of underrepresented minorities and women in the organization.

The statutory language and political intent of initial Title VII legislation did not include preferential treatment for nonwhites and women for employment and promotion considerations over white candidates (Glazer, 1975; Territo et al., 1977; Fallon and Weiler, 1985). Starting in 1964, however, federal and state case law, EEOC administrative rulings, and police agency employment practices determined that the statistical imbalances between the number of nonwhites represented in an organization and the determined labor pool constitute a *prima facie* case for discrimination. Remedies to address imbalances included quota systems and preferential treatment for nonwhites and women in employee selection.

Despite strong political and legal opposition by private- and public-sector labor unions and aggrieved individuals, these remedies were constitutionally upheld. The Supreme Court in 1979 upheld the use of a voluntary quota system for selecting black candidates for a training program over the objections of an unsuccessful white applicant who claimed that he had been the victim of discrimination (*United Steel Workers* v. *Weber*, 1979). In his majority opinion, Justice Brennan wrote that the intent of Title VII was to improve the economic plight of nonwhites through the use of preferred selection systems.

Before the *Weber* case, the use of quotas and preferential treatment had received judicial approval through a number of Supreme Court cases and EEOC rulings under the **disparate impact theory**. In the 1971 case *Griggs* v. *Duke Power Company*, the Court ruled that employment tests and practices that exclude a disproportionate number of nonwhites and women may be discriminatory regardless of whether there was intent by an employer to discriminate. If a situation of disparate impact exists, the employer must demonstrate that such tests and practices relate to a business necessity and the demands of the position. Disparate impact is any case where a civil service test, for example, admits more white male employees to the occupation than minorities or women, even if the white applicants have higher civil service scores on the test than those of the minority or female candidates. This legal reasoning raises complaints about reverse discrimination and the use of quotas when using civil service tests for the admission of new candidates for employment.

Disparate impact was applied to police departments because of their failure to recruit nonwhites and women in comparison to a statistical representation of these minorities in a designated community. Disparate impact formed the basis for court orders and consent decrees by which police agencies had to remedy the historical effects of discrimination through quotas. Agencies, under court orders, were forced to review their hiring and testing procedures in light of the principle of disparate impact. In the case of consent decrees between police agency employers and federal or state courts, there was no admission of intentional discrimination on the part of the employing agency.

When representation in a police agency matches minority representation in a defined community labor pool, affirmative action was said to be successful (Hochstedler, 1984). Quotas and preferred hiring have had a backlash effect because many qualified whites have complained that they were not considered for employment simply because of race. In police circles, this practice is known as **dipping**, and charges of reverse discrimination have been made in the following situations:

1. The use of racial preferences to prescribe the selection of candidates who otherwise appear less qualified than rival candidates
2. The use of preferences for candidates who have not proved that they were the victims of past discrimination
3. The use of targets and goals to determine the number of nonwhite candidates to be hired on the basis of race

Reverse discrimination related to employment was the basis of many lawsuits and public policy debates with regard to voluntary and court-mandated affirmative action plans and consent decrees. Disparate impact theory was challenged in the 1989 Supreme Court ruling in *Ward's Cove Packing* v. *Atonio*. Filipino and native Alaskan cannery workers employed at several companies charged discrimination on the basis of statistics because the majority of skilled jobs were filled by whites. Because of the unique seasonal nature of the work and the makeup of both the skilled and unskilled workforce, the court ruled that statistical imbalances alone could not be used to prove disparate impact discrimination. Instead, it had to be shown that the imbalance occurred because of the application of a particular employment practice. The court also added that it was the plaintiff's responsibility to prove discrimination instead of the company's having to defend its practices. This ruling led to others in a similar vein that appeared to halt statistical imbalance lawsuits. However, the 1991 Civil Rights Act restored disparate impact premises so that "neutral employment practices" that resulted in discrimination could continue to be challenged. Since 1990, federal and state court rulings regarding affirmative action discrimination cases have been very specifically applied to the employment practices and existing affirmative action plans of an agency or municipality.

Dramatic changes in affirmative action as a public policy occurred in 1995. The landmark case involving affirmative action was *Adarand Constructors* v. *Federico Pena*, which involved a lawsuit filed by a construction company. The company was the low bidder for a public works project and contested the work being awarded to a Hispanic-owned company. The main contractor for the project, in turn, received a monetary award by the federal government for furthering an affirmative action plan. The Supreme Court struck down the awarding of the contract, ruling that affirmative action plans that created racial discrimination must meet a strict scrutiny test according to the following guidelines:

1. There must be a compelling reason why a program was put in place.
2. The plan must be temporary, with a definite end in sight.

The End of Affirmative Action?

At the same time that the *Adarand* case was being argued, the California Board of Regents in 1995 dismantled its affirmative action–based programs, arguing that the set-aside programs in college admissions are discriminatory. In another closely watched higher education case, the U.S. Court of Appeals for the Fifth Circuit (Texas, Louisiana, and Mississippi) in 1994 found that admissions procedures at the University of Texas that promoted racial and ethnic diversity were improper (*Hopwood* v. *Texas*, 1994). In 1996, the Supreme Court announced that it would not review the decision. Although the ruling applies only to institutions of higher education in these states, it has prompted many colleges and universities to review their admissions standards and procedures.

As for policing, many agencies have ended their quota programs for recruitment and promotion, pointing out that the workforce was representative of the resident population. McWhirter (1996) argued that most state and federal government affirmative action programs created in the 1970s and 1980s that create quotas or set-aside programs will not stand this strict scrutiny test. Affirmative action as a governmental policy is not going to dissolve completely; however, many police agencies have readjusted their programs to consider affirmative action as a way to conduct proactive recruitment for underrepresented populations in the workforce and to review employment hiring practices that may be discriminatory.

Current affirmative action issues have arisen over promotions, especially when a department opts to use a quota system or some other initiative to achieve racial and ethnic diversity when statistical and historical evidence shows past discrimination. For example, in *McNamera* v. *City of Chicago* (1998), a special civil service list category, was upheld by a federal appeals court so that African American and Hispanic firefighters could achieve representation in the position of captain. However, on June 28, 2009, in a complex case involving disparate impact theory, the Supreme Court ruled in *Ricci* v. *DeStefano* that the City of New Haven could not toss out a promotional exam series where white candidates outperformed minority candidates. As a social policy, affirmative action continues to have a profound impact on many areas of human resource management, college admissions, and the awarding of contracts. Based on our experiences and observations in classroom discussions and agency personnel hirings over the past two decades, we can say the following about affirmative action:

- It created deep divisions in American society in that many whites could not understand why preferential treatment and quota programs were fair.
- It allowed women and people of various races access to police organizations that hitherto were not representative of their communities. Bergmann (1996: 19) states that the job market in many occupations remains stacked against African Americans and women.
- It challenged formal and informal methods of discrimination that had prevented women, African Americans, Hispanics, Asians, and members of other groups from becoming police officers.

THE ROLE OF THE POLICE HUMAN RESOURCE ADMINISTRATOR

The director of human resources and his or her staff hold key positions in determining employment practices and promotion qualifications. Although their judgments are based, in part, on myriad court cases, legislative acts, and administrative law rulings, their decisions will have a profound effect on the level of quality personnel in a department.

In a small agency, the chief police administrator, normally the police chief working with a human resource office performs most of the tasks of a personnel department in a larger agency. In some small agencies, the political unit, be it county, town, or village, has a personnel office that handles staffing for all municipal offices.

More than 70 percent of a police administrator's time is spent on human resource issues, such as recruitment, selection and training, promotions, evaluations, discipline, and quality-of-life issues. Because of the procedural and legal concerns that can arise, it is critical that the police chief have either a staff member or a key liaison at the municipal department of personnel with the expertise to assist in policy development and issue resolution. This expertise should include agency policies, the collective bargaining agreement (if applicable), and the wide scope of federal and state public employment law.

PERSONNEL SELECTION: ISSUES AND CONCERNS

Before 1965, the police personnel selection process generally consisted of a written examination, a physical agility test, a physical, and perhaps an oral interview. Based on these criteria, a list was established of successful candidates, and the police administrator picked new officers from this list. Various aspects of this process are continually under attack and revision because of the emergence of affirmative action. We will now review the police personnel selection process, especially those areas affected by Title VII.

Written Tests

The civil service procedures of the nineteenth century incorporated the extensive use of written tests as a chief criterion of selection. These tests were usually composed of multiple-choice questions related to the position being sought. But according to Schachter (1979: 86), "Traditional written examinations do not measure many of the skills and competencies which effective police work requires. In fact, a written test of this nature cannot really assess the entire range of skills and situations that are related to job competency."

The affirmative action movement of the 1970s resulted in legal attacks on written civil service testing for a wide variety of reasons. The major arguments center on the following issues:

1. The relationship between the test and the job (often called the *attitude/behavior relationship* in research literature on testing)
2. Content validity of the testing instrument
3. Reliability of test items

In 2013, regardless of how studied, appealed, sued, and dreaded the police entrance exam may be, the time-honored tradition is alive and well. In fact, it would be difficult to find a police agency in the United States that does not require a written exam as part of the hiring process for a full-time position. Still, so much emphasis is placed on that initial general knowledge exam, and with the masses of people who take any one exam, good luck comes into play. Candidates who would otherwise be highly qualified may not ever get a call to move on in the hiring process due to guessing wrong on one question. The authors discuss in the section below on *Educational Requirements* how higher educational requirements for new hires could make lessening the weight of the written exam a possibility.

Age

The normal age for application ranges from 21 to 29, although some agencies will accept recruits as young as 18. This lower age has been the subject of much controversy since many police administrators feel that this lower age limit will recruit police officers who lack mature judgment. At this time, no research data are generally available to document anything concerning this controversy. Although age requirements are published and adhered to in most cases, there are an increasing number of age exceptions.

Exceptions to the higher age limit are given to wartime veterans. The intent is to be able to recruit qualified future officers from the military without penalizing them for their years of military service. For example, if the veteran is age 32 and has 10 years' service in the military, he is qualified to enter a department with a maximum age limit for recruitment of 29 years of age. State civil service limits the number of veteran years that can be subtracted. In the past, especially during the early part of the twentieth century, former military men were considered prime candidates for the police department. At present, veterans' preference and exceptions are resented by many younger recruits who lack military service.

Why are there age limits? One reason is related to the physical requirements that are supposed to be justified in terms of the rigors of the job.

Another major reason for the age requirement is the lifetime of work of the police officer compared with retirement and training costs. This is an especially crucial point when considering the 20- and 25-year retirement programs. This means that the best and most experienced officers are often lost at the peak of their use to the department and only to receive half-pay for not working. Surprisingly, police agencies with these policies allow their best people to go at a time when private business would consider them to be in their prime productive years.

The Age Discrimination in Employment Act of 1974 extended coverage of age discrimination to state and local police agencies, and many state constitutions have developed antidiscrimination policies concerning age. There have been a number of cases throughout the nation concerning age discrimination by police departments, and these police agencies have had mixed results in defending their policies. At the moment, the trend seems to be a breakdown of the upper age requirement unless there is specific state legislation empowering the civil service department to set an upper age limit.

Educational Requirements

Between 1990 and 2003, the percentage of police officers working in agencies that required some amount of college credits increased threefold to 33 percent (Hickman and Reaves, 2006). Louis Mayo, Executive Director of the Police Association for College Education (PACE) reported that approximately 30 percent of police officers in 2012 had earned a four-year degree—a number that is growing at approximately 2–3 percent a year (Conciatore, 2000). A 1988 Police Executive Research Forum (PERF) study of nearly 500 police agencies found that over 44 percent of police officers had completed two or more years of college and 65 percent experienced at least one year of college (Breci, 1994; Roberg and Bonn, 2004).

While those numbers may initially appear encouraging, they are also deceptive. Less than 1 percent of the well over 17,000 state and local police agencies in the United States require a bachelor's degree (Hickman and Reaves, 2006). That statistic bears repeating; it is not *slightly less than 1 percent of police agencies in the United States DO NOT require a bachelor's degree*, it is *less than 1 percent* do.

As discussed by Walsh (2013), one of the benefits of increasing police hiring standards, and requiring college experience, is that doing so would reduce the mass number of people currently applying to become a police officer. With that reduced pool of applicants to process, it may be possible for agencies to consider alternative ways to the current process, which leaves the written entry exam, as discussed above, the primary gatekeeper for an applicant to move along to more important parts of the vetting, such as the background investigation.

Theron Bowman, Chief of the Arlington Police Department, which increased its educational requirement to a four-year degree nearly 30 years ago, noted that, not only has the educational requirement not hindered their efforts at diversity to reflect that of the community Arlington Police Department serves, but their agency experienced an increased pool of female and minority candidates (Bowman, 2001). Bowman also noted that students liked working for an agency that valued a college education.

Physical Fitness

Physical fitness concerns the health of the individual officer and is a measure of his or her physiological readiness to perform critical physical tasks when required. Physical fitness has been demonstrated to be a bona fide occupational qualification.

Historically, police officers have been expected to be physically fit. Preservice selection and training academy programs generally have some component for physical training and testing. The type of agility tests and courses vary from department to department. The types of tests commonly employed include running, an obstacle course, climbing ropes, barbell push-ups, chin-ups, scaling walls, and climbing through tubes. What is lacking in these tests, however, is applicability to the job of police officer.

To address job relatedness, the Cooper Institute for Aerobics Research of Dallas, Texas, developed a testing regimen that is being adopted by many departments. Based on national scores and a review of physical agility needs for the police officer, the Cooper method tests include the following competencies (Cooper Institute, 2014):

1. *Aerobic power.* A 1.5-mile run is scored to measure cardiovascular endurance or aerobic power. The run can be conducted on a treadmill or correlated to a 12-minute distance run.
2. *Flexibility.* A sit-and-reach test serves as an important measure of hip and back flexibility. *Flexibility* is defined as the range of possible movements in a joint or group of joints. These joints can be tested to determine their functional ability through a full range of motion indicated by the sit-and-reach test.

3. *Maximum strength.* This is defined as the amount of tension a muscle can exhibit in one maximum contraction. The one-repetition maximum bench press correlates well with total body strength.

4. *Muscular endurance.* The sit-up (with knees bent) is used to determine a person's endurance effort.

Because of the Americans with Disabilities Act (ADA), physical tests have come under greater scrutiny. Departments are required to address the following questions regarding their standards:

1. The relationship between the standard and the job performed by officers
2. The relationship between the standard and the training required for the basic academy and advanced schools
3. The applicability of standards to all members of the department

Another method to address physical fitness policy is the creation of a job–task simulation. In this scenario, the actual parts of a police officer's job are broken down to ascertain whether the candidate can perform various tasks within a specific amount of time. Such tasks might include running for several yards after alighting from a parked patrol vehicle, climbing a fence, climbing through a window, and moving a 150-pound dummy from one position to another. As the Cooper Institute (2006) discusses, a job–task simulation does not measure physical fitness but only a small percentage of the range of physical tasks performed by law enforcement officers.

Related to this issue is the reality that most departments do not enforce any physical standards on their officers once the officer has passed recruit training. By the end of a five-year period, many officers exceed recruit weight requirements and many must wear glasses. Sadly, many seasoned officers cannot run a mile. Should all officers who do not meet the rigid physical entering requirements be fired? Do you disqualify an officer because he or she becomes obese, develops flat feet or poor vision, or has heart problems?

Because of the protection afforded by civil service and union contracts, physically unqualified officers are able to retain their police jobs. Others go on permanent disability because of injuries that might have been avoided if the officer had been in top physical shape. As a result, many departments are initiating formal programs involving physical reconditioning and mandatory medical checkups. Some have gone so far as to issue letters to officers with unchecked obesity problems. Utilizing informal group relationships, other departments use peer pressure as an incentive for the officer to keep in physical shape.

EYESIGHT STANDARDS Traditional physical fitness standards related to vision are also being contested. Until the past decade, most departments required police recruits to have vision corrected to 20/20 and be free of color blindness. The theory behind these standards is that officers must be able to identify suspects, vehicles, and other items at a reasonable distance, to function without glasses in serious situations, and to correctly identify the color of objects like vehicles. A review of vision standards by Holden (1993) shows that these reasons cannot be supported by agency data or empirical research. A national review of vision standards by the author shows a wide range of variance, ranging from the traditional 20/20 corrected standard to no standards. He concludes that most standards are merely supported by what-if scenarios. These what-if situations are still used by agencies today.

There is still another aspect to this issue. In the future, we may see different physical requirements being specified for different categories of police jobs. It may be that officers on patrol must meet one standard and that older officers assigned to administrative tasks must meet a different standard. There may come a time when all officers will be physically certified in terms of the jobs they will be allowed to do within the department.

AMERICANS WITH DISABILITIES ACT   The **Americans with Disabilities Act (ADA)**, which became fully effective in July 1992, prohibits discrimination against persons with disabilities in employment, public services, transportation, public accommodations, and telecommunications. The law (PL 101–336) very broadly interprets *disability* as any impairment limiting a major life activity. Disability thus includes sight, hearing, suffering with a disease like AIDS (acquired immunodeficiency syndrome), and disfigurement that does not result in an actual impairment. Those who feel that they have been discriminated against on the basis of a disability may file complaints with the EEOC. Preceding the ADA was the Federal Rehabilitation Act of 1974, which prohibited discrimination by the federal government and its contractors against federal benefit recipients.

Title I of the ADA applies to all areas of police employment, such as testing, hiring, assignments, evaluations and disciplinary actions, training, promotions, sick leave, and termination. The immediate impact of ADA on police has already been felt in preemployment processes like physical medical tests. A department that disqualifies a person because of a disability must show why the rejection is job related and consistent with business necessity. Furthermore, the agency must be able to demonstrate that it cannot make a reasonable accommodation to enable the individual to perform the essential job functions or that the accommodation would impose an undue hardship. The concept of reasonable accommodation is quite broad. It ranges from making physical adaptations to the work environment to changing policies and work practices.

Returning to our civil service selection chart in Figure 12-1, it is important to note that qualified candidates cannot be screened out because of their disability before their actual ability to do the job is evaluated. Thus, police employers have to make a tentative job offer before medical testing is undertaken. Sometimes departments undertake initial background investigations before the conditional offer, which would include addressing issues on medical and psychological capacity to perform the duties of a police officer. In order not to violate ADA requirements, it is advisable to conduct preliminary testing such as written, physical agility, and an introductory review of the background investigation before the conditional offer is made. Once these steps are satisfactorily completed, then the entire background investigation and physical–medical–psychological exams may be undertaken. The ADA has prompted a review of preemployment medical and physical agility standards in terms of those factors necessary for performing the essential elements of police work. Each department or state regulatory agency, such as civil service, must define the minimum physical agility requirements that are needed. A person who is disqualified on the basis of a disability, such as impaired hearing or loss of a limb, can seek a challenge to see whether a reasonable accommodation can be made.

Alcoholics and recovered drug abusers are also considered to have a disability under this act. Certain cynics have charged that the ADA could force a department to hire a recovered drug abuser. Other observers point out that the ADA has no impact on character investigations or on physical agility tests. Thus, a substance abuser could be disqualified because he or she disobeyed the law in conducting his or her drug use.

Thus, the ADA has resulted in large numbers of unsuccessful candidates filing lawsuits addressing normally held medical and agility standards related to police employment. For example, in *Joyce v. Suffolk County*, the court rejected a candidate's contention that he had a disability within the definition of ADA because he failed eyesight and blood pressure requirements for the position of police officer. These conditions, the court ruled, might render him unfit for the position, but they in no way constitute a major impairment limiting major life activity. In 1999, this concept was further upheld in a number of cases reviewed by the Supreme Court. For example, in *Sutton and Hinton v. United Airlines* (1999), the Supreme Court ruled that correctable eyesight problems did not constitute a disability or a major impairment within the scope of the ADA.

This case and others demonstrate that the police department must be able to define the essential functions of the job and, on a case-by-case basis, determine whether the person's condition constitutes a disability within the legal definition of the ADA. It should be noted that assignment and staffing practices will be taken into consideration to ascertain whether reasonable accommodation can be made.

The main intent of the ADA is to combat discrimination against those with disabilities by attacking commonly held notions related to disability and matching disability with the essential functions of a job. ADA cases involving law enforcement operations have been involved mainly with disabilities such as back disorders and job-related injuries.

In some cases, civil service and the collective bargaining agreement may have an impact on the following questions:

1. Does the physical or mental injury or impairment affect a major life function, as defined under the ADA?
2. To what extent does the injury or medical condition affect the essential functions of the position?
3. Can the department provide reasonable accommodation, such as a light duty assignment?
4. To what extent is the accommodation reasonable and effective?

This does not mean that local remedies have to be exhausted before an ADA tort action. In *Wright* v. *Universal Maritime Service Corp.* (1998), the Supreme Court held that an employee could sue under the ADA without first using the grievance procedure contained in the collective bargaining agreement. To date, a majority of ADA legal complaints have been filed by police officers who have been injured on the job and have been rendered unable to perform the essential functions of the police officer position. Most cases are very fact specific, based on the injury and the history of the complaint, and in many cases, the officer attempts to return to alternative assignments other than patrol rather than take a disability pension and removal from the job.

Skin Piercings and Body Art

Skin piercings and body art have become more prevalent among the general population through media coverage of sports figures, especially in college and professional basketball, screen actors, popular singers, and military personnel. In the authors' former college town of 26,000 population, three skin piercing and body art establishments have been established over the past three years. Historically, body art or tattoos were common in the military to denote affiliation or pride for one's unit. At present, the popularity of skin piercing and skin art has impacted human resource management practices for policing in terms of the extent to which department personnel may have or show tattoos or skin piercings. The presence of an arm or neck tattoo on a police officer can be offensive to members of the general community; for example, "Death from the Skies." A general review of the issue by Dean (2008) shows that most departments forbid skin piercings and body art that can be seen while on duty. This becomes a major issue during warm months when uniformed personnel switch to short sleeve shirts. Regulations of this nature often negatively impact the labor pool from which candidates can be drawn since tattoo regulations can result in immediate disqualification. Thus, some applicants will resort to surgery on their own expense to remove the tattoo.

The Background Investigation

After a candidate has passed the written and physical portions of the selection process, a background investigation is conducted by the agency. The objective is to obtain information relating to the candidate's suitability (or nonsuitability) for police employment. Because of the mobility of today's population, the background investigation is an expensive long-term process that may cover a variety of locations in many states. Informal relationships among police agencies are tapped for this facet of police personnel selection since it is economically impossible for investigators to check every location.

The thoroughness of the background investigation varies from agency to agency. In some cases, it is perfunctory; in other cases, it is meticulous. Based on the candidate's application, each place of residence (usually within a 10-year period) and the immediate neighborhood are checked. Neighbors and landlords are asked questions related to the candidate's character that cover a wide range of topics (e.g., the number of parties held while the candidate lived on the premises; drinking habits; driving habits; relations with spouse, girlfriend, or boyfriend; and so on). Former and present employers are also questioned about the candidate's honesty and work habits. Other areas that are reviewed are educational and military history.

But the most important information that investigators wish to learn is the candidate's criminal history, especially incidents that were not included on the employment application. As a routine practice, information as to a possible criminal record is obtained from criminal computer banks maintained by federal, state, and local law enforcement agencies. A copy of the candidate's fingerprints is also sent to the Federal Bureau of Investigation and state criminal justice records division. During the background investigation, police investigators also wish to know of offenses for which the candidate was arrested that may not be classified as crimes, such as public intoxication, disorderly conduct, harassment, and various violations of local municipal ordinances.

Related to the check for criminal history is the driving record. Most police agencies have access to data on all aspects of motor vehicle operation and registration in just about every state through a computer terminal in the police station. Hence, this information is readily obtained. An important issue that comes to light with regard to background checks is the use of these investigations to

---

Essential Functions

What are the essential functions of a police officer position? Based on a job analysis, essential functions include arrest and detention of suspects, controlling civil disorder, collecting and preserving evidence, conducting a crime scene search, operating a motor vehicle, and using physical force. Under these general headings, there are a number of essential tasks that must be performed. For example, under the heading of "Using Physical Force," we have the following essential tasks:

1. Break up a fight between two or more people
2. Carry by yourself an immobile child
3. Pull a person out of a vehicle to effect rescue
4. Subdue an attacker
5. Use weaponless defense tactics
6. Subdue a person resisting arrest
7. Disarm a violent armed suspect
8. Pull a person, who is resisting arrest, out of a vehicle
9. Search for a person in a darkened building or environment
10. Strike a person with a baton

Equipment that a police officer must use to perform these essential tasks are baton, flashlight, flex-cuffs, and handcuffs.

"weed out" undesirable candidates. Having excessive traffic tickets is a common reason for rejection, as is falsification of any information.

Credit history checks are another area of review and are becoming an important part of the background investigation process. A candidate with a bad credit history or not being able to live within one's economic means gives an indication of one who is not able to take care of his or her personal affairs and thus a potential problem officer in performing everyday duties, such as arriving to work on time, completing reports, and obeying supervisors. He or she also becomes a risk for police misconduct and civil lawsuits by creditors.

There are a number of computer software programs specifically designed for these investigations in order to sort and store all of this information in an organized manner. These programs can also generate letters of inquiry to employers, police departments, and to those listed as references.

Residency

Many departments give preference to applicants who live within the boundaries of the local police jurisdiction. This is handled in a number of ways. In one approach, only citizens with prior residency in the local agency jurisdiction are eligible for police employment. Prior residency varies from a few weeks to many months. In other jurisdictions, residency is required only after employment. Others give a preference to prior residents on the hiring list; this means that local residents will be hired before the residents of any other jurisdiction will be considered. One of the author's students who placed fourth on a local civil service police examination discovered that he had been placed 64th on the list when the examiners found out that he lived about a mile outside the city limits. He had not been aware of these residency preferences when he took the examination, but he was certainly aware of them after the civil service lists were published.

Residency areas vary widely. They can be limited to the municipality in question or extended to contiguous counties or throughout the state. In one city, officers had to live no farther than "five air miles" from the police station in order to respond to emergencies. Some departments, such as those in Houston and Los Angeles, have nationwide recruitment programs with no prior residency requirements. They are looking for the best talent, nationwide, for their departments.

The issue of residency is related to the questions of (1) merit and talent versus the need for local knowledge and adherence to local customs that local citizens would have and (2) the wish to give preference in the spending of tax dollars to those who provide those tax dollars. Reform-minded police managers, especially those in the larger departments, prefer talented and meritorious candidates regardless of place of residence. Local conservative politicians appeal to home rule and local pride in establishing rigid residency requirements. If police departments are to upgrade their personnel, rigid residency requirements will have to be abolished since these requirements limit the talent pool from which potential officers can be drawn.

Psychological Testing

Personnel managers who use psychometric testing and clinical evaluation to assess police recruits look for a stable personality that is flexible enough to adjust to the stress of police work along with the complex peer relations. Police managers are especially concerned with having some idea as to whether that particular recruit is apt to "break" in a stressful situation in the future. If that is, in fact, a major concern, then the authors would recommend that personnel managers in police departments create a series of stress interviews to use in selecting recruits. One problem with this type of testing is that researchers have barely scratched the surface in testing the predictability of these tests in police performance. However, we do have an extensive research literature on industrial and business personality profile testing and have excellent empirical evidence in terms of predictability of performance and standardized group scores.

Psychological testing is useful in weeding out psychotic and potentially dangerous human beings. However, most professionals agree that psychological testing is useful only for rejecting the truly abnormal. In that gray area encompassing normal-neurotic-deviant, different kinds of judgments need to be made to be fair to the recruits.

What is rather scary is that some smaller police departments use no psychological screening for recruits. If, say, even 10 percent can be rejected for potentially psychotic behavior, then what we have created by not using this technique is a group of unguided missiles with great potential for harm. Industry and businesses have found these techniques to be useful and spend millions of dollars a year to employ them. Businesses would not go to this expense unless there was clear-cut evidence that these tests are useful in judging future performance. It is now time for law enforcement to catch up with the private sector by using personnel evaluation techniques of proven value.

Lateral Entry

Lateral entry allows recruitment for various levels in a police agency. It allows for mobility in that an officer can transfer at a rank above recruit and below such elected or politically appointed positions as chief, sheriff, and deputy chief. This means that a sergeant in one agency may be able to transfer laterally to another police agency, keeping his or her rank.

Of course, lateral entry is almost nonexistent. Mobility comes only to the lowest and highest levels of policing. In relation to the entry-level positions, it is normally a termination of one job and an entry into another job. Lateral entry at the bottom is difficult to distinguish from simple job mobility. This may mean an upgrading of the officer from a local police job to a more prestigious county, state, or federal law enforcement occupation. This is a simple case of upward mobility rather than lateral entry. At the top level, police executives move from one jurisdiction to another.

In smaller communities, state civil service commissions have created the civil service position of chief. The net result is normally freezing the chief in his position and reducing mobility. In fact, some small communities require through their police charter that the chief must come from the ranks regardless of qualifications.

There are a number of real restrictions on the creation of a lateral entry system: (1) nonuniform retirement systems, (2) differences in pay scales for the same positions, (3) residency requirements, (4) nonuniform training for different levels of staffing, and (5) differences in civil service requirements for the same management level. Generally, in many of these cases, it would take a major adjustment by local management and the police benevolent association's personnel policies and in some cases change in local and state laws to implement a lateral entry personnel system.

Data from the Bureau of Justice Statistics review of Local Police Departments (2003) show that lateral transfers are common among departments of less than 10,000 residents. Transfers often occur in order to obtain police officer candidates who have already completed state training and certification, which becomes an economic benefit for the hiring department (and a loss for the department that paid for the employment costs related to the training).

Polygraph Testing

A **polygraph** is an instrument that is used to measure physiological responses to questions. Three variables—breathing, blood pressure, and amount of perspiration—are monitored as the subject is introduced to stimuli by way of specific questions, such as, "Have you smoked marijuana in the past five years?"

Today, the polygraph is increasingly being used by law enforcement agencies as a preemployment screening device as well as an investigatory tool. The objective in utilizing the polygraph for police personnel selection is to uncover those aspects of a person's character that would be deemed undesirable for a career in law enforcement. These include excessive drinking, gambling, immoral sexual conduct, and criminal behavior that might not be uncovered during a background investigation. Police agencies that use the polygraph for their personnel selection point to the high number of applicants who are disqualified based on information obtained during the course of the polygraph test. Also, by publicizing the use of the polygraph for police selection, many agencies feel that this tends to deter candidates who would ultimately be found unsuitable.

Many important questions emerge on the use of the polygraph for selection purposes. First, the polygraphist must be well trained. This involves a rigorous course of some 600 hours, followed by refresher seminars to keep him or her abreast of new trends. Then the department has to establish criteria that would disqualify a candidate, that is, to determine what past or present behavior is unsuitable for police work. For example, should candidate Jones be disqualified because he smoked marijuana five years ago while in college? If Jones admits to stealing while he was a juvenile, what type of stolen property would result in his disqualification? A car? A fountain pen?

In essence, the use of the polygraph is based on the subjective judgments of the polygraphist and the overall policies of the department. While there has always been criticism of the usefulness and accuracy of polygraph testing, it is still the mainstay of testing for many police departments today. A study by Jefferson (2008) into fraudulent police applications for a major city department found that most disqualifications for negative background check findings were based on failure to report criminal arrests and use of controlled substances. It was the polygraph that was critical in uncovering this information, even after candidates had already passed several steps in the hiring process.

The Interview

Traditionally, the candidate is either required or invited to have an interview with the chief of police regarding his or her candidacy for employment. In states where civil service prevails, this interview may be perfunctory or an important part of the process if the department is able to select from a pool or a certified list of candidates. The purpose of the interview is for the administrator to meet the candidate and ask questions to determine whether he or she would be a good police officer and an asset to the department.

Many departments have turned the interview into a stressful group process whereby the candidate meets with three to six interviewers from the department, the community, or both. Difficult questions are asked, ranging from personal philosophy to judgment in police situations, and the candidate's responses are measured accordingly. This process gives the department something that no multiple-choice tests can ever give—the ability to examine the potential officer in a stressful situation; in the interview room, the candidate is required to make immediate judgments on the questions presented.

A review of group interview questions from a variety of sources yields the following examples:

1. What unique skills, strengths, and abilities will you bring to the department?
2. What do you expect from a supervisor?
3. What kind of call would be distasteful (or most stressful) to you?
4. Suppose that while you are on patrol, you receive a call to go to a residence where a baby is crying. There is a babysitter inside the residence, but no one comes to the door. What do you do?

The candidate is judged not only on his or her responses but also on his or her ability to communicate and to make judgments. Interviews range from structured questions that require the demonstration of specific types of knowledge to interviews that include a few structured questions but the interviewers are allowed to free-associate and probe the candidate's replies.

College Education Requirements

Of the many programs created by the Law Enforcement Assistance Administration, some that will endure are the college criminal justice programs that were created in response to the mandate of the President's Commission on Law Enforcement and Administration of Justice that all police officers must possess college degrees. In the 1970s, a trend began for police departments and civil service commissions to raise educational requirements from the traditional high school diploma to two or four years of college study with a major in criminal justice or a related field.

While this would appear to be a step toward creating a professional police force and attracting candidates who are able to think, write, and speak well about the social problems affecting the community, many police administrators and college educators question the value of a college education as it relates to police work. Detractors or those neutral to the idea point out that the realities of the police role (making arrests, seeing people at their worst) may nullify the value of classroom study (Weiner, 1976). Furthering this controversy, the National Advisory Commission on Higher Education for Police Officers (1979) concluded that many criminal justice college programs were no more than extensions of the police training academy, staffed by former police officers, that offered "how-to" courses (scoffed at as "Handcuffs 101") rather than courses related to important social and police managerial issues. Others have contended that college cannot teach common sense and that many college graduates do not know how to read and write well.

Some earlier educators replied that common sense is simply the sum total of the prejudices that one has developed over a lifetime. They also argued that much of this "common sense" is not 20 years of professional growth, but rather that same rookie year repeated 20 times with all the mistakes integrated into a rigid approach to law enforcement.

Stepping back from this argument, many criminal justice educators and police professionals recommend that learning be a combination of knowledge and experience. Those college and training programs that synthesize the two are generally lauded by police administrators. It makes no sense to reinvent the wheel each year because the recruit was never given the knowledge of how wheels operate.

In a textbook on the role of the police, Radelet and Carter (1993: 152) cite research that suggests that higher education provides a number of benefits for law enforcement personnel. In addition to learning more about history, law, and ethics, which contributes to an officer's information base, higher education benefits may include the following:

1. Developing greater empathy and tolerance for people with different lifestyles and ideologies; this in turn helps with communication skills
2. Helping officers make decisions and use discretion while handling individual cases without direct supervision
3. Permitting officers to be innovative and flexible while dealing with complex policing strategies, such as problem-oriented or community policing
4. Enabling officers to cope better with stress, resulting in more stable and reliable employees
5. Helping officers communicate and respond to situations and to the service needs of the public in a civil manner

According to the Bureau of Criminal Justice Statistics (2010), only about 16 percent of municipal departments have college education requirements for entry-level patrol positions. The report did indicate that approximately 38 percent of those departments serving municipalities of over one million residents required some college education. However, the number of persons holding degrees in patrol, supervisory, and senior leadership ranks has generally increased. Often departments will have unofficial norms for promotion that include college education at the graduate school level. Federal law enforcement agencies generally require a bachelor's degree or some combination of higher education and police/military experience.

The Assessment Center

While most agencies have continued to utilize the various traditional steps just discussed for police personnel selection and wrestle with affirmative action complaints, others have adopted selection models from private industry. One that shows promise is the **assessment center**, a concept first used by the German and British military in World War II for selecting service people qualified to perform special missions. After the War, the idea caught on in private industry in the United States. Some federal and municipal law enforcement agencies are experimenting with or are using the assessment center concept.

At the assessment center, the candidate participates in a number of activities, ranging from a structured interview to group simulation exercises. In the group exercise, the candidate must confront a problem that might be encountered on the job, such as intervening in a family fight. Trained assessors rate the candidate on how well he or she performs the assigned tasks.

Hale (2005) concludes that well-designed exercises simulate on-the-job behavior in a way that traditional pen-and-paper tests cannot. Moreover, a large amount of performance information can be obtained in a relatively short period of time. Although various methods are used, the exercises are constant for all candidates undergoing the process.

An assessment process, first cited by Gavin and Hamilton in 1975 and now used by the University of Wisconsin Police Department, might include the following steps:

Phase I

1. Written examination
2. Verbal screening
3. Psychological testing

Phase II

1. Oral board interview, composed of a senior police officer, a psychologist, and a community representative, in which questions are asked concerning the candidate's background and motivations for entering police work
2. Situational testing, in which the candidate is confronted with typical police situations (assessors watch the exercise behind a one-way mirror)
3. Leaderless group discussions, at which time the applicants are presented with a police-related topic (At the end of the discussion, the candidates present their conclusions. The assessors watch the discussions and rate the candidates on their participation.)
4. Individual psychological interview
5. Combining the data gathered from phases I and II and ranking the candidates

Phase III

Based on successful completion of phases I and II, the candidates then undergo a polygraph examination, background check, physical examinations, and police/staff interviews.

The assessment center can be expensive or even inaccessible for smaller departments because of geographic considerations.

Caldwell et al. (2003) also present a number of major issues that must be addressed to ensure assessment selection validity. These include undertaking a complete job analysis, preparing pretest evaluations, conducting complete assessor training, preparing exercises that reflect on-the-job tasks, and creating complete documentation and scoring. Hale (2005) also points out the need for pretest planning, which includes having backup role players and video equipment. Overall assessment processes are rarely used for recruit selection but have become someplace for supervisor and executive selection.

Social Media Sites

A number of agencies have begun to review social media sites either as a formal or informal method of evaluating candidates. In one department, candidates are asked to present their various social media sites to the investigator conducting the background check. The use of these sites to assess employment considerations is a controversial topic for both public and private sector organizations. Some feel that it is an intrusion into one's personal life whereas others decree that these sites are "fair game" in trying to determine the character and fitness of a person for police employment. At this time we have told our students to clean their social media sites up, including blogs, social network Web sites, and online videos. It is clear that no one is impressed to see a candidate throwing up at a party or acting in some other inappropriate manner for all to see.

RECRUITMENT TECHNIQUES

The basic considerations in recruiting are who you want to reach and the cost per sworn-in recruit. The department needs to provide funds for travel for the recruitment team as well as funds for printed materials. Any media messages should be produced by professionals for maximum impact. Professional organizations will be able to provide cost figures in terms of populations reached and numbers in those populations. The department needs to quiz new recruits in terms of how they found out about the available positions and use this information in charting recruitment costs.

The first step in any recruitment campaign is to make potential applicants identify with the organization. There are a number of ways that this can be achieved. Recruitment brochures, televised public service announcements, and Web sites should reflect the existing diversity of the department in terms of pictures and programs and have a direct link to recruiting/job opportunities. In some cases, personal vignettes can be presented. Candidates today use the Internet to review job openings and position requirements. Thus, it is important that the official Web site also reflect the diversity of the department. Similarly, the recruiters who are assigned to job fairs and recruitment details at high schools and colleges should recruit women and minorities. Because police agencies are defined by jurisdiction on the state, county, and local level, finding out what agencies are hiring is a full-time investigative endeavor. The International Association of Chiefs of Police and the Bureau of Justice Assistance have recently launched a Web site, discoverpolicing.org, that gives information on position openings by state and an overview of police careers and qualifications. This is a positive step in nationwide recruitment for departments in identifying potential recruits.

A number of departments, and in particular federal law enforcement agencies, have begun to accept applications over the Internet as the first step for application. While this provides easy access for applicants, we have found instances where candidates fail to present themselves in a professional manner and may use text-messaging shortcuts instead of preparing formal responses to questions.

Toward a Rational Model of Police Selection

The authors feel that the multistep traditional model of police selection has served its usefulness—in essence, the dictates of the 1883 Pendleton Act are still being employed as the chief criteria for selection. What we propose is a new model that attempts to include methodologies used for personnel selection both in the private industry and by some law enforcement agencies in the United States.

In reviewing this chapter, it becomes obvious that the traditional civil service selection process is outmoded on two bases. First, we are no farther ahead than we ever were in abolishing certain personnel abuses that existed before 1870, especially those related to the influence on the police by the community political establishment. Although the wholesale firing of police officers after Election Day has ended, the outright spoils system that existed in the nineteenth century has been replaced by a system that we call *sophisticated patronage*, in which party affiliation becomes a factor in who gets selected in a rule-of-three situation. Moreover, not all police departments use civil service. In many states, and even in those states that have civil service, some departments still use a selection process based on political influence and informal community relations (e.g., "I am a friend of the chief, and I have lived here all my life").

Many police administrators, moreover, are fed up with traditional procedures. Although there are many qualified candidates who wish to become police officers, these individuals are forced to put off career plans simply because they must take a pencil-and-paper test that may be scheduled only once a year. Frequently, too, the results of the test are not made known until months after the examination. When coupled with the other factors related to the selection process—interviews, background checks, polygraph examinations, and so on—it may take a year and a half, or more, from the time of the examination to eventual employment. Many departments have solved this dilemma by doing most of the process, excluding the background examination, within the specific time frame of a week or days.

Police administrators who desire a specific candidate are still able to find loopholes to further the cause of sophisticated patronage. One department studied, conducted its own selection process and hired a number of officers under the statute terms of provisional appointment. When the civil service test was held, the new officers, who had been on the job for a year, had to take the examination with other candidates. The results showed that some of the year-old appointees did not rank very high on the list. The administrator solved the dilemma by importing a residency requirement (again within the terms of the state law) that eventually eliminated all the applicants who had taken the examination except for the officers previously hired.

Against this background, many researchers employed by police departments, colleges, or research institutions are attempting to upgrade the existing process by answering diverse legal and methodological questions related to job performance and specific portions of the process. To date, this has resulted only in the allocation of time and monetary resources to upgrade the status quo.

New Police Recruit Selection Model

To address the issues presented, we propose a model for police recruit selection. This rational model for police selection is based on three premises:

1. There is a need for better designed entry-level, pencil-and-paper tests. Current tests often fail to predict on-the-job performance or the potential of the candidate.
2. The responsibility for police personnel selection rests with each state in terms of allocating financial and human resources for this objective. Since 90 percent of the police departments in the United States are small agencies composed of 15 officers or fewer, it is obvious that most agencies cannot afford to maintain an ongoing professional selection process.

At the same time, each police agency must abide by state requirements for the position of police officer.

3. Civil service personnel in existing departments need to be retooled to perform ably in this proposed model. The present personnel must be retrained, acquiring (1) new skills and (2) new attitudes toward their role as police officer. This entails the various tasks police officers perform.

To be considered for the position of police officer, based on this proposed model, a candidate should be able to fulfill the following requirements:

1. *Age.* A minimum age of 21 years is recommended. It is at age 22 that most people in the United States embark on careers. There is no set maximum age to give each department the flexibility to decide on what kinds of experience and skills potential employees need. At the same time, those departments with 20-year retirement systems will have to adjust their pension systems for the older worker. This would be a proportionate pension system based on years of service to the retirement age.

2. *Education.* Under this new model, each candidate would have to possess a bachelor's degree from an accredited college or university. The bachelor's degree is the accepted norm for most professional careers. It is assumed that routine and clerical tasks would be performed by civilian employees and that police officers would serve as professional law enforcement officers. Thus, the kind of education that allows one to deal with a large range of cultures and roles and that teaches one to write well would be of value. District attorneys have known for years that cases written up by college-educated police officers are better than those written by officers without a college education. A college-educated police force of professionals whose job description is related to professional skills and knowledge will be a superior police force. Jumping from a high-school diploma as the educational requirement for new hires directly to a four-year degree, however, may prove to be too much, too quick. Instead, to create the likelihood of greater support for the new initiative, it is recommended that the change be incremental, including starting with a 60 college credit requirement, as well as to set the effective date two years in the future to allow both the agency and the potential candidate to properly prepare.

3. *Physical requirements.* Each candidate must be in basic good health and physical condition according to a national standard like Cooper. Nevertheless, each department would have physical requirements for selecting officers for special units (e.g., special weapons and tactics [SWAT] teams, hostage negotiation, bicycle patrol, and emergency services). Candidates must be free of any disease or physical ailments that would keep them disabled for long periods of time or prevent them from performing police duties.

After fulfilling these three basic requirements, the candidate would then report to a regional assessment center. Here the candidate would undergo a variety of tests currently in use by many police agencies. The testing would include a battery of psychological examinations.

On successful completion of the assessment center review, the candidate would then be eligible to attend the regionally operated police academy. The academy curriculum would include the basic tasks related to police work: firearms, crisis intervention, law, introduction to the criminal justice system, and physical conditioning. Candidates who fail tests or firearms requirements would be eliminated.

On completing the assessment center and police academy stages, the candidate would then be issued a certificate making him or her eligible to be a law enforcement officer for state and local agencies. The officer would be notified of available openings in the various departments and would be required to notify the department of his or her interest in working for that agency. From this pool of applicants, the agency would select the police officers for its department. The selection process would be based on the desires of the department and the community.

OTHER PERSONNEL ISSUES

Sexual Harassment

The presidency of William J. Clinton and his interactions with a student intern prompted continued interest in the topic of **sexual harassment**, especially with regard to interpersonal relationships in the workplace. Sexual harassment consists of the following:

1. The supervisor demands sexual consideration in exchange for job benefit.
2. An employee makes unwelcome sexual advances toward another employee in the form of pressure for dates, stalking, love letters, and calls.
3. Activities or behavior by one or more employees creates a hostile work environment for the complainant regardless of the loss of economic or tangible job benefits. These activities might include pranks, jokes, and comments of a sexual nature.

Sexual harassment can include incidents between people of the same gender.

Prohibitions against sexual harassment are not new. In the 1980s, a number of federal and state court cases concluded that sexual harassment activities violated EEOC guidelines and Title VII of the Civil Rights Act of 1964.

The **hostile work environment** standard, however, is very complex and often depends on the pattern of behavior in the work environment. Employer liability with regard to fines also depends on the extent to which the employer knew or could have reasonably known and prevented the sexual harassing activity. In a number of noted cases, public and private companies were fined by either state or federal courts for failing to stop the activity.

Today, most police departments have policies prohibiting sexual harassment and have established processes by which employees can make complaints and seek resolution of sexual harassment. Many have conducted training sessions for employees and supervisors to discuss the various aspects of sexual harassment and its negative effect on the mission of the department.

The crux of police department efforts against sexual harassment remains departmental disciplinary processes insofar as investigations, hearings, and sanctions must be meted out according to due process standards. In situations where the department fails to address sexual harassment complaints, the employee may go outside the department and file a complaint through either a state or a federal regulatory agency. Policing remains a male-dominated occupation in many departments throughout the United States. While the number of female officers has increased in many large state and metropolitan departments, there remain few or often no women in small agencies. Regardless of agency size, sexual harassment and the "hostile work environment" remain a problem for male and female supervisors and agency heads because of the delicate, complex nature of interpersonal relationships. We suggest that sexual harassment is a problem that must be continually addressed through training seminars, roll-call training, departmental advisories, and efficient complaint/resolution procedures. On the next page is a model policy presented by the Massachusetts Commission Against Discrimination.

It is important to understand that other forms of harassment in the workplace are forbidden. Workplace harassment for reasons of race, national origin, physical or mental disability,

Sexual Harassment Policy of [name of employer]

I. Introduction

It is the goal of [name of employer] to promote a workplace that is free of sexual harassment. Sexual harassment of employees occurring in the workplace or in other settings in which employees may find themselves in connection with their employment is unlawful and will not be tolerated by this organization. Further, any retaliation against an individual who has complained about sexual harassment or retaliation against individuals for cooperating with an investigation of a sexual harassment complaint is similarly unlawful and will not be tolerated. To achieve our goal of providing a workplace free from sexual harassment, the conduct that is described in this policy will not be tolerated and we have provided a procedure by which inappropriate conduct will be dealt with, if encountered by employees.

Because [name of employer] takes allegations of sexual harassment seriously, we will respond promptly to complaints of sexual harassment and where it is determined that such inappropriate conduct has occurred, we will act promptly to eliminate the conduct and impose such corrective action as is necessary, including disciplinary action where appropriate.

Please note that while this policy sets forth our goals of promoting a workplace that is free of sexual harassment, the policy is not designed or intended to limit our authority to discipline or take remedial action for workplace conduct which we deem unacceptable, regardless of whether that conduct satisfies the definition of sexual harassment.

II. Definition of Sexual Harassment

In Massachusetts, the legal definition for sexual harassment is this: "sexual harassment" means sexual advances, requests for sexual favors, and verbal or physical conduct of a sexual nature when:

a. submission to or rejection of such advances, requests or conduct is made either explicitly or implicitly a term or condition of employment or as a basis for employment decisions; or,

b. such advances, requests or conduct have the purpose or effect of unreasonably interfering

with an individual's work performance by creating an intimidating, hostile, humiliating or sexually offensive work environment.

Under these definitions, direct or implied requests by a supervisor for sexual favors in exchange for actual or promised job benefits such as favorable reviews, salary increases, promotions, increased benefits, or continued employment constitutes sexual harassment.

The legal definition of sexual harassment is broad and in addition to the above examples, other sexually oriented conduct, whether it is intended or not, that is unwelcome and has the effect of creating a workplace environment that is hostile, offensive, intimidating, or humiliating to male or female workers may also constitute sexual harassment.

While it is not possible to list all those additional circumstances that may constitute sexual harassment, the following are some examples of conduct which if unwelcome, may constitute sexual harassment depending upon the totality of the circumstances including the severity of the conduct and its pervasiveness:

- Unwelcome sexual advances—whether they involve physical touching or not;
- Sexual epithets, jokes, written or oral references to sexual conduct, gossip regarding one's sex life; comment on an individual's body, comment about an individual's sexual activity, deficiencies, or prowess;
- Displaying sexually suggestive objects, pictures, cartoons;
- Unwelcome leering, whistling, brushing against the body, sexual gestures, suggestive or insulting comments;
- Inquiries into one's sexual experiences; and
- Discussion of one's sexual activities.

All employees should take special note that, as stated above, retaliation against an individual who has complained about sexual harassment, and retaliation against individuals for cooperating with an investigation of a sexual harassment complaint is unlawful and will not be tolerated by this organization.

III. Complaints of Sexual Harassment

If any of our employees believes that he or she has been subjected to sexual harassment, the employee has the right to file a complaint with our organization. This may be done in writing or orally.

If you would like to file a complaint you may do so by contacting [Name, address and telephone number of the appropriate individual to whom complaints should be addressed. Such individuals may include human resources director, manager, legal counsel to organization or other appropriate supervisory person]. [This person] [These persons] [is/are] also available to discuss any concerns you may have and to provide information to you about our policy on sexual harassment and our complaint process.

IV. Sexual Harassment Investigation

When we receive the complaint we will promptly investigate the allegation in a fair and expeditious manner. The investigation will be conducted in such a way as to maintain confidentiality to the extent practicable under the circumstances. Our investigation will include a private interview with the person filing the complaint and with witnesses. We will also interview the person alleged to have committed sexual harassment. When we have completed our investigation, we will, to the extent appropriate inform the person filing the complaint and the person alleged to have committed the conduct of the results of that investigation.

If it is determined that inappropriate conduct has occurred, we will act promptly to eliminate the offending conduct, and where it is appropriate we will also impose disciplinary action.

V. Disciplinary Action

If it is determined that inappropriate conduct has been committed by one of our employees, we will take such action as is appropriate under the circumstances. Such action may range from counseling to termination from employment, and may include such other forms of disciplinary action as we deem appropriate under the circumstances.

VI. State and Federal Remedies

In addition to the above, if you believe you have been subjected to sexual harassment, you may file a formal complaint with either or both of the government agencies set forth below. Using our complaint process does not prohibit you from filing a complaint with these agencies. Each of the agencies has a short time period for filing a claim (EEOC–300 days; MCAD–300 days).

1. The United States Equal Employment Opportunity Commission ("EEOC") One Congress Street, 10th Floor, Boston, MA 02114 (617) 565-3200.
2. The Massachusetts Commission Against Discrimination ("MCAD") Boston Office: One Ashburton Place, Rm. 601, Boston, MA 02108, (617) 994-6000. Springfield Office: 424 Dwight Street, Rm. 220, Springfield, MA 01103, (413) 739-2145.

religion, and age can form the basis for civil liability. According to Bagyl and Boyd (2009: 48), federal claims of sexual harassment have slowly declined, while complaints for other forms of harassment have increased. Examples of this conduct include jokes, physical contact, and written communications.

A complaint against an employer or a group of employees often creates a situation where retaliation is made against the complainant. While such actions are prohibited, the Supreme Court in 2006 also included provisions for an employee to be reassigned to another position without change of job title or terms and conditions of employment after filing a harassment complaint.

Drug Testing

Drug testing for police personnel became widely used in the mid-1980s in response to the widespread use of illegal substances by citizens coupled with the dramatic rise of drug-related police corruption cases. Policy makers, legislators, and police administrators reasoned that the so-called war on drugs could not be waged by police officers who use illegal substances. Apart from the negative effects on physiomotor skills, the use of illegal substances by police officers provides a wide range of moral and legal dilemmas regarding drug enforcement. Perhaps the most profound are those life-and-death implications for drug enforcement officers who are compromised or threatened by fellow officers "bought" by drug dealers. The Bureau of Justice Statistics (2003) reports that nearly 85 percent of all local police departments have some form of drug testing for recruit officers.

Despite widespread use, drug testing remains controversial among police officers and police unions because of the invasion of personal privacy and the legal consequences for personnel who test positive. Departments that have drug screening may use one or a combination of the following programs:

1. Random testing for all personnel on a routine basis
2. Mandatory testing for all preemployment applicants
3. Testing for preservice and in-service officers based on reasonable suspicion that the person is using illegal substances. (Reasonable suspicion may be based on (1) internal investigation in response to a complaint; (2) observation of behavior at work, such as slurred speech, unsteady gait; or (3) long-term work patterns regarding sick time and attendance.)
4. Testing of officers being considered for sensitive assignments, such as narcotics enforcement, helicopter operations, explosives, and special weapons and tactics
5. Voluntary testing by officers to show that they are above reproach

Legally, drug screening is based on the Fourth and Fourteenth Amendments regarding searches and procedural due process. By the end of the 1980s, both the U.S. Supreme Court and higher state courts ruled on the legality of certain kinds of searches related to drug testing. The most noted case was *Skinner* v. *Railway Labor Executives Association* (1989), in which the Supreme Court decided that drug testing undertaken for railroad workers after accidents and safety violations constituted a search within the confines of the Fourth Amendment. The Court reasoned that the need to regulate the conduct of employees for safety purposes was far greater than the need for individual privacy. The same logic was applied to drug screening for U.S. Customs officers assigned to law enforcement duties. In *National Treasury Employees Union* v. *VonRaab* (1989), the Court concluded that preventing the entry and promotion of drug users into sensitive positions outweighed privacy interests in view of the physical and ethical demands related to the position. In both cases, the Court also discussed the deterrence value of drug screening; in each situation, employees had fair warning that the tests would be conducted.

The upholding of drug testing in these cases does not mean that testing for all personnel will automatically be upheld. In either a court or an administrative hearing setting, the following key elements will be analyzed: the nature of the testing (random versus postincident), the preliminary notice given to employees who are to be tested, the laboratory procedures used and their validation, and the need for testing based on the particular functions of the job.

In 1988, the Police Executive Research Forum surveyed police chiefs around the country. The following are the policies the chiefs favored:

• Drug testing if reasonable grounds existed to suspect an officer using drugs (87.7 percent)
• Drug screening of police applicants (76.4 percent)
• Regular drug testing of officers during probationary period (66 percent)
• Random drug testing of officers in "sensitive" positions (64.7 percent)

These policies would be subject to legal and union contract considerations. In order to have credibility with the public, it is necessary to have specific alcohol and drug abuse policies that are enforced. Police unions favor drug and alcohol abuse policies geared toward rehabilitation, with sanctions as a last resort.

DRUG TESTING IN PRACTICE   The most common screening procedure used at this time is urine testing by way of the enzyme multiplied immunoassay technique (EMIT). In this procedure, a urine sample is analyzed for the presence of a single substance or a class of drugs or metabolites by separating the various enzymes. The procedure is inexpensive and, thus, widely used. The use of EMIT suggests only the presence of a substance; it does not show quantity and level of impairment. As Connors (1989: 165) suggests, there must be further testing and investigation through gas chromatography and mass spectrometry to address the problem of "false positives." The key elements in screening procedures are the safeguards used in this testing, including such variables as the quality of equipment, chain of custody of evidence, training of personnel administering the test, and the test site procedures.

For in-service personnel who test positive in random or periodic testing programs, the next course of action by management involves interrogation and disciplinary action. Most police unions have at this time negotiated a series of steps to protect the interests of employees in situations when an employee has been ordered to submit to drug testing and related interrogation. These steps—representation by counsel, written notice of charges, reasonable privacy during urination, and second-opinion testing of the suspected employee—are generally in addition to any other rights negotiated by contract. To support administrators in situations in which a complaint about drug use by an officer is based on the testimony of a confidential informant, language of the collective bargaining agreement often states that the employer does not have to reveal the name of the informant.

Police executives generally agree that termination of employment is perhaps the only fitting way to deal with confirmed illegal drug users. Connors (1989) points to the legal aspects of such situations, including possession of a controlled substance and association with known drug users. Some departments, in concert with their police unions, have started programs of drug abuse education and professional assistance for personnel who voluntarily declare that they have a substance abuse problem. The success and employee acceptance of these programs vary because police officers generally stay away from these programs if assistance offices are located in the police station or if confidentiality is not ensured. Some collective bargaining agreements declare that the officer will not be subject to drug screening if he or she voluntarily enters a rehabilitation program. Whether the officer is temporarily suspended or allowed to continue in another assignment varies from program to program.

This trend in drug screening and discipline will not change drastically as long as state court and administrative rulings continue to uphold valid screening programs and disciplinary sanctions for drug abuse committed in both on-duty and off-duty situations. Further, a related federal policy for drug-free workplaces and schools was ensured by the end of the 1980s. In 1988, the Federal Drug Free Workplace Act was signed into law. It requires employers with federal contracts in excess of $25,000 to certify that they will provide a drug-free workplace through the following: (1) providing publications and education about drug awareness, (2) requiring notification to the employer by the employee if he or she is arrested for criminal violations occurring in the workplace, (3) requiring convicted employees to participate in a drug abuse assistance or rehabilitation program, and (4) notifying employees of possible sanctions that might be taken against them by the company. The language and intent of the 1988 Act were also applied in the Drug Free Schools Act, which stipulates that financial aid can be withheld from students convicted of drug violations.

Contract Police Issues

Albert Reiss Jr. (1988: 9) produced three models of secondary employment that are still useful today.

1. The *officer contract model*. Each officer is a principal who independently contracts with an employer for a particular job.
2. The *union brokerage model*. An officer's union or association brokers the employment for its members so that they need not search for their own job and negotiate pay.
3. The *department contract model*. The department is the principal agent for officers and contracts their secondary employment.

There are many variations of the officer contract model. For example, Arlington, Virginia, restricts outside employment to the state of Virginia, county of Arlington, and the U.S. government. Cincinnati handles the billing and compensation of officers when the contracting party is the city; otherwise, it lets its officers contract on their own for employment.

According to Reiss, under the union brokerage model, the union sets conditions and pay for paid details and may bargain with the police department concerning status and condition of paid details. The Seattle Police Officers' Guild coordinates requests for off-duty employment, but the officers act as independent contractors. For special events held at the Seattle Center complex, off-duty officers "are employed by the complex's director of security and compensated by an outside accounting firm" (Reiss, 1988: 11).

Under the department contract model, the police department performs three major functions (Reiss, 1988: 11): It "(1) contracts with employers for paid details; (2) assigns officers to details; and (3) pays the officers from reimbursements by employers." The Metro-Dade Florida Police Department contracts for all police-related work, but "officers are allowed to contract independently for non-police related work on application for a specific job and under permit for that employment." Metro-Dade is unusual in that it subcontracts police services for private security. Boston, Colorado Springs, New Haven, and St. Petersburg operate primarily with the department contract model.

The three major issues that restrict employment of the public police are: (1) potential conflict of interest, (2) threat to the dignity of police as an occupation, and (3) "an unacceptable risk of temporary or disabling injury that would limit their [the police officer's] return to regular duty" (Reiss, 1988: 11).

Most departments have rules and regulations and issue work permits for all outside employment. Departments place even more stringent restrictions when the public police officer is employed in uniform. Many departments and police unions also restrict the rate of compensation that can be earned, for example, demanding a minimum rate. They also restrict the type of employment and the amount of time spent on secondary employment, such as a maximum number of hours outside work per week. The exact time of employment—for example, working prior to coming on duty—is also an area of concern. These restrictions are normally enforced by issuing or denying work permits to individual officers. All in all, the relationship between private and public police will continue to be a major concern of police managers in the public sector.

Police Overtime

Millions of dollars are spent annually on police **overtime**, yet there are practically no published studies on this topic. Since police normally deal with emergencies, disasters, mass demonstrations, murders, and major performances drawing thousands of fans, the public should expect police managers to plan for these events with a minimal use of overtime or with a program to recoup overtime costs from event sponsors. The lack of attention and planning on this issue can result in bloated budgets, an inefficient use of police personnel, police officer exhaustion, and unnecessary tension between line officers and police supervisors.

This is sometimes complicated if the department or unit is not adequately staffed. Many functions operating 24 hours a day require five or six people to carry out the duties of one position. A discussion on staff planning can be found in Chapter 14.

A nationwide study of overtime involving 2,183 police agencies found that the major reasons for overtime were shift extensions, court appearances, emergency situations, and contract requirements. Other reasons were briefings and roll calls, callbacks to duty, and meetings and training outside of work hours. In some departments, a homicide was treated as an emergency requiring overtime (Bayley and Worden, 1998: 3, 4).

Labor contracts and state and federal laws normally charge overtime at time and a half of an officer's hourly wage rate. These contracts can often create costly, artificial overtime charges. Some examples of excessive labor contract provisions are the following:

- Brief court appearances earning, by contract, three or four hours in overtime
- Standbys earning a minimum of three hours of overtime
- Overtime of 15–30 minutes given for roll calls
- Having all meetings outside the department charged for overtime

Removing these provisions from contracts should be a high priority in negotiations with police unions. It may be necessary to make these labor abuses public in order to eliminate them.

The high cost of overtime needs to be controlled through proactive police management, including recording, analyzing, managing, and supervision. The most vital issue is to have basic records of the following:

- Number of overtime minutes
- What the overtime was used for
- Officers and units performing the overtime work
- A daily computerized usage record in a retrievable form

Only 38 percent of the departments surveyed in the nationwide sample were able to provide the number of overtime hours worked.

Compensatory time is repaying overtime with time off at the rate of one and a half times more than straight time. This creates more problems when professional personnel are simply not available for normal duties because they are on "comp" time. As Bayley and Worden (1998: 3) stress, "Paid overtime increases policing activity while compensatory time results in less policing because every hour worked must be repaid by the department at time and a half time taken away from other activities."

Bayley and Worden found one department in which all overtime was paid in cash, overtime was tracked by unit and function, and a report was distributed to management every two weeks. Thus, it is possible to create a system that works in controlling overtime. With good records, overtime can be controlled by police management. Overtime cannot be totally eliminated given the nature of police work, but with proactive policies in place, millions of dollars can be saved.

Proactive Policies for Controlling Overtime

1. A program is required that notifies management any time a unit or officer is building up overtime so the reason can be looked into immediately.

2. An agreement should be reached with the courts to limit personnel needed in court, to eliminate the need for supervisory police personnel, and to create a court schedule that conforms to straight time as much as possible. With instant communications and computer scheduling available, police officers should be able to work other duties while awaiting court appearances.

3. Written guidelines are needed for instructing supervisors when to approve shift extensions. The overtime should be immediately entered into the overtime computer program, with the reason for shift extension, and the officers' names and units that were granted the extension.

4. Good records on overtime are mandatory. When elected officials consider the costs of police personnel, a report should be on their desks giving the reasons for overtime costs in understaffed police departments.

5. Emergency planning must be done with straight-time personnel. Emergencies can also be planned for with a mobilization plan and an interagency agreement with other police departments.

6. Special events, including traffic control, need to be planned well ahead of time, using special police officers on straight time, and should involve other agencies. Event sponsors may need to pay for extra police coverage.

7. Adjustable and flexible work schedules are a first line of defense. The schedules must be available to senior management, planning personnel, and line supervisors. A 2011 study by the Police Foundation found that officers assigned to 8-hour shifts earned five times as much overtime as officers assigned to 10-hour shifts, and three times as much as officers assigned to 12-hour shifts (Amendola et al., 2011).

8. All overtime should be through payroll financial compensation, never in compensatory time.

9. Departments should have adequate staffing to cover line and auxiliary functions and should not depend on overtime for basic coverage.

Proactive control of overtime through data analysis and an instantly available computer-based information system will give proactive police management the following:

- The tools to explain the use of overtime to legislatures
- The ability to eliminate costly labor contract provisions
- The ability to create an efficient system to monitor and control overtime

Stress Management

Police work entails high **stress**, and managing that work can produce a great deal of stress. Stress itself can be good or bad. "Manageable" stress is a positive factor in organizational life if it motivates employees to complete a job and act in a responsible manner. If stress leads to avoidance of work or creates a feeling of being overwhelmed by events, it can become a strong negative force.

More and more studies are being written on the subject of police stress. The major issues relate to stress created by the organization and stress created by the individual. Organizational stress is created by lack of communication or by miscommunication. A lack of consistency may cause the line officer and his or her immediate superiors to think that they lack control over their jobs.

Individual stress is often created by a personality type attracted to police work that has been labeled *type A*. Type A personalities tend to overcommit themselves to a wide variety of tasks and feel that they have to be doing something all the time. They feel that they must be in control of all situations affecting them. They often have insomnia, but they also accomplish a great deal of what they set out to do.

This is in contrast to *type B* personalities, who accomplish what they can, worry a bit about what they have control over, and do not worry about what they cannot control. If the job is not finished on one day, this individual feels that there will be other days to finish it. The type A personality, in contrast, would either finish the job in the time allotted or be overwhelmed by guilt. When stress management consultants do their task well, they are able to apply type A and type B personality profiles to individuals and work out specific exercises that strike a balance between the two personality types. This is a very real challenge that can make or break a police organization. Meditation, posture work, and a variety of exercises are excellent tools that have been used to deal with stress and stressors. Remember that stress, itself, is not bad. It is uncontrolled stress that is destructive.

Stress recognition and reduction techniques should be part of every in-service police training program. However, all the techniques in the world will not change stress-producing situations. By the nature of their work, police officers are often confronted by dangerous situations. However, perceptions of violence and techniques for handling violence can reduce stress on individual officers. An officer must have enough training and experience to handle and control stress-producing situations. That is why, for example, training in domestic crisis intervention is so vital for the patrol officer, as is specific training in riot and crowd control, the handling of juveniles, and so on. The more skills an officer has, the less stress he or she will experience.

Organizational structures can produce or diminish stress. In plain English, this means that police personnel need consistency of command, time to assimilate new orders, and a good feedback system that allows for modification of orders in terms of the needs of the line officer. Officers and managers, especially middle managers, need communication skills so that the line officer will feel that (1) someone up there in management land is listening and that (2) he or she has a real and responsible input into the orders that affect his or her everyday professional life. People need to feel in control of their lives. Capricious orders with no explanation destroy this feeling of control.

When a number of police officers from different departments are drinking coffee at 2:00 A.M. in the middle of a patrol assignment, what is the talk about? Is it about crime, forensics, or how to patrol more effectively? Not usually. The talk is normally about promotions, orders, personalities in the police force, and individual stories about police-related incidents. Good police managers know this and will take steps to assure line officers and supervisors some control over the affairs that dominate their lives.

Stress management is a major concern for police managers. Police have to make instant life-and-death decisions and face violence, and yet they are also stressed by boredom. Some stress-related factors in police work are the following (Niederhoffer, 1967; Stratton, 1984):

- Shift work
- Quasimilitary structure
- Need to repress emotions and keep a psychological distance
- Lack of promotions and very few lateral transfers
- Media image of the supercop to live up to
- Police cynicism
- Frustration and lack of input into the police bureaucracy
- Fear and danger (killing a citizen or having a fellow officer killed, especially your partner)
- Social isolation
- Retirement
- Excessive paperwork
- Frustration with the judicial system
- Impact of a profession stressing danger and imposing stress on the spouse and children

Police officers, despite the social solidarity of police, often do not trust one another. Unlike other professions, police officers do not like to show personal weaknesses. There is also a stigma of seeking professional counseling. Until recent years, many departments did not recognize or acknowledge the symptoms brought about by postcritical incident stress or PTSD.

John Stratton, former director of Psychological Services in the Los Angeles County Sheriff's Department, also gives many practical examples and suggestions in his book *Police Passages* (1984). These include counseling programs for spouses, police widows and widowers, officers approaching retirement, and the availability of a 24-hour crisis hotline for police officers.

Violanti (1983) showed that stress increases in what he calls the first two stages of a police career: 0–5 years, the alarm stage, and 6–13 years, the disenchantment stage. He recommends that programs on stress management be focused on these years. He concludes with this hopeful note (Violanti, 1983: 216): "Despite strong pressures and the imbalanced nature of the police functions, officers managed in time to reduce stress." He felt that "individual perception is the most important factor in determining stress levels." Thus, stress can be coped with both by the individual and by the police organization through positive intervention strategies.

One approach that large departments can use and smaller departments can create on a regional level is what Robert Loo, the first chief psychologist of the Royal Canadian Mounted Police, calls his proactive approach to psychological services. He recommends the creation of a center that will have a career-cycle perceptive on providing psychological services, including "recruit selection, support of force training programs, the support of members in the workplace and pre-retirement services" (Loo, 1985: 134). In the past, he felt that police agencies simply reacted to such problems as low morale, stress reactions, drug abuse by police personnel, and community/citizen complaints against police officers. He feels that this proactive approach will help police managers deal more adequately with these problems.

Family stress can be decreased by departmental intervention. At the training level, spouses and domestic partners should learn about the job and the stressors in the job, tour the police unit, and take part in a ride-along program. Emergency communication and debriefing procedures for critical incidents, along with counseling for families, need to be available. Counseling and support groups need to be created with the support of the police administration. These can provide stress management workshops, social affairs, and volunteer opportunities.

Officers need to be physically fit and should have good eating and sleeping habits in order to reduce stress. Departments need to set up nutritional guidelines and physical fitness programs that are related to an officer's age, work, and physical condition. Many departments consider this a frill. However, given the investment in training and work experience in the form of the human capital of police officer and police supervisor, the approach should be considered essential to the job.

In *Stress Management for Law Enforcement Officers*, Anderson et al. (1995: 283) show four major factors that affect officers' negative attitudes toward their work: "(1) the particular stresses they face, (2) the extent to which the legal system backs them and rewards them with convictions for the good arrests, (3) their zone of stability, and (4) their support system."

The zone of a person's stability is "the range of stimulation (excitement, arousal) from the least to the most an individual can handle without signs of distress" (p. 17). People operating below their zone of stability will be bored and uncomfortable; when operating above the zone of stability, they will feel stressed and pressured. Good police managers need to know their own zone of stability and their subordinates' zones of stability so that there is enough good stress to keep people moving without exceeding their comfort zones.

Supervisors, such as sergeants, lieutenants, or captains, who are trained in supervision techniques are less stressed and create less stress for subordinates. This approach improves the morale of the whole police department. As one lieutenant and shift commander stated, "The daily stressors associated with management . . . can produce the same kind of stress reactions among supervisors . . . as a domestic disturbances call might provoke among line officers" (Standfest, 1996: 10). Training and stress management is just as important for supervisors and managers as for any line officer.

Standfest has a four-stage approach:

1. *Assessment.* Through assessment, police executives learn which stressors are affecting their supervisors.
2. *Planning.* The police executives remove the stressors in a cost-effective manner. Standfest says that fundamental approaches, such as repairing station houses and vehicles, could reduce a great deal of stress at low cost.
3. *Action.* Police executives fully carry out any plan and let the supervisors know what is going on.
4. *Follow-through.* Police executives evaluate the action, making sure that the orders were fully carried out, and assess the outcomes.

Anderson and colleagues (1995: 130) show the nature of police role stressors and role overload. These recommendations can be summarized as follows:

1. Clear and current policies and procedures concerning work tasks reduce police role ambiguity.
2. A consistent expectation by supervisors concerning their subordinates, along with a clear two-way feedback system, is essential.
3. Officers and supervisors need to have a high tolerance for ambiguity.
4. Active participation by all authority levels in decision making provides a system of mutual responsibility that continually relieves stress.

The Cop Diet

We first heard the term *cop diet* during a discussion with Karen Collins (personal interview, August 1, 2005), a dietitian who writes for the American Institute for Cancer Research, MSNBC.com, and other media venues. Many police officers today are very health conscious and find that the doughnut shop jokes have been overplayed, but the dietary issues related to stress cannot be ignored. Police officers do eat horribly, with the two main food groups being caffeine and sugar. "It's usually fast food and eat fast," Collins states, especially patrol officers who eat between calls or very late at night. Popular items such as burgers and fries lead to weight problems, high blood pressure, high cholesterol, and diabetes.

What it all comes down to is personal choice, discipline, and a bit of food content knowledge.

Collins realizes that police officers cannot escape fast food establishments during patrol work, for these restaurants and diners are open all the time and have parking. "Avoid the super-size portions—those are killers," Collins states. "Go for water or diet cokes, salads, and grilled chicken sandwiches. Put fruit in the patrol car for snacking. Stay away from the doughnuts—an average portion has about 240–350 calories. Muffins are no better; some have as many as 600 calories, especially the 'big guys,' sold in delis."

Police managers, supervisors, and patrol officers must be aware of their diet and health, especially as they get older. Every area has registered dietitians who can do a personal review for anyone, Collins concludes.

Supervisors can reduce stress by "(1) teaching the officers 'verbal judo'; that is, how to use words to control citizens' behavior; (2) showing the officers the laws that apply and when to use them; and (3) explaining the nature and characteristics of the particular public they serve" (Anderson et al., 1995: 285). This is exactly what proactive participatory management and proactive community policing do when they are working effectively.

Fatigue Management

Scientists working at Walter Reed Army Institute report the following (Vila, 2000: 26):

> Sleep deprivation degrades the higher, more complex mental processes. Soldiers lose battlefield awareness. . . . They can shoot and shoot accurately but no longer can distinguish friend from foe.

Studies by Vila showed that officers identified as fatigued had slow reactions to various kinds of mechanical and speed tests and were high risks for motor vehicle accidents. Unlike truck drivers and railroad engineers, there is no **fatigue** standard for police officers. However, the alertness assurance program is a proactive approach that can help protect departments from lawsuits resulting from mistakes made by tired officers. Following are some elements of the program:

- Implementing a consistent and biocompatible work schedule with controls for overtime
- Teaching employees and their families about how to manage shift work
- Not letting employees drive home while fatigued by providing free rides and a place to nap
- Setting up a permanent employee/management task force to manage fatigue

Vila offers other recommendations for fatigue management (2000: 146):

- Minimize shift changes.
- Maximize work hour regularity.
- Never use weekly shift changes.
- Always rotate forward.
- Don't let tired cops hit the streets.
- Minimize mandatory overtime, and develop an overtime policy.
- Provide a bright, stimulating nighttime environment with opportunities to eat healthful food.

The research also found that most officers who took time off—that is, sick days, vacation days, or a regular number of days off between shifts—recovered from fatigue.

Behind some of these recommendations are useful training concepts, such as "alertness switches," which can affect an officer's performance during nighttime hours:

1. Spotting a suspect or finding people in crisis heightens alertness.
2. Dawn brings natural alertness and new energy. Midnight to dawn is a down time for the human body.
3. Not having enough sleep over more than a day drains your "sleep bank."
4. Coffee and doughnuts provide immediate stimulation but cause a crash within an hour.
5. Cold air from a car window brings alertness, whereas hot, humid air brings drowsiness.
6. When the hum of the car tires start to lull you to sleep, stopping and walking around will help.

This is the kind of knowledge supervisors must bring home to police officers. A carefully planned session on managing fatigue is needed both at roll call and during recruit training. Supervisors need to recognize the symptoms of fatigue, and police managers need to use the principle of managing fatigue when creating a work schedule. Controlling and minimizing overtime and off-duty jobs is essential to reducing officer fatigue.

Police Suicides

Much like it is outside of policing, a police officer committing suicide is a topic that few want to talk about or deal with. Yet, it is a reality that cannot be ignored. The past year, 126 police officers in the United States took their own lives. Of those, the average age was 42, and the average amount of time as a police officer was 16 years. Eleven percent of the 2012 police suicides were military veterans, 91 percent were male, and 63 percent were single (Clark and O'Hara, 2012). We will probably never be able to eliminate suicides from happening in law enforcement; however, as police leaders become more progressive and educated, we are likely to see increased emphasis being placed on recognizing the psychological impact of policing, and with that awareness, increased resources being placed in support of specially trained support units, such as the Employee Assistance Program discussed below.

Employee-Assistance Programs

During the past decade, police departments have learned the painful lesson that their employees have personal problems similar to those of the general population. This theme has been picked up by popular television programs that show police at their best and worst. From time to time, police officers have to cope with marital problems, alcohol and drug dependence, children with delinquency and academic problems, job stress, and burnout. The reasons police officers have these problems are the same as for people in any other occupation. What is different is the physically demanding task of adjusting to shift work and the mentally demanding task of seeing people at their worst or dying. One officer has a recurring nightmare about a drowning incident: "He comes to me at night when I sleep. Sometimes once or twice every week. His hand was above the water, but my supervisor held on to me to prevent me from going in after him. The water was electrified—there was not one goddamn thing I could do to help."

Many departments, under their own initiative or through union pressure, have begun employee-assistance programs (EAPs) to deal with these problems. Smaller agencies participate through regional arrangements or with state- or county-sponsored programs. Generally, these programs are staffed by fellow police officers who receive training in counseling and referral. Larger departments have the services of professional counselors and psychologists.

When these programs first began, many officers stayed away for fear of being thought crybabies or cowards or destined for the rubber gun squad. Confidentiality was and remains an issue, and many early programs were doomed to failure when their offices were located in central headquarters. Begrudgingly, police officers have accepted the value of these programs, and the stigma associated with going to EAP has declined somewhat.

The trauma associated with critical incidents like shootings, mass disaster, and gruesome death has received special attention in training and operations policies. In one seminar attended by one of the authors, a panel of veteran police officers recounted the following posttrauma experiences to a class of police recruits:

- Killing a person who was trying to choke an officer
- Responding to a car accident in which the officer's daughter died
- Search-and-recovery operations after a drowning
- Being gunned down by an armed suspect

An officer who takes another human life goes through a number of physical and mental reactions that will never entirely go away (Myles, 1986). He or she will be questioned by investigators, and his or her actions will be reviewed in grand jury proceedings, administrative hearings, and perhaps at trial. There will also be pressure on the officer's family and children. Thus, many departments have posttrauma policies (e.g., supervisory reaction and rules on interrogation) and counseling to deal with these problems.

Many departments have also initiated written line-of-duty death notification policies to address a number of concerns related to on- and off-duty deaths. Policies of this nature address guidelines for death notification and for working with the family for the wake and funeral ceremonies. Some policies address situations in which the family is taken to the emergency room. The key issues related to situations of this nature include review of insurance and workers' compensation benefits, media relations, assistance to out-of-town family members, and postfuneral assistance for survivors. At all times, the wishes of the family are paramount in terms of the department's involvement in these matters.

Conclusion

Personnel is a major expense in law enforcement, and personnel matters take up approximately 80 percent of an administrator's time. Once a recruit has completed probation, he or she stays on the job until retirement. The majority of police departments in the United States continue to have permanent appointment or tenure for officers, which means that the employee cannot be fired without a lengthy hearing unless he or she has been arrested for a crime or has made a series of grave mistakes. It is not surprising that police candidates are carefully evaluated during the probationary period; during this time, the employee serves at the pleasure of the department and often can be terminated without a formal hearing.

The first step in police hiring is the written test, which is administered either by the department or by state or local civil service units. This test measures the candidate's ability to understand written material and gives some indication of situational judgment. Oral interviews are commonly used, and they are very important for assessing interpersonal skills. The assessment center is particularly useful for candidate selection because of cost. Issues related to personnel selection and administration were presented, such as college education requirements, physical agility and medical standards, background checks, age requirements, drug testing, residency requirements, and the use of polygraph testing. In the absence of national or state hiring standards, each issue must

be evaluated according to local agency and state personnel practices and procedures.

Drug testing for new candidates has now become routine as a method of deterring drug users from becoming police officers. Recent court cases conclude that there is public support for reducing drug use by police officers. However, drug testing for in-service employees is subject to collective bargaining negotiations, and court cases have ruled that testing cannot be applied to all classes of employees. Commenting on random testing, Webster and Brown (1989: 6) conclude that mandatory testing programs have been upheld when there is evidence of a drug problem in the department.

Since 1970, affirmative action legislation and related court cases and administrative rulings have had the most profound impact on police candidate selection through judicial review of hiring processes and criteria. Police hiring processes underwent critical scrutiny based on the nonrepresentation of women and minorities in the police workforce. Certain agencies were forced to hire and promote under consent decrees or quota systems as a means of creating a diverse workforce, which led to allegations of lowered standards and reverse discrimination by white male candidates and veteran police officers. Nevertheless, the trend now is to end quota programs where statistical representation has been achieved.

The increased number of females in the police workforce has forced all departments to review sexual harassment complaints, referral policies, and impart training on this topic for all line and management personnel. In our experience, the most common complaints by female officers are related to hostile work environments that include pranks, jokes, and offensive comments.

The Americans with Disabilities Act (ADA) has had a profound impact on police hiring. This law has already forced police agencies to review medical standards and the actual duties performed by officers. At this time, many departments in the United States have precise medical and physical agility standards for candidates and police academy recruits but not for in-service personnel. Candidates disqualified because of eyesight, weight, or other standards will no doubt challenge their disqualification based on the relationship between the standard and the duties performed by in-service police officers. Court cases and administrative rulings will lead to medical and physical standards that will apply to all in-service officers, a situation that will require periodic medical and physical agility retesting.

Questions for Review

1. Compare and contrast police hiring practices of the nineteenth century with those of today.
2. What is the controversy surrounding affirmative action programs?
3. List the benefits of the following personnel selection tools: polygraph test, assessment center, interview, review of social media sites, and lateral entry. Also, give criticisms of each.
4. Explain why written tests have generated great controversy in police personnel selection.
5. Explain how the ADA affects assignment decisions.
6. How can management eliminate excessive overtime?
7. Produce a stress reduction plan for a midsize police department.
8. Explain the importance of drug testing for police personnel.

Class Projects

1. Role-play an interview. There should be no more than three or four interviewers. The interviewers may assume the following roles: a police personnel officer, a detective, a civilian who is the head of a local civil rights group, and a patrol officer. One member of the class will portray the police candidate. As the interviewers ask their questions, the rest of the class should rate the responses of the candidate. After the interview, the class members will discuss their reactions to the interview process, their assessment of the candidate, and various issues regarding interviews.
2. Review the officer hiring standards for a local or state police department. In the standards, list the qualifications for the position, which might include a written test, a physical agility test, a background check, and so on. What are the physical agility requirements for the position? Are there in-service requirements after you graduate from the academy? Do the standards reflect the Cooper Institute items or job-related tasks?

Web Works

Review the employment standards and processes for police officers in your state and area. These can be obtained by going to department sites or agencies that administer state criminal justice standards. What are the standards for physical agility, eyesight, background investigations, and so on? Is there a written examination as a first step?

References

Adarand Constructors v. *Federico Pena*, 132 L.Ed.2d 158 (1995).

Amendola, K., D. Weisburd, E. Hamilton, G. Jones, and M. Slipka. "The Shift Length Experiment." Retrieved from policefoundation.org/content/shift-length-experiment

Anderson, Wayne, David Swenson, and Daniel Clay. *Stress Management for Law Enforcement Officers.* Upper Saddle River, N.J.: Prentice Hall, 1995.

Bagyl, John, and Matthew Boyd. "Harassment Prevention." *Security Management* (January 2009), pp. 46–55.

Bayley, David H., and Robert E. Worden. *Police Overtime: An Examination of Key Issues.* Washington, D.C.: U.S. Department of Justice, 1998.

Bergmann, Barbara R. *In Defense of Affirmative Action.* New York: Basic Books, 1996.

Bowman, T. *Educate to Elevate: Academics Have Pushed Our Department to a New Level of Professionalism and Innovation.* Police Association for College Education (PACE), 2001. Retrieved from police-association.org/library/articles/educate_elevate.html

Breci, M. "Higher Education for Law Enforcement." *FBI Law Enforcement Bulletin,* 63, no. 1 (1994), 1–4.

Bureau of Justice Statistics. *Local Law Enforcement Departments, 2007.* Washington, D.C.: U.S. Government Printing office, 2010. Web posted at bjs.gov/content/pub/pdf/lpd07.pdf

Caldwell, Cam, George C. Thornton, and Melissa L. Gruys. "Ten Classic Assessment Center Errors: Challenges to Selection Validity." *Public Personnel Management,* 32 (Spring 2003), pp. 73–88.

"City to Pay $750,000 to Settle Claim Light-Duty Policy Demeaned Injured Cops." *Disability Compliance Bulletin,* August 4, 2005. Web posted at web.lexisnexis.com.www.utica.edu:2048/universe/document?

Clark, R., and A. O'Hara. "Police Suicides: The NSOPS Study," 2012. Retrieved from policesuicidestudy.com/id16.html

Conciatore, J. "D.C. Council Votes to Require Learning for Law Enforcement." *Community College Week,* 12, no. 20 (2000).

Connors, Edward F., et al. "Employee Drug Testing in Police Departments." In James J. Fyfe, ed., *Police Practice in the 90's.* Washington, D.C.: International City Management Association, 1989, pp. 160–171.

Cooper Institute. "Common Questions Asked About Fitness for Public Safety." Web posted at cooperinst.org/vault/2440/we/. Accessed on January 28, 2014.

Dean, Christina. "Skin Piercings and Body Art." Unpublished manuscript, Utica College, 2008.

Fallon, R.H., and P.C. Weiler. *Firefighters* v. *Stotts: Conflicting Models of Racial Justice: Supreme Court Review.* Chicago: University of Chicago Press, 1985.

Fogelson, Robert M. *Big City Police.* Cambridge, Mass.: Harvard University Press, 1977.

Gavin, James F., and John W. Hamilton. "Selecting Police Using Assessment Center Methodology." *Journal of Police Science and Administration,* 3, no. 2 (June 1975), pp. 166–176.

Glazer, N. *Affirmative Discrimination: Ethnic Inequality and Public Policy.* New York: Basic Books, 1975.

Griggs v. *Duke Power Company,* 401 U.S. 424 (1971).

Hale, Charles. "Pros and Cons of Assessment Centers." *Law and Order,* 4 (April 2005), pp. 18–20.

Hickman, M. and B. Reaves. *Local Police Departments, 2003,* 2006. US Department of Justice, Office of Justice Programs, Bureau of Justice Statistics. Retrieved from bjs.ojp.usdoj.gov/content/pub/pdf/lpd03.pdf

Hochstedler, E. "Impediments to Hiring Minorities in Public Police Agencies." *Journal of Police Science and Administration,* 12, no. 2 (1984), pp. 227–240.

Holden, James. "The Myths of Eyesight Requirements." *FBI Law Enforcement Bulletin,* June 1993. Web posted at www.fbi.gov/leb. Accessed on March 15, 2003.

Hopwood v. *Texas,* 861 F. Supp. 551 (1994).

Jefferson, Ebony. *Application Fraud: A Case Study of Credential Deception in Law Enforcement.* Utica, N.Y.: Utica College, 2008.

"Jury Awards $150,000 to Disabled Officer Who Was Denied Reinstatement." *National Public Employment Reporter,* June 1, 2005.

Kenney, Dennis Jay. "Intelligence and the Selection of Police Recruits." In Dennis J. Kenney and Gary W. Cordner, eds., *Managing Police Personnel.* Cincinnati: Anderson, 1996.

Loo, Robert. "Policy Development for Psychological Services in the Royal Canadian Mounted Police." *Journal of Police Science and Administration,* 13 (1985), pp. 132–137.

Manson, Patricia. "Court Rejects ADA Claim by Cop Who Can't Handle a Gun." *Chicago Daily Law Bulletin,* July 13, 2005.

Massachusetts Commission Against Discrimination. *Model Sexual Harassment Policy,* 2006. Web posted at mass.gov/mcad/harassment.html. Accessed on April 6, 2006.

McNamera v. *City of Chicago*, 959 F. Supp. 870 (N.D. Ill. 1998).

McWhirter, Darien A. *The End of Affirmative Action*. New York: Birch Lane, 1996.

Myles, Gregory. "Post Incident Trauma Seminar." Albany: New York State Police Academy, Summer 1986.

National Advisory Commission on Higher Education for Police Officers. *Proceedings of the National Symposium on Higher Education for Police Officers*. Washington, D.C.: Police Foundation, 1979.

National Treasury Employees Union v. *VonRaab*, 109 S.Ct. 1384 (1989).

Niederhoffer, Arthur. *Behind the Shield*. Garden City, N.Y.: Doubleday, 1967.

Radelet, Louis A., and David Carter. *Police and the Community*, 3rd ed. Upper Saddle River, N.J.: Prentice Hall, 1993.

Reiss, Albert J., Jr. *Private Employment of Public Police*. Washington, D.C.: National Institute of Justice, 1988.

Ricci v. *DeStefano,* Supreme Court of the United States, No. 07-1428 (2009).

Roberg, R., and S. Bonn. "Higher Education and Policing: Where Are We Now?" *Policing: An International Journal of Police Strategies & Management*, 27(4), pp. 469–486.

Schachter, Hindy Lauer. "Job Related Examinations for Police: Two Developments." *Journal of Police Science and Administration* (March 1979), pp. 86–89.

Skinner v. *Railway Labor Executives Association,* 109 S.Ct. 1402 (1989).

Standfest, Steven R. "The Police Supervisors and Stress." *Law Enforcement Bulletin*, 65, no. 5 (May 1996), pp. 7–10.

Stratton, John. *Police Passages*. Sandusky, Ohio: Gellon Publishing, 1984.

Sutton and Hinton v. *United Airlines*, 527 U.S. 471 (1999).

Territo, Leonard, C.R. Swanson Jr., and Neil C. Chamelin. *The Police Personnel Selection Process*. Indianapolis: Bobbs-Merrill, 1977.

United Steel Workers v. *Weber*, 443 U.S. 193 (1979).

Vila, Bryan. *Tired Cops*. Washington, D.C.: Police Executive Research Forum, 2000.

Violanti, J.M. "Stress Patterns in Police Work: Longitudinal Analysis." *Journal of Police Science and Administration*, 11 (1983), pp. 211–216.

Walsh, G. *Downsizing to a College-educated Police Force,* unpublished article, 2013.

Ward's Cove Packing Co. v. *Atonio*, 49 FEP 1520 (1989).

Webster, Barbara, and Jerrold Brown. *Mandatory and Random Drug Testing in the Honolulu Police Department*. Washington, D.C.: National Institute of Justice, October 1989.

Weiner, Norman L. *The Role of the Police in Urban Society: Conflicts and Consequences*. Indianapolis: Bobbs-Merrill, 1976.

Wright v. *Universal Maritime Service Corp.*, 119 S.Ct. 391 (1998).

CHAPTER

13   Training

KEY TERMS

blood-borne pathogen

civil liability

diversity

domestic violence

emergency management

field training officer (FTO)

hate crime

Homeland Security

less-than-lethal weapons

Taser

terrorism

virtual reality

weapons of mass destruction (WMD)

HISTORICAL PERSPECTIVES

Modern police training has come a long way since the early days when a police officer might have been told the following (Sullivan, 1971: 250) as part of his training by veteran police officers:

- When you hit a suspect, hit him hard.
- When you tell someone something, tell him only once because once is enough.
- Do not trust anyone—not even your wife.

Herbert Jenkins, an Atlanta, Georgia, police chief, described the full range of training when he entered the force in Atlanta:

> When I joined the Atlanta Police Department in the early thirties I was issued a badge, a revolver, blackjack, and Sam Browne belt, and sent out on patrol with a senior police officer. After one week of "training" I was a full fledged policeman on my own. (Jenkins, 1970: 1)

As late as 1952, Charles Reith (1975: 106–7), the well-known writer on police history, was able to comment, "Ignorance of police duties is no handicap to a successful career as a policeman." He went on to point out "in their handling of criminals and armed gangsters, ignorance and a lack of training and understanding are defined as being the causes of the frequency of police discomfiture." Although this was true of most departments in that era, based on personal visits to American police departments from 1915 to 1917, Raymond B. Fosdick related some outstanding examples of police training schools of that day:

> Probably the most ambitious police school at the present time is in Berkeley, California. Here the class, which meets one hour a day, takes three years to complete the courses included in the curriculum. The New York school involves two months of full-time instruction; in Chicago, Philadelphia, St. Louis, Detroit and Newark, the training period is four weeks; in Cleveland it is three. In Cincinnati and Louisville only part of the day is devoted to school work, the remainder being spent in the performance of regular duty. (Fosdick, 1969: 298–99)

The Berkeley police school had an extensive curriculum, including the following subjects over a three-year period: physics, chemistry, biology, physiology, anatomy, anthropology, criminal psychology, psychiatry, theoretical and applied criminology, police organization and administration, police practice and procedure, microbiology, microanalysis, public health, first aid, and elementary and criminal law (Fosdick, 1969: 299).

In 1970, one of the first extensive surveys on police training was published. It entailed a nationwide survey in which letters were sent to 360 agencies; 60 usable replies were received. Excluding Boston, which included extensive patrol operations in its 1,600 hours of training with 1,015 hours of its curriculum devoted to patrol and traffic training, the Chicago Police Department, with 1,085 hours of training, had the longest training period; Kalamazoo, Michigan—at 120 hours—had the shortest. In other words, the Chicago police recruit spent twenty-seven 40-hour weeks in training, whereas the Kalamazoo recruit spent three weeks (McManus, 1970: 175, 183).

Fast-forwarding a few decades, the Bureau of Justice Statistics (2009) completed an extensive survey on the organization, curriculum, and delivery of police training in 2006. It found that police recruits were required to complete approximately 19 weeks of classroom training, followed by 453 hours of field training. Based on a census of 648 state and local law enforcement academies, over one-half used a "military stress" environment, which involves marching, daily inspections, and a demerit or physical agility punishment system for rule infractions.

GENERAL NEED FOR TRAINING

Training at any level introduces new skills and also socializes personnel into their work roles. Lack of morale, surges of unnecessary grievances, and such factors as negative relations with citizen groups and ethnic communities often reflect a need for training. Officers who do not know how to handle situations are criticized by the press and victims. They become the subject of bad publicity for the department and may even be subject to civil suits by citizens. As will be discussed, if an officer deprives a citizen of his or her legal rights and civil liberties just because the officer has not been trained properly, then the citizen may have legal recourse to ask for compensation for this loss.

Poor judgment may not be the police officer's fault. It could be the fault of the department and the law. Two major causes may be the following:

1. Officers who have been on the force for less than a year may not have received any training, including training in the use of weapons. Most state laws let departments appoint officers and then give them a period of months for the officers to begin their training.

2. Some departments provide no more training than the state's minimum requirements. These programs lack trained instructors and modern curricula. The newly trained officer may not know what to do when a hostage situation develops or a domestic crisis looks like it will become violent.

These may not be the only reasons that an officer fails to respond in an effective and professional manner to stressful situations, but they are reasons that have been cited too often in the past. Many modern police administrators feel that lack of training should never exist because the department's reputation and citizens' lives are at stake. One mistake made by a poorly trained or untrained officer is one mistake too many.

Most states set minimum training standards. However, these standards normally deal with what has been called "nuts and bolts" training, dealing with a "how-to" approach to essential tasks. Such programs might include weapons training, report writing, basic criminal law, minor criminal investigation techniques, including some crime scene control, and so on. Most states also include training for human relations skills.

The following are issues in current training programs:

1. *Program content.* The core areas of the police training curriculum include operations, weapons/self-defense, legal issues, self-improvement, community policing and dealing with citizens, and special topics. The special topics often cover human relations, such as diversity, internal communication, victim/witness assistance, basic communication with citizens, terrorism, and adult and juvenile behavior. The question remains of how much content should be added and what should be the total number of hours.
2. *Quality control of instructors.* In days past, instructors were pulled from the field but did not know how to teach. Too often, "instructors" were command and supervisory officers who related stories about policing just to impress young recruits with their experience. Some modern police academies sometimes go to the opposite extreme, bringing in a professor who talks about research on violence in families, for example, without ever relating this research to practical skills. The goal is to strike a balance between the common practice of using police instructors from the field and basing instruction on the findings of academicians. The best instructors are needed, regardless of rank. The major question that must be asked about each instructor is this: Can this instructor communicate effectively and serve as a role model for the recruits? Data from the Bureau of Justice Statistics (2009, p. 3) study on police training indicated that 97 percent of full- and part-time instructors were certified by state-level authorities.
3. *Training facilities.* In the past, training has taken place in basements of jails, gyms, auditoriums, and so on. Most instruction was lecture style. Multimedia and small-group instruction, including role-playing activities, need to be made available for all instruction sessions. Facilities for weapons training and driving instruction are needed.
4. *Training equipment.* This is closely tied to the upgrading of facilities. Instructional technology and methodology should include the use of videotapes and DVD programs, PowerPoint equipment, and so on. Demonstrations and hands-on work have to be an integral part of the instruction.
5. *Certified instructors.* Training should be given by police instructors that are certified by state or national training agencies. Non-police instructors should have appropriate work and academic experience.
6. *Full-time attendance.* Ideally recruits should attend the academy full-time and have no other job-related duties. Part-time students and part-time work make for tired officers and half-trained students who fall asleep during instruction.

7. *Training before exercising police power.* All recruits should be made employees of their respective police departments but should not be permitted to use full police powers until they have graduated from the academy. This accomplishes two major goals of professional law enforcement: (1) It takes untrained officers off the street, and (2) recruits do not have to unlearn any bad habits from the street.

8. *Field training officers.* Specially trained officers who are experienced should be used to evaluate the recruit's work in the field after classroom training. A Bureau of Justice Statistics (2009) review reported that field training ranged from 255 to 1,875 hours depending on the type of training academy. For example, schools offering preservice programs before formal hiring had few field training hours in their program.

9. *Teaching methods.* Beyond driving, weapons, and defensive tactics, most topics are taught in the basic lecture format followed by a quiz or multichoice exam. Students memorize the material and, according to one old adage, forget it once the examination is over. Advanced programs have adopted the "student-centered learning" strategy, whereby students are presented with basic knowledge and then are asked to apply the information to operational problems. Assessment is based on how the student identifies and then solves the problem. The learning process often involves working with other members of the class. For example, in a burglary investigation class, the student would be introduced to the basic legal and investigative concepts. The instructor would then present a crime scene problem and ask the student group how they would address the situation. The group not only has to recall the information related to the burglary class but also other classes, such as criminal law, report writing, and interviewing techniques. The goal is to present the training information in an applied, realistic manner.

Unfortunately, there have been incidents where recruits and in-service officers have been seriously injured or killed during training. Sometimes this is related to the extent to which "boot camp" strategies are used to transform civilians into police officers with military bearing. In one case in Massachusetts, a recruit was denied water and died from dehydration. In other cases, instructors and students have been injured during firearms, arrest tactics, and defensive driving courses. Today instructor and officer safety should be of paramount importance in all training operations.

The use of military training tactics for police training applications is another issue under discussion. Outside of tactical operations and weapons training, the question is: To what extent should drill and protocol and sanctions be used for recruits who are being trained to make individual decisions for specific situations?

LOCATION AND TIMING OF BASIC TRAINING

When we discuss the police academy, we are talking about the three main types of police academies in this country: agency, regional, and college sponsored. Agency schools are generally found in large municipal areas or are established for the state police or highway patrol. They are staffed and operated by individual police departments and offer recruit training as well as a variety of in-service courses. Regional academies handle the training functions for both large and small departments located in a designated geographic area. Finally, there are training academies operated on the premises of postsecondary institutions, particularly community colleges. These college-sponsored academies allow a person to take police training and earn college credit. In some states, this can occur before appointment to the police department. As will be discussed, the curriculum for an academy must follow a state mandate for police training that is overseen by a training agency. Regardless of training model, police agencies have two basic objectives:

1. Train the recruit in the skills necessary to perform the functions of a police officer.
2. Socialize the recruit into the police profession, the insignias of the office—uniform, handgun, nightstick, shield—and what former New York City Police Inspector Arthur Neiderhoffer calls "the web of protocol and ceremony that characterizes any quasi-military hierarchy." (Neiderhoffer, 1969: 43)

The traditional model of recruit training consists of an officer being sent to the academy after appointment. Certain states allow nonsworn officers to fulfill basic training as a requirement before appointment at their own time and expense. This training allows the candidate to seek employment in a local department for a specific period of time. On appointment, the candidate must then complete field training and probationary requirements related to the department's rules and practices. Not all agencies in these states embrace this model.

The obvious advantage to the preemployment training model is that the appointing agency saves time and money for basic recruit training. Opponents of this practice, especially those in large departments, argue that the department would rather "train its own" in order to socialize and teach basic skills according to department dictates. They also argue that police training should only be given to people who have undergone a full background check as part of the police hiring process.

Field Training for Police Officers

Field training involves the evaluation of a recruit officer by a trained **field training officer (FTO)** as the new officer performs various patrol functions. The evaluation involves breaking down police tasks into distinct functions and behaviors.

Until the mid-1970s, the concept of field training was unheard of. Officers who graduated from the training academy were "turned loose" by themselves or perhaps were paired to a senior officer for a period of time without any formal evaluation or feedback. Soon departments developed checklists that listed the various duties that an officer should learn after the academy, but this training too was conducted without formal daily evaluation.

San Jose, California, had one of the first field training programs, which was established in 1972. It continues to serve as a model training program for other departments. In San Jose, "the Patrol Division administers the field training program: six-officer teams consisting entirely of FTOs and their sergeants conduct the training. . . . The recruit normally spends four weeks with three different FTO's."

There are three phases to the San Jose training program:

Phase I

Weeks 1–16 have 14 weeks of a standardized training academy; if the recruit passes, then there are two weeks of in-house classroom training.

Phase II

Weeks 17–30 consist of: (1) four weeks with one FTO, a district evaluation; (2) four more weeks with a different FTO on another shift, another district evaluation; (3) four more weeks with another FTO on yet another shift, a district evaluation; and (4) a final two weeks with the FTO that the recruit started with. There are daily observation reports by FTOs and weekly evaluation reports by supervisors. At the end of this stage, the recruit passes on to phase III, is given remedial training, or is dismissed from the force.

Phase III

Weeks 31–52 start with a solo beat outside the training district and biweekly evaluation reports by the supervisors. At the end of 10 months, there is a review board, and if the recruit is certified, he or she returns to the solo beat outside the training district. Then there are monthly evaluations by the supervisor. At the end of this period, the recruit is either certified as a permanent employee or phase III is extended. (McCampbell, 1986: 4)

Field training can be a valuable experience for both the recruit and the trainer. FTOs are encouraged to explore various ways of introducing the police recruit to fieldwork instead of waiting for situations to occur. For example, one of the authors used role playing during quiet times to simulate traffic accidents, robberies in progress, and so on. Gradually, recruits took on performing tasks by themselves after being introduced by the FTO to the specific skill. This was done under the dictum that the FTO would step in at any time if he or she felt that things were not going well.

McCampbell (1986: 6–7) presents a series of recommendations that still work for police managers who wish to use field training:

1. Chief executives should view the field training program as a normal part of the recruit selection process.
2. Administrative control of the field training program in larger agencies should be assigned to the patrol function.
3. All training in the field program should occur in a planned, organized sequence and be identified by clearly written policies.
4. Agencies should perform a task analysis for the job of patrol officer and use the analysis as the basis for evaluating recruits.
5. Agencies should use standardized evaluation guidelines to reduce FTO discretion.
6. FTOs should give recruits a written evaluation every day.
7. Each recruit should be assigned to several FTOs.
8. The FTO's role as trainer and patrol officer should be well defined [to avoid conflict between the two roles].
9. Agencies should conduct a job task analysis for the position of FTO.
10. FTOs should receive at least 40 hours of training before they are allowed to assume their duties.
11. Agencies should consider offering extra compensation to ensure that the most qualified personnel are attracted to and retained in the position of FTO.
12. Field training programs should be evaluated at least annually.

These recommendations have been used by Michael Payne (1999) in the *Police Field Training Officer Course*. Because individuals learn in different ways, there should be opportunities for remedial training. If a recruit officer does not achieve agency standards, then the person should be terminated in a process that is fair and consistent. It is obvious that the daily and weekly evaluation reports will be very important if there is a lawsuit contesting the termination.

Field training, if planned carefully, with special emphasis on having the most qualified officers as field training officers, can be an excellent way to train recruits, increase professionalism, and diminish police cynicism. It remains critical that police commanders put time into selecting field training officers, as they play a critical role in a new officer's career.

The Importance of Training to Police Managers

Police training is of paramount importance to both police supervisors and command personnel. Supervisors need to feel confident that their officers know the fundamentals of the job. They also have to be concerned that their officers develop skills in both the technical aspects of patrol operation and defensive tactics and in the area of human relations. On-the-job training of fundamental skills like these becomes dangerous since police are often dealing with people in tense situations.

If there are too many poorly trained individuals, command personnel cannot rely on the officers to carry out their commands because the officers do not know how to carry them out. Without trained personnel, investigations become error prone, paperwork becomes confused, and morale gets lower and lower as the officers become frustrated with their own inadequacies.

Modern managers realize that training their forces in modern police methods over a long period of time is a capital investment for a department with high morale. It takes years to train a whole force fully, including in-service training. The investment pays off as morale rises and the officers realize that they can handle situations that were formerly unnerving. Confidence breeds confidence.

HISTORICAL RECOMMENDATIONS FOR POLICE TRAINING STANDARDS

In 1973, the National Advisory Commission on Criminal Justice Standards and Goals, Task Force on Police, published a volume of policy recommendations titled *Police*. The recommendations reflected the consensus of professional opinion from the more advanced police departments of the day and national agencies concerned with the training of police. This report sparked a great deal of discussion and some change in police training methods, curricula, and basic organization.

Preparatory training is emphasized and a minimum of 400 hours of basic police training is recommended. Besides police subjects, law, psychology, and sociology as related to police–community relations are to be emphasized. Ongoing in-service training is mandated, as is a minimum of four months of field training.

The recommended curriculum, based on a variety of experiences from major cities, is as follows:

Introduction to criminal justice system	8%
Law	10%
Human values and problems	22%
Patrol and investigation procedures	33%
Police proficiency	18%
Administration	9%

Training before promotion as a policy was likely to produce some self-confidence and better efficiency if an officer knew what to do on the job before promotion. It was also felt that middle management training programs should be integrated with college and business programs (National Advisory Commission, 1973: 399).

In-service training was a significant part of the report, with the recommendation of a minimum of 40 hours per year up to and including captains. This was considered to be a routine, mandated procedure that would be a normal part of every police budget.

Instruction quality control, with certification for specific training subjects, was mandated to ensure that training performance objectives would be met. This included an annual review of instructional materials along with the use of up-to-date audiovisual and computer-assisted instruction.

Police training academies and criminal justice training centers were mandated, with 1978 being the target date for the availability of such training for every police officer in every state. In terms of quality control, there was state certification of the basic police training along with encouragement of the states for interagency cooperation. The authors feel that regional police academies make major contributions to police professionalism and efficiency of training:

1. They offer benefits from economies of scale. Classes can be large enough to justify expert instructors along with the use of expensive training equipment.
2. They begin the fight against parochialism and localism in law enforcement. By being trained regionally, officers, at the start, would look at the big picture of crime fighting and act in a more professional manner.
3. They encourage the formation of professional relationships and friendships with officers outside of the local department at the start of an officer's career. This leads to more cooperation, especially on a regional basis, which becomes increasingly important as recruits rise in rank and begin to cooperate on fencing rings, white-collar crime, and regional solutions to crime problems.

Other benefits may exist, but these begin to explain why this is a significant approach for management to use in the creation of a training program.

THE TRAINING CURRICULUM AT PRESENT

As discussed earlier, the average length for a police recruit training program today is 760 hours. Table 13-1 gives an overview of minimum training requirements for California law enforcement officers, as presented by the Commission on Peace Officer Standards and Training (POST). This curriculum lists classes and the number of hours devoted to each topic.

Nationally, most training programs can be divided into the following six areas:

1. *Administrative procedures.* Quizzes, graduation, and instruction on note taking
2. *Administration of justice.* History of law enforcement, police organization, probation, parole, and social services
3. *Basic law.* Constitutional law, offenses, criminal procedure, vehicle and traffic law, juvenile law and procedures, and civil liability
4. *Police procedures.* Patrol observation; crimes in progress; field notes; intoxication; mental illness; disorderly conduct; domestic violence; police communication; alcoholic beverage control; civil disorder; crowd and riot control; normal duties related to traffic enforcement, including accidents and emergency vehicle operations; criminal investigation, including interviews and interrogations; control of evidence; and various kinds of cases, such as burglary, robbery, injury, sex crime, drugs, organized crime, arson, and gambling
5. *Police proficiency.* Normal firearm training, arrest techniques, emergency aid, courtroom testimony and demeanor, and bomb threats and bombs
6. *Community relations.* Psychology for police, cultural diversity, news media relationships, telephone courtesy, identification of community resources, victim/witness services, crime prevention, officer stress awareness, law enforcement family, and police ethics

TABLE 13-1   Content and Minimum Hourly Requirements—California, 2009

Domain Number	Domain Description	Minimum Hours
01	Leadership, professionalism, and ethics	8
02	Criminal justice system	2
03	Police and the community	18
04	Victimology/crisis interventions	—
05	Introduction to criminal law	4
06	Property crimes	6
07	Crimes against persons/death invest	6
08	General criminal statutes	2
09	Crimes against children	4
10	Sex crimes	4
11	Juvenile law and procedure	3
12	Controlled substances	12
13	ABC law	2
15	Laws of arrest	12
16	Search and seizure	12
17	Presentation of evidence	6
18	Investigative report writing	52
19	Vehicle operations	24
20	Use of force	12
21	Patrol techniques	12
22	Vehicle pullovers	14
23	Crimes in progress	16
24	Handling disputes/crowd control	12
25	Domestic violence	8
26	Unusual occurrences	4
27	Missing persons	4
28	Traffic enforcement	22
29	Traffic accident investigation	12
30	Crime scenes, evidence, forensics	12
31	Custody	4
32	Physical fitness/officer stress	44
33	Arrest methods/officer tactics	60
34	First aid and CPR	21
35	Firearms/chemical agents	72

Domain Number	Domain Description	Minimum Hours
36	Information systems	4
37	Persons with disabilities	6
38	Gang awareness	2
39	Crimes against the justice system	4
40	Weapons violations	4
41	Hazardous materials awareness	4
42	Cultural diversity/discrimination	16
43	Emergency management	16
Minimum instructional hours		560

The minimum number of hours allocated to testing in the regular basic courses is shown below. Note that most academies exceed the allocated time by about 200 hours.

Test Type	Hours
Scenario tests	58
POST-constructed knowledge tests	40
Exercise tests	6
Total minimum required hours	664

Source: 2013.

TOPICAL ISSUES IN TRAINING

Some of the newer topics that have been covered in police training are discussed briefly in this section.

Terrorism, Homeland Security, and Emergency Management

As a result of the events of September 11, 2001, there has been recognition of the need for training in **terrorism, emergency management**, and the term that evolved from the 9/11 attacks: **Homeland Security**. Executives of U.S. law enforcement agencies have found that they must train their command staff and line officers in the following areas:

- Terrorist group identification
- Intelligence gathering and reporting
- Community threat analysis
- Response to incidents involving possible **weapons of mass destruction (WMD)**
- Security of critical facilities
- Legal issues related to counterterrorism
- Document fraud and identification (motor vehicle and immigration)

- Traumatic stress from WMD incidents
- Ethical issues related to post–September 11 policing
- The National Incident Management System (NIMS) and the Incident Command System (ICS)

As discussed in Chapter 9, most counterterrorist activities and investigations pre-9/11 were federal initiatives, with state and local law enforcement trained in an emergency response capacity to terrorist incidents after they happened. Post-9/11, every police officer in the United States plays some role in the nation's overall Homeland Security effort, and this abrupt change in policy requires the development of anti-terrorism training for state and local law enforcement.

Walsh (2011) found in his research on anti-terrorism training needs for state and local law enforcement that personnel assigned to terrorism-related responsibilities, whether full-time or part-time, foremost wanted to see the inter-agency rivalry, which in the past characterized routine law enforcement's inter-agency relations, be replaced with a more coordinated, cooperative effort to maximize the resources of all levels of law enforcement in order to better protect the United States from international terrorist attacks. Also, nearly half of the respondents held some level of dissatisfaction with post-9/11 anti-terrorism training effort, specifically in the areas of training availability, training variety, and training that addresses the respondents' needs. Terrorist origin and culture, as well as intelligence gathering techniques, were most commonly listed as desired training topics, while the amount of simulated training offered fell far short of that desired by respondents. Training would be most effective with some degree of federal coordination, held at various training locations in two- to three-day blocks, with multi-agency participation encouraged.

While such state and local initiatives were underway, federal law enforcement had to not only continue anti- and counter-terrorism initiatives, but improve them. Federal law enforcement and the various border control agencies must be able to identify and deter terrorist suspects from entering the country. In addition, under new and wide-sweeping surveillance and tracking statutes, such as the USA PATRIOT Act (2001), federal law enforcement must identify the sources of economic and operational support. For instance, certain Muslim social and religious organizations serve as recruitment and economic fronts for Al Qaeda. State and local law enforcement will be drawn into these investigations, which brings on a whole host of issues such as agency cooperation, intelligence gathering and sharing, and the use of local informants. Accordingly, many states have passed legislation that mirrors the USA PATRIOT Act in terms of obtaining roving wiretaps and enacting offense categories for crimes involving terrorism, possession or use of chemical or biological weapons, and committing hate crimes. This, of course, raises all kinds of ethical issues, such as racial profiling, related to the use of these new powers.

An important training agenda for federal, state, and local law enforcement has been in the areas of identifying targets and analyzing and responding to potential incidents of weapons of mass destruction. These include nuclear, biological, and chemical agents, as well as incendiary and explosive devices, that are weaponized and used to cause massive personnel casualties and property destruction. Responding to incidents of mass destruction has become very important since the attacks of September 11 and the anthrax-related criminal incidents that followed. As recently as April 2013, federal, state, and local investigators were responding to and investigating ricin being mailed to government officials, including President Obama and NY City Mayor Michael Bloomberg.

In threat assessment, police officers are trained to identify potential terrorist targets and to use enhanced patrol techniques to deter terrorist acts. Potential targets include transportation facilities, chemical installations, and water resource facilities. While all of this may seem like common sense, a detailed step-by-step analysis in one community found that there were potentially explosive chemical tank cars in a railroad yard adjacent to a major police station and that the local university had a nuclear reactor for academic research—and all of this was unknown to city emergency planners! Enhanced patrol for potential targets can range from prohibiting access to certain areas to having patrol units maintaining higher vigilance while performing routine duties. For example, an unmarked work truck parked under a major bridge or a person walking near a water reservoir requires further investigation.

AIDS and Other Blood-Borne Pathogens

Concern regarding acquired immunodeficiency syndrome (AIDS) and hepatitis B brought about safety regulations and training requirements from the Occupational Safety and Health Administration (OSHA) with regard to **blood-borne pathogens** (any microorganism or virus that can cause disease). Because police and other public safety personnel frequently come in contact with blood and other body fluids, the regulations call for agency control plans to limit direct exposure and to administer a vaccine for hepatitis B to affected employees. The regulations also call for training regarding measures one should take to prevent contamination. Stewart (1993) suggests the following training topics:

- Means of human immunodeficiency virus and hepatitis B virus transmission
- Suggested personal prevention practices
- Universal precaution strategies
- Protective equipment
- Specific workplace prevention practices
- Exposure management and treatment procedures

Domestic Violence

Every several years there is a major media event related to domestic violence. When celebrities find themselves in the middle of a domestic violence investigation, much attention is placed on the subject. For example, in 2009, the relationship between singers Rihana and Chris Brown came under scrutiny. On Thanksgiving Day, 2009, professional golfer Tiger Woods became subject to a domestic incident investigation that played out across media outlets around the world, costing him multi-million dollar endorsements. Events of this nature renew public policy discussion on **domestic violence**. Traditionally, domestic violence offenses occurred between married people and involved such crimes as assault and harassment. In a vast majority of cases, the victim is a woman. Murder, which frequently occurs in these situations, was usually not mentioned in earlier discussions of domestic violence.

Until the later 1980s, law enforcement and prosecution offices did not give these situations high priority or serious attention because they occurred behind closed doors, and the role of the wife was considered to be subservient to the husband. An instructor in one of the authors' basic recruit classes in 1973 called these situations "get in and get out calls" because complainants do not press charges the next day even if you make an arrest.

It was not until the early 1980s that this attitude changed. Research on violent crime and murder concluded that many cases were the result of domestic violence. The women's rights movement paid particular attention to the role of women in society and the "battered wife cycle." Presented in various ways, this cycle consists of stages that start with emotional abuse and then end up with serious physical assault. If, despite police intervention, the abuser and the victim make up, in many cases the cycle begins all over again. In response to this, many communities established 24-hour crisis hotlines and safe houses, where women with children can find refuge and obtain counseling. Police training programs include the topic of domestic violence calls as part of their training, especially because of the potential for serious physical injury against responding officers.

In the 1990s, many states changed their laws and arrest policies regarding domestic violence so that an officer could make an arrest for a petty offense without witnessing the act and without the express consent of the victim. In Florida, for example, a law enforcement officer in domestic violence situations may arrest the suspect and does not need to witness the abuse.

This proarrest policy is based on the theory that immediate intervention will stem the cycle of violence. In addition, the definition of *domestic violence* has been expanded by laws and police agency policies to include offenses in which the people involved have an intimate relationship and police intervention is requested (New York State Office for the Prevention of Domestic Violence, 1995).

In addition to reviewing laws and departmental response policies regarding domestic violence, training programs include such topics as protecting yourself against injury, listening skills, preparation of special reports, investigation of domestic violence complaints, procedures for the arrest and detention of offenders, and victim assistance programs.

Use of Physical and Deadly Physical Force

The use of physical and deadly physical force by police is a controversial topic in any community, particularly after an incident where force has been used. American police are expected to use a minimum amount of force to capture or subdue suspects. Force that is deemed to be excessive often results in negative media attention, civilian complaints, lawsuits, and (in some serious cases) civil riots. As illustrated by the Rodney King incident in Los Angeles in 1991, which is still widely discussed in police academies, incidents involving excessive use of force are easily captured today by civilians using video cameras and camera cell phones for public showing by media outlets, or for instant downloading and viewing through YouTube, Vine, and other venues. Thus, the use of force is an important topic for training and includes topics related to firearms, less-than-lethal weapons, and arrest tactics.

Training in these areas has vastly improved over the past 30 years. In the authors' experience, firearms training and qualifications at one time were simply a matter of officers shooting at a target at various distances from a standing position to show their accuracy and marksmanship. Today firearms training deals with officer safety, avoidance of risk to bystanders, decision making (using the right kind of force based on the situation), and accuracy.

A standard police firearms course will normally include topics on weapon familiarization, legal issues on the use of deadly physical force, range instruction, and scenario/simulation and postincident shooting protocols. Department policies involving the use of deadly physical force are also reviewed. The typical policy declares that deadly physical force may not be used unless the suspect presents an immediate deadly threat or will cause serious bodily harm to the officer or to another person. In addition, physical force may be used only to obtain control over a person who is resisting or who poses a threat to others' safety.

Key is scenario/simulation training whereby officers are introduced to street and active shooter situations and have to make decisions. This training may include case studies, role plays, and simulations. For example, at the Smith and Wesson Training Center in Springfield, Massachusetts, police trainees wearing protective clothing both shoot and are shot at in a training facility that has been constructed to resemble a wide range of combat situations, including rooms with little or no light. The bullets used are plastic covered with a low powder load, but as one trainee exclaimed, "They hurt like hell if you are hit."

Computer and Video Simulation

In the past five years, computer-aided training has been applied to police training. Borrowing from earlier technologies for airline pilots and driver education, computer and video instruction was developed for firearms training. Through video, students are presented with various street scenarios for which they must decide whether or not to shoot. The instructor can observe and evaluate the proper draw, stance, and shooting technique of each trainee. The computer evaluates whether the plastic round hitting the video screen hit the suspect or an innocent bystander and whether the officer fired within an appropriate time period. What is impressive about this type of learning is the noise and realism.

Simulation has unlimited potential for police training and other resources. For example, law enforcement is following the lead of the military in using simulation as posttraumatic stress therapy. Using 4D virtual simulators, veterans suffering the aftereffects of a traumatic incident, say an IED striking their vehicle or one in their convoy, are placed in models of a military vehicle very similar to the one they had been in at the time of the explosion. They are given props mimicking their issued weapon, and even the sounds and smells are piped in to make the simulation even more lifelike, as victims of a traumatic experience often have acute memory of senses, such as smell. Such simulation can easily be adapted to patrol officers having difficulty processing a traumatic incident, as well.

Computer-generated scenarios of this kind are very expensive, and many departments attempt to arrange shared services through regional training or interagency agreements.

Less-Than-Lethal Weapons

Less-than-lethal weapons include a wide range of devices that will, in most cases, not cause immediate death if used properly. Examples are the baton, pepper spray, and the "Taser." The purpose of these weapons is to cause pain and create compliance, thus allowing an officer to subdue and handcuff a suspect. Other less-than-lethal weapons used for crowd control are beanbag guns, tear gas, pepper fog, and pepper balls.

Each less-than-lethal weapon has certain applications and effects. The classic impact weapon is the baton, commonly called a nightstick. The weapon is used to strike a leg, arm, or shoulder and to disable a combatant. The standard baton measures 21 inches; newer versions are expandable after being released from a holster carried on the duty belt.

Pepper spray is the most common of the less-than-lethal weapons and is carried by both police and security officers. The spray, which is a mixture of pressurized alcohol/water and cayenne pepper, is shot into a suspect's face and causes intense pain in the eyes and in the mucous membranes in the nose.

Some suspects, particularly those under the influence of certain drugs, can withstand the effects of pepper spray. A recent addition adopted by many departments is Conducted Energy Devices or CEDs. The most popular of these is the Taser. The **Taser** shoots two barbs connected to the weapon into a suspect. These electric barbs contain 50,000 volts of electricity, which causes the person to be incapacitated. The Taser can be used only in close quarters (15–20 feet), and the officer generally has only one attempt. Under certain circumstances, the weapon may cause death to subjects with heart or drug-related physical problems.

Newer versions of the device have a small camera and audio feature to record the incident before the device is deployed. Before firing, a red laser dot is directed to the suspect's target area, which often in itself has a deterrent effect in ending suspect aggression. It is important to note that both probes must make contact with the violent subject in order for any CED to be effective.

The use of this type of nonlethal device is preferred by law enforcement personnel to deal with violent subjects in enclosed areas and in crowded area situations that discount the use of a firearm or pepper spray.

As presented by Croin and Ederheimer (2006), there are over 50 items that should be considered for training and field implementation. Many departments require a six- to eight-hour training course for an officer or supervisor to be considered an "authorized" user. The course includes nomenclature, officer safety, appropriate use in situations, use of backup cartridges, weapon limitations, follow-up actions to be taken according to department policy in treating suspects, and accountability review. CEDs are placed in a position comparable with that of Oleoresin Capsicum (pepper) sprays on a use-of-force continuum. The department policy must also include removal of the darts and the need for emergency care and evidence collection, particularly if a sensitive area is hit. In all cases, if the device is used, a written report must be filed for incident investigation and a department review on its appropriate use.

For use-of-force training, most police academies and police departments employ a use-of-force continuum whereby the officer must use the amount of force that is appropriate in a situation to overcome resistance or a threat to safety. The continuum ranges from the officer's presence and voice to the use of deadly physical force against an armed suspect. For example, an officer would not draw a weapon simply because a person is talking in a loud voice; it must be shown that the officer is threatened or the other person also has a weapon.

After a person graduates from the basic academy, the major management issue for departments involves annual retraining for weapons qualifications and review of department policies. The standard timing around the country for firearms requalification is twice a year, and once a year for less-than-lethal weapons. In all training situations, there should be a review of case studies on when and how weapons are used in various scenarios.

Tactical Operations

This is usually an in-service training course for veteran officers to review basic academy topics such as use of personal weapons, handcuffing techniques, high-risk vehicle stops, and building-entry techniques. The focus here is not only on review but also on encouraging a partner-team approach in high-risk situations. Courses of this nature include hands-on exercises, low-light situations, and even the use of blank or paint guns for realism.

Diversity

Cultural **diversity** is defined as having empathy toward other cultures and ways of life in order to explain why people feel the way they do. In the late 1980s, instruction in cultural sensitivity (sometimes called *cross-cultural training*) for officers was initiated to improve community relations and to reduce, in part, citizen or community complaints against police officers for unwarranted use of force or arrest powers on underrepresented members of the community. These issues are not new but a continuation of the historical animosity between the police and minority groups in the community. As discussed by Johnson (1992), the police represent the majority culture in a community and are often viewed as the defenders of the status quo or the ruling elites. Ideas, lifestyles, and people outside the mainstream are often viewed by the police with distrust, and vice versa. What happens, as recounted by Weaver (1992: 3), is a "clash between two icebergs," as typified in the following routine situation:

> A Nigerian cab driver runs a red light. An officer pulls him over in the next block, stopping the patrol car at least three car lengths behind the cab. Before the police officer can exit the patrol car, the cabbie gets out of his vehicle and approaches the officer. Talking rapidly in a high-pitched voice and gesturing wildly, the cab driver appears to be out of control, or so the officer believes.
>
> As the officer steps from his car, he yells for the cab driver to stop, but the cabbie continues to walk toward the officer. When he is about two feet away, the officer orders the cabbie to step back and keep his hands to his sides. But the cab driver continues to babble and advance toward the officer. He does not make eye contact and appears to be talking to the ground.
>
> Finally, the officer commands the cab driver to place his hands on the patrol vehicle and spread his feet. What began as a routine stop for a traffic violation culminates in charges of disorderly conduct and resisting arrest.

According to Weaver (1992: 4), the situation escalates out of control because of a breakdown in nonverbal communication. While most Americans are socialized into staying in their vehicles, the cab driver felt that it was a sign of respect to exit his vehicle and not trouble the officer to leave his patrol car. As the driver approached the officer, the social safe distance between the two decreased, and the driver ignored the "step back" command. The social distance for conversation in Nigeria is much closer than in the United States. In the mind of the officer, the lack of eye contact and the rapid, high-pitched voice denoted a person who was dangerous to the officer.

Training, according to Shusta and others (2005), prepares officers to deal with the various ethnic and cultural groups in their communities and with one another in a professional manner. Knowledge of words, gestures, and communication norms can increase communication and also enhance officer safety. Training must also include a review of common misconceptions and beliefs that are held between the police and various minority groups. This is very important today as all police departments must deal with a wide variety of ethnic groups, including Muslim groups that are often labeled as terrorists. Additionally, the legalization of same-sex marriages and the rise of equal rights for lesbian-gay-bisexual-transgender persons also require a review of stereotypes, discrimination, and harassment by police. It is important to note that this training must be undertaken before and not after an incident occurs. Too often we have seen training used as an intended panacea to address a community relations problem. Most after-the-event classes don't work because officers view them as disciplinary in nature.

Hate Crimes

The Bureau of Justice Assistance (1997: ix) gives the broadest definition of "hate crimes or bias motivated crimes as offenses motivated by hatred against a victim based on his or her race, religion, sexual orientation, handicap or national origin." In 1990, Congress passed the Federal Hate Crime Statistics Act, which helped focus law enforcement on **hate crimes**. In October 1998, the *New York Times* (Lyman, 1998: 6) reported that 41 states had hate crime legislation, including penalty enhancement (hate crime penalties added to criminal felonies, creating longer sentences). Typical hate crime organizations are the Ku Klux Klan, American Nazi Party, Church of Jesus Christ Christian, Aryan Nations, and White Aryan Resistance (Ridgeway, 1995; Potok, 2000). Their major means of communication is the Internet. There are other American and Arab groups.

Bias crime police units have problems sorting out hate crime from free speech and other types of crimes. Three questions asked by the New York Police Department's Bias Incident Investigating Unit might help (Jacobs, 1998: 155–156):

1. Is the victim the only member or one of the few members of the targeted group in the neighborhood?
2. Are the victims and perpetrator from different racial, religious, ethnic, or sexual orientation groups?
3. Were the real intentions of the responsible person motivated in whole or part by bias against the victim's race, religion, ethnicity, or sexual orientation or was the motivation based on something other than bias (e.g., a childish prank or unrelated vandalism)?

Today we need hate crime police training, police bias investigation units for larger departments, and prosecutors who understand hate crime legislation and can sort it out from free speech.

Americans with Disabilities Act

As discussed in Chapter 12, the Americans with Disabilities Act requires police departments to provide services to people with disabilities. Department policies and training must address ways for officers to deal with those with disabilities (e.g., a mugging victim who is blind or an arrestee who requires a wheelchair). Training programs should also include responses to routine and emergency calls for services for those with disabilities. Sometimes, people with disabilities or illnesses are not properly identified right away—for example, a diabetic suffering a seizure may appear to be a disorderly drunk but is actually in need of insulin.

Computer and Video Simulation

In the past five years, computer-aided training has been applied to police training. Borrowing from earlier technologies for airline pilots and driver education, computer and video instruction was developed for firearms training. Through video, students are presented with various street scenarios for which they must decide whether or not to shoot. The instructor can observe and evaluate the proper draw, stance, and shooting technique of each trainee. The computer evaluates whether the plastic round hitting the video screen hit the suspect or an innocent bystander and whether the officer fired within an appropriate time period. What is impressive about this type of learning is the noise and realism.

New Technologies

Through satellite communications and the Internet, many colleges, universities, and government agencies are able to sponsor teleconferences where participants can hear a presentation and phone in questions and comments. From the experience of the authors, a great deal of preparation is required, and the audience attention span for a teleconference is about two hours. Teleconferencing is ideal for transmitting information to multiple sites, thus reducing the time and cost for travel and lodging.

Online courses offered through the Internet are well established across the country, and make returning to school much more convenient for a police officer faced with unpredictable recall to duty and rotating schedules. With online learning, students are largely free to set the time of day to do school-related work as it best fits their individual schedule.

At this time there are over hundreds of degree programs that are offered online in the United States where students never enter into a traditional classroom. In fact, this text may be part of an online learning experience where learning is done through assigned readings, discussions, chat room seminars, and Web-based demonstrations. Then again there are other programs that are termed hybrid where courses are offered both in a face-to-face classroom residency and then completed online. At present, the most practical application for online learning for law enforcement agencies is in-service training, which avoids station supervisors having to schedule each officer to attend a training session physically. This provides several advantages, including not having to jockey the schedule of officers assigned to afternoon and midnight shifts to attend day-time training, and then backfill the loss of those officers with overtime. Also, agencies, in many cases, save the cost of transportation, and sometimes lodging for officers to attend training. An excellent benefit of online in-service training is that the officers remain available for emergency response, as they can take their online course while in uniform at the station.

There is also more specific training available for specialized units, such as special weapons and tactics (SWAT) teams, major felony squads, regional arson investigation teams, and so on. Instruction includes courses in computer security and electronic surveillance as well as emergency vehicle handling, "routine" traffic stops, and crowd control. A number of states have created training centers in abandoned airports and warehouses to create situational training for active shooter, hostage negotiations, and emergency vehicle driving. A number of scenarios are presented to the students, including the use of Airmunition, which is a cartridge that can be fired from a pistol.

Some time ago, one of the authors recalls entering an amusement arcade and finding customers pumping quarters into machines to play a game of shooting bandits in a Dodge City setting. While commonplace then, Playstation games like those have turned into classics with the release of games based upon **virtual reality**. Virtual reality is a computer-generated, three-dimensional environment that includes the senses of sight, sound, and touch (Hormann, 1995: 8). For police training, the computer creates environments that are viewed by a trainee in a helmet. The trainee is also connected to the computer by devices that deploy weapons. Unlike current computer-generated training, where one faces a screen and reacts, virtual reality allows the person to turn around, open doors, switch transmission gears, and perform other tasks while feeling the "action" as if it were real. In newer training versions, participants may get "shocked" from return fire. Then, there is a lot of noise from cars, helicopters, sirens, and so on (Griffith, 2009).

Computer simulations continue to improve with voice and sound and can be applied to a number of situations. Based on the technological advances in gaming and training, these simulation programs will be used for all kinds of field situations that are applicable for recruits to executives. There is always the issue of cost and maintenance and upgrade for this equipment. While larger departments, such as that in Los Angeles, can afford a number of units, other agencies have made arrangements for cost sharing on a regional basis.

Cyber Crime Investigation

In many basic training programs, an introductory course offered to police recruits is computer crime investigation. A course at this level typically reviews the basics of a computer and certain dos and don'ts for handling software and hardware for evidence collection and forensic analysis.

A computer can be an instrument for the commission of crime, such as stealing credit card information, destroying data, embezzling money, and stealing software. In a similar manner, a computer or a computer system can be the target of a criminal attack by a person or group seeking access to databases. Increasingly, police and prosecutorial agencies are now developing special units and investigations training programs for computer crime cases. The laws and search-and-seizure rules were not written for electronic data. Computer evidence can be easily altered and destroyed unknowingly by an unskilled investigator.

The increased popularity and access to mobile online devices has also increased criminal activity. One of the new orientation programs for college students is Internet privacy and security. The increased use of financial transactions over the Internet has also increased the number of crimes. These include the purchase of contraband, such as drugs, liquor, weapons, and child pornography. Some users have developed personal relations and sometimes marriages through introductions over the Internet. Not surprisingly, pedophiles view the Internet as a medium for making contact with potential victims via chat groups.

A specialized training for first responders and investigators to address computer crimes has become indispensable. Investigative and forensic capacity to deal with computer cases is readily available only to major federal and state agencies and major city and regional task forces.

Over the past several years, a number of training courses have been developed to address the wide range of cyber and Internet-related crimes.

Internet Crimes Investigation. This is an introductory course on the workings of online computer networks and investigative software tools. Courses of this nature include a review of Internet, Google, MySpace, and how to understand and trace IP addresses and prepare search warrants. Advanced courses address investigative strategies, case preparation, and recovery of evidence.

Computer Crimes Investigation. This course reviews the wide scope of computer crime, including illegal computer usage, identity theft, hacking, child exploitation, and phishing. Advanced courses include child exploitation.

Computer Examination. Once a computer is properly seized, the unit is subjected to forensic examination. Topics include duplicating hard drives, and dealing with encrypted data. The basics of digital evidence analysis are presented with a focus on forensic software. Courses of this nature also include a review of steganography and encryption.

Search and Seizure of Networks. The focus of this type of courses shifts from the individual computer to the network. Evidence can be obtained from the SOHO network. It deals with how to conduct electronic surveillance to identify wireless networks and access points.

Cell Phone Investigation. Most criminals today use cell phones and they often contain a wealth of information related to any criminal investigation. This course presents the basics of cell phone networks. Courses of this nature show how to obtain and analyze data and prepare cases for prosecution. (Bureau of Justice Assistance, 2009)

Programs delivered across the nation include courses related to cyber gangs, information security, data mining, and child stalking.

Another cybercrime that deserves attention is the investigation of financial crimes related to employee theft, misuse of funds, buying and selling of property, and a wide host of Internet-related scams. Financial investigation courses include information on evidence documentation, auditing, financial analysis, and case presentation. Advanced courses deal with the application of computers and the Internet to determine fraud activity (Bureau of Justice Assistance, 2009).

Related to the above topics is identity theft, which is the use of someone else's identity to commit a crime. This includes the use of another person's social security number, state-issued identification card such as a driver's license, credit card or financial account, or any biometric data. The Federal Trade Commission, which receives consumer complaints on identity theft, estimates from a survey completed in 2006 that over 8.3 million American citizens have been victims of this offense (Federal Trade Commission, 2007). This includes the use of the victim's identity to open a new financial account, the misuse of non–credit card accounts such as a checking or store account, and the misuse of a credit card or other financial account.

As discussed in the 2006 survey report, the cost to victims is both financial and the time spent in reclaiming one's financial reputation. Unfortunately, identity theft is not captured in UCR and NIBRS police crime reports as many victims resolve the issue with a financial institution. Because of the media attention on identity theft, there has been an increase in reports to police departments. Major governmental reports, including that of the President's Identity Theft Task Commission (2006), conclude on the need for law enforcement training and response policies for identity theft cases. Based on a review of training programs in New York and selected state police agencies, McCandlish (2009) summarized that few departments have response policies and training to deal with identity theft cases and recommends the following:

1. Preparation of a written police report
2. Assisting the victim in completing the Identity Theft Affidavit prepared by the Federal Trade Commission. This commonly accepted form allows the victim to provide necessary information for filing reports with financial institutions to address identity theft claims
3. Entering the complaint into the identity theft data site of the Federal Trade Commission
4. Initiating a training program that addresses the following topics:

    - Scope of identity theft
    - State and federal criminal statutes
    - Patterns of identity theft cases
    - Addressing victim needs, especially regarding filing reports with financial institutions and credit reporting agencies such as Trans Union and Equifax

As with any larceny case, identity theft cases are difficult to investigate and are often linked to organized groups. Reviewing over 400 cases investigated by the U.S. Secret Service, researchers from the Center for Identity Management and Information Protection found that the Internet was used in approximately one half of the cases where identity was stolen for financial gain during a financial transaction. Approximately one-third of the cases involved theft through employment situations (Gordon et al., 2007).

AREAS OF TRAINING

With the exception of basic recruit training programs, much of law enforcement training is haphazard at best. This is not to say that specific courses, seminars, or workshops lack quality. Indeed, most are very good. The problem is lack of goals, objectives, and coordination for the overall training program. In short, there is not enough planning, and training is usually funding-driven. When financial support dwindles, so too, often, does the non-mandated training.

Planning is the basic function of a manager. As the administrator of training, planning is no less important to the training director. Planning answers the questions what, when, where, who, and by whom and allows us to avoid the common mistake of "training for training's sake."

During the past decade, the expansion of law enforcement training has been phenomenal. Added to the ever-increasing demands that are placed on police officers are concerns about civil and vicarious liability.

A police career is divided into a number of stages or phases that require training. In addition to the recruit phase, a police officer may attain rank or job functions related to supervision, investigations, management, and various specialty areas. Therefore, he or she must undergo a training program to learn the new responsibilities and social roles of the function.

Specialist Training

Officers assigned to specialized units, such as criminal investigation, vice/narcotics, youth, traffic, or training, are provided seminars and workshops to develop their expertise in these areas. Primarily, external resources offering the needed training are used for these activities. These resources include the Northwestern University Traffic Institute, Southern Police Institute, FBI National Academy, and others. Refresher or advanced training in these areas may also be provided, depending on the length of the officer's assignment, job performance, new developments in the specialized areas, or other factors. Officers in specialized assignments will also be assigned to quarterly in-service training sessions.

Officers participate as members of special teams, such as a special response team, underwater recovery, or bomb squad. Instructors at the academy also fall within the realm of the specialist training phase and are provided any additional training required for this function.

Supervisory Training

Officers promoted to sergeant enter the supervisory training phase. As soon as possible, all newly promoted sergeants should be scheduled for a practical supervisor's course. In addition, they attend an in-house supervisory orientation program to familiarize themselves with specific departmental policies, programs, and procedures.

In addition to these programs, we recommend the following model for first-line supervisory training. Police first-line supervisors, meaning sergeants and lieutenants, are usually the first managers to arrive at the scene of critical field situations. The first responders, that is, the officers who first respond to service calls, are normally the department's line officers. Routinely, these first-line supervisors also make decisions on myriad issues ranging from employee discipline to civil liability. In many departments, peer pressure becomes an important issue since a promotion means that the new supervisor is now directing the activities of fellow officers whom he or she worked and socialized with previously as an equal. It requires special skills and talents to make this transition from a line officer to a management-oriented supervisor. Unfortunately, in some agencies some police officers wearing stripes are not really functioning as supervisors. The paper-and-pencil tests used for promotion in most departments cannot predict command presence or the attainment of communication and decision-making skills under stress.

A first-line supervisory training course must provide the knowledge and skills needed by the supervisor to function effectively, efficiently, and professionally. The course needs to provide a framework to assist the new supervisor in developing strategies aimed at dealing with the supervisor's critical role in the department's operation. The model proposed is a two-week or four-week intensive program. Departments may vary in their requirements and demand a more extensive course of study.

This is seen as an intensive residential program in which the student prepares for each class with out-of-class readings and other homework assignments. The students live and work together and, in addition to daytime classes, have additional evening classes. This training should be given before the officer assumes the duties of a supervisor as part of a one-year civil service probationary period before certification as a supervisor. If the officer fails the training program, he or she will return to line officer status.

A MODEL FIRST-LINE MANAGER'S (SUPERVISOR'S) COURSE   The following program covers the major things a first-line supervisor needs to know and provides an opportunity for supervisors to practice skills and be critiqued in this new role. A major portion of the program is presented in the classroom with daily quizzes and weekly comprehensive examinations. Students are expected to attend all classes, maintain an academic average of 70 or better for the daily quizzes, and achieve a score of 80 or better on the two comprehensive examinations.

The director of the program welcomes all students during an opening ceremony and informs them that they are supervising a mythical squad of line officers. Throughout the program, the students complete the following in-basket exercises with this mythical squad: (1) conducting briefings, (2) issuing orders, (3) planning events, (4) attending to routine administrative matters, and (5) dealing with a variety of personnel problems. The squad exists only on paper; however, it will be as realistic as possible, consisting of a number of police officers who will be described in vivid detail. Assignments will be linked to daily class topics, and the results will be graded on a pass/fail basis. All "fails" have to be repeated until the student passes.

The following are covered in the first-line supervisor's program:

1. *Registration and overview of the program.* This consists of a review of the academic requirements of the program and an introduction to the details of the mythical squad.
2. *Role of supervisor and leadership skills.* This course presents the role of the supervisor in the formal and informal organization. Leadership concepts and styles are defined. Important concepts covered are delegation, command presence, span of control, and formal and informal organization.
3. *Wellness program (every morning).* These morning physical exercises include running, aerobics, and team sports, along with physical examinations and counseling for any personal health problems.
4. *Supervisor communications and media relations.* The purpose of this part of the course is for the student to recognize effective communication channels. Methods for clearing obstacles from existing written and oral channels are discussed. The program uses role playing to demonstrate the effective flow of the communications grid and then goes on to deal with specific problems related to print and electronic media, general communications, and the use of computer-assisted communications.
5. *Civil liability.* This part of the course reviews major national and state tort law cases, with an emphasis on the liability of supervisors who fail to supervise or train subordinates properly. Liability issues related to legally high-risk police operations, such as high-speed car chases and the use of deadly physical force, are also reviewed. Included are a review of defenses with regard to negligence, failure to perform, and the purview of indemnification under prevailing public officers' law.
6. *Evaluation, counseling, and discipline.* This part of the course is composed of the following components: (1) review of existing collective bargaining contracts and departmental policies, (2) review of evaluation methods for employees by supervisors, (3) progressive discipline

based on departmental policies, (4) state common law, (5) techniques for dealing with problem employees, (6) conducting successful counseling sessions, (7) the role of the supervisor in documenting employee problems, and (8) preparation for administrative hearings. Preclass readings consist of collective bargaining agreements, along with departmental policies relating to discipline and grievances.

7. *Intermediate law.* This portion of the course of study reviews the rights of individuals in relation to (1) victim/witness rights, (2) employee rights, and (3) juvenile rights. The rights of the accused are analyzed through the case study method, along with a review of changes in the penal law, criminal procedure law, and search-and-seizure issues.

8. *Crime prevention and community relations.* The student is expected to develop specific crime-prevention and citizen-cooperation programs. Techniques for improving good cooperation from citizens in all areas are discussed.

9. *Stress management.* Major stressors are identified for supervisors and subordinates. Stress-reduction techniques are practiced.

10. *Incident and critical-incident management.* As frontline administrators, supervisors in their capacity as lieutenants and sergeants must immediately take command of crime scenes. Other incidents, such as demonstrations and parade details, need to be planned. The differences between an *incident* (a parade) and a *critical incident* (a homicide) are discussed, including the issue of the prioritization of incidents.

    In dealing with critical incidents like the use of deadly physical force, physical injury/death, hostage negotiations, and environmental safety accidents, emphasis is placed on protecting the crime scene and protecting personnel. Patrol operations related to the supervision of crimes in progress and sensitive crimes like sexual assault and child abuse are also reviewed.

11. *Personnel issues.* This section of the course develops an awareness and ability to deal effectively with a wide range of employee issues and problems, including sexual harassment, substance abuse, burnout, and prejudice.

12. *Use of deadly physical force.* The first part of this training deals with legal issues, while the second portion presents defense tactics, such as the proper techniques for handcuffing, takedowns, use of the baton, and use of mace.

13. *Report review.* Students are taught how to review reports of crime incidents, legal papers, and summonses. They are also taught corrective techniques.

14. *Supervisor as trainer.* Supervisors train recruits and veteran officers. The focus of this portion of the course is to have the supervisor identify training needs for his or her subordinates through observing firsthand, reviewing reports, and identifying the need for remediation.

Only first-rate instructors drawn from the field and from higher education institutions should be used. Each instructor needs to use a variety of classroom techniques that go beyond the normal lecture and discussion (e.g., role playing). Video recording devices provide an opportunity for immediate feedback for many of the exercises in the course of study. Many state police and regional academies have introduced computerized work board simulations where a miniature town is created and supervisors deploy resources as conditions change.

Management Training

Promotion to lieutenant and above marks the next phase of an officer's development. At this level, the officer functions primarily in a management capacity, and newly promoted lieutenants are scheduled for training in this area. After attaining the rank of captain, one is eligible to apply to the FBI National Academy for continued management training.

In addition to these major programs, officers who are lieutenants, captains, or majors may participate in a variety of seminars, workshops, and retraining conferences to stay abreast of changes and new developments in the field of law enforcement. Using this framework allows departments to anticipate the bulk of their training needs and plan accordingly, yet there is flexibility. Specific programs in any phase can be changed to meet the changing needs of the department. Entire phases can be deleted or others added. The concept is not intended as a rigid structure to be religiously followed; instead, it is a tool to be used in the planning process.

We are aware that police executive courses are needed. Despite the fact that law enforcement is an expensive business in terms of the impact that equipment and personnel costs have on the community, few police command officers have had the benefit and experience of executive police training. Police command officers are personnel in policymaking positions, such as chiefs, deputy chiefs, majors, captains, and directors of public safety. It is difficult to come to closure on the necessary training needed for a good police executive. Certain chiefs would even say that executives have the benefit of both experience as well as graduate education in administration, criminal justice, business, and law.

A number of courses are offered throughout the country on a departmental or regional basis. The National Academy sponsored by the Federal Bureau of Investigation offers advanced-level courses to police executives at Quantico, Virginia. Such topics as public administration, budgeting, forensic management, and critical incident management are covered. To qualify for this course of study, a candidate must apply to the FBI and be sponsored by the employing police agency. This is also a self-selected program, where either the student or his agency must assume the travel and living costs. It is the closest program to the police–college model that exists in many European countries and that offers required programs to command officials. Many departments use attendance at this program as a means of selecting future executives. Smaller departments sponsor the chief or assistant chief as a way to obtain formal management education.

Not all police executives have the opportunity to attend the National Academy. What, then, is the prerequisite formal training one needs in order to be a proactive police executive?

A model police executive course offers the following topics for:

- Introduction to public administration, with an emphasis on organizational and political survival theory
- Statistics for public policy analysis
- Leadership and ethics
- An introductory course in the use of computers
- Communication skills, with an emphasis on public speaking and organizational writing
- Research methods, with an emphasis on those common to police policy analysis
- Command-level courses in critical incident management, with an emphasis on planning
- An introductory course in accounting and budgeting, followed by an elective in public budgeting
- History of American policing through a review of the great books on police leaders, and social trends affecting police administration
- Human resource management, including crucial personnel topics related to hiring, discipline, and workplace liability
- Law for executives, with an emphasis on liability, human resource issues, and criminal law updates
- Marketing the service of the department

Summary

Training provides a number of benefits to the department. First, it helps to ensure that officers have the skills and knowledge to perform at each level of their development in the department. Second, the concept ensures that the officers continue career development on a timely basis. Third, officers know what they can expect from the department in the area of training and development. This can be very beneficial to officers' morale. Fourth, it provides for a fair and equitable system in which every officer receives approximately the same level of training. In addition to being a positive morale factor, this is also beneficial in administering the department's affirmative action plan. Fifth, an organized approach to training aids in the coordination and planning of the department's overall training program and helps to avoid many of the common pitfalls in administering the program.

CIVIL LIABILITY AND TRAINING

In the early 1980s, federal courts established that municipalities can be held liable for a police officer's negligence and intentional wrongdoing. During the Reconstruction period of the Civil War, Congress provided citizen access to the federal courts when their constitutional rights under the Thirteenth and Fourteenth Amendments had been infringed on. Before this change, the Sovereign Immunity doctrine stated that governments could not be sued. This was the first step in chipping away at this legal doctrine. Over time, state and local governments became civil defendants when citizens sought monetary awards and injunctive or declaratory relief based on allegations of unconstitutional acts.

These torts defined civil wrongs that resulted in lawsuits by the party being harmed. Currently, a majority of torts against state officials are filed under 42 Section 1983 of the United States Code (USC), which forbids any deprivation of constitutional rights by public officials acting in their official capacity or "under color of state law." In cases involving federal officials, these actions are begun under the Bill of Rights and are known as *Biven's actions* (Silver, 1993).

The landmark decision was a 1978 case involving a requirement for pregnant employees to take unpaid leaves of absence before medically necessary. In *Monell* v. *Department of Social Services* (1978), the Supreme Court ruled that government could be sued directly if it is held responsible for constitutional violations inflicted under the auspices of official policy in violation of Section 1983 USC. Local governments were also held liable for the attorney's fees of a successful complainant. Federal and state courts have ruled that municipalities are liable for action by employees and their supervisors who are directly involved in such incidents. The interpretation of what is official policy has ranged from written standards of a police department all the way to a series of unwritten practices over time.

Training has become an important legal issue in tort actions involving negligence and nonfeasance. Legally, training is an affirmative duty of police administrators. **Civil liability** exists in the failure to train a police officer or in training a police officer in a negligent fashion. In tort actions directly or indirectly related to training, questions will be asked that focus on state minimum standards regarding training and the scope of duties performed by trained or untrained employees. Certification of instructors and even lesson plans used in training have become legal issues. The following are six examples of the complex tort issues that have been raised:

1. *Sager v. City of Woodland Park (1982).* This is an example that is often used in police training liability discussions. A film used in a police academy training session in Colorado

showed how not to do something in a felony stop. A police officer who had been to this training academy, while attempting to handcuff a suspect, shot and killed the suspect. The burden of responsibility shifted from the municipality to the regional police academy conducting the training.

2. *Oklahoma City* v. *Tuttle (1985).* A single incident of police misconduct did not, in and of itself, prove a policy of inadequate police training or supervision in holding a municipality liable. Where the policy itself is not unconstitutional, there is a need for more proof than a single incident to establish requisite fault and the causal connection between "policy" and constitutional deprivation.

3. *Tennessee* v. *Garner (1985).* The U.S. Supreme Court held that the use of deadly force to prevent the escape of a fleeing, unarmed burglary suspect constituted an unreasonable seizure in violation of the Fourth Amendment. Review was conducted of department operational training policies related to the use of deadly force in these situations.

4. *Voutour* v. *Vitale (1985).* The police department was found liable for a wrongful shooting involving procedures that were supposed to be taught at a six-week training program. A 30-minute training film at roll call was substituted for the regular training.

5. *Kibbe* v. *City of Springfield (1985).* Reviewing the actions of officers involved in a high-speed chase that resulted in the death of the fleeing suspect, the Court of Appeals for the First Circuit found that the police officers involved were inadequately trained and that departmental policies on high-speed pursuits and alternatives to pursuits contributed to the death of the suspect. During the course of this event, there were three separate shooting incidents involving 10 officers. A kidnapping victim was also present in the suspect vehicle during the pursuit. The city of Springfield argued that civil rights liability litigation was not appropriate litigation for the actions of the officers. The Supreme Court dismissed the case as being improvidently granted.

6. *City of Canton* v. *Harris (1989).* In this landmark decision, the Supreme Court ruled that a failure to train might create municipal liability when there is deliberate indifference to the rights of citizens. In this case, a woman under police custody fell down several times and was incoherent. She could not respond when asked if she needed medical assistance. The police department had a policy whereby the shift supervisor could decide when to summon medical assistance. In this case, medical assistance was not summoned. She was later released and taken to a hospital by her family. After a year or so of hospitalization, the woman sued under Section 1983 USC, and a federal district court awarded monetary damages against the city since the actions taken by the supervisor were "shocking" and training in medical emergency procedures was lacking. The Court of Appeals upheld the decision of the district court but remanded the case for a new trial based on legal questions regarding jury instruction by the court judge.

   The case was heard by the Supreme Court, which remanded the case for a new trial based on new standards that were defined in its ruling. The Court ruled that a municipality may be held liable under Section 1983 when constitutional violations result from the failure to train its employees and when such "failure to train" results in a deliberate indifference on the part of the municipality to protecting the constitutional rights of its inhabitants. The concept of deliberate indifference was defined by the Court to mean that the municipality's failure-to-train policy results in intentional recklessness or gross negligence in protecting the constitutional rights of citizens. The municipality, moreover, must have notice of a training deficiency in either of two ways. First, notice may be implied where failure to train officers or employees is very likely to result in a violation of constitutional rights and that the need for training is obvious. The most common example is when a municipality issues firearms to its police officers but fails to train them on the proper use of force. The second example of notice is when a municipality is formally notified of regularly occurring situations that threaten the constitutional rights of citizens and of inadequate training or remediation to deal with the situation. A case in point might be not addressing recurring civil rights violations at the city lockup over a period of time after a series of complaints.

As first stated in *Tuttle*, one single incident does not constitute a policy (see *Gabriel* v. *City of Plano*, 2000). There must be a series of incidents resulting in direct constitutional injuries to citizens. The policy of deliberate indifference must also deal with constitutional issues. In *Collins* v. *City of Harker Heights* (1992), the Court ruled that the accidental death of a municipal sewer line worker for "failure to train" by the city was not a constitutional due process issue. In an expanded discussion of due process, the Court found that the lack of training was not a deliberate effort to deprive an employee of his civil rights but rather a state safety matter.

Based on the cases presented since *Harris*, there are a number of factors that departments should consider to address failure to train or deliberate indifference issues. The worst-case scenario would be when the police department does not address citizen complaints that deal with civil rights issues over a period of time. Another scenario would be failing to train supervisors and officers on basic police procedures, department operational guidelines, or issued weapons.

Interestingly enough, failure to train in canine use of force or to monitor the use of dogs has resulted in training-related tort actions. In *Kerr* v. *City of West Palm Beach* (1989), the deliberate indifference standard was used in a complaint against the department for failure to issue operational guidelines and to conduct training for its canine unit.

A more recent example occurred in Providence, Rhode Island, where an off duty police officer at night was accidentally shot as he attempted to assist two other officers who were focused on another suspect outside of a bar. As discussed by Ryan (2013), the case of *Young* v. *City of Providence* showed the need for departments to train in scenario-based situations and not simply requalifying once a year with stationary targets. For this case, the lawsuit was dismissed as the department showed that it did conduct scenario-based training, including shoot/don't shoot.

These are only a small sample of cases that have raised issues regarding training in tort actions. A review of state and federal cases reviewed by Silver (2008) shows that "failure to train" presents the first major issue in a civil proceeding. Proactive police managers need to realize that their police agencies, municipalities, and even individual employees may be sued and that issues in relation to training may very well be raised.

Following is a basic checklist that police managers should use to prevent such tort actions:

1. Do not allow untrained officers to perform any field police duties! An untrained officer is any officer who has not successfully completed basic school and field training.
2. Training academies need to keep accurate records, including (1) lesson plans, (2) attendance of all students, (3) instructor qualifications, (4) test scores, (5) all handout materials given to students, and (6) all films and videos shown to students. In addition, it might be a good idea in skill-related courses, such as the use of the baton, to videotape students to document their proficiency in the skill area.
3. Official departmental policies should be reflected in training. For example, the policy on using deadly physical force should be presented within the context of a course of instruction on deadly physical force.

4. Lesson plans, policies, and instructional techniques need to be reviewed and updated. A saying for instructors that is especially true in tort cases is "Do not laminate your lesson plans, for they will probably become obsolete next year!"

Conclusion

In the future, training will continue to play a key role in law enforcement; however, as we have seen, the training will become increasingly sophisticated. Law enforcement is attracting more and more college graduates. Human relations skills, including such topics as stress management, will continue to be emphasized and will become a larger part of the curriculum. At the same time, police training officials will attempt to fill in the technological gap with the use of personal computers, which are now part of the everyday life of police departments. Knowledge of communication has always been a significant need in training and will continue to be so.

One of the key innovations that have affected training around the country has been field training. When carefully planned and staffed with adequately trained and well-selected field training officers, field training combines theory and practice and has a significant impact on new police officers.

Civil liability is becoming an increasingly significant issue for both line officers and police managers. Solid, professional, documented training remains one of the best protections against civil liability.

More training is also needed for police executives as well as supervisory personnel. Major corporations provide hundreds of thousands of dollars for training their major executives, while police agencies are just starting to create training programs in this vital area.

It is hoped that we will also see more in-service training for middle management personnel. Newly promoted officers especially need to acquire new knowledge along with personnel, management, and administrative skills. A curriculum providing the technological and human relations skills to operate in a modern police department will take commitment on the part of a proactive management. Personnel can anticipate events that they have been trained to recognize as familiar situations. A truly proactive department will synthesize planning and training so that line officers and police supervisors will have a positive plan-ahead perspective on their respective roles in the police organization.

Questions for Review

1. What is the purpose of police training?
2. List four common deficiencies in many current training programs.
3. Why does the regional training concept offer many remedies to small police agencies?
4. Explain the importance of the following training topics: crisis intervention, first aid, firearms training, ethics, domestic violence, stress management, cybercrime, and terrorism.
5. What are the basic core areas found in recruit basic training?
6. What are the common topics found in supervisory and executive training courses?
7. To what extent can technology be used to replace traditional classroom courses for police training?

Class Project

Depending on size, the class is divided into a number of task forces. The instructor asks each task force to review the curriculum of a police academy either in the area or in the state. (If possible, the task force should visit the academy.) Compare and contrast the curriculum in terms of recommendations made in this text.

Web Works

Perhaps the most extensive review on the scope and delivery of police training can be found at http://www.bjs.gov/index.cfm?ty=tp&tid=77. Review the training materials found on this site and compare them to a police academy that is operated in your community. To what extent do the curriculum and hours match those presented by the Department of Justice Study and other items in this chapter?

References

Bureau of Justice Assistance. *A Policymaker's Guide to Hate Crimes*. Washington, D.C.: U.S. Department of Justice, 1997.

Bureau of Justice Assistance. *Law Enforcement Training Opportunities*. Washington, D.C.: U.S. Department of Justice, 2009.

Bureau of Justice Statistics. "State and Local Law Enforcement Training Academies, 2006." Washington, D.C.: U.S. Department of Justice—Office of Justice Programs, February 2009 (Revised April 14, 2009). Web posted at post.ca.gov/training-and-testing-specifications-for-peace-officer-basic-courses.aspx. Accessed on May 17, 2009.

California Commission on Peace Officer Standards and Training. Web posted at www.post.ca.gov/regular-basic-course-training-specifications.aspx. Accessed on August 1, 2014.

City of Canton v. *Harris*, 489 U.S. 378 (1989).

Collins v. *City of Harker Heights*, 503 U.S.115 (1992).

Croin, James M., and Joshua A. Ederheimer. *Conducted Energy Devices: Development of Standards for Consistency and Guidance*. United State Department of Justice Office of Community Oriented Police and the Police Executive Research Forum, Washington, D.C., 2006.

Federal Trade Commission. *Federal Trade Commission—2006 Identity Theft Survey Report*, 2007. Web posted at ftc.gov. Accessed on May 30, 2009.

Fosdick, Raymond B. *American Police Systems*. Montclair, N.J.: Patterson Smith, 1920, reprinted 1969.

Gabriel v. *City of Plano*, 202 F. 3d 741 (2000).

Gordon, Gary, Donald J. Rebovich, Kyung-Seok Choo, and Judith B. Gordon. *Building a Data-Based Foundation for Proactive Enforcement*. Utica, N.Y.: Center for Identity Management, 2007.

Griffith, David. "Virtual Reality Training." *Police Magazine* (April 1, 2009). Web accessed at policemagazine.com/channel/technolog. Accessed on December 22, 2013.

Hormann, Jeffrey S. "Virtual Reality: The Future of Law Enforcement Training." *FBI Law Enforcement Bulletin*, 64, no. 7 (July 1995), pp. 7–9.

Jacobs, James B. "The Emergence and Implication of American Hate Crime Jurisprudence." In Robert J. Kelly and Jess Meghan, eds., *Hate Crimes*. Carbondale, Ill.: Southern Illinois Press, 1998.

Jenkins, Herbert. *Keeping the Peace: A Police Chief Looks at His Job*. New York: Harper and Row, 1970.

Johnson, Roger. *Cultural Diversity*. Albany, N.Y.: Human Resources Training, 1992.

Kerr v. *City of West Palm Beach*, 875 F. 2d 1546 (11th Cir., 1989).

Kibbe v. *City of Springfield*, 777 F. 2d 801 (1985).

Lyman, Rick. "Hate Laws Don't Matter Except When They Do." *New York Times*, October 18, 1998, section WK, p. 6.

McCampbell, Michael S. *Field Training for Police Officers: State of the Art*. Washington, D.C.: National Institute of Justice, 1986.

McCandlish, Vernon. *Identity Theft Investigation Training for Law Enforcement First Responders in New York State*. Utica, N.Y.: Utica College, 2009.

McManus, George P. *Police Training and Performance Study*. Washington, D.C.: U.S. Government Printing Office/Law Enforcement Assistance Administration, 1970.

Monell v. *Department of Social Services*, 436 U.S. 658 (1978).

National Advisory Commission on Criminal Justice Standards and Goals. *Police*. Washington, D.C.: U.S. Government Printing Office, 1973.

Neiderhoffer, Arthur. *Behind the Shield: The Police in Urban Society*. Garden City, N.Y.: Doubleday, 1969.

New York State Office for the Prevention Of Domestic Violence. Updated Model Domestic Incident Policy and Domestic Violence Training Curriculum for Law Enforcement http://www.opdv.ny.gov/public_awareness/bulletins/spring2011/lawenfcurric.html

Oklahoma City v. *Tuttle*, 105 S.Ct. 2427 (1985).

Payne, Michael. *Police Field Training Officer Course.* Albany, N.Y.: Division of Criminal Justice Services, Office of Public Safety, 1999.

Potok, Mark, ed. *The Southern Poverty Law Center's Intelligence Report.* No. 97 (Winter 2000).

Reith, Charles. *The Blind Eye of History.* Montclair, N.J.: Patterson Smith, 1952, reprinted 1975.

Ridgeway, James. *Blood in the Face,* 2nd ed. New York: Thundermouth Press, 1995.

Ryan, Jack. "Legal Liability Issues in the Training Function," 2013. Web accessed at http://patc.com/weeklyarticles/liabilitytraining.shtml. Accessed on August 2, 2013.

Sager v. *City of Woodland Park,* 543 F. Supp. 282 (1982).

Shusta, Robert M., et al. *Multicultural Law Enforcement: Strategies for Peacekeeping in a Diverse Society,* 3rd ed. Upper Saddle River, N.J.: Pearson Prentice Hall, 2005.

Silver, Isidore. *Police Civil Liability.* New York: Matthew Bender, 1993.

_____. *Police Civil Liability.* New York: Matthew Bender, 2008.

Stewart, Jerry D. "Bloodborne Diseases: Developing a Training Curriculum." *FBI Law Enforcement Bulletin,* 62, no. 5 (May 1993), pp. 11–15.

Sullivan, John L. *Introduction to Police Science.* New York: McGraw-Hill, 1971.

Tennessee v. *Garner,* 105 S.Ct. 1694 (1985).

Voutour v. *Vitale,* 761 F. 2d 812 (1985).

Walsh, G. *State & Local Law Enforcement's Antiterrorism Needs.* Dissertation prepared for Fielding Graduate University, Santa Barbara, Cal., 2011.

Weaver, Gary. "Cultural Diversity." *FBI Law Enforcement Bulletin,* 61, no. 9 (1992), pp. 1–7.

Wood, Daniel E. "Phase Approach to Training." *FBI Law Enforcement Bulletin,* 49, no. 5 (May 1980), pp. 13–15.

14 Proactive Planning

KEY TERMS

budget

Compstat

contingency plan

emergency mobilization

extrapolation

forecast

forfeiture

infrastructure

instrumental planning

intuitive approach

line-item budgeting

macroforecasting

National Incident Management System
   (NIMS)

networking

normative planning

operational planning

patrol allocation plan

planned program budgeting system (PPBS)

terrorism

zero-based budgeting (ZBB)

P roactive police management is the result of effective planning. Police management teams need to develop the necessary control to manage future events and to anticipate future action. This control is developed through a planning function that draws on solid, empirical research. Police planners need to develop contingencies based on documented and known facts with conservative extrapolation indexes. **Extrapolation** is the ability to forecast future events based on current trends. The **forecast** is usually stated in terms of probabilities; for example, a 95 percent probability that a burglary will occur in a certain four-block area during the midnight shift. There is also **macroforecasting**, which is the attempt to give probability curves and indexes to large-scale events. One example would be an 80 percent probability that police manpower needs will increase during a major national disaster, therefore demanding an increased manpower budget and certain types of reorganization of the police structure to meet this demand.

PLANNING DEFINED

For our purposes, planning is defined as devising a strategy to apply equipment, fiscal, and human resources to address a defined particular issue or problem. The defined issue or problem becomes a set of operational objectives, such as planning to reducing robberies in a certain sector.

Hudzik and others, in their overview of personnel planning (1981: 133), reinforce this approach with their three-pronged definition of planning. Planning is seen as a continuing activity concerned with a set of interdependent parts, where a number of alternative choices are developed in relation to future events. Besides the concept of optimization of the means to achieve goals, another major contribution of this approach is the concept of developing alternate means of reaching the desired goals. Too often, police planning units tend to look for a single answer to a problem when the good management choice is to decide among an equal number of viable alternative means and be able to switch from one choice to another, depending on events. Here, *flexibility* is a key word, but it should be an organized flexibility with clearly spelled out parameters.

There is another major distinction between normative and instrumental planning. **Instrumental planning** occurs when choices are created in terms of the means of obtaining goals that have been stated and given. Normally, the goals, under instrumental planning, are not questioned. **Normative planning** occurs when the goals to be chosen are considered part of the planning process. Thus, planning, under normative planning, is clearly linked to public policy analysis and the creation and implementation of public police policy. Police agencies have no problem, in most cases, with the setting of certain public policy in relation to organizational goals. However, some managers consider this type of broad police-policy goal setting as part of the political process, and many feel that this should be left in the hands of local legislators and political executives. However, if a police manager is to deal with future events and have an understanding and feel for controlling these events, normative planning must be part of his or her particular management style. A forward-planning chief police executive must be able to develop policy alternatives and not feel locked into given policy goals and a constricted set of policy alternatives.

THE SIGNIFICANCE OF PLANNING

People talk about intuitive knowledge and hunches and often use such knowledge to achieve results. In some cases, this approach may seem reasonable, especially when decisions have to be made in the absence of essential data. However, if police management is going to operate at optimal efficiency, something more than hunches is necessary. Good police managers wish to operate in an organized and efficient manner and eliminate as many errors as possible. This does not mean that the **intuitive approach** should be eliminated but, rather, that the intuitive approach needs to be channeled and controlled. One of the major thrusts of proactive police management is to have an alert, rational, and efficient organization with the known purpose of controlling unknown variables and creating a reasonable base for future action.

A major objective of planning is to create consistency over time so that day-to-day police operations are uniform. Policies need to be made known to all the officers in the organization, and thus they need to be written and understood easily. Moreover, these policies must be applied in an even-handed manner to police personnel, citizens, and situations.

Police deal every day with many volatile situations, and officers need a secure base from which to operate if they are to reduce their feelings of stress in relation to the organization.

Consistent and forward-looking planning accomplishes reduced organizational stress for individual police officers as well as for managers and administrators and lets individuals in the organization know that policies will not change abruptly.

Planning also helps to define organizational roles for all ranks in the police department and the formal relationships between these roles. Since roles are often considered simply a pattern of expected behaviors, this will also reduce police officer and manager stress by creating a stable base of role expectations. It lets individuals in all ranks and positions know, within reason, what is expected of them in their organizational role. Police administrators often need to have the parameters of their jobs defined. This is done through organizational charts and standard operating procedures (SOPs).

A well-organized planning staff that works closely with management can help administrators and officers understand the limits of each position in the organization. It will also anticipate the need for advanced training and positive two-way communication whenever there is a need to change the parameters of the various roles in the organizational structure. For example, from time to time, training officers take on additional duties in relation to recruitment, especially in the area of affirmative action. Traditional departments without a planning component simply write an order and assign the additional duties to the head of the training sections. A proactive, planning-oriented department calls the officers in to discuss the additional duties with members of the management team. A plan of action is formulated with the planning unit, and any additional training that is needed begins before the officers have to take on the additional duties.

ACCREDITATION AND PLANNING

The International Association of Chiefs of Police, the National Organization of Black Law Enforcement Executives, the National Sheriff's Association, and the Police Executive Research Forum formed the Commission on Accreditation for Law Enforcement Agencies (CALEA). The Commission set up management guidelines that each member agency would have to address. These guidelines, which became known in law enforcement circles as *standards*, were divided into the following: (1) responsibilities and relationships, (2) organization and administration, (3) personnel structure, (4) personnel process, (5) law enforcement operations, (6) operations support, (7) traffic operations, (8) prisoner- and court-related activities, and (9) auxiliary and technical services, such as communications, evidence, and property management. For example, one standard related to administration calls for written directives that require the formulation, annual updating, and distribution to all personnel of written goals and objectives for the agency and for each organizational component within the agency (Commission, 1984: 1). Another example would be directive 33.3.2, on training instruction: "A written directive governs the tenure of instructors in all agency-operated training programs" (Commission, 1984: 33).

The Commission uses these standards to evaluate a police agency for accreditation. The evaluation itself comes at a considerable expense for the department and has to be budgeted for. To meet the standards, there may be additional expenses, and the local elected officials may not wish to spend money on upgrading the police agency. Although the standards are an excellent idea and go into enough detail to be operationalized, not all the standards apply to all departments, especially the smaller police agencies. However, given the increasing concern with civil liability for both individual officers and departments, the meeting of professional standards promulgated by respected professional associations may become more common in the future. The question of standards is often raised in civil suits.

The purposes of accreditation, according to CALEA, are to

1. Increase a department's capabilities to control crime
2. Enhance effectiveness and efficiency of services
3. Improve cooperation with citizens and with other agencies in the criminal justice system
4. Increase citizen and employee confidence in goals, objectives, policies, and practices

The accreditation process follows a similar program used by colleges, universities, and professional groups for regional and professional accreditation, which consists of (1) application and review of materials, (2) agency self-study to meet all standards, (3) site visit by accreditation team to review self-study and to interview officers and community representatives, (4) response by agency to team review, (5) final discussion on points of dispute, and (6) awarding or denial of accreditation. As Behan (1989) points out, the standards are not prescriptive; agency personnel must decide how to deal with such issues as personnel selection, training, and arrest procedures. Adopting state and national practices, however, is not a one-time deal. Within a period of five years, the agency must seek reaccreditation and go through a similar review process. Thus, the agency is responsible for maintaining both accreditation and its operating standards.

An endeavor of this nature involves much time and work, especially in the review of agency practices during the self-assessment period. Some may ask, "Why bother?" Proponents point out that accreditation is an important management tool. It allows the department to formally measure its strengths and weaknesses according to national norms with the goal of self-improvement. Accreditation also carries prestige for department members and the community. It is also reasoned that liability costs can be controlled since all high-risk activities will have operating and training guidelines. Further, it provides an opportunity to modernize certain equipment (provided budget support is available) as well as procedures and practices.

Not everyone is convinced that accreditation is all that it purports to be. It is very expensive and time consuming in terms of staff and department involvement. According to Oettmeier (1993), reports, policies, and directives have to be reviewed and rewritten. This can result in the paper-tiger syndrome, in which the process becomes more important than anything else. Further, the objectives of accreditation may not immediately result in the stated purposes for accreditation. In other words, an accredited department may not be that effective and efficient in controlling crime or in increasing cooperation with other agencies. Successful agencies, moreover, may not need accreditation since they are being proactive in addressing problems. What is lacking in the accreditation movement, Oettmeier feels, is the attention to the quality of services and other questions, such as employee satisfaction and creativity. More importantly, critics suggest that CALEA and other groups involved in accreditation should explore changes that can be employed in such areas as police training and practices.

CALEA does not hold a monopoly on accreditation. Because of the costs and an argument that CALEA standards cannot apply to all the states and to small departments (10 or fewer sworn employees), certain states, such as New York, Colorado, and Washington, have begun their own accreditation programs. In New York, the number of standards for the state's accreditation program has been reduced to comply with existing statutes, statewide practices, and collective bargaining agreements. Some associations, such as the International Association of Campus Law Enforcement Administrators, have created national accreditation programs for college and university police departments.

In summary, accreditation, whether national or state, is a useful managerial process for departments that want to measure their operations according to a set of professional standards. It is a necessary tool for departments that are attempting to deal with poor personnel practices, negative community relations, corruption problems, and administrative ineptitude.

THE NEED FOR A PLANNING OFFICER OR A PLANNING UNIT

Whether there is a planning officer or a separate planning unit naturally depends on the size of the department. Whatever the case, every department, regardless of its size, needs a specific location in the organizational chart in which planning activities are carried out. For the sake of brevity, we will speak of the planning unit with the realization that in smaller departments this planning unit will most likely consist of a single officer who does the bulk of the planning and research work of the department.

Basically, the planning unit provides staff services to the proactive police management team in five vital areas:

1. Dissemination of information
2. Preparation of orders
3. Long-range planning of departmental procedures
4. Development of legal and statistical information
5. Provision of specific and general assistance in the decision-making process

These services are performed in terms of the three basic functions of planning and research in any police department:

1. *Records and reports.* Maintain statistical records, rules, and regulations of the department; design, formulate, modify, and, when necessary, eliminate departmental forms.
2. *Data and fiscal analysis.* Assist in budget preparation both internally and for presentation to external funding sources, such as political executives and legislatures; provide trend analysis of crime statistics for both managerial planning and the line officer's daily needs; prepare annual reports; and so on.
3. *Legal.* Interpret recent court decisions for use by staff and line officers; assist in departmental hearings, provide information and database needed for future criminal justice legislation, provide copies of new laws that affect operations, and prepare explanations and analysis of new laws using ordinary English rather than legal jargon; provide explanations of new technical legal jargon that affects planning and operational activity.

With the exception of keeping some records and reporting data to the Uniform Crime Reporting Program, many of these needs are not met in many medium-sized and smaller departments. However, they are vital to both the short-range and long-range health of any police organization. Positive, effective management includes an information machine that digests enormous amounts of data into summarized and analyzed forms. The planning unit provides such uniform and timely information for the proactive management team.

STEPS IN THE PLANNING PROCESS

As in the development of any process, certain factors or conditions need to be determined to follow through logically to a successful conclusion. In the planning process, the following steps have been identified:

1. *Recognize and analyze the problem, specifying the need for a plan.* This is one of the most difficult steps in the planning process. There is a need to make sure that the problem really exists and is one that is relevant to the police organization. Is this a problem that is unique and simply needs to be dealt with on an ad hoc basis, or will there be a continuing need to deal with this problem in terms of future organizational activity? Planning

resources should be targeted toward problems that are relevant and significant to the police organization.

Ultimately, the problem needs to be defined so that it can be resolved through the use of empirical data. General questions of ethics or metaphysical notions cannot be resolved by planning units. Also, the problem needs to be stated in such a way that it can be resolved with the tools and resources that the planning unit has available. Specifics are also needed in terms of the resolution of problems and the creation of specific plans. For example, rather than an increase or decrease in crime rate in general as a problem, planning units should specify a narrower scope—such as the decrease in burglaries in a specific area of the police jurisdiction.

2. *Formulate a detailed set of objectives.* This goal-setting activity should be formulated in specific empirical terms—that is, be stated so that the data gathered are either directly or potentially verifiable through the five senses: seeing, hearing, feeling (touch), smelling, or tasting. A context for the verification has to be identified—that is, a laboratory procedure, gathering of statistical data, interviews, and so on. Also, a standard of goal attainment needs to be stated. Rather than simply a reduction in property crime, it would be better to state that there should be a 5 percent reduction in robberies in certain geographic locations within a specified time period. Internally, planning could propose a 10 percent reduction in personnel grievances against middle management. However stated, the goals, or behavioral objectives, must be (1) specific; (2) obtainable, that is, possible; (3) empirical; and (4) related to general goals of the police organization.

3. *Gather data.* Literally anything can be called *data*: gunshots and noises, gossip, scientific experiments, and even people crossing the street. The major test of the data gatherer is that of considering what is significant (relevant) in relation to the problem to be solved. If you use too fine a net to gather data, your time is wasted, and your files are filled with irrelevancies. If the mesh of your data-gathering net is too large, then significant facts may slip through and be lost to the investigation.

Data gathering is not simply looking at random events and choosing facts with little or no judgment. There is need for a crude but effective cost–benefit flowchart at this stage of the problem-solving planning process. For some data, cost is literally not a factor. In the solution of homicides, for example, both the police and the public are willing to sustain high costs. Data are collected that might be considered irrelevant in less important cases, on the off chance that something might be there that would lead to solving the crime. In a highly publicized multiple murder, for example, the data net is fine indeed, and costs are generally not even considered.

Increased availability of computer-generated information has stressed the need for personnel trained in analysis and the ability to make sound judgments concerning relevance. A major problem in current practices is not the lack of data but rather the existence of too much information. The secret of success is the ability to have enough analytic skills to use the significant data you have to solve the planning problem while discarding or, better yet, not gathering the irrelevant data.

4. *Operational plan.* This is where highly organized analytic skills come into focus, and may very well be the most important part of the effort. A strong planning effort often leads to very satisfying results. Technical data, for example, need to be digested, interpreted, and refashioned in such a manner that they become useful to planners and management. This might include the reorganization of statistical and evaluative data in clear English. Thus, conclusions can be drawn that can be used to organize and identify the plan of attack.

The operational plan needs to be specific enough that it makes sense to both line officers and supervisors. Orders have to be drawn and definite action commitments have to be made in terms of specific timetables. Definite procedural orders are needed so that line personnel know what they have to do to implement the attack plan.

This example was taken from a planning study of a police department of around 35 sworn personnel. The plan was designed to develop a unit that would take care of administrative detail and provide planning continuity for the police chief. The unit could have consisted of anywhere from one to three persons. The chief would decide which ones would be civilians and which ones would be uniformed.

Note: Post-9/11, agencies hoping for federal funding are expected to have all operational plans NIMS (the **National Incident Management System**) compliant. One of the criticisms to come from the 9/11 and Hurricane Katrina response was that many of the emergency response agencies working side by side spoke "another language." For example, a fire official might be giving out commands to multiple agencies, speaking in his or her own agencies' argo, or terminology. If that agency used a 10-code, it would be useless chatter to some of the non 10-code speaking agencies waiting for orders. For efficiency—and safety—one of the NIMS requirements is that all emergency response agencies refrain from codes, and use normal words. For this reason, all operational plans being put together should be NIMS compliant.

5. *Get the agreement of those involved in the plan (obtain concurrences).* In the military, *obtaining concurrences* means obtaining the agreement of those who are to be involved with the operationalization of the plan. In some cases, it would be valuable to obtain specific input from line officers. The obtaining of concurrences is an attempt to have the officers and agencies involved agree at an early stage on the details of how the plan is going to be carried out. If this is done, positive cooperation is more likely to occur. The reason for this positive feeling is that officers who are consulted concerning the implementation of plans will feel that they are part of the team and have something personal at stake in the success of the plan. In addition, involved officers are less likely to place obstacles in the way of implementing the plan.

A further practical reason for obtaining concurrence is the need to receive input from those who are most familiar with the fieldwork necessary to operationalize a plan. Without such input, necessary details may be missed. Concurrence should also mean that those carrying out the plan will have a better understanding of the need of the plan and its success. They will be able to anticipate problems and obstacles to implementation because of prior consultation. Involvement of this kind, in basic management decisions, normally increases morale among all levels of personnel.

6. *Evaluate.* Needless to say, unless the plan is actually made operational and there is a means of evaluating its success, much time and effort would have been wasted. Unfortunately, many good plans fail to reach the operational stage for a variety of reasons (e.g., administrative change, change of priorities, lack of budgetary support, and internal conflict).

TYPES OF PLANS

Planning, doing, and controlling are three phases of the management process. Total planning helps to ensure success of both the doing and the controlling. It is essential that planning be well thought out. In that regard, we have divided our discussion into long-range administrative/management plans, fiscal plans, and short-range operational/tactical plans.

Long-Range Strategic Plans

These are plans that concern the basic structure of the police organization. They are the responsibility of the jurisdictional officials who created the agency and of the department head that is charged with its daily operation. It is at this level that the policies governing the departmental activities are formulated. *Policy* is defined as a "may do" activity as opposed to lower level procedures, which usually are detailed and presented as "must do" activities. Special emphasis is placed on interfacing and overlapping areas of authority.

This long-term planning process is often called strategic planning. As outlined by King (2004), the department conducts a review of its strengths, weaknesses, opportunities, and threats (SWOT). This review focuses on the department's external environment in terms of impact of population decline or growth, economics, technology, national and world events, and relationship to the public. It involves participation by all units of the department and includes a review of the department's mission, vision, and major goals.

A mission statement is simply a summary statement of the main purpose of the department and a statement of purpose. Most departments have mission statements that involve serving the community by providing a wide range of quality police services. The mission statement should also be tied to specific problems that the organization tries to address, such as reducing crime, comforting victims, and providing emergency assistance.

Linked to the mission statement is the organization's vision. The vision is a higher level benchmark for the organization that centers on a motto such as "We want to be the best" or ways the organization will be successful. For example, the vision statement of the University of Illinois Police is, "This Division will be a model public safety organization in partnership with the community we serve."

Tied to both mission and vision are core values that reflect the organizational culture of the department and that hopefully are put into practice. Such values might include commitments to ethical behavior, innovation, honesty, quality services, and protection of the rights of citizens. Examples of all three items appear in the box discussing the New Hartford, New York, Police Department.

The planning process that is part of the strategic planning process includes a review of the following:

- Making internal and external assessments of major economic and political factors
- Evaluating key issues that the organization has to face through the SWOT analysis
- Developing strategies that address each issue
- Setting goals and implementing actions
- Monitoring and assessing results

Included in the process are survey and focus group research with community groups and other stakeholders to obtain their views on police services. Some departments use Internet surveys of their communities. Thus, the strategic plan outlines the department's major goals for a five- to eight-year period. Also included in the plan is a GAP analysis, which measures the gaps between what is needed and the resources of money, people, and equipment that are at hand. In strategic planning, the major areas that are addressed are economic future, staffing, major technology, and capital improvements or construction for police buildings. The plan needs to be flexible, as evidenced by events after 9/11, when attention had to be paid to security of community infrastructures and emergency management.

Mission and Values of the New Hartford (NY) Police

Our mission is to promote a sense of safety and quality of life in New Hartford by providing police services with integrity and commitment to excellence in partnership with our community. We view the people who live and visit New Hartford as our customers who deserve our concern, care, and attention.

The Department has five Core Values. The values are the yardstick by which we hold ourselves accountable. To be effective they must be universally understood, communicated, reinforced, and integrated into all our daily activities. They are as follows:

Ethical Behavior—maintain and enforce the highest standards of integrity and fairness in all our actions.

Continuous Improvement—embrace positive changes and maintain professional development through training.

Respect for People and Diversity—achieve success through mutual respect with the people we deal with, operating in an environment based on openness, trust, teamwork, innovation, diversity, and integrity.

Service Delivered in Partnership with the Community—recognize that the concept of community policing and crime reduction involves partnerships. These partnerships will result in an enhanced quality of life in our community and a mutual respect between law enforcement and the public.

Realistic Expectations and Management by Fact—the leadership of the New Hartford Police Department will establish and maintain realistic expectations of its employees. The leadership will seek accurate information to make sound decisions, establish clear realistic goals, monitor progress, and promote ongoing feedback.

Following are central issues to be considered in long-range plans:

1. *Changes in basic organization.* This may include the centralization versus decentralization issue but is much broader in concept. It could mean, for example, a shift in which major investigations take place in the detective division or among a team of field police officers. This includes a basic change in authority relationships and functions of different units of the police organization. A hard look at current organizational practices is taken in conjunction with the planning unit. Developing authority relationships are examined in the light of the need for an efficient department. Optimization of general administrative and managerial practices in conjunction with effective leadership styles is also examined. The question to be asked is: Do these relationships optimize the effective administration of the police organization, or is there a more effective mode of organization that should be implemented?

2. *Long-range personnel deployment.* This includes hiring, firing, grievance procedures, fringe-benefits negotiation and implementation, along with effective use and maintenance of the tools of the trade, such as vehicles, armaments, mobile communications, and so on. In a service organization like law enforcement, where up to 90 percent of the budget may be devoted to personnel and the servicing of personnel, effective planning in this area may have a serious impact on the police organization. Budgets have to be related to the optimizing of individual morale and efficiency, and this has to be related to the overall operations.

3. *Training needs and requirements.* In the budget-cutting process that police budgets experience at the hands of legislators, training is often considered a luxury. Politicians often fail to see the relationship between effective training and effective operations in the field. When training monies are cut and a plan is being implemented, there may not be enough

of a budget to train personnel in implementing the plan. Personnel might need new skills, a possible change in attitudes and perceptions, and new knowledge in order to facilitate the implementation of certain plans. When personnel are not able to acquire these effective tools for planning implementation, plans fail, not because the plans were bad, but because the training budget was cut. Without the implementation of the training function as part of the overall planning process, management may need to implement training in the middle of a plan and with less than adequate training personnel. What happens in such a situation is that the plan limps along at higher cost and with lower morale. The training plan should be implemented prior to and concurrent with the general plan of attack. Police managers have to educate legislators to the notion that effective training is essential to solid management planning. Training is not a luxury but is essential to every budget. Training needs to be regarded as essential to any change in organizational structure and in the implementation of new plans.

Strategic Planning in Practice

Zhao et al. (2008) examined, using a random sample of 3,639 departments in the Community Oriented Police base, to what extent police departments undertook strategic planning. They found that 105 departments indeed had a plan, and the initial survey was followed up with personal visits in the case of seven departments, which had sworn officers numbering from 66 to 2,900.

They found four major models from this exercise:

1. *Model 1: In-Depth Plan with Limited Application* In this category, there was in-depth planning for some divisions or precincts, with limited involvement by the rank and file. This resulted in an efficient use of limited resources with the officers involved. The divisions and precincts were aware of the goals of the planning and were supportive.
2. *Model 2: Top Leadership in Charge* In this model, the leadership had an extensive plan on where the agency was headed for in the next few years, and this became a basis to seek support from external resources. This resulted in incremental change with controlled planning but garnered little support outside of top administrators.
3. *Model 3: Management Model* Here the department had organization-wide planning with frequent updates. The plan became an effective management tool in the collection of data and crime control planning. Consensus was developed among commanders, and it demonstrated achievement to politicians and the community.
4. *Model 4: Total Implementation Model* Strategic planning was the engine that drove the department and produced proactive change. It demanded change in planning, organization, and performance evaluation. Consensus was developed, and officers at every rank were held accountable. Importantly, the community was aware of the strategic plan.

All of these models are part of the approach of proactive police management and are to be commended.

Fiscal Plans

Fiscal planning is a continuous departmental activity that requires the department to project a number of fiscal futures and live within its **budget**. A budget is the financial plan for the department for a period of time based on anticipated income and expenditures. Every police department develops an annual budget to deal with its specific needs. What is needed is long-range fiscal planning that is projected beyond the immediate needs of the annual budget.

Many police administrators lack training in fiscal planning. The normal approach of police administrators who lack budgetary skills or access to personnel who do have these skills is simply to add 10 percent to the old budget when they submit their new line budget and hope for the best. When these administrators run out of fiscal resources, they depend on crisis management to deal with the situation, often approaching the local government for more money. This type of approach is no longer feasible in this era of fiscal constraints. Police administrators have learned that they need to become more sophisticated about the budget process or be able to hire the experts needed. Of course, the top administrators must be able to understand the fiscal experts that they hire, or they will not understand their own budgets.

Most budgets can be broken down into three types:

1. Line-item budgeting
2. Planned program budgeting system (PPBS)
3. Zero-based budgeting (ZBB)

Most other types of budgets that are referred to in public management and police management texts are variations on these three approaches.

The approaches to budgeting under these systems include the following (Lewis, 1978: 229):

1. Open-end budgeting
2. Fixed-ceiling budgeting
3. Work measurement or unit costing
4. Increase–decrease analysis
5. Priority listings
6. Item-by-item control or line-item control

In an *open-end budget*, the manager submitting the budget attempts to justify the fiscal request in terms of services performed with few or no guidelines. In a *fixed-ceiling budget*, an executive or legislative body gives the police agency a dollar amount that it will fund and then tells the police management team to create a budget and justify it in terms of the given dollar ceiling. *Work measurement* or *unit costing* is more sophisticated and is often used with PPBS or ZBB, where each service performed by a police department is given a dollar value in terms of the cost of that service and then is justified for budgetary purposes.

In *increase–decrease analysis*, the funding body or executive in control asks for justifications in the police budget only where there is an increase or decrease in a budget request compared with the prior year's requests. In *priority listing*, the police management team lists budget items in order of most important to least important. This is especially useful to a local legislature that is interested in cutting the police budget. Finally, in *item-by-item control*, often called *line-item control*, the executive or funding body exercises control in terms of approval of specific fiscal decisions concerning certain line items in the budget during the fiscal year. The funding body actually exercises a veto over certain police management decisions concerning the spending of funds during the fiscal year. This last approach makes it difficult to exercise management control over the fiscal policies of a police department. It should be done only in times of fiscal emergencies or fiscal chaos.

Whatever approach is used for the budgeting process, every police manager must observe certain principles:

1. The focus should be on future as well as present problems.
2. Budgeting should be considered as one aspect of the overall planning process.

3. Budgets should be created in terms of an overall mission statement of the department, thereby enabling management to set general goals for the law enforcement agency.
4. Budgeting is a critical part of the law enforcement executive's role in terms of budget development and fiscal monitoring.

Keeping these principles in mind makes it easier to take a look at the different kind of budgets; many different approaches and types of budgets will fulfill these principles, but some types and approaches will work better than others.

LINE-ITEM BUDGETING   **Line-item budgeting** is the most widely used approach because (1) it is the simplest to construct, and (2) it is easily understandable by people who lack fiscal expertise and training. The line-item budget simply makes a list of all personnel in terms of rank and salary. This personnel list normally makes up 85–90 percent of the budget. Equipment, including such items as desks and laboratory equipment are listed with their costs. Next, fixed charges—heat, light, gas for buildings, gasoline for vehicles, pensions, and other fringe benefits—are listed with their costs. Most of these items are normally given as totals under these or similar categories. A sample line-item budget is shown in Table 14-1.

The line-item budget is normally passed from police administrator to police administrator and fiscal year to fiscal year with additional costs and requests simply added to the appropriate category. Some administrators may simply increase the requests by 10 percent over the last fiscal year when creating a new budget. Thus, this type of incremental budget often

- Lacks details of the specific costs of each operation.
- Does not relate costs to general goals and specific objectives.
- Lacks fiscal justification.

As a result, this is one of the hardest budgets to defend before a legislative body that wants to cut costs. It is also one of the easiest budgets to cut. Because of the broad categories involved, legislative bodies and fiscally hard-pressed executives may simply tell the police manager to cut the budget by an overall percentage or to eliminate certain categories. Since these budgets generally do not relate budget items to specific services performed for a community, it makes it difficult to justify the costs. Because of the nature of this budget, it is difficult for a police executive to say whether an increase or decrease in categories of the budget will lead to a *significant* increase or decrease in what the police executive considers a needed police service for the local community. Thus, what a police manager gains in the advantage of the ease of preparation of the line-item budget may be lost when it is cost-cutting time for the local legislature.

PLANNED PROGRAM BUDGETING SYSTEM   The **planned program budgeting system (PPBS)** is a more difficult budget to formulate because it demands an analysis of the organizational structure of the police agency and the individual units of the agency. In social science, this is a structural–functional approach. The planning unit or officer draws up an organizational chart of the agency showing the authority relationships. This is the structure part. Then the function of each unit is described, much in the same manner as the civil service would describe the services to be performed in a standard job description. This is the function part.

Once you know how the units relate to one another and what function each unit is supposed to perform in the law enforcement organization, it is possible to set specific objectives for each

TABLE 14-1	Basic School Costs		
		03/12 Students	04/13 30 Students
.01	Director ($1500/week)	$13,500	$14,400
.02	Temporary service for administrative assistance	3,000	3,500
.03	Books/equipment	900	900
.04	Recruit lodging	26,520	25,200
.05	Instructors' lodging	3,600	3,800
.06	Food	15,600	19,000
.07	Physical education uniforms	900	900
.08	Physical education instructor	4,000	4,200
.10	Travel for instructors	3,000	3,800
.14	Bus rental for crime prevention program	400	—
.20	Emergency vehicle operations course	400	—
.21	Emergency vehicle operations course equipment	400	350
.22	Defensive driving course training	350	345
.23	Psychological testing	1,500	1,200
.30	Classroom rental	3,250	4,825
.31	Honorariums for nonpolice personnel	800	800
.40	Telephone charges	120	300
.45	Miscellaneous	400	400
.50	Awards	—	500
.60	Composite class picture	—	500
	Totals	$78,640	$84,920

unit in light of the overall goals of the organization. These objectives are created in conjunction with middle management and supervisors in charge of each unit. The objectives are expected to be attainable and measurable, and all have to be justified in practical, empirical terms and related to all fiscal requests. The distribution of personnel and materials is identified with each planning unit or subsystem in the organization, and each unit is related to the structure of the total police organization to create the overall fiscal justification for the services that the police organization performs. This is a planning-oriented budget.

ZERO-BASED BUDGETING   The **zero-based budgeting (ZBB)** approach creates and justifies an entirely new budget each year; there is no reliance on precedent and incremental planning from previous years. The object is to force agency planners and administrators to create new justifications for every expenditure, thereby providing a comprehensive fiscal analysis of every unit of the agency in relation to (1) a justification for the very existence of the unit and the services it provides and (2) the relationship between the justification of the services provided and the cost of these services. The originators of this approach helped both to encourage comprehensive planning and to eliminate waste and inefficiency. As Wildavsky and Hammond state (1978: 243):

> The major purpose of the zero-based budget was to examine all programs at the same time and from the ground up to discover programs continuing through inertia or design that did not warrant being continued at all or at their present level of expenditure.

Monies saved by this analysis would then be used for programs of a higher priority than the ones defined as redundant or would simply be a means of reducing expenditure for the total budget.

The ZBB is part of a long tradition of comprehensive fiscal planning that fiscal experts have tried to have public agencies adopt for many decades in terms of making judgments on how scarce resources should be applied for the greatest good. This point needs to be emphasized when looking at any fiscal process. Because there are never enough resources to meet all demands—and is true of all public agencies, including law enforcement—the basic decision to be made is how to allocate these resources. This allocation, after all the fiscal experts have completed their budgets, may, in the end, be a political decision.

However, the ZBB has met full force one of the major points that V. O. Key Jr. made in his classic 1940 article (1978: 36):

> Whether a particular agency is utilizing and plans to utilize its resources with the maximum efficiency is of great importance, but this approach leaves untouched a more fundamental problem. If it is assumed that the agency is operating at maximum efficiency, the question remains whether the function is worth carrying out at all, or whether it should be carried out on a reduced or enlarged scale, with resulting transfers of funds to or from other activities of greater or lesser social utility.

This, in fact, is the basis of ZBB: Whether a function should be carried out at all is the real question. Also, a standard approach of ZBB is to ask the different units what kinds of services they would provide at different funding levels (e.g., a 90 percent funding level or a 70 percent funding level). This allows policy makers to cut their budgets in a logical manner with a reasonable awareness of the specific consequences of the budget cuts in the delivery of services by various units of the police agency. The ZBB, however, fell out of favor with managerial accounting practices, largely due to questioning whether the time commitment to conform to its guidelines was truly the most efficient practice. Elements of the ZBB, rather than the whole philosophy, are starting to be seen more frequently once again (Kavanagh, 2011).

THE BUDGET PROCESS   In all governmental entities, there is a budget process that consists of the following six parts:

1. *Budget or fiscal year.* This is the time period for planning the fiscal year. In some communities, it corresponds to the regular calendar year, but for others it may span two calendar years, such as July 1, 2014–June 30, 2015.
2. *Planning period.* This leads up to preparing the budget for the fiscal year. During this time, the police chief or the chief budget officer will request budget items from various internal departments and unit commanders and review fiscal expenditures for the year.
3. *Preliminary budget/public presentation.* At this time, the chief executive officer for the governmental entity (village, town, city, county, regional authority) calls for budget requests from all department heads, including police. This gives time for fiscal staff to pull all department budgets together for presentation to the legislative body that reviews the budget requests. In some cases, the police chief will be working with a budget subcommittee

from the legislature in preparing the request. After this information is collated, then the final budget for the police department is presented.

4. ***Budget review.*** During this time, the legislative body formally reviews the budget and may request further information or make additions or subtractions to requested items. This is all part of the political give-and-take between the executive branch that requests the funding and the legislative branch that approves the budget and its expenditures.

5. ***Final budget announcement.*** The formal budget is announced, and plans are made to make sure that tax revenues and state and federal subsidy programs will meet the proposed expenditures.

6. ***Audit.*** In essence, this begins the next budget cycle in that expenditures are monitored to see if they are spent according to previous estimates. As is often the case, monies are reallocated if there are savings or overspending in certain areas.

The main budget item is personnel, which encompasses anywhere from 70 to 80 percent of the police department's budget. Included in this general heading are salaries, increases created from union contracts or across-the-board increases, workers' compensation insurance, contributions for Social Security and Medicare, health insurance, contributions for retirement plans, and overtime. It is estimated that a benefit package can encompass 30–40 percent of personnel costs. The largest increases over the past five years for many departments have been in the areas of health insurance and overtime for security details. Thus, it is imperative that police managers have a handle on staffing for projected workload. It is also recommended that the department conduct comparative studies of personnel costs for both adjacent and like-size departments in the area and state. This is important for officer retention and collective bargaining negotiations.

The role of the police chief and major department heads is to monitor expenditures and to plan for the next budget cycle. Thus the budget for the current fiscal year becomes the benchmark for future budgets. For planning purposes, the police manager must anticipate what changes might occur in the future in terms of delivery of services, police service costs such as personnel costs, and economic changes in the economic environment. For example, the crisis in the housing market has forced many departments to think about the likelihood that they may have to reduce personnel and curtail services due to decreasing tax revenues caused by homeowners' defaulting on their mortgages.

Throughout this whole process, there are never-ending negotiations for either extra resources for those communities experiencing growth or maintenance of the status quo for those dealing with economic decline. The budget is a political document; it reflects the political dynamics of a community in terms of priorities and the range of services that can be provided. Thus the chief is constantly working on the budget on a daily basis in terms of expenditures. This involves having a close working relationship with the municipal finance officer or chief comptroller.

SUPPLEMENTING THE POLICE BUDGET   Throughout the country, police budgets are becoming pinched. This section points out some strategies that police managers may use to supplement their police budget while doing a great deal of good for their departments. The most successful strategies for law enforcement agencies to raise money outside the normal budget have been donation programs and forfeiture. Another strategy, the charging of user fees for police services (e.g., special patrols, copying of accident reports) is the least effective way and creates a great deal of resentment among citizens.

Donation drives often generate free positive publicity for police agencies either through private fund drives, donations by companies, or funds raised through police foundations. The most common items are body armor, vests and covers, tactical first aid kits, and crime scene equipment. These examples illustrate the two major approaches to this type of fund-raising: special-issue campaigns and ongoing foundations.

If the donation approach is going to work, it must be run and controlled by police managers rather than by professional fund-raisers. Professional fund-raisers are very commercial, often taking a large percentage of the gross (up to 90 percent) for overpriced services; in some cases, they have been indicted and convicted of illegal activity in the area of fund-raising. Donation programs can work, but only when they are controlled by police management and are part of a community effort.

Of great interest to police managers around the nation is the **forfeiture** approach, where goods and monies gained illegally are forfeited to the police department. Departments have seized such items as cars, airplanes, and yachts, and countless computers and other electronic equipment. The Florida Contraband Forfeiture Act allows for the forfeiture of any "instrumentality" used in the commission of a felony. Under this system, police departments get to keep everything they confiscate and can hire their own lawyers for the civil proceedings. In addition, local governments cannot reduce the police budget because of forfeiture income. The Fort Lauderdale Police Department in a two-year period seized 20 vessels, $1.4 million in cash, 89 vehicles, and two airplanes, with the total forfeiture amounting to over $3.3 million. In a three-year period, the amount rose to $5.5 million. Even the Delray Beach Police Department, a small department, in one year confiscated a $24,000 Formula boat, $240,000 in cash, a Mercedes-Benz, and a Cadillac. Between the years 2003 and 2011, the US Department of Justice's asset forfeiture fund grew from $500 million to $1.8 billion, $445 million of which went to local law enforcement (Riggs, 2012). Clearly, it can be argued that the asset forfeiture program, among its many benefits, helps pay for itself. An excellent example of this point was the $25 million New York State Police Forensic Identification Center, which was built entirely on seized assets from drug traffickers and was dubbed, upon its grand opening ceremony in 1996, "The house that crack built" (Parsavand, 2002).

If forfeiture is going to hurt the criminal element while helping the police department, it has to be planned carefully. First, the chief needs to be familiar with forfeiture laws in his or her jurisdiction. Many laws are needlessly complex, limit the monies that can go to the police department, or place all monies in a general fund. Second, the chief needs to protect the detectives from getting involved in entrapment and/or criminal soliciting. Third, there are costs involved: lawyers, storage, upkeep of property, advertising, and the selling of confiscated items. Finally, drug dealers are becoming more sophisticated and are keeping large loans attached to their property to protect themselves from the forfeiture laws. Forfeiture can work and has worked on the coast of Florida, but once again, good police management means proactive planning.

The imposition of fines, which are much like user fees, may prove useful. Many departments, especially those in expensive rich suburbs, have had to impose fines for false alarms coming from burglar alarms. Responding to false alarms is a waste of police time.

An example of a false alarm regulated program occurred in Seattle, WA. Because of the high number of false alarm calls, the city and the police department in 2011 required that all alarm companies be licensed. Additionally, false alarm calls for residents and businesses were charged to the alarm company: $230 for a false intrusion alarm and $115 for a technical false activation. If the dispatcher is notified to cancel the police response, then the alarm company is not charged. Interestingly, alarm calls at residences are given low priority; residents are encouraged to have the alarm company guard service respond (Seattle Police, 2013). It was reported by the department that alarm calls had been drastically reduced.

The object is to reduce the false alarm rate by making those people who create the unnecessary work pay for it.

Finally, the Internal Revenue Service gives a finder's fee to people who turn in tax evaders. The city of Atlanta found that it was able to turn in tax evaders uncovered during the investigation of racketeers. Atlanta has an arrangement whereby the finder fees are paid to the city through the comptroller for Atlanta.

Another area that raises income is grants. Grants are sums of money given by a state or private entity for a specific purpose during a defined time period. Grant funds are awarded to departments based on their application and eligibility for the funding. Examples of grants include funding for extra DWI patrols, the purchase of an expensive capital improvement item, or the hiring of extra police officers for community policing. Many large and mid-sized agencies have personnel dedicated to the application and monitoring of grant applications. According to Chief Raymond Philo (personal communication, 2009), grant funds should be considered as a one-time revenue source for a specific item or program and not part of continuous operating costs.

Risk Management and Liability

Part of strategic planning includes risk management, which is a comprehensive review of assets that could be damaged, stolen, or lost and countermeasures to prevent major occurrences (Curtis and McBride, 2005). In private business, assets include people, equipment, property, information, and reputation. Countermeasures can include a backup plan, removing the threat or obtaining insurance if such an event were to occur. For example, a risk manager would work with the department to devise a backup plan if a computer system were to fail or fall victim to a virus. The first step would be to take measures to prevent the occurrence through computer use policies and the installation of firewalls and other virus protection software; methods would also be explored to save operational files each day. The second phase would involve going to a backup or manual system if the whole system were to crash.

Part of the risk management process is to identify those areas where the organization or its members can be held legally liable for actions that were either taken or not taken by department personnel. Using a World War II naval warfare analogy, most police departments are slow-moving convoys when it comes to litigation activity on the federal and state court levels. There is also much regulatory oversight and legal activity that occur in such areas as operational standards and labor relations by various regulatory agencies. The most active litigated areas are internal employment practices, use of force, arrest situations, high-speed pursuits, and civil rights violations.

First is a primer on tort or civil liability. As discussed by Ross (2003), there are two forms of liability: criminal and civil. Criminal liability occurs when a person commits a crime in conjunction with his or her official duties. Supervisory personnel can also be held responsible if they are part of the occurrence. For example, patrol and supervisory personnel of a police department that routinely administers beatings to prisoners could be held criminally liable for these actions.

A civil action, or tort, is a wrong committed against another party. In these actions the offended party wishes to obtain damages or prevent further occurrences. Most tort actions are based on state law. A federal tort action, as discussed in Chapter 13 on training, often involves a violation of constitutional or statutory rights of a person under "color of federal law," as described in 42 U.S.C. 1983.

The three major areas in torts, or civil wrongs, are intentional conduct, negligence, and strict liability conduct. In an intentional action, it was the person's conscious choice to commit an act. Typical tort against police for intentional actions involves assault, defamation, false arrest, and malicious prosecution. In a case involving negligence, the officer or organization is alleged to have failed to perform an act or to exercise the care that a responsible or prudent person would exercise; for example, a department can be sued for failing to provide adequate medical treatment to an injured prisoner. In strict liability cases, the person is held to a tort proceeding regardless of intent or negligence; liability is imposed because the action occurred. The term *vicarious liability* is often discussed in civil actions. This occurs when the employer is also held responsible when the employee was acting as an agent of the organization.

Tort actions can be filed for a number of reasons by victims and prisoners. Employees can also file tort actions against the police department, and their reasons include the following:

- Unlawful search of property
- Discrimination
- Retaliatory discharge
- Freedom of speech
- Union or political activity
- Discipline or termination action
- Personal appearance or dress code
- Unfair labor practice
- Compensation for on-the-job injury

According to Robert J. Meadows (1999: 156), in his review of legal issues and police, the top eight litigation issues, based on a survey of police chiefs of 20 cities with over 100,000 in population, are as follows:

1. Use of force
2. Auto pursuit
3. Arrest/search
4. Employee drug test
5. Hiring and promotion
6. Discrimination based on race, sex, or age
7. Record keeping and privacy
8. Jail management

Newspaper or Web site articles that report the filing of a suit or the negotiation of a pretrial settlement against a police department reflect the adage that we are a litigious society in this country. The reality is that many civil actions are settled before a trial to forgo the cost of litigation or are dismissed for lack of evidence. An average claim will cost a municipality investigative time and defense expenses. Most major cities have a department of law that deals with tort actions, while state entities are indemnified by the office of the attorney general. Smaller towns and villages will have an attorney on retainer. In successful actions by a plaintiff, damages are paid by an insurance company or directly from the municipality's operating budget. Sad to say, many municipalities may have to borrow money through the issuance of bonds to pay for civil damages.

In certain civil rights cases or state criminal cases, the individual officer may also be sued if his or her actions are found to be outside the scope of police employment. Thus it is important in risk management exercises to explore the scope of indemnification for agency personnel. The risk manager then reviews those operations that are potential grounds for civil action and recommends corrective actions. This involves a review of policies and practices undertaken by the department that present the most liability exposure.

Short-Range Operational/Tactical Plans

Up to this point, we have been examining planning as a long-range endeavor. Of the types discussed, fiscal planning comes closest to short-range planning in that immediate needs in the fiscal year are normally analyzed in terms of function and performance. However, for long-range planning to work, specific objectives and even orders need to be created to carry out the plan. Long-range plans also need feedback-evaluation systems that can be used to modify the plan as it is operationally carried out.

OPERATIONAL PLAN   Long-range planning, including fiscal planning, sets the basic principles and the context for short-range **operational planning**. To carry out any planning, specific procedures have to be drawn up and implemented. Operational plans control the day-to-day activity of the police organization in a uniform manner. Specific procedures have to be created to carry out police duties in a predictable manner so that there can be accountability and consistency:

1. *The duty manual.* A major example of an operational plan, although many police chief executives do not recognize it as such, is the standard police duty manual. The duty manual creates SOPs for the department, including job descriptions and authority relationships. Specifics, such as procedures concerning the use of deadly force, may be a combination of law and operational procedures created in a standard order by the police agency. However, the list of operational procedures includes virtually every operation of the police agency (patrol procedure, evidence flow, civil emergencies, lineup procedures, and so on). Although often codified in a duty manual, operational procedures are changed according to condition. Thus, the duty manual is supplemented by both temporary operating procedures (TOPs) and SOPs. If these two supplementary procedures are in place, they may become part of the duty manual. However, one problem with this type of procedure is in keeping the SOPs and TOPs to a minimum so that the duty manual is a useful document. Another problem is to have the duty manual be comprehensive enough to cover operations but not so bulky that it loses its utility.

2. *Patrol planning.* Another major example of an operational plan and one that dominates a department is a **patrol allocation plan**. The overwhelming majority of resources in a police agency are devoted to patrol. Table 14-2 shows the general trends that have occurred in patrol planning through a comparison of traditional and recent plans. Items in the traditional categories really require no planning; the chief simply divides the patrol force into three shifts and maps out patrol zones based on the geography of the municipality and some personal rule of thumb. Plans reviewed by Levine and McEwen (1985: 9) involve obtaining activity data. Patrol personnel and vehicles are allocated according to calls for service, which include both service and crime incident responses.

PATROL STAFFING MODEL   There are a number of patrol planning models that are used in the United States. One developed by the International Association of Chiefs of Police involves measuring calls for service to determine the number of patrol posts and staff needed to fill these posts. This is done according to the following steps (McDougall, 1992):

1. The total calls for service for each tour of duty are obtained for one year (12 months).
2. The 12-month total is multiplied by the average time required to respond to a call for service and to complete the preliminary investigation. This provides the number of

TABLE 14-2	Trends in Patrol Planning	

Traditional	Recent
Equal staffing on three shifts	Staffing proportional to workload
	Overlapping shifts for extra coverage during peak demand periods
Little emphasis on scheduling	Overlapping and delayed shifts implemented
	Development of models to guide scheduling decisions
Enough patrol units available to provide an immediate mobile response to all calls for service	Enough patrol units available to provide an immediate mobile response to emergency calls for service
	Diverting calls for service to telephone reporting units, queuing calls for delayed response, setting appointments for taking reports, referring calls to other agencies
Time not spent on calls for service largely devoted to unstructured, random patrol (preventive patrol)	Time not spent on calls for service devoted to both routine patrol and directed patrol
	Directed patrol assignments planned in response to problems identified through crime analysis
Minimal analysis of patrol operations	Increased use of data processing for analysis
	Routine monitoring of reports generated for management
	Recognition of the integrated relationship of patrol with other police functions and inclusion of representatives from such functions in decisions that affect patrol

Source: Margaret J. Levine and J. Thomas McEwen. *Patrol Deployment*. Washington, D.C.: U.S. Department of Justice, 1985.

hours per year spent in handling calls for service. Previous studies show that the average time required to investigate adequately at the preliminary level by members of a patrol force is 45 minutes (0.75 hour). Note that we are focusing on patrol response and not follow-up investigations by detectives as a major crime will take hundreds of hours before it is "cleared."

3. The hours per year in calls for service are multiplied by 3. This is a "buffer" factor to account for the time spent on preventive patrol, inspectional services, vehicle servicing, and personal needs. This gives total patrol hours.

4. The total hours are divided by 2,920, the number of hours necessary to staff one post on one eight-hour shift for one year (8 hours × 365 = 2,920). The quotient equals the minimum number of patrol posts needed for the particular tour of duty.

This model was used to review staffing for a small police department. The first step was to determine the number of patrol posts, which is outlined in Table 14-3. What is done is to review the total number of calls for services by each shift. In general, shifts during the evening

TABLE 14-3 Determining Patrol Posts for a Police Department

Shift Hours	Actual Calls for Service
7 A.M.–3 P.M.	2,850
3 P.M.–11 P.M.	4,100
11 P.M.–7 A.M.	2,445

Next, these numbers were multiplied by 0.75 (75 minutes) to get the average time expended by officers on a call over the year.

Shift Hours	Approximate Time Expended
7 A.M.–3 P.M.	2,137.5
3 P.M.–11 P.M.	3,075
11 P.M.–7 A.M.	1,751,833.75

These figures are converted to include a buffer and time for routine patrol activity (×3).

Shift Hours	Projected Time Expended
7 A.M.–3 P.M.	6,412.5 hours/year
3 P.M.–11 P.M.	9,225 hours/year
11 P.M.–7 A.M.	5,501.25 hours/year

These numbers are then divided by 2,920, or the total hours needed to fill an eight-hour post for one year (356 × 8 = 2,920).

Shift Hours	Post Needed
7 A.M.–3 P.M.	2.19
3 P.M.–11 P.M.	3.14
11 P.M.–7 A.M.	1.88

to early morning hours generate the most calls because of the general rise of crime activity, heavy traffic, and human events. As the unit of analysis, a "call for service" can range from an actual reported crime to a request to check on the welfare of a person. Calls for service can be self-initiated such as issuing traffic summons or stopping a crime in progress. Thus it is important to have data generated by the communications unit, which can track calls for every shift throughout the year.

Once posts have been determined by the mathematic steps outlined in the figures, the next step is to obtain the number of personnel to staff these posts. Because of regular days off, sick days, holidays, personal leave, and other factors, an assignment availability factor must be determined. This is obtained by subtracting the number of "average hours off" from 2,920 hours, which is the total number of hours needed to cover a shift. Table 14-4 calculates the assignment/availability factor for this police department. As a planning tool, some calculations have to be made for "set posts" where an officer will normally be stationed for an eight-hour tour. These assignments might include court and airport security and are not based on calls for service but on an activity need. In urban populations or in hospital or campus environments, it may be that

TABLE 14-4	Determining Assignment/Availability Factor		
Factor	**Number of Days × 8**	**=**	**Hours Off**
Regular days off	104	=	832
Vacation	26	=	208
Personal leave	5	=	40
Sick/injury	15	=	120
Holidays	12	=	96.00
Court time	2	=	16
Training	12	=	96
Other	1	=	8
Total	177		1,416 average hours off

Hours in Staff-Year	**Average Hours Off**		**Hours Available**
2,920	− 1,416	=	1,504

Total Hours in a Staff-Year	**Hours Available**		**Assignment/Availability Factor**
2,920	÷ 1,504	=	1.94

Source: Theodore E. McDougall. *A Study of Police Operations at the SUNY Cobleskill Campus.* Albany, N.Y.: Bureau for Municipal Police, 1992.

several patrol personnel are allotted to one patrol post simply because of the high number of people at certain times of the day.

There are a number of questions that need to be raised when undertaking this analysis to take into account local needs. For example, in villages and towns, it might be that 30 minutes would be the average time to deal with a call for service that starts when the patrol unit is dispatched to the time it is clear for another call. Departments in rural areas may need to create another patrol post for safety reasons to provide a reasonable response time and for backup in emergency situations. Departments engaged in community policing activities might find that officer presentations and working with special populations will be difficult to calculate based on a number of time factors that go into these efforts.

The figure of 1,416 is the number of hours a typical officer is away from duty each year. This is subtracted from 2,920 hours to produce an hours-available figure of 1,504. An assignment/ availability factor is obtained by dividing the hours-available figure of 1,504 hours into 2,920 hours, which creates a factor of 1.94, the number of personnel needed to fill each post. Table 14-5 applied this factor to determine staffing for this department, which was found to need 14 people.

Although on paper this department may need 14 members from data calculations, the actual level of staffing is going to be based on a number of factors; the most important being budget. If the department is not fully funded, or has been forced to take either reductions or no hiring for replacement officers who have left for other positions or retirement, then understaffing will remain an issue. Tough choices have to be made to do more with less or to come up with innovative ways to get the job done through either non-sworn personnel for non-law enforcement tasks or through joint services with other departments in the area.

TABLE 14-5	Recommended Staffing for a Small Police Department				
Post	7 A.M.–3 P.M.	3 P.M.–11 P.M.	11 P.M.–7 A.M.	Raw Score	Staff Needed
Chief[a]	1.00	—	—	1.00	1
Lieutenant		1.00	1.00	2.00	2
Post #1	1.94	1.94	1.94	5.82	6
Post #2	1.94	1.94	—	3.88	4
Secretary	1.00	—	—	1.00	1
				Total =	14

Note: Supervisory ranks and administrative personnel are usually given a value of one. If the department wanted to include a sargeant rank for patrol supervision at all times, then it would include the 1.94. For communications personnel, a different calculation may be employed as they may not have the same number of hours for training and court activities.

THE MYTH OF RAPID RESPONSE   Although response time is part of the planning model, a word of caution must be exercised. Police managers have often felt that if their response was two minutes or less to service calls, this was a mark of an efficient department. The opposite may well be true. A two-minute response to every service call may mean that the patrol force is not properly distributed. Response is important to emergencies and crimes in progress. For most other service calls, the two-minute response is normally irrelevant.

There were a number of studies critical of response time in the 1970s (Bercal, 1970; Reiss, 1971; Meyer, 1976; Maxfield, 1979). Less than 20 percent of service calls are related to criminal matters, and emergency calls account for less than 15 percent of all service calls. Even in relation to crime, normally too much time elapses from the time the crime is committed and to when the police are called. Cohen and McEwen (1984: 4) report that "research [Farmer, 1981; Spelman and Brown, 1981] showed that police response time had no effect on the chances of on-scene arrest in 70 to 85 percent of serious crime cases." Are citizens dissatisfied with slower response time? The answer is that citizens are dissatisfied only if they expect rapid response time. However, "if callers were told to expect a delay, their satisfaction did not significantly decrease if response time was slower" (Cohen and McEwen, 1984: 4).

Response time may be helpful for emergencies and a few cases of crimes in progress; overall, departments should be careful not to place too much emphasis on providing rapid response for all service calls. Complaint clerks who take calls for service and dispatchers who dispatch the vehicles need specialized training. This includes training in telephone courtesy, screening, and referrals to other agencies. All agencies need to use a priority classification dispatching system.

The operational plans serve as control mechanisms for management by providing guidelines for employees, both civilian and uniformed. Operational plans give supervisors a means of evaluating personnel in relation to specific duties that are clearly defined and in writing. Evaluation and discipline can take place only in the light of written guidelines that both supervisory personnel and line officers understand. They have to be clearly stated, unambiguous in content, and practical enough to be carried out daily. They also have to have internal consistency and be in line with the long-range goals of the department, including the philosophy of social utility and law enforcement that is demanded by the community in which the police agency is located.

CONTINGENCY PLANS   **Contingency plans** are made for specific events and occurrences but are not part of the daily duties of police department personnel. This type of planning demands some specific detail in terms of procedures, but because of changing conditions in the field, it often demands more flexibility than do other types of planning. There are two major types of contingency plans:

1. *Tactical plans.* These are plans for major events, such as crowd control at athletic events and VIP escorts.
2. *Emergency plans.* These are plans for general situations with the specifics to be inserted when the emergency occurs. When done in conjunction with other agencies, this type of planning is often termed *planning for emergency mobilization.*

Tactical plans are formulated based on what is expected to take place. A recurrent event is one that is expected to happen again; however, the time and place of the event may not be known. Tactical plans are made for mundane events (parades, political rallies) as well as for natural disasters (blizzards, floods).

Emergencies come and go, and no one can predict when they will strike. However, contingency plans offer a general framework for action. Emergency planning has been considered by some police managers as a type of tactical plan for unusual occurrences and crisis situations.

EMERGENCY MOBILIZATIONS AND THE FEMA MODEL   **Emergency mobilizations** are the response by local, state, and federal authorities to natural disasters, riots, civilian disorders, terrorism, and large events that disrupt the normal flow of commerce and life in a community or region. The police department is one important group that has to be organized as part of an overall plan for mobilization. This generally calls for specific contingency planning under the auspices of a governmental entity or a regional emergency authority, such as a state or county emergency planning commission.

To develop a reasonable plan for emergency and crisis management, departments, in concert with other agencies, should focus on overall planning efforts to four specific crisis or emergency levels:

1. *Crisis intervention.* An emergency situation is localized to one person or a small group of people.
2. *Community emergency.* An emergency affects a community and involves disruption of services caused by fire, large crowds, criminal event, or weather.
3. *Regional emergency.* An emergency is larger in scope and caused by human or environmental factors.
4. *Major emergency.* An emergency affects a state or an entire region, such as storms, nuclear accidents, and civil disturbances.

A planning model developed by the Federal Emergency Management Agency (FEMA) calls for the following planning strategy for dealing with these emergencies (FEMA, 2003):

Step 1: Establish a Planning Team

Form the team

Establish authority from the chief executive

Issue a mission statement

Establish a schedule and budget

Step 2: Analyze Capabilities and Hazards

Where do you stand right now?

Review internal plans and policies

Meet with all "stakeholders" and agencies: fire, EMS, Haz-mat

Identify codes and regulations

Identify critical services and operations

Identify resources and capabilities

Conduct a hazard analysis

List potential emergencies (both natural and human made)

Estimate probability

Assess the potential human impact

Assess the potential property and business impact

Assess the potential business impact

Assess internal and external resources

Address terrorist situations

Step 3: Develop the Plan

List the plan components

Executive summary

Emergency management team identification

Emergency response assignments and call-up

Functional annexes for operational responses

Map out the development process

Identify challenges, and prioritize activities

Write the plan

Establish a training schedule

Continue to coordinate with outside organizations

Review, conduct training, and test the plan

Step 4: Implement the Plan

Integrate the plan into agency operations, and conduct training

Distribute the plan

Conduct training activities

Evaluate and modify the plan

Further information on emergency response planning can be found at FEMA's Web site at fema.gov. Those interested in this important field can take self-paced certification courses offered by FEMA and the Department of Homeland Security. In light of the tragic events in New Orleans and the Gulf Coast area in the fall of 2005, you may also wish to see if your community has an emergency response plan.

National Incident Management System (NIMS)

The attacks of September 11, 2001, on the World Trade Center and the Pentagon illustrated the problems that occur in an emergency response to a major disaster in terms of command, coordination, and communications. As discussed in Chapter 3 (in the section on managing in chaos) and further discussed in the 9/11 Commission Report (National Commission on Terrorist Attacks Upon the United States, 2004), there needs to be a unified response by fire, police, and emergency medical units, especially when an event becomes multiagency or multijurisdictional. On February 23, 2003, President Bush issued an executive order to the Secretary of Homeland Security to develop a national response plan.

The backbone of such a system had already been created by a program called Incident Command System (ICS), which was used by the U.S. Forest Service and many California agencies for fighting forest fires. Variations of ICS were already employed by many police and fire agencies for dealing with major emergencies, including weather catastrophes, chemical spills, fires, major crimes. In March 2004, NIMS was adopted by the Department of Homeland Security, which created a national standard for response, planning, training, and equipment needs for local, regional, and national disasters (Office of Homeland Security, 2009). Updated executive orders for national command and control systems were signed in March 1996 and September 2006 (Figure 14-1).

The core of NIMS centers on the following functions:

Preparedness—this means that government and interested private sector organizations must assess and prepare to deal with major emergencies.

Resource Management—includes identifying, storing, and tracking the personnel, equipment, and related supplies for eventual deployment in a major emergency.

Command and Management—the three parts of command and management are found in the Incident Command System (ICS), Multiagency Coordination System, and Public Information.

Management and Maintenance—the creation of standards, credentialing, and training are undertaken by the National Integration Center and the Incident Management Systems Integration Division under the FEMA.

An important factor for NIMS is the ICS, which consists of the following components:

1. *Command.* The command function for an incident may consist of one person who is the incident commander and operates from a command post. Unified command occurs when there are different agencies responding to an event. The goal here is to overcome duplication of effort, share information, and develop a common set of goals to deal with an incident. Each agency head will be located in the command post. In major events that cross state boundaries, there may be an area commander who oversees separate commands by state or region.

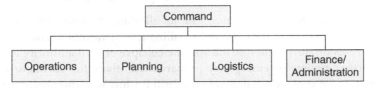

FIGURE 14-1 Incident command system: command staff and general staff. *Source:* Department of Homeland Security (2004). National Incident Management System. Web posted at dhs.gov. Accessed on September 6, 2005.

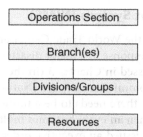

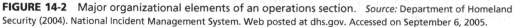

FIGURE 14-2 Major organizational elements of an operations section. *Source:* Department of Homeland Security (2004). National Incident Management System. Web posted at dhs.gov. Accessed on September 6, 2005.

Included in the command function are the public information officer (PIO), a safety officer, and a liaison officer to deal with secondary agencies. In most cases, the PIO conducts news briefings and also reports to the command post any questions and information regarding the incident. The safety officer basically sits on the sidelines and evaluates how the event is going and whether a course of action will endanger personnel. For example, in a hazardous condition, various chemicals may be present, and the safety officer ensures that operations personnel have the correct equipment.

2. *Operations.* This area coordinates first responders to deal with a situation and save lives and property. The operations section follows a deployment model because in a wide-area emergency, various branches may have to be established because of geographic conditions (see Figure 14-2).

3. *Planning.* This section presents information and intelligence gained from any sources. Planning functions for NIMS include obtaining information on the situation, possible resources, and technical support and preparing documentation for later evaluation. Planning may also include air operations, vehicle traffic, evacuation of civilians, waste management, decontamination, and investigative and evidence recovery.

4. *Logistics.* This section is responsible for locating and transporting personnel, communications, and medical and safety equipment.

5. *Finance and administration.* This section is often overlooked but is terribly important. This group keeps cost estimates and records related to any fiscal expenditure. It also keeps documentation for eventual billing purposes for federal or state aid or private recovery efforts. For example, FEMA will compensate agencies for personnel and equipment costs in a major disaster; however, the agency requires a detailed expenditures report as part of the application.

6. *Information and intelligence.* This function has been added to the model since March 2004. As discussed in Chapter 8, intelligence is the process of obtaining various bits of information and making some sense of them. Depending on the nature of the incident, information and intelligence may be assigned to planning or directly to command.

It must be emphasized that planning will not alleviate crisis situations unless there are adequate resources, drills, preparations, and a willingness of various agencies to share ideas. No doubt the events of Hurricane Katrina and the collapse of civil authority in New Orleans will lead to further review of emergency preparedness plans for all major cities, as will responses seen as more successful, such as to the 2013 Boston Marathon bombings. One of the critical components of the four-pronged Emergency Management wheel: Planning, Response, Recovery, and Mitigation, is mitigation, where emergency response personnel review the most recent response for lessons learned—both good and bad. The goal of mitigation is to first try to avoid a similar emergency from ever happening again, and if it does, to make its effect less impacting.

POLICE RESPONSE TO SPECIAL POPULATIONS   Police have been called for assistance with special populations, such as the public inebriate, the mentally ill, and the homeless. However, these are not police problems but problems that really demand a human services solution. Deinstitutionalization of the mentally ill and alcoholics has left many of these people on the street, often without adequate housing. It makes sense for police to use the human service agency network when it is available. However, **networking** cannot be done at random. Police managers need to do the following (Finn and Sullivan, 1987: 6):

1. Develop a formal agreement to collaborate—preferably a written document that commits each group to the partnership.
2. Describe the specific activities in the agreements that each party in the network will undertake.
3. Sooner or later involve every important agency and facility that provides emergency services to the target population.
4. Make sure that the arrangements benefit every participant.

Los Angeles has created a special relationship with the county department of mental health, while the Boston police work with the Pine Street Inn, which serves 3,000–4,000 homeless each year, and San Diego has a seven-minute dropoff for public inebriates at an inebriate reception center. The sheriff in Washtenaw County, Michigan, has developed a two-tier approach to assisting the mentally ill. The executive directors of the sheriff's department, community mental health department, community services agency, county planning department, department of social services, public health department, and the United Way formed a policy team. At the same time, midlevel managers from these agencies formed an operational team to oversee day-to-day operations.

These are just a few examples. Police agency networking can range from just one agency to multiple agency agreements. The benefits of the approach are many, as shown in Table 14-6.

TABLE 14-6 Benefits of Networking	
For Law Enforcement	**For the Social Service System**
Saves time by reducing or eliminating the need to	*Saves time* by reducing or eliminating the need to
Stabilize the situation at the scene	Evaluate, treat, or transfer inappropriate referrals
"Shop" for an available facility	
Wait at the facility	
Book the individual	
Make repeat runs for the same individual	
Testify in court	
Reduces danger because	*Reduces danger* because
Trained staff take over volatile situations	Officers come quickly to help in situations involving violence in the facility or in a home

(continued)

TABLE 14-6	Benefits of Networking (*continued*)	
For Law Enforcement	**For the Social Service System**
Social workers warn officers about potentially dangerous cases	
Officers receive training in handling problem individuals	
Increases job satisfaction because	*Improves job performance* because
Fewer repeat cases are handled	Clients are referred to facilities that have treated them before
Feedback on case results is provided. Positive relationships with social service workers develop	Trained officers testify at commitment hearings
Homicides involving problem individuals and jail suicides are reduced	Agency's image in the community improves
Municipal police department working relationships improve with jail officials concerned about overcrowding	Positive relationships develop with law enforcement officers
Dispositions are available that are more appropriate than jail or doing nothing	Client contact with criminal justice system is reduced
For Local Government Officials	
Increases political support because	
Constituents are pleased to see a serious community problem addressed	
Businesspeople are pleased to have the downtown made more attractive to customers	
Embarrassing incidents are less likely to occur	
Prevents political crises and unexpected expenses because	
Chances of a lawsuit are reduced	
Jail overcrowding is alleviated	

Source: Peter Finn and Monique Sullivan. *Police Response to Special Populations.* Washington, D.C.: National Institute of Justice, 1987, p. 7.

POLICING TERRORISM: PROACTIVE HOMELAND SECURITY

The object of **terrorism** is to disrupt a community and implant fear in order to advance a political, social, or religious agenda. Terrorists are radical ethnic, religious, or political ideologues. Examples are anarchists, Marxists, racist hate groups, anti-Semitic groups, ethnic and tribal groups, extreme nationalists, ecoterrorists, political extremists, and religious fanatics. In 1789, Robespierre used the terror of public executions by "Madame Guillotine" during the French Revolution to instill terror, and in 2001, Osama bin Laden used bombings to attack the United States for political and religious reasons.

Proactive planning is the best way to contain a terrorist agenda. Proactive police managers plan ahead, anticipate events, and act to prevent terror and crime. This approach calms the local community and lets the world know that the elected and appointed representatives of the citizens are in charge.

Proactive police departments need to deal with terrorism in four specific stages:

1. Preventing terrorist acts through planning, investigation, and the gathering and sharing of local, regional, and national intelligence
2. Handling terrorist acts through cooperation with and coordination of local, regional, and national agencies with a planned agenda of activity
3. Dealing with the aftermath of a terrorist act, including the coordination of posttrauma human service, physical reconstruction, and the uplift of the community in an integrated effort
4. Learning from previous terrorist acts and working with community groups to prevent another—the essence of the proactive approach

For American law enforcement, terrorist groups fall into two main categories:

1. *Domestic groups.* The American terrorist groups are small in number but occasionally extremely violent in behavior. The 400-lb bomb that destroyed the Murrah Federal Building in Oklahoma City in 1995 was set off by members of the Michigan Militia. Domestic militia and hate groups have to be monitored by state and local police agencies.
2. *Overseas political/religious groups.* At the moment, the overseas terrorist groups that affect the United States are mainly anti-American Muslim fundamentalists with international support. The 1993 and September 11, 2001, bombings of the World Trade Center in New York City are the most dramatic examples of their actions. Domestic concerns are heavily focused on Islamic splinter groups and "lone wolves," or individuals acting on their own accord after being inspired by others or events.

Criminal Groups versus Terrorist Groups

Terrorists are members of groups who use planned violence for their own ends. Some terrorist networks work with domestic and cross-national organized crime groups and commit crimes for money, but their objectives are ideological rather than motivated by profit. Cross-national organized crime groups launder money and sell arms and other support items to terrorist groups (Grennan et al., 2000; Lyman and Potter, 2000).

The "Black Hand" was a Sicilian immigrant group that terrorized small businesses in the early twentieth century to extort money. They beat people up, torched businesses, and poured acid on store goods. In the 1990s, the Dominican Republic C&C gang controlled a whole neighborhood in the Mott Haven section of the Bronx in New York City. The gang extorted money from drug dealers by charging them "rent" (Grennan et al., 2000). Asian gangs have traditionally extorted money from small businesses in Chinatowns throughout the United States. This is all done for money. When Willy Sutton was asked why he robbed banks, he explained that that's where the money is. Extortionists may use terror to obtain money, but they have no ideological agenda.

In contrast, when the Taliban worked its lucrative heroin business, the money was used to buy arms and to support fundamentalist Muslim terrorist groups in the Central Asian states of the former Soviet Union. When Al Qaeda, Hamas, and Hezbollah looted Muslim charities, the money was funneled to terrorist activities (Wechsler, 2002). In the 1980s, a racist, anti-Semitic hate group called the Order robbed two armored trucks, netting $1.3 million. They used the money to finance various terrorist activities, including burning a synagogue, assaulting homosexuals, and killing a Jewish talk show host, Alan Berg. They were hunted down by the FBI, which employed an informant, among other tactics (Zellner, 1995). The group's leader, Jay Matthews, was killed in a shootout. Most of the other members are now in prison. It took good police work to do this, and it was a police job, not a military effort. The groups that made up the membership of this violent band reads like a who's who of hate groups in the 1980s: Aryan Nation, Aryan Brotherhood, National Alliance, Ku Klux Klan (KKK), and the Covenant, Sword and Arm of the Lord (CSA).

The same tactics of intelligence gathering and use of informants are used for investigating organized criminal groups and terrorist groups. Up to now, the FBI has been a reactive agency that investigates criminal organizations after a terrorist act or crime has been committed. The FBI has been criticized for refusing to share information with local police agencies. Historically, the FBI has done a fine job of intelligence investigation and prosecution of a few major organized crime figures. The bureau is now targeting new cross-national organized crime and terrorist groups that exist in the United States. The Central Intelligence Agency (CIA), set up to coordinate foreign intelligence, has never really cooperated with any police agency in the United States, even when the criminal or terrorist activity was of foreign origin. As discussed in Chapter 13, 9/11 changed how federal, state, and local law enforcement address international terrorism.

Hate Groups and Militias in the United States

Hate groups are intensely biased against specific groups of people based on their race, ethnicity, religion, disability, or sexual orientation. They use violent, bigoted language against these groups and have resorted to criminal violence, which includes destroying property and human lives. Immigrants have historically been a focus of domestic hate groups. Closely related are militia groups who own firearms and practice military techniques.

Floyd Cochran, a spokesman, recruiter, and strategist for Aryan Nation, said in 1993 that there are "500 card-holding members, from Ku Klux Klan, Nazi skin heads, 366 hate web sites, 1,200 jailed members, 40,000 active members among all white supremacy groups and 200,000 people that order literature which supports the Aryan Nation" (Cochran, 1993). Not much has changed. The Southern Poverty Law Center, which sponsors Klanwatch and Hate Watch, has a Web site that provides a map of the location of hate groups and reports on militia groups throughout the United States at splcenter.org. The Center reports that militias are on the rise because of the economy, illegal immigration, and the election of an African American president (2009).

Proactive police intelligence units in local, state, and federal police agencies can easily access this information, locate and infiltrate local hate groups, and keep track of them. Police agencies that refuse to do this are simply irresponsible. We can no longer afford to ignore the responsibility of national and local police agencies to share intelligence.

Domestic hate groups are always communicating and organizing. Hate groups also join with militia and survivalist groups. The militia and survivalist groups have hundreds, possibly thousands, of hidden weapons and ammunition. Nobody knows their real membership numbers. The worldwide Internet is a major means of recruiting and advertising hate groups in the United States. Lee and Leets (2002) surveyed adolescents on the effect of hate Web sites and concluded that they were effective in getting their hate message across but that the effect was short-lived. The Boston Police Department has a special hate crime unit enforcing Massachusetts's hate crime laws.

Proactive Policies for Combating Terrorism

1. National authorities must share terrorism intelligence with state and local police agencies whenever there is a local credible threat. The CIA was originally created to coordinate and be a central gathering point for all the federal intelligence agencies. It should do what it was created to do. Homeland security needs the funds and authority to coordinate terrorism intelligence. The focus should be on terrorist attacks on America and on American assets at

home and abroad. The FBI and the CIA need to give up their decades-long feuding and coordinate their intelligence on terrorism. The FBI also needs to assist and share intelligence with state and local police.

State offices of antiterrorism are currently spending millions to establish, among other needs, a counterterrorism network that will transmit intelligence data from the state and federal level to local police departments. In New York State, for example, computers transmit filtered data—from suspect profiles through bioterrorism threats—to each of the state's 543 police agencies (Reaves, 2007). The objective is to involve local police agencies in preventing future terrorism and create a standardized warning system that will work all the way down to the beat cop. Maryland is currently establishing a statewide emergency response communications system to facilitate early warning and integration of police communications ("NYS Office Takes the Point against Terror," 2002: 11).

2. Local police must be given the authority to deal with foreign-based terrorist threats within their jurisdiction. Police outside of Tallahassee, Florida, stopped a rental truck full of 26 men and women who did not speak English and had no documentation. They called federal immigration officials, but none showed up. The illegal immigrants had to be let go. Florida has proposed that 35 local and state police officers who operate on antiterrorism teams be given federal training by the U.S. Immigration and Naturalization Service and the authority to arrest illegal immigrants. Business and Hispanic interest groups that wish to protect illegal immigration to the United States are opposing this approach ("Give Us Your Tired," 2002: 1, 14).

3. An office of intelligence must be created in every major police agency. It should also coordinate the protection of major terrorist targets. Local and state police budgets will have to be part of the federal homeland defense funding and federal training resources.

There also needs to be intense coordination between public and private police. Private police protect major corporate properties and executive personnel, but they have no powers to arrest. Professional standards created by state law and enforced by state agents have to be in place.

Public police will also have to coordinate with the National Guard and the armed forces in protecting national monuments, bridges, reservoirs, nuclear energy units, airports, tunnels, ports, and power grids. This is already being done in every modern industrial country in the world. With overtime and the need for specially trained units and extra personnel, new funding may be required, such as the home security bond California is proposing. The National Conference of Mayors has estimated that additional security will cost municipalities $2.1 billion in 2002 ("From Coast to Coast," 2002: 11).

4. Proactive police defensive and offensive coordination and plans for terrorist attacks have to be in place, and private and public agencies should be at the same or better level as civil defense in time of war. Much of this civil defense, critical incident, and disaster planning is already in place. Now local and regional police agencies and police coordinating bodies will have to look at these plans in the light of a terrorist attack, from blowing up buildings to bioterrorism. FEMA is the lead agency in times of widespread natural disaster and would normally be the federal agency to help coordinate any crisis. The FBI has a Nuclear Incident Contingency Plan and a Chemical/Biological Contingency Plan. These plans need to be shared with other police agencies. The armed forces, including the Reserves and the National Guard, have had contingency plans since 1998 for dealing with weapons of mass destruction and the subsequent cleanup. Biological, radiological, and chemical defense preparedness has been a priority of the armed forces for many years and can be of great help in civilian and police planning and coordination.

Critical Infrastructure Assessment and Protection

Protection of the community **infrastructure** should be part of the planning agenda for every police department. Critical infrastructure includes bridges, power lines, and electric generation plants, including nuclear plants. Police responsibility extends to the protection of banking, finance, energy, transportation, vital human services, and physical assets.

James K. Kallstrom (2002), a special adviser to a state governor on counterterrorism immediately following 9/11, recommended a "prevention, detection, response, and recovery" approach when considering a terrorist attack. He is especially concerned with a cyberattack and has set up a cybersecurity task force, which includes experts from federal and state governments, universities, and private corporations and businesses. It is establishing a list of private vendors to call on in case of a cyberattack.

Planners are concerned with "catastrophic loss of life, disruption of essential services, and incapacitation/destruction of critical infrastructure." The worst-case scenarios being considered are the following:

1. The malfunction of air traffic control equipment
2. The circulation of poisonous gas through the heating and air-conditioning systems of a large office complex
3. Interruption in 911 telephone communications
4. Electrical blackouts
5. The destruction of power dams, causing major flooding and endangering thousands
6. The disruption of financial markets

Local police departments, in cooperation with other government agencies, need to do a survey of critical infrastructure within their jurisdiction and consider whether they have the necessary expertise and resources to protect this infrastructure. Law enforcement departments cannot do everything and be everywhere. Risk assessment, the identifying of crucial assets, and priority planning focus scarce resources on the essentials. The questions to be answered in this police emergency planning process are the following:

1. What are the major elements of the infrastructure in the local community?
2. What private and public protection is needed for this infrastructure under various levels of threat?
3. What are the most essential and important targets to the community, and how do we prioritize them?
4. What private and public assets are available to protect this infrastructure, and how do we mobilize these assets?

Proactive planning will allow law enforcement to focus its scarce resources to maximize their efficient use for public protection.

Summary: Police Planning for Terrorism

In some ways, it is business as usual in planning for domestic and cross-national organized crime and drug syndicate investigations. Civil defense and natural preparedness planning should be a normal part of police planning.

In other ways, after September 11, 2001, proactive policing is an Orwellian "brave new world." Militia and hate group members blow up a federal building and go on killing rampages, killing even children. Muslim terrorist groups blow up major New York City buildings and the Pentagon after learning to fly airplanes and living in America. Money to fund terrorism comes from our "allies" in the Middle East and from "charities," some of which are located in the United States. We worry about our privacy and civil liberties in this post-9/11 world, but we don't want our friends and families killed by these fanatics who come to our towns and cities.

To protect both our civil liberties and our nation from terrorism, we must have calm, careful, proactive police planning, the elimination of interagency rivalries, and further integration of services. Coordination and communication will give the American civilian police forces a way of professionally and democratically protecting our local community from future terrorist acts.

COMPSTAT AS A PROACTIVE PLANNING TOOL: A REENGINEERING, DATA-DRIVEN APPROACH

In Chapter 7, **Compstat** is presented as a management tool for reducing crime. Compstat is also a strong technological innovation because of its "on-time" data retrieval of crime statistics, its geographic mapping of neighborhood crime data, its use in operational planning, and the results-oriented evaluation of police supervisors. Vincent Henry, who was the major developer and operational planner for Compstat, discusses in his book, *The Compstat Paradigm* (2002), how this planning took place.

In 1994, Compstat and reengineering were used to turn the New York City Police Department around. Focus groups and a general survey of police officers showed what the officers thought important and what they thought the management thought important. The major revolution was creating goals to match what the officers wanted as goals for the department (Henry, 2002: 201):

Goals Officers Considered Most Important to Management	**Goals Officers Considered Most Important to Themselves**
1. Write tickets	1. Reduce crime, disorder, and fear
2. Hold down overtime	2. Make gun arrests
3. Stay out of trouble	3. Provide police services to those who request them
4. Respond quickly to radio calls	4. Gain public confidence in police integrity
5. Report police corruption	5. Arrest drug dealers
6. Treat supervisors with deference	6. Correct quality-of-life conditions
7. Reduce crime, disorder, and fear	7. Stay out of trouble

Ten crime-control and quality-of-life strategies were developed over the years. The following revisions apply those strategies to a more general audience (Henry, 2002: 227–29):

1. *Get guns off the streets.* In New York, this included training and resources to investigate and identify gun traffickers.
2. *Curb youth violence in the schools and on the streets.* Included school safety plans, increased number of youtth officers, and having patrol officers return truants to school. Planning data showed a significant relationship between truancy and delinquency.

3. ***Drive drug dealers out of the city.*** Increased patrol officer involvement in narcotic investigations, with the focus of the department on more midlevel and high-level drug deals and increased forfeiture of drug dealers' assets.

4. ***Break the cycle of domestic violence.*** Used databases to track violence and to intervene proactively, providing a proarrest policy along with cooperation with social services.

5. ***Reclaim public spaces.*** A "broken windows" quality-of-life approach, using loitering, public nuisance, and noise ordinances. Sound meters were distributed.

6. ***Reduce autorelated crime.*** Included sting operations of "chop shops" that dismantled autos, identification of license plates of stolen cars, and increased training and intelligence gathering.

7. ***Root out corruption and build integrity.*** Included the use of local commanders and took internal affairs out of dealing with petty complaints so that its focus would be on major corruption.

8. ***Reclaim the roads of the city.*** Established a traffic control unit to plan and analyze reasons for congestion and incidents and increased the response time of personnel.

9. ***Heighten courtesy, professionalism, and respect.*** Increased training and set performance goals and measures to evaluate how well the principles were practiced.

10. ***Bring fugitives to justice.*** Strengthened patrol officers' capacity to track down court absconders and warrant violators.

These goals would be useful for many police departments. Having the whole department involved in planning for these goals is part of the reengineering approach. In New York, the responsibility, authority, and resources for carrying out these policies were brought down to the supervisor's level, and the supervisors were evaluated using data from the Compstat computer program. Organizational lines were flattened, and the command structure was brought down to the borough level. In departments around the country, this would bring the flattened bureaucratic structure down to a multineighborhood and neighborhood level.

Jack Maple (1999: 246–47) demonstrated how Compstat works operationally once major planning has taken place. Operations at every level must be guided by the four steps of Compstat:

- Accurate and timely intelligence that is clearly communicated to all
- Rapid, concentrated, and synchronized deployment
- Effective tactics and strategies
- Relentless follow-up and assessment

Performance in relation to the four steps must become the subject of regular crime meetings at four different levels—between the executive corps and the field commanders, between the field commanders and their lieutenants, between lieutenants and sergeants, and, most significantly, between sergeants and their officers.

Henry (2002: 235) also describes the basic process of communication, information, accountability, and result. He says it can be used for organizational diagnosis, which we would consider as a planning tool (Henry, 2002: 229–30). In the basic form organizational diagnosis involves reviewing the entire structure of the agency, including operating policies and coming up with new approaches and solutions. In essence it is another form of reengineering discussed in Chapter 3.

As a planning tool, computer mapping combined with the principles of reengineering can redesign police departmental structures and operations. Besides crime data, traffic, housing, and demographic variables can be added to the basic Compstat program and be used for advanced forward city, county, and police planning.

Conclusion

Planning is an important tool that enables proactive police managers to anticipate events and, in some sense, respond. A number of definitions were offered regarding planning, which in essence consists of developing a method for achieving organizational goals.

As we noted, all police agencies, consciously or unconsciously, engage in planning. Planning is useful to the police organization in that it operationalizes rational decision-making procedures for organizational policies. It also assists in defining organizational roles for all members of the agency. Whether there is a formal planning unit or one officer or manager assigned to the planning task, planning involves disseminating information and assisting in the managerial decision–making process.

The planning process for our purposes consists of six functions: (1) recognizing and analyzing the problem; (2) setting objectives; (3) gathering data; (4) making a plan of attack; (5) getting the agreement of those involved in the plan; and (6) conducting an evaluation. Various types of plans were discussed.

Specific attention was devoted to fiscal planning. Three widely used budgets—line-item, PPBS,

and ZBB—were presented, and their strengths and weaknesses were analyzed.

The chapter examined some innovations in the planning process: (1) procedures to supplement the police budget, including donation programs, forfeiture, user fees, and fines; (2) a model for patrol planning: automated resource allocation; and (3) responses to special populations, such as the mentally ill, the homeless, and the public inebriate through networking with social service agencies.

We also looked at the myth of rapid response. This example showed the need to plan with specific goals in mind and not waste limited resources on responding to all service calls within two minutes. Rapid response should be limited to crimes in progress and emergencies. While the chapter emphasized long-range planning, we included short-range, contingency, and emergency mobilization planning, as they are also important to all police agencies.

The economic realities of the twenty-first century demand responsible fiscal and contingency planning. Expertise, anticipation of events, evaluation, and the responsible supervision of personnel are the traits that will characterize police managers of the future.

Questions for Review

1. What are the benefits of planning for police organizations?
2. List the duties of a planning officer or a planning unit.
3. What are the main steps of the planning process?
4. Discuss three types of plans.
5. What are the differences between long-range and short-range planning?
6. Why is budgeting an important part of the managerial process?
7. What are the main attributes of emergency mobilizations?
8. How do you plan proactively for terrorism?
9. How can Compstat be used as a planning tool?

Class Projects

1. Police budgets are public documents. Obtain from a local agency an operating budget for the past fiscal year, and answer the following questions:
   a. What portion of the budget is devoted to personnel costs (e.g., salaries, benefits, overtime), equipment, training, and miscellaneous items?
   b. What is the fiscal year for this department?
   c. Does this budget represent an increase or decrease in police costs compared with the budget for the year before? If a large increase or decrease is noted, in what areas did it occur? What do you suspect are the reasons for the increase or decrease?

2. Suppose the police department of your community has asked your class to help with the planning of a Fourth of July parade. According to the mayor, this will be the biggest parade ever. Considering the geographic variables in your community, prepare a plan to provide police coverage for this parade. Your instructor will supply the needed additional information (proposed number of marchers, units, general route). Your plan must take into account all factors related to police operations during the event and the costs for this coverage. Follow the guidelines in this chapter.

Web Works

The most ambitious reorganization of American policing took place with the creation of the Department of Homeland Security in 2002. The agency was formed to provide comprehensive protection and enforcement of federal laws related to the protection of the United States against crime and terrorism. Listed below are a number of sites that students may review for information on policing, homeland security, and emergency management. The main site is located at dhs.gov. Other links to agencies that are under Homeland Security include the following:

Bureau of Citizenship and Immigration Services	immigration.gov
Bureau of Customs and Border Protection	cpb.gov
Federal Emergency Management Agency	fema.gov
Federal Law Enforcement Training Center	fletc.gov
Federal Protective Service	gsa.gov
National Domestic Preparedness Office	ndpo.gov
Office of Domestic Preparedness	http://www.fema.gov/pdf/media/factsheets/2011/cdp.pdf
U.S. Secret Service	secretservice.gov

Further information on emergency response planning can be found at FEMA'S Web site. Those interested in this important field can take self-paced certification courses offered by FEMA and the Department of Homeland Security. In light of the tragic events that have occurred over these past years, you may also wish to see if your community has an emergency response plan.

References

Behan, Cornelius J. "The Accreditation Process." In James J. Fyfe, ed., *Police Practice in the '90s: Key Management Issues.* Washington, D.C.: International City Management Association, 1989.

Bercal, Thomas E. "Calls for Police Assistance: Consumer Demands for Public Service." *American Behavioral Scientist*, 13, no. 5/6 (May/June 1970), pp. 681–691.

Cochran, Floyd, "Hate Groups." *Appearance on Good Afternoon with Art Levy*. WCNY, Liverpool, NY, September 28, 1993.

Cohen, Marcia, and J. Thomas McEwen. "Handling Calls for Service: Alternatives to Traditional Policing," *NIF Reports*, no. 187 (1984), pp. 4–8.

Commission on Accreditation for Law Enforcement Agencies. *Standards for Law Enforcement Agencies.* Fairfax, Va.: Commission, 1984.

Curtis, George, and R. Bruce McBride. *Proactive Security Administration.* Upper Saddle River, N.J.: Prentice-Hall, 2005.

Farmer, Michael T., ed. *Differential Police Response Strategies.* Washington, D.C.: Police Executive Research Forum, 1981.

Federal Emergency Management Administration. *State and Local Guide 101: Guide for All Hazard Emergency Operations Planning.* Washington, D.C.: FEMA, 2003. Posted at fema.gov/rrr/gaheop.shtm. Accessed on March 15, 2003.

Finn, Peter, and Monique Sullivan. *Police Response to Special Populations.* Washington, D.C.: National Institute of Justice, 1987.

"From Coast to Coast, Anti-Terror Plans Take Shape." *Law Enforcement News,* February 28, 2002, p. 11.

"Give Us Your Tired, Your Poor. . . . Fla. Cops May Get Immigration Enforcement Powers." *Law Enforcement News,* March 15/31, 2002, pp. 1, 14.

Grennan, Sean, et al. *Gangs: An International Approach.* Upper Saddle River, N.J.: Prentice Hall, 2000.

Henry, Vincent. *The Compstat Paradigm.* Flushing, N.Y.: Looseleaf Publications, 2002.

Hudzik, John K., et al. *Criminal Justice Manpower Planning: An Overview.* Washington, D.C.: U.S. Government Printing Office, 1981.

Kallstrom, James. Statement to the Committee on Science, U.S. House of Representatives—Homeland Security, Utica, New York, June 24, 2002.

Kavanagh, S. *Zero-based Budgeting: Modern Experiences and Current Practices,* 2011. Retrieved from gfoa.org/downloads/GFOAZeroBasedBudgeting.pdf

King, John. Strategic Planning. Presentation at Executive Training Institute, International Association of Campus Law Enforcement Executives, Whittier, Calif., November 2004.

Lee, Elissa, and Laura Leets. "Persuasive Storytelling by Hate Groups Online." In Harvey W. Kushner, ed., *Cyberterrorism in the Twenty-First Century.* Thousand Oaks, Calif.: Sage, 2002.

Levine, Margaret J., and J. Thomas McEwen. *Patrol Deployment.* Washington, D.C.: U.S. Department of Justice, 1985.

Lewis, Verne B. "Toward a Theory of Budgeting." In Albert C. Hyde and Jay M. Shafritz, eds., *Government Budgeting: Theory, Process, Politics.* Oak Park, Ill.: Moore, 1978, pp. 221–235.

Lyman, Michael D., and Gary W. Potter. *Organized Crime,* 2nd ed. Upper Saddle River, N.J.: Prentice Hall, 2000.

Maple, Jack, with Chris Mitchell. *The Crime Fighter.* New York: Doubleday, 1999.

Maxfield, Michael G. *Discretion and the Delivery of Police Services: Demand, Client Characteristics and Street Level Bureaucrats in Two Cities.* Ann Arbor, Mich.: University Microfilms, 1979.

McDougall, Theodore E. *A Study of Police Operations at the SUNY Cobleskill Campus.* Albany, N.Y.: Bureau for Municipal Police, 1992.

Meadows, Robert J. "Legal Issues and Police." In Rosyln Muraskin and Albert R. Roberts, eds., *Visions for Change.* Upper Saddle River, N.J.: Prentice Hall, 1999, pp. 145–164.

Meyer, John C. "Empirical Analysis of Police Service Tasks: Antecedent for Management Planning." *Journal of Police Science and Administration,* 4, no. 3 (1976), pp. 264–273.

National Commission on Terrorist Attacks Upon the United States. *The 9/11 Commission Report.* New York W.W. Norton, 2004.

"NYS Office Takes the Point against Terror." *Law Enforcement News,* February 14, 2002, p. 11.

Oettmeier, Timothy. "Can Accreditation Survive the '90s?" In John W. Bizzack, ed., *Issues in Policing: New Perspectives.* Lexington, Ky.: Autumn House, 1993, pp. 96–112.

Office of Homeland Security, New York State. NIMS Components. Retrieved from security.state.ny.us/training/NIMS/components.html. Web accessed on May 18, 2009.

Parsavand, S. *Forensic Center Takes on Work of DNA Testing,* 2002. Retrieved from old.dailygazette.com/911/stories.htm

Reaves, B. *Census of State and Local Law Enforcement Agencies, 2004,* 2007. Retrieved from bjs.gov/content/pub/pdf/csllea04.pdf

Reiss, Albert J., Jr. *The Police and the Public.* New Haven, Conn.: Yale University Press, 1971.

Riggs, M. *Federal Asset Forfeiture Continues to Skyrocket Under Obama,* 2012. Retrieved from reason.com/blog/2012/07/31/federal-asset-forfeiture-skyrockets-under

Ross, Darrell. *Civil Liability in Criminal Justice.* Cincinnati, Ohio: Anderson, 2003.

Seattle Police Department, False Alarm Program. Retrieved on August 2, 2013 from seattle.gov.

Southern Poverty Law Center. "Return of the Militias." Web posted at splcenter.org/news/item.jsp?aid=392. Accessed on September 17, 2009.

Spelman, William, and Dale K. Brown. *Calling the Police: Citizen Reporting of Serious Crime.* Washington, D.C.: Police Executive Research Forum, 1981.

Stellwagen, Lindsey D., and Kimberly A. Wylie. *Strategies for Supplementing the Police Budget.* Washington, D.C.: National Institute of Justice, 1985.

Wechsler, William F. "Strangling the Hydra." In James F. Hoge Jr. and Gideon Rose, eds., *How Did This Happen?* New York: Public Affairs, 2002, pp. 129–144.

Wildavsky, Aaron, and Arthur Hammond. "Comprehensive versus Incremental Budgeting." In Albert C. Hyde and Jay M. Shafritz, eds., *Government Budgeting: Theory, Process, Politics.* Oak Park, Ill.: Moore, 1978, pp. 236–251.

Zellner, William W. *Counter Cultures.* New York: St. Martin's Press, 1995.

Zhao, Jihong "Solomon," Q.C. Thurman, and Ling Ren. "An Examination of Strategic Planning in American Law Enforcement Agencies." *Police Quarterly*, 11, no. 3 (January 4, 2008), pp. 4–24.

15

Collective Bargaining and Police Management

KEY TERMS

agency shop

binding arbitration

blue flu

Boston police strike

collective bargaining

community of interest

grievance

impasse

improper practice (IP)

injunction

lobbying

mediation

negotiator

seniority

strike

Police unions have a major influence on daily police operations and basic management decisions in those states and municipalities that allow collective bargaining. Unionism has led to the following:

- The use of job actions to attain goals after negotiations have stalemated
- Activism reflected not only at the bargaining table but also in outside political lobbying over various issues affecting police services to the community
- The wide variety of items found in labor contracts that were once deemed areas of management decision
- Increased emphasis on contract administration and the use of municipal or state resources to deal with union grievances before arbitrators and labor boards

In this chapter, we examine the development of police unionism and its effect on the police manager. Specific attention is given to collective bargaining, for this is one of the most important managerial processes affecting the police organization today.

COLLECTIVE BARGAINING DEFINED

According to Bowers (1973: 6), **collective bargaining** is the process by which representatives of labor and management negotiate wages and working conditions for a given employment entity. For both the public and the private labor sectors, bargaining is chiefly an economic enterprise in which two sides negotiate over how much money management will give employees for their work. For the private labor sector, collective bargaining is a bilateral process in which the management and the union representing the employee unit are the two factions that determine the wages and benefits that union members will receive. While economic issues remain significant, job protection, employee work rules, and benefits like health insurance are important concerns in the current collective bargaining forum.

In the public sector, politics enters the situation as a third force. The addition of this third factor leads to what is termed a *multilateral labor relationship*; that is, more than two parties are involved. For example, in the preparation of a departmental budget, the budget planner must obtain information from a number of sources before presenting the final proposal. Moreover, in government, many people must have their say to protect their own interests. In the case of public labor unions, the chief effect is on the range and cost of services provided to the community. The length of time that public managers remain in their positions is often determined by how effectively and economically these services are provided to the community.

Other interest groups also enter into the collective bargaining relationship. Often labor negotiations are expanded not only to the political administration but also to public pressure. Outside actors include the judiciary, the governor, and the civil service commission. Nevertheless, politics remains an important factor in the multilateral relationship between the police union and municipal or state management.

The strong political influence of collective bargaining on the municipality or state becomes particularly apparent around election time. This was highlighted in the study of a county election in which the candidate for district attorney made a concerted effort to receive endorsements based on his position of law and order from every police benevolent association in the county. The endorsements received were used in public relations and in a media campaign directed at voters.

HISTORY OF POLICE UNIONISM

In 1919, the Boston Police Department went on strike in an attempt to increase officers' wages. Although other police departments had used the strike tactic as a means of protest, the **Boston police strike** gained nationwide attention, in large part because of the looting, robberies, and general disorder that occurred after it was apparent that there were no patrolmen on the streets. Massachusetts governor Calvin Coolidge eventually ordered the state guard into Boston to police the city and replaced the striking officers with auxiliaries.

Observers of the Boston police strike (Gammage and Sachs, 1972; Juris and Feuille, 1973) agree that the actions taken by state authorities in quelling the strike retarded the development of unionism in American police forces for the next 50 years. Prior to 1919, many metropolitan police departments had formed social clubs to serve as liaisons between the officers and the municipality for the purpose of improving wages and conditions of employment. In Boston, an invitation had already been tendered to the Boston Social Club by the American Federation of Labor to join the national organization. This invitation was withdrawn soon after the strike. The wave of public support toward Massachusetts authorities in their blanket dismissal of the strikers signaled to other budding police labor unions that union militancy would not receive support either from the public or from national labor organizations.

Police unionism in the United States remained dormant until the 1960s, although a few police benevolent associations did join national labor groups for public employees. This general trend held not only for police officers but also for all public employees. That is, in the public sector between 1920 and 1950, unionism was opposed by both public management and public employees. While wage scales for public employees generally lagged those of private workers, significant benefits were earned by government workers in the form of job security via civil service and a generous system of vacation and personal leave.

After World War II, three main developments altered this trend:

1. An expansion of government services was coupled with an increase of government employees.
2. A continued policy by the federal government supported the right of public and private workers to unionize and bargain collectively. For the public sector, this culminated in 1962 with President Kennedy's signing of Executive Order 10988, which allowed most federal employees to organize unions and bargain collectively. Further refinements of Executive Order 10988 were signed by Presidents Johnson, Nixon, and Ford.
3. There was a significant decline of union membership in the private sector. This trend forced many private union organizations to look for new membership, readily available in the public sector.

It became apparent to many public employees that there was no reason why they should not receive salaries and conditions of employment similar to those earned by their private counterparts in an affluent society. Unions, which were at one time spurned by public employees, were now welcomed as a means by which to achieve employee demands. Private and public union organizations welcomed these new members with open arms to boost sagging union membership. Lobbying efforts were initiated to have cities and states enact comprehensive collective bargaining statutes modeled on existing federal statutes. Starting in the late 1950s, such statutes were enacted by New York City (1956), Wisconsin (1959), and New York State (1967).

It is not surprising that the trend to unionize by public employees was readily accepted by many police officers at this time. These officers felt that they were underpaid and the frequent object of public abuse and criticism for a variety of social problems, particularly the rise in crime. While low pay became the chief determinant for the rise of police unions, an equally significant factor arose from the poor personnel practices that were commonplace in many police organizations. According to Juris and Feuille (1973: 21), the following practices were often cited as a source of contention:

Lack of internal civil and constitutional rights for officers being investigated for misfeasance and malfeasance

Lack of a functional grievance procedure

Being called to duty and held on standby or called to court, for no compensation

Having to lose a day's pay as penalties for rule infractions

No premium pay for overtime work

Being transferred from one shift or job to another with little or no advance warning

Physical and verbal intimidation and degradation by superior officers

The demand for higher wages and improved working conditions can also be traced to the influx of younger officers, many with college degrees, who balked at a militaristic bureaucracy that demanded blind obedience. Moreover, the militancy that is often attached to police unionism should come as no surprise. This attitude reflected the mood of the 1960s, in which protest and activism were the main tactics of generally all social change groups, ranging from students to minority groups. It is no wonder that many police unions became particularly adept at protest tactics (calling in with **blue flu**, wearing sneakers while in uniform, not shaving, engaging in street protests) by simply borrowing such methods from groups that they had fought against.

OVERVIEW OF POLICE UNIONS

According to the Bureau of Labor Statistics (2014), approximately 11.3 percent of all wage earners are union members, which equates to 14.5 million workers. In 1983, the union membership rate was 20.1 percent with approximately 17.7 members. Workers in government services comprised about 35.3 percent of union members. Within this sector, personnel in the protective service (police and fire) represented 35.3 percent of the membership.

Most police unions in the United States today are local organizations that may or may not be affiliated with a national or state parent organization. The reason for this local orientation is that wages, benefits, and conditions of employment, including promotions, are heavily dependent on local economic and political conditions. The police department is the arm of local county or state government. Unlike multinational corporations, those who control the destinies of the nation's police are clearly tied to the local community, and in police matters, their concerns end at the community boundary.

However, police unions affiliated with national groups have received valuable assistance from outside consultants during negotiations and work actions. The national unions have developed strong campaigns to interest local police in national union affiliation. However, the response has been mixed nationally because of the strong community control over law enforcement.

State legislation on public unions has performed a significant role in the type of unions that have developed in law enforcement. The state legislation on collective bargaining can be divided into two major categories:

1. Those states that have comprehensive statutes allow police officers to bargain collectively in some manner.
2. Those states that make it illegal for police to form a union and absolutely forbid union membership to police officers.

The rule in both of these cases is that states, in the light of the 1919 Boston strike, generally forbid police to strike.

In place of this no-strike rule is the concept of **binding arbitration**, in which unresolved issues or contract disputes go to a neutral arbitrator who makes a decision that is binding on both sides. The use of an arbitrator is frequently seen as an attractive mechanism by which unionized police personnel can obtain equal footing with the employer.

States that do not allow bargaining by police usually allow state agencies and municipalities to "meet and confer" with police representatives to discuss employees' issues and grievances. Despite the existence of no-bargaining statutes, many officers have joined national unions in a first step toward organizing.

More and more police officers have formed benevolent organizations for social and athletic purposes. Eventually, the organization takes on many, if not most, of the characteristics of a union, and these no-union state laws are being either tested or ignored. In general, nonunion states provide some form of binding arbitration. One of the major problems with these binding-arbitration clauses is that the final decision on the contract is made by local and state legislatures.

In states that have comprehensive collective bargaining statutes, such as New York, Ohio, California, Wisconsin, Michigan, and New Jersey, the members of each police department are allowed to form a union. The process begins with a large number of employees expressing their interest in forming a union. This generally involves the presentation of a petition or signature cards to the county or state labor board indicating this goal. Often, a state or national police union will provide professional assistance in the hopes of having the employees join the larger organization. This is followed by an election in which the employees formally decide to form a union and select a collective bargaining agent and affiliation. This decision could result in the formation of a local bargaining unit or affiliation with a national police union. After this occurs, the state labor board certifies that the bargaining unit is the exclusive representative for the job titles that created the unit.

The key elements are that the union is the only recognized body to negotiate with the employer and that the union has the right to collect dues. In certain states, such as New York, legislation allows for the **agency shop**, where the union collects dues from all employees, members and nonmembers alike. The rationale is that all employees should share the cost of negotiating contracts with the employer.

During the past decade, courts have consistently ruled that nonunion members must pay that portion of their dues directed to collective bargaining purposes, which might include political lobbying, national conferences, and other activities related to union business. However, in *Lehnert v. Ferris Valley Faculty Association*, the Supreme Court ruled in 1991 that nonunion public employees did not have to pay dues that were directed to ideological causes. An example of an ideological cause would be support for a political candidate or **lobbying** for a certain bill in the state legislature that union members might not support.

Another important element in the establishment of the union is the question of the categories of employees that will be represented, otherwise known as the **community of interest**. For example, in large metropolitan police departments, separate union groups represent patrol officers, supervisors, and middle managers. The community-of-interest question was complicated when detectives formed their own organization, breaking away from the police benevolent association. In other cities and states, all members of the department, including the chief of police, are represented by one union. In some cases, especially in smaller departments, this presents problems since the chief and his or her friends may be able to control the union and, of course, control the collective bargaining process.

Although one union is recognized as the sole representative for collective bargaining, state laws allow for a designated time period when a rival organization may solicit petitions and, if receiving a certain percentage of votes, conduct elections to contest representation. This is an important aspect for police unions that wish to become affiliated with national groups when consensus does not exist in the union membership for such a move.

Finally, states with comprehensive statutes provide **mediation**, fact finding, and arbitration to deal with disputes that cannot be resolved during the course of collective bargaining or the administration of the contract:

- *Mediation.* This is a noncoercive process in which a neutral third party studies the issues in dispute between the two parties. This mediator works behind the scenes with the parties and attempts to act as a go-between in settling the dispute.
- *Fact finding.* This is another noncoercive procedure by which a third party gathers evidence from the two parties and then offers a solution. The recommendations may be publicly released in an effort to have community pressure enter into the settling of the dispute.
- *Arbitration.* This is a third-party process in which an official body or representative of a state arbitration board studies the issues in dispute and then makes a ruling. This decision may then be binding on both parties, depending on statute.

These three processes are used to settle disputes between labor and management during the course of collective bargaining when an **impasse** occurs. An impasse is generally understood to occur when labor or management or both have determined that no further progress will be made through negotiations at the table.

For police unions, binding arbitration is often used as a method to forestall a strike. Arbitration can also be used to settle grievances that arise during the administration of the union contract. Basically, a **grievance** occurs when either management or the union feels that the contract has been violated in some way. Grievances can also arise from a violation of the rules and regulations involving employee health, safety, physical facilities, materials, or equipment. Consider the following example of a grievance procedure:

1. A time limit of 10 working days is set as a limit in which a grievance may be filed after an officer becomes aware of the event constituting the alleged grievance.
2. Informal discussion usually marks the next step. Here the employee verbally presents his or her claim promptly to the immediate supervisor, and both parties attempt to solve the situation.
3. If the grievance is not resolved in the informal stage and the employee wishes to continue into the grievance process, a written notice is forwarded to a higher command officer. Again, a time limit is set between the final determination made by the supervisor and the filing of written notice.
4. Within a specific period of time, the ranking supervisor must process the grievance and schedule a hearing. At the hearing, the employee presents written and oral statements on his or her position.
5. Within a specific time frame, the command officer answers in writing his or her course of action on the grievance.
6. If the grievance is still not adjusted at the command officer level, the grievance is filed with the head of the agency. In some departments, the sheriff or the chief of police has the final say as to the determination of the grievance. In states that have comprehensive collective bargaining statutes, the grievance is handled by a public employee relations board.

A fifth method of conflict resolution is through litigation. Since the courts are the traditional forum for solving disputes between public agencies, many unions, especially those in large metropolitan jurisdictions or affiliated with national organizations, have a battery of attorneys on the payroll. Litigation sponsored by police unions has produced various noteworthy cases involving drug testing, discipline, and off-duty employment.

Major Police Union Organizations

The trend in policing today appears to be increased unionization, especially in those states that as yet do not allow police officers to form unions. Nonunion police departments are the rule rather than the exception in the South and the Midwest, whereas unions are especially strong in the Northeast and on the West Coast, as states in those areas have comprehensive collective bargaining statutes.

There is also the additional trend for many local police unions to affiliate with national groups to strengthen their bargaining position and to increase union benefits to members. The main national union groups are as follows:

- *International Union of Police Associations (IUPA).* Founded in 1953 as the National Conference of Police Associations, this union was originally organized for networking and legislative lobbying purposes among various police organizations in the United States and Canada (Swanson et al., 2001). In 1978, the organization—then known as the International

Conference of Police Associations—split apart after a decision was made to affiliate with the American Federation of Labor and Congress of Industrial Organizations (AFL-CIO). Many departments were opposed to the higher dues and the greater percentage of money that went to the national organization. In the following year, the AFL-CIO granted a charter to the IUPA. Today, the group represents approximately 80,000 officers through 480 local organizations.

- *Communications Workers of America (CWA).* Originally founded to represent telephone and communications technology workers, the CWA decided in the 1990s to expand into the public sector to organize workers in various areas, such as graduate students, medical workers, and police officers. The National Coalition of Public Safety Officers (NCPSO), the CWA affiliate for police and public safety officers, represents about 35,000 police officers, deputy sheriffs, probation officers, and correctional officers. What is significant about the NCPSO is its statewide organization of public safety workers in the population growth states of Texas, Arizona, and Florida.

- *Fraternal Order of Police (FOP).* This is the oldest police organization in the United States. The FOP is basically a professional organization that emphasizes collective bargaining in some areas and exists mainly as a social organization in others. Each lodge is independent of control from the national organization. There are now over 2,100 lodges and nearly 300,000 members.

- *International Brotherhood of Teamsters.* This private union was quick to see the potential for government workers to increase membership. Estimates of police officer membership range as high as 15,000. Many police union officials (and management as well) distrust the Teamsters because of its long history of organized crime influence and mismanagement of pension funds via low-interest or no-interest loans to gangsters. Nevertheless, the Teamsters are aggressive in seeking public sector membership and are presently conducting recruitment and organization drives in those southern states that forbid police to form unions. Today, the Teamsters represent officers at 297 police departments in 19 states.

- *International Brotherhood of Police Officers (IBPO).* Founded in Rhode Island in the late 1960s, the IBPO was organized to deal with collective bargaining issues among local police unions in New England. In 1970, the IBPO became affiliated with the National Association of Government Employees, which in 1982 became affiliated with Service Employees International Union, a large collective bargaining group of public sector service employees that is affiliated with the AFL-CIO. Today, the IBPO continues to represent police officers in New England and has expanded to many states in the western United States.

- *American Federation of State, County, and Municipal Employees (AFSCME).* Affiliated with the AFL, this union for public employees was founded in 1936. AFSCME was the first organization to make serious attempts to enroll public employees in the decades before the rise of union membership in 1960. Today, AFSCME is perhaps the largest public sector union, representing over 1.3 million members. Police unions are organized under AFSCME as separate councils for state and local police departments. Approximately 35,000 police officers are represented by this organization. There are also thousands of federal workers who are in staff and clerical positions in various federal law enforcement agencies. Federal law enforcement officers, such as Secret Service, Federal Bureau of Investigation, Drug Enforcement Administration, and others, do not have union representation but have job-related due process rights and salary benefits enacted by Congress. Exceptions to this are the U.S. Marshals, the Border Patrol, and various federal security personnel who are represented by the American Federation of Government Employees, an AFSCME affiliate.

- **Black Officer Associations.** These have been formed in police departments that have a high percentage of minority officers as well as a record of prejudice and discrimination against these officers in terms of recruitment, promotions, or job assignments. Examples of these associations are the Guardians in New York City and Hartford, Connecticut; the Afro-American Patrolmen's League of Chicago; and the Oakland, California, Black Officers Association. These associations usually remain apart from the union structure of their departments and attempt to settle differences between their members and management by direct negotiations and political lobbying.

The long-term organizational goal for many of these groups is the creation of a national police union. This appeared to be a real possibility in the 1970s with the large increases in membership and activism associated with police unions. The decentralization of American police, the state of the economy, and the changing nature of American unionism make a national union less likely today and in the future. However, various local unions do join formal and informal state and national networks and conferences to lobby for officer-related legislation and collective bargaining rights.

MANAGEMENT RIGHTS AND COLLECTIVE BARGAINING: A DILEMMA

The most crucial factor facing the police administrator—managing the agency—arises from the emergence of collective bargaining and police unionism. Union contracts today contain a variety of clauses affecting police operations. For example, the union contract may specify that two troopers must be assigned to patrol vehicles during the midnight watch. Decisions of this nature would appear to be the prerogative of management. Yet there are two general reasons why such clauses appear in union contracts.

First, the police management role in collective bargaining in the 1960s was generally characterized as either negligent or nonexistent. Because of the multilateral nature of the process, negotiations often were carried on by a member of the state or municipal personnel office who may or may not have advised the police agency affected by the outcome of the contract. On the other side of the table, union negotiators were generally better prepared to argue their demands, strengthening their position with the use of outside consultants for expertise on issues and tactics.

Second, not all infringements on managerial prerogative occurred through the collective bargaining process. In some cases, police departments were forced to comply with union demands via binding arbitration rulings or court litigation. Arbitration and legal rulings forced many law enforcement administrators to undertake participatory management in the formulation of policy within their agencies. In many cases, grievance and litigation proceedings may be avoided by having union input as a part of the policy decision-making process. On the other hand, militant unions may harass management through their use of grievances at every turn.

The first step in hindering union infringement on managerial rights lies with a management rights clause in the contract. A traditional model clause prepared by the National League of Cities (Rynecki et al., 1978: 7) states that topics not presented in the contract are given to the employer and that the union agrees to file a grievance against management on the topics.

Such rights include the right to do the following (Geller, 1991: 303):

1. Establish departmental rules and procedures
2. Schedule shifts, tours of duty, and work assignments
3. Discipline and discharge for cause
4. Lay off employees if the need arises

5. Transfer employees and governmental operations
6. Consolidate the operations of two or more departments or reorganize the operations within a department
7. Set hiring and promotional standards
8. Set education and training standards

The reality is that despite the existence of this clause, unions will grieve on any topic if it is important to the membership. The existence of a management rights clause is not the final solution in the problem of managing without union interference. Unpopular decisions still may be the basis for a lawsuit or for resistance by personnel. Yet there remains the need for such a clause, as it is the first line of defense if a decision is grieved and reaches arbitration. Management can point to this clause as part of the contractual agreement.

THE COLLECTIVE BARGAINING PROCESS

The goals and objectives of police management and labor in the collective bargaining process are similar, although they may differ somewhat in detail and substance and substantially in the means to obtain these goals:

Management Goals	Labor Goals
1. Provide fair and adequate pay for all employees, including a reasonable and competitive compensation package for management	1. Provide fair and adequate pay for all employees in the bargaining unit, along with a solid fringe benefit package
2. Maintain managerial efficiency, producing an efficiently run police department	2. Respect police officers as individuals and as part of an efficiently run police department
3. Preserve the public interest in policing the community	3. Preserve the public interest in policing the community
4. Have employees identify with managerial and departmental objectives, along with a positive esprit de corps and high morale	4. Have a positive esprit de corps, with high morale and the creation of departmental objectives that are mutually beneficial to both the department and the sworn officers
5. Have adequately trained officers who respond in a professional manner to management's needs, objectives, and specific orders	5. Have adequately trained officers who have good working conditions and who respond in a professional manner to reasonable requests by management personnel

These objectives are complex because police personnel relations are complex and often not as clear as this chart would indicate (Klotz, 1978).

The language of the goals for management and labor differ, along with some of the meaning of this language. The matter of definition is paramount for good management–employee relations. The municipality setting wages and fringe benefits may differ considerably in what it considers to be adequate and fair pay; this may well be below what the union considers fair and adequate and even below what the management considers fair and adequate. The same holds true for (1) conditions and benefits of employment, (2) reasonable orders or requests, (3) mutually beneficial objectives, and (4) an efficiently run department. A major problem is the existence of three groups—police management, sworn officers and other police department members of the bargaining unit, and municipal politicians and governmental officials—using differing definitions.

Although bargaining has been likened to horse trading, certain preparations must be made before the horse trading begins. Effective use of the collective bargaining process means that the police management team has an organization that collects data and does extensive homework on a year-round basis. The basic issues that are normally reviewed are as follows (Klotz, 1978):

1. A review of prior contracts with key administrative personnel to see what items need to be updated or revised. Special attention should be given to items that have poor language or have been the source of problems or grievances with the union.

2. A review of current union agreements with other area police agencies and agencies of similar size facing similar problems. This should be looked at in terms of remaining competitive in the market, keeping the officer's morale high, and being able to make reasonable offers in light of union demands.

3. Collection and analysis of economic data concerning what the municipality can afford to pay and is willing to pay, given political and economic realities. This could include informal discussions with local decision-making leaders concerning what they feel is a reasonable increase in wages and benefits.

4. A thorough study and analysis of arbitration decisions awarded under the current contract or awarded to police unions.

5. Checking out rumors informally as to what items are important to the union and to members of the bargaining unit and what areas of dispute might be unknown to management. By checking informally before bargaining is begun, management may offer compromises, and settlement may be possible before either party takes a solid position.

The next step in the bargaining preparation is the selection of the bargaining team. The key person of this team, the chief **negotiator**, has the authority and prestige to represent the department with credibility. The negotiator has to be able to have frank discussions with the chief concerning all issues, especially those deemed undesirable or contrary to management's best interest. He or she also has to enjoy the chief's confidence. Assisting the chief negotiator are other members of the team who generally provide two major services: (1) information retrieval and research and (2) expertise in areas with which the chief negotiator might not be familiar.

In small police agencies with limited budgets and personnel, the chief often takes an active role in the bargaining process. While it is imperative that police management be represented at the bargaining table, it is *not* recommended that the chief become a chief negotiator. By becoming personally involved in the bargaining process, the chief may foster future morale and personal repercussions that would be detrimental to management. For example, if the chief is seen as not supporting his or her people on the issue of higher wages, this could be a blow to morale.

Some municipalities have been hiring professional negotiators, and most have found them well worth the expense. These negotiators are familiar with the labor laws and the expenses of such items as health and dental insurance. They have gone through the process thousands of times and are familiar with the rituals and customs of collective bargaining in relation to the membership, the government, and the press. National unions often send professional negotiators to unions in the field when a contract is about to end. Since literally millions of dollars and the basic welfare of the department are involved, the negotiating process is no place for amateurs.

Contract Administration

The signing of the contract is only the continuance of the collective bargaining relationship. The contract reflects new guidelines between the employer and the union that will be subject to future review by both sides. The most important aspect of administering the contract involves the dissemination of information to all members of the agency on policies, programs, and equipment affected by the new agreement. Those items affected by the contract will still have to be worked out between management and union representatives. For example, while the contract may specify that all officers will receive a new caliber of weapon, the actual issuance of the weapon will not occur overnight.

Between the signing of the new contract and the initiation of the next round of negotiations, a chief portion of contract administration by union and management involves handling and monitoring formal and informal deviations arising from situations and interpretations not covered in the existing document. The most effective manner in which to work out these disputes is to have one person or officer administer the contract and keep records concerning these differences or disagreements. What often happens is that over the life of the contract, these differences become agenda items for the new contract negotiations. Unresolved issues often become agenda items during the next round of bargaining or may become major grievance items. These issues are summarized in the following sections.

SENIORITY   **Seniority**, meaning the number of years or days that an officer has served, remains the cornerstone of collective bargaining agreements for such items as shift and special detail assignments. Grievances that arise over this issue are, in fact, very complicated in terms of the calculation of seniority time. For example, depending on the locality, "time on the job" may begin the first day the person walks through the front door, after graduation from the training academy, or after the probationary period. From the management view, seniority is a hindrance in terms of assigning the best person to the best job, and seniority often interferes with the administration of the daily operation of the agency.

After September 11, 2001, efforts in Massachusetts to create an elite antiterrorism team at Boston's Logan Airport became stalled as the union for state police officers wanted this assignment made on the basis of seniority (Daniel, 2002). In another agency, a major grievance emerged over training school assignments based on management decision rather than the existing seniority list. The calculation of the seniority list is most important in those police agencies facing employee layoffs, as it is well known that the last hired is the first fired.

GRIEVANCE PROCEDURES   The reasons and guidelines for a grievance procedure have been discussed in detail. Grievances can arise from disputes over administration of the contract relating to wages, benefits, and conditions of employment. Conditions of employment pose an open-ended arena for grievances. Police officers in states with comprehensive collective bargaining statutes can grieve anything and everything, and they do! A typical batch of grievances in one large state agency for a six-month period includes the following:

- Lack of interior or writing-light replacement bulbs in patrol vehicles
- Administration of first aid to a person suspected of having AIDS
- Transportation of prisoners by only one officer in an "uncaged" vehicle
- Responding to fires without proper equipment and going inside to locate the cause of the alarm before the arrival of fire-service personnel
- Not being allowed to wear leatherlike athletic shoes in place of the prescribed leather shoes
- The presence of rats in a locker room

The reader, no doubt, will ask why these items could not have been settled by open, face-to-face communication. The reality is that mundane and seemingly simple issues should be worked out either through informal communication or formal labor–management meetings. Although necessary and important, formal grievances take time and bruise egos in terms of win-lose-or-draw outcomes between management and labor. Most of these issues could and should be worked out through direct and frank discussion.

IMPROPER LABOR PRACTICES   An **improper practice (IP)**, occurs when an employer does one or more of the following:

- Interferes with, restrains, or coerces employees who wish to form or join a labor union
- Dominates or interferes with the formation or administration of a labor union
- Discriminates against any employee for the purpose of encouraging or discouraging membership or activity in the union
- Refuses to negotiate in good faith with the recognized or state-certified representatives of the union
- Assigns work performed by union employees to nonunion employees

Charges of improper practices can also be alleged against employees for similar reasons: (1) failing to negotiate in good faith with management, and (2) interfering, restraining, or coercing fellow employees from exercising their rights as union members, for example, seeking new representation from another labor organization. In most cases, IP complaints are handled at the local administrative level up to a final resolution at a state employee relations hearing board.

Charges of improper practices by both labor and management often occur when contract negotiations reach a stalemate. They also seem to arise when officers of a department begin to organize a union under prevailing legislative guidelines. Invariably, in these situations, there are outright or implied threats by command personnel or the civilian administration about abolishing jobs, cutting back on existing benefits, and sometimes abolishing the entire department. An IP is often filed when it is felt that the internal grievance process set up by the contract is not working or is taking too long.

Another rich area for IP complaints involves instances when management attempts to hire or use outside consultants or employees for work that is normally done by police union members, for example the use of civilians for dispatching or for writing parking tickets or bringing outside police officers in to handle an event. The basis for these complaints is the contention that management is discriminating against union employees by having civilians do the jobs of sworn officers.

At the state level, improper practices are resolved through a state level employee relations board. As with grievances, attorneys for both sides will attempt to work with the state level law judge. If the matter cannot be resolved then the issue goes before an administrative law judge for final determination.

DISCIPLINE PROCEDURES   In states with comprehensive collective bargaining statutes, disciplinary procedures invariably appear in the collective bargaining agreement. Contract language often defines the process by which discipline is imposed in terms of written charges, the parameters for interrogation, and union representation during interrogation. An important element is the time frame by which the employer should have known that a rule or law was violated.

Contracts often have prohibitions against the use of chemical or polygraph tests unless voluntarily agreed to by the suspect employee. Employees may also demand a review by an outside arbitrator on the punishment that the agency has imposed or seeks to impose. As with IP complaints, employee-discipline procedures follow a grievance-type process involving a local hearing and then review of the charges and punishment by a state labor relations board. The desire by the employee to dispute either the notice of discipline and/or the punishment must be made within a specified period.

Union contracts vary with regard to representation of members by union-paid attorneys for charges filed by other police agencies and civilians. With some contracts, the union defends all officers against charges, while in other jurisdictions, paid-for legal defense is optional or non-existent. As discussed in Chapter 10, the police administrator must know by heart the rules and conditions for discipline that appear in the union contract and the relevant civil service law. The police manager needs to follow the common law that evolves through the administration of a contract or contracts over time. Although many say that every case is different, state arbitrators have dismissed charges because of the following:

1. Lack of proper and complete investigations and proper documentation
2. Too severe punishment in relation to the offense (e.g., suspension for failing to wear the uniform)
3. Lack of just cause in initiating discipline (e.g., a personality clash rather than a legitimate issue)
4. Lack of consistency in enforcing department rules

Thus, a labor agreement is not a static document but, rather, changes as the organizational needs change. Also, conditions change and fringe benefits are looked at differently from one year to the next. One general rule: It is easy to add a benefit to a contract but extremely difficult to take one away, even if the benefit proves too costly.

Fair Labor Standards Act

An important element in the collective bargaining relationship is the payment of money for work performed. The Fair Labor Standards Act (FLSA), passed by Congress in the 1980s with strong support from police union groups, proscribes that employees must be paid overtime at a rate of one and one-half times the regular wage rate for over 40 hours of work. For many years, state work practices exempted law enforcement agencies because operational needs required personnel to work shifts that would fill 24 hours without any gaps. However, in 1986 this concept was tested in *Garcia* v. *San Antonio Metropolitan Transit Authority*; the Supreme Court ruled that FLSA was applicable to state and local law enforcement agencies.

Since that time, police unions and employers have addressed a number of complicated issues related to the law, either through labor/management discussions or lawsuits. Law enforcement officers must be compensated for overtime, with either pay or compensatory time off, at a rate of not less than one and one-half hours for each hour over 43 hours per week, or 171 hours for a 28-day work period. The notion of work performed includes all activities that provide a benefit to the employer, such as preshift briefing, finishing reports from the previous tour, and travel to and from training courses. The rules for overtime apply to investigators who may work for days on one case. When the FLSA is violated, law enforcement officers may sue for back wages, attorneys' fees, and punitive damages.

There are exceptions to these standards. As McCormack (1995: 29) discusses, the FLSA does not cover law enforcement agencies that employ fewer than five officers within a workweek. Elected officials, such as the sheriff, or volunteers or management officials who are paid on a yearly salary are FLSA exempt. Those who are attending a training academy may not be covered because they are not considered regular employees. The issue of who is an exempted employee is always problematic for law enforcement managers who hold command rank. For example, if the manager can have hourly wages deducted based on a fine imposed by the department, then he or she is not FLSA exempt.

THE POLICE STRIKE

Even though most states prohibit strikes or work slowdowns by police, police **strikes** (stoppages of work) sometimes do occur. Short of a strike, police unions may resort to job actions such as blue flu (not reporting to work for alleged sickness), slowdowns, and the initiation of "Fear City" campaigns over police cutbacks.

There have been fewer police strikes and job actions in the past decade than in the previous decades. A major reason for this is the economics of local municipalities that have suffered decreased tax revenue along with cutbacks in federal and state aid. In the light of the many austerity budgets, there has been a new tendency for many police unions to cooperate with administrative and legislative leaders and managers in order to retain job security.

What has arisen in many contracts is the concept of givebacks, where the union gives back certain benefits negotiated and won in the past. There have also been many cases where unions have agreed to wage freezes or to work free for a specific number of days in order to continue job security.

While the Boston police strike remains an important historical event, a police strike in Montreal in 1969 should also be considered. Soon after it was realized that police were not on the streets, there was a rash of robberies and looting in the central area of the city. The absence of police led many observers to conclude that perhaps there was some validity to the "thin blue line" philosophy in that the police are the last defense against total anarchy.

Even though most contracts and state statutes forbid strikes by police and firefighters, it is important that all agencies have prepared plans to maintain essential police services. Most police agencies rely on outside assistance and the use of supervisors and nonstriking officers to fill this need. A court **injunction** is often used in halting a strike. Because of the no-strike clauses in labor contracts and state legislation, the injunction forces the officers back to work under the threat of contempt of court. In some strikes, court injunctions have been successful, and strikers have returned to work under threat of jail or huge fines levied against the union treasury.

After the dust has settled and the police officers return to work, there are the follow-up issues of disciplinary proceedings against the strikers. There are no precise answers to this dilemma simply because each strike has different variables. However, a no-penalty or no-punishment clause in some contracts helps to stop petty punishments that serve only to damage morale and undermine employee–employer relations. A general rule that might be applied is that punishments do not deter future strikes and do a great deal of damage to the organization in terms of creating resentment among the employees.

POLICE UNIONS AND THE POLITICAL PROCESS

As police union contracts are tied to local and state economic issues, it is no surprise that local, state, and national politics often becomes enmeshed with union activity. Politicians running for office routinely request the endorsement and sometimes the economic support of police unions. The candidate's views on crime control and his or her previous support for police-sponsored bills become an important consideration before political support is given.

Police unions often present themselves as good community citizens by sponsoring community events, crime-prevention programs, and sports teams for youth. Community activity is often devoted to fund-raising to augment fiscal resources obtained from member dues. Fundraising can lead to a number of issues and concerns. It is not uncommon for local unions to contract with national fund-raisers to conduct phone campaigns for money. In one month, the author received two requests from telemarketers to support local police benevolent associations and their antidrug education. Further investigation found that less than 10 percent of the money raised actually went to the union.

Another related activity is the police union yearbook, which consists of police activity photos, crime-prevention tips, and many advertisements. It's the advertisements that often become a sore spot. When businesses are asked to buy space for advertising, some observers complain that this may become a form of shakedown if there is any hint of reprisals for not supporting the campaign.

Major police unions, or confederations of local unions, maintain offices in state capitals and Washington, D.C., to monitor legislation and to lobby for support of union-sponsored bills. For example, the Fraternal Order of Police urged its members to write to their elected representatives to have Congress pass a bill that would allow police officers to carry firearms on or off duty anywhere in the United States. The rationale for this legislation is that current homeland security efforts may require emergency mobilization of off-duty and retired police officers who may have to cross state lines. After much lobbying, H.R. 218—the Law Enforcement Officer's Act—was signed into law on July 22, 2004, for qualified law enforcement officers employed by government agencies. A controversial portion of the act also includes retired police officers who are issued documentation stating that they have met agency standards for firearms training. Details on this act can be obtained at fop.org.

If anything, police unions have become more active in defending their members, especially those who have been arrested for crimes. It is not unusual for the local union or the national group to set aside funds for the legal defense of officers accused of criminal misconduct, as contracts do not, as a rule, provide legal indemnification for union members who are accused of a crime.

Declining economic conditions starting in 2008 have made labor negotiations very contentious, especially with regard to health benefits, pension plans, and the reality of possible layoffs of police officers. An internal union memo gathered from one dispute in California showed the "order of battle" in dealing with the issue, which included the following:

1. Have the entire membership show up at meetings of the government council
2. Go public with billboards and handout flyers
3. Get commitments from elected officials

Sometimes these tactics have a reverse effect. One such paper handout showed a group of Latino gang members on the cover with the caption "On the streets gang members outnumber Escondido police officers by almost 6 to 1. . . ." Community reaction toward the police union was negative based on the focus on one ethnic group that represented a significant number of the overall community population (Lynch, personal communication, 2009).

In the Midwest, a number of states such as Indiana and Ohio, passed "right to work" legislation, which meant that employees could decide whether or not to join a union and pay dues. This was a complete opposite from states that had agency shop requirements, whereby all employees are required to join a union and pay dues.

In 2012, this controversy came to a head in Wisconsin, which ironically was one of the first states to authorize collective bargaining for public employees. In January of that year, newly elected Governor Scott Walker, in an effort to balance the state budget, added an addendum to a budget bill that limited the scope of union negotiations to wages that became known as Wisconsin Act 10.

Moreover, employees would have to vote every year if they wished to remain in a union. Another major facet was that dues would not be automatically deducted from all employees 'wages unless the individual employee chose to join the bargaining unit. Without this important requirement, the bargaining unit would not be allowed to collect dues from employee paychecks. Although the measure did not affect the majority of police and fire unions officers of the University of Wisconsin Police and the Capitol Police were impacted.

As reported by Stein and Marley (2013) days after this announcement, a wide range of public and private sector labor groups and employees from all over the state descended on Madison, the capital, and occupied the statehouse. They were joined by national union supporters from all over the country and for the next 30 days, the issue became a focus of national media attention. Wisconsin State Capitol Police were overwhelmed and had to be assisted by police personnel from the University of Wisconsin and from local municipalities from all over the state (Riseling, 2013). Through a series of legislative maneuverings in the Republican controlled legislature, the bill was passed and signed into law on March 11. A subsequent move to recall Governor Walker from office was also defeated.

The events in Wisconsin were seen as a move to reduce the power of unions in the state and their traditional alliance with the Democratic Party. Indeed, the measure had an effect on public unions as membership declined in those bargaining units representing workers in public service, education, and transportation. The significance of this was not lost on national observers of the political process and collective bargaining, who viewed this as the first step for other states to follow suit to reduce the political power and collective bargaining rights for their own public unions including fire and police. Whether this will occur remains to be seen.

Conclusion

Collective bargaining is an important process for law enforcement agencies throughout the nation. Professionals who manage police departments see it as a step toward easing some of the strain between employees and employer, as written contracts help to eliminate misunderstandings. A fair grievance procedure, one that is fair both to management and to labor, if used as intended, can settle disputes before they worsen. Disputes settled at the informal stage of the grievance procedure can help a department grow and adapt to changing times and conditions. However, disputes that go through the formal machinery assure all officers that they can have their day before a neutral hearing officer.

In all, collective bargaining is seen as a generally powerful force in upgrading police agencies. However, contracts do give management less flexibility in exercising the necessary authority to administer an agency. This problem will be met when management is willing to use the civil service and/or contract machinery to fire undesirable employees. Many managers feel that it is not worth the trouble; however, inaction means that the department will have to live with that undesirable employee for many years.

One new concept concerns givebacks, that is, returning or giving up certain benefits that have been previously earned at the bargaining table (e.g., agreeing to give up uniform cleaning). This stems from the dire economic state in which many municipalities find themselves because of a national economy in recession, budget cuts, and a declining tax base.

Overall, there is a quiet change that is taking place with collective bargaining. The majority of officers in states where collective bargaining is allowed belong to local police unions that focus on the terms and conditions of employment for their city, town, or county members. The idea of a national police union for all officers remains abstract. However, the political powers of public sector unions in such states as Wisconsin and Indiana have been reduced. It remains to be seen whether a similar change will take place in other states.

Questions for Review

1. What were the major issues surrounding the rise of collective bargaining for police in the United States?
2. Define the following terms: *blue flu*, *binding arbitration*, and *management rights*.
3. Identify four major national police unions in the United States. Why are many local police unions reluctant to join national organizations?
4. Define *collective bargaining*. How does public sector collective bargaining differ from that found in the private sector?
5. Explain the significance of the following strikes: Boston (1919) and Montreal (1969).
6. Give three reasons why police should have the right to strike. Give three reasons why police should not have the right to strike. Give one reason why you choose one side or the other.

Class Project

The city of Jonesville will be negotiating a contract with the newly formed Jonesville Police Benevolent Association (PBA). At present, the overall conditions of employment for Jonesville officers are as follows:

1. Salaries are $40,000 for patrol officers, $50,000 for sergeants, and $60,000 for lieutenants. All personnel receive a $1,500 pay increase every two years.
2. The following holidays are allowed: July 4, Christmas, Thanksgiving, and Memorial Day.
3. There is one week of paid vacation for all personnel.
4. All officers must contribute toward their own pension fund.
5. All officers receive major health and dental care benefits from the city.
6. Uniforms are provided, except for leather and handguns.
7. There is no pay for overtime or call-in time.
8. All grievances are handled by the chief of police.

The city of Jonesville might be located anywhere in the United States. As with many American cities, Jonesville is showing a deficit, in this case $2 million, for this fiscal year. There is talk of layoffs for municipal workers. General unemployment for the area runs roughly 6 percent.

GAME PLAN

The class will be divided into two teams. One team will represent the Jonesville Police Benevolent Association; the other, the city of Jonesville. We suggest that teams be limited to eight students each. Each team must select a chief negotiator. The chief negotiator will then assign each member specific research tasks. For example, one

team member might be assigned to research the costs of pension programs for municipal employees, another member would deal with the issue of salaries, and so on.

ROLES OF NEGOTIATORS

The instructor will assign various team members to play specific roles. During one role-play session, one of the authors had the following characters:

For Jonesville PBA

Bill Griffith—recently elected as chief negotiator. Bill has promised to "bring home the bacon" and improve working conditions.

Wayne Freeman—a veteran patrol officer who sees this whole process as "chicken s—t" stuff. Freeman advocates the use of blue flu and strikes.

Linda Tomley—the first female officer in the department. Officer Tomley wants such things as lockers for female personnel and paid family leave.

Jack Smith—presently serves as public relations officer for the PBA. Among other things, he feels that the PBA should go "national" and get some clout to improve salaries and working conditions.

For City of Jonesville

Bill White—recently hired as director of personnel for the city. This is his first job since graduating from the School of Labor Relations at the state university. White has promised the mayor and the city council to "kick ass and take names" when it comes to increasing personnel costs for any group of city employees. White hopes to make a name for himself here in Jonesville before moving on to a larger city.

Susan Brown—deputy director of personnel relations. She has great concern for the role of women and minorities in city personnel practices. Brown also handles complaints filed against city workers, including the police. She feels that too many members of the police department are overpaid and are unfit to be police officers.

James Castle—city councilman who is assigned to the Public Safety Committee. Castle received an endorsement from the PBA in the last election. He is known as a "cop lover" by other politicians.

OBJECTIVES

The Jonesville PBA must try to improve its present wages, benefits, and other conditions of employment. The city of Jonesville must attempt to keep the status quo lest it plunge itself deeper into debt.

PLAYING THE GAME

Both sides must organize and prepare themselves for the bargaining session. Review this chapter and follow the processes presented by the authors. There should be enough time to complete the game, but your instructor may have to impose some time constraints. In one bargaining session, the class spent over 40 hours and still was at an impasse before the role-play was terminated.

Web Works

Review a Web site of one of the unions cited in this chapter. Many sites, such as the Fraternal Order of Police (fop.org), have links to various state and local sites.

Review the vast array of services and information offered at these sites.

References

Bowers, M.H. "Contemporary Police Employee Organizations and the Labor Relations Process." In *Crucial Issues in Police Labor Relations*. Gaithersburg, Md.: International Association of Chiefs of Police, 1973.

Bureau of Labor Statistics. *Union Members Summary— Union Members in 2013*. Washington, D.C.: U.S. Department of Labor, January 2014. Web posted at bls.gov/news.release//union2.nr0.htm. Accessed on January 30, 2014

Daniel, Mac. "Massport Hoping to Create Elite Police Unit at Logan." *Boston Globe,* retrieved from Lexus/ Nexus, September 4, 2002.

Gammage, A.Z., and S.L. Sachs. *Police Unions*. Springfield, Ill.: Charles C. Thomas, 1972.

Garcia v. San Antonio Metropolitan Transit Authority, 29 U.S.C. Sections 201–262 (1986).

Geller, William A. *Local Government Police Management* (3rd ed.). Washington, D.C.: International City Management Association, 1991.

International Association of Chiefs of Police. *Crucial Issues in Police Labor Relations*. Gaithersburg, Md.: International Association of Chiefs of Police, 1977.

Juris, H.A., and P. Feuille. *Police Unionism: Power and Impact in Public Sector Bargaining*. Lexington, Mass.: D.C. Heath, 1973.

Klotz, R. "Ground Rules." *Police Law Reporter*, 5 (1978), pp. 13–16.

Lehnert v. Ferris Valley Faculty Association, 111 S. Ct. 1950 (1991).

McCormack, William U. "Law Enforcement and the Fair Labor Standards Act." *FBI Law Enforcement Bulletin*, 64, no. 5 (May 1995), pp. 28–32.

Riseling, Susan. *A View From the Interior: Policing the Protests at the Wisconsin State Capitol*. Milwaukee, WI: Maven Mark, 2013.

Rynecki, Steven, D.A. Cairns, and D.J. Carnes. *Police Collective Bargaining Agreements: A National Management Survey*. Washington, D.C.: National League of Cities, 1978.

Stein, Jason, and Patrick Marley. *More than They Bargain For: Scott Walker, Unions and the Fight for Wisconsin*. Madison, WI: University of Wisconsin Press, 2013.

Swanson, Charles R., Leonard Territo, and Robert W. Taylor. *Police Administration: Structures, Processes, and Behavior* (5th ed.). Upper Saddle River, N.J.: Prentice Hall, 2001.

16 The Future of Proactive Police Management

KEY TERMS

consolidation

consultative management

evidence-based policing

flat world

global policing

global positioning system (GPS)

Google

home rule

new technology

proactive community police

proactive management model

voice over Internet protocol (VOIP)

A SCENARIO FOR THE FUTURE

Captain Ryan Ortega put on his virtual helmet as his command vehicle came to a stop. His partner, Mary Fung Kan, looked at the swirling crowds in the low-income housing area. Drone aircraft transmitted clear pictures of the housing project directly to Ortega's helmet. The computer screen in the car and smart phone were alive with probability curves of potential crimes and disturbances in the 10-block area surrounding the car. Lieutenant Kan was doing an asset array, including undercover assets and firepower potential, on her laptop. The GPS chip imbedded in every police weapon and vehicle tracked police personnel via satellite. Ortega opened the command channel, which included a digitized encrypted line to the community police section headquarters.

Captain Ortega calls the sergeant, through his voice-over chip, for the community policing unit in the area and requests information on the causes for the gathering. According to Sergeant Anthony Smith, a rumor has started that the housing project is scheduled to be closed because of the collapse of federal and state housing auxiliary funds. The project, which used to be a brick city in the 1990s, was turned into a neighborhood with townhouses, trees, and gardens. The majority of the population here is over 50 years old. According to the rumor, everyone will be forced to move, and the area will be turned into a manufacturing nanochip site owned by a multinational corporation. What has sparked this event is that private police officials from the Euro-Pacific and Space Transportation Company have been doing crime-prevention surveys to see whether the area can become a repair station for earth and space transport ships.

Smith asks Ortega to contact the mayor's office and ask representatives to come and talk to the crowd. "The organizers have promised not to hurt the public community police officers, but they will take out property owned by Euro-Pacific that is in the area," Smith reports.

The information is transmitted directly to the executive team at headquarters and becomes part of a database for the district community policing team. A riot is forming. Riot-control dispersal experts are called in while the burglary-prevention team secures the majority of homes in the project. A notification via 3D holograms goes to the homes in a computer-generated address list of the neighborhood, overriding all other broadcasts. In the meantime, military command headquarters for the state begins mobilizing its Rapid Response Strike Force (RRSF), which was created to assist federal and state police forces in addressing high crime, domestic riots, and border areas with illegal immigration problems. Drones spread throughout the target area, preparing to immobilize any citizen pinpointed through satellite-controlled imagery. An analysis for this area shows several languages and cultures based on recent immigration. All police programs and communicators are equipped with translation devices for handling these different groups.

All these events and actions have been anticipated by the central police agency planning team, which works out of the regional planning, hiring, training, and laboratory center. The metropolitan department had just been given high marks for its training/education, community involvement, and police service. The rapid response team was one of the department's highlights.

ANTICIPATING THE PROACTIVE POLICE UNIVERSE

While the above excerpt is fictional, current economic, political, and technological trends in the United States and the global environment give the scenario a great deal of reality for police managers. These trends include the following:

- Increased costs for energy fueled by global demands from new economies in the Far East and South America
- Growth of inexpensive technology with instant communication through smart cell phones and miniaturized personal computers such as iPads and cell phones
  - Greater use of social media on the Internet for persons of all ages
  - The adoption of new police technologies that include droids for surveillance and robots for tactical situations such as barricaded suspects and suspicious packages
- Increasing economic and social division and barriers between rich and poor individuals and countries
- Changes in population demographics, with the increase in the cultural and ethnic diversity of the population creating ethnic, lifestyle, and social class enclaves and neighborhoods throughout the country
- Career equity regardless of gender, race, and ethnicity pushed, in part, by the immigration into North America of highly educated professionals from Third World and former Soviet countries
- Increased multinational organized crime and cybercrime activities preying on individual neighborhoods and businesses through illegal drugs, extortion, and theft of major goods and services, partially sponsored by Third World governments

- Decline in the overall crime rate but increased concern with offenses committed by violent juveniles and individuals with modern weapons, gangs, terrorism, cybercrimes, and threats against the infrastructure, such as the disruption of communications by cybercrime or terrorist bombings
- Increases in planning and allocation of domestic resources for homeland security and protection from domestic and international terrorist groups
- Increasing powers of multinational corporations, many of which hail from the United States, Brazil, China, and India, and the mix of competition and cooperation from private police controlled by the same corporations, with target hardening and executive protection becoming major concerns
- Increasing professionalization of public and private police, and community involvement with public police, but the growing numbers of armed private police who augment public police
- Universal smart credit cards based on imbedded microchips, DNA identification, and **global positioning system (GPS)** technology, with data transmitted to central banking and public databases, which can be used to track the movements and transactions of almost everyone
  - Interactive global sites becoming personally, politically, and commercially important
  - The growth of a generation that is very socially interactive via Web sites and concerned about what people are talking about them. Teenagers in all areas of the world with advanced cell phone service are comfortable with technology and totally interconnected through Twitter, Facebook, YouTube, and other services.
  - Greater use of predicting software that can review criminal activity based on social media transactions, crime reports, and the mining of diverse data sets such as surveillance cameras, license plate readers, and gang intelligence reports.

Formal reports by futurists, such as *Levin and Jensen* (2007) and *Schafer* (2007) by the Futures Working Group of the FBI and Police Futurists International, address the above trends and add scenarios related to privacy rights, increasing technology, the inability of public governments to address long-standing problems, the use of military forces for domestic issues, and the aftereffects of domestic terrorism incidents. The purpose of all these discussions is to try to look into a crystal ball to see what American policing might look like for the future.

The Proactive Community Police Response

The **proactive community police** response is a series of strategies that includes cost-effective concentration of administration, human resources, laboratory services, corruption and police brutality intervention, and training services for police departments. It includes the following:

- Deployment of community policing, including giving more authority to remote unit supervisors; human service/communication training for officers, supervisors, and police managers
- Proactive planning and intelligence to anticipate planned and unplanned events, including critical incidents and intelligence and hot spot management; centralized rapid-response teams with maximum equipment and human relations experts organized for instant deployment
- Greater interactions with private police, auxiliary police, and community volunteers

- Major police executives who are highly educated and professionally trained and move from one major police department to another—whether public or private—throughout the country

All this is the extrapolation of current trends. This is done by becoming thoroughly familiar with current police management data, policies, and concepts. Ours is a rapidly changing society. Adults from the World War II and Korean War generations can still remember a childhood without electricity. The car became important to policing in the 1920s, before television. Anomalies exist. As we did in the nineteenth century, we still use horses for effective crowd control. Computers became available to the general public only during the past two generations. Cyber activity and technology will dominate future policing trends.

The global world is here to stay with instant communication and affordable transportation. The pace of change for the postindustrial generation is staggering. This is a scenario for America and other industrial and postindustrial countries. The overwhelming majority of the world's population lives in preindustrial conditions, with access to modern communications. Thus they have jumped into the twenty-first century with cell phones, Wi-Fi, satellite communication services, and flat screens. Being wired today has come to mean having wireless communication through Skype, wireless smart phones, and inexpensive notebook computers. Thus, we must never forget that policing is global and both private and public. That globe is shrinking every day.

Nevertheless, the human condition will always be with us despite the rapid changes. Law enforcement is still a human service agency, a people agency. Of course, the realistic view is that the future is now.

What does the future hold for law enforcement managers? Given current trends, it is expected that police departments may be changed or organized along the lines presented in this chapter in the not-so-distant future. We believe that this will result in effective community policing, given the socioeconomic, political, and technological trends. However, the major thrust for change will be the demands made by cost-conscious municipal governments to continue to provide the police services demanded by citizens.

POLICE DEPARTMENT CONSIDERATIONS

This abundance of forces is the historical result of our federal system of government and the wish of local communities to have control over their police. These realities of a democratic republic produce common problems of concurrent jurisdiction and duplication of effort. While citizens in cities can generally identify their police department, citizens of the many townships across the country have two or more options when they need the police. The selection includes the state police, town police, county sheriff's department, or village police. As a result, there exist these organizational realities in American policing today:

1. Active competition exists between police organizations for calls, resources, and, at times, personnel.
2. De facto spheres of influence are arranged by formal and informal agreements between agencies. For example, while the state police have statewide jurisdiction, many will normally not answer calls in a village that has a police department; the village police, in the same light, will not go outside municipal limits except in pursuit of an offender.
3. Informal relationships, usually based on how well certain officers or agency heads get along, determine the distribution of intelligence information, assistance to other departments during emergencies, and the success or failure of interagency projects.

Some economists and social scientists might argue that this is healthy since it allows for competition, selection, and other market variables used by consumers for private sector products. Some feel that police services can be provided by private contractors as long as the legal questions and cost-for-services formulas are worked out.

The number of law enforcement organizations would undoubtedly continue to increase were it not for the recent sharp demand for cost-effective police services and constraints on public sector costs. As municipal and police managers dealing with annual budgets know, costs for police personnel, benefit packages, pensions, equipment, technology, and buildings have escalated in the past decade. Most of the funding is derived from taxation, and taxpayers and many lawmakers do not want future tax increases and want to reduce budget deficits at the federal, state, or local level. Political officeholders know that if taxes escalate in their communities, it will be a hard sell. The message to "hold down costs" has been relayed to all municipal department heads. And so the story goes all over the country.

This financial crisis of 2008 has reached new proportions created in part by a number of policies on the federal level—such as housing—which reduced aid to state and local municipalities. When funding is tight, vehicles are overhauled rather than replaced, plant maintenance and rehabilitation are deferred, and wage and benefit increases are forestalled either by contract or by mutual agreement. In some cases, there are layoffs of police officers. All in all, proactive police managers of the future will have to offer police services in an effective and economical way; that is, they will be required by their citizenry and elected officials to do more with less. State and federal governments may have to respond with creative ways of raising money for policing. For example, we may see a tax on certain services, such as responding to home or building alarms in private businesses. Already, parking fines are returned either directly or indirectly to police budgets; other forms of revenue may be generated outside of the tax structure. Probation departments, for example, charge their clients for certain services such as vehicle immobilizers (for drunk-driving defendants), ankle GPS bracelets, and other technological services.

The Jurisdictional Dilemma

The existence of too many police departments results in duplication of services for many areas in the United States. Many argue for this, especially small-town politicians and police chiefs, who use the **home rule** argument to keep this jumbled, inefficient system intact. We predicted in the first edition of our book that many municipalities would merge their police department with other governmental units or abolish the department outright. This has not occurred, mainly because of home rule.

In many parts of the United States many local schools have been closed or merged because of the decline in the number of children who have to be educated. When such an action is announced, there is often community protest and some delay, but usually the change is effected. This, however, has not taken place in municipal government. In some situations, municipal entities have debated on merging or simply going out of business but there is not much activity across the country.

Police departments are now subject to similar action, but there are some alternatives available for communities that wish to retain their local police. One common way is to share centralized services; for example, computerized record keeping, communications, vehicle acquisition and repair, supplies, equipment, and even laboratory and training facilities. In many instances, this type of sharing results in an upgrade of the present system of equipment currently in use by the local department.

A trend that is always discussed is police **consolidation,** as when two or more departments are disbanded and merged into an area or county metropolitan police department. Departments that have undergone this process include those in Nassau and Suffolk Counties in New York; Riley County, Kentucky; Jacksonville, Florida; Charlotte-Mecklenburg, North Carolina; Las Vegas, Nevada; and Toronto, Ontario. While this may sound easy, consolidation can be a very arduous process and is always based on the political will to meet an objective.

Although there is potential for increasing police efficiency by reducing duplication of effort, consolidation does not always result in economy. From the outset, it can be expensive. Officer and command officials of previously existing departments are often given new pay raises based on the highest wage scale paid in one of the "older" departments. New equipment has to be purchased on a mass scale for distinctive uniforms, department patches and logos, vehicles, and weapons. New station houses have to be rented, purchased, or constructed. Aside from implementation, there are some other long-term managerial ramifications. Regarding the collective bargaining issue, smaller police unions are eliminated and reformed into one or more powerful union(s) because of increased membership. Former chiefs of police are "demoted" to ranking administrative officers. New organizational charts and duties have to be prepared. Interestingly enough, departmental subculture is revised with the creation of a consolidated police force, which results in new patrol zones, shifts, duty assignments, and attitudes in dealing with situations. But for lower-ranking administrators and patrol officers, consolidation presents all kinds of opportunities for professional and career advancement. Importantly, the public has to be educated on how to contact or where to go for services with the new department.

What this all means is that the concept of consolidation can be feasible where there are high concentrations of people or businesses that create a single socioeconomic municipality. Consolidation, moreover, may reflect another trend whereby municipalities merge as political entities resulting in a merger of police, fire, and other public services.

Many communities in the United States contract for police services from another municipality. The basic considerations in determining contractual services are the following:

1. Statutory provisions related to contract agreements
2. Formulas to be used in charging for such services as patrol, traffic, criminal investigations, and so on
3. Planning and resolving various issues that come with normal policing (e.g., interruption of services, liability, physical plant needs, personnel requirements)
4. Determining performance criteria for continuance of the contract (e.g., lower crime rate, citizen satisfaction with services)

Since the 1970s, a number of feasibility studies were undertaken over the issue of contractual services. According to the National Sheriff's Association, there are the following types of contractual arrangements:

- *City to city.* Police service is provided by one city to another.
- *County to city or county to region.* Perhaps the most common contractual arrangement in the United States occurs when a county sheriff or police department provides police services to municipalities in the county on a shared-expense or contributory-expense arrangement.
- *Resident officer program.* Small towns that do not have a police department may contract for one or more full-time police officers from the state police or county sheriff's department. Expenses paid for these officers by the township are usually one-half the total cost of each person. In some cases, the officers receive a bonus if they reside in the contractual area.

In 2003, the International Association of Chiefs of Police (IACP) undertook a review of consolidation case studies and focused on consolidation efforts in the cities of Sparta and Tomah, Wisconsin, and the City of Belvedere and the County of Boone, Illinois. From this review, the following consolidation models were presented (2003: 1–2):

Functional—functional units such as dispatching or crime scene analysis being combined for two or more agencies.

Cross Deputization/Mutual Enforcement Zone/Overlapping Jurisdictions—sworn officers are pooled so that personnel from one department can make arrests and provide backup in another adjacent jurisdiction. This often occurs with campus police departments that have a large student population living off-campus.

Public Safety—fire, police, and emergency medical services are combined under one agency. This public safety model was a rage in the early 1970s when some newly created jurisdictions were set up in the west and southwest of the United States.

Local Merger—two or more agencies combine their police operations.

Regional—a number of agencies are combined into a new police regional entity based on geography.

Metropolitan—two or more agencies combine into one large agency for a major metropolitan area. This is what occurred in Toronto, Ontario, and Las Vegas, Nevada.

Government—the entire governments of two or more municipalities are combined into one new political unit.

One of the main findings of the IACP study is the need to gauge community opinion and to air the strengths and weaknesses of consolidation. A "focus group approach" was created whereby community members can meet and address the following questions:

1. Who will oversee the new department?
2. How will the chief and other command personnel be chosen?
3. What will be the initial and long-term operating costs?
4. How will officers from the "old" departments be merged and deployed in the new agency configurations? Will there be new or continued special units?
5. How will citizen involvement and review be achieved?
6. How will the new department be evaluated in terms of providing services and reducing crime?

A major issue that also needs to be addressed is the many state and local laws and regulations that relate to the creation of a police department. This also includes addressing collective bargaining or personnel work agreements related to wages, benefits, and conditions of employment that were explored in Chapter 15.

In all, there is a renewed interest in consolidation based on current economic conditions and the need to reduce the various layers of government. As the case studies cited show, consolidation is a long process that requires careful planning, public discussion, and political support if actual change is to occur. What may drive the move for consolidation or shared services in many communities are the costs for pensions and medical care. At this time, these costs account for about 30 percent or more in addition to the regular salary. The reality is that many states and communities cannot afford to fund these immediate and long-term expenses, as shown in the case of Detroit, Michigan, which went into bankruptcy.

Technology

The technological revolution continues to revise police practices. Even the smallest of departments have embraced microcomputing systems and workstations. We see no end in sight to the various adaptations that can be accomplished. Nevertheless, police managers have to be informed consumers of this **new technology**.

Although managers are not expected to know how to tear apart a computer terminal system, they should know the strengths and weaknesses of implementing a computerized records system for a department or division. They need to know about basic programming to experiment with new methodologies that deal with budgets, crime trends, personnel records, and so on. The same is true for other forms of technology, such as video units, which can be used for long-term surveillance of target areas, thereby freeing personnel for other duties.

As we talk about technology and policing, we must not lose sight of the need for greater interaction between citizens and their police officers. One program that has assisted in this endeavor is bicycle patrol (some might say a rather low-tech program), which on college campuses and in densely populated areas has received high marks for increasing visibility and officer–citizen interaction.

Patrol methods may change dramatically from the preventive brand that is employed today. It is now possible for every patrol vehicle to be equipped with a miniature computer-augmented mobile radio that relays an automatic signal back to the communications center giving the location of the vehicle on an electronic map of the metropolitan area. Computerized crime analysis also permits this map to be keyed to show a great variety of characteristics to facilitate planning. Some of these are the following:

1. Street and map response time grid
2. Modus operandi grid related to demographic characteristics and time of crime commitment
3. Time, place, and nature of crimes shown by number and color for easy identification, with listings of burglaries, robberies, traffic deaths, juvenile crimes, and other grids available at the punch of a button
4. Demographic vehicles: density, distribution, and vital statistics of population
5. Trend-analysis grids for traffic control, civilian disasters, and energy blackouts available for planners if a disaster or traffic stoppage occurred
6. All this available on encrypted, handheld palm computers

Reflecting the state of the art for cable television, all homes and businesses can be linked to a central dispatch system in a police-approved, computer-based remote linkage system. This combines burglar and fire alarms operating through landlines and cable television circuits. As discussed by Orange (2009) and Plotkin (2009), everyone has a "data cloud" that can be pinpointed through cell phones and other devices, and these data are publicly available. Once data leave your person through the Internet or other means, they become public rather than private. This data cloud or data mining can become available for police departments and, unfortunately, also for criminals.

Personnel Standards

Given the current trends in positive personnel selection, it is possible that we may see the following personnel standards in the future:

1. Associate's or bachelor's degree being demanded of all recruits.
2. Men and women being assigned to all facets of the police mission and promoted to specialty units and command and supervisory positions—all on an equal basis.

3. The police recruit selection process placing less emphasis on pencil-and-paper tests and more emphasis on testing by role-play, interview, aptitude, and other assessment-center methods.

More lateral entry between police departments on a state and national level would increase the pool of available candidates for line, staff, and managerial positions. If this becomes a reality, there will be renewed emphasis on the quality selection of police managers since the available pool will increase competition. At this time, due to the recession, there are a greater number of college-educated candidates who would be attracted to a career in law enforcement.

While running the risk of criticism for being too general, it can be said that the "typical police chief" of today has the following characteristics:

- Is 45–52 years of age
- Has worked through the ranks of a department
- Has had little experience in either public or private administration prior to appointment or selection as chief and has training consisting of some police academy seminars and learning by the ropes, with formal education limited to high school, augmented by courses taken at the local community college, or an associate's degree
- Was selected as chief by written civil service examination, political appointment, or election

With the organizational and milieu changes that we see occurring in American policing, it comes as no surprise that the credentials of future managers will also be undergoing some change. Reflecting current trends in patrol officer selection, police managers of the future will also be the products of advanced managerial training and higher education. In the future, the selection of police managers will correspond to that already practiced by many private sector enterprises for executive talent. Psychological testing, role-plays involving managerial problems, and oral review boards will be the rule for selection rather than the exception. This cadre of police executives will be highly mobile in that a police executive could be "chief" at a number of departments during a law enforcement career, with minor or extended excursions into industry and teaching.

Selection for supervisors and administrative staff members will also reflect some changes. Again, less reliance will be placed on pencil-and-paper tests and years of experience. Requirements for future hiring might be the following:

- A master's degree in police administration or a related field
- Three years of experience in police planning, patrol, or investigations
- Successful completion of the state-certified training academy for police patrol officers and supervisors, with some states issuing licenses that have to be renewed on a timely basis

Individuals who show administrative talent would be "tracked" into a departmental executive development program that would provide for future executives a rational combination of in-class training and field exposure to all facets of the police mission.

WHAT WORKS AND EVIDENCE-BASED POLICING

Twenty-first-century technology gives the proactive police manager the tools to control events. This technology is being improved and becoming less expensive almost on a daily basis. The first principle of the **proactive management model** is that police management is always in charge of technology. Technology should never be allowed to drive police management policy.

Police management in the twenty-first century will be both data driven and based on the rapid communication of information. This means that all justifiable policies and procedures will be computer based. Police officers deal with human beings, often in stressful situations. Officers will need to be grounded in the social sciences and human behavioral studies.

Let's take a look at the state of affairs that meet professional proactive standards for the twenty-first century. As a community-based criminal justice social service, police departments and police management need the latest in technology for both communications and planning. With scarce resources, the police manager needs to keep doing what works and stop doing what does not work.

Unlike the rigid computer mainframe technology of the past, the twenty-first-century approaches, focused on the individual officers and field units, change rapidly and are extremely flexible. To make full use of this new technology, police management will have to decentralize daily decision making down to the line officers, their immediate supervisors, and individual field units. Centralized communications, a solid feedback system, and proactive, flexible written departmental rules will make this system work.

Written rules and records include stored electronic communications and some limited use of hard copy. Digital technology is now available in every police car. Individually, personnel communication and recording devices will be carried by every officer in the near future.

A proactive department is a data-driven department, with its human side being provided by community policing. This department (1) lowers crime through good management and the proactive use of technology and (2) has the community set the agenda for the police department. A community-based problem-solving approach will create the twenty-first-century proactive police department. This department will be goal oriented, focusing on the same goal as the first nineteenth-century professional police department. The 1829 Metropolitan London Police Department's goal was the prevention of crime rather than just the apprehension of criminals. Prevention is proactive, while apprehension is reactive because apprehension comes after the crime has been committed.

The major proactive police management and technology tools to bring about this successful approach involve crime mapping. Compstat is viewed as the most successful use of crime mapping. It is available to other departments now, and will work even more effectively in the future when combined with the newest laptop and cellular information technology with continuing feedback.

Crime-mapping approaches can also enhance community policing when community policing guidelines are added. Crime maps can be made available to citizen groups to provide crucial information to crime problems in specific neighborhoods, towns, and villages.

Two major documents published in 1998 by Larry Sherman help set the stage for this new approach: *Preventing Crime: What Works, What Doesn't, What's Promising* and *Evidence Based Policing*. This approach, which is enhanced by computer mapping, is to base crime-reducing strategies on hard data and scientific evidence.

Preventing Crime (Sherman, 1998b) was based on a review of 500 prevention programs using standard data-based scientific criteria. Some of the nonpolice programs that diminished criminal behavior were antibullying campaigns in schools, teaching social competence and stress management skills, ex-offender job training for older males, and therapeutic community treatment programs in prisons for adult drug addicts.

Going after landlords who allow drugs on their property works. Working with public housing authorities to drive out the drug dealers and penalize the landlords works. Focusing extra police presence on what Sherman calls "hot spots" works. Hot spots, or places where crime is concentrated, may be determined by the high percentage of police calls to a bar or public housing project, for example. Arresting employed suspects for family violence who live in the suburbs works, but arresting unemployed, minority suspects in the inner city increases family violence and does not work.

Some favorite police programs do not work. Mobilizing inner-city residents to stop crime, gun buy-back programs, Drug Abuse Resistance Education (DARE), neighborhood watch, storefront police offices, and police newsletters with local crime information do not work. Crime prevention that is based on data works. Crime prevention that is based on good feelings is a public relations program rather than a crime prevention program.

This is partly what is meant by a proactive data-driven police department: Do what works based on data, not on public relations or good feelings. This also means that police departments need to evaluate police policy based on data and scientific evidence.

According to Sherman (1998a: 3–4), "Evidence-based policing is the use of the best available research on the outcomes of police work to implement guidelines and evaluate agencies, units and officers .... Evidence-based policing uses research to guide practice and evaluate practitioners." He wants to create a feedback loop using the evaluation of outcomes to change police practices. For example, if DARE does not work, put your limited resources into hot spot policing. If gun buy-back programs do not work to control youth homicides, create an interagency drug task force focused on youth homicides, like the one that worked in Boston. Use some of the resources that you had to fund storefront police and instead fund programs for controlling homicide by gang members. We cannot continue to fund police programs that are documented as failures while we have police programs that have been documented as successes. This is how an evidence-based police department works to justify choices by police managers.

Sherman (1998a: 5) shows what data he would refer to in **evidence-based policing**: "offenses per 1,000 residents, repeat victimization per 100 offenders, and so on." If you complain about how an officer handles a call but have no data, it is a negative remark with negative outcomes. If you have a program that can be placed on a graph concerning callbacks by officers and units, you have, at least, one data-driven evaluation. This would have a positive effect on future police management decisions. Management would have to analyze the reasons for the callbacks and the rate of callbacks by each unit for specific events.

Sherman's evidence-based policing and proactive data-based police management focus on outcomes. If police managers want to have a police department that actually solves ongoing community problems, part of every problem-solving approach needs to include data-based evaluations (Goldstein, 1990). Sherman says that successful approaches to problem solving have to be generalized. Police management can no longer consider each problem to be unique to every police department.

Sherman (1998a: 6) says that most police practices are "still shaped by local custom, opinion theories and subjective impressions." He is looking for a new data-driven approach based on implementation evaluations as well as experimental evidence.

One study conducted by Sherman found that offenders who felt that the police did not treat them fairly committed 60 percent more incidents of family violence than those who felt that they were treated fairly. Sherman recommended creating guidelines for police procedure concerning the fair treatment of suspects in family violence incidents. The success of these guidelines and their implementation would be evaluated using county- or citywide data on family violence.

If the police management goal is to decrease repeat instances of family violence, then different procedures and policies have to be tried until police management identifies the ones that work. From time to time, the new policy will have to be evaluated to see (1) whether it is still working and (2) what may be hindering and helping the implementation of each successful policy.

GLOBAL CRIME AND THE NEED
FOR A GLOBAL POLICE ORGANIZATION

Have we reached a time when there is a need for a global police organization? We already have a history of transnational police cooperation for the transmission of intelligence. In 1992, the European Union established Europol to combat "illicit drug trafficking, trafficking in human beings, terrorism and money laundering" (Reichel, 2002: 181). Interpol has facilitated an international exchange of criminal information since the 1920s (Footner, 1985). The International Narcotics Control Board of the United Nations has established international exchange of police information and cooperation. National police agencies now need to move beyond this sharing of information and extradition treaties to something far more universal, however.

Global policing is the next step needed to investigate and arrest both cross-national criminals and terrorists and to destroy cross-national criminal and terrorist organizations. A global police organization would assist and train local, regional, and national police departments in investigations across national borders.

Consider the following. Conspiracies involving drugs, stolen property, illegal immigration, and terrorism with roots in other parts of the world have profound economic and political effects on the United States. For example, the attacks on September 11, 2001, continue to have an impact on the American economy in terms of homeland and transportation security costs. Terrorist and transnational crime organizations buy and sell arms and explosives throughout the world. Money laundering worldwide is an important enterprise of illegal drug cartels and international groups. It is well documented that cross-national drug enterprises are organized and supported by terrorist groups as a major source of funding. Often these groups engage in murder and kidnapping of high-ranking public and corporate officials. Right now, the current emphasis is on the Al Qaeda terrorist group, which continues to be a worldwide network reaching out from the isolated regions of Pakistan to the urban areas of Europe and the United States. While attention is focused on the training and transit of terrorists, the real dilemma is the extent to which Al Qaeda accumulated fiscal resources through legitimate businesses in Europe and the Sudan. There is even the theory that the group attempted to manipulate airline stock prices and profits before September 11.

While terrorism and narcotics trafficking gain much official and media attention, there are other important issues. On the global level, rapidly increasing population trends and civil war inevitably lead to overcrowding of urban areas, large areas of poverty and hunger, and concentrated movements of people and goods across national boundaries. These unstable conditions attract transnational criminal organizations to provide weapons for competing political factions. Conditions of this nature, as evidenced in Africa and the former communist state of Yugoslavia can lead to state-sponsored genocide, which is the elimination of ethnic groups.

Adding to the problem is the issue of "rogue countries." A rogue country is one that actively supports international offenses ranging from drug smuggling to terrorism. In some cases, the country is unable to deal with criminal cartels because official corruption has rendered law enforcement efforts ineffective, as appears to be the case in Nigeria, Jamaica, and Mexico.

Another important issue is the large number of financial transactions that escape all formal foreign exchange regulations imposed by national governments. The billions generated by drugs, money laundering, and illegal arms purchases have a destabilizing effect on many countries in terms of lost tax revenue and official corruption.

The Link between Global Terrorism and Global Crime Organizations

Financing for terrorist activities is generated with the help of organized crime and involves the illicit drug trade, the smuggling of weapons, kidnapping, and extortion. These terrorist activities have reached global dimensions. There is a clear link between many terrorist organizations and cross-national crime, but there is no effective proactive global police organization available to combat this activity.

Many politicians and bankers are involved in global money laundering that escapes all formal foreign exchange regulation imposed by the national governments. Due to the nature of the transaction and the lack of any traceable records, it is very difficult to detect or prove these criminal violations. Profits generated through these transactions are often used to purchase arms across borders. These illegal transactions create political and economic instability in the country of origin and in neighboring countries. The billions generated by drugs, money laundering, and illegal arms purchasing and smuggling has had a destabilizing effect on Third World countries and regions.

Obstacles to International Police Cooperation

The great rates of transnational criminality have laid the foundation for new guidelines for various forms of international police cooperation at the global level. There are, however, some major obstacles.

SOVEREIGNTY   At present, no country wishes to give up territorial and political sovereignty to a world centered police force. With the exception of extradition procedures based on treaties, borders and jurisdictions are jealously guarded. Foreign police forces are not allowed to formally conduct investigations unless "invited" by the host government. The exception, of course, are espionage operations carried out by a nation's secret or intelligence service.

LANGUAGE BARRIERS   The lack of a universal language is a major communication problem for regional, national, intercontinental, and international levels of policing. This can range from investigative practices to arrest and apprehension of transnational criminals. Associated police agencies inevitably have to rely on interpreters. Following in the footsteps of the airlines and the World Wide Web, the adoption of English as the major language for international police cooperation would simplify communications and eliminate a major source of misunderstanding and expense.

POLICE CORRUPTION   Police personnel in many countries still lack elements of professionalism, receive meager remuneration, and are equipped with weak technology. This leads to police personnel's involvement in many direct and/or indirect forms of corrupt activities. In some situations, the corruptive practices are linked with fellow governmental officials and some political leaders. Problems of corruption and unethical behavior plague law enforcement agencies the world over. In all countries in the world, there are informal relations and the exchange of favors between the police, political leaders, governmental officials, and private citizens.

International training centers with high professional and ethical standards administered by a cross-national police service would be a major step in fostering a positive attitude toward the elimination of police corruption. A highly ethical cross-national police service would serve as a standard and model to professionalize Third World police forces.

The presence of everyday citizens with cell phones is also another factor. It is no secret that many departments in the United States are keen that every move officers make can be recorded by a cell phone. In the same light, many departments are already using video cameras in patrol cars and it is just a matter of time before officers will be wearing patrol cameras on their uniform lapels.

LACK OF PERMANENT FUNDING FOR GLOBAL POLICING ACTIVITIES Police organizations face obstacles in recruiting, training, and paying for global policing services. These factors are highly disproportionate from country to country. This has a negative impact on the quality of personnel selected for policing. Many poor countries lack appropriate electronic and other technical equipment that is needed to detect crimes, especially when investigating homicides, drug transactions, and fraudulent documents, which include illegal passports, visas, and counterfeit currency. Forensic analysis laboratory facilities are often either inadequate or nonexistent.

POLITICAL HOSTILITY AND INDIFFERENCE It is important that politicians support the policing functionaries when compared to other social and economic problems of the respective countries. The criminals and terrorists have become organized in the world. The time is ripe for legitimate countries and global corporations of the world to defend their citizens and customers against these criminals and terrorists by establishing a cross-national police service.

The Need for Cross-National Police Services

Most countries participated in international police cooperation as early as 1923 (Footner, 1975). Most countries, including those that gained independence only recently, have shared and extended various informal and formal mechanisms for apprehending crimes and criminals and have confronted three major problems: illegal drug trafficking, terrorist activities, and various forms of social, political, and economic upheavals.

International cooperation is crucial in addressing transnational crimes. Rapid changes in countries provide many new opportunities for transnational criminal activities. Cooperation has become functional at (1) formal and informal levels; (2) regional and national levels; (3) intercontinental levels; and (4) international levels. The process of police cooperation at the global level is continuing. A coordinated effort between developed and underdeveloped countries is required for the establishment of treaties, agreements, and conventions on extradition, legal assistance, transfer of criminal proceedings, transfer of penal sanctions, and transfer of prisoners (Anderson, 1989; Sessions, 1990; Nadelmann, 1993).

Nevertheless, several factors point to the need for international police cooperation:

1. Current travel facilities enhance offenders' mobility and thus their ability to escape detection of crime.
2. The present technologically advanced world of electronic transactions allows transfer of illegally obtained funds and profits to overseas financial institutions, thus reducing the possibilities of detection.
3. Transnational criminals are able to harm individuals, organizations, and neighboring countries through technological transactions without entering the victimized countries. Thus, transnational law enforcement has become enormously complex.
4. Due to the transparency of national boundaries, criminals can easily "lose" themselves, thereby making detection and apprehension difficult if not impossible. The rapid reorganization and boundary changes witnessed recently in Eastern Europe have also made it easier for fugitives to escape detection and apprehension.

5. Although many countries have developed and introduced treaties to extradite offenders, many still lack identical definitions and punishments for similar crimes (Anderson, 1989; Nadelmann, 1993).

The global economy needs a cross-national police organization that will deal with criminal problems that cross national boundaries.

The Investigation of Cross-National Crime

A global police organization would provide expert personnel in various areas of cross-national crime, including drugs, money laundering, extortion, international kidnapping, terrorist organizations, banking, and computer crime. This takes sophisticated technology and personnel that many countries cannot afford. Global police services would provide access to these specialized services through treaties and private contracts by signing on countries and global corporations.

Regional cross-national crime laboratories could provide both analysis of evidence and transnational criminal patterning. Communications would be both land and satellite based. Sophisticated imaging would provide digital results of chemical and other physical tests.

A global police training center is needed to focus on forensics, crime investigation, cybercrime, organized and organizational crime, tracking across borders, money-laundering techniques, banking protocols, proactive police management techniques, budgeting, hostage negotiation, and terrorist organizations and methods. Courses would be online and on campus. Certain courses would only be taught on campus, with limited and carefully screened enrollments for security reasons. Experienced faculty would be borrowed from national police academies to augment the training center's permanent core of full-time faculty. They would need the appropriate academic credentials and field experience.

Cross-national criminal and terrorist groups are organized with the latest technology. They are more profitable and have more money than many Wall Street corporations. They do not respect national boundaries, legitimate governments, or police agencies. Rogue nations protect these criminal and terrorist groups, providing them with safe havens and legal documentation.

It is now time for the legitimate countries and global corporations of the world to set up a counterforce to fight these criminal and terrorist groups.

THE WORLD IS FLAT IN THE TWENTY-FIRST CENTURY

In 2005, *New York Times* columnist Thomas Friedman published a book entitled, *The World Is Flat*. The **flat world** continues to increase in complexity because of the global use of information technology. Today over two billion people are connected through the Internet. In a like manner, the number of wireless phone users continues to increase to over six billion users (Schmidt and Cohen, 2013). Fiber optics and cable have made it inexpensive to communicate, exchange data, and coordinate the delivery of goods and service, including police services, worldwide. This flat Web-based world means that China, India, the European Union, Eastern Europe, and Russia are on a level playing field with the United States because of the World Wide Web. For law enforcement management, this twenty-first-century level playing field includes the following reality: *Crime and terrorism are global while law enforcement is local.* This should be above the desk of every police chief in the nation.

Trends in Cyber Crime

The cyber cloud, cybercrime, and the Internet recognize no national boundaries. These trends will result in major changes in police culture. It has been well documented that cybercrime, including millions of stolen debit and credit card, is costing Americans billions of dollars a year. No major police department can afford to ignore this crime and still say it is serving to protect the public. Interdepartment cooperation at all levels is the only way to investigate these crimes. In addition, agencies will need to adapt to ever-evolving technology, such as:

1. More transparency because of the involvement of the department and individual officers in increasingly intrusive social media through the Internet, such as Facebook, Twitter, and Instagram.
2. Financial transactions have become mobile, wireless, and based on the cyber cloud with financial servers being placed at any place in the world.
3. Successful individual encryption of 13 alphanumerics and longer, allowing individuals, businesses, and criminals to remain anonymous in their global and local communications including e-mail.
4. Almost all documents, music, media, and leased software will have a monthly fee and will be stored in the cyber cloud, including various encrypted lockbox approaches.
5. Today's most valuable commodity is information, including data related to infrastructure, financial, and technology.

These are not future predictions. These are changing realities for police departments and police culture as insular norms will weaken and disappear.

Twenty-First-Century Facts for Proactive Police Managers: Context Is Everything

"America remains the world's biggest manufacturer producing 75% of what it consumes though that is down from 90% in the mid-90s" (Friedman, 2005: 127). Wal-Mart imports goods worth billions of dollars from China to the United States each year, making Wal-Mart China's major trading partner. Wal-Mart tracks its goods from factory to shelf with radio frequency identification (RFID) chips embedded in shipping packages. These devices would be useful in keeping track of police department inventory, including weapons and other equipment. The UPS smart-label bar code can track packages globally and can be printed on your personal computer and tracked on your screen. Police can now do this for evidence.

Only a third of searchers on **Google** are United States based, and 50 percent of Google's content is in English. Remember even police officers can Google anything from almost anywhere; for example, Google-earth can give anyone a satellite image of anywhere on the earth. Google is also digitalizing a number of the world's libraries for free, with free access. Google is now developing the use of driverless vehicles so that one could drive on expressways on auto pilot.

An Apple computer 30-gigabyte iPod photo can hold most faculty text files for the past 10 years, or up to 7,500 tunes and up to 12,500 photographs, and play on any FM radio. A photo cell phone can send photographs, text, and word messages throughout the United States and Europe from a boat in the Caribbean. Both these devices weigh a few ounces and fit in the palm of a hand. Police departments should provide officers with these devices to be used with suspects, crime scenes, and investigations, to name a few. The iPod will add storage for the officers' digital police camera; police information, such as penal laws, departmental rules, and stolen cars, can be downloaded and instantly available. The officer can even do a digitalized photo lineup for a witness with a slideshow and a departmental download of the faces of active local criminals.

How Did This Flat World Happen?

Friedman argues that it was the fall of the Berlin Wall on November 9, 1989; the initial public offering (IPO) of Netscape on August 9, 1995; and workflow software offering a way to coordinate parts and services from around the world. Computers have been built and are being used all around the world. As a result, many service jobs in the insurance, banking, and credit card industries have been the topics of outsourcing, open sourcing, and offshoring, and more recently, sourcing in overseas areas such as India, Ireland, the Far East, and certain countries in South America. As many who work in international operations know only too well, knowledge and work can be done without regard to geography and distance.

Reality Check

The following are realities for the twenty-first-century proactive police manager:

- The **voice over Internet protocol (VOIP)** connects your telephone and personal digital assistant (PDA) to the global Web, letting you telephone the world. PDAs are becoming wireless Web-connected cell phones, and every police officer should have one. Third World countries will never need telephone lines.
- Virtual worlds invented for video gaming can create a revolution in police training.
- Virtual private networks are secure and can link all officers in a police department anywhere.
- There are millions of migrant workers in the world today, most of whom send money from rich countries to poor countries, depleting the capital of rich countries. Foreign students have dominated the computer, mathematics, and engineering graduate schools.
- Pod casting should reach 12.3 million households by 2010.
- The police departments of 170 nations share information on terrorists, and 55 nations have changed their domestic laws to accommodate the global pursuit of terrorists.
- Most major cities have surveillance cameras in public areas and in public transportation centers. These eventually can be used with face identification technology for investigations.

The National Security Agency has been collecting daily records of Internet communications between the United States and various overseas areas. This has been used to obtain wiretap information to obtain intelligence information on suspected terrorist plots.

- Lasers using photoluminescence spectroscopy casting light on objects will make the detection of explosives easier.
- Light-emitting diodes will replace 90 percent of lighting by 2025 and will cut in half the cost of lighting. This will be important for crime prevention.
- Fluency in English is rising around the globe, especially in China. Spanish remains the second most popular language in the United States.
- Every police vehicle needs to be tagged with a GPS identification device and have one in the car loaded with the specific details of local jurisdictions as well as police information such as the location of hot spots and crack houses. The latest Magellan has points of information such as gas stations, etc.

- This digital flat world is available to criminals and terrorists, and its technology is being used every day.
- Major terrorist threats to the United States are listed by the Department of Homeland Security:
  - Blowing up chlorine tanks
  - Spreading disease at airports, sport venues, and train stations
  - Infecting livestock with disease
  - Detonating nuclear devices in a major city
  - Releasing nerve gas in office buildings
  - Bombing sports arenas

How Does This Flat World Affect Police Managers?

This is not just a matter of new technology; this is a different worldview for policing. Police managers in the twenty-first century need the worldview, education, and tools to deal with global crime and terrorism in every police department in the nation. This means the need for collaboration between police agencies and the sharing of knowledge as they work to combat global terrorism and crime without being overwhelmed. More state and federal funding and better integration of information and coordination of resources are necessary.

Proactive Rural Policing

Meanwhile, rural communities will become less isolated as the Internet and communications systems link them with the worldwide network of work/communications. Rural police will have the means through communication and technology to adapt to the standards of the proactive police departments in metropolitan areas. Regional academies and services for rural agencies will upgrade the professionalism of these police officers. Their enlightened communities will also demand a higher level of community policing.

Rural communities have existed in the United States since its early years as an agricultural society. Police were already part of these communities even before the idea of community policing had been formed. The sense of community that urban areas are searching for was established in small-town America. Since police in these areas are considered part of a greater community, it is a fairly simple step to establish the proactive community policing of the twenty-first century.

Technology will provide a vast communications network; distance and weather are no longer barriers to instant communication. Virtual communities have already been established. These virtual communities will welcome a professionalized proactive community police force.

The Proactive Community Policing Management Model in Summary

It will take time to establish proactive community police norms as part of police culture. Police still cherish their social isolation and their perception of public hostility. Reality and political pressure will play an important part in the transformation of the traditional police department into the technologically aware, proactive, professional police force of the future. Since the creation of the London Metropolitan Police Department in 1829, police culture has had to solidify its present subculture. It will take time and a great deal of effort to transform our police forces into a paradigm. However, it will happen. The new generation of police officers, supervisors, and managers who are reading this textbook will make it happen. But it will not be easy.

The combination of centralized administration and internal services for the police agency and remote community-based decision making will work. The extensive use of technology and communication makes this possible. The educated line officer will take on more responsibilities with community enforcement as a major approach to street and neighborhood crime. Training in communication and human services and the use of technological services and collective behavior will become of paramount importance to the proactive police officer, manager, and supervisor. As more responsibility for anticipating events and taking proactive action is embraced by every level of command, morale will improve along with responsibility. Communities will take back their neighborhoods with the help of their proactive police department.

A **consultative management** model is demanded by the new generation of professional police line officers and supervisors. They are college educated and are taking their place in police departments throughout the nation. These police officers and supervisors will demand more responsibility and autonomy. The promise of present and future technology, along with an attitude change brought about by the proactive community police model, will make this possible. The major characteristics of a proactive management model for community police are the following:

1. Participatory management with more responsibility and autonomy given to supervisors in the field.
2. Centralized rapid response for critical incidents and emergencies.
3. The community sets the agenda for proactive policing in every neighborhood, town, village, and community center.
4. Police managers, supervisors, and line officers actively working with the community to prevent and contain crime, property theft and damage, and community violence.
5. Proactive, planned, and limited patrolling. The split force will have a section responding to 911 calls and a section for planning, hot-spot targeting and community policing, and so on.
6. Planning, forecasting, and anticipating events taking place in every part of every department. This will be conducted from a centralized planning unit to an individual team of officers making plans with a community neighborhood. Anticipatory planning will be central to the proactive community police department.
7. Training and education will take place side by side. After extensive background checks and testing, including psychological testing, the college-educated police officer will enter a highly professional training program. This program will emphasize police ethics, community involvement, technological and communications expertise, and human service skills along with the traditional subjects. In-service and clinical training will persist throughout an officer's career, including supervisory and management training at promotion. Human resources will include stress management for all levels from line officers to major managers and their families.
8. This will be a "smart" police force that will use technology extensively. However, the educated proactive police manager will use technology as a tool and never let technology drive policy. Human beings will be in charge of technology, which will be extensively used in a community-oriented human service department.
9. This proactive department will use this planning and technology to reduce crime and to solve crimes for its communities. Solid investigative work will use the latest techniques, including DNA identification and hair/drug testing. Departments will employ their own lawyers to make cases prosecutable and to protect them against unreasonable plea bargains. Everyone, from line officer to police manager, will take a proactive approach to creating the best prosecutable cases possible.

Will this happen? This is the model that we reach for. If we reach for it, it can happen. If we do not reach for it, it will never happen. It can and will happen as the new generation of police managers, supervisors, and line officers work with the communities they have sworn to protect.

Questions for Review

1. Do you agree or disagree with the societal changes in the twenty-first century that appear at the beginning of this chapter? Add two changes to the list.
2. Is the proactive police response realistic or just science fiction?
3. State the pros and cons of police consolidation. What do you think will happen in the future, and why?

4. What would you add to personnel practices for the future, and why?
5. Analyze the characteristics of the proactive community police model, and explain why you think it will or will not work.

Class Project

Based on your review of this chapter, design a police vehicle for the year 2020. How will it be powered?

What kinds of equipment might be "standard" by this time?

References

Anderson, Malcolm. *Policing the World*. Oxford: Clarendon Press, 1989.

Footner, Michael. "INTERPOL: Global Help in Fight Against Counterfeiters, Drugs, and Terrorists." *National Institute of Justice—Research in Action* (September, 1985), pp. 1, 5.

_____. *Inside Interpol*. New York: Coward, McCann and Geoghegan, 1975.

Friedman, Thomas L. *The World Is Flat*. New York: Farrar, Straus and Giroux, 2005.

The Futurist. Washington, D.C.: World Future Society, 2005.

Goldstein, Herman. *Problem-Oriented Policing*. New York: McGraw-Hill, 1990.

International Association of Chiefs of Police. *Consolidating Police Services: An IACP Planning Approach Executive Brief*. Alexandria, Va.: International Association of Chiefs of Police, 2003.

Kelling, George, and Mark H. Moore. "The Evolving Strategy of Policing." In Victor Kappler, ed., *The Police and Society*. Prospect Heights, Ill.: Waveland Press, 1995, pp. 3–28.

Levin, Bernard and Carl J. Jensen. Homeland Security in 2015. Web posted at futuresworkinggroup.cos.ucf. edu/docs/Volume2/vol2Levin&jJnsen.pdf. Accessed February 7, 2014.

Nadelmann, Ethan A. *Cops Across Borders: The Internationalization of U.S. Criminal Law Enforcement*.

University Park: Pennsylvania State University Press, 1993.

Orange, Erica. "Mining Information from the Data Clouds." *The Futurist*, 43, no. 24 (July–August, 2009), pp. 17–21.

Plotkin, Robert. "The Automation of Inventing." *The Futurist*, 43, no. 24 (July–August, 2009), pp. 23–27.

Reichel, Philip L. *Comparative Criminal Justice Systems* (3rd ed.). Upper Saddle River, N.J.: Prentice Hall, 2002.

Schafer, Joseph A. (Ed). *Policing 2020: Exploring the Future of Crime, Communities, and Policing*. http://futuresworkinggroup.cos.ucf.edu/publications/Policing2020.pdf

Schafer, Joseph, ed. *Policing 2020*. Quantico, Va.: United States Department of Justice, Federal Bureau of Investigation, 2007.

Schmidt, Eric, and Jared Cohen. *The New Digital Age: Reshaping the Future of People, Nations and Business*. New York: Knopf, 2013.

Sessions, William S. "International Crime in the 90's and the Twenty-First Century." *Vital Speeches of the Day*, 57 (November 15, 1990), pp. 69–70.

Sherman, Lawrence. *Evidence Based Policing*. Washington, D.C.: Police Foundation, 1998a.

_____. *Preventing Crime: What Works, What Doesn't, What's Promising*. Washington, D.C.: National Institute of Justice, 1998b.

INDEX